KARMIC TAROT

KARMIC

BY WILLIAM C. LAMMEY

TAROT

A Profound System
for Finding and Following
Your Life's Path

Revised & Expanded Edition

Newcastle Publishing, North Hollywood, California

Revised edition edited by Ed Buryn and Gina Renée Gross
Charts by William C. Lammey
Cover and interior design by Michele Lanci-Altomare

ISBN: 0-87877-136-0
A Newcastle Book
First printing 1988
Revised edition first printing 1993
10 9 8 7 6 5 4 3 2 1
Printed in the United States of America.

DEDICATION

Karmic Tarot is dedicated to those truly fortunate people
whose lives have been and will be touched by the transformative wisdom and power
of the mysterious wonder we know as the Tarot.
To you, the reader—may this book make a healthy contribution
to your steady growth along your spiritual path
and reveal to you the confidant, the advisor/counselor,
the in-house best friend waiting for you in the Karmic Tarot.

CONTENTS

LIST OF CHARTS

FOREWORD

I am deeply moved and gratified by Bill Lammey's work on Tarot. It is a comprehensive synthesis of Tarot symbolism with certain fundamental philosophies in the areas of human consciousness research and transpersonal psychology. As a student and teacher of transpersonal psychology, the Tarot has been especially significant to me, both personally and professionally, during my own journey into the depths of the Self. Tarot is the metaphysical system that has given me the key to understanding and transcribing portions of "the mystery of the Self" in my work. I honor its wisdom, its humor, and its incredible accuracy. But the Tarot requires an interpreter who is highly trained in the intuition and integrity of The Higher Self for its wisdom to fully materialize. Bill Lammey is such an interpreter, and he evidences high degrees of understanding in this excellent work of synthesis and correspondences.

I began reading Tarot cards when I was a child. The first time I "connected" with a Tarot deck was one of my first mystical experiences. There was a familiarity I could not explain. It was as though I was reconnecting with a very old friend! I carried the cards around with me for awhile and would lay out spreads spontaneously when I needed guidance. Along with going to church on Sundays and Wednesdays and praying to Jesus, I now also consulted The Hermit, The Emperor, The High Priestess, and The Hierophant when I needed help. The Star and The Sun held special importance for me, as they always told me when I was "right on." (Later, I learned I am a Leo Sun sign with Aquarian Moon and Aquarius Rising, which correlate with The Sun and The Star.) I did not know this at the time, but what I had done was to find a way to connect with my essence through the symbolic energies of these powerful cards.

Then, one day when I was in my teens, a cousin of a friend of mine was visiting and informed me quite dramatically that the Tarot was "evil." I was shocked! But being a compliant Baptist, I promptly put them away, feeling confused and somewhat embarrassed. It was not until 1974, when I met a Hermetic philosophy teacher/initiate, that I again came upon this symbolic system of ancient wisdom. Under her tutelage I studied metaphysical systems, including Tarot, and I re-experienced that feeling of familiarity. I became a Tarot reader myself, but have reserved its use for special times and for people passing through chaos during those moments of great inner change.

I recognize the Major Arcana as a source of understanding the archetypal energies available to the Self and necessary for the Self to attain in order to become fully human in this realm. The powers of the Self, the laws of the universe, and the stages of initiation every soul must undergo to return to its Source are all profoundly made personal through the symbols of the Tarot. I am excited about the current merging of ancient wisdom, modern science, and psychology that gives access once again to this system of universal truth.

Karmic Tarot is not only a sourcebook of ancient wisdom but a transformative journey that will touch the very core of your psyche. Bill Lammey's knowledge of metaphysics and psychology is impressive. It is accurately transcribed according to the laws of correspondence and parsimony that determine uncontaminated thinking and the movement toward wholeness—which both science and the mystical tradition adhere to.

As spirituality and science become unified again, the use of symbols as a way to connect with truth is becoming more accepted, even within the mainstream of psychology. Symbols are containers of meaning and energy. They can accelerate the process of awakening that automatically becomes activated in the psyche once you make contact with the true Self that is the core of your being. "Seeing is believing" is more true than you realize. What you believe, modern physics teaches us, becomes your reality! And when you "see" a thing, or "see through" a situation, you come to the light of truth that was buried under the web of illusion you have woven around your experiences here on earth. Tarot will teach you the incredible transformative power of the symbolic world, the world Plato considered real.

As you study the characters and situations in the cards, you will notice that certain ones will present themselves to you over and over during particular phases of your circumstances, as though they are trying to tell you something. These constantly recurring visitors can become your teachers, or your symbols for meditation, to be used for guidance or for power. Over time, the recurring symbols will change and others will assume dominance in your readings. You will be able to see progress, lessons learned or failed, illusions becoming less powerful, warnings, pats on the back, and other types of messages containing wisdom beyond your ego's ability to "see." The cards will give you a broader view than the one most of us usually live with. All of this is available with a comprehensive system like Tarot when you have an interpreter like Bill Lammey, who operates from a deep intuitive understanding of the wholeness of the Self and its entire journey through time. Bill is not an "exoteric" teacher (one who only teaches on the surface), but an "esoteric" teacher—one who is tapped in to the mysteries of the Self and its journey.

One time I had a vision of how Tarot came to be. I saw that people were being punished and tortured for being carriers of wisdom. The world had become fearful of truth, and of the power of responsibility we feel when we realize "the God within." So one day a representative of each spiritual school met in secret and placed the seeds of the their wisdom into a simple deck of playing cards. These cards retained all the archetypal wisdom of the ages in a picture story that tells of the hero's journey, the story of the prodigal son, the ancient mariner, the traveler through the realms, the descent and ascent of the soul, the pilgrim. They had found a way to store their oral traditions until they could be brought out in a safe and accepting world of the future. Whether or not this vision is truth or fiction, I know that the Tarot (Rota, Tora) becomes symbolic of the "wheel of life" that transcends the religious dogma or psychological reductionism by honoring all paths. I think we now have a safe environment in the world for these truths to emerge and blossom again.

Our possibilities as humans sharing an incredible experience together here on earth are told by the cards. I hope you will get to know them. Each card will teach you who and what is, and how it came to be.

—Jacquelyn Small,
author, *Transformers/Personal
Transformation: The Way Through*
and *Awakening in Time*

ACKNOWLEDGMENTS

How books come to be written is a magical process and much of that magic comes in the form of concrete assistance from family, friends, associates, and even strangers. One of my pet concepts is that we are each other's guardian angels. We tend to cross paths with those people who carry the appropriate message, who offer the needed assistance, for the lesson that we are presently learning.

I want to first acknowledge the many people for whom I read the Tarot during the year and a half that this book was being written. Every reading brings new knowledge to the reader as well as the readee (also known as the querent), but many of the readings during this period were sources of extraordinary insight. I'm most thankful for the product of those wonderful exchanges. Much of this Tarot work took place at the Renaissance Festival in Magnolia, Texas, in fall 1986. It was a six-week event where the energies of so many strong and dedicated souls created an especially healthy environment for growth.

Special acknowledgment goes to Gary Lee, of Gary Lee Associates, who, besides being a Class A friend, happens to be a computer genius. Not only did he provide me with my word-processing program, he taught me how to use it and then was available whenever I needed help—which was more often than I'd like to admit.

Most special thanks go to Gary McLeod, my good friend and business partner, for taking time away from his yoga and meditation classes whenever I needed to try out an idea or phrase on him. He gave my project equal priority with his own interests. I am eternally grateful for his support.

There remains one more thank you of an extraordinary nature. In 1972, when I was still a practicing architect, I took part in a Silva Mind Control workshop. As part of a meditation exercise, I was introduced to the notion of spirit guides, and much to my amazement, to my own guide, Jámí. I was shocked that such a clear image of this man, young and handsome, would impose himself and his name on my consciousness so simply and directly. I was even more surprised that the name and the image stayed with me.

If I were to recount all the instances of my relationship with Jámí, this would be a book on spirit guides and not on the Tarot. Suffice it to say that since I met Jámí, I have had a best friend, an advisor and a confidant on whom I could call at any time, in any situation.

I began my work with the Tarot also in 1972, and fifteen years later, when I decided to write this book, it was only natural for me to ask Jámí to share the experience with me. I don't really talk with Jámí as much as I ask for his attention and guidance, to reassure myself that he is still there. One way or another Jámí has always enriched the situations in which my consciousness has included him. This book is the strongest example of that.

In March 1987 I took a Sufi chanting class as part of my interest in the origins of sound and language. During a break I was leafing through a copy of The Way of the Sufi *by Idries Shah. I found a chapter called "Hazir Jámí"—and was reintroduced to my spirit guide and friend of fifteen years!*

Jámí was born in Mullá Núrud Dín Abdur-Rahmán Jámí in Khurásán on Shabán 23, 817 (November 7, 1414) and died at Herát on Muharram 18, 898 (November 9, 1492). According to Edward G. Browne's A Literary History of Persia: Vol.111 1265-1502, *Jámí "... was one of the most remarkable geniuses whom Persia ever produced, for he was at once a great poet, a great scholar, and a great mystic. Besides his poetry, which, apart from minor productions, consisted of three* Díwáns *of lyrical poetry and seven romantic or didactic* mathnawís, *he wrote on the exegesis of the* Qurán, *the evidence of the Divine Mission of the Prophet Muhammad, traditions, lives of the Saints, Mysticism, Arabic grammar, Rhyme, Prosody, Music, acrostics* (muammá) *and other matters. In the* Tuhfa-i-Sámí *forty-six of his works are enumerated, and I do not think this list is exhaustive .... By his most illustrious contemporaries he was regarded as "so eminent as to be beyond praise and so well known as to need no detailed biography."*

Thank you, Jámí, for being my friend.

I would like to share with you Jámí's "Prayer for Spiritual Enlightenment" that I uncovered while researching his life.

My God, my God! Save us from preoccupation with trifles, and show us the realities of things as they are! Withdraw from the eyes of our understanding the veil of heedlessness, and show us everything as it truly is! Display not to us Not-Being in the guise of Being, and place not a veil of Not-Being over the Beauty of Being. Make these phenomenal forms a Mirror of the Effulgence of Thy Beauty, not a cause of veiling and remoteness, and cause these phantasmal pictures to become the means of our knowledge and vision, not a cause of ignorance and blindness. All our deprivation and banishment is from ourselves: leave us not with ourselves, but grant us deliverance from ourselves, and vouchsafe us knowledge of Thyself!

ACKNOWLEDGMENTS FOR REVISED EDITION

First, thanks to my publisher Al Saunders for his support since the first edition of Karmic Tarot, *and for the opportunity to make these considerable additions presenting the results of the last five years of my research and teaching. To Kelly Younger, the editor of the first edition, there simply is no way I can thank you enough for your friendship and advice these five years on my other books and projects. To two of my graduate students, Pat Morgan and Lee Sabrsula, thank you for your dedicated work and feedback in weekly classes over the past three years during which the 3432 card definitions in the Karmic Spread were generated, interpreted, written, and rewritten. To Ed Buryn and Gina Renée Gross, my editors, to Michele Lanci-Altomare, the book's designer, and everyone at Newcastle Publishing who has worked to make this book what it is, I am one very grateful author.*

INTRODUCTION

Many people first become aware of Tarot cards when they see them used in a motion picture or television drama. The Tarot reader uses the cards to reveal the possibility of a future event which would strongly influence the life of the person receiving the reading, the "readee." Rarely in such dramas is any information given about the questions that come up: How does a Tarot deck differ from a playing card deck? What is the history of the Tarot cards? What do the cards mean? What are the qualifications for being a reader? How much value is there in the information given in a reading?

A typical deck of playing cards has fifty-two cards divided into four suits (clubs, diamonds, hearts, and spades) of thirteen cards each; a suit contains cards numbered from 1 to 10, ("Pip" cards), and three "Court" or face cards. A traditional Tarot deck has seventy-eight cards, divided into the Major Arcana and the Minor Arcana. The Major Arcana consists of twenty-two cards numbered from 0 to 21; each one is rich in pictured symbols. The Major Arcana can be likened to an extra suit of cards with more power than trumps or wild cards. The Minor Arcana consists of fifty-six cards divided into four suits, called Pentacles, Cups, Swords, and Wands; each suit contains cards numbered from 1 to 10 and four Court or face cards. All are illustrated, but to a lesser degree than the Major Arcana.

The history of Tarot cards does not reveal any specific origin. Written records indicate that the cards have existed for at least five centuries. When the process of printing cards from wooden blocks became popular in the fifteenth century, Tarot cards became common throughout Europe. The European ancestry of many Tarot decks is apparent both from the illustrations on the cards and the references in accompanying books to physical characteristics most common among people of European descent. Some modern decks have a much more cosmopolitan appearance through the illustration of symbols and people from a variety of cultures.

The meanings of the cards are not fixed, but vary from book to book and system to system. Each author tends to make his own interpretations, changes, and additions based on whatever sources that author finds acceptable. These sources may include everything the author finds in print on Tarot, intuition, speculation, imagination, and information obtained from paranormal sources.

Anyone who is interested can become a Tarot-card reader. The process consists of acquiring a Tarot deck and a book or pamphlet that assigns a set of meanings to the cards. The reader-to-be studies both and learns one or more ways to lay out the cards in a spread for a reading. Then there is a period of becoming familiar with the process with practice readings until the reader becomes adept.

The value of a reading can only be determined by the readee, sometimes only after enough time has passed for the information received to be evaluated and examined in terms of the readee's experience and awareness. Most readers know that they are not infallible. A Tarot reading is a combination of art and craft; it is strongly influenced by a number of factors, including the abilities of the reader, the rapport between the reader and readee, the feedback from the readee during the reading via words, facial expressions, body language, or any other means, and the receptiveness of the readee. The reader uses knowledge and intuition to explain the patterns, choices, and probabilities in the readee's life as revealed by the reading, in an effort to aid the readee. The best way to evaluate the reading is to see how successful the aid is for the readee. Readers can evaluate the reading they do to gain insight about their own lives.

Bill Lammey takes a mystical, metaphysical approach in *Karmic Tarot*. He presents the Tarot and his reading system as a divinely inspired tool to be used by people to better their lives. Readers who approach this system openmindedly will find much useful information here, regardless of the extent of their Tarot experience and knowledge.

The book is divided into three parts. Part One is concerned with the meaning and purpose of the Karmic Spread, which is the author's way of laying out the cards for a reading. Part Two defines the meanings of the cards as determined by the author. Part Three provides information on how to do readings and the process of becoming a Tarot reader.

Chapter One provides an introduction to the cards and to the book.

In Chapter Two, Karmic Tarot is described as a system of reading in which every question, large and small, is answered in the context of the master plan for the readee's life. This Karmic master plan is revealed by the Tarot. Bill Lammey shares his insights that the master plan is a contract between a person and the Divine about the life to be lived; the person exercises free will in the choices made about how to fulfill the contract and thus find personal satisfaction.

Chapter Three describes the spread or layout of the cards that Lammey has created for Tarot readings. Each position in the layout is important because the meaning of the card plus the meaning of the position help determine the message for the reading. There is a grid with four horizontal rows and seven vertical columns, making twenty-eight potential positions; because six of these are for "swing" cards, the total number of positions is actually twenty-two. Twenty-two cards are laid out on this grid as shown in Charts 1 and 1A.

Chapter Four is about the four horizontal rows of the spread, which represent the four Planes of the Self: Physical, Emotional, Mental, and Spiritual. These are correlated respectively to the four suits of the Minor Arcana: Pentacles, Cups, Swords, and Wands. Lammey also explains how the four Planes are related to many other disciplines, including numerology, colors, Aristotelian concepts, Rosicrucian teachings, channeled material about ancient races, Yoga, physics, psychology, and other frames of reference. These correlations can be extremely helpful in establishing rapport between reader and readee when both share knowledge, belief, or acceptance of a correlated discipline or concept.

Chapter Five gives information about the seven columns of the spread, which represent two separate progressions simultaneously. Each column shows a period of time, e.g., birth, childhood, recent past, present, near future, mid-future, and long-term future. These seven columns also represent seven levels of evolving consciousness: physical, emotional, mental, spiritual (awakening), higher mental, higher emotional, and higher physical. Lammey correlates these seven Stages of progression in time and consciousness to the Minor and Major Arcana, and to other disciplines such as sound, the concept of spiritual hierarchy, philosophy and religion, the seven chakras, the seven stages of a Sufi story, the seven stages of life in Shakespeare's *As You Like It*, Theosophical ideas, and more.

Chapter Six describes the meanings of the twenty-two positions in the Karmic Spread. Bill Lammey summarizes his sources for the position definitions. For those readers who want more than the summary, details on the sources are presented in the Appendix. One of the most valuable pieces of information given here is the procedure for seeing time factors accurately in a reading. Many readers have difficulty determining the timing of events revealed by the Tarot. The author instructs the reader to select as a time frame either the full life or a seven-month period that begins three months before the month of the reading. The reading period can just as well be seven weeks or seven days. Applying this technique to a reading makes it much more specific and potentially more meaningful to the readee. Before doing any readings with a more immediate time frame, Lammey always does a full-life spread/reading first, to frame the more specific questions within the karmic purpose.

Chapter Seven presents the author's meanings for the twenty-two cards of the Major Arcana. He derives these meanings from his analysis of the four Planes, the seven Stages, and their interactions. In addition to the overall meanings of the cards, each of the Major Arcana is interpreted in each of the twenty-two positions of his Karmic Spread.

The meanings for the fifty-six cards of the Minor Arcana are presented in Chapter Eight. The author believes that the numbered cards of the Minor Arcana represent the life experiences required for us to learn the lessons of our life path. These lessons are symbolized by the Major Arcana, the archetypes of universal truths. Lammey sees the Court (face) cards of the Minor Arcana as the people or spiritual guides involved in the readee's life. One of them can also represent the readee. In addition to the overall meanings of the cards, each of the Minor Arcana is interpreted in each of the twenty-two positions of the Karmic Spread.

Chapter Nine tells how to give an actual Tarot reading. It describes the reading process as consisting of five objective factors—the reader, the readee, the Tarot deck, the layout, and the environment—and one subjective factor, the Provider. Lammey discusses the importance of using a Tarot deck that has seventy-eight cards conforming to the standard or classical deck; he mentions his favorite, the Rider-Waite deck, but feels that other decks are certainly acceptable. He defines the subjective factor, the provider, as the divine source of all knowledge.

One of the most important points made in Chapter Nine is that it is perfectly valid for readers to offer different meanings for the same card or position. Like many readers, the author sees the Tarot as a language of symbols subject to individual interpretation and shades of meaning. In this concept, each reader develops an individual dialectic based on individual experience. Each reading gives the reader shades of meaning and interpretation that enable them to periodically update the Tarot information held in memory.

This development of an individual dialectic is what most readers experience as they begin to gain enough expertise to give a reading without recourse to charts and text. To aid in this development, many readers have a deck that they alone will use, thus allowing their interpretations to apply to the individual cards in that deck based on their own experiences.

Bill Lammey stresses the importance of preparing the readee for the reading by providing them with a framework for accepting the information. The reader should give the readee a simple, brief explanation of how the Tarot works as the reader understands it. Readees who have never had a Tarot reading previously may need a lengthier explanation than readees with experience. If the readee does not have at least an open mind about Tarot readings, the effectiveness of the reading may be greatly reduced.

In the final chapter, Chapter Ten, the author focuses on aids for the reader outside the reading process. He discusses a number of ways for a continuing study of Tarot to deepen the reader's understanding. All of the study methods presented are designed to help the reader be more specific in readings.

This book can be used by beginners or by experienced Tarot readers. The information here can benefit any reader in the quest to provide useful information to the readee, which is the primary goal of Tarot reading. But, Lammey shows us that the bonus in studying the Tarot goes far beyond the ability to do a reading, for the Tarot is a repository of the universal truths that permeate all creation. He stresses that by studying the images and structural relationships of the cards, the student is internalizing those truths and will always have them available when needed.

This book will be a welcome addition to the library of anyone who has a serious interest in the Tarot. You will find that the charts are especially valuable tools in both personal study and readings. Adding your own index tabs to these charts will make repeated reference much easier.

—Camden Benares,
author, *Tarot for Pleasure,*
Zen without Zen Masters

PART ONE

THE
MEANING
AND PURPOSE OF
THE KARMIC SPREAD

CHAPTER ONE

A Beginning

This is a book for anyone, beginner to advanced, who wants to understand and read the Tarot. It has a newly revealed layout and card interpretations that will excite the serious student and presents an easy new system that avoids laborious memorizing. It is deliberately intended to encourage beginners to take up the subject of Tarot.

Everything that happens in your daily life is part of the unfolding of your divine purpose. The more you can grasp the essence of that purpose, the more harmonious that unfolding will be. The system of Karmic Tarot includes ways of broadly discerning your chosen lifetime purpose. But it is also highly useful in your day-to-day affairs. You can gather rich information about specific issues and time factors affecting your current situation. A Tarot reading with the Karmic Spread is not only diagnostic but prescriptive. You are getting answers to the questions you are asking in your heart.

To be rich in meaning and valid in its insights, a reading must be both passive and active; passive in the emotional and spiritual planes in order to listen and receive information—and active in the physical and mental planes in order to validate and interpret all messages.

The system of Karmic Tarot guides the reader to see the underlying principles and patterns at work in Tarot, rather than having you memorize what numerous others say given cards mean. It is designed to kindle knowledge hidden deep within you as a potential reader. If you can discover the essence of the cards and their relationships in the deck, the meanings you need will always be there when you need them. They will bubble up from deep inside you with little or no effort during a reading.

The Tarot is both a rational and an intuitive system, a marvelous blend of right-brain and left-brain thinking. It is a logical system of archetypal symbols and structured layouts on which the intuitive right brain can play its half of the game. So it's an excellent tool for exercising and training the *whole* brain, for study of any kind in any field.

The Tarot is also an excellent and friendly introduction to metaphysics, as it embodies so many of the underlying mysteries of the universe. *Karmic Tarot* focuses on your movement through your own universe, the evolution of your personal consciousness.

I believe that Tarot is a gift from God to help us on this path, and to help us create our future—rather than merely predict it. I think the Tarot was conceived as a tool to aid us in fulfilling our divine purposes. It is my sincerest hope that this book will give you a working knowledge of that tool and the people for whom you read.

This book does not address the history of the Tarot per se; that has already been well documented. Rather, it is concerned with the origins of the Tarot, with looking at it intensely and from many viewpoints, so that you can see its underlying principles at work.

The Tarot is a living, "written" (visually symbolical) language. Despite the fact that the oldest deck found to date is from the late fourteenth century,[1] Tarot may well be the oldest of all written languages. For Tarot's symbology could well have been born in that magical, ancient moment when man invented the first alphabets to capture the sounds of his speech. This, in fact, was the moment symbology itself was born—the original stuff from which archetypes have derived. This brought the sense of sight into the ability of man to communicate, and what is referred to in this book as the mental plane of man was born. This is why archetypal symbology moves us in such a deep and mysterious way. Even now it is hard to express many of these "messages" in words.

Up until now, much Tarot work has been limited to forecasting the future, placing it side-by-side with mediums used primarily for fortune-telling, such as palmistry, tea leaves, and the crystal ball. Other, more serious Tarot work, such as correlations with the Hebrew alphabet, the Kabbalah, astrology and various mythologies, have centered around only the main twenty-two cards of the deck, the Major Arcana. Even when the emphasis of such work has been on using the Major Arcana to discover the pathways of the evolution of consciousness, the result has been little more than enriched meanings for those twenty-two cards.

All Tarot card references in this work are to the classical Tarot deck, i.e., a deck of seventy-eight cards. Such a deck consists of a twenty-two-card Major Arcana and a fifty-six-card Minor Arcana (four suits of fourteen cards each—ten numbered or "Pip" cards, and four "Court" or face cards).

This new spread reflects the journey that your four-fold self (physical, emotional, mental, and spiritual) takes through the seven Stages of evolutionary consciousness, beginning with your Karmic Contract at birth, i.e., what you have chosen to do in this lifetime. It uses the increasing similarity and harmony of Eastern and Western philosophies, exemplified in Eastern terms as the seven chakras in the unfolding of the *kundulini,* and in Western terms by the transpersonal psychologists as the seven Stages of evolutionary consciousness.

A unique interpretation of inverted cards is part of the Karmic Tarot's facility as a centering mechanism, to help you walk the middle path, a path that is literally a journey through all the dualities that threaten to pull you off course. Upright cards are interpreted as the central, root message of that archetype; while inverted cards are seen to be an imbalance of that root, involving either too much or too little of that principle.

In *Karmic Tarot*, you'll see for the first time how the Minor Arcana are used along with the Major Arcana to define the path of evolving consciousness. A structure within each of the Arcana, as well as a structural relationship between the two, is uncovered. So a wealth of new information is revealed, creating a new spread and expanded meaning for all the seventy-eight cards.

You will also see how each Arcanum can be used to deepen your understanding of the meanings of the cards in the other Arcanum—much as words in a dictionary send you back and forth but with increasingly better definitions each time. Just as you use words to define other words in conventional language, you can use cards to define other cards in the language of the Tarot. This is important for growth in interpreting the Minor Arcana. The more you can see into the mechanics behind and within the Tarot, the less you will depend on blind memorization of cards and arbitrary layouts and the more you will see where each card fits into the whole. Once you see the fit, your mind automatically fills with interpretations.

The Tarot is a system that enables your intuitive Soul/Spirit self to communicate with your objective Mind/Emotion/Body self. There is unlimited information available to you from your intuitive level, and the Tarot is an excellent way of reaching and working with it. Given a good deck, a good reader, and the proper setting, the possibilities are limitless.

ENDNOTES

1. Richard Cavendish, *The Tarot* (London: Harper & Row, 1975), p. 11: "The household accounts of King Charles VI of France show that in 1392 a payment was made to 'Jacquemin Gringonneur, painter, for three packs of cards, gilded and colored, and ornamented with various devices, supplied to the King for his amusement.'" Also, from p. 1: "In the Bibliothèque Nationale in Paris there are seventeen magnificent cards, sixteen of the Tarot Trumps, which were long believed to have been made by Gringonneur for Charles VI, but which are now thought be Italian and to date from about 1470."

CHAPTER TWO

Karmic Tarot

SOME BASIC DEFINITIONS

Karmic Tarot is a Tarot convention that uses the rich philosophical treasures inherent in the concepts of reincarnation and karma. Every question, no matter how simple or complex, is considered within the context of the underlying purposes of the present lifetime.

"Reincarnation" is the belief that the essence of your being, the soul, never dies. It is reborn in new bodies in a series of lifetimes, which is the process of "evolution of consciousness"—from the very separateness of man to the very oneness of the Divine.

Karma is the belief that the soul's agenda for a given lifetime is determined by your progress on the path of your evolving consciousness.

CLARIFICATION OF KARMA

The concept of Karma that most people have is that you are making up for what you did in past lifetimes. This is a negative interpretation, implying that every lifetime begins with some sort of karmic punishment.

Such a negative slant is an inaccurate understanding of metaphysics. There are no handicaps. You do not begin life with punishment by God for poor past performances any more than you begin with any advantages for good performances. As you will soon see, all negativity and pain is part of the process whereby you choose and learn your lessons on the path. Every lifetime for every soul begins on an even keel. The soul, however, does choose its agenda for the present lifetime with the full knowledge and understanding of its progress so far—the results of past actions. It will therefore choose an identity and tasks that take into consideration that progress. From the overview available to the soul it will choose what it needs to accomplish to best go forward on the path—the soul's evolution of consciousness. To the soul, no identity or task is any better or worse than any other. It is simply a question of what is best for the progression of the soul.

THE KARMIC CONTRACT

Fundamental to the concept of a discernible Karma at work in the Tarot is the belief that each of us, as our soul is preparing to be born, decides on a master plan for the lifetime ahead. This is the "Karmic Contract," an outline or framework agreed upon with the Divine. You could say that at this point the God "within" agrees with the God "without" on the framework. The degree to which you satisfy this contract is the degree to which you will be happy and successful. In other words, you feel fulfilled when you are fulfilling your contract. You feel most angry when you are not meeting the terms of your contract, because you are violating an agreement you have made with yourself.

FREE WILL AND THE KARMIC CONTRACT

Prior to birth your free will is expressed by the choices your soul makes for your Karmic Contract. After your birth your free will is expressed by the choices you make within the framework of that contract. You have an apparent infinity of choices, but those choices must fall within the agreed upon path if you are to have a satisfying life.

Imagine your life as the process of building a tower, a tower with four columns as foundation and structure. The construction of this tower represents the first of many paradoxes that will mark your path. These columns represent the four aspects of your contract—the physical, the emotional, the mental, and the spiritual givens. Stated positively, they are the parameters for your lifetime; stated negatively, they are the limitations, which must be accepted and used in order to succeed. And they are the lesson in paradox, for if you accept your limitations, you will be unlimited in what you can put into your tower and in how high you can build it. The intention is for you to be able to reach the heavens, to return to God with all your lessons learned. To a Hindu this would be the end of the cycle of reincarnations.

Only by accepting and working with the givens of any situation can you hope to build on it, to change it. The paradox again. Only by accepting can you effect change. First you must be passive to the will of God; then you can be active with the will of Man. This universal lesson of the contract at your moment of birth is what moves through life with you in every situation of every moment of every day. Accept and give thanks for what you have, and then you can change. You must build on your foundation.

STAYING CENTERED ON THE PATH

You are born with complete knowledge of your Karmic Contract and the lessons it includes. Your challenge in life is to see how efficiently you can bring those lessons, which you know intuitively, into fruition in your conscious existence. God communicates with you continuously to remind you of the pressing requirements of your Karmic Contract. A "centered" life path is one on target with the soul's obligations. These are the people whose lives seem charmed, who always appear happy, healthy, and of course, extremely lucky. These are the people that test us via the sin of envy.

God communicates with all of us equally, but we do not listen with equal attention. Centered people are good listeners. Those of us who are less than perfect listeners must be reached in more concrete ways. These can be from minor to major attention-getters. Initially, you may be nagged by recurring thoughts, dreams, or daydreams. Headaches can be thought of as information heating up, trying to get out. Headaches can also be thought of as your heavenly telephone ringing...God calling you, saying you should slow down, find a quiet corner, and listen. If necessary the message will be externalized. It may be in the form of unsolicited advice from family and friends. Or, new people may be introduced to you, seemingly out of the blue. Illness and accidents are at the extreme end of the ways you are spoken to. They can be avoided by paying attention and learning your lessons earlier in the process.[1]

GOD DOES NOT SPEAK ENGLISH

You have probably noticed that God does not usually communicate directly in the English language. That is why the study of archetypal symbology is so important. Tarot and language are born out of the same symbology...the same archetypes. More specifically, Tarot symbology was most likely born at the same time as alphabets. When man first felt the need to create visual symbols of his verbal speech, he created the first alphabets.

The Tarot is a symbolic externalization of spiritual-level input from God. Western man finds it easiest to work with such "external" input—information that comes in through the five senses. We have not been conditioned to acknowledge and interpret the sixth sense, the "internal" voice, very well. However, with the impact of Eastern philosophies and practices, this is rapidly changing.

PRAYER VERSUS MEDITATION

When Western man turns his attention toward God, he prays. When Eastern man turns toward God, he meditates. In prayer, the major form is interrogatory. And we are not just asking questions, we are asking *for* things. But the main point here is that *we* are doing the talking. In meditation, the major form is silence, so that we may listen.

The Tarot is a form of listening wherein the inner message is externalized and then taken back in through the sense of sight. Tarot stops the mind and gives it focus. It provides a means of centering yourself on the path. It supplies specific information to correct your course and is an efficient and painless way of "getting the message."

THE NATURE OF PROBLEM-SOLVING IN KARMIC TAROT

There are no "bad" cards in the Tarot, only lessons to be learned. That which is flowing and already bringing you joy is the result of lessons already learned or in the process of being learned. That which is not flowing begins to present itself, by definition, as a problem—something negative. This negativity is an illusion designed to draw your attention to a lesson you need to learn. The instant the lesson is learned and internalized, the problem disappears.

All of the so-called "negative" experiences you have are nothing more than such lessons. It can be hard to accept this in the midst of intense pain or sorrow, but acceptance is the first step toward converting the illusion of negativity into the joy that is rightfully yours.

The trick is to realize and consciously assert that, in the midst of the apparent negativity, there is something very positive. That positive something is the lesson to be learned. It can seem like a catch-22 to search for the positive while the negative has you numbed with pain. Negativity and pain draw your attention because you want the pain to stop. But the moment you discover the positive lesson, the problem is solved and the negativity is gone. And you haven't done anything except allow a change of awareness.

Tarot can save you a lot of pain. It shows you the lessons you are facing—the potential negativity—and if you can learn what lesson that potential problem has for you, learn it in a reading, you will not need to experience it. You can go on to the next lesson. In other words, you do not need to actually experience any pain, you just need to do your homework and learn your lessons. This is true no matter what the karmic carryover may be.

Remember, initially all guidance for what we need to be doing comes to us intuitively at the spiritual level. We are given the opportunity to learn then and there and if we do so there will be no negativity, no pain. We simply become bigger and better, and we will have to remind ourselves to acknowledge this growth and to say thank you. People who are especially adept at getting the message at the spiritual level are like those who live in the caves and on the mountain tops in the Himalayas. A quick glance into their eyes reveals the speed at which they are assimilating God's messages. For those of us less efficient at learning, the message will have to descend first to the mental level, where it must be grabbed by the conscious mind. If not learned at the mental level, it will have to descend to the emotional level. If not learned through emotional experience, it will descend to the level of physical experience.

The function of the duality of positive/negative follows that of all dualities, i.e., hot/cold, up/down, good/evil, God/Devil; they exist/do not exist. And you must deal with them in both respects. They exist as apparent extreme points, so that you can conceive of what is in between those limits. The points themselves exist only as an abstract concept. What really exists is everything that is in between. Duality is a mental tool for defining things.

The Tarot teaches the illusions and realities of duality and paradox. Especially, and most importantly, it teaches the duality of good and evil, and more specifically, that of God and Devil. These, too, are abstract points at the extremes of conceptual limits. What exists is everything in the middle and it is all God.[2]

In interpreting readings with the Karmic Spread, upright cards are interpreted to be centered, root meanings that lie between various duality pairs. The duality pairs themselves are the signposts of the extremes of that central meaning carried to either too much or too little of that concept. The duality pairs are much the same as channel markers that describe the left and right boundaries of safe travel in and out of a harbor. The closer we get to the markers themselves, the closer we are to being out of the channel of safe passage.

KARMIC TAROT IS AN EVOLUTION OF CONSCIOUSNESS

All the questions you have, all the decisions to be made, the problems to be solved, can be brought to the Karmic Spread, because all your questions relate to your progress on the path...and the path is your evolution of consciousness.

At various speeds we are all waking up to the reality of what we really are. Modern physicists are now finally saying and proving what metaphysicians have always known: Everything is Energy! I believe that the Tarot, both Major and Minor Arcana, was conceived with this knowledge of "all is energy" in mind.

The two Arcana can be seen to be energy patterns. They are actually sine curves, visibly pulsing to numerous rhythms that you can study in their symbology and that give valuable information to the meanings of the individual cards while suggesting a new layout for their interpretation, the Karmic Spread. In addition, the structure of each of the Arcana lends itself to the definition of the other. This becomes very clear later, in the explanation of how the Karmic Spread works, for the spread is literally a graphic grid of the interaction of the two Arcana.

There have been several workable concepts of the Major Arcana as symbolic of your path through life, your evolution of consciousness.[3] What has not been recognized until now is that the Minor Arcana, too, are directly involved with this path, this evolution of consciousness, and not simply as characters and events on the path.

ENDNOTES

1. The premise here is that you are dealing with individual karma, but part of that individual karma includes aspects of the groups into which you were born. The requirements of your group karma are internalized as part of your individual package in the Karmic Contract.

2. Read the definition of position 15 in the Karmic Spread and of card 15, The Devil, in the Major Arcana to see this phenomenon of duality at work in the Tarot.

3. Here are three examples of studies on the journey through the Major Arcana:

    A. Juliet Sharman-Burke, *The Complete Book of Tarot* (New York: St. Martin's Press, 1985).

    B. Liz Greene, Juliet Sharman-Burke, and Tricia Newell, *The Mythic Tarot* (New York: Simon & Schuster, 1986).

    C. Clifford Bias, ed., *The Way Back* (York Beach, ME: Samuel Weiser, 1985).

CHAPTER THREE

The Karmic Spread

HOW THE MAJOR AND MINOR ARCANA INTERACT WITH EACH OTHER

The Karmic Spread is a structure that accommodates and uses information generated by the karma at work in an individual's lifetime. The two Arcana uniquely interact to reveal four aspects of the Self, moving through seven Stages of life. The Karmic Spread represents the full range of possibilities in a lifetime. This spread is shown as Chart 1 and Chart 1A, at the end of this Chapter.

The spread has twenty-two positions that can contain very specific messages. It has new meanings for all of the cards and, more importantly, ways of deriving meanings.

The Karmic Spread has four horizontal rows and seven vertical columns, but because of the unique function of the six "swing" positions, the number of positions is twenty-two, not twenty-eight. The nature and function of the "swing" positions are a key part of the magic in the Karmic Spread.

THE SEVEN STAGES OF THE EVOLUTION OF CONSCIOUSNESS

These seven vertical sub-divisions, called columns, in the Karmic Spread include the twenty-two positions, which represent the way-stations on your path of evolving consciousness. The meanings assigned to these positions correspond to the Major Arcana and are in agreement with the order ascribed to Arthur Edward Waite.[1]

But the greater power of these positions comes from the impact on them of the Minor Arcana, which contain a complete profile of your being—your physical, emotional, mental, and spiritual selves. You can see these four aspects of yourself projected across the seven symbolic Stages of your lifetime. These four Planes in the Karmic Spread are generated by the same energy that forms the four suits of the Minor Arcana; i.e., the physical (Pentacles), the emotional (Cups), the mental (Swords), and the spiritual (Wands).

In the Karmic Spread the term "Karmic Contract" refers to a profile created by the first four cards, one each at the Physical, Emotional, Mental, and Spiritual Planes (positions 1 through 4). This is your selected package of "givens" at the time of your birth.

READINGS WITH THE KARMIC SPREAD

Readings are a result of the interaction of the cards, the spread, and the reader. Readers bring a double aspect to the situation. First is their objective knowledge of the meanings of the cards and positions. Second is their intuitive ability to derive the specific meanings of those cards on those positions at this one never-to-be-repeated point in time. While Karmic Tarot cannot improve on the intuitive ability of the reader, it does give the reader an excellent easy-to-learn system for learning the Tarot.

The cards and the positions are memory devices, triggers for messages to the reader. The stronger the spread and the greater the reader's pre-knowledge of the cards and positions, the more opportunity there is for a more specific, helpful reading.

The Tarot is both rational and intuitive. It links the mental and spiritual worlds and operates under the rules of both at the same time, just as we do.[2]

Most Tarot systems are based on memorizing, similar to the memory systems in various religions and other disciplines in which large amounts of information need to be routinely accessed. The two most common examples of these are prayer beads, like the Catholic Rosary and the Sufi *Taspi*.

In Karmic Tarot it is not necessary to memorize the abstract meanings of seemingly unrelated bits of information. There is an immediately apparent logic to the organization of the spread, i.e., to the grid of interaction between the four Planes of the Self and the seven Stages of Life. So, once you understand the four-fold profile of the Self (the four Planes) and the seven Stages of Life (the seven Stages of the evolution of consciousness), you have a ready-made reference system that yields over 3,000 meanings that you don't have to memorize.[3] More importantly, while this system does offer up immediate and obvious archetypal meanings, it is an open system that continues to suggest more possibilities every time it is accessed.

The Karmic Spread enables you to use the Tarot for questions about straight-forward everyday problems like decision-making, relationships, or work, as well as about your deepest psychological and philosophical concerns. And this spread is particularly well-suited to defining the questions themselves. That is important, because often you just *know* something isn't quite right but have no clue to what's wrong—just a feeling that things could be a lot better. Often, the solution to the problem appears with the definition of the question. The answer then lies in realizing what the question is.

The Karmic Spread provides a layout that is meant to be interpreted on two levels. The seven columns are to be read as Stages of both consciousness and time. The Stages of evolving Consciousness emphasize the karmic progress on your life path. The Stages in Time emphasize the meter of real time to which we march.

STAGE	CONSCIOUSNESS	TIME
Stage One	Physical	At Birth
Stage Two	Emotional	Early Childhood
Stage Three	Mental	Recent Past
Stage Four	Spiritual (Awakening)	Present
Stage Five	Higher Mental	Near Future
Stage Six	Higher Emotional	Mid-Future
Stage Seven	Higher Physical	Long-term Future

The TIME column shown above spans the entire lifetime from birth to death. However, as you will see later in this book, you may use the spread for other time spans—seven years, seven months, or seven days, for example—but in every case Stage Four remains the present moment; i.e., the time of the reading. Notice also that this always coincides with Spiritual Awakening. A reading brings you the information that you have been missing through other means, and as such is a centering process awakening you to your full potential.

DIVINATION—WHAT IT IS; WHAT IT ISN'T

Time itself is a duality. Your Present is the meeting point of what we call your Past and your Future. The Present itself can be seen to be the mid-point of an infinitely large Present and an infinitely small Present. At its infinitely small end, what you are about to say becomes what you have just finished saying. At this extreme, there is no present moment at all, only the future becoming the past. But at its infinitely large end, the present is so big that it includes all of your past and all of your future. At the extremes, that even includes all of your past lives and all of your future incarnations. When the present moment pulses between its extremes of infinitely small and infinitely large, the reading glimpses the future.

But here again is the magic of paradox, for the future the reader sees is not a predestined fait accompli without free will. The future it sees is dependent on the present moment, on your free will and your sincere desire to maximize your life potential.

THE CHARTS OF THE KARMIC SPREAD POSITIONS

Chart 1 shows the Karmic Spread positions with the twenty-two governing Major Arcana in place. This is the pattern shown on the cover of this book. In a reading, of course, there will be twenty-two cards chosen at random from the entire pack of seventy-eight cards. They will be the cards looking up at you from this pattern, not the Major Arcana as shown here. Meditate on this chart to plant firmly the picture of the Major Arcana marching in this sine curve pattern across the page, for they are the clues to the meanings of the positions in the Spread. Remember that the Major Arcana derive their meanings from the same place that the positions of the Spread derive theirs.

Chart 1A shows the Karmic Spread positions with the Major Arcana cards removed. Each position is noted with its functional meaning, as well as the appropriate governing Major Arcana card. When doing a layout using the Karmic Spread, each of the twenty-two cards selected at random is interpreted as the response to the meaning of its respective position.

Chart 1
THE KARMIC SPREAD POSITIONS
(With Governing Major Arcana Cards)

The Seven Stages on Two Levels: In Time and in the Evolution of Consciousness

Note: The Major Arcana are shown here in their related spread positions as they derive their meaning from this interaction of horizontal planes and vertical stages just as does the spread itself, and they govern the respective positions. The meanings of the positions themselves are summarized in Chart 1A. When you do a reading, you will select twenty-two cards at random from the deck of seventy-eight cards and arrange them in this order beginning at position one and ending at position twenty-two.

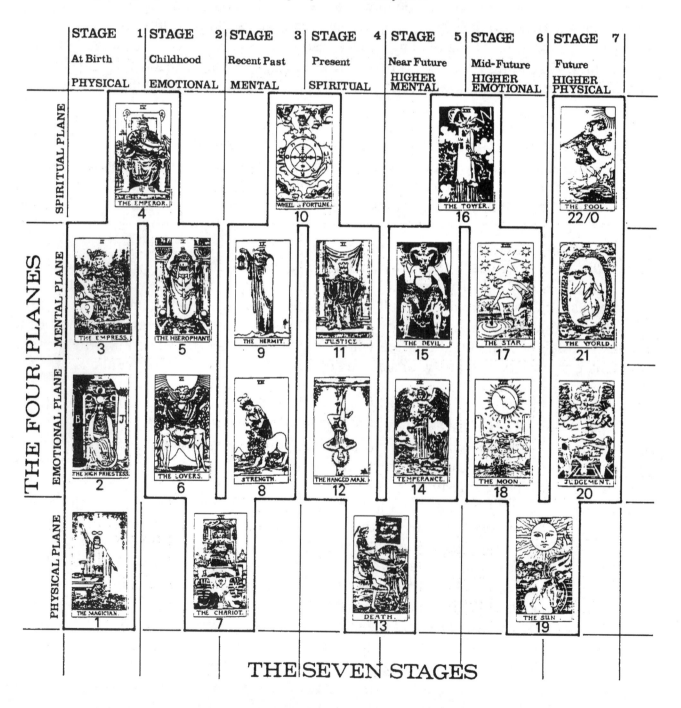

Chart 1A
THE KARMIC SPREAD POSITIONS
(With Position Meanings)

The Seven Stages on Two Levels: In Time and in the Evolution of Consciousness

Note: With your pattern of twenty-two randomly selected cards laid out in the pattern shown below, you may proceed to do your reading, interpreting the meaning of the card itself superimposed on the meaning of the position in the layout. Sample interpretations of all of the cards in each of these positions are given in Chapter Seven (Major Arcana) and in Chapter Eight (Minor Arcana).

	STAGE 1 At Birth PHYSICAL	STAGE 2 Childhood EMOTIONAL	STAGE 3 Recent Past MENTAL	STAGE 4 Present SPIRITUAL	STAGE 5 Near Future HIGHER MENTAL	STAGE 6 Mid-Future HIGHER EMOTIONAL	STAGE 7 Future HIGHER PHYSICAL
SPIRITUAL PLANE	4 governed by THE EMPEROR — Spiritual Givens, Life Purpose		10 governed by WHEEL OF FORTUNE — Central Message, Theme of Reading		16 governed by THE TOWER — Next Lesson, Grace of God		22/0 governed by THE FOOL — Soul's Fulfillment, Evaluation
MENTAL PLANE	3 governed by THE EMPRESS — Mental Givens, Intellectual Predisposition	5 governed by THE HIEROPHANT — Systems Born Into, Life Purpose	9 governed by THE HERMIT — Belief System, Basis for Decisions	11 governed by JUSTICE — State/Content of Mind, Plans	15 governed by THE DEVIL — Temptation/Challenge, Fears, Near Future	17 governed by THE STAR — Aspirations of Ego, Goals, Maximum Expectations	21 governed by THE WORLD — Ego's Fulfillment, Evaluation
EMOTIONAL PLANE	2 governed by THE HIGH PRIESTESS — Emotional Givens, Out of the Mother	6 governed by THE LOVERS — Emotional Tapes, Basis for Relating	8 governed by STRENGTH — Emotional Resources, Energy	12 governed by THE HANGED MAN — State of Emotions, Subconscious	14 governed by TEMPERANCE — Emotional Test, Near Future	18 governed by THE MOON — Aspirations of Heart, Compassion	20 governed by JUDGEMENT — Heart's Fulfillment, Evaluation
PHYSICAL PLANE	1 governed by THE MAGICIAN — Physical Givens, Out of the Father	7 governed by THE CHARIOT — Physical Resources, Means to Achieve		13 governed by DEATH — Physical Situation, Hard Reality		19 governed by THE SUN — Material Fulfillment, Evaluation	

THE FOUR PLANES

THE SEVEN STAGES

ENDNOTES

1. Arthur Edward Waite, *The Pictorial Key to the Tarot* (Secaucus, NJ: Citadel Press, 1959).

2. Ken Wilber, *Eye to Eye: The Quest for the New Paradigm* (Garden City, NY: Anchor Press/Doubleday, 1983). Wilber stresses the importance of understanding that the various planes of self-experience (principally for him, spirit, mind, and matter) operate accordingly to different realities, and that many of our problems derive from unknowingly applying the laws of one plane to another. The Tarot knows this and keeps things separate in the four Minor Arcana suits.

3. See Chapter Ten for the 3432 System, an example of the function of a memory system for the Tarot.

CHAPTER FOUR

The Four Rows of the Karmic Spread: The Planes

This chapter explains the derivation and meaning of the four horizontal rows of the Karmic Spread, which are called *Planes*. Each of these Planes is correlated to several different frames of reference, so that you can understand it fully. Chart 2 shows these correlations, at the end of this Chapter.

CORRELATION OF THE PLANES WITH THE FOUR ASPECTS OF SELF

These four horizontal rows, the Planes, represent the four aspects of the personality or self commonly referred to in metaphysical and yogic literature and in modern psychology, beginning with such concepts as Abraham Maslow's "hierarchy of needs." These Planes are:

Plane One:	The Physical
Plane Two:	The Emotional
Plane Three:	The Mental
Plane Four:	The Spiritual

Life's progression can be seen as from the lowest to the highest: "...matter is spirit at the lowest point of its cyclic activity, and spirit is matter at its highest."[1] At the root of it all is your physical existence, your biological package. This is the level of concern with being and staying alive. Herein lies the basic fear of death translated into the urge for survival. This is the source of all fears. Once you become secure enough about your physical self, you can begin relating to things outside the self, and the Emotional Plane starts to open up and develop. Here you see your progress with love and relationships. Only when the

Physical and Emotional Planes are reasonably developed does the Mental Plane come into its own. And with the conceptual abilities of the Mental Plane you are then capable of dealing on the Spiritual Plane.

CORRELATION OF THE PLANES WITH THE FOUR LEVELS OF THRUST

At the bottom, on Plane One, are the instincts that are part of your selection package at birth. They are fixed and operate below your conscious awareness, i.e., below the Mental Plane. How you react to and with your instincts is a function of the next three, higher, levels.

At the top, on Plane Four, are the insights, the intuitive communication with God which comes to you every moment of every day of your life. This is the Spiritual Plane.

CORRELATION OF THE PLANES WITH THE FOUR MINOR ARCANA SUITS

The four Planes are respectively affected by the four suits of the Minor Arcana in the spread.

Pentacles:	Activity in the "lowest" Plane, the Physical
Cups:	Activity in the second Plane, the Emotional
Swords:	Activity in the third Plane, the Mental
Wands:	Activity in the "highest" Plane, the Spiritual

There are many other alignments of the four suits and their characteristics. This alignment is unique, particularly in the context of this spread and in how the Minor Arcana relates to the concept of your evolution of consciousness.

CORRELATION OF THE PLANES WITH THE OTHER FOUR ELEMENTS

Plane One:	Pentacles = Earth
Plane Two:	Cups = Water
Plane Three:	Swords = Air
Plane Four:	Wands = Fire

The Earth is at the bottom. Water sits on the Earth. Air is above the Water and Earth. Fire is above all, as that which transforms the physical reality of the lower three—Fire as the transformative power of the Spirit.

CORRELATION OF THE PLANES WITH THE ARISTOTELIAN CONCEPTS

Aristotle said that all that exists can be divided into four categories or conditions. These distinctions support and further divide the four Planes:

Plane One:	Fixity represents the Material, the matter of the thing.
Plane Two:	Liquidity represents the Efficient, action external to the thing, the start of the process.

Plane Three: Fluidity represents the Formal, forming activity, development and differentiation, the cause of the growth of things.

Plane Four: Radiation represents the Final, the design of the thing, consciously held in mind through thought.

CORRELATION OF THE PLANES WITH ELEMENTARY PHYSICS

Plane One: Solids

Plane Two: Liquids

Plane Three: Gases

Plane Four: Ether

CORRELATION OF THE PLANES WITH PSYCHOLOGY

Plane One: Pre-Conscious

Plane Two: Subconscious

Plane Three: Conscious

Plane Four: Super-Conscious

CORRELATION OF THE PLANES WITH NUMEROLOGY

Plane One: Carries all the power and significance of the number One.

Plane Two: Carries all the power and significance of the number Two.

Plane Three: Carries all the power and significance of the number Three.

Plane Four: Carries all the power and significance of the number Four.[2]

CORRELATION OF THE PLANES WITH COLOR

Plane One: Influenced by Green.

Plane Two: Influenced by Blue.

Plane Three: Influenced by Yellow.

Plane Four: Influenced by Red.

CORRELATION OF THE PLANES WITH VARIOUS DUALITIES

RELATED ALTERNATING ENERGIES

Plane One/Physical/Pentacles: Rational

Plane Two/Emotional/Cups: A-Rational

Plane Three/Mental/Swords: Rational

Plane Four/Spiritual/Wands: A-Rational

The same applies for masculine/feminine, extrovert/introvert, and positive/negative, and you can make quite a long list, to some advantage.

CORRELATION OF THE PLANES WITH ROSICRUCIAN

The "Rosicrucian Cosmo-Conception,"[3] within its presentation of the complex order of the world, speaks of the following four-fold aspect: Physical World, World of Desire, World of Thought, and Pure Spirit.

CORRELATION OF THE PLANES
WITH OLDER CHANNELED MATERIAL ABOUT THE ANCIENT RACES

Lemurian Man was of the Physical polarization, awakening to the Emotional. Atlantean Man was of Emotional polarization, awakening to the Mental. Aryan Man (our present civilization) is of Mental polarization, awakening to the Intuitive/Spiritual.[4]

CORRELATION OF THE PLANES WITH DISCIPLINES OF YOGA

There are numerous and subtle distinctions among the many yogic disciplines. Of note are four major types of yoga which parallel the four Planes and further define them. These are: Hatha Yoga, which is predominantly physical; Bhakti Yoga, which is devotional; Raja Yoga, which is mental; and Agni Yoga, which is spiritual.

CORRELATION OF THE PLANES WITH OTHER TAROT SYSTEMS

Paul Foster Case, in *The Tarot: A Key to the Wisdom of the Ages*, lists the elements as follows: Earth = Material World, Water = Creative World, Air = Formative World, Fire = Archetypal World.[5] Eliphas Lèvi (real name, Alphonse Louis Constant) uses the same order as *Karmic Tarot* in his explanations of the elements and suits,[6] as does Eden Gray.[7]

A SUMMARY DEFINITION OF THE FOUR PLANES

To help you keep the concepts of these planes in mind, here is a summary taken from Matthew Oliver Goodwin's Numerology: The Complete Guide, Volume I:[8]

> The Physical component is represented by the body, deals with the senses. The Physical viewpoint is concerned with tangible form, material matters, practical affairs, physical adventures.

> The Mental component is represented by the mind, deals with thinking, reasoning, logic, facts. The Mental viewpoint is concerned with mental activities, business enterprises, political affairs.

> The Emotional component is represented by the emotions, deals with feelings. The Emotional viewpoint is concerned with feelings, affection, artistic endeavors, creativity, imagination.

The Intuitive Component is represented by the spirit, deals with inner awareness. The Intuitive viewpoint is concerned with sensitivity to non-material experience—spiritual, religious, psychic, metaphysical—and ultimate wisdom.

EVOLUTION OF SELF ALONG EACH OF THE FOUR PLANES

Although your evolution of consciousness follows the progression of positions 1 to 22 by stepping up and down through the four Planes, you can also look separately at the progression along each of the Planes. This gives you a clear look at your progress physically, emotionally, mentally, and spiritually. It helps you know what to look for in your problem-solving. This is done in detail in the next chapter. As you study these progressions, it will help to remember that:

Our emotions are how we come to grips with the relationship between two or more things on the physical plane.

Our mentality is how we come to grips with the relationship between two or more things on the emotional plane.

Our spirituality is how we come to grips with the relationship between two or more things on the mental plane.

Chart 2
CORRELATIONS OF THE FOUR HORIZONTAL ROWS: THE PLANES

	ASPECT OF SELF	QUALITY	MINOR ARCANA SUIT	ELEMENT	ARISTOTLE	PHYSICS	PSY-CHOLOGY		
PLANE FOUR	SPIRITUAL	INTUITION	WANDS	FIRE	RADIATION	ETHER	SUPER-CONSCIOUS		−
PLANE THREE	MENTAL	THOUGHT	SWORDS	AIR	FLUIDITY	GASES	CONSCIOUS		+
PLANE TWO	EMOTIONAL	FEELING	CUPS	WATER	LIQUIDITY	LIQUIDS	SUB-CONSCIOUS		−
PLANE ONE	PHYSICAL	INSTINCT	PENTACLES	EARTH	FIXITY	SOLIDS	PRE-CONSCIOUS		+

ENDNOTES

1. Aart Jurriaanse, *Bridges: Basic Studies in Esoteric Philosophy* (Somerset West, Capetown, South Africa: Sun Center School of Esoteric Philosophy, 1981), p.55.

2. See Chapter Eight: the Pips, for the effects of numerology.

3. Max Heindel, *The Rosicrucian Cosmo-Conception*, 28th ed. (Pasadena, CA: Wood & Jones, Printers/Lithographers, 1977).

4. See Chapter Five: correlation with the concept of the Seven Root Races held by the Theosophists, for a fuller explanation of the concept of the Ancient Races.

5. Paul Foster Case, *The Tarot: A Key to the Wisdom of the Ages* (Richmond, VA: Macoy Publishing Co., 1947).

6. Eliphas Lévi, *Dogme et rituel de la haute magie* (Paris: Germer Baillière, 1856).

7. Eden Gray, *The Tarot Revealed* (New York: Crown, 1971).

8. Matthew Oliver Goodwin, *Numerology: The Complete Guide, Vol. 1* (North Hollywood, CA: Newcastle Publishing Co., 1981), pp. 173-174.

CHAPTER FIVE

The Seven Columns of the Karmic Spread: The Stages

This chapter explains the derivation and meaning of the seven columns of the Karmic Spread, which are called Stages. If any of the correlations seem confusing, concentrate only on the ones you understand somewhat; the others can follow later. Each of the correlations helps define the others in the long run. Part of their value is that they are different ways of saying the same thing. Chart Three summarizes these correlations.

THE MEETING OF EAST AND WEST

The seven vertical columns represent the seven Stages in the evolution of our consciousness. With this pattern of the four-fold self (Physical, Emotional, Mental, Spiritual) moving through seven Stages of consciousness, we can see the Tarot in relation to the wide body of thought, Eastern and Western, that addresses consciousness and the development of mankind. This body of knowledge embraces mythology, religion, and philosophy.

Of particular significance in bringing rich meaning to the seven Stages of the spread is the work of transpersonal psychologists like Jacquelyn Small and Ken Wilber.[1] Much of the terminology used for discussing the seven Stages is based on Jacquelyn Small's book, *Transformers/Personal Transformation: The Way Through.*[2]

Equally important in understanding these Stages are the Eastern schools of thought, where the levels of consciousness are symbolized by the seven chakras and the *kundulini*.

You can observe the meshing of Western and Eastern philosophies in many fields. For example, the importance of the number seven in man's development has been recorded by Western metaphysicians for centuries, and that information has also directly or indirectly come out of the Far East, in particular the Himalayas, in the works of people like H. P. Blavatsky and Alice Bailey. Metaphysicians feel that the schism between East and West never materialized.

Chart 3
CORRELATIONS OF THE SEVEN VERTICAL COLUMNS: THE STAGES

INFLUENCES ON STAGES	STAGE ONE	STAGE TWO	STAGE THREE	STAGE FOUR	STAGE FIVE	STAGE SIX	STAGE SEVEN
TIME FACTOR	AT BIRTH (KARMIC CONTRACT)	EARLY CHILDHOOD	RECENT PAST	PRESENT	NEAR FUTURE	MID-FUTURE	LONG-TERM FUTURE
LEVEL OF CONSCIOUSNESS	PHYSICAL	EMOTIONAL	MENTAL	SPIRITUAL	HIGHER MENTAL	HIGHER EMOTIONAL	HIGHER PHYSICAL
MINOR ARCANA SUITS	PENTACLES	CUPS	SWORDS	WANDS	SWORDS	CUPS	PENTACLES
COLOR	GREEN	BLUE	YELLOW	RED	ORANGE	INDIGO	PURPLE
SOUND	DO	RE	ME	FA	SO	LA	TI
DAYS OF WEEK	MONDAY MOON	TUESDAY MARS	WEDNESDAY MERCURY	THURSDAY JUPITER	FRIDAY VENUS	SATURDAY SATURN	SUNDAY SUN
CHAKRAS	ROOT/ANAL	GENITAL	SOLAR PLEXUS	HEART	THROAT	THIRD EYE	CROWN
SENSES	HEARING	TOUCH	SIGHT	TASTE	SMELL	ASTRAL/MENTAL	POST-MENTAL
PHILOSOPHIES	MARX	FREUD	SOCRATES DARWIN	PATANJALI RAM DASS WILBER	EINSTEIN BOHM	MOSES ST. PAUL KIRPAL SINGH	KRISHNA BUDDHA CHRIST MUHAMMAD
ELEMENT	EARTH	WATER	AIR	FIRE	AIR	WATER	EARTH
	1 +	2 −	3 +	4 −	5 +	6 −	7 +

THE SEVEN STAGES AND THEIR TWO LEVELS

Each of the seven Stages operates on two different levels. First, each represents a time period in the individual's life. Second, each Stage represents a phase of their evolving consciousness. It is this second level that interacts most richly with the Planes to give us the meanings of the twenty-two positions in the spread.

TIME FACTORS OF THE SEVEN STAGES

Stage One:	At Birth (the Karmic Contract)
Stage Two:	Early Childhood
Stage Three:	Recent Past
Stage Four:	Present
Stage Five:	Near Future
Stage Six:	Mid-Future
Stage Seven:	Long-Term Future

At the beginning of any reading, six of the time periods may be adjusted to represent any desired units of time. However, Stage Four must always represent the Present. A valuable alternative is the seven-month period (read with the present month plus three months preceding and three months following). Greater time specificity is available using a seven-week or seven-day period.

ASPECTS OF CONSCIOUSNESS FOR THE SEVEN STAGES

Stage One:	Physical
Stage Two:	Emotional
Stage Three:	Mental
Stage Four:	Spiritual (the Awakening)
Stage Five:	Higher Mental
Stage Six:	Higher Emotional
Stage Seven:	Higher Physical

A detailed set of descriptions of the aspects of consciousness for the seven Stages is shown on Chart 3A. These definitions are from Jacquelyn Small's book, *Transformers/Personal Transformation: The Way Through*. Chart 3A is a condensation of Table 1 from that book: "A Model of Human Nature."

Chart 3A
ASPECTS OF CONSCIOUSNESS FOR THE SEVEN STAGES

	STAGE ONE Physical	STAGE TWO Emotion'	STAGE THREE Mental	STAGE FOUR Spiritual	STAGE FIVE Higher Mental	STAGE SIX Higher Emotion'	STAGE SEVEN Higher Physical
Force	WILL TO LIVE	WILL TO FEEL	WILL TO KNOW	AWAKEN-ING	LOVE OF TRUTH	LOVE OF LIFE	LOVE OF GOD (SELF)
Quality	SELF-PRESER-VATION	SELF-GRATIFI-CATION	SELF-DEFINI-TION	HARMO-NIZING HIGHER WITH LOWER NATURE	COMPRE-HENSION/ AUTHEN-TIC EXPRES-SION	INTUITION/ ALTRUISM	SELF-MASTERY
Level of Consciousness	ORDER/ INSTINCT	PLEASURE DEVOTION	ANALYSIS/ COMPARI-SON	HARMONY THROUGH CONFLICT	ACTIVE INTELLI-GENCE	LOVE/ WISDOM	LOVE/ WILL
Basic Urge	FEAR	PASSION	IDENTITY SEEKING	ACCEPT-ANCE/ HARMON-IZING	UNDER-STANDING	COMPAS-SION	UNITY
Pitfall	ISOLATION	DUALITY	FRAGMEN-TATION	ATTACH-MENT TO CONFLICT	ABSTRAC-TION	OVER IDEN-TIFICATION WITH SUFFER-ING	INDISCRI-MINATE USE OF WILL
Mastery	RIGHT ACTION	RIGHT FEELING	RIGHT THOUGHT	SELF-CREATION	ILLUMINA-TION	REVELA-TION	TRANS-FORMA-TION

CORRELATION OF THE SEVEN STAGES WITH THE MINOR ARCANA SUITS

Stage One: Influenced by Pentacles

Stage Two: Influenced by Cups

Stage Three: Influenced by Swords

Stage Four: Influenced by Wands

Stage Five: Influenced by Swords

Stage Six: Influenced by Cups

Stage Seven: Influenced by Pentacles

In this evolving sequence from Pentacles to Wands and back to Pentacles again, you can see the energy at work in the Tarot—a polarity, a pulse, a rhythm; the concept of involution/evolution; the spiral (everything returns to its beginnings, but at a different, higher level). You begin at the Physical and it is to the Physical that you return. But you are not the same, you are transformed. This pulse can be seen in the pattern of the twenty-two Major Arcana cards stepping up and down through the four horizontal Planes of life experiences (see Charts 1 and 1A).

CORRELATION OF THE MAJOR ARCANA WITH THE SEVEN STAGES

The twenty-two Major Arcana move through the four Planes in seven Stages. Each of the seven Stages has a four-step cycle. The fourth step in each cycle serves a dual function as the end of one Stage and the beginning of the next. (In numerology this is acknowledged as a natural function of the number four).[3]

In Stage One: The positions are 1, 2, 3, and 4, with 4 being the resolution of the series 1 to 3. However, besides doing duty as the end of Stage One, position 4 is also the beginning of Stage Two.

In Stage Two: The positions are 4, 5, 6, and 7, with 7 as the resolution of the series of 4 to 6; and also the beginning of Stage Three.

This phenomenon is true through all seven Stages:

Position 10 ends Stage Three and begins Stage Four.

Position 13 ends Stage Four and begins Stage Five.

Position 16 ends Stage Five and begins Stage Six.

Position 19 ends Stage Six and begins Stage Seven.

Position 22 is both the end and a beginning. It is 22 as the end of Stage Seven and as such it represents the end of the present lifetime.[4] However, as 0 it represents the beginning of the next lifetime. The Fool becomes the Magician in that next lifetime.[5]

PROGRESSION OF THE POSITIONS IN EACH OF THE SEVEN STAGES

Stage One: Magician(1) ↔ High Priestess(2) ↔ Empress(3) ↔ Emperor(4)

Stage Two: Emperor(4) ↔ Hierophant(5) ↔ Lovers(6) ↔ Chariot(7)

Stage Three: Chariot(7) ↔ Strength(8) ↔ Hermit(9) ↔ Wheel(10)

Stage Four: Wheel(10) ↔ Justice(11) ↔ Hanged Man(12) ↔ Death(13)

Stage Five: Death(13) ↔ Temperance(14) ↔ Devil(15) ↔ Tower(16)

Stage Six: Tower(16) ↔ Star(17) ↔ Moon(18) ↔ Sun(19)

Stage Seven: Sun(19) ↔ Judgement(20) ↔ World(21) ↔ Fool(0/22)

THE SWING CARD POSITIONS

The "swing" card positions are: Emperor(4), Chariot(7), Wheel(10), Death(13), Tower(16), Sun(19). They represent the swing from the end of one cycle to the beginning of the next.

CORRELATION OF THE SEVEN STAGES WITH COLOR AND SOUND

STAGE	COLOR	SOUND (MUSICAL SCALE)
Stage One:	Green	Do
Stage Two:	Blue	Re
Stage Three	Yellow	Mi
Stage Four	Red	Fa
Stage Five	Orange	So
Stage Six	Indigo	La
Stage Seven	Purple	Ti

If you are already a student of the characteristics and effects of color, you can readily apply your understanding to the seven Stages. Otherwise, I encourage you to study the metaphysics of color as a top priority. The sources referenced in Chart 3B would be a good place to start.

In Western music, compositions are based on the diatonic, or whole-tone scale of seven notes. In Indian music there are also seven basic tones called *suars* which expand to twenty-two basic intervals called *shrutis* in their "octave."[6] Our seven tones expand to twelve tones called the chromatic scale. The study of sound readily augments the study of Tarot in relation to the evolution of consciousness. Remember the many theories and mythologies relating the birth of creation to the one Sound—the sound of origin behind the "om." Remember also the idea that when sound as speech first became symbolized and gave us the earliest alphabets, symbology itself was born; what we know today as archetypes, such as those classically preserved in the Tarot, are the logical evolution of that early core of symbols.

There seems to be little agreement in assigning the aspects of color and sound to the seven Stages. See Chart 3B for a listing of various opinions.

CORRELATION OF THE SEVEN STAGES WITH THE CONCEPTS OF THE HIERARCHY

The idea of the spiritual Hierarchy has been a question which has always been discussed in all ages, and especially at this time, when people have their conceptions much more separate and different along spiritual lines than before. The spiritual Hierarchy is not man's imagination; it is not only a poetic idea, but it is as real as one's own being.[12]

Chart 3B
COLOR AND SOUND FOR THE SEVEN STAGES

		STAGE 1 Physical	STAGE 2 Emotional	STAGE 3 Mental	STAGE 4 Spiritual	STAGE 5 Higher Mental	STAGE 6 Higher Emotional	STAGE 7 Higher Physical
SOUND	Allan Bennett[7]	C	D	E	F	G	A	B
COLOR		RED	ORANGE	YELLOW	GREEN-YELLOW	BLUE-GREEN	INDIGO	MAGENTA
SOUND	William David[8]	C	G	E	D	B	F	A
COLOR		RED	ORANGE	YELLOW	GREEN	BLUE	PURPLE-VIOLET	INDIGO
SOUND	Alex Jones[9]	C	D	E	F	G	A	B
COLOR		RED	ORANGE	YELLOW	GREEN	BLUE	INDIGO	PURPLE-VIOLET
SOUND	Parama-hansa Yogananda[10]	C	D	E	F	G	A	B
COLOR		GREEN	RED	GOLD	YELLOW-WHITE	BLACK	YELLOW	ALL COLORS
SOUND	H.P. Blavatsky[11]	C	D	E	F	G	A	B
COLOR		RED	ORANGE	YELLOW	GREEN	BLUE	INDIGO	VIOLET
COLOR	Lammey	GREEN	BLUE	YELLOW	RED	ORANGE	INDIGO	PURPLE
		At Birth	Early Childhood	Recent Past	Present	Near Future	Mid-Future	Long-term Future

An excellent compilation of the content of channeled information from the various members of the Hierarchy can be found in the book *Bridges,* by Aart Jurriaanse. Belief in the Hierarchy and the work of its Masters is fundamental to the work of many metaphysicians. This concept is worth exploring more fully. Here is a brief excerpt from Bridges:

> The Masters are members of that group of "illumined minds" which is guided by love and understanding, and by deep compassion and inclusiveness towards humanity. They are striving towards a comprehension and translation of the Divine Purpose, and are illumined by knowledge of the Plan; they are also characterized by a readiness to sacrifice their own immediate spiritual progress if thereby they can assist humanity in its upward struggle.[13]

THE HIERARCHY AND THEIR COLORS

STAGE	COLOR		MASTER
Stage One:	Green	=	Dwal Khul
Stage Two:	Blue	=	Kuthumi (Koot Hoomi)
Stage Three:	Yellow	=	Serapis

Stage Four:	Red	=	El Morya
Stage Five:	Orange	=	Hilarion
Stage Six:	Indigo	=	St. Germain
Stage Seven:	Purple	=	Jesus

CORRELATION OF THE SEVEN STAGES WITH THE SEVEN DAYS OF THE WEEK

STAGE	DAY	ORIGIN
Stage One:	Monday	from the Moon
Stage Two:	Tuesday	from Mars
Stage Three:	Wednesday	from Mercury
Stage Four:	Thursday	from Jupiter
Stage Five:	Friday	from Venus
Stage Six:	Saturday	from Saturn
Stage Seven:	Sunday	from the Sun

CORRELATION OF THE SEVEN STAGES WITH PHILOSOPHY

These comparisons were inspired by two of Ken Wilber's books, *Up from Eden and A Sociable God*. In *Up from Eden* he says: "...the eventual core of a truly unified, critical sociological theory might best be constructed around a detailed, multi-disciplinary analysis of the developmental-logic and hierarchic levels of exchange that constitute the human compound individual."[14] This reference to a "hierarchic level of exchange" introduces a discourse on the contributions of major thinkers who have strategically affected the course of events in world history, and places these thinkers in levels that roughly parallel the seven Stages in the Karmic Spread. This provides another valuable source of information for a further definition of these Stages.

Again quoting from *Up from Eden*:

> (1) The physical-uroboric level of material exchange, whose paradigm is food consumption and food extraction from the natural environment; whose sphere is that of manual labor (or technological labor); and whose archetypal analyst is Marx. (2) The emotional-typhonic level of pranic exchange, whose paradigm is breath and sex; whose sphere is that of emotional intercourse, from feeling to sex to power; and whose archetypal analyst is Freud. (3) The verbal-membership level of symbolic exchange, whose paradigm is discourse (language); whose sphere is that of communication (and the beginning of praxis); and whose archetypal analyst is Socrates. (4) The mental-egoic level of the mutual exchange of self-recognition, whose paradigm is self-consciousness or self-reflection; whose sphere is that of mutual personal recognition and esteem (the culmination of praxis); and whose archetypal analyst is Hegel (in his writings on master/slave relationship). (5) The psychic level of intuitive exchange,

whose paradigm is *siddhi* (or psychic intuition in its broadest sense); whose sphere is shamanistic *kundulini;* and whose archetypal analyst is Patanjali. (6) The subtle level of God-Light whose sphere is subtle Heaven (Brahma-Loka); and whose archetypal analyst is Kirpal Singh. (7) The causal level of ultimate exchange, whose paradigm is radical absorption in and as the Uncreate (*samadhi*); whose sphere is the Void-Godhead; and whose archetypal analyst is Buddha/Krishna/Christ.[15]

Taking the above analysis from Wilber, with the exchange of levels 4 and 5 (the mind acted upon by the spirit becomes the enlightened higher mind), we can apply the best thinking in history to our seven Stages. You are encouraged to extrapolate on this brief outline:

Stage One:	Marx
Stage Two:	Freud
Stage Three:	Socrates/Darwin
Stage Four:	Patanjali/Ram Dass/Wilber
Stage Five:	Einstein/Bohm
Stage Six:	Moses/St. Paul/Kirpal Singh
Stage Seven:	Krishna/Buddha/Christ/Muhammad

CORRELATION OF THE SEVEN STAGES WITH THE CHAKRAS

Stage One:	Root/Anal	=	Self-Preservation (Fear and Paranoia)
Stage Two:	Genital	=	Sensuality and Sexuality
Stage Three:	Solar Plexus	=	Domination and Submission
Stage Four:	Heart	=	Empathy
Stage Five:	Throat	=	Nurturance and Expression
Stage Six:	Third Eye	=	Seat of Intuitive Knowledge
Stage Seven:	Crown	=	Highest State of Consciousness

These attributes for the seven chakras are taken from *Yoga and Psychotherapy* by Swami Rama.[16] There are many subtle variations to the significance of the chakras and the development of the *kundulini*, and all of them can provide insight into the definition of the seven Stages in the Karmic Tarot Spread.

CORRELATION OF THE SEVEN STAGES AND THE MAJOR ARCANA WITH A SUFI STORY

There are numerous examples from the classical literature of many countries that refer to man's development through "seven stages." A beautiful and amazing correlation is found in a Sufi story written in 1899 under the title, "The Mystic Rose from the Garden of the King: A Fragment of the Vision of Sheikh Haji Ibrahim of Kerbela." The author was Sir Fairfax L. Cartwright, who later became British Ambassador to Vienna.

> In my wanderings in the Strange Land, this did I see: A Temple built like a Tower rising to a great height, surrounded at its base by a circular colonnade. Impelled by a desire to learn, I knocked at the Gate of the Temple and prayed for admittance. A venerable old man—the Sage of that Temple—opened the Gate and said to me, "What seekest thou?" I replied, "Knowledge." He said, "Hast thou the strength and determination to climb to the topmost chamber of the Tower?" I said, "The desire have I if thou wilt be my guide to show me the way." Then he stretched out his hand and raised me up, saying: "If thy heart is stout, cross the threshold of the Temple of Human Knowledge." ...The Tower is high and it containeth *seven levels* [italics mine], and on each level are three Chambers and above all lieth one Chamber....[17]

The story goes on to describe the twenty-two chambers, one by one, and they represent explicitly the Major Arcana! Even more interesting is the fact that they follow the order presented in this book, except that the nineteenth chamber is the World and the twenty-first is the Sun, a reversal of the order ascribed by Waite.[18] Chamber one is The Magician and Chamber twenty-two is The Fool.

CORRELATION OF THE SEVEN STAGES WITH SHAKESPEARE

What more pointed example can be imagined than Shakespeare's "Seven Ages of Man" soliloquy from *As You Like It*, Act 2, Scene 7:

All the world's a stage,	
And all the men and women merely players.	
They have their exits and their entrances,	
And one man in his time plays many parts,	
His acts being seven ages. At first the infant,	(Stage 1)
Mewling and puking in the nurse's arms.	
Then the whining schoolboy, with his satchel	(Stage 2)
And shining morning face, creeping like a snail	
Unwillingly to school. And then the lover,	(Stage 3)
Sighing like furnace, with a woeful ballad	
Made to his mistress' eyebrow. Then a soldier,	(Stage 4)
Full of strange oaths and bearded like the pard,	
Jealous in honour, sudden and quick in quarrel,	
Seeking the bubble reputation	
Even in the cannon's mouth. And then the justice,	(Stage 5)
In fair round belly with good capon lin'd,	
With eyes sever and beard of formal cut,	
Full of wise saws and modern instances;	
And so he plays his part. The sixth age shifts	(Stage 6)
Into the lean and slipper'd pantaloon,	
With spectacles on nose and pouch on side;	

His youthful hose, well sav'd, a world too wide
For his shrunk shank; and his big manly voice,
Turning again toward childish treble, pipes
And whistles in his sound. Last scene of all,   (Stage 7)
That ends this strange eventful history,
Is second childishness and mere oblivion,
Sans teeth, sans eyes, sans taste, sans everything.

CORRELATION OF THE SEVEN STAGES WITH THE THEOSOPHICAL CONCEPT OF THE SEVEN ROOT RACES

H. P. Blavatsky, in her monumental work, *The Secret Doctrine*,[19] put forth the concept that mankind is evolving through seven great epochs. The first and second were so long ago, and man so undeveloped, as to be irrelevant to our purpose here. Bur the third epoch is called Lemurian, the fourth, Atlantean, and the fifth, our present age, is called Aryan. The sixth epoch, which we are in the process of entering, is to be called the Aquarian Age. The seventh is yet to be named.

Blavatsky suggests that each of the epochs is intrinsically linked with the external senses: 1 = Hearing, 2 = Touch, 3 = Sight, 4 = Taste, 5 = Smell, The sixth epoch, the Aquarian, will be our Astral/Mental sense; the seventh will be Post-Mental/Spiritual.

We are looking at the developmental evolution of mankind through these seven epochs for their implications to the evolution of consciousness of man in a single lifetime, and as such they will impact our definition of the seven Stages for our Karmic Spread.

Blavatsky also says that each of these seven epochs has seven stages. With that in mind, if we apply the definition of the transpersonal psychologists to these epochs and stages, here's what we get for the period of time we are living in now: Blavatsky says that we are in the third stage of the fifth epoch. In the transpersonal language of Jacquelyn Small, that means that we are in the "Mental Stage of the Higher Mental Epoch." This means that our epoch is operating under the basic *Force* of the Love of Truth; the basic *Quality* of Authentic Expression; the basic *Level of Consciousness* of Active Intelligence; the basic *Urge* for Understanding; the basic *Pitfall* of Abstraction; and the *Mastery* of Illumination. And it means that our specific stage is operating under the basic *Force* of the Will to Know; the *Quality* of Self-Definition; the *Level of Consciousness* of Analysis/Comparison; the basic *Urge* of Identity-Seeking; the *Pitfall* of Fragmentation; and the *Mastery* of Right Thought.

It's interesting to observe that in the Karmic Spread the positions that make up Stage Five are: Death(13), Temperance(14), The Devil(15), and The Tower(16). We will hold the analysis of this series of card positions until Chapter Six.

Yogic tradition also tells us..."that the Grand Cycle of Man's life on the Earth is composed of Seven Cycles, of which we are now living in the third-seventh part of the Fifth Cycle."[20]

ENDNOTES

1. See the following for more on transpersonal psychology:
   A. Ken Wilber, *The Spectrum of Consciousness* (Wheaton, IL: Theosophical Publishing House, 1985).
   B. _____, *Up from Eden* (Boulder, CO: Shambhala, 1981).
   C. _____, *No Boundary* (Boston & London: Shambhala, 1981).
   D. _____, *The Holographic Paradigm* (Boulder, CO & London: Shambhala, 1982).
   E. _____, *Eye to Eye: The Quest for the New Paradigm* (Garden City, NY: Anchor Press/Doubleday, 1983).

2. Jacquelyn Small, *Transformers/Personal Transformation: The Way Through* (Marina del Rey, CA: Devorss, 1982).

3. See Chapter Eight: the Pips, for the effects of numerology.

4. See Chapter Six: analysis of positions up/down each of the four Planes.

5. Ibid.

6. David Tame, *The Secret Power of Music* (New York: Destiny Books, 1984).

7. Proposed originally by Allan Bennett (Frater Iehi Aour), a member of the Golden Dawn, per Nevill Drury, *Music for Inner Space*, p. 141.

8. William David, *The Harmonics of Sound, Color and Vibration* (Marina del Rey, CA: Devorss, 1980).

9. Alex Jones, *The Seven Mansions of Color* (Marina del Rey, CA: Devorss, 1982).

10. Paramahansa Yogananda, *Autobiography of a Yogi* (Los Angeles: Self-Realization Fellowship, 1975).

11. H. P. Blavatsky, *The Esoteric Writings of Helena Petrovna Blavatsky* (Wheaton, IL/Madras, India/London: Theosophical Publishing House/Quest Books, 1980), p. 379.

12. Hazrat Inayat Khan, *The Unity of Religious Ideals* (New Lebanon, NY: Sufi Order Publications, 1979).

13. Aart Jurriaanse, *Bridges: Basic Studies in Esoteric Philosophy* (Somerset West, Capetown, South Africa: Sun Center School of Esoteric Philosophy, 1981).

14. Ken Wilber, *Up from Eden* (Boulder, CO: Shambhala, 1981).

15. Ibid.

16. Swami Rama, Rudolph Ballentine, M.D., and Swami Ajaya, Ph.D., *Yoga and Psychotherapy: The Evolution of Consciousness* (Honesdale, PA: The Himalayan International Institute, 1981).

17. J. D. Blakeley, *The Mystical Tower of the Tarot* (London: Watkins, 1974).

18. Arthur Edward Waite, *The Pictorial Key to the Tarot* (Secaucus, NJ: Citadel Press, 1959).

19. H. P. Blavatsky, *The Secret Doctrine, Vols. I & II* (Adyar, India: Theosophical Publishing House, 1978).

20. Yogi Ramacharaka, *Lessons in Gnani Yoga* (Chicago: Yoga Publication Society, 1934), p. 234.

CHAPTER SIX

Definitions of the Positions in the Karmic Spread

Chart 1 and Chart 1A (The Karmic Spread Positions) show the twenty-two position layout itself. Chart 4, at the end of this chapter, is a summary of the definitions of the twenty-two positions. Within the spread, you may take the position definitions provided in these charts, and the charts on Planes and Stages, and have rich, effective readings with the Karmic Spread before you go on to the detailed sections below. Later, if you take the time to see the origin of the definitions discussed here, you will gain a deeper understanding of the entire system.

DERIVATION OF THE POSITION DEFINITIONS

The meanings of the twenty-two positions in the Karmic Spread are derived principally from the general characteristics of the Planes and the Stages in which the positions fall. Of special significance to position definition is the effect of the interface of the Planes and Stages, i.e., the grid of meanings generated by the intersections of the horizontal rows and the vertical columns. A summary list of these sources of influence follows: (See the Appendix for Source Definitions.)

SUMMARY OF THE SOURCES FOR POSITION DEFINITIONS

1A. Numerology

This refers to the number of the position for all the positions, from 1 to 22. The position is first considered for its actual number and then for the effect of the numerological reduction of the number.[1] For example, the number 17 is first considered as just that, the number 17. Second, it is considered in its theosophically reduced form, which is 8.

1B. Numerology

This is the part the position number plays in the analysis of the seven sequences of 1 to 4 that make up each of the seven Stages. The seven groups of four are: 1,2,3,4... 4,5,6,7... 7,8,9,10... 10,11,12,13... 13,14,15,16... 16,17,18,19... 19,20,21,22(0). Thus you can see that the number 17 is also the sixth #2. Number 19 is the sixth #4 and the seventh #1.

2. Corresponding Major Arcana Card

Each position corresponds to a Major Arcana card and the influence of that card.

3. Consciousness Grid

The aspects of the personality (the Planes) interface with the levels of consciousness (the Stages). For example, looking at Chart 1, you can see that position 17 is in the Mental Plane and the Higher Emotional Stage. Therefore, in the Consciousness Grid, position 17 is where the mental aspect of the personality goes through the higher emotional level of consciousness. In short form this is shown as Mental/Higher Emotional. For another example, position 6 is shown as Emotional/Emotional; position 21 is shown as Mental/Higher Physical. For positions 4,7,10,13,16, and 19, as they are swing positions and play the dual function of ending one phase and beginning another, there will be two sets each on the Consciousness Grid to consider for a position meaning. For example, position 10 is first considered as Spiritual/Mental (for its function as the end of Stage Three) and second considered as Spiritual/Spiritual (for its function as the beginning of Stage Four).

4. Minor Arcana Grid

This grid works much as does the Consciousness Grid, except that the interface factors are the suits of the Minor Arcana. Charts 2 and 3 show the assignment of influence of the suits to the Planes and the Stages, respectively. For example, position 11 is the interface of Swords/Wands; position 14 is Cups/Swords. Again you see the swing cards 4,7,10,13,16, and 19 with two sets each in the grid. For example, position 7 is first considered as Pentacles/Cups and second as Pentacles/Swords.

5. The Elements Grid

This grid is an interface of the characteristics of the four elements as applied to the Planes (Chart 2). For example, position 8 is the interface of Water/Air; position 5 is Air/Water. Again you see the swing cards 4,7,10,13,16, and 19 with two sets each in the grid. For example, position 13 is first considered Earth/Fire and second Earth/Air.

6. Real Time Factor

This source is the effect of real time marching across the seven Stages. Any units of time may be applied to any given reading prior to the laying out of the cards. The selection of the overall time frame chosen for the reading and the subsequent division of that overall time frame into seven time units for the seven Stages is fundamental to the definition of the positions. Some major options are:

STAGE	FULL LIFE	SEVEN MONTHS
Stage One:	At Birth	3rd Month Past
Stage Two:	Early Childhood	2nd Month Past
Stage Three:	Recent Past	1st Month Past
Stage Four:	Present	Now
Stage Five:	Near Future	1st Month Future
Stage Six:	Mid-Future	2nd Month Future
Stage Seven:	Future	3rd Month Future

Instead of SEVEN MONTHS above, you may use seven years, or seven weeks, or seven days. Once you select a time frame, you can interpret four card positions for each of the seven Stages, one in each of the four Planes.

7. Chakras

Application of the characteristics of the chakras to the seven Stages adds rich meaning to the positions, especially regarding health. Chart 3 shows the correlation of the chakras across the seven Stages.

8. Senses

Application of the characteristics of the senses to the seven Stages adds to the spread positions the capability of analyzing questions about the operation and efficiency of the senses themselves, and adds to the sensory source and content of important information. For example, it may be significant to pay special attention to what you will be eating; or to what you hear or say; or to periods of meditation.

9. Color/Sound

These aspects affect the four positions in each of the seven Stages as shown in Chart 3B. While the effects of color and sound on the positions are fundamental and profound, here the reader must study and meditate in order to get meaningful, useful, personal information. Color and sound are at the roots of archetypal symbology and the ability to communicate. Each reader must come to grips with this category personally. Color and sound can be studied, but in the long run, they must be internalized through direct experience. Assign colors to the positions and then let your intuition take over.

10A. The Major Arcana Journey

Your path through the twenty-two cards generates significant meaning for the positions. In the Karmic Tarot the major journey from 1 (Magician) to 22 (Fool) is actually seven mini-journeys, with way-stations at 4, 7, 10, 13, 16, and 19.

10B. The Journeys through the Planes

While your journey is seen primarily as a path through the Major Arcana that weaves its way up and down through the planar effects of the Minor Arcana, additional insight for the meaning of the positions is gained from looking at the horizontal journeys within the level of the Planes themselves.

This generates four mini-Journeys, at the levels of the Physical, Emotional, Mental, and Spiritual Planes, which are as follows:

Physical: (1)Magician (7)Chariot (13)Death (19)Sun
Emotional: (2)High Priestess (6)Lovers (8)Strength (12)Hanged Man (14)Temperance
                     (18)Moon (20)Judgement
Mental: (3)Empress (5)Hierophant (9)Hermit (11)Justice (15)Devil (17)Star (21)World
Spiritual: (4)Emperor (10)Wheel of Fortune (16)Tower (22)Fool

DESCRIPTIVE DEFINITIONS OF THE TWENTY-TWO POSITIONS

Each position gives first the basic function and then the maximum potential of the position.

Position 1—Governed by The Magician

Here are the Physical/Material aspects of the Karmic Contract: your disposition toward the Physical Plane, matters of health and well-being. Beginning, origin, birth of all aspects of existence. The beginning aspects of beginnings. Specifically, the Physical Birth, the effect of the Genetic Father, your masculine heritage. Your package of instincts. The absolute physical individual before any environmental influences. From this position all the life will evolve. Your propensity for fears and anxieties. Financial roots. Basic resources. Sustenance. Fuel. The will to live. From here everything is possible (Magician), everything is the future, as this is your first stop on the journey, specifically, the Physical/Material journey.

Position 2—Governed by The High Priestess

Emotional aspects of the Karmic Contract. Your disposition toward the Emotional Plane. Emotional beginnings. Specifically, the Emotional Package at the time of physical birth, your feminine heritage, the effect of the Genetic Mother. The effect of the Feminine Principle (High Priestess). Origin of passions. The absolute emotional individual before any environmental influences. Feelings toward self. Your Sexual Drives. Energy. Motivation. The will to love. This is the second stop of Stage One (Physical), where you pick up your emotional baggage for the trip. From this position your emotional life will evolve.

Position 3—Governed by The Empress

Mental aspects of the Karmic Contract. Your disposition toward the Mental Plane. Mental beginnings. Specifically, the Mental Package at the time of physical birth. Your Mental Heritage and primary reference to the cumulative effects of past lives that impinge on this incarnation. The will to know. Capacity to learn and teach. Ability to communicate. The origin of your philosophies and belief systems. Drive for achievement. The ego. This is the third stop of Stage One (Physical), where you pick up your mental baggage for the trip. From this position your mental life will evolve.

Position 4—Governed by The Emperor

Spiritual aspects of the Karmic Contract. Your disposition towards the Spiritual Plane. Spiritual beginnings. Your Spiritual heritage. This position indicates the level of service of this incarnation and the composition and direction of this service. The card that falls in this position, together with those in the previous positions, 1, 2, and 3, completes the Karmic Contract and will give an indication as to the age of the soul and the nature of this lifetime. This is the fourth stop of Stage One (Physical), where you pick up the envelope with your instructions from the soul for the trip. From this position your spiritual life will evolve, and it is at this level that you will find your intuition at work, interpreting the messages about the lessons at hand. This is also the first stop on Stage Two (Emotional). You begin your approach to life based on how you "feel" about things. You leave the birth/infant Physical Stage behind.

Position 5—Governed by The Hierophant

You are open and vulnerable here as your Mental Plane reaches Stage Two (Emotional) and you receive your environmental imprinting on the intellect. Early in life you tend to adopt the belief systems of your family and surroundings. This is how you "see" things as a young child/adult, your earliest mental "tapes." Attitudes that affect sexuality. The choices for the lifetime begin to materialize at this fifth stop on your life journey. Here the effect of the Spiritual first impacts the Mental Plane, as symbolized by the card of influence for this position, The Hierophant.

Position 6—Governed by The Lovers

Here your Emotional Plane reaches Stage Two (Emotional), and here you see the greatest emotional experience and impact of your formative years. This shows the effect on your heart of your early attempts to relate to your environment. This may be a physical, mental, or spiritual experience, as well as the emotional experience that has had an impact on the heart. Your childhood high may have been winning the spelling bee (mental); or a visit to a monastery where priests were chanting (spiritual); or hunger (physical); or a storybook-type crush on the little boy or girl in the seat next to you in the first grade (emotional). Your earliest emotional "tapes." The card of influence here is The Lovers. In lives that have advanced efficiently and smoothly in the Emotional Plane, you may see strong relationships and marriage here as the background for the emotional future, as these will undoubtedly be the strongest "tapes" in the emotional past. Just remember—and particularly for this position—that positions in the past will present lessons learned or yet needing to be learned relevant to the question(s) of the reading.

Position 7—Governed by The Chariot

Here your Physical Plane reaches Stage Two (Emotional) and prepares for the shift to Stage Three (Mental). This is where you get your "wheels" and you can see the effect of the card of influence, The Chariot. This is what lies just behind you in the Physical Plane, such as your health, financial, or environmental histories. This is your physical/material situation as you entered the period for control of your own life. This can show the degree to which you have balanced your will and assertiveness with your environment. Whereas your emotional drives have dominated heretofore, pushing you to interact, mate, and propagate, you begin to see the effect of the will to know and achieve, in order to support the emotional packages your feelings have established. This is the result of the extroverted drive of Stage Two and the basis of the thrust to provide for self and extensions of self.

Position 8—Governed by Strength

Here your Emotional Plane reaches Stage Three (Mental); the thrust here is a maturing, a settling down, and you see how well you cope with such a demand on the heart. This is what lies just behind you in the Emotional Plane. The card of influence is Strength and you see the effect of the mind harnessing the emotions. The heart begins to think. Gut feelings about the past. Frequently, if you have seen information about marriage in position 6, you may see children here, as completion of the most significant emotional past. This is your "emotional temperature."

Position 9—Governed by The Hermit

Here your Mental Plane hits Stage Three (Mental) and you see the status of your independent philosophy, your belief systems, and your way of approaching issues. This is what lies just behind you in the Mental Plane. This is you separated from everything else and observing it. The mind looks at the self as something separate. The card of influence is The Hermit. This is the epitome of the rational, subjective/objective, dualistic view of your world. It is what the "lower brain" thinks. This is the state of mind that brings you to the present moment.

Position 10—Governed by the Wheel of Fortune

Here your Spiritual Plane reaches Stage Four (Spiritual) and you see the impact of an awakening, the result of the opening of the Heart Chakra. The mental focusing submits itself to the higher spiritual input, in the ending of Stage Three and the beginning of Stage Four. This is the first position for the reading of the present. The card of influence is The Wheel of Fortune, signifying the strategic necessity of faith in getting the message from God concerning the lesson of the moment. This is what you should be most involved with in this reading. It is the key to the subject of the reading.

Position 11—Governed by Justice

Here your Mental Plane reaches Stage Four (Spiritual) and you see your state of mind at the present moment. To the left of this card lies your mental past; to the right, the possibilities of your mental future, your plans and goals. The card of influence is Justice. As the Mental Plane impacts the spiritual effects of Stage Four, the mind wants its philosophies and strategies to be empirically correct and just. The power of the number 11 in metaphysics is evident here. As this is the fourth stop on your progress through the Mental Plane, here the mind must stabilize and provide a foundation for the future. It must include the message from position 10 in the plan. Here you will see yourself striving for harmony through the conflict of accepting both your lower and higher mentalities; accepting the identity-seeking, self-defining of the past, while embracing the understanding, authentic expression of active intelligence in love with truth which paves the way for your mental future. The pitfall to watch for in this position is the attachment to abstraction, which can lead to fragmentation.

Position 12—Governed by The Hanged Man

Here your Emotional Plane reaches Stage Four (Spiritual) and you see your emotional state at the present moment. All the positions in Stage Four—10, 11, 12, and 13—are in the present, and it is apropos that the absolute moment is the now of the Tarot reading and represents an awakening. To the left of this card lies your emotional past; to the right the possibilities of your emotional future. The card of influence is The Hanged Man. This aspect of your transformation is the opening of your Heart Chakra to include many more people than heretofore. Your emotional world is to be larger. You are able to handle all existing emotional commitments and obligations and more. Everyone can have the same size piece of your emotional pie, but your pie has become miraculously bigger. Here you will see yourself striving for harmony through the conflict of accepting both your lower and higher emotions; accepting the passionate self of your past, while embracing the compassionate self of your future. The conflict here should be in the nature of a clearing, an acceptance. The pitfall to watch out for in this position is the attachment to conflict and duality, although any conflict here is a means to an end, not an end in itself.

Position 13—Governed by Death

This is the physical foundation of the present moment, and as such, the base on which your future is to be built. This is the end of Stage Four (Spiritual) and the beginning of Stage Five (Higher Mental). Energy, shifts from the Heart Chakra to the Throat Chakra, a shifting from the emphasis on the will to that of love. You see the effect of learning to build constructively in your Physical Plane and to achieve physical harmony out of physical conflict. You begin to express yourself in your environment, applying active intelligence and inner knowledge to your surroundings and support systems. Here you want to accept the lower physical, the you as you are, limited, separate, and full of fears; with that acceptance comes the awareness of the higher physical, with its underlying unity and love of God (Self). Your love affair with truth begins.

Position 14—Governed by Temperance

Here your Emotional Plane reaches Stage Five (Higher Mental) and you see your emotional state in the near future. You see the demand for truth, honesty, and authentic expression towards others as well as true comprehension of others' actions and feelings towards you. You gain a higher understanding of your passions. Your higher mind gives you an active intelligence in your emotional affairs. Any propensity to intemperate behavior, to addictions of any kind, will appear here. This is a barometer to your emotional balance and the establishment of emotional support systems. The pitfall here is the possibility of being too mental/abstract about emotional affairs.

Position 15—Governed by The Devil

Here your Mental Plane reaches Stage Five (Higher Mental) and you see your mental state in the near future. This is a position of raw mind at work. The card of influence is The

Devil. Here you find confirmation in the Tarot that evil is a construct of man, and of man's mind at that. You know that until you come to the level of man in the hierarchy of creation, there is no evil; rocks are not evil, trees are not evil, dogs are not evil, and man's physical body and heart are not evil. The capacity for evil resides solely and completely on the mental level of man. This position shows you at your very best or worst. This is independent man. These are the temptations that your mind can attract to you like a magnet. This is where your will to know and love of truth lead you to confront aspects of evil you were heretofore unaware of. For complete growth you must have knowledge of, if not experience of, evil. This is the influence and integration of the shadow side of the personality. You do not have to be a perpetrator or a victim, but you must be knowledgeable.

Position 16—Governed by The Tower

Here your Spiritual Plane reaches Stage Six (Higher Emotional) and you see the next major input from the Spiritual. This is the end of Stage Five, the series of 13, 14, 15 and 16 near-future positions, which can be interpreted as the next year. You are shifting from the Throat Chakra to the Third Eye and sensing via the Astral/Mental. The card of influence is The Tower. This is indeed your next burst of intuition from the Divine and is intended as a backstop after your spurt of independence at position 15, feeling some mental prowess. If you feel overextended, here is the message of how to get back on track. You see revelations and are instilled with wisdom to help you with the challenge of compassion required of this higher emotional stage and the daily demands of altruistic behavior. The message here will be meant to show you how to end your struggle with and for truth. You have decided at what level you will participate in the life of truth...and you begin to live. You no longer struggle with the question of right or wrong and are no longer preoccupied with consequences. There is an inner confidence that has come from the lessons learned at previous stops on the journey. Increasingly smaller and simpler things in your objective reality begin to reveal increasingly grander lessons, as you literally fall in love with every being, every thing in your physical reality, your tangible universe.

Position 17—Governed by The Star

Here the Mental Plane reaches Stage Six (Higher Emotional) and you should begin to consciously know many things that your heart has known for quite awhile. This position is the resolution of things begun in position 15 and moderated by the Divine in position 16. This is the mind in the mid-future. The mind pushes and motivates. This is what you want to be doing to feel good about yourself, your vision of potential accomplishment. You become ambitious and are beginning to get very emotional about your achievements. You want to feel that you have made a difference. This is the ego level mixed with compassion. You see "causes" and dedication. You begin to take stock of your progress to date. If all goes well, you begin to see with the help of the Third Eye. The card of influence is The Star, indicative of the fireworks the heart creates as it lights a fire under the conscious mind; but underlying this apparent explosion of thought is a new order and stability of selflessness setting the tone for the rest of the journey. The ego is bigger than ever, but it is more mature and dedicated to the even bigger picture that has been revealed. You can no longer think in the vacuum of the personal ego. The mind presses forward with a sense of service and duty. One of the major pitfalls here is a sense of self-righteousness.

Position 18—Governed by The Moon

Here the Emotional Plane reaches Stage Six (Higher Emotional) and your emotions grow up. You are emotional but with a higher love and wisdom. Self-gratification is mature and altruistic. This is emotion in the mid-future. You begin to feel with the help of the Third Eye. The card of influence is The Moon, and you see the results of feeling things deeply. Deep creativity surfaces. Just as you were able to see the potential pitfall of too much thinking in position 15, here you must be aware of the pitfall of too much emotion.

Position 19—Governed by The Sun

Here the Physical Plane enters Stage Six (Higher Emotional) and represents the transition to Stage Seven (Higher Physical). It is the shift from your mid-future to your long-term future. The card of influence is The Sun, which ends the lessons begun by the Tower in position 16 by shining so brightly that you can no longer bear to look outward and upward. You can no longer direct your energies toward the deep emotional interaction with the tangible universe. So you look inward (the true "upward"), and there The Sun is blazing brighter than ever you have seen before. Somehow, even though The Sun is so brilliant, you can see perfectly, for here its light is not rejected (reflected) by what it falls upon; rather, it is absorbed. And where before you only saw things that rejected the light of The Sun, now you see things which embrace it. And as you, too, have stopped rejecting The Sun and now absorb its light, the old physical self (Stages 1 to 6), in a sense disappears. The impact of the revelations of the Higher Emotional Stage have relieved the pressures and fears of the Physical Plane. You simply are less and less concerned with the status and condition of your physical self. You are shifting from the Chakra of the Third Eye to that of the Crown. This is the physical set for the final phase of your lifetime. Whereas in Stage Six you have had right feeling leading to revelation, here in Stage Seven you have right action leading to transformation, and vice versa. The Death card(13) can mean physical death if received in this position.

Position 20—Governed by Judgement

Here is the last position in the Emotional Plane. This is the heart's report card on how well you have fulfilled the emotional aspect of your Karmic Contract. The card of influence is Judgement and as such reminds you that judgement is an emotional issue...judgement/acceptance/forgiveness. Here the Tarot reveals that judgement is not an action by an external God with the potential to punish. Rather, is is the judgement of your own heart on your affairs. It is the last number 2, the final antithesis in your journey. The duality of passion/compassion disappears, melts into a spirit of oneness. Your drive for self-gratification becomes self-mastery. Your will to feel becomes a love of

God(self). The pitfalls here include the negativity being judgemental, unaccepting, and unforgiving toward self and others.

Position 21—Governed by The World

Here is the last position in the Mental Plane. This is the mind's report card on how well you have fulfilled the mental aspect of your Karmic Contract. The card of influence is The World, reminding you that your concept of the world and the universe is just that—a concept. If all has gone well at your previous stops on the journey, your mind now has a working concept of the non-duality behind duality, of the God "within" and the God "without," and you begin to know by identification, instead of by your will to know. You begin to know that you know. Identity-seeking becomes unity, self-definition becomes self-mastery. Right thought has contributed to transformation and vice versa. The pitfall here is fragmented, indiscriminate use of the will, for here there is great knowledge and power and great responsibility to use your understanding via transformation of non-dual reality in your everyday world of duality-dominated consciousness. This is the test of tests for the incarnated soul in the physical body.

Position 22/0—Governed by The Fool

Here is the last position in the Spiritual Plane and the last position in the spread. As such, it is the culmination of all aspects of the journey. The last card of the physical incarnation is read in position 21. Here you have the Soul's report card on how well you have fulfilled your entire Karmic Contract. How efficient has this incarnation been? Are there any clues as to what your next incarnation will be like? The card of influence here is The Fool. The significance of the additional numbering of The Fool as 0 is that, just as the numbers 4, 7, 10, 13, 16, and 19 must all do double duty as 4's and 1's in their respective Stages,[2] so too must 22 be considered as the fourth step in the last stage of this lifetime and also the first step in the first stage of the next lifetime. The Fool that represents the end of this incarnation becomes The Magician in the next; 0 becomes 1. The zero of The Fool, which symbol is the *ouroboros* (the snake eating its own tail), becomes the *lemniscate* (the symbol of infinity, a figure eight on its side) of The Magician.

THE JOURNEYS THROUGH EACH OF THE FOUR PLANES
Plane One: The Physical Journey
Magician(1) ↔ Chariot(7) ↔ Death(13) ↔ Sun(19)

The Magician(1)

Your physical birth, the given biological package and the very earliest aspects of material existence. Everything appears to be magic. You have no rationale, no basis for judgement. There are sensations, but no emotions. This is simple existence. Everything is seen in wholes, then in big chunks as the sense of self develops and begins to differentiate self versus other. Behavior is predominantly instinctive and dominated by fear and survival mechanisms.

The Chariot(7)

"The Emperor gets a set of wheels." You have truly realized yourself as a distinct entity apart from other people and things and have tasted the sweets of passion in relationships with your fellow man. Your physical body has passed from puberty to young adulthood. You may have mated. You have developed a hunger for more. You begin to compare in order to make choices, and comparison is analysis. You have truly begun to think. Your mental phase is beginning. You are getting organized and wanting more, and having more, develop security systems to protect your possessions, your new extended self. You begin to communicate and interact with society.

Death(13)

You really die long before your physical death. This is recognized in most philosophical systems, but the fact that there are aspects of that "death" (before your actual physical death in this lifetime) that are indeed physical is not stressed. If all is going well on your path there is marked physical change here at the end of Stage Four, an awakening that propels you into the higher mental phase. If all is not going well and there is a struggle within your biological package, you experience what is known as "mid-life crisis." I believe there is even a fundamental change of polarity at this point in preparation for the second half of the physical life. There is so much more to come, to learn, but somehow you are different now, more ready for what lies ahead.

You do feel turned upside down, and indeed you have experienced The Hanged Man(12) in your Emotional Plane. At this point enough should have fallen into place for you to know the difference between right and wrong action. What you do with this knowledge constitutes the remainder of your lifetime. Physical existence from this point on should be a harmonized blend of the lower and higher self. The underlying fears and survival instincts that dominated the first half of your lifetime should give way to a calm, inner peace derived from the inner knowledge that death is an illusion...as well as a reality. All the lessons of Phase Four, the spiritual awakening, are lessons in duality. In a sense you awake to the fact that you are leading two lives at once—an inner and an outer life; a higher and a lower existence. "At once" is the key phrase. You do not have to wait until your physical death to gain the "reward" of the higher life. It is here, it is now, as Ram Dass tells us.

The Sun(19)

With the Magician(1) there was the sense of oneness with everything in the innocence of not knowing, before the ego developed. With the Chariot(7) there was the early ego development and extensions of the self into the environment. With Death(13) there was mature ego development, a peaking of the externalization of ego, and generation of support for the individual self. Here is the process whereby the personality begins to recapture the other side of the duality of existence, the oneness of everything, even in the most apparently separate of all the levels, the Physical Plane. And now at the later stage of life, this is an awareness derived from experience and knowing as opposed to the unknowing sense of oneness at the beginning of the lifetime. Oneness/innocence has become oneness/experience.

Plane Two: The Emotional Journey
High Priestess(2) ↔ Lovers(6) ↔ Strength(8) ↔ Hanged Man(12) ↔ Temperance(14) ↔ Moon(18) ↔ Judgement(20)

The High Priestess(2)

Your Emotional Plane at your physical birth, the given emotional package, and the very earliest aspects of emotional existence. Importance of the female to you at birth, the character and condition of nurturing, the fact that your earliest emotional "tapes" spring from the physical mother and in physical form...the milk, the warmth, the protection. The duality of your life is clear here in the moment of birth. One minute you are one with universe (mother), warm and secure; then you are separate and confused—your first lesson in "letting go." Mainly, you learn that you will need to depend on others as you depend on your mother for milk, warmth, and protection. Somewhere, too, in this earliest nurturing lie the seeds of love that will blossom into the full-grown passions and compassions of your closest relationships.

The Lovers(6)

Here is the lesson that can only be learned by placing as much value on another entity as on yourself. You realize the true blessing of the sex drive and passion but do not intellectualize it. It comes as part of your instinctual package and once you have experienced it, you know it. You are beginning to care for things outside the self, but are still for the self, an extension of the self. The degree to which one-on-one relationships can transcend this barrier of self-interest is what determines the depth and truth of the love experience. The reality of duality begins to assert itself on you.

Strength(8)

The emotions begin to build a support system. Your heart wants to "know" things. You want reliability, predictability in your emotional affairs. You rationalize, systematize, and legalize the things you feel most deeply about. Here the application of right thought to right feeling leads to true strength and an emotional base that generates the energy needed to fuel your projects and realize your goals.

The Hanged Man(12)

Here you experience an awakening at the Emotional Level. The dividing line between the self and everything else begins to soften as the second side of duality, the "all is one," comes into play. But now it is through the power of knowledge that comes from experience. You can still enjoy the passions made possible by the excitement of relationships between separate entities, but superimposed over and around these relationships is a feeling of unity at the same time as the separateness. You literally begin to feel duality.

Temperance(14)

Now awakened, the emotions move into the Higher Mental Stage. Emotional potential is greater than ever before and so is emotional control, somewhat like a controlled reaction in a nuclear reactor. Much of the test at this Stage is to see how well you can manage and control your emotions. With proper control you have the energy and drive to achieve your wildest dreams. Without proper control you can literally be destroyed with your own energy, by your own doing, from within.

The Moon(18)

The earlier emotional drive of passion has now become a drive of compassion, as the less secure sense of the lower self has given way to the more secure sense of the higher self. This secure sense of self extends far beyond the boundary of the physical body, out into the community at large. You are able to feel things at ever-increasing distances and with ever-increasing intensity. Under control this is a very rich sensory experience full of rewards, as you feel more and more alive, more and more part of everything around you. Life is exciting, but you feel indiscriminately and you can be overwhelmed if you are not prepared and do not maintain the balance you learned from your Temperance(14) stage.

Judgement(20)

Here you see that the emotional duality has melted into the one, the universal love, of God, of self. Anything you desire for the self at this point is for the universal good as well; they are one and the same. Major lessons have been internalized, such as love without attachment. Forgiveness fills your hearts as guilt melts away. Here is where you actually can change the past, by how you choose to remember behavior and events long gone. As you replay the memories for new lessons to be learned from your relationships, you "forgive your debtors" and are in turn forgiven. Then, emotionally you are truly here and now, centered in the present moment, free. Here is the true meaning of Judgement Day, the culmination of the emotional journey, when your own heart takes stock of your life experience. There is no punishment from the God "without"; only assessment from the God "within." How well did you realize your God-given gift of Love?

Plane Three: The Mental Journey
The Empress(3) ↔ The Hierophant(5) ↔ The Hermit(9) ↔ Justice(11) ↔ The Devil(15) ↔ The Star(17) ↔ The World(21)

The Empress (3)

Here is the mental plane at your physical birth, the given mental package, and the very earliest aspects of mental existence. This is the virgin mind. Here then is the birth of the ego and the origin of your identity package. The sense of self as separate is not developed and you are dependent on the maternal physical support systems. Instinctively, the earliest mental programs will be ways to increase the self, its size, its worth, its security, its tenure; in short, its ownership and control over things external. But this is prior to truly understanding the duality of things. Here the ego is ever hungry.

The Hierophant(5)

You begin to feel, to understand duality and its set of givens and requirements. You begin to decide how you can fit in with everything that already exists. It is the dawn of your conscience, your knowledge of right and wrong. Here are your earliest belief systems, but they come from the pages of other people's books. The ego sizes up the situation. This is where you see the function of organized religion and how it is used to train the minds of youth. This is the environment you are born into, what your parents hand you.

The Hermit(9)

Here is where you mentally set yourself apart from the herd. You have established what you think and believe and you rely on that, rather than on what others think. You now have the ability to analyze and compare; not just feel differences, but to know them. The ego develops a solid sense of being separate and makes plans that will satisfy its every imaginable whim. This is you, not just seeing yourself at the center of your world, but quite possibly seeing yourself *as* the center of the world. This stage is as necessary as all the others, but as it is not currently the fashion to favor the ego, healthy development at this stage is frequently aborted. Unless you fully experience this separate half of duality, you will not get very far later when you need to experience the togetherness, the oneness. You have to bring a whole, developed you to the party if you are going to have any fun.

Justice(11)

Here the fully developed mind with its fully developed, healthy ego becomes consciously aware, albeit with help from spiritual insights, of the flip side of duality in the Mental Plane. Having externalized and experienced the major lessons of the consciousness of separateness, you see the need to internalize and experience the lessons of togetherness/oneness. You begin to see and understand the similarities in things where before you saw only differences. Where you used to define, you now refine. The lower and higher (outer and inner) minds are in harmony.

The Devil(15)

First on the list of things to bring within your expanding sense of self is the shadow, or inner, side of your own persona. Only when you neglect the reality of this half of your being do you risk the runaway lack of mental direction of the will that we describe as evil. Evil cannot exist unless you refuse to accept this half of your mental duality. Acceptance and integration at this stage are strategic. When they are accomplished, you are prepared to receive revelations and spiritual insights that will raise your level of mental activity to new heights, as you are called upon to apply your intellect to the common good.

The Star(17)

Bursts of insight and inspiration now excite the prepared mind and confound the unprepared, as information from the Spiritual Level descends into your conscious awareness. To the ego side of your mental duality these are opportunities of a lifetime for concrete achievements and are meant to be used to your advantage. To the post-ego (or ego-evolved) side comes the ability to direct those opportunities for the benefit of others. Here your minds seem to push you; you become extroverted and active, for you have seen that there is so much that needs to be done. There is a drive to achieve. The intellect is excited. You want to make a difference. (See the duality at work in this last sentence: the "you" is the ego that wants to act, but the "difference" is one that will be of benefit to mankind in general, not the self alone.) All of this type of activity with The Star shows the impact of the Stage of Higher Emotions on your thoughts. You are motivated for the common good.

The World(21)

Your mind establishes a functioning link with the universal mind. You have identified with the collective will. The intellect realizes that apparent free will has brought it to this point, but it also realizes that the will has been guided and that individual will and collective will are now one and the same. Your thoughts are very powerful now, and only through the lessons of responsibility and universal concern are you able to exercise appropriate restraint. To the fully developed intellect there is no restraint necessary, as all thoughts are proper and no checks are required.

Plane Four: The Spiritual Journey
The Emperor(4) ↔ The Wheel(10) ↔ The Tower(16) ↔ The Fool(22/0)

The Emperor(4)

Here is the Spiritual Plane at your physical birth, the given spiritual package, the very earliest aspects of your spiritual existence. You see the embryo of the Divine in the individual soul. Instinctively, at birth, you know your divine purpose, but it slides further and further away from your conscious awareness as the ego develops. This Emperor is the concept for the "divine right of kings" and is your guide for the achievement of "on earth as it is in heaven," or the hermetic "as above, so below." Here is the blueprint, the major lesson, for the lifetime.

The Wheel of Fortune(10)

At this point you have experienced the limitations of the Physical, Emotional, and Mental Planes and have been given the opportunity via the lessons of The Hermit(9) to comprehend the meaning of your spiritual existence. You are aware that there is more than your material existence. Here you awaken to the fact that you can spin of The Wheel of Fortune with complete faith in your fate; faith that what you signed up for—the Karmic Contract your soul has chosen for you—will indeed bring you fulfillment, happiness, and success. Once you demonstrate your faith, once you commit your trust, you are immediately reassured and given a healthy glimpse of what lies ahead on your path. Faith is unmanifested fulfillment. This act or condition of faith is synonymous with being a neophyte, accepting at all levels of consciousness that you have chosen a definite spiritual path. At this point the neophyte knows that he or she is on a path and consciously acknowledges the fact that what lies ahead is the inner part of the path and that the incline is much steeper. There are options of degrees of difficulty and achievement which must be decided upon at this Stage.

The Tower(16)

As you expressed your status as neophyte at The Wheel of Fortune(10), so you express here your status as initiate. The revelations here are at once rewards for your performance as neophyte and challenges to your status as initiate to enter the Stage of Higher Emotions. You are very conscious of the duality of your existence and conscious in both states at the same time. As you open up more to the underlying oneness, your struggle with the overlying separateness eases. The struggle with truth, with right and wrong, ceases. You do not see all the pieces, but the pieces you do see are falling into place. You are literally falling in love with everything in your tangible universe. Life seems relatively automatic and natural, as events flow gently from one to the next. Time still moves, but it is not quite as linear as it once was, and it has lost its power over you. You are able to enjoy both sides of the coin. You can enjoy the sensations brought back to the separate self, as the separate self. But the process of identifying with the universal has gone far enough so that you can sense what it is really like to be other things as well as yourself. You can feel a falling leaf, not just see it. You can feel the sound of the surf, not just hear it.

The Fool(22/0)

In Karmic Tarot, this position is the soul's viewpoint after death. Upon dying, whatever remains on your list of lessons to be learned, on your Karmic Contract, is revealed to you. Thus the soul here knows everything about the lifetime and you are able to see how efficiently you moved up your path, how far your consciousness evolved. This represents, of course, the final step of the Spiritual Level, but it is also the final step at the Seventh Stage of Higher Physical Evolution and suggests correctly that there is a physical aspect to the soul itself. There is a physical continuity from lifetime to lifetime, albeit residing on the spiritual level.

ENDNOTES

1. This is the process in numerology known as "Theosophical Reduction." It consists of reducing all numbers of two or more figures to a single figure. To accomplish this, all of the figures that make up the number are added together until only one figure remains.

2. This phenomenon is explained in Chapter Five.

Chart 4
KARMIC SPREAD POSITION DEFINITIONS — A SUMMARY

POSITION IN SPREAD	MEANING OF POSITIONS
1 MAGICIAN	Physical package at birth . . . influence of parents esp. Father . . . Part of Karmic Contract. **Fears will to live** Disposition of physical health . . . our biological package . . . Inheritance (wills) How we approach material things. Our instincts as survival mechanisms . . . Our disposition toward fear/paranoia . . . Our physical safety . . .
2 PRIESTESS	Emotional package at birth . . . Influence of mother . . . Part of Karmic Contract. **Passions will to feel** Disposition of emotional health . . . Attitude toward touch/physical love . . . Toward self/then others
3 EMPRESS	Mental package at birth . . . IQ . . . Part of Karmic Contract. **Concepts will to know** Disposition of mental health . . . Mind applied to self preservation . . . Our ability to learn/to analyze . . . begins here . . . at the physical level
4 EMPEROR	Spiritual package at birth . . . Part of Karmic Contract . . . Key card of the four Contract Cards. **Faith will to will/to believe** Our spiritual "health" . . . How we begin things . . . Our approach . . . Our style End of Stage One: Physical . . . Beginning of Stage Two: Emotional
5 HIEROPHANT	Our earliest philosophy/ideology package . . . The system(s) of thought that we are born into . . . Mental impact of early environment . . . Earliest effect of feelings on thought . . . The ego begins to develop . . . and as we begin to see ourselves, we begin to see others . . . The dawn of duality in our consciousness . . . The birth of conscience.
6 LOVERS	Emotional impact of early environment . . . Earliest and most profound emotional experience . . . Earliest attachments . . . Our emotions raw and uncovered . . . We begin to feel things . . . Attitude of others toward us . . .
7 CHARIOT	Our physical support systems . . . Physical extensions of the self . . . End of Stage Two: Emotional . . . Beginning of Stage Three: Mental
8 STRENGTH	Our emotional support systems . . . The emotional package gets rationalized/systematized . . . Mental side of emotions Status of formalized relationships/marriage . . . Emotional growth . . . We begin to know and understand our feelings . . . Our heart tells us what to do . . .
9 HERMIT	Our philosophy . . . Attitude . . . Approach . . . Our game plan . . . Our rules . . . Our thoughts about our thoughts . . . Caterpillar before the butterfly . . .
10 WHEEL	Spiritual Stage of Spiritual Plane . . . The present moment . . . Major message from God . . . Present super-conscious The awakening . . . The butterfly emerges . . . We have the courage to spin The Wheel of Fortune . . . Turn to faith . . . What we must get on with . . . Major aspect of this reading . . . No way to know until we commit, then we are told . . . End of Stage Three: Mental . . . Beginning of Stage Four: Spiritual
11 JUSTICE	Conscious mind at the present moment . . . Plans for the future . . . Major decisions appear here . . . Mental decisions . . . Ability to communicate verbally Status of Throat Chakra
12 HANGED MAN	Present state of emotions . . . Present sub-conscious . . . Innermost desires Decisions of the heart appear here . . . Disposition of Heart Chakra and/or Solar Plexus and/or Genital Chakra
13 DEATH	Physical situation at present moment . . . The effect of Higher Mind and the love of truth on the body . . . Status of Root/Anal Chakra . . . End of Stage Four: Spiritual . . . Beginning of Stage Five: Higher Mental . . .
14 TEMPERANCE	Effect of Higher Mind on Emotional near future . . . Higher understanding of Emotional nature . . . Taking Emotional stock . . .
15 DEVIL	Devil is Mental/Mental position . . . Evil as total mental fabrication by man's conscious level . . . Where our will-to-know and love-of-truth lead us to a confrontation of aspects of evil heretofore unaware of. For complete growth we must have knowledge of evil . . . but not necessarily direct experience of evil. Major potential temptation/detour off our intended path . . . Off our Karmic Contract . . . Status of the ego . . .
16 TOWER	Flashes of intuition from Higher Mind at the Spiritual Level . . . How we shift from love of truth to love of life . . . How to begin our Higher Emotional Stage . . . Next major input from God . . . End of Stage Five: Higher Mental . . . Beginning of Stage Six: Higher Emotional
17 STAR	Revelations of right thought . . . Effect of love of life and compassion on thought . . . Effect of our philosophy at work . . . Outcome of temptations of position 15 and input from God, position 16 . . . Ability to communicate feelings . . . Major new ideas . . . Emotional evaluation of our achievements . . .
18 MOON	Our compassionate nature . . . Our attitude toward others . . . Mid-range future of our Emotional Nature . . . This position is Emotion/Emotion . . .
19 SUN	Physical harvest . . . Ego begins to melt under heat of sun Disposition for final Stage in life . . . Ultimate evolution of the five senses . . . Long-term physical health . . . Physical legacies (wills) End of Stage Six: Higher Emotional . . . Beginning of Stage Seven: Higher Physical
20 JUDGEMENT	Emotional harvest . . . Our heart's review of life's performance. Long-term what we will feel the most . . . Care the most about . . . What will rule our hearts . . .
21 WORLD	Mental harvest . . . Mental review . . . as we begin to see, know and understand the universe and melt into unity again . . . Mental legacies . . . Teachings . . . Creative works
22 FOOL	The Karmic Contract . . . The "Report Card" on how well we fulfilled our contract

P = Pentacles   C = Cups   S = Swords   W = Wands

Chart 4A
KARMIC SPREAD POSITIONS THROUGH THE SEVEN STAGES

To strengthen your understanding of the Karmic Spread here is Chart 4A to show how the aspects of consciousness operating in the seven Stages (shown in Chart 3A) relate to, and help define, the meanings of the 22 spread positions.

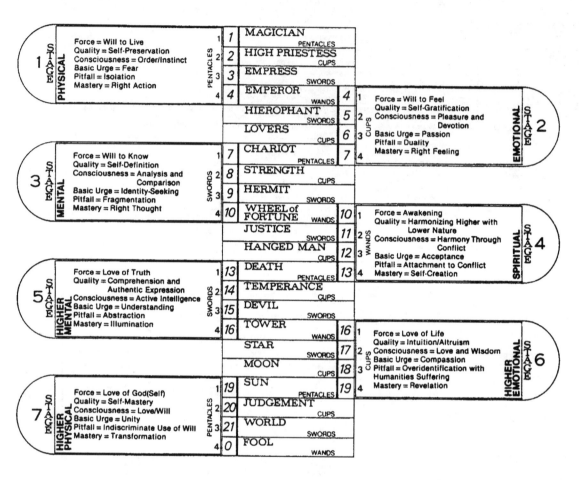

PART TWO

THE

MEANINGS

OF THE CARDS

CHAPTER SEVEN

The Major Arcana

In this chapter and the next are definitions of the seventy-eight cards. First, the card's general meaning is given; then specific interpretations for its location in each of the twenty-two Karmic Spread positions. These definitions will connect you with the roots of each card, opening doors for further personal interpretation.

Although 3,432 definitions are provided, intuition is still paramount given the enormous probabilities for the relationships of the 22 cards in the Spread. The potential relationship of 22 cards is equal to the number 22 factorialized, which is 1,124,000,727,777,607,680,000. The actual number is larger, since the 22 cards are selected at random from a possibility of 78 cards, not just 22.

Let my definitions be your training wheels and then leave them behind as the archetypes speak to you directly about their nature and how they interact. Then you will discover more than any number of definitions could ever divulge. And, you will not be memorizing.

Whether a card is upright or inverted is an indicator for keeping the readee more centered on their path. Knowing that karma is not negative, in Karmic Tarot an inverted card is not negative any more negative than an upright card is positive. An upright card represents the central meaning of the archetype of that card. An inverted card represents too much or too little of that principle. For example: The Queen of Cups, in her centrally defined role, signifies the nurturing female. At one extreme, she may be so overprotective that she never lets her young son go out to play; on the other, she may not know where he is at ten o'clock at night. Even though the extremes are to be avoided in principle, in a given reading the readee may need to move toward one extreme—toward one half of a duality pair—in order to balance the other. The inverted card, representing excess or deficiency, is an invaluable tool, giving signposts for walking the middle path.

As you read the definitions of the Majors, remember that their meanings are generated by the interaction of the Planes and Stages in the same way as the meanings of the positions of the Karmic Spread.

The meanings of the Major Arcana are summarized on Chart 5 at the end of this chapter.

THE MAGICIAN.

1 THE MAGICIAN

UPRIGHT: Beginning of beginnings—first stop of 22 way-stations through the Seven Stages in the evolution of consciousness. This first stop in Stage One (Physical) is also the beginning of the Physical Plane aspects of the personality. Here as life begins, all things are possible. One can make the future. This is the One before the birth of duality, representing both masculine and feminine energy behind all things, God incarnate. Here are all four Minor Arcana suits, symbolized on the table—the elements of Earth, Water, Air, and Fire. "As above, so below," seen in the right hand raised skyward with receiving wand, and in the left hand pointing to the ground. Spiritual Teacher. Master. Guide. Centered awareness. A good listener as well as communicator. Interpreter. His belt is the ouroboros, a snake eating its own tail, alpha to omega, the symbol zero, every ending a beginning, the duality inherent in the non-duality of the zero. The link between life incarnate and life in death (outer and inner life). Twisted, the pre-unity of zero becomes the infinite and eternal (space and time) of the lemniscate, seen above his head. Concerns of the physical earth. In the duality pair of The Magician(1) with The Fool(22/0), The Magician is the Will of Man while The Fool is the Will of God. The Magician is The Fool reborn in this life. ***INVERTED:*** Distortion by way of too much or too little in the above meanings. Difficulty with balancing the Will of God and Will of Man, of passive and active.

In This Spread Position...Interpret The Magician Meanings to Include:

1 GOVERNED BY THE MAGICIAN: PHYSICAL GIVENS, OUT OF THE FATHER
UPRIGHT: Advantageous beginning. Great physical potential. Good genetic package. Action oriented. Physically talented and charmed. Rich, accurate instincts. Drawn to earth disciplines. Masculine in stature and interests. ***INVERTED:*** More power and talent than you can handle or use. Dominated by earthly instincts, elementals. Too many or not enough physical advantages.

2 GOVERNED BY THE HIGH PRIESTESS: EMOTIONAL GIVENS, OUT OF THE MOTHER
UPRIGHT: Great creative potential. Fertile. Energetic. Charming. Persuasive. Extroverted. Assertive in relationships. Emotionally identified with masculine. ***INVERTED:*** Could be manipulative, or having tendency to be manipulated. Perhaps driven to lose oneself in work or the material.

3 GOVERNED BY THE EMPRESS: MENTAL GIVENS. INTELLECTUAL PREDISPOSITION
UPRIGHT: Mentally disposed to masculine archetype. Assertive. Pragmatic thinker, yet highly original. Can-do attitude. Self-expressive. Ability to see things through. ***INVERTED:*** Aggressive. Prone to theory and fantasy. May be too far ahead of field. Tendency to dominate, manipulate, seek control.

4 GOVERNED BY THE EMPEROR: SPIRITUAL GIVENS, LIFE PURPOSE
UPRIGHT: Spiritual teacher. Gift of prophecy. Spiritual identification with the Father energy of the divine. Ability as well as responsibility to perform proper magic. Here is Hermes having to help the Above be as Below, and the Below be as Above. ***INVERTED:*** Same as upright but to more or less extent.

5 GOVERNED BY THE HIEROPHANT: SYSTEMS BORN INTO, SOCIETAL INFLUENCE
UPRIGHT: Self-reliance encouraged. Perhaps born into a patriarchy, male oriented. Highly independent family. ***INVERTED:*** Over or under reliance of family on family, or of self on self. Too male-oriented, or not oriented toward male where appropriate. Taught to use power or magic without proper understanding.

6 GOVERNED BY THE LOVERS: EMOTIONAL TAPES, BASIS OF RELATING/CREATING
UPRIGHT: Confidence in love, relationships, in your ability to create. Enamored of the prophet, moral leader, shaman, weaver of dreams. ***INVERTED:*** Too much confidence, or too little. Tendency to worship an idol, to create a superior or false image in one's heart.

7 GOVERNED BY THE CHARIOT: PHYSICAL RESOURCES, MEANS TO ACHIEVE
UPRIGHT: Confidence in work, health. Excellent support systems over broad base. Flexibility. Prepared. Superb foundation. ***INVERTED:*** Overconfident or needlessly pessimistic about physical conditions. Misuse of resources. Building on wrong or inadequate foundation.

8 GOVERNED BY STRENGTH: EMOTIONAL RESOURCES, ENERGY
UPRIGHT: Proper love and appreciation of independence and own talents. Resourceful. Amazing amounts of energy, even Samsonesque if needed. In control of relationships and creative endeavors. ***INVERTED:*** Over or under-involved with own talents. Perhaps too independent. Too much energy? Abusing others with your way?

9 GOVERNED BY THE HERMIT: BELIEF SYSTEM, BASIS FOR DECISIONS
UPRIGHT: The ultimate optimist. Anything is possible, for self and for others. If it can be conceived of, in time it can be done. Belief in your ability, ability of man. ***INVERTED:*** Overly optimistic, or pessimistic. Distorted understanding of magic, of the duality of Will of Man versus Will of God.

10 GOVERNED BY THE WHEEL OF FORTUNE: CENTRAL MESSAGE/THEME OF READING
UPRIGHT: Faith is strong, a healthy balance of your willpower and that of the divine. A good combination of active and passive. You have reached the plateau of understanding wherein knowledge is balanced with responsibility. ***INVERTED:*** Either too reliant on yourself being much too active, or waiting for God to take care of everything being much too passive. Problems with knowledge/responsibility. Must learn this before more progress is possible.

11 GOVERNED BY JUSTICE: STATE/CONTENT OF MIND, PLANS
UPRIGHT: Positive. Energetic. Forceful. Full of original ideas and determination. Overview of situation. Acceptance of your role and responsibility. Application of gifts. ***INVERTED:*** Difficulty applying personal dynamism to life situation. May seem like forcing a round peg into a square hole. May not be fully accepting your role or potential. Abusing your role?

12 GOVERNED BY THE HANGED MAN: STATE OF EMOTIONS, SUBCONSCIOUS
UPRIGHT: Healthy, vibrant relationships. Good sex life. Abundant energy and creativity. In love with life. Happy with yourself and others. Enjoyment of your abilities. ***INVERTED:*** May get somewhat lost in yourself and the ambiance of your situation. Don't try to freeze the moment. Keep an eye on of the source of your pleasure.

13 GOVERNED BY DEATH: PHYSICAL SITUATION, HARD REALITY

UPRIGHT: Good circumstances. Well-positioned. In control. Strong, capable body. *INVERTED:* Things so good—where to from here? Manipulation, abuse of situation. Not taking full advantage of moment. Not rising to full potential.

14 GOVERNED BY TEMPERANCE: EMOTIONAL TEST, NEAR FUTURE

UPRIGHT: Impact of more and more knowledge/capability on personal and public life. Your abilities are pushing you upward and outward, changing your relationships, deepening your creativity. Acceptance of responsibility. *INVERTED:* Your potential is overriding all other aspects, some unnecessarily. Give more of your present a chance to move with you into the future. You may not be opening honestly to the call, fearing the changes it will bring.

15 GOVERNED BY THE DEVIL: TEMPTATION/CHALLENGE, FEARS, NEAR FUTURE.

UPRIGHT: Integration of your strength and capacity to engineer change is appropriate. Accept that you are exceptional and plan to use all your gifts to the maximum, and with humility. *INVERTED:* Perhaps you fear yourself, what you may do with your knowledge. Or, perhaps you do not have enough respect for your position and your power to affect others and may be planning selfishly.

16 GOVERNED BY THE TOWER: NEXT LESSON, GRACE OF GOD

UPRIGHT: Intervention by or influence of a major personality. Realization of your inner magician. Acceptance of your physical gifts and their desire to be used to the maximum. *INVERTED:* This may be traumatic, or easily integrated—it's up to you.

17 GOVERNED BY THE STAR: ASPIRATIONS OF EGO, GOALS, MAXIMUM EXPECTATIONS

UPRIGHT: Desire to be an effective cause agent, maker of miracles, guide to life on a higher plane. Seeing yourself at the forefront of civilization's progress. Responsible power. *INVERTED:* May desire control for control's sake, personal aggrandizement, gain. Or may not yet be capable of setting goals commensurate with your full abilities, selling yourself short.

18 GOVERNED BY THE MOON: ASPIRATIONS OF HEART, COMPASSION

UPRIGHT: Desiring power, but altruistically, to help others. Sensual, genuine appreciation of the material side of life. Rich aesthetic sensibility. Intimate with your environment. Desire to feel deeply, without fear. *INVERTED:* Tempted to distort the means for the ends, which you see as noble. Perhaps myopic towards one thing because your sights are on another. May want to do good only because of possible rewards.

19 GOVERNED BY THE SUN: MATERIAL FULFILLMENT/EVALUATION

UPRIGHT: You reap the benefits of efficient programming, creative visualization, or other means of accepting responsibility for oneself and others. Physically healthy and active throughout lifetime. You will be self-made, having done it your way. *INVERTED:* You could overdo it on the self-will side, while missing many messages from the Will of God side that would make life even more rewarding. You will be in a position to abuse your abilities.

20 GOVERNED BY JUDGEMENT: HEART'S FULFILLMENT/EVALUATION

UPRIGHT: Heart will swell at the fullness of successful involvement with many, many people. Success at the family, and the public, role. Peacemaker. Many will benefit from your touch. *INVERTED:* While achieving good, may overstep your bounds, intruding on others' karma. Too forgiving.

21 GOVERNED BY THE WORLD: EGO'S FULFILLMENT/EVALUATION

UPRIGHT: Fame. Recognition as a good force, shaper of destiny. Satisfaction with considerable legacy you leave to future generations. Highly efficient life of major achievement. *INVERTED:* Perhaps unable to see achievements as others see them. Maybe more notorious than famous. A difficult legacy?

22/0 GOVERNED BY THE FOOL: SOUL'S FULFILLMENT/EVALUATION

UPRIGHT: A lifetime of active service. Proper use of all talents and potential. A worker of miracles. *INVERTED:* Perhaps under or over-use of talents and power, a worker of inappropriate magic.

THE HIGH PRIESTESS

2 THE HIGH PRIESTESS

UPRIGHT: Here is the birth of duality, of energy, of prana, the feminine, of choice, of nurturing, of potential. It is the second stop on the journey of 22 way stations through the seven Stages in your evolution of consciousness. This is the physical origin of your Emotional Plane. The beginning of life in the emotional body. Physical aspects of your emotions. Reproduction. Birth of rhythm and flow. Mother of Mothers. The ultimate female. In any position this may be a figure of great importance to the readee, such as a teacher or guide. The root of all feminine principles. Subjectivity. Guardian of alternatives. Knowledge of the other. Concerns of the element Water. Motivation. Fertility. This is the Gaia principle in the Physical Plane of Earth, from which comes our concept of mother Earth as the source of life. **INVERTED:** Distortion in the form of too much or too little in the above meanings. Too much or too little physicality in the emotions, sex.

In This Spread Position...Interpret The High Priestess to Include:

1 GOVERNED BY THE MAGICIAN: PHYSICAL GIVENS, OUT OF THE FATHER
UPRIGHT: The root female principle dominates all affairs in the Physical/material Plane, but here is through the Father. This is maleness that is extremely sensitive to feminine energy and skills historically thought of as feminine in Western culture. Sensitivity to earth and nature. If the readee is a man, may indicate homosexuality or bisexuality. Also, a gift for the esoteric or occult through the father. **INVERTED:** Integrating the feminine principles into this plane will bring an aesthetic quality to your material world, but not without challenges.

2 GOVERNED BY THE HIGH PRIESTESS: EMOTIONAL GIVENS, OUT OF THE MOTHER
UPRIGHT: The root female principle is dominant just where we expect it to be, in the affairs of the emotional/creative plane, but here reinforces its strength many fold. Especially strong gift for the esoteric and the occult, nature and herb crafts, the healing arts, psychic abilities, female shamanism, channeling and the like, through the mother's line. **INVERTED:** These givens will either be much stronger or somewhat moderated.

3 GOVERNED BY THE EMPRESS: MENTAL GIVENS, INTELLECTUAL PREDISPOSITION
UPRIGHT: The Mental Plane will be inclined to support the programs of interest to the High Priestess. Much of what we call New Age philosophy fits under this influence due to its recognition and re-inclusion of the feminine, the inner aspect of the Godhead, and an integration of Eastern religions into Western culture and religion. **INVERTED:** The mind must be on guard not to exclude the masculine in the way that the masculine exclude the feminine for so long.

4 GOVERNED BY THE EMPEROR: SPIRITUAL GIVENS, LIFE PURPOSE
UPRIGHT: This is a lifetime dedicated to the work of the High Priestess. The main thrust of the next century, even the next millennium, is to balance the feminine with the masculine, by reasserting the feminine. Women must do this as well as men, for the effect of the masculine is in them also, and indeed was brought about by both men and women. We have done this to each other in partnership, and we must undo it together. **INVERTED:** This work is already done in you for the most part and you must now help others to their balance.

5 GOVERNED BY THE HIEROPHANT: SYSTEMS BORN INTO, SOCIETAL INFLUENCE
UPRIGHT: This early environment was rich in female imagery and example. In some instances this was a virtual matriarchy, ranging from the home with a strong mother and/or other female figures (grandmother, aunts, sisters) to groups or communes literally governed by women, or in rare circumstances by men according to female principles as in some native societies. **INVERTED:** At one extreme here, too much feminine compared to masculine.

6 GOVERNED BY THE LOVERS: EMOTIONAL TAPES, BASIS FOR RELATING/CREATING
UPRIGHT: This passion in this young heart was to be the classical heroine or mythic proportions, and prior to its reduction by male dominated civilization. This is the heroine/hero which can live in both woman and man waiting for their talents to be called on to save the day. Perhaps there is even a historical, or imaginary, feminine hero figure living in your dreams. **INVERTED:** All heroine/hero worship must have its limits. Such tapes must be our guides, not our task masters demanding the letter perfect apery.

7 GOVERNED BY THE CHARIOT: PHYSICAL RESOURCES, MEANS TO ACHIEVE
UPRIGHT: You are rooted in natural principles and can fall back on a storehouse of excellent instincts. Natural foods, natural medicines, keep you and your loved ones fit. Female energy is the main force in your environment, health, work, and perhaps even your exercise/leisure athletics. A significant part of your foundation may derive from a person embodying The High Priestess. **INVERTED:** To be even stronger here, do not allow too much or too little of this archetype.

8 GOVERNED BY STRENGTH: EMOTIONAL RESOURCES, ENERGY
UPRIGHT: You are comfortable with and able to use and benefit from basic feminine energy and disciplines. This gives you abundant creativity in expressing your talents, and sensitivity in your relationships. Your psychic facility makes you efficient in this plane. **INVERTED:** Center your feminine energies and integrate them to avoid extremes of too much or too little. Do not try to generate more energy than you can use properly.

9 GOVERNED BY THE HERMIT: BELIEF SYSTEM, BASIS FOR DECISIONS
UPRIGHT: Goddess or feminine-based religions fit here. Emphasis on the God-within more than the traditional God-without, hence shifting to the forgiving, nurturing aspect of the Divine. Affinity for Eastern traditions and religions. **INVERTED:** At one extreme, a disrespect for the feminine. At the other extreme, a tendency to worship the feminine to the neglect of the masculine. You must do both. From your skin outward to the infinitely large is the God-without, worshipped as a male God—the strong and punishing side of divinity. From your skin inward to the infinitely small is the God-within, the female half of God—the caring and nurturing side of divinity.

10 GOVERNED BY THE WHEEL OF FORTUNE: CENTRAL MESSAGE, THEME OF READING
UPRIGHT: You are being washed with universal feminine truths. Valuing all creation is uppermost, respecting nature and man's place as part of nature,

working in harmony with the environment instead of trying to dominate it. Great sensitivity to life. *INVERTED:* The lessons of the High Priestess are especially important to you now. Study her meanings and meditate on the card itself.

11 GOVERNED BY JUSTICE: STATE/CONTENT OF MIND
UPRIGHT: You have tremendous inner confidence in making decisions at this time, partly because intuitive right-brain functions are so accessible. Great capacity to listen and learn. *INVERTED:* You may have received more information through right-brain, psychic/intuitive input than is helpful for you and your purposes. Consult objective references and/or apply affirmation techniques before acting.

12 GOVERNED BY THE HANGED MAN: STATE OF EMOTIONS, SUBCONSCIOUS
UPRIGHT: The heart is immersed in the feminine world, in appreciation of nature and the natural. There is great love of the Mother, with complete trust in her judgement and ability to soothe your cares. *INVERTED:* There may be a block to this feeling, it being unreachable to the extent that you would like or need. As with all positions, the High Priestess here could be a person. Remember also to examine the possible effect of too much or too little.

13 GOVERNED BY DEATH: PHYSICAL SITUATION, HARD REALITY
UPRIGHT: You are awash with healthy energy, creative projects on line and productive. Mysticism is a positive force in your affairs. Environmental issues may be dominating the moment. *INVERTED:* Inefficient or poor use of feminine energy, a distortion of esoteric or occult traditions.

14 GOVERNED BY TEMPERANCE: EMOTIONAL TEST
UPRIGHT: In the near future, put more time and attention on yourself first and then loved ones. This can also mean a creative project crying-out for completion. Look to your deepest desires and bring them into the light. *INVERTED:* Your emotions and desires may run deep for a short while. Many outside energies vie for your attention, most not worthy of your time. Do not begin major new relationships or creative projects until your heart clears.

15 GOVERNED BY THE DEVIL: TEMPTATION/CHALLENGE, FEARS
UPRIGHT: Work to integrate the subconscious more fully with the conscious mind. Begin or increase your study of the occult, mysticism, esoteric philosophy, and/or metaphysics. *INVERTED:* Possible confusion about how your mind wants to pursue its interest in these subjects. Be both objective and intuitive in your selection and proceed accordingly.

16 GOVERNED BY THE TOWER: NEXT LESSON, GRACE OF GOD
UPRIGHT: Here is the protecting umbrella of the Mother. A burst of creative energy for you, and enough revelation to know what you are supposed to do with it. *INVERTED:* By grace, there will be a cutting back on the level of feminine energy, a little gift of balancing from the divine, like a spiritual rolfing or massage session.

17 GOVERNED BY THE STAR: ASPIRATIONS OF EGO, GOALS, MAXIMUM EXPECTATIONS
UPRIGHT: Your goal is the nobility of the feminine in all its glory, to have its intellect and courage, to be guided by its loving nature and sense of responsibility. To be a female leader or a leader in the cause of the female. *INVERTED:* This may be a desire for female power over women that is too much in the interest of the ego.

18 GOVERNED BY THE MOON: ASPIRATIONS OF HEART, COMPASSION
UPRIGHT: The heart desires to achieve the full energy and power of the female, with maximum effectiveness and nurturing support for many. *INVERTED:* Look for distortions here so that the aspiration can be strengthened.

19 GOVERNED BY THE SUN: PHYSICAL FULFILLMENT/EVALUATION
UPRIGHT: By realizing female goals in the physical plane, you are surrounded by healthy, natural extensions of the self.. Your habitat is a living testimony to man's creativity, as much a laboratory as a home. Many like to visit, and most would like to stay if you let them. *INVERTED:* Work the best of Mother Nature and her principles into your material world.

20 GOVERNED BY JUDGEMENT: HEART'S FULFILLMENT/EVALUATION
UPRIGHT: Here the arms of the Mother open wide to embrace her loved ones. Ultimate sense of belonging and togetherness. The feminine principles have been achieved in the emotional plance, her shrine. *INVERTED:* Ask the High Priestess to help you to realize this archetype in your life.

21 GOVERNED BY THE WORLD: EGO'S FULFILLMENT/EVALUATION
UPRIGHT: Here is the equivalent of the Mother's pride, in the participation, the contribution, the success of her children, of others, as part and parcel of her own success. This is the mind's satisfaction at having implemented a program of root female values. *INVERTED:* Remember to embrace the masculine as well, and the success of the feminine will be surer and sweeter.

22/0 GOVERNED BY THE FOOL: SOUL'S FULFILLMENT EVALUATION
UPRIGHT: This has been a lifetime of energetic creativity. Feminine strength, the proper understanding and use of power, has been achieved. *INVERTED:* The lessons in this reading are guides to this fulfillment.

THE EMPRESS.

3 THE EMPRESS

UPRIGHT: Here is the third stop on the journey. It is the physical origin of your Mental Plane. The beginning of life in the mental body. Education. Knowledge. Teacher of teachers. Student of students. Chief of scribes and communication. Record-keeping. History. Oracles and prophets report here. Head administrator. Administration and government. Confucianism (professional, ordered control of society). Principles of civilization. Mental guide. Birth of logic and reason. Correctness. Original child of original duality: As the number 1 is thesis and the number 2 is antithesis, so the number 3 is synthesis. Mother of resolve and resolution. Embodiment of the male and female intellect. Authority figure. As opposed to the nurturing side of the female, here is the organizing and ambitious side aspiring to the best for herself and her brood. Remember that The Empress represents these qualities in all of us, female and male alike. The gentlewoman/lady. **INVERTED:** Too much or too little of the above principles lead to imbalances that must eventually be corrected. Imbalance in teacher/student principle—must input and output information equally so that we must all find our teachers and our students. Over or under administration. Too much or too little authority in a given situation. Objective information must be balanced with intuition. Too much logic, or not enough. Over or under-organized.

In This Spread Position...Interpret The Empress Meanings to Include:

1 GOVERNED BY THE MAGICIAN: PHYSICAL GIVENS, OUT OF THE FATHER
UPRIGHT: Your Physical Plane will be ordered and efficient, and your best work will involve mental disciplines under the auspices of The Empress. You will have concern for your appearance and public image. Nothing will get lost around your house. You like games involving logic. **INVERTED:** Organized people may be a trial for those they live with.

2 GOVERNED BY THE HIGH PRIESTESS: EMOTIONAL GIVENS, OUT OF THE MOTHER
UPRIGHT: Your Emotional/creative Plane will be organized and under control if you have anything to say about and you will. You have a knack for acting and entertaining in general. There is an interest in performing arts. Writing and speaking are good possibilities. **INVERTED:** It is not that you want to control everyone's lives; it's just that you would be so much better at it than they would.

3 GOVERNED BY THE EMPRESS: MENTAL GIVENS, INTELLECTUAL PREDISPOSITION
UPRIGHT: The Empress is in her home position and therefore centered and especially powerful. You know how to plan and achieve goals. A natural-born leader, administrator. Education fascinates you, whether teacher or student. You are an excellent teamplayer, although happiest as chairman. **INVERTED:** If they are on your team, they had better be ready to work.

4 GOVERNED BY THE EMPEROR: SPIRITUAL GIVENS, LIFE PURPOSE
UPRIGHT: Your abilities are needed to bring greater efficiency to bear. There is strong discipline here as you feel the calling to further the progress of civilization along the ideal of the Greeks, especially Plato. Education and knowledge are your tools. Your motivation—mental acumen must strive for understanding of God and the nature of spirituality if man is to progress. **INVERTED:** You will be passing on much of what past lives have taught you.

5 GOVERNED BY THE HIEROPHANT: SYSTEMS BORN INTO, SOCIETAL INFLUENCE
UPRIGHT: Your early environment was very organized and highly disciplined. The Empress may represent a female figure who was especially important in setting your young mind on the path. You may have spent considerable time in school, even a boarding school. If not, then school was at home with your parents. **INVERTED:** At one extreme, too much discipline, schooling, and adultness—not enough time being a kid.

6 GOVERNED BY THE LOVERS: EMOTIONAL TAPES, BASIS FOR RELATING/CREATING
UPRIGHT: Here is a love for the ideal of Empress/Princess—the establishment, all-capable female—not the damsel in distress. **INVERTED:** Keep this ideal as a guide, not a firm blueprint demanding exact construction to measurement.

7 GOVERNED BY THE CHARIOT: PHYSICAL RESOURCES, MEANS TO ACHIEVE
UPRIGHT: Your physical foundation rests on stability itself—good habits and a regimen of daily rituals that serve you well, keeping you healthy and fit. Your education will serve you wherever you go. **INVERTED:** Your physical foundation is your best resource, but needs some work to restore it to good order.

8 GOVERNED BY STRENGTH: EMOTIONAL RESOURCES, ENERGY
UPRIGHT: There is great clarity and awareness in your emotional house, with your relationships and your creative projects. You have acted very responsibly and with admirable control. **INVERTED:** Too much control will have stifled some opportunities and too little may have let them slip away.

9 GOVERNED BY THE HERMIT: BELIEF SYSTEM, BASIS FOR DECISIONS
UPRIGHT: Your beliefs may be almost Confucian. You believe in concrete knowledge and absolute order and a society based on just that. For you, reason must win out. You are very systematized. Your school of thought is probably more academic/philosophical than it is religious/spiritual. **INVERTED:** Perhaps the knowledge you admire is too concrete and the order too absolute. On the other hand, you may aspire to a freer system, an ideal without formal organization and order, a form of non-civilization.

10 GOVERNED BY THE WHEEL OF FORTUNE: CENTRAL MESSAGE, THEME OF READING
UPRIGHT: This is your call to accept leadership and responsibility, to organize and move forward with mental goals. Meditate on The Empress to find guides who may want to use this archetype in this reading. **INVERTED:** Much of this call may be for the benefit of others rather than yourself.

11 GOVERNED BY JUSTICE: STATE/CONTENT OF MIND
UPRIGHT: At this time you are clear headed, a good judge of character and situations with keen self-awareness. Others are sensing and trying to avail themselves of your spirit of cooperation. A person, The Empress, may be giving you good advice. **INVERTED:** You do not think that you are very prepared at the moment and this will affect your decisions.

12 GOVERNED BY THE HANGED MAN: STATE OF EMOTIONS, SUBCONSCIOUS
UPRIGHT: You appreciate yourself and your abilities, your power and position in this well-deserved moment. Your heart may be disposed to the person of The Empress. *INVERTED:* At one extreme, you may be disappointed in how well you have done the business of The Empress. Or, you may be less than pleased with your position of authority.

13 GOVERNED BY DEATH: PHYSICAL SITUATION, HARD REALITY
UPRIGHT: The Empress may actually be on the scene, or at least her energy is here. Your position is strong and defensible if necessary, for she is who the army fights for. To some she is the Archangel Gabriel and guides the suit of Swords. Your karmic purpose is on-line and productive. *INVERTED:* You are not as prepared as you can and should be.

14 GOVERNED BY TEMPERANCE: EMOTIONAL TEST
UPRIGHT: As you take on more knowledge and responsibility in the near future to satisfy your hunger for self-improvement and advancement, you must make the necessary adjustments in your Emotional Plane. Do your loved ones want the same things for you that you do? *INVERTED:* At this time you may not be prepared emotionally for a big push in the mental plane.

15 GOVERNED BY THE DEVIL: TEMPTATION/CHALLENGE, FEARS
UPRIGHT: You feel the time might be right to seek additional authority and power for your proper growth and for the benefit of others. You know you may have to acquire more knowledge or stretch a bit. *INVERTED:* In one extreme, you may have more doubts and hesitation about moving up the ladder than you would like to admit. In another extreme you may actually want to step back for awhile.

16 GOVERNED BY THE TOWER: NEXT LESSON, GRACE OF GOD
UPRIGHT: The near future shows many windows of opportunity opening for you, but with considerably more responsibility than at present. The Empress may be a woman figuring significantly in this. Here comes the status you have waited for. This can be a reassertion of the mental aspect of your karmic contract. *INVERTED:* Others look to you for opportunities, knowledge, and other things from the Empress's grab bag. Yes, you.

17 GOVERNED BY THE STAR: ASPIRATIONS OF EGO, GOALS, MAXIMUM EXPECTATIONS
UPRIGHT: You aim to be good at what you do and in a position to do it well, with good support and little interference. You expect to maximize your abilities and help others to do likewise. You need to seek power, for the right reasons, to get things done. *INVERTED:* You like being part of a system with higher authority than yourself, just not over your immediate affairs. In a shorter range reading this can suggest your desire to overturn the authority of someone else, or take their place.

18 GOVERNED BY THE MOON: ASPIRATIONS OF HEART, COMPASSION
UPRIGHT: This is an aspiration to capability and leadership out of a passion for a people or a cause and the need to get something done that requires your particular talents. This is a call to leadership that the heart must answer. *INVERTED:* Look carefully here, for in some circumstances this suggests that the heart is pulled to the wrong cause or misjudges its role.

19 GOVERNED BY THE SUN: PHYSICAL FULFILLMENT/EVALUATION
UPRIGHT: Things look like they went much the way you wanted them to; at least they ended up that way. You are very much in charge of your world as you reach those senior years. *INVERTED:* There is much more to be done if you want the degree of order and reason this archetype suggests, but it is yours for the having with work.

20 GOVERNED BY JUDGEMENT: HEART'S FULFILLMENT/EVALUATION
UPRIGHT: Much seems to have fallen on you in the affairs of family and loved ones, but there is good understanding between all the major players as you finish the business of this plane. There was much shared intellectually that helped bind you together to work out problems. There are no loose ends. *INVERTED:* Your loved ones may have to compete for your time against your intellectual interests and obligations, but you can manage your responsibilities to achieve this archetype.

21 GOVERNED BY THE WORLD: EGO'S FULFILLMENT/EVALUATION
UPRIGHT: You may be the intellectual's intellectual. You have ended your mental path with much knowledge about knowledge. Such is the mark of a hard working philosopher. *INVERTED:* Now that you know this is where you are headed, just do it.

22/0 GOVERNED BY THE FOOL: SOUL'S FULFILLMENT/EVALUATION
UPRIGHT: Wisdom is the able management of knowledge and there is much of that here. *INVERTED:* Work with the interpretations in this spread to better fulfill your Karmic Contract.

THE EMPEROR.

4 THE EMPEROR

UPRIGHT: Here is the fourth stop on the journey. It is the physical origin of the Spiritual Plane, and it represents the concept of the divine right of kings. This is the earthly part of the link between "As above, so below." Here is obedience of The Emperor to God, and obedience by man to God through the earthly administration of The Emperor. Here is the origin of duty and conscience. A master at the science of influence, the political spirit. Male authority figure with ultimate responsibility for making things work in the physical world. There is no earthly authority higher, and no responsibility greater, than this archetype. The buck stops here. Here is structure, foundation. This archetype is the magnet that holds society together. All that applies to 4's in the four suits of the Minor Arcana is applicable here. Here is the person in the Earth plane on whom we can rely for fair judgement and intuitive common sense. He is the leader, and a leader among leaders. The epitome of self-sufficiency, so efficient that he can provide for the needs of his loved ones and all others who require his help. Here is the Eastern discipline of Zen. Discipline and foresight to accomplish goals in the here and now, with keen awareness of past, present, and future. Here is the interplay between dependence and independence, the one and the all. The gentleman. **INVERTED:** History records the distortions that materialize with too much or too little of what this archetype represents. Excess brings despots and tyrants who abuse their power. Dearth brings weak, ineffectual kings who let anarchy and lawlessness take their toll. The gamut is from totalitarianism to anarchy; societal and personal health lies in taking the middle path.

In This Spread Position...Interpret The Emperor Meanings to Include:

1 GOVERNED BY THE MAGICIAN: PHYSICAL GIVENS, OUT OF THE FATHER
UPRIGHT: Your Physical/material Plane will be healthy and hearty. From a prominent role in the field of medicine to wearing the helmet of a general, there is need for your natural leadership ability. You may have inherited many strengths and much responsibility, possibly an estate or the rarity of a title, through your father's line. **INVERTED:** While many are drawn to your strength and position, others run the other way.

2 GOVERNED BY THE HIGH PRIESTESS: EMOTIONAL GIVENS, OUT OF THE MOTHER
UPRIGHT: Your Emotional/creative Plane will write its own rules. Many will be drawn to your strength and decisiveness. Natural leader and focal point in the creative arts. Your shoulder will see many a tear. You may have inherited many strengths and much responsibility, possibly an estate or the rarity of a title, through your mother's line. **INVERTED:** Beneath that authoritative posture beats a heart of gold, but some lack the courage to risk finding it.

3 GOVERNED BY THE EMPRESS: MENTAL GIVENS, INTELLECTUAL PREDISPOSITION
UPRIGHT: A mind dedicated to society, politics, management, and running through all of them—discipline and order. This is the rationality of mind at its pragmatic best, working to improve life for all of the outcasts of Eden. **INVERTED:** This could well have been the origin of the phrase, "This is going to hurt me more than it is you," for you must make many take their medicine.

4 GOVERNED BY THE EMPEROR: SPIRITUAL GIVENS, LIFE PURPOSE
UPRIGHT: Here is the Emperor card in his home and the meanings are at their strongest. You must accept that you are born to be a leader of leaders, the five star general amongst a host of generals. Your willpower will be central in all that you do. **INVERTED:** You have learned many of these lessons of leadership in past lives and much of what you do here is to assist others with these same lessons. In effect you may be teaching leadership.

5 GOVERNED BY THE HIEROPHANT: SYSTEMS BORN INTO, SOCIETAL INFLUENCE
UPRIGHT: Your early environment was clear, purposeful, controlled, a perfect boot camp for a future emperor. Whether your parents were ambassadors or giants of industry here at home, you were in and around the corridors of power and influence. **INVERTED:** At one extreme, this was far too much adult responsibility in lieu of toys and games. At the other extreme, you may have had little guidance or role modeling to go by.

6 GOVERNED BY THE LOVERS: EMOTIONAL TAPES, BASIS FOR RELATING/CREATING
UPRIGHT: Power and authority are attractive to many people, but for you, this archetype makes this serious business. You have a conventional desire for love and sex, with courtship, engagement et al, probably with an older, but certainly an established, mate. **INVERTED:** At one extreme, you may have more than enough ambition for you, your mate, and your entire family.

7 GOVERNED BY THE CHARIOT: PHYSICAL RESOURCES. MEANS TO ACHIEVE
UPRIGHT: You are a master at the game of life. You are strong physically, financially, politically, socially. You are the Duke in his hilltop castle surrounded by loyal attendants. **INVERTED:** Check your resources as a general would check his men—their physical condition (health and equipment), their emotional well-being (sex life), and their state of mind (loyalty).

8 GOVERNED BY STRENGTH: EMOTIONAL RESOURCES, ENERGY
UPRIGHT: You draw much of your strength from within and above, accepting responsibility, but you also gain strength from the very people depending on you. You are loved and admired by many. **INVERTED:** You may depend on someone else for your strength, but be wary of taking advantage. Nor can you let another control you or assume your responsibilities.

9 GOVERNED BY THE HERMIT: BELIEF SYSTEM, BASIS FOR DECISIONS
UPRIGHT: Here is the system player, guided by faith in collective thinking, the actions of a group. It is faith in the idea of society itself, and so at root very Socratic. You look for people with whom you can share an ideology. **INVERTED:** At one extreme, there is rejection of the group, the society, and advocacy of supreme individuality. Your ideal home may be a remote cabin in the woods. At the other extreme, too much faith in collective thinking hinders the individual path. This has been seen in radical socialism/communism in the twentieth century.

10 GOVERNED BY THE WHEEL OF FORTUNE: CENTRAL MESSAGE, THEME OF READING
UPRIGHT: This is a time for order, discipline, rules. You must assert yourself, taking more responsibility and an active leadership role. You might be tempted to go a bit easy except that other people depend on you and helping them is the best thing you could do for yourself as well. **INVERTED:** Look to the leadership of someone obviously capable to help you with your responsibilities. Your goals can best be met by teaming up with another person or group, perhaps more established and experienced than you/yours.

11 GOVERNED BY JUSTICE: STATE/CONTENT OF MIND
UPRIGHT: You are prioritizing, establishing procedures, making important decisions, confronting reality head-on and taking control. The person of the Emperor may be putting in an appearance as an advisor. **INVERTED:** At one extreme, you may be conjuring up more than the situation needs and should loosen up some. Do not assume more responsibility than necessary.

12 GOVERNED BY THE HANGED MAN: STATE OF EMOTIONS, SUBCONSCIOUS
UPRIGHT: Your heart is opening up to the idea of having power and control. You are beginning to trust yourself. You are comfortable with the cast of characters, the politics of the moment, whether internal in the family or external in business. The person of the Emperor may be entering your heart. **INVERTED:** At one extreme, the heart is not only opening up to this archetype, it is over enthusiastic to a fault. At the other extreme, the heart is closing on the idea of responsibility and power, too much so for good balance.

13 GOVERNED BY DEATH: PHYSICAL SITUATION, HARD REALITY
UPRIGHT: You are very much in charge and on top of the situation. Your authority is recognized and complied with. **INVERTED:** You may be overstepping your bounds for this situation. The opposite extreme has you not stepping in where you should.

14 GOVERNED BY TEMPERANCE: EMOTIONAL TEST
UPRIGHT: Here is the impact of position and power in your emotional house in the near future. If you are beefing up your act, how are others reacting? **INVERTED:** The person or influence of The Emperor may be asserted over you, testing your true strength and the depth of your motivations.

15 GOVERNED BY THE DEVIL: TEMPTATION AND CHALLENGE, FEARS
UPRIGHT: You are being pulled toward more leadership and power. There will be stability in your mental program, a base from which you assert your willpower to assure ordered progress. **INVERTED:** At one extreme, you may be tempted to accept a position simply for status. At another extreme, The Emperor puts in an appearance as someone you are tempted to follow or emulate. Think twice, maybe three times.

16 GOVERNED BY THE TOWER: NEXT LESSON, GRACE OF GOD
UPRIGHT: You are about to become a significant part of a strong system. You will be asked to accept a position of leadership that is right for you. It may be so right that you seem to be inheriting it. You will begin here your move toward maximum power and responsibility for this lifetime. **INVERTED:** Even though this opportunity is correct for your karmic path, you may be more influenced by a sense of duty because it seems so right for so many others, for so many reasons, that you cannot say no to it.

17 GOVERNED BY THE STAR: ASPIRATIONS OF EGO, GOALS, MAXIMUM EXPECTATIONS
UPRIGHT: Almost everyone starts out wanting their playmates and friends to pick them as captain of the team, or to nominate them for class office, because it was a way of knowing you were liked and belonged. But they picked you because you were good and it would be best for them, the team, the class if you had the job. And they picked you because they sensed you wanted the job and would work hard at it. And today your goal is the same, to have the number one job and to do a number one job on the job. This is the goal of an ordered society. Correct political ambition. **INVERTED:** The distortions here include the ego trips for power and prestige. Power is considered essential to success.

18 GOVERNED BY THE MOON: ASPIRATIONS OF HEART, COMPASSION
UPRIGHT: The expression "natural-born leader" applies to you, and you are more than aware of it, you accept it wholeheartedly. People gravitate to you because they know that it is always in their best interests to do so. You want to be in charge, simply because you know that you can get things done that will improve people's lives. Pulled toward the concept of an ideal commune. **INVERTED:** The need to be loved and admired can be too great and distort this archetype and its effectiveness. A benevolent dictator. Distortions on the idea of a utopia.

19 GOVERNED BY THE SUN: PHYSICAL FULFILLMENT/EVALUATION
UPRIGHT: You are much in control in your senior years, a patriarch/matriarch of family or business. There is independence and self-sufficiency as you age. Everything around you will bear your mark. **INVERTED:** If you want to wear emperor's clothes that other people can see, then follow the lessons of the Tarot to fulfill this archetype.

20 GOVERNED BY JUDGEMENT: HEART'S FULFILLMENT/EVALUATION
UPRIGHT: You have been affected by many people, as indeed you have affected many. To be a leader and a follower, to find the balance of individuality and group identity, is a must on the path and you have achieved it. A special bond develops between leader/follower just as between teacher/student that cannot be explained any more than that between lovers, but you have achieved it. **INVERTED:** If you want to be able to take off the emperor's clothes and still be visible, follow this archetype to its fulfillment at the end of your emotional path.

21 GOVERNED BY THE WORLD: EGO'S FULFILLMENT/EVALUATION
UPRIGHT: Here is a legacy of pattern, of organization, of a system that will continue long past your time, exactly as you would have it. For your leadership was such as to make people independent of you, rather than dependent on you. You know fully that your followers followed what was in their best interests. They of course think they followed you. **INVERTED:** If you wish to deserve to wear the emperor's clothes study this archetype carefully and the interpretations of this reading, especially of the mental plane.

22/0 GOVERNED BY THE FOOL: SOUL'S FULFILLMENT EVALUATION
UPRIGHT: This soul has faced the duality of personal and group karma squarely and successfully. In being a good citizen, a good governor, you have been both a good servant of your karmic purpose, and of course God. **INVERTED:** Work to balance the inner and outer aspects of the will of God and you will serve both self and fellow man well.

5 THE HIEROPHANT

UPRIGHT: Here is the fifth stop. This is the spiritual as comprehended by the intellect, and at this stage usually an acceptance of the external/collective intellect as opposed to your own. Organized religion and other systems of belief, ethics and morality. Or, any strong philosophical belief structure within which you are operating. Faith in the earthbound aspects of spirituality. Thought forms and ideologies that you become attached to because they are bridges to your own. This is the young and/or undeveloped mind attracted to and studying the thoughts of others. This is a link between ordinary worldly consciousness and the intuitive knowledge of God's law. Here then is the establishment, the norm, the administrative arm of the Emperor to administer the laws by which a "below" can be established to the "above." Aristotle taught, like the Tarot here, that in any society/state, the form of religion practiced was fashioned after the form of government. Here we have consensus reality, society, "common" sense, organized religion, bureaucracy. The Hierophant presides over the realm of the number 5, and should be studied with the four 5's of the Minor Arcana which tell four stories about freedom/uncertainty. **INVERTED:** Distortions of this archetype can be over-attachment and blind acceptance/following. But, just as you are eventually kicked out of your mother's physical/emotional nest, so too will your own mind kick you out of an outdated mental nest that is no longer comfortable. To the neurotic, this looking outside of the self for the accepted norm of behavior can become literally "the voice of God." Hegel argued that we exist only as part of a system; he called it organicism. The only problem here is Hegel's use of the word only. We exist in a system, by the grace of that system into which we are born, but then we must decide for ourselves how we want to use, to adapt, to change that system and so pass it on to the next generation. Some of us choose a personal system very much like our parent/predecessors, but we must choose it not blindly follow it. Others of us strike out on very different paths from the map handed to us.

In This Spread Position...Interpret The Hierophant Meanings to Include:

1 GOVERNED BY THE MAGICIAN: PHYSICAL GIVENS, OUT OF THE FATHER
UPRIGHT: The Physical/material Plane will show the impact of beliefs through the father's line. Behavior may be rooted in the religions of the West, principally the Judaeo-Christian and/or the Islamic traditions. **INVERTED:** There are physical challenges and lessons which come with being born into any elaborately detailed way of looking at the world.

2 GOVERNED BY THE HIGH PRIESTESS: EMOTIONAL GIVENS, OUT OF THE MOTHER
UPRIGHT: The Emotional/creative Plane will show the impact of beliefs through the mother's line. Behavior may be rooted in the religions of the East, such as Hinduism and Buddhism. **INVERTED:** There are emotional and creative challenges and lessons which come with being born into any historically rich view of the world.

3 GOVERNED BY THE EMPRESS: MENTAL GIVENS, INTELLECTUAL PREDISPOSITION
UPRIGHT: You will be intellectually comfortable with formal religious teachings, and find society and its demands on its citizens presents no formidable barriers to your personal development. You are especially good at logic and ethics. Your mind will work to explain and to administer "as above, so below." **INVERTED:** Your challenge will be to help others fit as easily into the system, or to shape a system to their liking, as it is for you.

4 GOVERNED BY THE EMPEROR: SPIRITUAL GIVENS, LIFE PURPOSE
UPRIGHT: This path is to administer and administrate the word of God, to help society function according to divine truth and law. Even the venerated professor of law or philosophy professor is at home here. **INVERTED:** Whether or not you are a defacto priest is a moot point, for you will serve communion to your fellow citizen.

5 GOVERNED BY THE HIEROPHANT: SYSTEMS BORN INTO, SOCIETAL INFLUENCE
UPRIGHT: This early environment was highly structured and peopled with many adults with very strong, well formulated ideologies. A clear message was presented in word and deed. **INVERTED:** At one extreme, the belief system may have been overly restrictive, and it may have been far from the mark of accuracy in witnessing God's truth. At another extreme, there may have been either little clear ideology or a hodgepodge of thinking and much inconsistency in ethics.

6 GOVERNED BY THE LOVERS: EMOTIONAL TAPES, BASIS FOR RELATING/CREATING
UPRIGHT: Here is an early passion for formal religion, such as a desire to join an order or become a priest. Also, here is the passion for the nation-state, such as a desire to run away and join the Marines. The love is for the group and the group belief. This is the mark of an early disciple to any system of thought or love. **INVERTED:** If acted on too early, these passions may prove to be less than long lasting. At another extreme the passion may be a hatred for a given belief system.

7 GOVERNED BY THE CHARIOT: PHYSICAL RESOURCES. MEANS TO ACHIEVE
UPRIGHT: You have aligned yourself, your time and your habits, with others, with establishment and established ways of doing things. You have enjoyed doing the expected, pleasing yourself and your group. **INVERTED:** Should you need to do something very out of the ordinary, you may have trouble getting the resources you need.

8 GOVERNED BY STRENGTH: EMOTIONAL RESOURCES, ENERGY
UPRIGHT: The beliefs of your parents, your early environment, have been comfortable and worked well for you. You are therefore surrounded by people who have been able to rely on you and vice-versa. This gives you the confidence and energy you need to grow. **INVERTED:** You may be wanting a new car that will no longer use your old brand of gasoline. Something has to give.

9 GOVERNED BY THE HERMIT: BELIEF SYSTEM, BASIS FOR DECISIONS
UPRIGHT: Your beliefs are most likely very similar to what you grew up with, but not necessarily. And most likely you are a practicing member of an organized religion, but not necessarily. But, you are an advocate of convention, if not the conventional. You insist on a healthy system for society's business and with a strong enough backbone of ethics to raise it above simple law and order to a belief system and some form of reliance on higher law. **INVERTED:** At one extreme, you would not touch organized religion with a twenty-foot pole. At the other extreme, you are such a devotee that you follow the letter of the church law, even when you know better. Also, here are alienation from a group or belief system and revolutionary ideologies.

10 GOVERNED BY THE WHEEL OF FORTUNE: CENTRAL MESSAGE, THEME OF READING
UPRIGHT: This is an opportunity to avail yourself of an established source, such as a given religion or philosophical school of thought. Truth is being presented in a package that is highly palatable. Babette's Feast, a cornucopia, is at hand. Do not miss it. It has been cooked especially for you. ***INVERTED:*** All of the above is true, but it may be hard for you to get you hands around it because it is yet too ethereal. Nevertheless, this is a group to which you want to listen and participate with. It will become more concrete with time; that is why you are to be involved.

11 GOVERNED BY JUSTICE: STATE/CONTENT OF MIND
UPRIGHT: Your mind is not on frivolous things, but on the rudiments of what makes you tick, of what makes everything tick. You are centered on your personal belief system, evaluating the group to which your personal beliefs adhere, and the universal systems to which that group adheres. This centering exercise cum evaluation is in preparation for some major work and you want the horses to be lined up just right. ***INVERTED:*** Do not waste your time or the horses' in trying to get them lined up precisely before you think you can act. Life is an organic process.

12 GOVERNED BY THE HANGED MAN: STATE OF EMOTIONS, SUBCONSCIOUS
UPRIGHT: You are immersed in your faith, your belief system, and the people sharing it with you. This is worship—what we want most, and when we do it right, what we get the most out of. This is the balance of give and take, from above to below and back again. And done right it does not matter which came first, the chicken or the egg. ***INVERTED:*** Too much immersion in a belief is actually a suspension of that belief, just as much as if you had refuted that belief to begin with. The heart will help you balance between belief and non-belief, between faith and doubt, between yourself and your group.

13 GOVERNED BY DEATH: PHYSICAL SITUATION, HARD REALITY
UPRIGHT: Your belief group is the most prominent, pre-eminent aspect of your material life. You may well be making your living on-line serving up God's reality in portions that people can swallow. You are putting your spirituality out there with others where people can touch it and try it on for size themselves. ***INVERTED:*** You can lead a horse to water but you can't make him drink is not a lament; it is as it should be.

14 GOVERNED BY TEMPERANCE: EMOTIONAL TEST
UPRIGHT: The heart's biggest question in the near future regards its relationship to the heart of the society to which it belongs. Do they beat as one? ***INVERTED:*** Ask yourself whether your belief system, your adherence to the collective faith, is opening your heart or closing it.

15 GOVERNED BY THE DEVIL: TEMPTATION/CHALLENGE, FEARS
UPRIGHT: Your mind runs society's mores up the flagpole to test them in the wind of truth. Are they alive, flexible, inclusive? Can they be projected into the future without stretching the imagination? ***INVERTED:*** Neither ask questions when you have none, nor not ask them when you have one.

16 GOVERNED BY THE TOWER: NEXT LESSON, GRACE OF GOD
UPRIGHT: Listen to these guides of grace shedding new light in old corners. You may view this as a new turn on an old truth, or as a new pattern of truth speaking an entirely new language. It will expand your awareness by giving you new friends to play and study with. Pay more than usual attention to dreams, channeling, meditation, all inner resources, as well as the marvel of serendipity in everyday events. ***INVERTED:*** Much of what you receive will be for others.

17 GOVERNED BY THE STAR: ASPIRATIONS OF EGO, GOALS, MAXIMUM EXPECTATIONS
UPRIGHT: This is aspiration to a faith, a means of accessing and acknowledging the divine, that is shared by many. Here is the hope to be effective in establishing and forwarding a set of thoughts. ***INVERTED:*** While the above is proper, one should not aspire to the surface content, or to the satisfaction of numbers, rather than to the essence of the belief itself. It is one thing to share with others a belief held by one's soul. It is altogether different to mislead one's group or oneself for the sake of comradery.

18 GOVERNED BY THE MOON: ASPIRATIONS OF HEART, COMPASSION
UPRIGHT: Your beliefs are central in all of your relationships. You relate well in and through organizations. You are demonstrative of your beliefs. There is importance here in the ability to communally worship, to observe in like manner and ritual, at common times and in common places. You wish to raise your voice with many others. ***INVERTED:*** While the above is proper, one should not aspire to the surface content, or to the satisfaction of numbers, rather than to the essence of the belief itself. It is one thing to share with others a belief held by one's soul. It is altogether different to mislead one's group or oneself for the sake of comradery.

19 GOVERNED BY THE SUN: PHYSICAL FULFILLMENT/EVALUATION
UPRIGHT: Your Physical Plane has been rich with ritual, with living observance of your most fundamental beliefs. Even if your faith requires no overt materiality to support it, it will be obvious to all but the least sensitive eye that spirituality has pervaded your every step. ***INVERTED:*** Continue to walk your talk and this will be your just reward.

20 GOVERNED BY JUDGEMENT: HEART'S FULFILLMENT/EVALUATION
UPRIGHT: You and your fellow travelers have enjoyed the game with a given set of rules that have worked well for you and many. You are filled with a sense of reward for your choices, and an extra special warmth at having traveled the road together. ***INVERTED:*** Caravans are relatively safe saving us from many a misfortune, but still we must travel together not out of fear, but out of our shared interpretation of love, our common destination.

21 GOVERNED BY THE WORLD: EGO'S FULFILLMENT/EVALUATION
UPRIGHT: You have contributed to the establishment and/or the maintenance of a belief group, the advancement of a cause to which many are linked. You have intimately connected your personal view with that of an organized body, or a school of thought. ***INVERTED:*** This is hard work you have chosen, but all the better the sense of satisfaction when all is said and done.

22/0 GOVERNED BY THE FOOL: SOUL'S FULFILLMENT/EVALUATION
UPRIGHT: Your life has been dedicated to finding a way of seeing the good, a view that is shared now by many others. Your contribution makes possible a continuation of a valuable lineage of thought and belief. ***INVERTED:*** The lessons addressed in this reading bear witness to your work.

6 THE LOVERS

UPRIGHT: Here is the sixth stop on the overall journey, and the second stop on the Emotional Plane. It represents an important emotional growth step to the desire for, and acceptance of, an extension of yourself. It is the birth of duality in the heart as the self discovers the other. Emersion out of the self; immersion in the other. It teaches you emotional partnering, how to share the basic components of human activity with one other person in particular. You voluntarily alter your course of needs and wants to accommodate those of another. Without the passion and sexual drives to spur you, you might never make this "compromise," but it is the first major lesson to the ego of the necessity to go beyond the separate, physical self. Here are the choices, the trials, the decisions created by desire. This emotional partnering may in some cases not be with another person, in which case that other something (possibly a place, a thing, or even a personal talent of yours) must be thought of as a surrogate for what would otherwise be a lover or mate. As long as the lessons to be learned at this stage are in fact being addressed and learned, this presents no problem. But if there is no partnering and no surrogate and no lessons being learned, watch out! The Romance Legends, such as the Arthurian tales where love predominates over the state, show the evolution of society from the Emperor(4) and Hierophant(5), i.e., from the belief systems which are handed to us by our elders, into the thrusts of desire of the Lovers which sends us on our individual quest. Hence, it takes the birth of duality in love to make us assert our individuality. **INVERTED:** Distortion in the way of too much or too little of the above meanings. Sex tied solely to reproduction. The previous lessons of the Hierophant(5), i.e., of society and the group may dominate the individual yielding: a female who looks to the society/state for her hero-mate and the male becomes an intruder and can even be considered evil...or, a male who looks to the society/state for his heroine, his source of civility and stability, and the female is reduced to a toy, an object, an obstacle or burden rather than a source of energy. Marriage of convenience rather than marriage of love (also seen in the Two of Cups, inverted).

In This Spread Position...Interpret The Lovers Meanings to Include:

1 GOVERNED BY THE MAGICIAN: PHYSICAL GIVENS, OUT OF THE FATHER
UPRIGHT: The Physical Plane will be full of energy and vitality from beginning to end and throughout all activities—health, work, leisure. Your amorous nature comes principally through your father's line. **INVERTED:** Be aware that others may not have your stamina or range of appreciation of the subtleties of your senses.

2 GOVERNED BY THE HIGH PRIESTESS: EMOTIONAL GIVENS, OUT OF THE MOTHER
UPRIGHT: The passions and depth of feeling possible with this predisposition of the heart offers you the level of creative ability that fills galleries, as well as a chance for love and intrigue to rival the classics of romantic literature. **INVERTED:** You may have an unfair advantage over mere emotional mortals, so be gentle.

3 GOVERNED BY THE EMPRESS: MENTAL GIVENS, INTELLECTUAL PREDISPOSITION
UPRIGHT: This mind is especially gifted in the affairs of the heart, of relationships. Such intellectual understanding of our emotions is rare and invaluable. Counselors will be found here. But such knowledge paired with this level of creative passion also produces great writers, especially poets, and communicators speaking through their arts. **INVERTED:** You can have a lot of fun if you play this card right.

4 GOVERNED BY THE EMPEROR: SPIRITUAL GIVENS, LIFE PURPOSE
UPRIGHT: Here is a life that will be dedicated to the discovery and expression of love, the play of divine energy in the worldly sphere. Here is raw motivation, the stuff that pushes all of us through the hoops with enough height and speed not to be burned by the ring of fire. **INVERTED:** Much of your energy will go to helping others find their energy and the motivation to use it.

5 GOVERNED BY THE HIEROPHANT: SYSTEMS BORN INTO, SOCIETAL INFLUENCE
UPRIGHT: While many youngsters do not see much overt affection and energetic display from the adults around them, such was not the case in your early environment. Here was an extroverted atmosphere of sociability and sensitivity fostering creativity. **INVERTED:** At one extreme, there may have been much too overt an attitude toward and display of affection, even sex. At the other extreme, there would have been much too little, conveying a more puritanical attitude—that not only sex, but affection and openness are somehow bad for us.

6 GOVERNED BY THE LOVERS: EMOTIONAL TAPES, BASIS FOR RELATING/CREATING
UPRIGHT: The ideal of love. You have a classic, fairy tale view of the successful love story—the princess and the white knight—as the base for your emotional program. You may have had a true love at a very tender age that stays with you as a feeling to be recaptured, or in those rare cases held onto. **INVERTED:** At one extreme, this tape is so ideal as to be deliberately, if subconsciously, unattainable. At the other extreme, you may have the non-ideal, the impossibility of true love, or an actual distaste for intimacy and pairing as your tapes. This latter is serious, as it blocks all growth, emotional and spiritual, and must be surmounted sooner or later, with less or more pain.

7 GOVERNED BY THE CHARIOT: PHYSICAL RESOURCES, MEANS TO ACHIEVE
UPRIGHT: The energy and verve with which you do things has given you great prowess. You are sexy; romance and creativity figure prominently in your overall scheme of things. Your work itself may deal with this archetype, ranging from an aerobics instructor to lifestyle magazine editor. **INVERTED:** At the extreme you may be burning the candle at both ends, an easy way to get burned.

8 GOVERNED BY STRENGTH: EMOTIONAL RESOURCES, ENERGY
UPRIGHT: You are a healthy romantic who understands the magic of give and take in the emotional world. You are at ease with your body, with intimacy and sex, and with people in general. There is a fluid ease in this plane that keeps you at the top of your form. Some would say you are lucky in love. **INVERTED:** Openness may not be that easy for you, but you can improve with conscious effort. At the other extreme, you may be letting it all hang out and may not be able to find it when you need it.

9 GOVERNED BY THE HERMIT: BELIEF SYSTEM, BASIS FOR DECISIONS
UPRIGHT: Here is the rule of Dionysian rather than Apollonian spirit, in the most positive sense. Life is to be lived, enjoyed, and therein at the core is the appreciation of the divinity in everything, in the absolute ecstasy of awareness. Only when we distort the pursuit of these things do we pull up short and get into ethical problems. **INVERTED:** At one extreme, there is the more popular conception/misconception that the bacchanal approach to life is to be avoided at all

costs, hence pleasure itself is a danger if not an outright no-no. At the other extreme, the confidence in pleasure as the route to all things is carried to the limits, or past them.

10 GOVERNED BY THE WHEEL OF FORTUNE: CENTRAL MESSAGE, THEME OF READING
UPRIGHT: Heads up for love. Pay attention to all the signs, and they should be aplenty. Honor your creative talents for now is the time to extrovert your feelings, sharing with others who may need your inspiration and prodding to free their feelings. **INVERTED:** Rare it is that we are told to let a love go, but such may be the case now. This may be a period where introspection and self-love is called for. To the artist, this means back to the studio rather than the gallery.

11 GOVERNED BY JUSTICE: STATE/CONTENT OF MIND
UPRIGHT: Love, relationships, creativity—such is the nature of your mind's activity at the moment. You are planning around your heart's desire, for here are the types of thoughts we have when we are in love. **INVERTED:** This is where the word preoccupied comes into good use. The mind needs more than this one track. At another extreme, these thoughts are against this archetype.

12 GOVERNED BY THE HANGED MAN: STATE OF EMOTIONS, SUBCONSCIOUS
UPRIGHT: When we say we are in love, this is the feeling we are trying to express. This is the personal passion and pleasure felt in the depth of the heart. **INVERTED:** Here may be the pain of intense love felt, not lost. At the other extreme, is the agony of unrequited or lost love.

13 GOVERNED BY DEATH: PHYSICAL SITUATION, HARD REALITY
UPRIGHT: Here love, the birth of duality in love, is doing its magic of pulling the self out of its shell by having it come to need another as much as it needs self. The self is growing to include this other in its idea of what it must be in order to continue its physical existence. Marriage. **INVERTED:** At one extreme, the process will subvert itself in progress by trying to possess or even consume the very other it has come to "love." Separation. Divorce.

14 GOVERNED BY TEMPERANCE: EMOTIONAL TEST
UPRIGHT: Love, an important relationship, acceptance of creative inspiration, is intensifying, demanding greater definition and expression. The external must be integrated into the heart. That which is integrated must be externalized and shared. **INVERTED:** Too much or too little, both can cause disappointment and sadness with the sense of loss, as a piece of self missing. Accept this twist on an old parable: Like the shepherd who leaves his entire flock to find the one lost sheep, the heart may neglect what is at hand to search for what is lost.

15 GOVERNED BY THE DEVIL: TEMPTATION/CHALLENGE, FEARS
UPRIGHT: In the near future you may face the challenge of integrating a relationship, a new and unexpected passion, into your life game plan. **INVERTED:** At one extreme, here comes true temptation. The impact of a full and throbbing heart on the rational business of mind. The advice here is to temper your emotions if you can find the wherewithal. At the other extreme, your libido is too low and you may be ignoring something that very much deserves your attention. Remember that this can be your own gifted talents.

16 GOVERNED BY THE TOWER: NEXT LESSON, GRACE OF GOD
UPRIGHT: You should not have to ask anyone about this when it happens. The phrase "love of your life" will come to pass your lips. In this position the suggestion is that it may come as quite a surprise as in "across a dark and crowded room," or "love at first sight." **INVERTED:** You may be the very instrumental agent in someone else's magic moment. In an extreme, this can be the amicable ending by grace of a relationship that has completed its course—"and they parted friends."

17 GOVERNED BY THE STAR: ASPIRATIONS OF EGO, GOALS, MAXIMUM EXPECTATIONS
UPRIGHT: Your mind is focused on the ideal of love, in a more immediate sense to be married. This may be a personal goal surpassing all others, or it may an intellectual fascination with the archetype which motivates your work, especially if you are making your living in a highly creative field. **INVERTED:** Too much of this ideal could lead an otherwise healthy mind down the garden path. Too little can be a self-limiting, pessimistic pit from which little of life can be seen, much less enjoyed.

18 GOVERNED BY THE MOON: ASPIRATIONS OF HEART, COMPASSION
UPRIGHT: Such aspirations as these do best sellers make. This is complete dedication to the object of love, and through that object the realization of the greater love of many learning the lesson of compassion through the guiding light of passion. Here the heart fully expects to lose itself in a worthy other, then in the universal other. **INVERTED:** At one extreme, the lonely heart expecting to remain lonely. Such a lack of faith in basic love reveals a lack of faith in God's love. At the other extreme, the projected love of the object of passion/compassion has swallowed the love of self which must remain at the core.

19 GOVERNED BY THE SUN: PHYSICAL FULFILLMENT/EVALUATION
UPRIGHT: A youthful vigor and relevancy carry through this plane to the end with the help of love and an openness to others. There is a love of life in its simplest and most meaningful sense that keeps you strong. This can show marriage late in life. **INVERTED:** Use the upright interpretations of this archetype to maximize your fulfillment here.

20 GOVERNED BY JUDGEMENT: HEART'S FULFILLMENT/EVALUATION
UPRIGHT: This has been a life so dedicated to love that it may be called the "art of love." Here has been complete surrender to the ideal of love, be it one person, many, a cause, or the love and honoring of your own talent. **INVERTED:** Keep your heart open and this will be your karmic fulfillment.

21 GOVERNED BY THE WORLD: EGO'S FULFILLMENT/EVALUATION
UPRIGHT: Your mental achievement centers on your understanding of love, of energy, of motivation, and your ability to share that understanding with many others. **INVERTED:** An open heart will provide your mind with all the material it needs to reach this goal.

22/0 GOVERNED BY THE FOOL: SOUL'S FULFILLMENT/EVALUATION
UPRIGHT: Here was a true lover. **INVERTED:** Here was a true lover.

THE CHARIOT.

7 THE CHARIOT

UPRIGHT: Here is the seventh stop on the overall journey, and the second stop on the Physical Plane. As such, you see the physical ways and means of extending your physical package, your physical growth. Here are the wheels for the Emperor/Empress. Physical transportation/movement. Travel. Relocation. Physical strength and capability, prowess. Construction. Physical action taken to increase your personal package. Physical extensions of the self and support in your environment. Material aids to achieving goals. Building and feathering the nest. Asserting physical independence. Creating your personal, physical world as a laboratory for your life's work. Getting things done on the Material Plane. Efforts to improve your health, especially your physical condition. Change and control in diet. Financial investment. Physical investment of time and energy. Harnessing of energy to appropriate physical ends. To achieve anything one must somehow harness the extremes of opposites, of dualities. Our chariot will go neither where the left horse would take it, nor where the right would have it, but where we steer it, straight ahead down the middle path just as Plato's Charioteer steered his two steeds. Here too is the archetype for the caravan, carrying not just the self, but the self with extended family. In one analogy the two horses are Temperance(14) and Temptation (Devil/15), one pulling us back, the other pushing us forward. ***INVERTED:*** Distortion in the way of too much or too little of the above meanings. Spinning your wheels. Moving in the wrong direction, too quickly, too slowly, not at all. Lack of flexibility in movement. Running away, or running headstrong into a messy situation—retreat or a foolish attack. Changing jobs too often, not often enough. Not enough, or too much, physical exercise. Building too much, too fast. Tearing down, reducing means. Accumulation of too much baggage, too heavy for your needs. Over feathering the nest. Physically over extended, or not extended enough. Overly independent or much too dependent.

In This Spread Position...Interpret The Chariot Meanings to Include:

1 GOVERNED BY THE MAGICIAN: PHYSICAL GIVENS, OUT OF THE FATHER
UPRIGHT: Physical ability, mobility, prowess, comes primarily through the father's line. Extension and growth of the self, enlargement, will be based mostly on physical talents and material progress. You will want to have a large extended family and many friends. ***INVERTED:*** Almost everyone admires this archetype at work in a person, but some will be envious of your physical/material success and try to give you a hard time.

2 GOVERNED BY THE HIGH PRIESTESS: EMOTIONAL GIVENS, OUT OF THE MOTHER
UPRIGHT: Physical ability, mobility, prowess, comes primarily through the mother's line. Extension and growth of the self, enlargement, will come mostly through the Emotional Plane and innate talents. You may want a large family. Creativity is a means for material security and success. ***INVERTED:*** Many people will want to play on your team. It will be hard for you to say no when there is no more room.

3 GOVERNED BY THE EMPRESS: MENTAL GIVENS, INTELLECTUAL PREDISPOSITION
UPRIGHT: You have an active, extroverted mind. Enterprising, self-starting, highly ambitious. Extension and growth of the self, enlargement, will be achieved through your mental agility, and a busy intelligence. ***INVERTED:*** Your ideas always seem to be the ones that get adopted, that take hold and generate activity. This pleases most people, but there will be some natural resistance from those who dislike change or wish to move more slowly.

4 GOVERNED BY THE EMPEROR: SPIRITUAL GIVENS, LIFE PURPOSE
UPRIGHT: This lifetime is to be centered on growth and enrichment. Much is to be accomplished in the hard reality of the Physical/material Plane. There should be much social activity as well as business and trade. This is a path of increase in the foundation of the self to include the well-being of others under its mantle of protection. Here is assumption of responsibility for a self that includes others. ***INVERTED:*** Much of this lifetime may be in the provision for others more than for self, and to help them with their growth.

5 GOVERNED BY THE HIEROPHANT: SYSTEMS BORN INTO, SOCIETAL INFLUENCE
UPRIGHT: This early environment was very do-it-yourself oriented and full of ambition and drive. This family was very much on the go, even when they were settled in one place. But there could have been a healthy amount of movement. In days gone by, this may have even been a nomadic lifestyle. ***INVERTED:*** At one extreme, this may have been a corporate or military family with so many location changes that continuity for children was difficult. At the other extreme, this may have been a family that was very inactive and not in a growth mode, so that an implosion of sorts was taking place.

6 GOVERNED BY THE LOVERS: EMOTIONAL TAPES, BASIS FOR RELATING/CREATING
UPRIGHT: These are the tapes of a very impressionable youth, eager to adopt heros and heroines of larger than life proportions. The more exotic and far reaching the better, such as science fiction. The underlying fascination here is in the figure/idol who is so physically strong that he/she can always get the job done, so that everyone ends up not only secure, but with more than they started out with. ***INVERTED:*** It is not good to feel that you can, or even should, always come out ahead, especially if that means ahead of everybody else. But neither should you feel you need to lose out so that someone else can get what they need.

7 GOVERNED BY THE CHARIOT: PHYSICAL RESOURCES. MEANS TO ACHIEVE
UPRIGHT:Here is the Chariot card in the position of the Chariot and so it is very centered and strong. Do you own your own trucking company, or run your own construction company? It would seem that you have the resources and the ability to do what needs doing. The strongest of foundations has been laid for the accomplishment of your Karmic Contract. ***INVERTED:*** On the one hand, you may have been stretching too much, too soon. On the other hand, you may not have been stretching enough, or not at all.

8 GOVERNED BY STRENGTH: EMOTIONAL RESOURCES, ENERGY
UPRIGHT: Your relationships have depth in quality and in number, having been built up in layers, one leading to another and another. This has bred status and thus confidence. You are emotionally stronger too because of your physical and material strength. ***INVERTED:*** At one extreme, this suggests an emotional plane that may be somewhat unwieldy for future requirements. The cast of characters, or the number of plays being attempted, is too ambitious. At the other extreme, there is not enough emotional ambition and so not enough energy. This heart waits too much, acts too little.

9 GOVERNED BY THE HERMIT: BELIEF SYSTEM, BASIS FOR DECISIONS
UPRIGHT: This is a "can do" philosophy, pragmatism personified. If it needs doing, do it. It has an air of Zen in its very centeredness in the eternal now, always the job at hand. It is self-reliance, believing that if it is worth doing at all, then it is worth doing well. This is deliberation in mind and spirit that insists on very deliberate physical action to match. Julius Caesar speaks here. ***INVERTED:*** Karmic Tarot teaches over and over again that too much of a good thing is

no longer good, and this is no exception. As long as the now event under consideration takes into consideration as much of the past and the future as it can grasp while intent on the moment at hand, then the action in the present will be spiritually correct and worthwhile. Otherwise, the present moment is tiny indeed and will not satisfy; it will bring decrease, not increase.

10 GOVERNED BY THE WHEEL OF FORTUNE: CENTRAL MESSAGE, THEME OF READING
UPRIGHT: The time is appropriate and the means are at hand for growth, a major step forward/outward. ***INVERTED:*** Your help may be needed in someone else's move ahead, especially if you are a key player in their affairs.

11 GOVERNED BY JUSTICE: STATE/CONTENT OF MIND
UPRIGHT: You are considering means of expansion, with detailed plans reviewing resources and logistics. A concrete strategy is necessary. ***INVERTED:*** Plans may be too optimistic, too grand. Or, you may be holding back being overly conservative.

12 GOVERNED BY THE HANGED MAN: STATE OF EMOTIONS, SUBCONSCIOUS
UPRIGHT: You are opening up to the need for growth, and to the means to achieve it, to the tools that are available or being offered, to new processes. ***INVERTED:*** You may be opening up to more growth than is appropriate, even into the realm of experimentation. Or, you may be far too closed to opportunities and means of growth that are appropriate.

13 GOVERNED BY DEATH: PHYSICAL SITUATION, HARD REALITY
UPRIGHT: Movement is underway or will be in the near future. Things such as home or job relocation make their appearance here. If one can actually see growth it is visible under these circumstances. ***INVERTED:*** Either there is far too much movement and expansion/relocation, or there is not enough.

14 GOVERNED BY TEMPERANCE: EMOTIONAL TEST
UPRIGHT: Your near future will see an expansion in your emotional house, a physical opening and inclusion of greater numbers, greater activity. You will be physically more demonstrative. ***INVERTED:*** On the one hand, your opening and extroversion here is greater than best suits your karmic purpose. On the other hand, you are holding back at a time when you should be moving forward.

15 GOVERNED BY THE DEVIL: TEMPTATION/CHALLENGE, FEARS
UPRIGHT: Here is an extroversion, an assertion of the self that is fully appropriate. A broadening of your mind, your plans, your beliefs, with a willingness to be outspoken about your conclusions. A decision to go for it. ***INVERTED:*** At one extreme, there is a hesitation, perhaps even fear, of putting yourself forward. At the other extreme, there is an overconfidence that should be brought into line.

16 GOVERNED BY THE TOWER: NEXT LESSON, GRACE OF GOD
UPRIGHT: Here is a gentle message to get moving; the status quo has reached its limit. If you take action now, the ball will be in your court. Wait and others will be doing the acting and you the reacting. This is grace offering an extra push/pull, the needed physical assistance to help you get things started. ***INVERTED:*** You may be called into action as a guardian angel to help someone else get their show on the road. While it is good metaphysics to wait until asked to intervene, the asking rarely comes in the form of an overt call for help. People with great needs often find it next to impossible, for a host of reasons, to ask for assistance.

17 GOVERNED BY THE STAR: ASPIRATIONS OF EGO, GOALS, MAXIMUM EXPECTATIONS
UPRIGHT: The goal is physical growth, to see the garden produce more each year adding to the security of its dependents. From the farmer who tries to buy up adjoining farms or improve per acre yield to increase output, to the explorer who courageously ventures into the unknown to add to the knowledge and resources of his society—here is man seeking to be more. ***INVERTED:*** At one extreme, this is man blatantly seeking to have more rather than to be more. At the other extreme, this is a goal of non-growth, a misunderstanding that catches many who correctly want man to be more harmonious with nature. Non-growth is not the solution; proper growth is. Our cycle is one of evolution, not involution.

18 GOVERNED BY THE MOON: ASPIRATIONS OF HEART, COMPASSION
UPRIGHT: The heart's desire is to see everyone and everything grow to its ultimate potential; this is an ultimate accommodation of the root feminine principle, here on earth of Gaia. This is the improvement of all nature and the general lot of society as part of nature. ***INVERTED:*** Distortion possibilities here are numerous. One possibility is to seek growth too quickly, even for compassionate reasons, such as building a dam to provide power to improve standards of living and in the process to destroy an entire ecosystem that devastates the economy of a region.

19 GOVERNED BY THE SUN: PHYSICAL FULFILLMENT/EVALUATION
UPRIGHT: There is agility and facility into old age, no infirmities here. The physical plane has been one of making things happen, from hands on physical assistance to venture capitalism. ***INVERTED:*** The potential of this fulfillment will energize you to make it a reality.

20 GOVERNED BY JUDGEMENT: HEART'S FULFILLMENT/EVALUATION
UPRIGHT: The heart is well satisfied with conduct of physical/material affairs. Your resources and energies have been well spent. Here is the path of a true lady or gentleman. You, your family, and extended family have been socially involved and are deeply rewarded for your participation in the pragmatic needs of people. ***INVERTED:*** Continuous, intimate involvement with the growth of others is hard but rewarding work.

21 GOVERNED BY THE WORLD: EGO'S FULFILLMENT/EVALUATION
UPRIGHT: The ego is filled with proper pride at your contributions to the greater well-being of society, for through your efforts not only are individuals encouraged but the very system we call our civilization has been advanced. ***INVERTED:*** With so much going on and so much important work being done, it would be easy to falter, but use this archetype as your guide and this will be your fulfillment.

22/0 GOVERNED BY THE FOOL: SOUL'S FULFILLMENT/EVALUATION
UPRIGHT: Here was a real mover, a shaker. This has been the successful balancing act of a healthy respect for the system, for what the past has achieved but with a respect as well for what needed to be done to meet the needs of people today and tomorrow. Your motto : In order for things to remain the same, they must change. ***INVERTED:*** As you internalize the lessons of your path, this will be your soul's fulfillment.

8 STRENGTH

UPRIGHT: Here is the eighth stop. Properly channeled and controlled emotions. You are on solid ground, centered. Strong self-image and self-respect. Confidence. There are extensions of self in place and functioning, i.e. family/extended family and creative projects. A feeling of invincibility. An emotional sense of the eternal, of permanence. Loyalty. Constancy without stagnation. A harnessing of our lower energies to support/generate higher energies. Here is the source of courage, the assumption of responsibility for one's own existence, hence emotional independence. The feeling of duality is strong but the self is in harmony with all extensions of the self, and with nature. Your heart has begun to know things for itself, with the help, but independent, of mind. (The hypothalamus is that aspect of mind, of reason, belonging to the heart.) Here ideas are generated in the gut, the Solar Plexus, before reason and perspective of higher mind get a crack at them. Conversely however, it is proper to say that this is the effect of mind in the emotions. We see here that true strength lies in our hearts, in our emotional stability. **INVERTED:** Distortion in the way of too much or too little of the above meanings. Feeling a need to be strong can prevent us accepting from others when it is their turn to give. Everyone must take as well as give. Too much strength can be part of a tendency toward complacency and stagnation. Too much strength can lead to abuse of power.

In This Spread Position...Interpret the Strength Meanings to Include:

1 GOVERNED BY THE MAGICIAN: PHYSICAL GIVENS, OUT OF THE FATHER
UPRIGHT: Your fortitude and stamina in the affairs of the Physical/material Plane may be legendary before this leg of your journey is over. The male lineage in your family is very strong, significant. You have been gifted with an exceptional physical, genetic package. **INVERTED:** Strong people generally are asked to carry heavy loads, but then that is because they can.

2 GOVERNED BY THE HIGH PRIESTESS: EMOTIONAL GIVENS, OUT OF THE MOTHER
UPRIGHT: Your fortitude and stamina in the affairs of the Emotional/creative Plane will turn many a head in awe before you reach the end of this path. The female lineage in your family is very strong, significant. You have been gifted with an exceptional emotional/creative package. **INVERTED:** While you can feel more deeply than most, you can handle more as well.

3 GOVERNED BY THE EMPRESS: MENTAL GIVENS, INTELLECTUAL PREDISPOSITION
UPRIGHT: Yours is a rich intellectual heritage, enabling you to withstand enormous pressures in mental affairs, keeping many games afloat at the same time. Your addition to any debate team virtually assures its success. There is a likelihood that you are meant to carry on the work of this mental heritage, from a family member or karmic group predecessor. **INVERTED:** With such a good memory and large capacity for information, you are in great demand when the computer is off-line.

4 GOVERNED BY THE EMPEROR: SPIRITUAL GIVENS, LIFE PURPOSE
UPRIGHT: Your emotional ties are very important. This lifetime may be centered on or within your origins, family, heritage. Your personal and group karma are closely related. Your abilities with people, the social graces, manners figure prominently in this lifetime. **INVERTED:** Your personal karma may be very much devoted to the karmic needs of your group.

5 GOVERNED BY THE HIEROPHANT: SYSTEMS BORN INTO, SOCIETAL INFLUENCE
UPRIGHT: Here is the solidity of a family, or family-type network. The emphasis here was on people and relationships. The exchanges of energy were frequent and substantial. Also, here is the equivalent network of creative enterprise in the social setting. **INVERTED:** If this group was too internalized this will have been draining rather than empowering. Likewise, if the family existed virtually for itself, but in an extroverted way and required an inordinate amount of attention from the outside, as in a traveling circus family, there would be a distortion here.

6 GOVERNED BY THE LOVERS: EMOTIONAL TAPES, BASIS FOR RELATING/CREATING
UPRIGHT: The desire here is to be strong and capable whenever and wherever one might need to be, for oneself and for others. From this derives your easy way with people, one on one and in groups. **INVERTED:** It can be difficult discerning which relationships and situations are most deserving of your attention. Without the ability to prioritize and say no when appropriate we become drained by participating in the wrong shows.

7 GOVERNED BY THE CHARIOT: PHYSICAL RESOURCES, MEANS TO ACHIEVE
UPRIGHT: Your social prowess, your credits with people, facilitate your getting what you need. Thus far, your personality has been your greatest asset. There is a constancy in your affairs that stands you well. **INVERTED:** Neither be too patronizing nor aloof in working with people. You can be direct and honest and still be considerate. Work to be part of the solution, not part of the problem.

8 GOVERNED BY STRENGTH: EMOTIONAL RESOURCES, ENERGY
UPRIGHT: Your strength is your strength. Like the proverbial cat, you always seem to land on your feet. You are the quintessential extrovert, maximizing all contacts, enjoying people genuinely as they enjoy you. Your loyalty to yourself is available to others. **INVERTED:** At the extreme, strength can be a weakness. If you swing a bat too hard it breaks. Also, even in strength you must be able to receive in like portion that which you give. Give and take have nothing to do with strength and weakness. Many who wish to help others, as in counseling and healing, may in lesser or greater degree be drawn to the equation out of a need and as a means of feeling stronger themselves; i.e. if I can help you then I must be doing alright. Wrong!

9 GOVERNED BY THE HERMIT: BELIEF SYSTEM, BASIS FOR DECISIONS
UPRIGHT: Your beliefs are rooted in gentility, manners, and ultimately the Golden Rule—Either the negative Confucian phrasing of "Do not do unto others what you do not want them to do to you," or the positive Christian phrasing of "Do unto others as you would have them do unto you." The honoring of relationships and your word is important, as is group consensus. This is a good belief system for an honorable politician. **INVERTED:** At an extreme, this can distort into a fear of taking and action, for in doing anything one might be hurting someone, or something.

10 GOVERNED BY THE WHEEL OF FORTUNE: CENTRAL MESSAGE, THEME OF READING
UPRIGHT: Your strength now must come from and go into existing relationships and creative enterprises. Use your social gifts to the maximum. **INVERTED:** Group karmas are asserting themselves.

11 GOVERNED BY JUSTICE: STATE/CONTENT OF MIND

UPRIGHT: You should be consciously dealing with your emotional systems, the effectiveness of all your relationships and your creative thrust. Here is analysis of therapies. **INVERTED:** You may be either too immersed in these questions, or not enough.

12 GOVERNED BY THE HANGED MAN: STATE OF EMOTIONS, SUBCONSCIOUS

UPRIGHT: There is a good sense of belonging as your heart is centered in a very healthy emotional world, immersed in relationships that are productive and rewarding. As a result you are highly energetic and motivated. **INVERTED:** The heart is not at its strongest; you may have put too much energy out, not gotten enough energy back.

13 GOVERNED BY DEATH: PHYSICAL SITUATION, HARD REALITY

UPRIGHT: You are in the right place at the right time and can deal from a position of strength. You are surrounded by what you need and yet you are free to move as the need arises. This is a healthy balance between attachment and non-attachment in the Physical/material Plane. **INVERTED:** Too much strength might deter others or you from some opportunities. Too little, for the purposes you may have under consideration.

14 GOVERNED BY TEMPERANCE: EMOTIONAL TEST

UPRIGHT: The near future will find you centered and strong within your relationships and your creative processes. The balance between self and other, between humanity and nature is healthy. **INVERTED:** Caution against complacency. Must marshal forces to an even greater extent. This may be a testing of loyalties, of yours, of others.

15 GOVERNED BY THE DEVIL: TEMPTATION/CHALLENGE, FEARS

UPRIGHT: Exploration of the depths and loyalties of relationships, of the rightness of your creative interests. Are you as strong as you could be, as you want to be? Here is the exercise of both losing and finding yourself in your relationships with others, with your group, and in the immersion in your talents. **INVERTED:** You may fear your own strength in what you are considering, or of course your weakness.

16 GOVERNED BY THE TOWER: NEXT LESSON, GRACE OF GOD

UPRIGHT: Here is the grace of emotional calm, a taming and focusing of energies in relationships or in creative matters. You will be more confident in social situations as you will be armed with emotional extensions to back you up. Failure is irrelevant, if not out of the question. You have nothing to lose. **INVERTED:** This strength is to enable you to help others, perhaps your group more than yourself.

17 GOVERNED BY THE STAR: ASPIRATIONS OF EGO, GOALS, MAXIMUM EXPECTATIONS

UPRIGHT: Your goal is the reliability, faithfulness, constancy, continuity, that emotional fortitude affords the mental plane, in the perpetuation of the personal ideology. With this goal achieved there is extension beyond the limits of this lifetime. The mind here believes successful achievement of this archetype would go a long way to satisfying the eternal nature and purpose of the soul. **INVERTED:** Mental fortitude and continuity to an extreme smack of totalitarianism and stagnation. On the other hand fear of that possibility can lead to the opposite effect of desiring everyone to be toothless tigers eating pablum and sitting on pillows avoiding interaction.

18 GOVERNED BY THE MOON: ASPIRATIONS OF HEART, COMPASSION

UPRIGHT: This goal is the reliability, faithfulness, constancy, continuity, that emotional fortitude affords the emotional plane itself, in the perpetuation of the personal creative seed, be it children or projects. The heart here believes successful achievement of this archetype would go a long way to satisfying the eternal nature and purpose of the soul. **INVERTED:** Too much of this archetype here breeds an introversion at some level between the self and the universal other.

19 GOVERNED BY THE SUN: PHYSICAL FULFILLMENT/EVALUATION

UPRIGHT: The emotional and creative stability that has been yours has made your Physical/material Plane appear to be the Rock of Gibraltar on which your success has been built. You can depend on yourself, and others on you, as long as you live. **INVERTED:** This archetype keeps everything you have worked for intact and is worth striving for.

20 GOVERNED BY JUDGEMENT: HEART'S FULFILLMENT/EVALUATION

UPRIGHT: Your heart is pleased with the firm hand you have employed in your Emotional/creative Plane. There was no funny business here as you did what you were supposed to do and expected no less from everyone else around you. As a result, you can rest assured that your family/extended family will be harmonious and productive long after you are gone. **INVERTED:** Let the lessons of this archetype bring efficiency and happiness to your emotional world. Face all issues squarely.

21 GOVERNED BY THE WORLD: EGO'S FULFILLMENT/EVALUATION

UPRIGHT: Your ability to stand firm even while changing and growing, while being open and fair, has endeared you to many and established a pattern for others to follow. You have been able to tackle ideas and issues and work them into the mainstream where they could do some good. **INVERTED:** Your mind will devour the principles of this archetype if you let it.

22/0 GOVERNED BY THE FOOL: SOUL'S FULFILLMENT/EVALUATION

UPRIGHT: This soul has magnified the self and others through its ability to nurture and sustain relationships and the creative enterprises of the heart. Here is a master of love in friendship and mutual understanding. **INVERTED:** Use this reading to help you understand your karmic purpose and to reach this fulfillment.

9 THE HERMIT

UPRIGHT: Here is the ninth stop. A withdrawal in order to get a wider and more objective perspective. This is both the mind's ability to create duality and the acceptance of responsibility to resolve it. An "eye" for an "I," the ability of self to see self, which is impossible without the background of other. Proper memories of the Past balanced with proper projections for the Future. The ability to see inward as well as outward, and in equal portions. Formulation of personal philosophy and goals. An important mental pause, a plateau after a significant period of development (assimilating others' views), before going on. Wisdom gained through solitude and silence; the sage in mental seclusion. The gifts of patience and prudence. The impact of instincts on mental processes abates and the impact of intuition increases. Where you have leaned heavily on the situations surrounding your birth package and the conditions of your environment, you now take charge and consciously begin to affect and effect your own future. Your sense of time and purpose is strong as you seek to know and implement the purpose of this incarnation. You begin to realize the contents of your Karmic Contract and to plan and act accordingly. Foundation of the healthy Ego. Autonomy. Formulation of beliefs. **INVERTED:** Anomie, which is social or personal unrest due to a lack of purpose or ideals. The word "hermit" comes from the Greek "erimos" meaning "desert." Man is anything but a desert unless in the process of separating in order to find himself he gets lost. Then, he must depend on the light of another, ultimately in grace, to bring him back.

In This Spread Position...Interpret The Hermit Meanings to Include:

1 GOVERNED BY THE MAGICIAN: PHYSICAL GIVENS, OUT OF THE FATHER
UPRIGHT: The Physical/material Plane shows the impact of the father's belief system. Your beliefs are rooted in the religious traditions of western society, principally those of the Judaeo-Christian and Islamic traditions. Your physical life may be very private, even conducting your means of livelihood out of the public eye. **INVERTED:** No one will be tougher on the conduct of your physical/material affairs than yourself.

2 GOVERNED BY THE HIGH PRIESTESS: EMOTIONAL GIVENS, OUT OF THE MOTHER
UPRIGHT: The Emotional/creative Plane shows the impact of the mother's belief system. Your beliefs are rooted in the religious traditions of eastern society, principally those of Hinduism and Buddhism. Your emotional life may be very protected from the collective eye. **INVERTED:** Your emotions have chosen a tough task master for this leg of your journey. No energy will be allowed to be wasted here.

3 GOVERNED BY THE EMPRESS: MENTAL GIVENS, INTELLECTUAL PREDISPOSITION
UPRIGHT: You have a highly independent mental disposition. You must see and prove everything for yourself. But this is the ideal mind for the work of the mind, for there is a drop of patience for every drop of persistence. **INVERTED:** No one will mess with your mental affairs more than you will. You will undo almost as much as you do before turning loose of the net product.

4 GOVERNED BY THE EMPEROR: SPIRITUAL GIVENS, LIFE PURPOSE
UPRIGHT: Here is the philosophical detective. Chronus, Father Time himself, with his hourglass to check on the rhythm of things. You may well be an ascetic, if such is the severity of your search for the truth. But you may also be in the mainstream, as principled teacher or objective researcher. **INVERTED:** The work of this mind may be you on loan as guardian angel, steering others to important goals.

5 GOVERNED BY THE HIEROPHANT: SYSTEMS BORN INTO, SOCIETAL INFLUENCE
UPRIGHT: There is an intellectual, academic influence early on, and possibly in a very esoteric or eccentric environment. This can also be the mark of an intellectual prodigy, with the earliest influences of consequence already coming from the self rather than from one's elders. It suggests that the basics of the belief system on which you rely today was formulated at a very early age. **INVERTED:** You may have been an unruly, difficult child with a strong distaste for authority. At another extreme, the environment itself may have been overtly anti-establishment, revolutionary.

6 GOVERNED BY THE LOVERS: EMOTIONAL TAPES, BASIS FOR RELATING/CREATING
UPRIGHT: Here was born a love of knowledge and an appetite for the search. The dominate passion is intellectual, fostering a love of books, computers, and the like. **INVERTED:** This can be a sign of narcissism and emotional introversion to the extreme. This is a preference to be completely alone. At the completely opposite extreme is a hatred for knowledge and things intellectual. Any distaste for the activities of the mind bode ill for the self as it is our birthright and an inevitability that we progress, which is to learn, and that cannot be done by the heart alone.

7 GOVERNED BY THE CHARIOT: PHYSICAL RESOURCES. MEANS TO ACHIEVE
UPRIGHT: Your material environment has been personalized to a tee and fits you like a glove. When you shift, so does your entire environment, so natural an extension of you is it. This also means that you are lean and mean, having nothing that you do not require to support your beliefs. Thus in a very pragmatic sense, efficiency is your great resource and the physical foundation on which you build. **INVERTED:** Your environment and support system may either not be a good fit, or it is too tight, not allowing room for others or sufficient flexibility for contingencies.

8 GOVERNED BY STRENGTH: EMOTIONAL RESOURCES, ENERGY
UPRIGHT: The ability of your mind in the Emotional Plane, to profoundly understand the game of love, the trials of family, and the pangs of creative stretching gives you your endurance. Your strong intellect has guided your creative program and the results have drawn others to you generating confidence and giving you a school of admirers to work and play with. **INVERTED:** An overzealous mind may be intruding on the major responsibility of the heart for the affairs of the Emotional/creative Plane. You may be far too independent and self-righteous in your relationships and/or creative projects.

9 GOVERNED BY THE HERMIT: BELIEF SYSTEM, BASIS FOR DECISIONS
UPRIGHT: There is purity of thought here, a classical thinker, metaphysician, philosopher. This mind believes in mind itself, in its ability to lead the ship safely to harbor. Here there are always new ways of seeing the world, breakthrough concepts and paradigms. Here is Diogenes (of Apollonia), the 5th cent. Greek philosopher, who held that air (the Mental Plane) was the basic element. Known as a cynic, always looking for the irony, the humorous twist that duality puts on the reality we experience. **INVERTED:** The purpose of withdrawal is to get the other, and therefore make clearer, our view of things, and so properly even in seclusion we are inclusive in our thought. The purpose of leaving is to rejoin. Even the ascetic living alone for years in the mountaintop cave is deeply involved and working on the collective need. His is the least selfish path of all, for he has foregone all other experience save the work of mankind and nature as a whole.

10 GOVERNED BY THE WHEEL OF FORTUNE: CENTRAL MESSAGE, THEME OF READING

UPRIGHT: The arrival of a guide/teacher. And be prepared to meet yourself, for this can be one of your past lives, in effect you coming to guide yourself with this matter at hand. Whatever the personification of the source of this message, this brings you closer to the belief system that is specifically correct to carry you forward on your path. This is the dialect of the philosophical language of truth which will best suit you. *INVERTED:* This reading will help you identify the spiritual group/family with which your karma is most closely linked. Take a look at your personal beliefs and justify them with those of the group.

11 GOVERNED BY JUSTICE: STATE/CONTENT OF MIND

UPRIGHT: You have come to the realization of your position, of what you have to teach. You accept that you are in the vanguard of the school of thought to which you subscribe. You are mentally in business for yourself, actively pursuing your own course. A declaration of independence. You may think of yourself as a scribe. *INVERTED:* On the one hand, you may be a bit smug about your awareness of your awareness. On the other hand, you may have doubts about your position. You could be suffering from anomie—social or personal unrest due to a lack of purpose or ideals.

12 GOVERNED BY THE HANGED MAN: STATE OF EMOTIONS, SUBCONSCIOUS

UPRIGHT: Your heart is surrendering to the assigned task, the responsibility that has come with the knowledge. You have been efficient learning your lessons and now as a reward, you have an expanded role. This corresponds to the sense of a walk-in with whom we share/trade tasks as with members of our group, in some cases devoting ourselves to self purpose from past lives. The heart here is dedicating itself to helping fulfill the beliefs. *INVERTED:* The distortion here is complex. One extreme is the heart's abandoning itself to an ideology that it is not in love with.

13 GOVERNED BY DEATH: PHYSICAL SITUATION, HARD REALITY

UPRIGHT: Your ideology is changing your life fundamentally as it comes to the forefront. You may or may not be seeking actual isolation, but your are going through changes in things like diet, exercise, routine, clothes. In short, much of your taste is being transformed by your beliefs. You are beginning to walk your talk, becoming a living witness to your truth. You may even begin to make your living directly from your beliefs. *INVERTED:* Sometimes the Physical Plane takes quite a beating as you try to catch up for lost time. Be gentle with yourself and others. In another extreme, you may do all the above, thinking these are your beliefs, but they are really someone else's.

14 GOVERNED BY TEMPERANCE: EMOTIONAL TEST

UPRIGHT: The heart agrees with mind, and you see the effect on relationships, on sex, on your creative projects. The heart may even be putting pressure on the Emotional Plane and its contents to conform to beliefs. *INVERTED:* The effect of the heart either disagreeing with mind, or agreeing much to easily and/or completely.

15 GOVERNED BY THE DEVIL: TEMPTATION/CHALLENGE, FEARS

UPRIGHT: Your belief system comes together in a stronger way than ever before. Now you can draw up your master plan in ink. Or, if they have solidified before now, here are the trials of sustaining, amplifying, expounding your theories and seeing if they stand the test of time and life. *INVERTED:* You may discover a crack in your system, or a new way of looking at things that transcends and replaces the old altogether.

16 GOVERNED BY THE TOWER: NEXT LESSON, GRACE OF GOD

UPRIGHT: Getting The Hermit at the spiritual level is suitably paradoxical, for it means that no seclusion of any kind is needed—no physical dropping out and wandering naked in the wilderness like the Hindu avadhutas in India, no emotional hiding from loved ones by changing our names and moving to Alaska, and no retreat into a mental fog impenetrable even at a busy faculty tea. Why? Because all of the lessons that are learned by such physical, emotional, and mental seclusion are being handed to you by grace. *INVERTED:* Whether this signals the above mentioned, or that you are to be coming out of seclusion with these lessons learned, the reason is that you are too busy yourself testing the waters with all your insights. So much for getting the theory worked out. Now, to the laboratory, Watson!

17 GOVERNED BY THE STAR: ASPIRATIONS OF EGO, GOALS, MAXIMUM EXPECTATIONS

UPRIGHT: The goal here is not so much to arrive at your belief system as to see it become established, validated, and so you must record it, write a book, teach it, share it by any means, and then it will become an epistemology and live. *INVERTED:* If your beliefs are valid and they have helped you, then they must be able to help others. This goal, in getting your thoughts before others, is actually to refute your own doubts.

18 GOVERNED BY THE MOON: ASPIRATIONS OF HEART, COMPASSION

UPRIGHT: The heart aspires to agree with mind and to provide the energy and motivations to sustain it and see it grow. The heart does this because it is convinced of the benefits that will accrue to the self, loved ones, the extended family and the realization of universal harmony. *INVERTED:* At one very extreme, is the heart which does not believe in the mind's game plan, and will not support it, and may even work to subvert it.

19 GOVERNED BY THE SUN: PHYSICAL FULFILLMENT/EVALUATION

UPRIGHT: As this trip draws to a close, your mind and its projects are everywhere in evidence in your material world, for the physical plane is the embodiment of your belief system. *INVERTED:* This is your fulfillment if you make the right turns, and there are good signposts.

20 GOVERNED BY JUDGEMENT: HEART'S FULFILLMENT/EVALUATION

UPRIGHT: The heart is greatly pleased with the contribution of mind to the affairs and programs of the Emotional/creative Plane. This was a productive teamwork of mind and heart that carried both to new heights. The heart made sense and the mind had depth of feeling. *INVERTED:* Neither let the heart rule the mind, nor the mind rule the heart and you will see this archetype realized.

21 GOVERNED BY THE WORLD: EGO'S FULFILLMENT/EVALUATION

UPRIGHT: The mind has succeeded at what it does best, getting a grip on illusion and reality. You are happy with your world view, its apparent accuracy and impact. *INVERTED:* Neither let the heart rule the mind, nor the mind rule the heart and you will see this archetype realized.

22/0 GOVERNED BY THE FOOL: SOUL'S FULFILLMENT/EVALUATION

UPRIGHT: This has been a life as a functioning ascetic. Whatever the nature of your ivory tower, you have used intellect to a worldly purpose. *INVERTED:* Let the Tarot help you choose the right forks and you will be here in good time.

WHEEL of FORTUNE.

10 WHEEL OF FORTUNE

UPRIGHT: Here is the tenth stop. Discovery of true faith/trust in God, and thus in Self. Acceptance. The mind begins to know the spiritual, as the mind and heart cooperate and you pay attention. Until now, your attention has been mainly on the external environment and input from the five outer senses, but here you realize that you must give equal time to your internal "environment" and its sensory input. This generates a new level of energy and inspiration. This is voluntary change, a submission of the self after introspection to higher authority. You are turning from a limited, self-serving life to an expanded self-directed to serving others. You only reach this point after you have served yourself well and are as strong and capable as you are willing. Here is the will (ingness) to take a chance, to spin the Wheel, for you have realized there is no such thing as chance. Einstein was right when he said, "God does not play dice with the universe." Man must not do so either. Faith is not a suspension of doubt. Faith is the quest itself. The Wheel suggests the appropriateness of the up and down of cycles, and the reciprocity of opposites even in faith. For even as this is a healthy letting go of will, it is the assertion of will that is in that very act of letting go. Remember how a spinning wheel appears to reverse direction as its speed increases. Here is the main gate to the series of courtyards and inner courtyards leading to the garden of Eden. It is the cusp from self-assertion to self-transcendence. A balance of give and take at the spiritual level. It is the wheel of Law, of Dharma, and we must turn it, alternating the flow up and down, between the will of man (inner aspect of divinity) and the will of God (outer aspect of divinity). We see here in the Wheel of Fortune primarily what man needs to do in relation to God, what he should be invoking, whereas in The Tower we mainly see grace, the action of God in relation to man. Here the God in man speaks to the man in God. **INVERTED:** You may be ill prepared for the chance you are considering. Or, you may be invoking divine providence to intervene inappropriately. Gambling is an example of this, if you are expecting something for nothing. It could also show an improper "I deserve this" attitude. Here are problems that come from depending solely on luck or fate (on the outer will of God with no balance of the inner will of God/man). Also, problems that come from depending solely on man's will (on the inner will of God with no balance of the outer will of God). The latter is a mistake made in many of the mind-over-matter schools of thought.

In This Spread Position...Interpret The Wheel of Fortune Meanings to Include:

1 GOVERNED BY THE MAGICIAN: PHYSICAL GIVENS, OUT OF THE FATHER
UPRIGHT: You are predisposed to do well in the Physical/material Plane; what is conventionally interpreted as lucky. But there will be little need for your harder lessons to descend to this plane, with the givens of the Wheel, the lessons of faith, the balancing of inner/outer will already internalized here. **INVERTED:** Some will consider you a magician and ask you to help them achieve what comes so easily for you.

2 GOVERNED BY THE HIGH PRIESTESS: EMOTIONAL GIVENS, OUT OF THE MOTHER
UPRIGHT: You are predisposed to fare well in the Emotional/creative Plane, and will be thought lucky in love. The lessons of the Wheel are with you in this plane from the beginning and help you deal with potential problems as they arise, heading them off at the pass. You trust people because you feel secure. **INVERTED:** You will be in great demand as you appear to be so on top of everything. You have a way of turning things around in your favor.

3 GOVERNED BY THE EMPRESS: MENTAL GIVENS, INTELLECTUAL PREDISPOSITION
UPRIGHT: You are confident in your mental gifts. You have the ability and willingness to look at all sides of an issue. The mind is linked fundamentally with the spiritual plane and therefore highly intuitive. **INVERTED:** You will get and learn most of your lessons here, leaving the lower planes open for enjoyment and productive service for others with the excess of energy from your efficiency as a student.

4 GOVERNED BY THE EMPEROR: SPIRITUAL GIVENS, LIFE PURPOSE
UPRIGHT: Here you are at the main gate, and a magnificent gatekeeper you make indeed. For entrance into this outer courtyard requires the passing of the word by gatekeeper and traveler alike. This is a life based on the true understanding of faith as the key to the word and therefore its passing. **INVERTED:** You will work to help others find their personal understanding of faith.

5 GOVERNED BY THE HIEROPHANT: SYSTEMS BORN INTO, SOCIETAL INFLUENCE
UPRIGHT: You were born into an environment that was fair and open, dominated by an atmosphere of trust. Many people came and went through your house. It may have been hard for a child to tell where family left off and outsiders began. The opportunities for early self-expression were limitless. **INVERTED:** At one extreme, the open door policy could have been too liberal and little was actually being accomplished. At another set of extremes, too much or too little will power.

6 GOVERNED BY THE LOVERS: EMOTIONAL TAPES, BASIS FOR RELATING/CREATING
UPRIGHT: Here was an early understanding of the nature of faith and therefore of the duality of will. And so, this young heart was able to dedicate itself to God at a tender age, innocent yet experienced and mature beyond its years. **INVERTED:** Distorted, this dedication may be to only half of the Godhead and so prostrate itself before the altar of the external will of God, or the internal will of man.

7 GOVERNED BY THE CHARIOT: PHYSICAL RESOURCES, MEANS TO ACHIEVE
UPRIGHT: The Physical/material Plane has been structured to accommodate spirituality in the routine of everyday life. Whether overt or subtle, there is ritual observance of your beliefs as you facilitate communication with God through your Spiritual Plane. You may spend most of your time and even make your living in these pursuits. **INVERTED:** There may indeed be observance and ritual, but with some imbalance of this archetype here, such as mistaking presumption for faith, or assuming faith is a lack of doubt. In severe extremes, on the one hand everything is left up to the external God; on the other hand there is rampant self-will presuming that God approves of everything it does, in effect assuming the entire role of God.

8 GOVERNED BY STRENGTH: EMOTIONAL RESOURCES, ENERGY
UPRIGHT: As the Wheel enabled you to see the message of God in everything, your emotions filled and broadened and you became much stronger. Identification with others has been easy and you are no longer quite as separate and vulnerable. As a rolling stone gathers no moss, so the Wheel gathers no problems, with its ability to adjust quickly. **INVERTED:** While you do not want problems to stick to you, you must be intimately engaged in all that you do.

9 GOVERNED BY THE HERMIT: BELIEF SYSTEM, BASIS FOR DECISIONS

UPRIGHT: This is belief in divine dialog, a confidence in the interchange between self and other. This is faith in life itself. It may be something akin to Descartes's "Cogito ergo sum (I think therefore I am)." But to it we would have to add, "God thinks therefore I am," and to that we would also then add, "I think therefore God is." ***INVERTED:*** Here would be a variety of imbalances ranging from the absolute God to the absolute Self and any of the tendencies to place ends before means.

10 GOVERNED BY THE WHEEL OF FORTUNE: CENTRAL MESSAGE, THEME OF READING

UPRIGHT: Exercise your vote, stretch the muscles of your free will, for the will of God is favorably disposed. These two aspects of divine will are aligned. Ask and you will receive. But think carefully of all the ramifications of your request. Remember King Midas. ***INVERTED:*** Even though this is your vote and your free will, it is suggested that you use this opportunity for invocation for the benefit of others.

11 GOVERNED BY JUSTICE: STATE/CONTENT OF MIND

UPRIGHT: The mind is focused on God. A state of prayer, invocation, intercession for self or others. Voting your will. A conscious attempt to merge self-will with the will of God. ***INVERTED:*** The timing of this process, the method, or some other factor may be less than it could be. There may be a mental act of worship that is inappropriate. Too much talking to God.

12 GOVERNED BY THE HANGED MAN: STATE OF EMOTIONS, SUBCONSCIOUS

UPRIGHT: The heart is focused on God. A state of meditation. Acceptance of grace. ***INVERTED:*** Too much listening. For now, all that is to be said has been said. Your turn.

13 GOVERNED BY DEATH: PHYSICAL SITUATION, HARD REALITY

UPRIGHT: Here is faith infused action. Courageous behavior. Leaps of faith. The ability to move when your exact destination is unknown, to jump when it is impossible to see the other side. ***INVERTED:*** At one extreme, there is a lot of action and bravado as if to defy the odds. At the other extreme, is an inability to spin the Wheel for fear of where it may stop.

14 GOVERNED BY TEMPERANCE: EMOTIONAL TEST

UPRIGHT: What do you do when the Wheel lands on Go? Here you are becoming a devotee, discovering the full meaning of love. This is falling in love with love, when there is recognition of God in self and self in God and life starts to really take on meaning. ***INVERTED:*** Still waiting for someone or something to spin the Wheel for you?

15 GOVERNED BY THE DEVIL: TEMPTATION/CHALLENGE, FEARS

UPRIGHT: Test of faith in the near future. A chance to encounter the ineffable and make some sense out of it afterwards. ***INVERTED:*** There will be difficulty in getting the message and/or getting the message across, as you have trouble rationalizing the irrational. A hint: Keep the wheel in plain view for awhile and let it talk to you. It is a transformer that brings the higher energy of the Spiritual Plane down into the energy of language in the Mental Plane just below it.

16 GOVERNED BY THE TOWER: NEXT LESSON, GRACE OF GOD

UPRIGHT: One overhears as the gods speak to the gods. There is an ineffable presence. ***INVERTED:*** The messages here may very likely be for you to pass quickly on to someone else, if you can just find the words.

17 GOVERNED BY THE STAR: ASPIRATIONS OF EGO, GOALS, MAXIMUM EXPECTATIONS

UPRIGHT: This is a noble goal, The Wheel, and it is a wise one, for once achieved it makes all other goals easier. It is perhaps the simplest and the hardest of all possible goals, for it requires only that the mind stay focused between inner and outer will/desire. ***INVERTED:*** At one of its extremes, this archetype distorts into the complete lack of any personal will or goal, ever yielding to the other. At the other, this can be the horror of a mind that aspires to original cause, to make everything the result of its will.

18 GOVERNED BY THE MOON: ASPIRATIONS OF HEART, COMPASSION

UPRIGHT: The heart wants to dance. Desire exists to motivate will. Will exists to fulfill desire. Such are the partners in the dance of love, and which is leading which? The beauty of this aspiration is that it doesn't matter who leads; the dancers both finish the dance at the same time, when the music ends. ***INVERTED:*** This aspiration runs aground when one or the other of these partners tries to lead all of the time. To only desire is to never be satisfied even for a moment. To only will is to be doing merely for the sake of doing.

19 GOVERNED BY THE SUN: PHYSICAL FULFILLMENT/EVALUATION

UPRIGHT: The inner sun is matching the outer sun and you are happily sitting in a material world balanced between them. You have experienced God in the superb materiality of nature in all her glory. You have tasted the divine in the food of God's handiwork all around you. Your sunset is truly golden. ***INVERTED:*** Let the wheels of your Chariot bring you to this Wheel of Fortune, this feast of life.

20 GOVERNED BY JUDGEMENT: HEART'S FULFILLMENT/EVALUATION

UPRIGHT: Here is absolution as the heart forgives and is forgiven all. Cleansed from all guilt the heart swoons, spinning faster and faster until it is visible no more, dissolved in the love of God. ***INVERTED:*** To help reach this fulfillment, look especially to the interpretations of the other cards in this row—Positions 2,6,8,12,14, &18.

21 GOVERNED BY THE WORLD: EGO'S FULFILLMENT/EVALUATION

UPRIGHT: The merging of self-will with the will of God has been completed to the degree that divine law permits an incarnated soul. And you have been able to share your experiences as you were meant to do. ***INVERTED:*** To help reach this fulfillment, look especially to the interpretations of the other cards in this row—Positions 3,5,9,11,15, & 17.

22/0 GOVERNED BY THE FOOL: SOUL'S FULFILLMENT/EVALUATION

UPRIGHT: Gnosis has been achieved. ***INVERTED:*** You need no one to tell you what your work is.

11 JUSTICE

UPRIGHT: Here is the eleventh stop, the fulcrum of the mind, illuminated and educated. You know that you know. There is now a code of ethics, a basis for appropriate action. This is rational mind in its equilibrium, balancing a host of dualities and paradoxes, principal among them—matching the below and the above—and giving equal time to both past and future. This is balancing give and take at the mental level. Here too must be decided the balance between the rights of the individual and the rights of society, the struggle Plato describes in "The Republic." "You can't demand absolutely perfect justice for yourself if the community is to survive. You moderate your desires, your claims on being treated with absolute fairness." Here is the mental link of dualities, as symbolized by the yoking of two oxen (Libra in astrology). To bring balance to all is to bring about a state of dynamic balance, action satisfying all the forces concerned. This is what is meant in the Hindu non-violence concept of Ahimsa— the state of mind, the dynamic balance of dualities that balances without stasis. Mental balance is peace. This is the centerpiece of civilization for there is knowledge of appropriate behavior, and the ability to be the gentleman or lady. Clarity. Decisiveness. Decisions can be difficult in spite of the clarity, as you now have a bigger picture with more factors to consider. The mind has been touched by the heart, by the spirit, but may or may not act accordingly. There is a working knowledge here of the order of things, and an intellectual understanding of "what the game of life is, what the rules are, and how to play." The drive for reconciliation of opposites; the resting place of opposites. Organization. Justice is change at the mental level, for the better.

INVERTED: Distortion in the way of too much or too little of the above meanings. This can indicate improper use of this knowledge, or a "Do as I say, but not as I do" person. A distortion of idealism into the unrealistic, dogmatic, uncompromising, and the overly critical. At one extreme, permissiveness; at the other, intolerance. On the principle of balance, at one extreme too much balance yields mental stasis, rigidity, inertia. At the other extreme is not enough balance, or imbalance, and we can see prejudice, bias, and favoritism. Unresponsiveness. Lack of attention. Dishonesty. Too much peace vs. too little peace (war), with others/with self.

In This Spread Position...Interpret the Justice Meanings to Include:

1 GOVERNED BY THE MAGICIAN: PHYSICAL GIVENS, OUT OF THE FATHER
UPRIGHT: Principles of this archetype coming through your father's line. Here is a Physical/material Plane insistent on equilibrium. You may be kept very busy keeping all things in their right places. There is a penchant for order and the law according to the highest of ideals. Physical equilibrium of the highest order with a delicate sense of touch—excellent qualifications from surgeon to tight rope walker. ***INVERTED:*** You will be around to break up your share of fights.

2 GOVERNED BY THE HIGH PRIESTESS: EMOTIONAL GIVENS, OUT OF THE MOTHER
UPRIGHT: The drive for these principles of Justice come through the mother's line. Creative talents may be channeled to deliver or foster these messages. Relationships will be handled with such diplomacy and equality that you must make special efforts to be demonstrative to those you love the most. ***INVERTED:*** Your insistence on honesty and forthrightness in your emotional affairs is discomforting to many.

3 GOVERNED BY THE EMPRESS: MENTAL GIVENS, INTELLECTUAL PREDISPOSITION
UPRIGHT: This is a mind free, capable of the purest objectivity. Ideal for the legal profession and naturally for judgeship. There is an amazing ability to manipulate large amounts of information dispassionately and yet with intense care. Your eye for detail is unmatched. ***INVERTED:*** You make a delicious friend and a formidable enemy.

4 GOVERNED BY THE EMPEROR: SPIRITUAL GIVENS, LIFE PURPOSE
UPRIGHT: This lifetime will be dedicated to balancing views. It falls to you to work toward the reconciliation of opposing forces. ***INVERTED:*** The balancing, the reconciliation you must bring about may be on a world scale, certainly large. And may the forces be with you as you complete your task, Mr. Ambassador.

5 GOVERNED BY THE HIEROPHANT: SYSTEMS BORN INTO, SOCIETAL INFLUENCE
UPRIGHT: Your earliest influences were from adults with sound secular ethics guiding their lives. To have this card suggests that they did not derive their morality base from religion as such, and may or may not have attended church. More than likely not. But a sense of fairness, equality of opportunity, and a tolerance for others' views was prevalent. ***INVERTED:*** At one extreme, these ideals may have been championed to a degree that were distorted and misapplied. At the other extreme, this environment would have been intolerant and not at all egalitarian.

6 GOVERNED BY THE LOVERS: EMOTIONAL TAPES, BASIS FOR RELATING/CREATING
UPRIGHT: The passion here, the guiding tape, is for equality, for fairness, and it grows up to be ideals like that of democracy in its purest form, and the text book heroic form of socialism in which all of God's children are treated well. ***INVERTED:*** At one extreme is the nirvana ideal that sounds good but proves to be a nightmare in disguise as heaven. At the other extreme is a distorted preference for inequality, for favoritism and advantage, the card player who prefers a stacked deck to the challenge of having to play against equal odds and winning by sheer ability.

7 GOVERNED BY THE CHARIOT: PHYSICAL RESOURCES, MEANS TO ACHIEVE
UPRIGHT: The balance you have achieved in your Material Plane is a marvel to behold. Balance, as much as sheer quantity and mass, is fundamental to a good foundation. Of course your ability to judge situations and make correct decisions in business matters has not hurt. ***INVERTED:*** Your resources, while they may add up on paper, may not be reliable when you need them. You have even distorted them to yourself so that you probably don't know where you really stand.

8 GOVERNED BY STRENGTH: EMOTIONAL RESOURCES, ENERGY
UPRIGHT: The even-handedness with which you have approached your relationships and people in general has given you a network on which you can depend. Objectivity in the Emotional Plane can multiply energy. ***INVERTED:*** At one extreme, you have treated everyone so much the same that those who feel they have a closer relationship and claim on your affections may feel slighted, even betrayed. At the other extreme, you have a varied scale of treatment, even including mistreatment and may have generated some resentment, even enemies.

9 GOVERNED BY THE HERMIT: BELIEF SYSTEM, BASIS FOR DECISIONS
UPRIGHT: Your beliefs are very secular in origin and character, maybe even a model similar to that of Socrates. In your list of observances we might find law

and order, a Bill of Rights, humanism/humanitarianism, and a golden rule of some sorts, but most likely not religion. ***INVERTED:*** Distortions here can include an extreme in which order and equality are sought after within a given group but not extended to another, as in one race to another, one nationality to another, one sex to another, or of humans to their fellow occupants of earth (animals, plants, etc.). In another extreme, the belief is in hierarchies rather than equalities with attendant rights and privileges.

10 GOVERNED BY THE WHEEL OF FORTUNE: CENTRAL MESSAGE, THEME OF READING
UPRIGHT: This is as the sword of Gabriel and the chakras are to be aligned for the work ahead. Here in the Tarot you see the necessary alignment of the Spiritual, Mental, Emotional, and Physical Planes. Hurry and get your seat on the correct side of the hall for the procession is about to begin. ***INVERTED:*** You must be more opinionated, self-directed, and expressive. Others need you to be centered and assertive and cannot wait as long as you think you can.

11 GOVERNED BY JUSTICE: STATE/CONTENT OF MIND
UPRIGHT: Here is an opening of the throat chakra, with an attendant increase in communicative abilities. Your mind is centered, clear, decisive, and responsible, as it works to resolve a host of dualities. There is a Zen presence of mind. ***INVERTED:*** At one extreme, the opening can be too great and should be tempered. At the other extreme, there is closure, poor communications, cloudiness and indecisiveness. Very little is being resolved, certainly no major dualities.

12 GOVERNED BY THE HANGED MAN: STATE OF EMOTIONS, SUBCONSCIOUS
UPRIGHT: The heart's gut reactions are on target; trust your instincts here. The heart has noble concerns about egalitarian issues. Justice must prevail. ***INVERTED:*** The heart's conclusions may be so correct as to be painful or to bring about a great reaction/change. Justice is prevailing but at a painful cost to this heart. At another extreme, there is distortion here with much inaccurate noise clouding the facts of the situation. Injustice is the hour of the day.

13 GOVERNED BY DEATH: PHYSICAL SITUATION, HARD REALITY
UPRIGHT: Physical situation balanced, under control. Peace. Fairness all the way around. Favorable legal decision in your material plane. ***INVERTED:*** Time for resolution of differences in the Physical Plane. At an extreme, a time of war. At another extreme is the more difficult problem to see, that of too much justice, too much control, too much leveling out, too much stasis. Legal decision unfavorable. Stop, take a breath, and get back on track.

14 GOVERNED BY TEMPERANCE: EMOTIONAL TEST
UPRIGHT: Here is the effect of a leveling hand on relationships and creativity, productivity. Legal decisions affecting relationships, in your favor. The Emotional Plane is making good sense. The heart is moving into more universal waters, caring about the effect of ethics and the lack thereof. ***INVERTED:*** Adverse legal decisions in the Emotional/creative Plane. The leveling hand may prove to be a bit heavy. Heart not up to code in matters of ethics. There may be a subconscious distortion of the truth.

15 GOVERNED BY THE DEVIL: TEMPTATION/CHALLENGE, FEARS
UPRIGHT: Trust your evaluations in the near future. Go with the facts, the truth. Legal resolutions in your favor. You have to make things add up before you can make much more headway. You may have to kill a sacred cow or two, but you will get those scales to balance. ***INVERTED:*** Temptation may be to neglect or distort the truth.

16 GOVERNED BY THE TOWER: NEXT LESSON, GRACE OF GOD
UPRIGHT: A mental calm washes over you. There is a pervading sense of correctness. Here is the answer to a mental conundrum. This sets the stage for your crusade. ***INVERTED:*** All this good feeling, and it is so that you can share it with and use it for others.

17 GOVERNED BY THE STAR: ASPIRATIONS OF EGO, GOALS, MAXIMUM EXPECTATIONS
UPRIGHT: The desire to be a lawyer or a judge is the most obvious, a politician only a little less so, but these professions are direct stems from this archetype. You wish to be instrumental in the equal distribution of opportunity and its rewards. The system by which society governs itself, its regulations and laws, dominates your thoughts. ***INVERTED:*** The means of governance may appeal to you for very personal reasons. At another extreme, your goal could be to overturn law, preferring revolution or anarchy.

18 GOVERNED BY THE MOON: ASPIRATIONS OF HEART, COMPASSION
UPRIGHT: Heart aspires to the stability of a well-functioning society and what it can guarantee its citizens. This can be the goal of the dedicated social worker, counselor, government worker, and other roles offering a creative contribution to the social system. ***INVERTED:*** In one extreme, this aspiration can be distorted toward an ideal such as a full welfare state. At the other extreme, this heart longs for the unfettered freedom of a laissez-faire system of Darwinian survival of the fittest, literally.

19 GOVERNED BY THE SUN: PHYSICAL FULFILLMENT/EVALUATION
UPRIGHT: You have been a member in good standing of the establishment, not in the elitist sense, but that of a solid, contributing citizen. You are pleased with the order in your physical/material house. ***INVERTED:*** You must exert a great deal of self-control, as well as healthy influence of those closest to you, to reach this fulfillment.

20 GOVERNED BY JUDGEMENT: HEART'S FULFILLMENT/EVALUATION
UPRIGHT: In the scales of death/judgement held by the Egyptian god Anubis, yours is the heart whose weight matches the lightness of the feather of truth in the opposing scale, for you have accumulated no guilt and no debt of remorse. Your relationships and creative enterprises have been deeply rewarding with the added play of your focused mind to enrich the game. ***INVERTED:*** It is hard to be fair in some matters of the heart, but where is it more important?

21 GOVERNED BY THE WORLD: EGO'S FULFILLMENT/EVALUATION
UPRIGHT: As did the Egyptian god Thoth/Hermes, so have you recorded the deeds of the lifetime, those of others as well as your own. ***INVERTED:*** This is a tough job, but somebody has to do it.

22/0 GOVERNED BY THE FOOL: SOUL'S FULFILLMENT/EVALUATION
UPRIGHT: You have understood that this sword of Justice is a sword which unites as well as divides, and used it well. It has carved a path of alignment through the lower planes of mind, heart, and body for the light of the spirit to follow, enlarge, and heal. It is the maypole around which you have danced. ***INVERTED:*** Use this reading and this time to meditate on the beauty of this potential fulfillment.

THE HANGED MAN.

12 THE HANGED MAN

UPRIGHT: This, your twelfth stop, is the midpoint of your emotional development as you swing from a passionate to a compassionate nature, from inner to outer, from self to other. It is the fulcrum of the heart, the opening of the heart chakra, allowing may people easier access. Life becomes much more public as you externalize and extend yourself into your environment. Extroverted personality. Here you can see a major emotional shift. With this major emotional change, you can be literally turned upside down as the spiritual descends to your emotional level. Voluntary self-sacrifice to a greater good, without sacrificing the self. As the self gives, it gets larger. As the heart gives, it grows. And so, there is an ability and willingness to accept suffering. The open heart is a trusting heart. Here too, is a change of heart. The fulcrum of the heart is working vertically as well to balance mind and body (the Mental Plane with the Physical Plane). **INVERTED:** Introverted personality. Clinging to the past. Attachment. Immaturity. Refusal to accept responsibility. Selfishness. Emotional suspension. Anxiety. Guilt. A traitor, as one who has turned his back to friends and loved ones, and in effect on himself in the process.

In This Spread Position...Interpret The Hanged Man Meanings to Include:

1 GOVERNED BY THE MAGICIAN: PHYSICAL GIVENS, OUT OF THE FATHER
UPRIGHT: There is good balance, an openness and ease with people in the affairs of the Physical/material Plane. The mark of an excellent salesperson, the gracious host, the life of the party. You may have been born into a high or active social position through your father's line. **INVERTED:** You must be careful to assure that your facility with people does not work against your physical and material objectives.

2 GOVERNED BY THE HIGH PRIESTESS: EMOTIONAL GIVENS, OUT OF THE MOTHER
UPRIGHT: There is good balance, an openness and ease with people in the affairs of the Emotional Plane. Relationships come easy as does creative expression. The mark of a good artist, but especially a great actor. You may have been born into a high or active social position through your mother's line. **INVERTED:** You must be alert to assure that your facility with people does not work against your emotional and creative objectives.

3 GOVERNED BY THE EMPRESS: MENTAL GIVENS, INTELLECTUAL PREDISPOSITION
UPRIGHT: This is a very open mind, disposed to and for others. Good at working with groups. A humanitarian. A democratic leader. You are dedicated to causes that extend your beliefs. **INVERTED:** You must be cautious to assure that your facility with people does not work against your mental objectives.

4 GOVERNED BY THE EMPEROR: SPIRITUAL GIVENS, LIFE PURPOSE
UPRIGHT: People, relationships, expression are central in this lifetime. Creative juices must flow. An open heart must prevail. **INVERTED:** Such openness is not without its risks, but for you and this path, closure is much more dangerous.

5 GOVERNED BY THE HIEROPHANT: SYSTEMS BORN INTO, SOCIETAL INFLUENCE
UPRIGHT: "Free spirit" is the more commonly used term, but here "free heart" is the more appropriate expression of the early environment in which you lived. The atmosphere may have been Bohemian, artistic, and free ranging with little dogma to tie you down. You were encouraged to just be yourself and to do your thing. **INVERTED:** There may have been too much of a good thing here.

6 GOVERNED BY THE LOVERS: EMOTIONAL TAPES, BASIS FOR RELATING/CREATING
UPRIGHT: Yours is a love of people and the give and take that social interaction affords. The more activity, the more people, the better. But, you are serious and sincere. This can also be complete openness and dedication to an innate talent that will be the centerpiece to your life. Here again though,...it will take you outward and upward on an extroverted course. **INVERTED:** At one extreme, you are the party animal who cannot sit still for a minute. There is very little that you prefer to do alone. You may marry many times. At the other extreme, here is the true loner, perhaps shy and introverted, but not necessarily. But, the preference is for your own rather than another's company. If you marry at all it will hopefully be to a very understanding and self-sufficient person.

7 GOVERNED BY THE CHARIOT: PHYSICAL RESOURCES. MEANS TO ACHIEVE
UPRIGHT: Your network of supporters and fellow team players is strategic in your Physical/material Plane. Social life figures prominently in your family, business, and your leisure activities. It may be difficult to draw the line where the social ends and the rest begins. **INVERTED:** There may be little contingency should your network fail. Ask what you alone could achieve if the need arose.

8 GOVERNED BY STRENGTH: EMOTIONAL RESOURCES, ENERGY
UPRIGHT: Your ability to balance give and take is your strong point. It allows you a tremendous range of relationships and creativity. You are never low on energy when you need/want to give, because you have been able to take when you needed to. **INVERTED:** You are less strong than your potential if you are not balancing this influx and outgo of your emotional fuel.

9 GOVERNED BY THE HERMIT: BELIEF SYSTEM, BASIS FOR DECISIONS
UPRIGHT: This suggests a highly devotional nature to your search, and in the most positive sense, a method of trial and error, an experiential, sense-reactive system. "Run it up the flagpole and see if it flies." Disciplines such as Bhakti or Tantra Yoga may be your bag. **INVERTED:** Devotional approaches are rooted in the emotional plane and, to be valid as guiding philosophy or belief system, there must be a healthy amount of mind at the helm as well, or the ship is going in circles at best, sinking at worst.

10 GOVERNED BY THE WHEEL OF FORTUNE: CENTRAL MESSAGE, THEME OF READING
UPRIGHT: This is an infusion, even a bombardment with the force of God's love in answer to your devotion. Preparation for a kundalini experience, or the opening of the heart chakra. **INVERTED:** You may be bombarded with social opportunities as the walls of your box come crashing down.

11 GOVERNED BY JUSTICE: STATE/CONTENT OF MIND
UPRIGHT: You are intellectually involved with devotional disciplines, such as Bhakti or Tantra Yoga, or other pathwork using the heart as guide. Here the

mind is yielding to the influence of heart wisdom, the intelligence also of the solar plexus. This is a poetic state of mind. ***INVERTED:*** With input from your heart, your gut reaction, you may be reversing your opinion on a subject.

12 GOVERNED BY THE HANGED MAN: STATE OF EMOTIONS, SUBCONSCIOUS
UPRIGHT: Here is the Hanged Man at its strongest as it sits in its home position. This is the opening of the heart chakra and any or all of the above general meanings may apply. Complete trust. Complete sacrifice. Little if anything is held back, and yet as you offer your blood you are strengthened with every drop taken. A positive, correct change of heart. A reversal or clearing of a prejudice. ***INVERTED:*** A change of heart that needs more attention. Hesitation in an aspect of opening that is slowing your progress. Closing of the heart chakra.

13 GOVERNED BY DEATH: PHYSICAL SITUATION, HARD REALITY
UPRIGHT: New dimensions are opening on the Physical Plane. There is an increase in opportunity in material matters. There is a deeper appreciation of the arts, of the emotional side of life, of that illusive yet ever available thing called beauty. ***INVERTED:*** At one extreme, there may be too much going on, confusing matters as most of it has nothing to do with you. At the other extreme, there is too much closure and not enough is going on. Decrease or increase contact until things even out.

14 GOVERNED BY TEMPERANCE: EMOTIONAL TEST
UPRIGHT: The heart will be opening further in the near future, and you will have many emotional balls in the air at the same time. This is a chance for a breakthrough in relationships or in a creative project. A great deal of energy will be available for your use. ***INVERTED:*** A time out may be the order of the day soon.

15 GOVERNED BY THE DEVIL: TEMPTATION/CHALLENGE, FEARS
UPRIGHT: Here you will have to integrate input from your higher emotions into your mental package. This may be in the form of a creative burst, or the impact of others, guides/teachers/loved ones. The smaller ego self is becoming the larger transformed Self. ***INVERTED:*** You must override your fear of openness and contact with people. It is stopping you from reaching your mental goals.

16 GOVERNED BY THE TOWER: NEXT LESSON, GRACE OF GOD
UPRIGHT: You are now strong enough, having learned well the efficiency of give and take. You are ready for the major shift from the predominance of taking, required on the first part of your journey, to a predominance of giving required on the second half. Many more of your vehicles are being opened by grace to participate in pathwork on a much larger scale than ever before. ***INVERTED:*** At first, this process may feel like it is only benefiting others, but be patient. This process benefits many others, but it is indeed for you.

17 GOVERNED BY THE STAR: ASPIRATIONS OF EGO, GOALS, MAXIMUM EXPECTATIONS
UPRIGHT: You aspire to have the creative intellectual ability and the social savvy to be instrumental in the advancement of your group, the culture of your society. ***INVERTED:*** At one extreme, this dips into the potential of inappropriate sacrifice of personal goals to group causes.

18 GOVERNED BY THE MOON: ASPIRATIONS OF HEART, COMPASSION
UPRIGHT: You long to be immersed in the very heart of your culture, your people, to be one with them in their greatest trials and sorrows as well as their greatest triumphs and joys. ***INVERTED:*** At one extreme, this can lapse into unnecessary martyrdom.

19 GOVERNED BY THE SUN: PHYSICAL FULFILLMENT/EVALUATION
UPRIGHT: This can be the mark of a late bloomer, or even of a form of conversion in senior years. But most likely, it reveals an active life with a high public profile. Most of what was done involved a large number of people. ***INVERTED:*** Be open.

20 GOVERNED BY JUDGEMENT: HEART'S FULFILLMENT/EVALUATION
UPRIGHT: This heart gave itself and everyone else every opportunity for full expression and appreciation. Creative talents were honored and, in turn, honored you with the beauty of honesty in form. ***INVERTED:*** Be open.

21 GOVERNED BY THE WORLD: EGO'S FULFILLMENT/EVALUATION
UPRIGHT: Your re-awakening figures prominently in the subject matter of your legacy. Openness is to be credited with your success. ***INVERTED:*** Be open.

22/0 GOVERNED BY THE FOOL: SOUL'S FULFILLMENT/EVALUATION
UPRIGHT: "I never met a man I didn't like." Will Rogers said it, but now you can claim it too. ***INVERTED:*** Be very open.

13 DEATH

UPRIGHT: Here is the thirteenth stop on your journey. This is fundamental, irreversible change of a physical/material nature. The interpretation of cessation of life, actual biological death is of course one possible meaning, but only one out of many others outlined here. One of the major metaphysical purposes for our aging and eventual death is to stop our material stockpiling, to stop us from putting all that energy into lateral growth at the physical level. The fact that we cannot take it with us is the blessing and fundamental lesson of death. With death, everything that we have done, collected, is in the long run for others, not for self. This is the Physical Plane's lesson of progress from self to other that matches the parallel lesson of self to other in the Emotional Plane (passion to compassion), and in the Mental Plane (little ego to super Ego). Death must be thought of as the mean, the middle, not the end. The phrase "in the dead of the night" means "in the middle of the night." New beginnings. New phases. New directions. This is the spiritual descended to the physical level, and can show reversals of ill health. Acceptance of physical endings and physical lessons. All fears center around change at the physical level. The positive function of fear shows here in its role of preserving life. But, when fear climbs up from the physical level of protection through the emotional and into the mental, it takes on the cloak of irrationality and works against our welfare. Here then is courage, derived from an intimate knowledge of the myths and realities of death. **INVERTED:** This can mean no change where change is needed, therefore a block. Here death represents the negative face of fear. Eventually all fears can be traced to the root fear of death. Physical insecurity, which is most closely linked with matters of health, work, and home. At one extreme, cowardice; at the other extreme, false courage.

In This Spread Position...Interpret the Death Meanings to Include:

1 GOVERNED BY THE MAGICIAN: PHYSICAL GIVENS, OUT OF THE FATHER
UPRIGHT: Many of the issues of death are literally behind you, learned in the lineage of your father. **INVERTED:** Earth spirits (elementals and gnomes) are assertive, but you are very much in tune with them, and there is little or no fear of nature.

2 GOVERNED BY THE HIGH PRIESTESS: EMOTIONAL GIVENS, OUT OF THE MOTHER
UPRIGHT: Many of the lessons surrounding death are behind you, learned in the lineage of your mother. **INVERTED:** Water spirits (undines) are assertive, but you are very much in tune with them, and there is little or no fear of water, of emotions, or creative energy.

3 GOVERNED BY THE EMPRESS: MENTAL GIVENS, INTELLECTUAL PREDISPOSITION
UPRIGHT: Many of the lessons surrounding death are behind you, learned in the succession of your past lives. **INVERTED:** Air spirits (sylphs) are assertive, but you are very much in tune with them, and there is little or no fear of air, of heights, of mind and its products.

4 GOVERNED BY THE EMPEROR: SPIRITUAL GIVENS, LIFE PURPOSE
UPRIGHT: There is no fear of death for there is a profound understanding of immortality, of the relationship of life to afterlife as the most complex and elusive of the dualities man is left to resolve. There is no fear of fear, but fear is respected and preserved in its proper place as a friend in need. **INVERTED:** Fire spirits (salamanders) are assertive and you are very much in tune with them.

5 GOVERNED BY THE HIEROPHANT: SYSTEMS BORN INTO, SOCIETAL INFLUENCE
UPRIGHT: Early environment dealt with issues of death in a forthright way, so that many of these lessons were integral to your early upbringing. Warrior peoples expose their young to rites of passage with tests of bravery and the like paving the way. The death of many family members, and the proper rituals associated with their passing, teach here. **INVERTED:** Improper death/killing and ritual sacrifice are distortions doing disservice to the honor that belongs to proper dying. Here could have been an inordinate fear of death impressed on youth.

6 GOVERNED BY THE LOVERS: EMOTIONAL TAPES, BASIS FOR RELATING/CREATING
UPRIGHT: To be in love with the archetype death in its purest form is simply to love, to welcome change with an open heart. This is the stuff of bravery, or chivalry. **INVERTED:** To love or to welcome death in its extremes of too much or too little leads to some of humanities most disturbing potentialities. An over fascination and embrace of death leads, on the lighter side to a love of danger with greater and greater risk to life, such as practiced by the dare-devil, and on the darker side to things like necrophilia, murder, and suicide. To welcome death too little is to fear death and leads to weakness, cowardice, and in the extreme a fear of the least little thing, and eventually life itself.

7 GOVERNED BY THE CHARIOT: PHYSICAL RESOURCES. MEANS TO ACHIEVE
UPRIGHT: You have been in harmony with life's basic cycles, aligned with the seasons. There may have been an issue of death in the past which is serving as backdrop to the question at hand, but as a positive element. You are brave, having a history of courageous deeds, perhaps even death defying. **INVERTED:** Perhaps you have not been in tune with nature and basic rhythms. Death as an issue behind you is unresolved.

8 GOVERNED BY STRENGTH: EMOTIONAL RESOURCES, ENERGY
UPRIGHT: Death has made you stronger as you have emotionally resolved its impact, its major lessons. **INVERTED:** Perhaps the loss of a loved one still grieves you. Loss, or fear of loss, lessens your effectiveness with others.

9 GOVERNED BY THE HERMIT: BELIEF SYSTEM, BASIS FOR DECISIONS
UPRIGHT: "Plus ca change, plus c'est la meme chose." This old French saying, "The more things change, the more they stay the same," probably says it all for you. The Greek philosopher Heraclitus said, "You can't step into the same river twice." Parmenides, his successor, said, "You can't step into the same river once." Everything changes but change itself. **INVERTED:** How is it we can be bored, bored being our reaction to a lack of change, of newness and variety, when we fight so hard against change all the time? And when we are bored, we seem to work even harder to keep things the same.

10 GOVERNED BY THE WHEEL OF FORTUNE: CENTRAL MESSAGE, THEME OF READING
UPRIGHT: Deal with the matters directly at hand. Physical and material matters predominate. Check on health, security. Be courageous. Welcome change with open arms. Direct prayers for change, not for the status quo. Invoke change. **INVERTED:** The matter at hand requires your participation, but you are not the principle character.

11 GOVERNED BY JUSTICE: STATE/CONTENT OF MIND
UPRIGHT: You are aware of, or you are planning, major change at the physical level. Courageous state of mind. *INVERTED:* Death, fear may be playing on the mind in a very counterproductive way. Do not avoid the subject; air it, face it.

12 GOVERNED BY THE HANGED MAN: STATE OF EMOTIONS, SUBCONSCIOUS
UPRIGHT: Heart accepts/desires major physical change. It can be the heart's acceptance of a death, of the lessons of death. *INVERTED:* A fatalistic heart. Heartache over change. A reluctance or inability to internalize a death, the lessons of death. At the other extreme, there can be an over-enthusiasm for this archetype, embracing too much change too quickly.

13 GOVERNED BY DEATH: PHYSICAL SITUATION, HARD REALITY
UPRIGHT: A major, irreversible physical/material change is taking place now or in the near future. Here is the physical aspect of the phenomenon of re-birthing, of being born again spiritually. The body undergoes a formidable change in chemistry and in general appearance. *INVERTED:* Change has been stalled, or its effects rejected, not internalized.

14 GOVERNED BY TEMPERANCE: EMOTIONAL TEST
UPRIGHT: Heart must make adjustments to the radically new physical/material situation. Things will no longer be as they were and that must be accepted, eventually even welcomed, if that is not the case initially. *INVERTED:* At one extreme, the heart may want to look back too much. Or, it may be ignoring the past and what has happened instead of integrating it.

15 GOVERNED BY THE DEVIL: TEMPTATION/CHALLENGE, FEARS
UPRIGHT: The mind embraces major physical/material change. Adapting to and integrating the new reality at the mental level. *INVERTED:* There may be fear of this change. If the mental fear is great enough, it can stall the effects the change was meant to implement. The change cannot however be reversed, or even compensated for; it must be embraced.

16 GOVERNED BY THE TOWER: NEXT LESSON, GRACE OF GOD
UPRIGHT: Here is the gift of courage just when it is most needed. The ability to rise above all fears to achieve the tasks at hand. *INVERTED:* The fears you are experiencing are legitimate and you will be able to navigate safely having heeded them. No need to put on a face of false courage.

17 GOVERNED BY THE STAR: ASPIRATIONS OF EGO, GOALS, MAXIMUM EXPECTATIONS
UPRIGHT: Here is the willingness to face the ultimate of death in the honoring of one's beliefs. It is a goal and an expectation of a major change in the world of the self, or if idealistic and grand enough, the world. The mind will not rest until it sees the sun rise on a new situation. *INVERTED:* At one extreme, here is the mental drive to martyrdom, having decided that death is an important link in the fulfillment of the cause. At another extreme, such as in Hinduism, is the desire to end the cycle of reincarnation, and so a permanent death is ideologically embraced.

18 GOVERNED BY THE MOON: ASPIRATIONS OF HEART, COMPASSION
UPRIGHT: Your heart aspires to the courage necessary to face the ultimate sacrifice of self for the sake of others. Again the martyr, but here it is the martyred heart. *INVERTED:* At one extreme, the heart is aspiring to disappear into the universal one and never return. At another is the less extreme, if more dramatic, desire to die for the love of another. This does not necessarily presuppose being reincarnated.

19 GOVERNED BY THE SUN: PHYSICAL FULFILLMENT/EVALUATION
UPRIGHT: Here is irreversible biological change in the future, and in this position we must look at this possibility of death as the cessation of life. The cards surrounding this position (and in the overall reading) address what can be done to avoid this eventuality, or what can be done to best accommodate and prepare for it. There is nothing to fear here. *INVERTED:* Neither be too eager for physical change so as to not enjoy the present, nor be too reticent refusing even the inevitable and worthy change.

20 GOVERNED BY JUDGEMENT: HEART'S FULFILLMENT/EVALUATION
UPRIGHT: This heart fully embraced change as the primary motivator for life, energizing relationships and creative output. *INVERTED:* Love will lead the way if you but follow. It is both the beacon in the lighthouse and the wind in your sails.

21 GOVERNED BY THE WORLD: EGO'S FULFILLMENT/EVALUATION
UPRIGHT: The mark of this mental path was its healthy restlessness, the appetite for constant renewal. This is the prerequisite for true awareness— for the restlessness and appetite come from a respect for what has already been learned, the questions that have already been answered. But the true answer to every question is itself the seed that grows into the next question. If there is no fertile seed in an answer, then that answer is not correct. *INVERTED:* Let the mind use updated charts to navigate and you will not sail off the end of the earth.

22/0 GOVERNED BY THE FOOL: SOUL'S FULFILLMENT/EVALUATION
UPRIGHT: This soul has existed because of what preceded it, and because of what is to follow it. That is what has made it "it." The success of this life is that this soul has known "it." *INVERTED:* Discover your rightful place between cause and effect, between all the duality pairs. Incarnate again; it is the thing to do.

14 TEMPERANCE

UPRIGHT: Here is the fourteenth stop on your journey, where you begin to appreciate the lessons of the higher emotions. This is a mature emotional constitution, where consideration for self and others strive to balance. This is Stage Four and the effect of higher mind on the Emotional Plane guides us to thoughtful behavior. Recognition and practice of both give and take in equal proportion, even as the opening of the heart chakra has elevated the emotions to the higher level wherein compassion transforms us into willing givers moving happily toward universal love. Temperance is the exercise of emotional balance horizontally in the earth plane, to generate movement vertically from below to above. Here is authentic expression and a higher understanding of your passionate nature, which must grow even as you become more compassionate. **INVERTED:** Distortions in the way of too much or too little of the above meanings. Sufi master, Hazrat Inyat Khan put us on notice that "love in its lower manifestations turns into law by forming habits." Intemperance. Emotional imbalance. Addictive behavior. A problem of giving or taking in healthy proportions. In a sense this card functions as an emotional barometer. Not being able to take is a problem for many, and is little recognized in modern society, where giving has received a "good" label and taking has received a "bad" label. You must learn to be a good taker or you will be denying others their right and pleasure in giving. There can be too much mentality creating abstraction and limiting heart. Too little mentality in the emotional.

In This Spread Position...Interpret the Temperance Meanings to Include:

1 GOVERNED BY THE MAGICIAN: PHYSICAL GIVENS, OUT OF THE FATHER
UPRIGHT: Yours is a calm and steady nature, evenhanded and sure in your work as well as your play. A positive presence. You seem to know how to balance things in your physical/material plane, and to keep it in check with your emotional and mental planes. **INVERTED:** You may be prone to extremes in matters of health, business, and other material matters.

2 GOVERNED BY THE HIGH PRIESTESS: EMOTIONAL GIVENS, OUT OF THE MOTHER
UPRIGHT: You are by nature a relaxed and easy going person that people like to be around, as your cool seems to rub off on them. A healing presence. You know how to keep things flowing smoothly in your Emotional/creative Plane, using energy for productive purposes rather than in putting out forest fires. **INVERTED:** You may be overly sensitive, easily swayed, or intemperate in your emotional and creative affairs.

3 GOVERNED BY THE EMPRESS: MENTAL GIVENS, INTELLECTUAL PREDISPOSITION
UPRIGHT: You are mentally stable, a peacekeeper by nature, within yourself foremost, but also in the conventional sense of self with other, of other with other. Here is a mind eminently capable of working with emotional issues, i.e. counseling on issues of imbalance which create disfunction and/or discomfort. Addictions, habits out of control, crumble before your awareness. **INVERTED:** You may be quick to make up and/or to change your mind and will need to practice the art of patience to achieve your mental goals.

4 GOVERNED BY THE EMPEROR: SPIRITUAL GIVENS, LIFE PURPOSE
UPRIGHT: Here is ecumenical awareness personified. Everything means everything. Nothing means nothing. Everything makes sense, and nothing makes sense. "Avec de la patience on arrive a tout." (With patience one arrives at everything.) A natural born diplomat. **INVERTED:** This emotional insistence on balance gives this path a steadfast quality that will help it weather many a storm.

5 GOVERNED BY THE HIEROPHANT: SYSTEMS BORN INTO, SOCIETAL INFLUENCE
UPRIGHT: This early environment was tolerant and openminded, but within expressed preferences. There was great strength here but it rarely had to bare its teeth. **INVERTED:** At one extreme, there was intemperance and imbalance took its toll, with irrational mood swings and self-indulgent behavior from irresponsible adults. At the other extreme, there was too much temperance and where there is not temper there is no fire, no progress. That is where temptation enters the picture. We are not allowed to be so content that we are complacent. The trick is to be happy but not blithely content.

6 GOVERNED BY THE LOVERS: EMOTIONAL TAPES, BASIS FOR RELATING/CREATING
UPRIGHT: This passion for emotional balance and harmony will insist on equality in relationships, as close to 50/50 as it can get. This equality does not infer role swapping or the like, just that energy of participation be equal regarding both energy in and energy out from each partner (or from all participants in groups). **INVERTED:** At one extreme, this can demand a sameness as opposed to an equality, or be intolerant of imbalances in the short run, destroying rather than fostering caring love.

7 GOVERNED BY THE CHARIOT: PHYSICAL RESOURCES. MEANS TO ACHIEVE
UPRIGHT: You have been so efficient in how you accomplish your tasks in the physical arena that you are rested and ready. You avoid the extremes in work, diet, and exercise. **INVERTED:** At one extreme, you are over concerned about doing too much and do not allow yourself enough range for experience. You may be considered dull because you simply refuse to do anything extraordinary. At another extreme, you are inconsistent and your actions cover a wide span.

8 GOVERNED BY STRENGTH: EMOTIONAL RESOURCES, ENERGY
UPRIGHT: You have a knack at making relationships work, at keeping all parties concerned satisfied. This is social diplomacy at its best. There is an abundance of creative talent that manages to avoid the normal tendency of an artist to be a loner. You are creative in conjunction with others. **INVERTED:** You may be calm and predictable to the point that people take advantage of you . But at another extreme, you are unpredictable and your moods can cover a lot of territory. Habits, addictions may have weakened you.

9 GOVERNED BY THE HERMIT: BELIEF SYSTEM, BASIS FOR DECISIONS
UPRIGHT: Your beliefs may resemble the Buddhist middle path, with the accompanying thought that control of desire is the solution to man's discomfort. Here we can also see the confidence in love's ability to solve everything, to heal all through the flow of energy in and out, cleansing the soul. **INVERTED:** At one extreme is a misunderstanding of desire and the attempt to negate it. To be born is to be given the blessing of desire. It is the desire to be one with God that energizes every action creating movement, life itself. It is the nature of our desires and our actions to fulfill them that carry the dis-ease. At another extreme, this can become philosophy of non-action, wherein the will of man lies fallow waiting upon the will of God.

10 GOVERNED BY THE WHEEL OF FORTUNE: CENTRAL MESSAGE, THEME OF READING
UPRIGHT: Ask for Temperance for that is the archetype needed at this time. Let it descend from this, the Spiritual Plane down through the Mental, Emotional,

and Physical Planes, to heal where imbalance has left its mark. ***INVERTED:*** This energy of Temperance will work through you for someone close who needs its healing balance. Direct your mind and heart to this task.

11 GOVERNED BY JUSTICE: STATE/CONTENT OF MIND

UPRIGHT: You are planning how to correct an imbalance in the Emotional Plane. You may want to shift the weight from one area to another. The issues may already be on the table for discussion. ***INVERTED:*** The mind can only address the issues here; the real work will still have to be done by the heart. The mind may be subverting or distorting knowingly the emotional issues at hand, and contributing to the problem.

12 GOVERNED BY THE HANGED MAN: STATE OF EMOTIONS, SUBCONSCIOUS

UPRIGHT: This heart understands that it will only get stronger if it can equalize the flow of energy in and energy out. It is in the process of redistributing energy at this very moment to achieve that balance. There may be a shift in the amount of normal giving, or taking, the desire to cooperate, to compromise. ***INVERTED:*** With temperance, timing can be a problem. As we identify an imbalance we want to correct, we may not wait for the appropriate situation. Give and take requires willing parties on both ends whose souls have complimentary needs at the same time.

13 GOVERNED BY DEATH: PHYSICAL SITUATION, HARD REALITY

UPRIGHT: You are having to temper your actions, saying and doing less (or more as the case may demand if you have been too passive). Reconciliation may be underway. Redistribution of material resources with high emotional content. ***INVERTED:*** Your action may be an over reaction. Reconciliation may be inappropriate or it may not be going well. Physical habits may be out of control; substance abuse appears here, with resulting damage to the body.

14 GOVERNED BY TEMPERANCE: EMOTIONAL TEST

UPRIGHT: This is Temperance in its home base and the effect will be especially strong. The reading may center to a great degree around this card here. In the near future you will be delicately balancing give and take. Remember that proper giving/taking does not require sacrifice from either party. ***INVERTED:*** An imbalance of this principle may put your relationships, or your creative endeavors, to the test. Habits may become destructive. As a preventive measure ask someone on whom you can rely to give you brutally honest feedback on your behavior for awhile, and then listen to them.

15 GOVERNED BY THE DEVIL: TEMPTATION/CHALLENGE, FEARS

UPRIGHT: Here may be a concern with the heart content of information, of words and ideas. Be as objective and fair as possible and still satisfy your goals. ***INVERTED:*** You may think of temperance as a weakness. You may even have a fear of compromise.

16 GOVERNED BY THE TOWER: NEXT LESSON, GRACE OF GOD

UPRIGHT: You will be washed with the emotional balm you need, suggesting you need the efficiency of all your energy directed toward a worthwhile endeavor of great benefit to you. ***INVERTED:*** The above is true, but in order for you to have the energy and motivation to help someone else get their project accomplished on time.

17 GOVERNED BY THE STAR: ASPIRATIONS OF EGO, GOALS, MAXIMUM EXPECTATIONS

UPRIGHT: Let there be peace on earth. If you could have your way, this is your greatest wish. As an operating principle you fall back on the Golden Rule, hoping others will do unto you as you do unto them. You may achieve this in many ways, from being a marriage counselor to an ambassador. ***INVERTED:*** You may practice "do as I say do, not as I do." At one extreme, this penchant for peace can distort and turn on itself like a scorpion, yielding something akin to the parents vow that "this is going to hurt me more than it is you."

18 GOVERNED BY THE MOON: ASPIRATIONS OF HEART, COMPASSION

UPRIGHT: Let there be wholeness on earth. You want to be able to heal where there is need. The desires for self and for others are merging, each feeding the other. Paradoxically, in order for these to merge well they must each be maximized in their own turn. Neither may be sacrificed for the other. ***INVERTED:*** Aspire to be helped as much as to help and you will be so efficient at learning the lessons of the higher emotions that you will have energy left over. It is this excess energy that has the innate power to heal. And it comes only through efficiency in learning, and that only from a balance of concern for self and for others.

19 GOVERNED BY THE SUN: PHYSICAL FULFILLMENT/EVALUATION

UPRIGHT: Your Material Plane shows the benefit of years of emotional stability, flexibility, patience, and perseverance. ***INVERTED:*** Let the archetype Temperance lead you to this fulfillment.

20 GOVERNED BY JUDGEMENT: HEART'S FULFILLMENT/EVALUATION

UPRIGHT: If at the moment of giving you have received and at the moment of receiving you have given, then no greater efficiency is possible for the emotional plane. Of your relationships it must be said that they are interwoven, for even the word interdependent suggests an aura of obligation that has already been paid. ***INVERTED:*** Emotions are like the water which will flow into the form of its container and unto its filling. The shape and size of your heart will determine the form and extent of your emotions.

21 GOVERNED BY THE WORLD: EGO'S FULFILLMENT/EVALUATION

UPRIGHT: You have been able to talk well and to listen well, and to know when to do which. Higher mind has been both a wise guide to the lower emotions keeping you from the errors of mistaken passion, and a wise follower of the higher emotions to the needs of compassion. ***INVERTED:*** Let holding back of temperance be the natural companion to the pushing forward of temptation.

22/0 GOVERNED BY THE FOOL: SOUL'S FULFILLMENT/EVALUATION

UPRIGHT: You have correctly used Temperance to make you stronger, not to weaken and slow you down. ***INVERTED:*** Like water poured into a jug, your emotions take the shape of your heart.

THE DEVIL.

15 THE DEVIL

UPRIGHT: Here at waystation fifteen the Mental Plane hits the fifth Stage of your evolution of consciousness, the Higher Mental, and your mind is given full reign, for this is the cutting edge of your intellect. Your full potential comes into awareness here as you pull out all the stops, for here is temptation to push you forward just as it was the function of Temperance(14) to hold you back. This is the realization that anything is possible but that you must be careful, for it is the mystery of alchemy. Remember King Midas and his fulfilled wish for everything he touched to turn to gold; it included his food. You too can have anything you wish, but alone you rarely have the overview and complexity of insight to know what to wish for correctly. The concept of good and evil, like every other mental concept and set of word-opposites, is just that, an abstract concept. There is no absolute good or absolute evil, any more than there is an absolute hot/cold or up/down. These are limits which help us define reality, the middle ground between all pairs of opposites. We have a popular concept of God as the point of extreme goodness at the end of our "directional" concept of good, and the Devil at the end of our "directional" concept of bad, but these are abstract points. What we actually have to work with is everything between these two points. And all of that is one thing...God. This archetype/card shows this is a time for understanding and integrating upper and lower self, inner and outer personality, and for accepting the whole that you are, not the half. **INVERTED:** This is the paradox of the practical side of what we call evil. It is the denial, the lack of recognition and acceptance that gives it its power, its very existence. Only when you cut off an integral part of yourself do you create your Dr. Jekyll and Mr. Hyde. Be cautious of what you deny. Only what you push into the dark can grow unnoticed, reappearing later in disguised form to terrorize you. This can be in the form of immoral or illegal acts by others directed at you, or by you at others. When the mind hangs onto its separateness, refusing the opening of the third eye, the lifting of the veil, the resolution of dualities, then balance is impossible. Evil occurs only when too much attention has been paid to one half of a duality pair without enough attention to the other.

In This Spread Position...Interpret The Devil Meanings to Include:

1 GOVERNED BY THE MAGICIAN: PHYSICAL GIVENS, OUT OF THE FATHER
UPRIGHT: You have inherited an assertive nature through your father's line. Mental challenges compel the body, the Physical Plane, to move forward, be it at work or at play. The blood of the adventurer/explorer runs in your veins. **INVERTED:** People like having you on their team; that way they are assured you are not on the other team. It is possible that you were conceived in violence.

2 GOVERNED BY THE HIGH PRIESTESS: EMOTIONAL GIVENS, OUT OF THE MOTHER
UPRIGHT: You have inherited an assertive nature through your mother's line. Mental challenges compel you in creativity and relationships. The blood of a creative trailblazer and an emotional whirlwind runs in your veins. **INVERTED:** People will be attracted to you because of your fiery spirit, and the sense of adventure you exude. It is possible that you were conceived in promiscuity.

3 GOVERNED BY THE EMPRESS: MENTAL GIVENS, INTELLECTUAL PREDISPOSITION
UPRIGHT: You are mentally a tiger, quick and alert for every opportunity, highly ambitious. Your intellect is powerful and quite capable of influencing people. **INVERTED:** Anyone who tries to keep this mental genie in a bottle will be in for a few surprises.

4 GOVERNED BY THE EMPEROR: SPIRITUAL GIVENS, LIFE PURPOSE
UPRIGHT: Born with the ability to see through the veil when necessary as the Devil(15) is the death of the duality that began with the Lovers(6). In this lifetime you are one with the energy of Prometheus who brought man the gift of fire, and hence spirit which is the gift of life as we know it now. Your deep innate understanding of metaphysics gives you a dual package of great knowledge attached to great responsibility. **INVERTED:** You will be called upon often to be the devil's advocate, to champion the underdog, to side with the uncomfortable viewpoint, to help keep the cutting edge of society sharp.

5 GOVERNED BY THE HIEROPHANT: SYSTEMS BORN INTO, SOCIETAL INFLUENCE
UPRIGHT: This early environment was most likely unconventional, non-conforming, and maybe even revolutionary, if it was really on the cutting edge. The guiding hand here was mind, not religion, and could have been agnostic or atheistic, which is not to say anything regarding ethics and morality. **INVERTED:** At one extreme, the mental influence may have been very narrow, identifying with very little in society, and could have been overtly anti-establishment and/or anti-religion. At the other extreme, it may have been trying to sample everything with the walls of duality-reality torn completely down, as if trying to live on the other side of the veil.

6 GOVERNED BY THE LOVERS: EMOTIONAL TAPES, BASIS FOR RELATING/CREATING
UPRIGHT: Here in the position of the birth of duality, The Lovers(6), is The Devil card indicating the death of duality. Thus your passion, the basis of your emotional tapes, is nothing less than an intellectual fervor for all things to be united, for the veil to be lifted. This is the heart of a dedicated metaphysician, beating with the same intensity that fired history's leading philosophical thinkers. This is a love of adventure of the most challenging and daring sort, seeking nothing less than the unknown, the unexperienced. **INVERTED:** At one extreme, the love of adventure here crosses into danger. Another, is the detached passion for the unknown simply for the sake of the unknown. Also, the desire to stir the pot for the sheer unpredictability of the results, to make trouble. Another possibility here is incest, or abuse.

7 GOVERNED BY THE CHARIOT: PHYSICAL RESOURCES. MEANS TO ACHIEVE
UPRIGHT: The extent of your knowledge and experience, the range of your activities, has given you the edge in material matters. Few can move as quickly and with such a clear sense of purpose as you. **INVERTED:** At one extreme, you may have sewn too many oats in too many fields. You are experienced, but can it be marshalled into what you need now? In some cases, penance will be necessary to fix the cracks in your foundation before going on.

8 GOVERNED BY STRENGTH: EMOTIONAL RESOURCES, ENERGY
UPRIGHT: You are comfortable with the out-of-ordinary, with strange settings, strange people, and even strange ideas. Thus, you are at ease when you are in the minority, or even in the enemy camp. All this is because you thrive on the edge of the unknown. **INVERTED:** This suggests a persona that has been too friendly with the other side, someone who may want to stay on the other side of the veil. A bad case of "the grass is greener on the other side." Perhaps Aleister Crowley was such a personality.

9 GOVERNED BY THE HERMIT: BELIEF SYSTEM, BASIS FOR DECISIONS
UPRIGHT: "There is nothing good or bad but thinking makes it so," says Shakespeare's Hamlet, and you agree. Any act of and by itself is not evil; it is the

intellect which underlies and surrounds the act which can generate the evil. Gnostic beliefs appear here, in their insistence that duality is the only game in town and that we had better learn how to play, starting with getting our hands on a set of rules. ***INVERTED:*** At one extreme, the erratic beliefs of a schizoid-ish personality. Another is straightforward amorality. Here too is the mind that has bought into the false extreme–of an ultimate evil up against an ultimate good— a mind that has a penchant for liking only one half of a duality pair. This is a mind that literally cannot get it together.

10 GOVERNED BY THE WHEEL OF FORTUNE: CENTRAL MESSAGE, THEME OF READING
UPRIGHT: Pay attention to the other side. Avoid complacency. Allow yourself to be tempted. ***INVERTED:*** Consider the radical opposite to your present belief or position. Review your methods, your means to your ends.

11 GOVERNED BY JUSTICE: STATE/CONTENT OF MIND
UPRIGHT: You are reviewing all the other viewpoints affecting your plans. The mind is open and expansive as it should be. ***INVERTED:*** You may be under the influence of viewpoints which are not favorable to your karmic purpose. This may be considered to be your lower self and the noise of elementals, or it may be improper guides eliciting your energy and talents for their group purposes rather than for your own.

12 GOVERNED BY THE HANGED MAN: STATE OF EMOTIONS, SUBCONSCIOUS
UPRIGHT: Your heart and the subconscious are disposed to new ideas and challenges. They want a broader range of feelings. ***INVERTED:*** At one extreme, you are being too adventurous, moving into unchartered waters best left alone. At the other extreme, you may be too inflexible, limiting much of what is intended for you.

13 GOVERNED BY DEATH: PHYSICAL SITUATION, HARD REALITY
UPRIGHT: Perhaps you are experimenting with your lifestyle, even trying things you've never liked before. You may be up to your ears in an adventure already, pushing for new sensations, new thrills. ***INVERTED:*** Here you might be possessed of your possessions. The cart may be pulling the horse, as materiality pulls the human around by the nose.

14 GOVERNED BY TEMPERANCE: EMOTIONAL TEST
UPRIGHT: In the near future your Emotional/creative Plane is introduced to new worlds and the certain feeling that there is more, much more than you ever imagined. ***INVERTED:*** Pay close attention, more may turn out to be less in this case.

15 GOVERNED BY THE DEVIL: TEMPTATION/CHALLENGE, FEARS
UPRIGHT: This in your near future will see you through the most important gate on your path, for it marks the boundary between inner and outer courtyard. Everything in the inner courtyard is the same as the outer, and yet it is different in its degree of intensity as all senses are magnified. This is the hidden validity behind all views that becomes obvious as the veil is lifted, and you are able to focus with the singular vision of the Third Eye bringing duality to its death. ***INVERTED:*** The big mistake that is made here is the attempt to stay on the other side beyond the veil, avoiding the very purpose of your incarnation, to find and bring this very awareness into your everyday reality, to see that the outer courtyards become as beautiful as the inner.

16 GOVERNED BY THE TOWER: NEXT LESSON, GRACE OF GOD
UPRIGHT: You always knew that there was more to it than this. Right? Well, here comes the proof. You can certainly handle it, but you may want to fasten your seatbelt. Lights! Camera! Action! ***INVERTED:*** Don't try anything that requires great balance, not until you quit using only half of your brain.

17 GOVERNED BY THE STAR: ASPIRATIONS OF EGO, GOALS, MAXIMUM EXPECTATIONS
UPRIGHT: Maybe this is what took Admiral Byrd to the North Pole. This goal, this drive, is to always know more. Its intention is to never be satisfied, as the answer to each question becomes the next question. ***INVERTED:*** Here too is intellectual snobbery, sometimes with a twist, the desire to manipulate rather than discover. This is knowledge turning its nose up at the coequal responsibility. And since responsibility is concomitant, integral with the knowledge, once removed the knowledge is no longer valid and breeds only evil, only halves of duality pairs.

18 GOVERNED BY THE MOON: ASPIRATIONS OF HEART, COMPASSION
UPRIGHT: This is the heart which aspires to feel everything, just as the mind which aspires to know everything. As presumptuous as this sounds, it is correct for it seeks not to replace or consume, but to fulfill its karmic purpose of contribution/dedication to universal mind and universal love. ***INVERTED:*** At one extreme, there is presumption which will lead to consumption and distortion, not contribution and dedication. At another extreme, the heart is attracted not to order but to chaos.

19 GOVERNED BY THE SUN: PHYSICAL FULFILLMENT/EVALUATION
UPRIGHT: This life was lived with its finger on the pulse of reality, intensely aware and involved. ***INVERTED:*** Now, why would you want to go to the lecture and not take notes?

20 GOVERNED BY JUDGEMENT: HEART'S FULFILLMENT/EVALUATION
UPRIGHT: Your heart realizes that, in truth, there is nothing to forgive, all is forgiven, all forgives all, and that our forgiveness of self and others comes when we realize that. ***INVERTED:*** Sometimes it is very hard to get the heart to agree with what the mind tells you is right; it is so much more stubborn than the mind.

21 GOVERNED BY THE WORLD: EGO'S FULFILLMENT/EVALUATION
UPRIGHT: Here was intimate, hands on awareness of the power of the mind. (Einstein) ***INVERTED:*** If you look for the Devil, he will find you.

22/0 GOVERNED BY THE FOOL: SOUL'S FULFILLMENT/EVALUATION
UPRIGHT: This man had to go see the mountain top for himself....and for others. ***INVERTED:*** It's one hell of a climb, but worth every aching minute of it.

THE TOWER.

16 THE TOWER

UPRIGHT: Here, on the sixteenth stop of your journey, is the profound impact of spiritual input, of grace, of completely unexpected intuitive insights. This does not necessarily indicate any physical change, much less disaster, but there can be radical learning in any or all of the Four Planes as a derivative effect of this revelation. For example: At the spiritual level—a profound revelation. At the mental level—a breakthrough idea. At the emotional level—a sudden change in a relationship. At the physical level—sudden change at work, an accident, or illness. All of them carry instant lessons which represent "musts" in our Karmic Contract which have reached the last window of opportunity and have to be learned post haste. Deeply mystical or religious experiences are anticipated with this card. You are not the same after you receive this information. You may see things differently, with the benefit of the holistic vision of the Third Eye. Life will somehow be fuller as well as more demanding. It can be a glance beyond the veil as you begin to function with more than just your five external senses. As unexpected as these deeply moving flashes seem at the time, they are usually the result of a period of intense and honest reflection in which you confront your hidden selves. The Tower symbolizes what happens to your existing structures when you begin to insist that they carry the weight of your whole being, not just half. And in a very real sense you do have to rebuild, but this will be solid construction on a foundation designed for the task. This card is about listening and getting the message. ***INVERTED:*** An inverted tower can suggest that the major lesson involves someone else, someone most likely close to you, but you are involved in them getting this message, and/or in the lesson itself.

In This Spread Position...Interpret The Tower Meanings to Include:

1 GOVERNED BY THE MAGICIAN: PHYSICAL GIVENS, OUT OF THE FATHER
UPRIGHT: Life may have begun with a shock on the father's side, a moment of revelation, trauma. ***INVERTED:*** Physically gifted or handicapped—through the father. Rape, abandonment, orphaned. Genetic defect.

2 GOVERNED BY THE HIGH PRIESTESS: EMOTIONAL GIVENS, OUT OF THE MOTHER
UPRIGHT: Life may have begun with a shock on the mother's side, a moment of revelation, trauma. ***INVERTED:*** Physically gifted or handicapped—through the mother. Hyperactivity. Autism, Savant. Genetic defect.

3 GOVERNED BY THE EMPRESS: MENTAL GIVENS, INTELLECTUAL PREDISPOSITION
UPRIGHT: Prophetic mind, impressed/attuned at birth. ***INVERTED:*** Mentally gifted, or handicapped. Dyslexia. Down Syndrome. Epilepsy.

4 GOVERNED BY THE EMPEROR: SPIRITUAL GIVENS, LIFE PURPOSE
UPRIGHT: You are a lightning rod for your fellow traveler. A transformer to prepare God's messages for man, and to prepare man for God's messages. ***INVERTED:*** You have been provided a strong constitution for many will reject the messenger as well as the message.

5 GOVERNED BY THE HIEROPHANT: SYSTEMS BORN INTO, SOCIETAL INFLUENCE
UPRIGHT: Early family, and perhaps the larger community, was influenced by significant events and/or revelations, either to members of the group directly or indirectly to the group through an outside medium. Messages healthy and constructive to the adults and through them to the children. ***INVERTED:*** Volatile early environment with periodic disturbances after input from poor sources. Perhaps born into a cult atmosphere. At another extreme, valid revelations were received and ignored with dire consequences.

6 GOVERNED BY THE LOVERS: EMOTIONAL TAPES, BASIS FOR RELATING/CREATING
UPRIGHT: Here was identification at an early age of a voice, a source of inspiration and guidance within. Love for a spirit guide. Strong relationship with self from a past life. Also, strong identity with group karma and therefore some members of the group. ***INVERTED:*** There can be an over romanticized view of the messages and/or the messenger. At another extreme, someone can become emotionally over-dependent on moments of crisis attaching to the burst of energy felt. An inability to process an early trauma.

7 GOVERNED BY THE CHARIOT: PHYSICAL RESOURCES. MEANS TO ACHIEVE
UPRIGHT: Physical health or work, building on a profound event in the past that brought fundamental change, such as the prison experience of Malcom X. ***INVERTED:*** Either too much or too little attention to a message or event, affecting the physical/material plane in the past.

8 GOVERNED BY STRENGTH: EMOTIONAL RESOURCES, ENERGY
UPRIGHT: Your source of strength is the energy and creativity released in your relationship with your guide, your source of inspirations, ultimately your on-line communication with the divine. ***INVERTED:*** At one extreme, you are too dependent on your guides, on your process for getting information, and that is independent of whether the information is good or not. At the other extreme, the suggestion here is that you would be much stronger if you paid more attention to your guides, to meditation, to listening.

9 GOVERNED BY THE HERMIT: BELIEF SYSTEM, BASIS FOR DECISIONS
UPRIGHT: You believe in prophecy and revelation, and the content of your beliefs has been shaped by them. Perhaps you received your inspiration all at once as opposed to a slow building up over time through trial and error. ***INVERTED:*** At one extreme, you are too carried away by the source and/or the information for healthy self-development. The process may be more important than the content. At the other extreme, you may reject altogether the idea of any source of value outside of you, and possibly reject the idea of God as an extension of that. Existentialism makes a home here.

10 GOVERNED BY THE WHEEL OF FORTUNE: CENTRAL MESSAGE, THEME OF READING
UPRIGHT: Spiritual awakening. Listen closely to your inner voice. This reading itself is a profound part of your revelation. ***INVERTED:*** The information you are receiving is not for you. You are an important link in someone else's lesson.

11 GOVERNED BY JUSTICE: STATE/CONTENT OF MIND
UPRIGHT: Your mind has been jolted. There has been a mental breakthrough. A creative rush. Things are adding up. ***INVERTED:*** You may still be in shock with the effect of an event or revelation. Instead of clarifying your situation, you may be somewhat muddled. Let nature help steady you and bring the right

message through—take a walk outdoors, a bicycle ride or other light exercise, where you can combine the physical and mental planes. Meditation alone to still the mind will most likely compound the problem.

12 GOVERNED BY THE HANGED MAN: STATE OF EMOTIONS, SUBCONSCIOUS

UPRIGHT: Your heart has been jolted and one of the possibilities is love at first sight. Emotions are intense as a result. But the nature of this revelation is to cause a change in your emotional house. After this, there should be little doubt as to what the change is, if it hasn't already taken place.
INVERTED: This heart may be in shock, possibly overwhelmed, but rest assured the feeling will pass. You may be compounding the problem by resisting the obvious.

13 GOVERNED BY DEATH: PHYSICAL SITUATION, HARD REALITY

UPRIGHT: This is abrupt change, without forewarning, in the Physical Plane. And upright, we can see some of these as being nothing short of miraculous.
INVERTED: These changes are abrupt and without warning. They can include accidents, illnesses, loss of employment. If something of this sort has already happened, let this reading be an integral part of your healing process. And, if nothing of note has occurred yet, this reading is part of your ability to turn that event away from your doorstep, not a fixed fate.

14 GOVERNED BY TEMPERANCE: EMOTIONAL TEST

UPRIGHT: This is a jolt in your Emotional Pane in the near future in order to get things where they really want to be. It will be a welcome shakeup.
INVERTED: This jolt may at first not be a welcome one, but time will change your mind. The tendency will be either to over or under react. Simply deal with it as objectively as possible and get on with your life.

15 GOVERNED BY THE DEVIL: TEMPTATION/CHALLENGE, FEARS

UPRIGHT: This could be the mental breakthrough you have been waiting for. *INVERTED:* It could also be a jolt that challenges your ego, and perhaps as a test of your resolve toward your goals. Such shocks can be tests and training to increase your ability to handle fear.

16 GOVERNED BY THE TOWER: NEXT LESSON, GRACE OF GOD

UPRIGHT: This is The Tower in its home position and its main message is—listen to your intuition. Do not fear information and shut it out before it can get to you. Let the mind and heart go to work with their processes of validation when you have the message in hand. Every message from God is both specific to your personal needs and general to universal needs. The Tower delivers the messages you have missed and need most to hear. *INVERTED:* Work harder to improve your validation of sources and messages.

17 GOVERNED BY THE STAR: ASPIRATIONS OF EGO, GOALS, MAXIMUM EXPECTATIONS

UPRIGHT: Your goal is to make a major innovative discovery with the power of your intellect. Upright, this has no burden of ego or lust after power and fame to taint it. It is simply recognition and acceptance of having been born to one especially significant moment of insight, as perhaps Jonas Salk was to the discovery of the polio vaccine. *INVERTED:* This mind may be waiting inappropriately for the moment when God will bless it with the big idea, much as some unemployed wait eternally for the right job.

18 GOVERNED BY THE MOON: ASPIRATIONS OF HEART, COMPASSION

UPRIGHT: Your heart aches for the divine spirit to enable it to be in the right place at the right time to do a maximum of good. It is not seeking to become a martyr, but it longs to save people estrangement from universal love in any way it can. *INVERTED:* Your heart may be overly dependent on God's grace. Together with its deep identification with others' problems, it may be stunned into inaction, turning off because the world isn't perfect. Your heart may ironically become part of the problem rather than part of the solution. God's grace is not something one waits on. It is already there. Use it.

19 GOVERNED BY THE SUN: PHYSICAL FULFILLMENT/EVALUATION

UPRIGHT: The finish of this Physical Plane will be a grand finale with a twist, as though you were waiting to the very end for your crowning achievement. It has to be a dilly to top all of the others. *INVERTED:* Remember to clean up between parties.

20 GOVERNED BY JUDGEMENT: HEART'S FULFILLMENT/EVALUATION

UPRIGHT: All of your best emotional/creative pieces fall together late in life, or at the very end, topped with whipped cream and a bright, red cherry, the very best in a long line of distinguished desserts. *INVERTED:* Don't eat too many desserts.

21 GOVERNED BY THE WORLD: EGO'S FULFILLMENT/EVALUATION

UPRIGHT: It isn't as though you haven't had your share of bright ideas, but even you will be surprised at the sparkling finish you have arranged. *INVERTED:* Don't forget to turn out the lights.

22/0 GOVERNED BY THE FOOL: SOUL'S FULFILLMENT/EVALUATION

UPRIGHT: This life was a revelation revolution, as you lurched from marvel to marvel. *INVERTED:* It may have been a bit bumpy, but what a ride.

THE STAR.

17 THE STAR

UPRIGHT: Here is the seventeenth stop. This is the state of mind after profound insight, mind illumined by the heavens. Fireworks. As The Tower is God's grace, The Star is what you do with that grace. Here is the mind's acceptance of responsibility for packaging and filtering spiritual input down to the Emotional and Physical Planes, the symbolism of pitchers of fluid knowledge pouring into water and land alike. Meaning is distilled after the fall of The Tower. This may seem like antiseptic poured on an open wound; there can be pain as the medicine effects its cure. There is undoubtedly major change in the offing and you must decide how to implement it in everyday life. Hope derives from our acceptance of the pain of the moment, which grows into an understanding of the present situation from a broader and longer range perspective. The Star offers hope, optimism, aspirations, productive mental growth, dedication to an ideal, and maximum expectations. Here are outer goals, the Moon will give inner goals. To think of our fate as being in the Stars is to say that our fate is in our highest expectations, our highest ideals. If something can be thought of, then it is possible. The mind is excited, active, with its taste of the future. Here you find the content of the message from a wide assortment of sources—from dreams, spirit guides, guardian angels in the guise of friends/family or complete strangers, synchronous events, books falling off shelves, and the list is literally endless. Here too is the recognition, the fame that accompanies the talent of expression, the embodiment of good ideas well executed. The star on earth is just so because of his/her ability to emulate the beauty of the stars in the heavens. **INVERTED:** At one extreme, we have pessimism; at the other extreme, there is over optimism. If pessimism dips low into depression, despair, complete lack of hope, then there is need for outside help. This reading itself may be a sign from God for the readee to seek such help. There may already be more information than you have been able to process on your own. Such an overload, if not handled, can lead to serious mental, emotional, and/or physical problems. Under normal circumstances, and certainly in metaphysical matters, you do not intervene unless requested. Requests need not come in words, and in this case an overt call for help may be beyond the person's ability.

In This Spread Position...Interpret The Star Meanings to Include:

1 GOVERNED BY THE MAGICIAN: PHYSICAL GIVENS, OUT OF THE FATHER
UPRIGHT: The activities of the Physical/material Plane will be your vanguard. You may be guided by the same goals as your father, and have been gifted with the same talents. Your unbounded optimism and high expectations in this plane will bring health and abundance here and serve as a solid base to the affairs of your other planes. You begin here as a star. **INVERTED:** To some your goals may seem overly materialistic.

2 GOVERNED BY THE HIGH PRIESTESS: EMOTIONAL GIVENS, OUT OF THE MOTHER
UPRIGHT: The affairs of the Emotional/creative Plane will be your vanguard. You may be guided by the same goals as your mother, and have been gifted with the same talents. Your unbounded optimism and high expectations in this plane will assure you successful relationships and creative endeavors serving as a centerpiece for the lessons of the other planes. You begin here as a star. **INVERTED:** To some your goals may seem overly romantic, or too altruistic, or both. To those with special gifts, there will be some who find you too self-centered.

3 GOVERNED BY THE EMPRESS: MENTAL GIVENS, INTELLECTUAL PREDISPOSITION
UPRIGHT: Here is the mark of the truly inventive mind. Ideas abound. A positive frame of mind on everything. You receive information continuously and from a vast array of sources. You may or may not attribute much to spiritual sources, to spiritual inspiration as such, because your conscious mind grabs hold of ideas so quickly that it does not pause to ask, Where did this come from? You begin here as a star. **INVERTED:** To some you will seem preoccupied in your ivory tower of a mind, maybe only interested in your ideas.

4 GOVERNED BY THE EMPEROR: SPIRITUAL GIVENS, LIFE PURPOSE
UPRIGHT: This lifetime asks that you use the formidable intellect you have been given to process the information that needs to descend from the spiritual into the Mental, Emotional, and Physical Planes. Be that as channeler, writer, translator, inventor or professional friend to many. Also, that you are simply destined to be among the best at whatever you do, and to be well known for it. You have been given the means to convey to others the hope that you feel in every fiber of your body, because you know how beautiful things can be; you have seen how beautiful they already are. **INVERTED:** You may have extra work with those who have the longest road to travel from pessimism to optimism, with those who have the least expectations from self rather than the most.

5 GOVERNED BY THE HIEROPHANT: SYSTEMS BORN INTO, SOCIETAL INFLUENCE
UPRIGHT: You were born into a world of ideas and plans, of dreams and enthusiasm. Mentally at least, this was no holds barred. Parents may have been noted. **INVERTED:** Perhaps the early environment was overly ambitious, driven to the extreme. In another extreme, there may have been an atmosphere of pretense and fantasy with little interest in bringing things down to earth. Also, the plain difficulties of growing up around a number of people at the top of their form, and perhaps with a lot of publicity.

6 GOVERNED BY THE LOVERS: EMOTIONAL TAPES, BASIS FOR RELATING/CREATING
UPRIGHT: This is an early passion for success, for being the best and being recognized as such. In love with your own dreams and certainly with very high expectations of realizing every one of them. **INVERTED:** This can be a fascination with success and its attendant glamour, but without the expectation that you will achieve it personally. This could lead you to a profession that keeps you near the inner circle but not in the spotlight yourself. At the other extreme, you may be obsessed with stardom in its abstract and unrealizable form.

7 GOVERNED BY THE CHARIOT: PHYSICAL RESOURCES. MEANS TO ACHIEVE
UPRIGHT: You have already laid the foundation of a long-term goal and are very much working toward it, so that there is great efficiency in your physical/material world. Everything contributes to the big picture. You may be working with the information received in a prophetic dream or another rich source. Also, simply that you have been very busy and productive. **INVERTED:** You may be working on an old idea, or a broken dream that has outlived its usefulness. Look for new additional sources of validation. You may have tried for the payoff a bit too early.

8 GOVERNED BY STRENGTH: EMOTIONAL RESOURCES, ENERGY
UPRIGHT: You are vibrantly alive, integrating well your Mental and Emotional Planes. Your relationships and professional goals are mutually supportive. **INVERTED:** You are not as strong as you could and should be, because the personal and professional tracks may not be parallel.

9 GOVERNED BY THE HERMIT: BELIEF SYSTEM, BASIS FOR DECISIONS

UPRIGHT: Here is belief in self, self-esteem in its most admirable form, the desire to be and to do the best that you possibly can with your God given talents. If you find the essence of that self and nurture it, you cannot help but succeed and on a grand scale. Here is innate faith in that kernel of greatness in each and every one of us. This is man's faith in man on a par with God's faith in man. This says, "I am good; I am very good. If you don't believe me, stick around and watch." *INVERTED:* There may be difficulty with thinking long-term. Or, there may be a tendency to forever revise or extend goals. At one far extreme, this is the philosophy of nihilism.

10 GOVERNED BY THE WHEEL OF FORTUNE: CENTRAL MESSAGE, THEME OF READING

UPRIGHT: You need to be optimistic and set your goals at the highest conceivable level. Avoid any tendency to sell yourself short. *INVERTED:* Look at your long-range goals. They may be inappropriate for this lifetime. Review Karmic Contract for your strengths and predispositions, your talents. There is such a thing as picking a goal that is out of reach. For instance, very short men should not aspire to becoming professional basketball players, but maybe a coach.

11 GOVERNED BY JUSTICE: STATE/CONTENT OF MIND

UPRIGHT: Much has already come your way but you are setting your sights, lining up your goals. Your mind is on top of things. Let your present optimism establish your benchmark for the future while you are thinking big. *INVERTED:* At one extreme, there is disappointment, pessimism. But at the other extreme, there is too much optimism for the question at hand. Don't overshoot.

12 GOVERNED BY THE HANGED MAN: STATE OF EMOTIONS, SUBCONSCIOUS

UPRIGHT: The heart is centered on the mind's directives. Desire is supporting the will. *INVERTED:* The heart may not be in favor of the program. Or, the heart is neglecting much of its own business to support the mind's programs.

13 GOVERNED BY DEATH: PHYSICAL SITUATION, HARD REALITY

UPRIGHT: Much of your goal is unfolding right now. You are living your dream in realtime. You are the center of attention and rightly so. *INVERTED:* You may be living in a dream, avoiding reality. Or, your plans have just gone up in smoke.

14 GOVERNED BY TEMPERANCE: EMOTIONAL TEST

UPRIGHT: Integrate those dreams, those goals and wildest expectations into your relationships so that they support each other. Here could be a test for the heart as the ego succeeds with its program. Will you enjoy your success? Will those who supposedly love you, love your success? *INVERTED:* This can be the effect of a mental disappointment, or general mental malaise on your emotional plane, your relationships, and creative output.

15 GOVERNED BY THE DEVIL: TEMPTATION/CHALLENGE, FEARS

UPRIGHT: It is time to give your ego its just due. This year wants to see you open up all the stops. You will be drawn outward in the limelight of recognition, and you should go more than willingly. *INVERTED:* You may exhibit one or both of these extremes, vacillating back and forth. On the one hand, there is a fear of exposure and publicity, of success. On the other hand, there is the easier to understand fear of failure.

16 GOVERNED BY THE TOWER: NEXT LESSON, GRACE OF GOD

UPRIGHT: Your goals, even your greatest expectations, will present themselves clearly and begin to unfold in your reality. Your star is arriving and it will be up to you to sustain its glow. *INVERTED:* Your success will be strategic to, and/or dependent on, that of another. Your Karmic Contract is closely intertwined with others and you should be able to work consciously with this fact from now on.

17 GOVERNED BY THE STAR: ASPIRATIONS OF EGO, GOALS, MAXIMUM EXPECTATIONS

UPRIGHT: There is a potent redundancy here. Your goal is to have a goal. And while this sounds weak at first, on observation it is as strong or stronger than setting one's sights on a hard and fast target. For it is a hope for hope itself. You accept that all goals are worthy in their right time and place and ask of God only that you be blessed with the ability and dedication to do well something of value. *INVERTED:* This is a desire for success that brings recognition from others as well as self. Recognition may be more important that the content of the achievement.

18 GOVERNED BY THE MOON: ASPIRATIONS OF HEART, COMPASSION

UPRIGHT: This heart is dedicated and passionate about its objectives, which are those of the mind as well. Success and its attendant notoriety are hoped for here so that you can get more done for more people. *INVERTED:* This heart wants the mind to maximize its potential because it will reap some delicious benefits down in the emotional department. Better relationships, better sex, creative juices flowing.

19 GOVERNED BY THE SUN: PHYSICAL FULFILLMENT/EVALUATION

UPRIGHT: There is material evidence everywhere of your mental goals having been reached par excellence. Your mind has provided well for your and yours. *INVERTED:* If you show up on time, bring your mind with you, and listen carefully, you will hear everything you need to reach this fulfillment.

20 GOVERNED BY JUDGEMENT: HEART'S FULFILLMENT/EVALUATION

UPRIGHT: The business of the heart has been served well by the mind and its goals, for this mind shaped its goals only around the inspired messages it attended to. *INVERTED:* If the heart does not like the goals of the mind, it must seduce the mind to like those of the heart.

21 GOVERNED BY THE WORLD: EGO'S FULFILLMENT/EVALUATION

UPRIGHT: This plane goes out with a bang, the fireworks of worthy celebration. You may have timed things so that your greatest achievement and critical success comes at the end of a long line of work. How nice of you to save the best for last. *INVERTED:* Let the stars that we see only at night brighten your days as well to bring you more surely to this archetype.

22/0 GOVERNED BY THE FOOL: SOUL'S FULFILLMENT/EVALUATION

UPRIGHT: On this man the sun has shined, and he has shined back. You thought about it, you decided to do it, you did it...all of it...and well. *INVERTED:* Let this reading help you toward this archetype.

THE MOON.

18 THE MOON

UPRIGHT: Here is the eighteenth stop. You see the emotions grown up, capable of intelligent love and compassion, as the self begins to merge with the other. Also, passions that are intricately and harmoniously woven into the overall fabric of the lifestyle and life's purpose. Here you have floodgates to work in concert with the ebb and flow of The Moon's attractiveness. Your mature emotions help equip you for the journey of your expanded sense of Self, the Self that has begun to feel as one with its environment and nature, the Self that will feel the larger joys and larger pains brought to it by its larger heart. This can indicate a sense of emotional mission. A dedicated humanitarian. Altruism. The Moon is the cool, silver, reflective mirror of the Sun. It gives us the ability to see ourselves and our effect on the selves of others. Here are the inner goals to match the outer goals shown by The Star(17). "The person who has deep compassion is not going to be bothered whether he tells a lie or the truth. All Buddhas have lied. They have to because they are so compassionate. The whole truth will be too much." (Indian guru Bagwhan Rajneesh) *INVERTED:* The pitfall of overidentifying with humanity's suffering. It can indicate incomplete or inadequate accommodation of elements of the subconscious, such as the shadow personality alluded to in the description of The Devil(15). Lack of awareness of emotions. This would indicate an emotional "Achilles' heel." Behavior will be vague, erratic, illusive, impersonal, confused, unpredictable, or uncertain. Here as with The Star(17) inverted, you may feel a need for outside intervention.

In This Spread Position...Interpret The Moon Meanings to Include:

1 GOVERNED BY THE MAGICIAN: PHYSICAL GIVENS, OUT OF THE FATHER
UPRIGHT: Your sensitivity will be very evident in your Physical Plane. Your clothing, your home, your work, will all reflect a closeness to the rhythms of the earth and moon. Your preference is to be out of doors, close to animals and nature. *INVERTED:* There is both an air of wisdom and an air of innocence and naivete about you. Your sensitivity is your strength and your weakness.

2 GOVERNED BY THE HIGH PRIESTESS: EMOTIONAL GIVENS, OUT OF THE MOTHER
UPRIGHT: Your sensitivity will pervade the affairs of this plane, making you an ideal lover and mate, and a friend to beat all friends. And it will steer the depth of creative talent that is yours toward very noble projects. *INVERTED:* The depth of your emotions leaves room for misunderstanding by those who are not closest to you.

3 GOVERNED BY THE EMPRESS: MENTAL GIVENS, INTELLECTUAL PREDISPOSITION
UPRIGHT: Your mind is predisposed to the programs of the higher emotions. It is familiar with the language of the heart and attuned to listen to its sources. *INVERTED:* To some you may appear smug, or out of it at times, when your mind is content to play in the less rational world of the emotions.

4 GOVERNED BY THE EMPEROR: SPIRITUAL GIVENS, LIFE PURPOSE
UPRIGHT: This is a lifetime for love, for hands-on sensory experience of people and the environment, of animals and nature. You are interested in virtually everything in one way or another. But this is a blending of passion within compassion. The motivation here is one of deep caring. *INVERTED:* You will depend on others even as they depend on you. Your heart will lead the way and many will follow.

5 GOVERNED BY THE HIEROPHANT: SYSTEMS BORN INTO, SOCIETAL INFLUENCE
UPRIGHT: Your early environment was emotionally full and rewarding. You were exposed to a fullness of life that many adults do not experience very often. The level of awareness here was very high. *INVERTED:* At one extreme, there may have been too much maturity and exposure. At the other extreme, there may have been insensitivity and immaturity.

6 GOVERNED BY THE LOVERS: EMOTIONAL TAPES, BASIS FOR RELATING/CREATING
UPRIGHT: Here is a love of love, a very mature emotion at such an early age. It is the spark of innocent, open-hearted longing for the world at large that grows into universal love in the mature heart. Many feel something like this when they are young only to lose it and have to rediscover it again. Your spark has grown into the full flame that burns in your heart to this day. *INVERTED:* Universal love cannot replace personal love. Each is needed to enhance the other. At another extreme, there is personal passion here without the balance of the universal, and it can be a detached and limiting love/sex.

7 GOVERNED BY THE CHARIOT: PHYSICAL RESOURCES. MEANS TO ACHIEVE
UPRIGHT: Yours is a highly creative, sensitive lifestyle. You are living your principles and there is a natural flow and ease in your environmnet which is a healthy extension of your personality. When you come home, you can relax and refuel. *INVERTED:* You may have been too involved with too many and too much, burning the candle at both ends.

8 GOVERNED BY STRENGTH: EMOTIONAL RESOURCES, ENERGY
UPRIGHT: Your strength is your ability and willingness to feel, to empathize and sympathize, for you get like energy back when you give energy to others. Your openness to loving and being loved keeps open the channels for creative inspiration that fuels your projects. *INVERTED:* Your strength can be your weakness if you overdo it. When you're tired, slow down.

9 GOVERNED BY THE HERMIT: BELIEF SYSTEM, BASIS FOR DECISIONS
UPRIGHT: This belief system is one based on direct experience, which includes inner senses as well as those of the five external senses (sight, hearing, touch, taste, & smell). It wants to touch and be touched. So in one aspect it is Dionysian, Bohemian, full of rich right-brain activity. But this is also a quality possessed by the great researcher, sociologist, anthropologist, doctor/healer. It is a belief in the power of love to move mountains. *INVERTED:* At one extreme, it is impossible to believe without having the experience. The experience is the belief, and is all that one lives for.

10 GOVERNED BY THE WHEEL OF FORTUNE: CENTRAL MESSAGE, THEME OF READING
UPRIGHT: Paying attention to others and their needs, acting out of love, should be part of daily life. Do not wait to be moved; move yourself. When you give, give wisely, and within your means. To give more, work to increase your means. *INVERTED:* Love yourself before you attempt to love others. It will save you much time. When others give to you to fulfill your need, take wisely and only from within the means of your benefactor.

11 GOVERNED BY JUSTICE: STATE/CONTENT OF MIND
UPRIGHT: Your mind is occupied with the heavy work of your heart; it is so full of love and compassion. The wheels are turning for ways to use the energy

generated by the rapid flow of blood through your veins. Passion harnessed to compassion is the stuff of creative genius that benefits all of mankind. ***INVERTED:*** The mind may be preoccupied with the heat of the moment more than the heart.

12 GOVERNED BY THE HANGED MAN: STATE OF EMOTIONS, SUBCONSCIOUS

UPRIGHT: The heart has discovered how to combine compassion and passion, how to offer life's blood to save others without sacrificing self. In such moments as this when the transfusion of give and take is simultaneous, something new is brought to life. This is the miracle of creativity. ***INVERTED:*** One can get lost temporarily in the power of exchange that is love and creativity.

13 GOVERNED BY DEATH: PHYSICAL SITUATION, HARD REALITY

UPRIGHT: The thoughts of the mind, the feelings of the heart—all are combined in the immediacy of your surroundings. The physical reality of the power of higher emotions is yours for the having. This is ultra sensitivity. ***INVERTED:*** This is too sensitive, maybe too sweet, maybe too sour, but whichever, you should do what you can, if you can, to temper the situation.

14 GOVERNED BY TEMPERANCE: EMOTIONAL TEST

UPRIGHT: Here comes the test of integrating the deeper, the higher emotions into your existing relationships and creative work. This is not the same stuff you have known so far. This is a softer and sweeter candy than you have ever tasted. And it is harder and more bitter. Your soul is heeding the call of more and more members of your group. ***INVERTED:*** You must be sure that you understand the similarities as well as the differences between compassion and passion. The heart must keep pure its motivations.

15 GOVERNED BY THE DEVIL: TEMPTATION/CHALLENGE, FEARS

UPRIGHT: Here is the mental test of maintaining a steady pace on a sure footed path as your heart increases its emotional commitments. ***INVERTED:*** The emotional goal and mental goal will eventually overlap completely, but for now you must guard against too much of the lower ego affecting the purity of balance between give and take.

16 GOVERNED BY THE TOWER: NEXT LESSON, GRACE OF GOD

UPRIGHT: Look at the next full moon and do exactly as it tells you. This is a time for letting go. Without thinking whether your actions are for yourself or for someone else, just act and react as events unfold, without premeditation, but with honesty. The magic of the moon will weave passion and compassion into one continuous silver thread of reward. ***INVERTED:*** This process may be more for another than for yourself, but you are still a key player.

17 GOVERNED BY THE STAR: ASPIRATIONS OF EGO, GOALS, MAXIMUM EXPECTATIONS

UPRIGHT: You want more than anything else to know what love—deep feeling and intense caring for others—is like. It isn't that you don't want to actually feel in the process, but your goal is more intellectual than it is emotional. That does not make it less noble. ***INVERTED:*** Here the goal becomes less noble in that it may want the power or the satisfaction that knowledge of love, involvement with others, service to others, might bring. Here there is the expectation of getting something in return.

18 GOVERNED BY THE MOON: ASPIRATIONS OF HEART, COMPASSION

UPRIGHT: Here is the aspiration to the power of love for universal good, for healing. The power of love is very real, but especially at the level of higher emotions, where the heart of self is aligning with many hearts toward universal love. ***INVERTED:*** Here is the potential for error in the exchange of energies, the distribution of the power of love, because of the intensity and number of emotions involved.

19 GOVERNED BY THE SUN: PHYSICAL FULFILLMENT/EVALUATION

UPRIGHT: You have had a natural intimacy with nature, with your environment. A healthy romantic, in love with life itself. You have been a shaman, a healer, whether in fact you practiced as such or not. ***INVERTED:*** Let the moon work its tidal magic on the shores of your beach and watch it grow bigger and more beautiful every year.

20 GOVERNED BY JUDGEMENT: HEART'S FULFILLMENT/EVALUATION

UPRIGHT: You have been intimate with your world, savoring every minute of every encounter, creating much where there was little. ***INVERTED:*** Be intimate with your world. Hide nothing from yourself and you will always be able to find what you want.

21 GOVERNED BY THE WORLD: EGO'S FULFILLMENT/EVALUATION

UPRIGHT: With this mind, the heart was able to come as close as ever to being able to talk for itself. That is creativity that speaks for itself. ***INVERTED:*** Help your heart to speak its mind in this lifetime.

22/0 GOVERNED BY THE FOOL: SOUL'S FULFILLMENT/EVALUATION

UPRIGHT: Here was a lover of love, a free spirit that allowed itself to be captured over and over again, without losing an ounce of its beautiful freedom. ***INVERTED:*** With the grace of God and your willpower this will be your epitaph.

THE SUN .

19 THE SUN

UPRIGHT: Here is your nineteenth stop. Things are bright and clear in the Physical/Material Plane. The four aspects of the personality have been balanced and are healthy and functioning well. Realization of physical and material goals. Identification with the Earth, her products and offspring. Harmony with Nature. Productivity. Preparedness. Abundance. Physical perfection. Approaching the sense of at-one-ment with the world/universe. There is a growing awareness of God in all material things, and materiality takes on a very spiritual sense for you. Life can seem to move in slow motion as you extract the nuances of pleasure from each minute you are awake. Split personality limitations are left far behind. The dispelling of fears, casting away of shadows. The power of conscious awareness to dispel darkness and fear. There is a physical urging toward even greater consciousness. Your physical conditioning pushes you forward; there is momentum. Your body is confident; you have faith in yourself. Here we will see happiness. Here there is victory.
INVERTED: Distortion in the way of too much or too little of The Sun here. For example, there may be too much exposure for your condition or circumstances. There may be risk of a burnout. This can mean a lack of realization/appreciation of your physical/material success and well-being, an overly conservative evaluation of your Physical Plane. Over production or under production.

In This Spread Position...Interpret The Sun Meanings to Include:

1 GOVERNED BY THE MAGICIAN: PHYSICAL GIVENS, OUT OF THE FATHER
UPRIGHT: A robust beginning in your physical and material house, drawn from your father's line. Your inheritance may not have been limited to your physical genetic package. There may have been material inheritance as well. **INVERTED:** At one extreme, if your package has been extraordinarily strong, it will be your challenge to use such gifts well. At the other extreme, even if your package has been weak, this given will prove to be a blessing, as it guides you into the proper channels for your path.

2 GOVERNED BY THE HIGH PRIESTESS: EMOTIONAL GIVENS, OUT OF THE MOTHER
UPRIGHT: A robust beginning, drawn from your mother's line, which begins your emotional and creative house with abundant energy. You literally have a strong heart and excellent circulatory system. **INVERTED:** At one extreme, you may have been given an extra layer of emotional muscle to help you carry much more, and so will be predisposed to do so. At the other extreme, you may be able to carry less, but only in quantity, not quality.

3 GOVERNED BY THE EMPRESS: MENTAL GIVENS, INTELLECTUAL PREDISPOSITION
UPRIGHT: Your mental and nervous system is constructed of the strongest materials, predisposed to handle an enormous amount of work with optimism and without tiring easily. Your academic achievements can be formidable. **INVERTED:** At one extreme, your capacity is much above average. You may be as the main frame to many others' desktop terminals. Much will be expected of you. At the other extreme, you may be able to handle less pressure than most in the mental plane, and should look to the other planes for your major work and rewards.

4 GOVERNED BY THE EMPEROR: SPIRITUAL GIVENS, LIFE PURPOSE
UPRIGHT: This is the personality born to a life of active participation, with as much time spent out of doors as possible. You are drawn to fields in which there is much visible growth, productivity, and beneficial results. **INVERTED:** With your abundance of energy and resources you will be asked to help others find their place in the sun.

5 GOVERNED BY THE HIEROPHANT: SYSTEMS BORN INTO, SOCIETAL INFLUENCE
UPRIGHT: Your early environment was active, extroverted, upbeat, and supportive—literally nutritious. Things were geared to growth and productivity. **INVERTED:** At one extreme, things may have been almost too perfect with a tendency to spoil you. At another, things may have been moving too fast and been pushed too hard. But at another extreme, the atmosphere was introverted and not conducive to growth; there may have been many more rainy than sunny days.

6 GOVERNED BY THE LOVERS: EMOTIONAL TAPES, BASIS FOR RELATING/CREATING
UPRIGHT: This passion is for life, for all things living, for people, animals, plants, for creation itself. **INVERTED:** At one extreme, even this worthy passion can suffer distortion in the extreme, for spirituality must have its abstract components as well as hard reality. God is to be found inside as well as outside. At the other extreme, there is a dispassionate cloud over the heart toward people and/or nature.

7 GOVERNED BY THE CHARIOT: PHYSICAL RESOURCES. MEANS TO ACHIEVE
UPRIGHT: The Sun has been achieved and stands behind you and with you as a ball of energy to help with your physical chores. **INVERTED:** At one extreme, there may have been a tendency to overdo things in the past. At the other extreme, there has been difficulty with completion.

8 GOVERNED BY STRENGTH: EMOTIONAL RESOURCES, ENERGY
UPRIGHT: There has been much confidence here, justifiable as relationships and creative projects have flourished. You approach everything in this plane with boundless energy and enthusiasm. People are drawn to you simply because they feel better when they are with you. **INVERTED:** At one extreme, you may have more energy than you know what to do with, and need to channel it better. Or, you may have either too much or too little confidence coming into the present situation.

9 GOVERNED BY THE HERMIT: BELIEF SYSTEM, BASIS FOR DECISIONS
UPRIGHT: You could be Norman Vincent Peale for all your confidence in the power of positive thinking. For you, if you can throw enough energy at a situation, you can make things happen. Here is creative visualization, Silva Mind Control, and other disciplines that focus the mind's ability to help the lower Emotional and Physical planes. **INVERTED:** At one extreme, the ego can go overboard on the realm of mind as being the pinnacle, which once surmounted, can solve all problems. This either neglects or ignores the spiritual level above the mind, from which inspiration fuels and enables mind. Mind of self (individual mind) simply does not have the overview of universal mind at the spiritual level. At the other extreme, there can be a distortion here that makes the material world the end all, be all.

10 GOVERNED BY THE WHEEL OF FORTUNE: CENTRAL MESSAGE, THEME OF READING
UPRIGHT: Now is the time for you to concentrate on the blessings of health and welfare in the material plane. Many gates are opening and it is for you

to chose. It is proper for you to determine what you want and to ask for it. Otherwise, Santa Claus will just pick something at random from his bag of goodies. Think positive, you will be amazed at what is possible now. ***INVERTED:*** Others need your optimism and energy to help them realize this is their time to shine.

11 GOVERNED BY JUSTICE: STATE/CONTENT OF MIND
UPRIGHT: You are upbeat and using your mind well, with proper use of intellect to help maximize efficiency at all levels. Good use of creative visualization, mind control, positive thinking, and the like. Energetic about present plans. You are correct in your evaluation of your karmic purpose and have chosen appropriate goals. ***INVERTED:*** At one extreme, you may be downbeat in your evaluation. At another extreme, you may be using your mental techniques to ill effect.

12 GOVERNED BY THE HANGED MAN: STATE OF EMOTIONS, SUBCONSCIOUS
UPRIGHT: You are happy about the state of your emotional affairs, your relationships, and/or your creative projects. Things are probably going well down in the physical plane too. ***INVERTED:*** At one extreme, this may be forced or false joy. Or, you are not appreciative enough of your situation.

13 GOVERNED BY DEATH: PHYSICAL SITUATION, HARD REALITY
UPRIGHT: Can things really be going this good? Yes, of course! And there seems to be plenty to go around. Hope you are enjoying every minute as you well deserve it. ***INVERTED:*** Too much energy; no need to over do it. Whether it's too much exercise, or too much food, or too much work—slow down. At the other extreme, there may be too little energy. You can actually increase your energy by doing more of the right activities, a little at a time.

14 GOVERNED BY TEMPERANCE: EMOTIONAL TEST
UPRIGHT: Here comes the sun. This will test how your Emotional Plane handles the good stuff. What will your heart do when everything goes right? Can you recognize and maximize good fortune? ***INVERTED:*** Same test, but with greater extremes. Here your relationships, or your creative affairs, must weather either outrageous good fortune beyond all expectations, or something much less than expected in your Physical Plane.

15 GOVERNED BY THE DEVIL: TEMPTATION/CHALLENGE, FEARS
UPRIGHT: Here the sun shines brightly on your mental affairs. If you are ahead of schedule, you will be put to the task of expanding your maximum expectations. ***INVERTED:*** Here can be a fear of too much light, too much exposure, too much success, a fear of happiness itself. What to do when all the enemies have been conquered, all the battles won? At the other extreme, can be the easier to understand fear of failure, of physical or material loss.

16 GOVERNED BY THE TOWER: NEXT LESSON, GRACE OF GOD
UPRIGHT: Here within this next year, physical and material blessings will fall to you. Much will seem as if by chance, but all is part of your karmic purpose unfolding and will bring its share of lessons to be learned. ***INVERTED:*** You will be instrumental in the good fortune of many others.

17 GOVERNED BY THE STAR: ASPIRATIONS OF EGO, GOALS, MAXIMUM EXPECTATIONS
UPRIGHT: Your goal is to be the absolute best you can be at a physical or material goal. You will pull out all the stops to succeed, but by honorable means, for the motivation here is to simply "be all that you can be," just like the U.S.Army. ***INVERTED:*** At one extreme, the goal to win is distorted and seeks the defeat of others as much or more than victory. The goal is definitely one of superiority. At the other extreme, here is the hard to understand, but unfortunately not rare, goal to lose.

18 GOVERNED BY THE MOON: ASPIRATIONS OF HEART, COMPASSION
UPRIGHT: The heart's goal is for all the world to be enjoying abundance, a compassionate call for a heaven on earth. This is the material aspect of the goal of the Bodhisattvas, who although they have reached enlightenment with completion of all karmic instruction, choose to return in further incarnations of service until all souls are enlightened. ***INVERTED:*** Here the heart's aspiration is similar, but pessimistic, grieving that universal love is not yet achieved. At another extreme, here is concern for the health of Gaia, Mother Earth, herself.

19 GOVERNED BY THE SUN: PHYSICAL FULFILLMENT/EVALUATION
UPRIGHT: The material goals have been achieved and things are exactly as you would have them. Everything around you is a proper extension of the self for fulfillment of your physical/material karmic purpose. ***INVERTED:*** If it feels right and you truly appreciate having it, keep it; if it feels wrong and you do not appreciate it, give it to someone else. Everything must appreciate in value.

20 GOVERNED BY JUDGEMENT: HEART'S FULFILLMENT/EVALUATION
UPRIGHT: There has been a wealth of pleasure from your Physical/ material Plane to help strengthen and enrich your relationships and creative work. Your heart finishes all of its heavy work well in advance of your finale. ***INVERTED:*** Let your heart enjoy the benefits of well-motivated pleasure.

21 GOVERNED BY THE WORLD: EGO'S FULFILLMENT/EVALUATION
UPRIGHT: The ego is properly content with the degree of physical and material success you have achieved, for it played no small part in the game. This mind steered a wise course to the deeper understanding of the material blessings of Earth as the foundation on which our God stands. ***INVERTED:*** Let your mind study even the simplest of things.

22/0 GOVERNED BY THE FOOL: SOUL'S FULFILLMENT/EVALUATION
UPRIGHT: For this soul, the garden of Eden has been here and now. ***INVERTED:*** Always look for the light, the light of God shining in your everyday reality.

20 JUDGEMENT

UPRIGHT: Here is the twentieth stop. This is the emotional clearing, the acceptance, the forgiving of others and of self necessary for completion. It is the emotional reward or the punishment felt in your own heart—the reward is being able to accept and move on; the punishment is being unable to overcome your past. This is the covenant of Jehovah— "if you forgive one another your trespasses, so Jehovah shall forgive you, that he himself may dwell among you." Correct, workable feelings about things. All duality at the emotional level is resolved, as all differences with your fellow man and creatures are forgiven, not forgotten; they must be remembered well as lessons lest you repeat your mistakes. In burying the dead the Egyptians did not remove the heart like they did the other organs. A text was inscribed on a scarab and placed over the heart imploring the heart not to testify against the deceased in the judgement before Osiris. Remorse/penitence. The making of emotional peace. Atonement. Confession and repentance of sins. Human salvation as man-god. Conscience (together-knowing, thus a sensing together). Impact of grace on the heart. Mercy. "Having no ill will for any living being, in all manners possible and for all times is called Ahimsa, and it should be the desired goal of all seekers."(Patanjali Yoga Sutras 2:30). **INVERTED:** It will not be uncommon to find this card inverted, for this is a very difficult step in your evolution of consciousness. There may be a serious flaw, clearing has not been achieved. Guilt, which is part of not forgiving self, can be the result of assuming more responsibility than is one's lot. This is seen as an aspect of the sin of pride, for it is presumptuous of us to assume too much responsibility. In so doing, we presume to be God. Amorality. Lack of remorse. Inability to forgive others or self.

In This Spread Position...Interpret the Judgement Meanings to Include:

1 GOVERNED BY THE MAGICIAN: PHYSICAL GIVENS, OUT OF THE FATHER
UPRIGHT: You have a healthy respect for your heredity, for your place and responsibility in the continuity of life. Your sense of fair play pervades your activities whether at work or play. You are a master at facilitating win-win situations seeing no reason why anyone should lose. **INVERTED:** Your directness may seem harsh at times.

2 GOVERNED BY THE HIGH PRIESTESS: EMOTIONAL GIVENS, OUT OF THE MOTHER
UPRIGHT: The emotional lessons of past lives have been well assimilated. This is a sophisticated heart, full of love but with the wisdom of Solomon. This heart walks a straight path unbending to the pressures of the moment. It will have no catching up to do as no guilt accrues over time. This heart never skips a beat. Creative projects will be to the point and clear of angst. There is the potential to create great beauty here. **INVERTED:** Your freedom from guilt may be taken by some who know you less well for a cold heart or amorality.

3 GOVERNED BY THE EMPRESS: MENTAL GIVENS, INTELLECTUAL PREDISPOSITION
UPRIGHT: You have been gifted with a clear, unbiased mind with the strength to remain fair and impartial. You are an excellent tactician because you can look at vast amounts of information objectively, evaluating each piece on its own merits. **INVERTED:** This capacity you have for good judgement and depth of insight will discomfort some people, and even frighten those who may have something to hide.

4 GOVERNED BY THE EMPEROR: SPIRITUAL GIVENS, LIFE PURPOSE
UPRIGHT: Atonement (At-one-ment). Universal love is the force through which everything is judged to be of God and therefore worthy of God, as self is worthy of self. You will walk this leg of your journey being open to any who would be your friend, and to those who would not, you will even be their lover. **INVERTED:** You will be called upon to teach many by your example.

5 GOVERNED BY THE HIEROPHANT: SYSTEMS BORN INTO, SOCIETAL INFLUENCE
UPRIGHT: Your early environment was marked by an ecumenical air of good will. Relationships were open and sharing. Creativity was free flowing. **INVERTED:** At one extreme, there can appear a harsh atmosphere of rigid opinions and a stunting of creativity. At another extreme, there may have been a false polyanna approach that insisted that everything was perfect, sweeping reality and its inevitable problems under the rug.

6 GOVERNED BY THE LOVERS: EMOTIONAL TAPES, BASIS FOR RELATING/CREATING
UPRIGHT: Your early emotional imprint on which you build even today is virtually utopian, but the realizable Utopia of universal love (brought to the West by the Christ) and understanding (brought to the East by the Buddha). **INVERTED:** These tapes may have been someone else's version of what was good, and in one extreme you are trying still to work with that version, in the other extreme you are rejecting it.

7 GOVERNED BY THE CHARIOT: PHYSICAL RESOURCES. MEANS TO ACHIEVE
UPRIGHT: You are surrounded by reliable situations in your material world because of your direct and efficient manner. Communication has been honest and everyone knows where they stand with you in business. Your health has prospered because there is little stress with nothing to hide. **INVERTED:** At one extreme, you could be on shaky ground because you have made and/or allowed things to become unduly complicated. At another extreme, you may have been unduly hard on those around you and there is little motivation for them to help you.

8 GOVERNED BY STRENGTH: EMOTIONAL RESOURCES, ENERGY
UPRIGHT: Your ability to understand yourself and others has lent an air of candor to your relationships and your creative projects. What you see is what you get. You will be able to weather the storms of everyday living because you are centered in your world, not someone else's. **INVERTED:** Candor does not go around looking under rugs or stirring up dirt. In another extreme, you may have tried to set the standards for everyone else while working on your own. Just work on your own.

9 GOVERNED BY THE HERMIT: BELIEF SYSTEM, BASIS FOR DECISIONS
UPRIGHT: Here is a positive eschatological world view, a conclusion in which universal heart establishes once and for all the common value of its component capacities for love. Positive means will yield positive ends. **INVERTED:** You may be distorting the means to achieve given ends. At one extreme, there are the numerous distortions of punishment and reward at the end of time, when a divided world of good and bad will go to their respective heaven and hell.

10 GOVERNED BY THE WHEEL OF FORTUNE: CENTRAL MESSAGE, THEME OF READING
UPRIGHT: This is a time for conscious resolution in your emotional house. Progress can be made in forgiveness of yourself and of others. The overtures are yours for the making. **INVERTED:** Accept the overtures of others to heal the past and prepare the future.

11 GOVERNED BY JUSTICE: STATE/CONTENT OF MIND

UPRIGHT: You have a good objective grasp of the situation. You are seeing things clearly and what you are planning is fair to all concerned. Now just keep it all out in the open where you can keep your eye on it and deal with it. **INVERTED:** Your view of things may be a bit skewed. Another possibility is that you have decided that others have things wrong.

12 GOVERNED BY THE HANGED MAN: STATE OF EMOTIONS, SUBCONSCIOUS

UPRIGHT: There is a mature, long-term look at the world in your creative output. Your heart is reviewing, as it likes to do often, the magic in its relationships in order to nurture it and make it grow even more, never satisfied that it has done enough, acting out of intense love not guilt. **INVERTED:** At one extreme, this heart may be struggling with itself over its track record. At the other extreme, there is the opposite of no struggle, even less no concern, with the flame of friendship and love barely flickering.

13 GOVERNED BY DEATH: PHYSICAL SITUATION, HARD REALITY

UPRIGHT: The peace pipe is being passed. Resolution of problems in your material affairs, centering around how people have handled each other. **INVERTED:** You may be passing judgement on someone at this time. And what's more, it may not be correct.

14 GOVERNED BY TEMPERANCE: EMOTIONAL TEST

UPRIGHT: The issues of judgement hit your Emotional Plane in the near future. The more universal character of higher emotions both demands and enables you to seek level ground in the give and take of your relationships. No energy debt can accrue, much less multiply, if giving and taking are according to need and ability to share. **INVERTED:** You will be feeling an inequity in your emotional house, a discomfort that you can ease by letting love and grace heal you, or you can exacerbate the problem further with self-pity or self-righteousness.

15 GOVERNED BY THE DEVIL: TEMPTATION/CHALLENGE, FEARS

UPRIGHT: Here is an opportunity for mind to help the heart with its karma. Mind can frequently identify an imbalance in your Emotional Plane, where a need for forgiveness of another or of yourself is clear, but the heart in its capacity of lower emotions will still find it difficult to clear the matter. The heart may even feel completely unable to clear. The higher mind, here in the function of a healthy conscience, is given the power to take action, to make a call or write a letter, to find the words it needs to say, and in time too the heart will believe the words the mind has found for it. **INVERTED:** One distortion here is that you may be planning revenge, or you may be anticipating and fearing it. Here the mind may be making matters worse under the influence of the lower ego.

16 GOVERNED BY THE TOWER: NEXT LESSON, GRACE OF GOD

UPRIGHT: Here comes a big dose of grace that helps the heart over the hurdles of disappointment, resentment, and anger. Listen, as the music of the spheres plays the notes that resonate in all hearts and the sense of alienation you feel will surely subside. **INVERTED:** You cannot do the work of others in this business of forgiveness, but you can do your part by forgiving yourself if you have wronged another. Confrontation, or face to face retreading of the issue, is not always the correct choice of resolution, and even when it is appropriate, forgiveness must have already taken place in the heart before the meeting. The meeting here is not the means to resolution, but merely an acknowledgement of the fact.

17 GOVERNED BY THE STAR: ASPIRATIONS OF EGO, GOALS, MAXIMUM EXPECTATIONS

UPRIGHT: This goal is to be able to see clearly with the heart on the level of higher emotions so that you do not have to be rescued from emotional quagmires by the conscience of mind, in other words to be ethically on the mark. **INVERTED:** This goal is to be among those saved, to be among the righteous. At one extreme, this can be the low ethics of a get-even mentality, that will jump from one enemy to the next, creating one in the mind if necessary.

18 GOVERNED BY THE MOON: ASPIRATIONS OF HEART, COMPASSION

UPRIGHT: Here is the aspiration to the Golden Rule, to do unto others as we would have them do unto us, but purged of the inference of not causing pain because we do not want to feel pain. This would be a form of selfishness, not selflessness. We must act fairly out of our love for all creation and a desire to honor it and raise it higher, not out of fear of retribution from our fellow man, from God. **INVERTED:** This desire is to be among those saved, but with a counter desire not to be among those damned. The element of fear taints this aspiration.

19 GOVERNED BY THE SUN: PHYSICAL FULFILLMENT/EVALUATION

UPRIGHT: You have acted in good faith and there is a relaxing rightness to your material house and all your surroundings. **INVERTED:** Clean living is to be thorough and complete in all your activities leaving no hidden residues to become sticky and clog the gears.

20 GOVERNED BY JUDGEMENT: HEART'S FULFILLMENT/EVALUATION

UPRIGHT: Your relationships are balanced, issues of forgiveness having been dealt with, and you are long since free from guilt and fear. **INVERTED:** The mind and heart must be able to learn from one another if your spirit is to be truly light and rising.

21 GOVERNED BY THE WORLD: EGO'S FULFILLMENT/EVALUATION

UPRIGHT: Here there is peace of mind possible only with peace of heart. **INVERTED:** The mind and heart must be able to learn from one another if your spirit is to be truly light and rising.

22/0 GOVERNED BY THE FOOL: SOUL'S FULFILLMENT EVALUATION

UPRIGHT: "I take from you the gift of life; I give to you a life of giving.
        I take from you your love so freely offered; I give to you my love to be freely enjoyed.
        I take from you, drawing on your infinite wisdom; I give to you, drawing from my lessons learned.
        I take that I might give; I give that I might take.
        I repeat the spiraling cycles, In and out, in and out,
        Until my spirit knows not the difference, Until day and night and we are one."
        (The poem "Until We Are One," from the author's book "The Perennial Philosophy")
INVERTED: "There is no heaven for those who run from hell."
        (Title of poem from author's book, "Living the Perennial Philosophy")

THE WORLD.

21 THE WORLD

UPRIGHT: Here is the twenty-first stop on your overall journey. There is worldly knowledge and attainment of your mental goals, as expressed in the maximum expectations of The Star. A well-rounded education has been achieved. The World is at your doorstep even as you are at the doorstep of the universe. This is another "anything is possible" status point similar to that represented by The Magician (1), except that it is not "anything is possible" as pure potential at the beginning of beginnings, it is "anything is possible" after many tests and lessons learned. This is experiential intelligence. Here are theories that have been proven in the laboratory of life. Wholeness. There is a full understanding of the pattern of the whole in every little piece, the holographic principles underlying our perception of reality. Here is the hermaphrodite dancing, uniting Hermes and Aphrodite as dualities are resolved; the limited lower self of the separated ego is now the unlimited higher Self of the superego united with the other, with universal mind. This is the full realization of achievement, as the mind is aware of completion of the Karmic Contract and so is justifiably and properly proud. Here, to not be proud would be to err, for the self-ego is meant to become fulfilled as self-esteem. **INVERTED:** Naivete. Sin of Pride. Having missed the mark, and either aware or unaware of that fact. At one extreme, hubris, arrogance. At the other extreme, lack of confidence, poor self-esteem/self-worth, inability to accept a compliment, praise, a reward.

In This Spread Position...Interpret The World Meanings to Include:

1 GOVERNED BY THE MAGICIAN: PHYSICAL GIVENS, OUT OF THE FATHER
UPRIGHT: You will be very comfortable in the activities of the Physical/material Plane. In many instances there will be a sense of deja-vu that lends confidence. Instincts are sharp. You could well be an outdoorsman as you have an affinity for nature. Survival courses would be your cup of tea. **INVERTED:** Some will interpret your confidence as cockiness until they know you and see you deliver.

2 GOVERNED BY THE HIGH PRIESTESS: EMOTIONAL GIVENS, OUT OF THE MOTHER
UPRIGHT: You will be very comfortable in the affairs of the Emotional/creative Plane. Deja-vu will be common. You have a natural way with people and can be captivating, even mesmerizing. There is a flair for entertaining. **INVERTED:** Your worldly manner in dealing with people may lead some to be suspicious of your intent.

3 GOVERNED BY THE EMPRESS: MENTAL GIVENS, INTELLECTUAL PREDISPOSITION
UPRIGHT: You will be very comfortable in the business of the Mental Plane. Knowledgeable at an early age, and surely multi-disciplined, a generalist, even though you may be a specialist in many categories as well. Perhaps multi-lingual. The qualities of a good diplomat, or a university president. **INVERTED:** Keep knowledge as a tool, not a weapon, and you will avoid what some will say tends toward smugness, arrogance.

4 GOVERNED BY THE EMPEROR: SPIRITUAL GIVENS, LIFE PURPOSE
UPRIGHT: Yours is to be a world player, an international figure, even if you never leave your home town. There are many paths to universality. You will be dedicated to large issues and resolution in the long run of metaphysical conundrums. **INVERTED:** It may fall to you to focus that large overviewing intellect of yours on very specific issues that need intense work. The specific cannot be valid unless it knows where it fits in the bigger picture.

5 GOVERNED BY THE HIEROPHANT: SYSTEMS BORN INTO, SOCIETAL INFLUENCE
UPRIGHT: This early environment may have been in or near the arenas of formal religion, government, or administration on a large scale. The subject matter would have been ecumenical, worldly philosophical, possibly science and cosmos oriented, and certainly highly intellectual. **INVERTED:** At one extreme, information resources and subject may have been overwhelming. At the other extreme, this environment may have been information poor, with a decidedly small world view and is common in communities sheltering themselves from larger truths.

6 GOVERNED BY THE LOVERS: EMOTIONAL TAPES, BASIS FOR RELATING/CREATING
UPRIGHT: Here was an early love of adventure, as a facet of hunger for knowledge and worldly experience, a healthy desire to know what was on the other side of the fence. This may have centered around heros of mythic proportion, as you wanted to emulate their ability to get things done benefiting not just themselves but whole nations or races. **INVERTED:** At one extreme, this is a dream for a limited, probably a fantasy, world or a piece of the real world to be frozen in time. At the other extreme, there is a distortion in the vein of "save the world" or of wanting to conquer the world, to possess it.

7 GOVERNED BY THE CHARIOT: PHYSICAL RESOURCES. MEANS TO ACHIEVE
UPRIGHT: The world may be in front of you, but it is also behind you. You have a broad base of experience, in some cases extensive travel. This is as solid as a foundation can get. You could do your thing anywhere, succeed with any group of people. **INVERTED:** The world that you have depended on may not be as you left it; it may be changed, perhaps smaller. At another extreme, the suggestion is that you need to pare down the size, the contents of what has been your world.

8 GOVERNED BY STRENGTH: EMOTIONAL RESOURCES, ENERGY
UPRIGHT: The scope of your awareness and level of sophistication, together with the sheer number of people that you relate to successfully, give you emotional bulwark that you can rely on with confidence. Your creative output is prodigious. **INVERTED:** You may be in the wrong setting, trying to center yourself in someone else's world rather than your own. At another extreme, you could well be overextended, and would be stronger if you could cut back on responsibilities and on the length of your supply lines.

9 GOVERNED BY THE HERMIT: BELIEF SYSTEM, BASIS FOR DECISIONS
UPRIGHT: Your beliefs are rooted in the real world, in the approach the Greeks called stoicism, the acceptance of the world and one's place in it as fact, as reason, as good, and to work from there. Here too are the roots of Gnosticism, for this faith in the world is at once both faith in self-will and God's will as facets of universal will, here symbolized as will of The World. The search for knowledge of the other, of what is beyond the veil, is in order to use that knowledge/gnosis for the betterment of creation, not to escape it. **INVERTED:** Here are numerous distortions which twist, or altogether disavow, the hermetic dictum "as above, so below." The viewpoint may be of a world bigger or smaller than it actually is—i.e. on the one hand, a material world that is everything, the universe itself, no afterlife, no above; and on the other hand, a diminution of the material world putting it down as something much inferior, much less than the divine, when in fact it is God personified.

10 GOVERNED BY THE WHEEL OF FORTUNE: CENTRAL MESSAGE, THEME OF READING
UPRIGHT: Look up to see the image of the world to which you want to belong. You are being filled with the inspiration, the knowledge which could transform the world in man's image, in your image, of those things which are best in you. Here then is a look at what is best in man, in you. *INVERTED:* The world can be no better or no worse than we make it.

11 GOVERNED BY JUSTICE: STATE/CONTENT OF MIND
UPRIGHT: There is a justifiable sense of accomplishment, as you reap the rewards of success for past efforts, for having done the right things at the right time. Much of your mental Karmic Contract has been achieved and you will now put the icing on the cake. Your awareness of the bigger picture is astounding, to you as well as to others, for your pride is also humble. *INVERTED:* At one extreme, is the recognition that your world is a little smaller. At the other extreme, your world is much bigger than you realize. There may be hubris here. Ironically, sometimes the achievement is noteworthy only to be spoiled by a sense of pride or arrogance that is bigger than the accomplishment.

12 GOVERNED BY THE HANGED MAN: STATE OF EMOTIONS, SUBCONSCIOUS
UPRIGHT: The heart is embracing large scale goals, identifying with the agenda that includes universal mind. Heart is happy with the ego and its programs and is lending it energy for its growth and transformation into the superego of higher mind. There is enjoyment of success. *INVERTED:* Heart is not pleased with the world situation, it aches to see things otherwise, and this in spite of your achievements. In another extreme though, the heart does not agree with your mind's view of the world.

13 GOVERNED BY DEATH: PHYSICAL SITUATION, HARD REALITY
UPRIGHT: Your present situation is invigorated with healthy ideas, and you may feel literally on top of the world. You are centered on your personal path to fulfillment of your Karmic Contract. *INVERTED:* This may feel like someone has turned your world upside down. Some of your old world may survive this flood, but you should be prepared that some of it will not. What remains is as it should be and you must begin to rebuild on that. In some cases, this is primarily a matter of scaling back.

14 GOVERNED BY TEMPERANCE: EMOTIONAL TEST
UPRIGHT: The near future is a time for great emotional and creative expansion. Your geographical playground may actually improve, but even if you stay close to home, your emotional environment will be huge. The heart is accepting its part of the drive of mind toward universality and resolution of dualities. The barrier between self and other is coming down in heart as well as mind. *INVERTED:* With spiritual initiates the tendency can be to attempt working on the whole world rather than the part of it applicable to your path. You must work on universality by working in your little corner. You can only improve the world by improving yourself and the extensions of yourself in your surroundings.

15 GOVERNED BY THE DEVIL: TEMPTATION/CHALLENGE, FEARS
UPRIGHT: You are externalizing, putting more of self into the other. This has you broadening your scope of interest and involvement. But you are also internalizing, accepting/embracing more of the other into the self. This is the process wherein the ego transcends self, turning the death of the ego into rebirth. *INVERTED:* As the barrier between self and other comes down and the self becomes larger, filled with the other, it must still deal with the habits of the old ego which will try to see itself as not only larger, but in its separate state of mind larger and therefore better. This lays the basis for an ego power trip.

16 GOVERNED BY THE TOWER: NEXT LESSON, GRACE OF GOD
UPRIGHT: Look up to see your new world as it descends to become your new reality, transforming your environment into a perfect fit, a suit of armor in which you can ride forth with confidence to find your holy grail. *INVERTED:* With a slight twist on the preceding, here you are part of the transformation of someone else's environment, and you will be a strategic part of their new world.

17 GOVERNED BY THE STAR: ASPIRATIONS OF EGO, GOALS, MAXIMUM EXPECTATIONS
UPRIGHT: Metaphysically, this goal is nothing less than the merging of self in universal mind. In more exoteric terms, these are worldly goals on a large scale—world peace, environmental harmony, and the like. This is ambition with a healthy capital A. *INVERTED:* Distortions of the extremes of this archetype include a penchant for utopian solutions, an escapement rather than immersion in reality, anti-environmentalism on the order of "and God gave man dominion over the Earth."

18 GOVERNED BY THE MOON: ASPIRATIONS OF HEART, COMPASSION
UPRIGHT: Here is the aspiration to love The World. Metaphysically, this goal is nothing less than the dedication of heart which is the necessary compliment in the merging of the compassionate self into universal mind. It contains the heart of universal love, loving all of God's creation. *INVERTED:* At one extreme, the heart can internalize too much, taking too much into itself, of a more consuming rather than witnessing love. While this may disguise itself as compassion, it may actually be emotional gout. At the other extreme, the heart can externalize too much, putting itself into the world and neglecting the home fires.

19 GOVERNED BY THE SUN: PHYSICAL FULFILLMENT/EVALUATION
UPRIGHT: The material world and your physical body have been both temple and laboratory for you and you richly deserve all that has come your way. *INVERTED:* When tasting life remember to ask where the taste comes from.

20 GOVERNED BY JUDGEMENT: HEART'S FULFILLMENT/EVALUATION
UPRIGHT: Your relationships have both contributed to and benefited from your mind's good projects and determination to know the secrets of the universe. This has been a healthy as well as educational journey for the Emotional Plane. The at-one-ment of the emotions that comes with the lessons of Judgement has been amplified by the at-one-ment that comes with the mental lessons of The World. *INVERTED:* The heart of the world is in your heart. Feel it.

21 GOVERNED BY THE WORLD: EGO'S FULFILLMENT/EVALUATION
UPRIGHT: This is as much as mind can know of the worldly side of gnosis. It is full intellectual recognition of the divine spirit that infills every morsel of reality and outpours every morsel of non-reality. *INVERTED:* Keep yourself hungry and you will never starve to death.

22/0 GOVERNED BY THE FOOL: SOUL'S FULFILLMENT EVALUATION
UPRIGHT: "As webs come out of spiders, or breath forms in frozen air, worlds come out of us." (William Irwin Thompson in "Imaginary Landscapes," p.129) *INVERTED:* For just this little while, let this reading be your world.

THE FOOL.

22/0 THE FOOL

UPRIGHT: Here is the immortal mortal. Invincibility. The Magician has learned all his lessons. Complete lack of fear, through innate knowledge of death. Understanding of death, both as illusion and hard reality, that at birth we begin to die; at death we begin to live. Here is complete balance, centered awareness. Transcendent of space/time. To earthly knowledge has been added much of the knowledge beyond the veil, and the ability to see beyond earthly duality while living it. The ultimate optimist. Appears very lucky to onlookers, and is indeed charmed. There is much good humor in all things. Unmitigated joy, walking on air, as here is the ability to see the positive lesson inherent in any presentation of negativity, to transform pain into pleasure. Here is The Fool as representation of God's Will in the duality with the Magician (Man's Will). The Fool in knowing that he knows, also knows what he does not know. His reaction is "Oh, but of course!" When opposites reveal themselves to be but two sides of the one, the same, whenever we discover the surprise in what was before so hard to see, there is a relief, a lightening of the spirit that comes with the enlightening of the mind. **INVERTED:** Indiscriminate use of knowledge. Irresponsibility. Misplaced humor. Foolishness. This is someone who knows better and yet for reason of whim or malice, or simple neglect, chooses to go against his own knowledge.

In This Spread Position...Interpret The Fool Meanings to Include:

1 GOVERNED BY THE MAGICIAN: PHYSICAL GIVENS, OUT OF THE FATHER
UPRIGHT: Excellent instincts. Quick reflexes. Easy going. Carefree. Confident. A survivor. Physically lucky. Good gambler. Divinely protected. **INVERTED:** Too sensitive, or insensitive. Tendency toward laziness, or irrational spurts. Lack of direction, motivation. Too silly, or too serious. Clumsy. Careless, especially about health, well-being.

2 GOVERNED BY THE HIGH PRIESTESS: EMOTIONAL GIVENS, OUT OF THE MOTHER
UPRIGHT: Highly creative, original. Excellent with people. Lucky in love. Psychically active, alert, receptive, and accurate. Gifts will be used wisely. A sensuous persona. Universally attractive and appealing. **INVERTED:** Talents will be extraordinarily challenging. Could be unsteady, frivolous, with unnecessary affectation. Hard to sustain energy and creative focus. Difficult deciding which of natural talents to pursue most.

3 GOVERNED BY THE EMPRESS: MENTAL GIVENS, INTELLECTUAL PREDISPOSITION
UPRIGHT: Inventive, independent mind. May apply intellect in any field you choose, but humor will always be uppermost, however serious the subject. Everything is funny, yet also serious. Philosophical, yet most likely not the overt philosopher. Knowledge is woven into the fabric of everyday life. **INVERTED:** Given to being either too serious, or not serious enough in mental affairs, maybe even to mood swings between the two. Responsibility is difficult. A penchant to tease, and to play one-upsmanship solely for ego rather than to achieve a worthwhile goal.

4 GOVERNED BY THE EMPEROR: SPIRITUAL GIVENS, LIFE PURPOSE
UPRIGHT: Lifetime as witness to lessons already learned, to help others move more efficiently. Outwardly, you seem one of life's chosen, lucky in all you do. Actually, this is to leave you with energy for others' problems. You are sophisticated and wise, as well as a pleasure to be with, and so people seek you out. **INVERTED:** Must strive to maintain interest, avoid a blase attitude, learning to enjoy the efforts of others to learn what you already know, while avoiding patronizing them. Path may be difficult as you must work side by side with those having problems.

5 GOVERNED BY THE HIEROPHANT: SYSTEMS BORN INTO, SOCIETAL INFLUENCE
UPRIGHT: Your early environment was full of natural wisdom and healthy influences. There was an easy order, an inherent organization to how things got done. Good humor predominated. You had ready access to good guides. The ethics inferred here did not come from any organized religion per se. **INVERTED:** Early influences somewhat erratic, maybe loose, irresponsible, yet good examples were available if you could read between the lines. A good environment in spite of itself.

6 GOVERNED BY THE LOVERS: EMOTIONAL TAPES, BASIS FOR RELATING/CREATING
UPRIGHT: You are a free spirit, with a raw love for life and the freedom to live it as you please. You love everything virtually equally and to the maximum. Here is the kernel of the adventurous heart. **INVERTED:** Perhaps here is too much admiration for the free spirit. (You would say, "How is that possible?") But maybe carefreeness leading to extremes, i.e. problems with constancy. Hard to be serious about your emotions?

7 GOVERNED BY THE CHARIOT: PHYSICAL RESOURCES, MEANS TO ACHIEVE
UPRIGHT: Fortunate circumstances behind you. Natural ability to provide, resourceful. Material ease. Good health. Prowess. **INVERTED:** Things may have gone too well, leaving you spoiled. Have you used resources well enough, to full advantage? Physically, you may be capable of much more. Value more highly your roots.

8 GOVERNED BY STRENGTH: EMOTIONAL RESOURCES, ENERGY
UPRIGHT: Direct, open expression in relationships and creative work. Love and commitment while honoring the lesson of non-attachment (unselfishness). Great potential for growth and expression of feelings. Use of talents wisely and to great effect. **INVERTED:** Perhaps misunderstanding, misusing lesson of non-attachment. Non-attachment is not non-responsibility. Lack of respect. Insincerity. Flippancy. Avoidance.

9 GOVERNED BY THE HERMIT: BELIEF SYSTEM, BASIS FOR DECISIONS
UPRIGHT: Highly independent, yet universal in outlook. Pragmatically idealistic. Platonic. Here is the philosopher's philosopher. Your ideas work not only for you, but for others because you have identified with cosmic truth. Your belief system is on line and working well. **INVERTED:** Independent to a fault. Impatient with others, perhaps the world as a whole. Overly idealistic. False ideal of the "perfect." Perhaps somewhat dogmatic and imposing. May lack personal will to match ideology. Spiritually lazy, unwilling or unable to share your path very well.

10 GOVERNED BY THE WHEEL OF FORTUNE: CENTRAL MESSAGE, THEME OF READING
UPRIGHT: Hear ye! Hear Ye! Listen to your soul. Yes, you can walk your talk. Make your moves now. Use the full force of your personality. Be yourself by letting your talents express themselves. Let up on yourself, be more carefree and ironically in so doing you will meet and accept true responsibility for your Karmic Contract. **INVERTED:** Too serious about the wrong things; not serious enough about the right things.

11 GOVERNED BY JUSTICE: STATE/CONTENT OF MIND, PLANS

UPRIGHT: Complete confidence. Self-respect. Optimism. Resolution. Plans on-line and integrated in present affairs. Continuation of present course, only more so. Very much on track. Ideals mixed with healthy pragmatism. Implementing principles into worldly affairs. ***INVERTED:*** Too much or too little confidence, check the facts. Overly optimistic, or pessimistic. Impatience. Avoidance or complete escapism. Mentally lethargic. Need to prioritize and simplify. Self-analysis, redirection for gaining self-esteem.

12 GOVERNED BY THE HANGED MAN: STATE OF EMOTIONS, SUBCONSCIOUS

UPRIGHT: Enjoyment of life situation. Love of self and others. Open to relationships. Creative juices flowing in support of Karmic Contract. The subconscious is an ally, not an enemy, of the conscious self. ***INVERTED:*** Too light-hearted, or too heavy, for the present situation. Too light—you may be missing some of the deeper possibilities of the situations at hand. Too heavy—you may be forcing or projecting on situations more than is appropriate. Subconscious may be screaming for attention. What about your dreams now?

13 GOVERNED BY DEATH: PHYSICAL SITUATION, HARD REALITY

UPRIGHT: You are well-positioned. Living your principles, walking your talk. Well-mannered, Pleasant, entertaining. Highly ethical, a role-model. Your spirituality is main-lined in your life, although you may not be conventionally religious at all. Your work may literally be spiritually oriented, helping teach others what you have already learned. ***INVERTED:*** Off center from your ideal. Feel uncomfortable. Behavior may be anti-social, even rude. Take charge of yourself. You, as Chairman of the Board over all that constitutes you, of all the elementals in your body, need to pull rank and set some new ground rules for where you are going. Time for tough self-love.

14 GOVERNED BY TEMPERANCE: EMOTIONAL TEST, NEAR FUTURE

UPRIGHT: Integration of higher emotions and spiritual ideals into day to day affairs, relationships, and creativity. May have actual teacher/guide at hand, learning first hand how to be in the clouds and on the ground at the same time. Balancing love of God, love of guru, love of self, love of others as different and necessary aspects of the same love. ***INVERTED:*** Do not lose yourself in the clouds. Be prudent. Guard against pessimism in creative and personal relationships. Do not let the facility you have with creativity and relationships diminish their importance to you.

15 GOVERNED BY THE DEVIL: TEMPTATION/CHALLENGE, FEARS, NEAR FUTURE

UPRIGHT: Time to balance prudence with daring. Feeling the pull to excellence by your higher mind, toward living fully in truth. Facing the demands of your karma more fully than ever before. ***INVERTED:*** Guard against letting your search for authenticity make you overly harsh on others. They have their path, their timing; you have yours. Do not seek mastery; it will come to you. Avoid the pitfalls of abstraction and false idealism. Ego struggles as veil lifts and duality wanes, revealing the program of the universal ego living in your soul.

16 GOVERNED BY THE TOWER: NEXT LESSON, GRACE OF GOD

UPRIGHT: Much the same as for position 10, but also— Listen and hear as you speak to yourself, urging your soul on its true course. Accept your tasks and your load will be light. Deny them and your burden will be heavy. ***INVERTED:*** Be more serious where you have been much too frivolous. Be much more light-hearted and light-minded where you have been much too serious.

17 GOVERNED BY THE STAR: ASPIRATIONS OF EGO, GOALS, MAXIMUM EXPECTATIONS

UPRIGHT: To be on your true path, being both free and tied at the same time. Proper responsibility. Acceptance of Karmic Contract brings no loads that are too heavy. Desire for personal and universal goals to coincide. To have courage of convictions. ***INVERTED:*** Goals may be abstract, unrealistic, or immature fantasies. Enlightenment as goal, but with lack of understanding that such is not a nirvana or heaven, rather a full knowledge and acceptance of all that is. Element of escapism clouds true work. Personal and universal goals may be at odds.

18 GOVERNED BY THE MOON: ASPIRATION OF HEART, COMPASSION

UPRIGHT: Desire to profoundly affect, and be affected by, others. Intimate involvement with your world. Heart is light in spite of intense involvement in your surroundings, your creativity. Ability and energy to help others without subverting or destroying self. ***INVERTED:*** Over-identification of self with universal emotions, with humanity's suffering. An element of compassion may be distorted, false, improper. The adoration trap—making a person or a figurehead the centerpiece of your emotions, and much too personally.

19 GOVERNED BY THE SUN: MATERIAL FULFILLMENT/ EVALUATION

UPRIGHT: Discipline will have given you complete freedom. You will be in your world, as you would have it, doing your thing. A romantic adventurer, yet with strong purpose. Physically very able and flexible even as you age. Active throughout life. Here is the holy man who knows/selects the exact hour of his death. ***INVERTED:*** Somewhat rootless, difficulty settling down in this lifetime. Perhaps a wanderer, even a hobo. Avoidance of duty, of self. Stuck, unable to fly. So overwhelmed by your own knowledge and potential, you may be staggering before the immensity of it all.

20 GOVERNED BY JUDGEMENT: HEART'S FULFILLMENT/ EVALUATION

UPRIGHT: Full love of life, of all living things. Openness and sharing will sprout wings on your heart in the realization of true universal love. ***INVERTED:*** Still unable to accept completely the apparent unfairness of life, especially of man's treatment of man, and of man's abuse of fellow creatures and nature. At the extreme, this is an inability to reconcile the harsh realities of life with God. This is an inability to love God., and likewise an inability to love self. You may not be able to seriously trust others or yourself enough to benefit from relationships, groups, or to maximize your own creativity. Problem with emotionally giving or taking could keep you out of much of the game.

21 GOVERNED BY THE WORLD: EGO'S FULFILLMENT/EVALUATION

UPRIGHT: The small ego transformed as it merged into universal mind/awareness. Self-mastery has been achieved. You realize that you will leave a considerable legacy to help others avoid the traps that you have mastered. ***INVERTED:*** Whether your achievements have been great or not, your ego senses that you could have done better. Perhaps, for one reason or another, there will be little or no legacy even if your achievements were many. You may not have taken yourself seriously enough.

22/0 GOVERNED BY THE FOOL: SOUL'S FULFILLMENT/EVALUATION

UPRIGHT: Here was learning with a fully attentive mind and a full heart. Nothing was wasted on this path. ***INVERTED:*** Much was expected by the self of the self in this lifetime and there may be some disappointment. Use the messages of this reading to reach this archetype.

Chart 5
A SUMMARY OF MAJOR ARCANA MEANINGS

CARD	MEANING

1 **THE MAGICIAN**....................Beginning of beginnings. All things possible. Start of your path, your evolution of consciousness. A spiritual teacher. Father of fathers - Adam. Master of the material plane. Guide through physical reality, physical sensation.

2 **THE HIGH PRIESTESS**..........Mistress of Emotional Plane. Mother of mothers - Eve. The ultimate female. Guide through emotional reality, emotional sensation and feelings. Origin of energy, prana. Birth of rhythm and flow.

3 **THE EMPRESS**.......................Guide through mental reality. Female authority figure. Birth of logic and reason. Education. Knowledge. Teacher of teachers, and student of students. Record keeping and history. Communication. Administration and government.

4 **THE EMPEROR**......................Guide through intuitive reality. Male authority figure. The divine right of kings - implementation of the hermetic dictum "as above, so below." Origin of duty and conscience. Responsibility. Obedience.

5 **THE HIEROPHANT**................Spiritual as comprehended by the intellect. Organized religion, the clergy. Established link between worldly consciousness and intuitive knowledge of God's law, universal truth. Collective belief systems.

6 **THE LOVERS**.........................Marriage. Emotional partnering. Passion. Birth of duality in the heart as self discovers other. Acceptance of others' desires to complement your own.

7 **THE CHARIOT**.......................The ways and means of physical/material growth. Physical movement - relocation, transportation, travel. Expansion. Construction. Asserting physical independence. Competitive drive. Efforts to improve health, strength.

8 **STRENGTH**.............................Properly channeled and controlled emotions. Strong self-image and self-respect. Confidence. Emotional independence. Extensions of self (family and creative projects) firmly in place and functioning. Loyalty, constancy.

9 **THE HERMIT**.........................Withdrawal to gain perspective, objectivity. Formulation of personal philosophy and beliefs. Mental independence. Autonomy. The gifts of patience and prudence. Foundation of the healthy Ego.

10 **WHEEL OF FORTUNE**.........Trust in God, and thus is Self. The leap of faith. Will(ingness) to take a chance, to spin the Wheel. The cusp from self-assertion to self-transcendence. Balance of the will of man and the will of God. Acceptance.

11 **JUSTICE**.................................Balanced, rational mind. Balance of give and take mentally. Civil behavior and action. Clarity. Decisiveness. Mental peace.

12 **THE HANGED MAN**.............Heart chakra opening. Major emotional change. Birth of compassionate heart. Trust. Balance of give and take emotionally. Energy of cross balancing horizontally and vertically, i.e passion with compassion, spirit with body.

13 **DEATH**...................................Major, irreversible change at the physical/material level. Here will come new beginnings, new phases, new directions. The root of all fears. Acceptance of physical endings and physical lessons.

14 **TEMPERANCE**......................Emotional balance, progressing., growing. A mature emotional constitution, where consideration for self and others strive for balance. Cooperation. Harmony. Improved relationships. Humility.

15 **THE DEVIL**............................Temptation pushes you forward, just as heart pulled you back with Temperance. Lifting of the veil separating all dualities. Opening of the third eye. Exposing the shadow personality.

16 **THE TOWER**..........................Revelation. Profound impact of spiritual input. Unexpected, out-of-the-ordinary change bringing instantaneous learning of a lesson. Collapse of old forms.

17 **THE STAR**..............................Hopes. Mental aspirations. Goals. Optimism. Exciting and productive mental growth, results. Flashes of awareness, mental breakthroughs. Messages from spirit guides, guardian angels, dreams, astral travel, etc.

18 **THE MOON**............................Mature emotions. Sophisticated passion. Compassion/altruism. Subconscious desires. Heart's aspirations. Individual boundaries dissolving as heart seeks universal love to parallel the maturing seeking universal mind.

19 **THE SUN**................................Productivity. Realization of physical and material goals. Abundance. Health. Harmony with Nature. Positive outcomes. Overcoming of fears, casting away of shadows. Physical legacy.

20 **JUDGEMENT**........................Making of emotional peace. Atonement. Impact of grace on the heart. Mercy. Forgiveness of others and self. Emotional reward. Emotional wisdom. Emotional legacy.

21 **WORLD** ....Worldly knowledge, experiential intelligence. Attainment of mental goals. Well-educated, well-rounded. Wholeness, resolution of dualities. Full realization of achievements. Mental legacy.

22/0 **THE FOOL** ....Lack of fear, invincibility. Magician with all lessons learned. Apparently charmed and lucky as result of being centered, grounded in spirit. Balance, humor in all things, all situations. Both innate and experiential knowledge. Wisdom.

Note: See the individual definition sheets earlier in Chapter Seven for more detailed upright meanings and for inverted meanings.

CHAPTER EIGHT

The Minor Arcana

You have seen the evidence of your evolutionary path of consciousness in the study of the Major Arcana and the definitions of the Karmic Spread positions derived in part from that path. There is as well an evolutionary path of sorts through the Minor Arcana. And whereas the Major Arcana were the archetypal lessons of the universal plane, the Minor Arcana are the everyday occurrences through which we get our chance to practice and perfect those archetypes. In another sense, we can say that whereas the Major Arcana are our inner experiences, the Minor Arcana are our outer experiences. You will see, however, that in the definitions I speak of the Minor Arcana as archetypes in their own right.

In studying the Minors you observe your existential growth from lessons learned in your interaction with your environment. In a sense you are marching through the physical lessons of the Pentacles, the emotional lessons of the Cups, the mental lessons of the Swords, and the spiritual lessons of the Wands. While this "march" is not an iron-clad linear progression, it is a progression in the general sense that you can only go so far in each of the "higher" suits without completing the lessons of the "lower" suits.[1] But remember that the Minors are highly interactive and interdependent. A given reading may show, for example, that certain emotional lessons need not be learned before further growth on the physical level.

The fifty-six cards of the Minor Arcana are divided into groups in two different respects. First, there is the division into four groups of fourteen cards each called *suits*. As you have seen in the earlier chapters, these are the Pentacles, the Cups, The Swords, and the Wands. Second, there is the division of each of these suits into the *Pips* and the *Courts*. Each of the four suits has ten Pips and four Courts, for a total of forty Pips and sixteen Courts. The Pips are numbered 1 to 10. The Courts each contain a King, Queen, Knight, and Page. Chart 6 summarizes the meanings of the Pips.[2] Chart 6A summarizes the meanings of the Courts.

The Pips represent what you experience during your lifetime to learn the major lessons on your path as represented by the cards of the Major Arcana.

The Court Cards represent the cast of characters with whom you act out those experiences.

They are the guardian angels bringing you concrete manifestation of the messages that your intuition would have you acknowledge and learn. Information as to physical characteristics, personality, lifestyle, and livelihood are also conveyed. The Courts obviously represent people that are incarnated with you in this plane of reality. The Courts can also represent activity and assistance from spirit guides.[3] The section "Identifying Guides" in Chapter Nine offers more on this subject.

The derivation of major meanings for the Pips comes from a review of the significance of the suit in question, interfaced with the meaning of the number itself. There is indeed much to be learned from following the progression of the numbers 1 through 10 within a given suit; for instance, from studying the Ace, then the 2, the 3, etc., of Pentacles (and then the other three suits), because the Minors represent an evolution of events and experiential knowledge for the four aspects of the personality.

But of additional and perhaps more significant help in defining the Pips is emphasizing the study of the numbers vertically. That is to say, to study all the 2's, the 3's, and so on, emphasizing what the numbers have in common and then allowing for the differences from suit to suit. This will be our method, as opposed to the usual emphasis on the progression of 1 to 10 within each suit.

The thorough knowledge of the suits gained from the review of the origin of suit meanings, such as that presented in Chapter Three, must be integrated with a sound knowledge of the numbers 1 to 10.[4] A working knowledge of these numbers is presented a little later in this chapter. The study of Numerology is an important compliment to a serious study of the Tarot. More is said about this in Chapter Ten.

THE FOUR SUITS: PENTACLES, CUPS, SWORDS, AND WANDS

Here are the characteristics of the four suits:

Pentacles represent: The Physical, Matters of Earth, Material Affairs, Business, Work with Hands, Instincts, Physical Health, Crafts, Farming, Sustenance, Possessions, Physical Activity/Achievements, Industry, Hatha Yoga, Physical Handicaps, Physical Prowess, Physics, Chemistry, Biochemistry, Anthropology, Things Green.

Cups represent: The Emotional, Matters of Water, Relationships, Work with Heart, Emotional Health, Passion/Compassion, Caring, Creative Expression, Theater, Dance, ReBirthing, Sentimental Activity, Lower Psychic, Tantra and Bhakti Yoga, Things Blue.

Swords represent: The Mental, Matters of Air, Work with Mind, Mental Health, Communications, Writing, Mental Activity, Logic, Mathematics, Information, Politics, Mental Businesses, Professions, Psychology, Philosophy, Government, Civil Service, Raja Yoga, Things Yellow.

Wands represent: Spiritual, Matters of Fire, Spiritual Work, Creative Insights, Intuition, Metaphysics, Higher Psychic, Centering Work, Gnani (Agni) Yoga, Things Red.

Inventor, mathematician, philosopher Arthur Young has pointed out the use of the four elements as verbs:[5]

To earth = to get down to earth, to materialize

To water = to nourish

To air = to make known

To fire = to arouse, to start, to throw out

THE PIPS

The aspect of Tarot as energy, oscillation, pulsation, rhythm, represented in mathematics as the sine curve, is visibly at work in the Pips. Just as you have seen the effect of the four levels on the Suits—Pentacles/Physical, Cups/Emotional, Swords/Mental and Wands/Spiritual—so, too, you can see their effect on the series of numbers 1 to 10. Take a quick look at Chart 6 and take particular note of the headings of the number columns showing the assignment of Physical, Emotional, Mental, and Spiritual to the numbers.

In Graph form it looks like this:

Spiritual.....................4's................................10's.
Mental.................3's........5's...................9's.
Emotional........2's...................6's........8's.
Physical ......1's.............................7's.

In Pips 1 through 4 the self is primarily engaged in establishing its existence within its heritage and proclaiming its individuality. In Pips 4 through 7 the self begins to enlarge its frames of reference and identity through the extensions of biological family and then the extended family of friends and associates. In Pips 7 through 10 the self enlarges further to include the family of man, the world.

1...........................4.............................7...........................10

Self   Self as extension   World as extension
                              of self   of self

In addition to providing summary meanings for all the Minor Arcana Pips, Chart 6 shows the grid interaction of the effect of the Planes of the personality (Physical-Emotional-Mental-Spiritual) on the suits and the numbers. This displays the energies these meanings derive from. For instance, look at the Ace of Swords. Because Swords are the Mental Plane, and because Aces are influenced by the Physical, this card is governed by Physical/Mental. It is the physical beginning at the mental level. As a second example, look at the Four of Pentacles. Because Pentacles are the Physical Plane, and because Fours are influenced by the Spiritual, this card is governed by Spiritual/Physical. It therefore represents centering (physically and materially), security, stability and well-being.

The characteristics of the Pips, which have been summarized in Chart 6, are listed below:

All ONES Contain:

Beginnings, Roots, Unity, Totality, Independence, Solitude, Singularity, Thesis. Ones represent the primary Physical aspects of everything, and as such show the origins of all four Planes—Emotional, Mental, and Spiritual, as well as Physical.

All TWOS Contain:

Duality, Choices, Cooperation, Antithesis. Twos represent the primary Emotional aspects of everything, and as such show the beginnings of partnerships and other matters of duality, for all four Planes—Physical, Mental, and Spiritual as well as Emotional.

All THREES Contain:

Resolution, Fruition, Expression, Creation, Synthesis. Threes represent the primary Mental aspects of everything, and as such show the beginnings of expansion, productivity, and resolution, and other aspects of tertiality, for all four Planes—Physical, Emotional, and Spiritual, as well as Mental.

All FOURS Contain:

Foundation, Stability, Reliability, Centering. Fours represent the primary Spiritual aspects of everything, and as such show the beginnings of order and solidarity for all Planes—Physical, Emotional, and Mental, as well as Spiritual.

All FIVES Contain:

Uncertainty, Freedom, Multiple Choices. Fives represent the secondary Mental aspects, and as such show the in-progress mental effects, the mental antitheses, for all four Planes.

All SIXES Contain:

Movement, Duty, Service, Externalization. Sixes represent the secondary Emotional aspects, and as such show the in-progress emotional effects, the emotional antitheses, for all four Planes.

All SEVENS Contain:

New Beginnings, New Directions. Sevens represent the secondary Physical aspects, and as such show the in-progress physical effects, the physical antitheses, for all Planes.

All EIGHTS Contain:

Compassion, Order, Selflessness. Eights represent the tertiary Emotional aspects, and as such show the resulting emotional effects, the emotional syntheses, for all four Planes.

All NINES Contain:

Healing, Forgiveness, Tolerance, Philanthropy, Idealism. Nines represent the tertiary Mental aspects, and as such show the resulting mental effects, the mental syntheses, for all four Planes.

All TENS Contain:

Completion, Perfection, Maximum Achievement. Tens represent the tertiary Spiritual aspects, and as such show the resulting spiritual effects, the spiritual syntheses, for all four Planes.

THE COURTS

First, let's examine the suit-generated characteristics of the Court cards in two respects: by physical characteristics and by personality. Physical descriptions are based on Caucasian references, but equivalent comparisons can be made for non- Caucasian peoples.

Then, we will look at characteristics generated by the Court cards as groups: the Kings, Queens, Knights and Pages.

Suit-Generated Characteristics

Pentacles' Physical Characteristics: Dark hair and dark complexion. The exception is a very fair complexion with very black hair, the skin being almost translucent. Eyes are dark brown, green, or violet.

Pentacles' Personality: Sturdy, reliable, down-to-earth, can-doers, good instincts.

Remember that Pentacles are the element Earth; the color green; and concern matters Physical.

Cups' Physical Characteristics: Light brown to sandy blonde hair and medium complexion, sometimes olive, with brown, blue, or gray-blue eyes.

Cups' Personality: Sensitive, emotional, moody, dedicated when motivated, creative. Remember that Cups are the element Water; the color blue; and concern matters Emotional.

Swords' Physical Characteristics: Blonde to light blonde hair and fair complexion with blue, blue-gray or greenish-brown eyes.

Swords' Personality: Active, strong, direct, extroverted, mentally alert, assertive, philosophical, studious.

Remember that Swords are the element Air; the color yellow; and concern matters Mental.

Wands' Physical Characteristics: Red to reddish-blonde or reddish-brown hair and fair or freckled complexion with green or blue eyes.

Wands' Personality: Vibrant, keen, fiery, introspective, intuitive, humorous, spiritual.

Remember that Wands are the element Fire; the color red; concern matters Spiritual/Intuitional.

Characteristics Generated by the Court Groups

The Kings: Mature males. They predominate over things Physical. Fatherhood. Male Leadership. Responsibility. The drive of necessity. The Kings are of the element Earth; the color green; influence Physical.

The Queens: Mature females. They predominate over things Emotional. Motherhood. Female Leadership. Nurturing. The drive of the heart. The Queens are of the element Water; the color blue; influence Emotional.

The Knights: Young adults (age 12 up) of both sexes. They predominate over things Mental. Communication and new ideas. The drive for expansion. The Knights are of the element Air; the color yellow; influence Mental.

The Pages: Children of both sexes under age 12. They predominate over things Spiritual. Exuberance and vitality. Innocence. Intuition. Creativity. Freshness. The drive for transformation. The Pages are of the element Fire; the color red; influence Spiritual.

The Royal Court

A look at Chart 6A will show the grid interaction of the two aspects of the Court defined above. Notice that the King of Pentacles is Earth/Earth; the Queen of Cups is Water/Water; the Knight of Swords is Air/Air; and the Page of Wands is Fire/Fire. This is *The Royal Court*. Each of these respective Court cards has by definition the same characteristics and responsibilities as its suit. The prototypical "providing" figure is the king of kings, the King of Pentacles, the father of fathers. The prototypical "nurturing" figure is the queen of queens, the Queen of Cups, the mother of mothers. The prototypical "protecting" figure is the knight of knights, the Knight of Swords, the expansive drive present in all the knights whereby the kingdom, led by the King and Queen, is enlarged. The prototypical "transforming" figure is the page of pages, the Page of Wands, the new potential inherent in all the pages.

ACE OF PENTACLES

UPRIGHT: Here are the physical, the material, beginnings of things. Also, the ultimate and successful completion of physical and material matters to the highest standards. Material fulfillment, perfection, blessings. Good fortune. Excellent health. New business ventures. New physical regimen, of diet and/or exercise. Physical prowess and/or superiority. Material independence and self-sufficiency. Ability to provide, to produce. Great physical potential. Physical, material thesis. This can also show the opening and development of the First Chakra (Root/Anal) and the handling of basic, debilitating fears.
INVERTED: Can suggest some difficulty getting a project started or finished on time, or to satisfaction. Also, there may be a physical block at an elementary level. Too much or too little of any of the above. Many examples of these appear in specific positions detailed below.

In This Spread Position...Interpret the Ace Of Pentacles Meanings to Include:

1 GOVERNED BY THE MAGICIAN: PHYSICAL GIVENS, OUT OF THE FATHER
UPRIGHT: Physically/materially blessed. Good inheritance. Healthy beginning from the father's side. Strong body able to support you throughout life.
INVERTED: Physical/material givens may be so strong as to paradoxically cause difficulty, such as through the envy of others, of things coming too easily, or the problem of conceit. Or, the reverse, that these givens at birth may not be very strong. Or, that development in this Plane begins slowly, i.e. physical maturation coming late, or the colloquial "late bloomer."

2 GOVERNED BY THE HIGH PRIESTESS: EMOTIONAL GIVENS, OUT OF THE MOTHER
UPRIGHT: Emotional fortitude. Good inheritance—genetically or materially, from the mother's side. Body will support creative endeavors, especially those requiring physical endurance. Especially suited to succeed financially in professions drawing upon the emotions and creativity, such as the arts. You may marry well. **INVERTED:** The magnitude of these gifts may be so great as to bring their own set of problems. Or, the reverse, that these givens at birth may not be very strong. Or, that development in this Plane begins slowly.

3 GOVERNED BY THE EMPRESS: MENTAL GIVENS, INTELLECTUAL PREDISPOSITION
UPRIGHT: An imminently practical thinker. A healthy mind, perfectly suited for earth professions, those of the Physical/material Plane (i.e. agriculture, science, architecture, health care, nature and the environment, manufacturing, military strategy, manual trades, crafts.) **INVERTED:** Could be overly practical, thereby prone to limiting vision. May be too heavy a thinker. Or, that this mind is more impractical, or less interested in things of a physical/material nature.

4 GOVERNED BY THE EMPEROR: SPIRITUAL GIVENS, LIFE PURPOSE
UPRIGHT: Life will require substantial achievement in physical and material matters. **INVERTED:** Part of your lesson may be in how well you handle the outstanding degree to which you succeed, how you handle wealth. Or, it could concern how you succeed without abundance.

5 GOVERNED BY THE HIEROPHANT: SYSTEMS BORN INTO, SOCIETAL INFLUENCE
UPRIGHT: Family, early environment, materially abundant with physical plane of utmost importance. Possibly very athletic and active. Resourceful. Pragmatic.
INVERTED: This influence of success in the Physical Plane may be overwhelming or at the expense of the other Planes. Or, it may be an atmosphere of striving for perfection materially/physically that is distorted.

6 GOVERNED BY THE LOVERS: EMOTIONAL TAPES, BASIS FOR RELATING/CREATING
UPRIGHT: Desire to be first, to make things happen, to be successful materially/physically. A fortune hunter. A passion for setting records, for physical perfection. **INVERTED:** Drawn to success for the sake of success. Or may be subconsciously drawn to failure, as a negative misunderstanding of the positive role of passivity.

7 GOVERNED BY THE CHARIOT: PHYSICAL RESOURCES, MEANS TO ACHIEVE
UPRIGHT: Abundant resources. Fresh, at-the-ready. Good health record. Support systems in place and working. **INVERTED:** Resources may be so strong, or prior physical success so great, that it may be somehow counterproductive for future needs. Or, resources/means may be inadequate or inappropriate for present/future needs.

8 GOVERNED BY STRENGTH: EMOTIONAL RESOURCES, ENERGY
UPRIGHT: Physical heritage and track record is your strength. Material situation has shored up your relationships and secured your creative enterprises. Ability to see and take advantage of real opportunities quickly. **INVERTED:** Relationships/creativity may be tested by blockage on the physical/material level. Are your relationships based on deeper love or on physical assets, be they money or beauty? Physical well-being must be a means to an end, not an end in itself.

9 GOVERNED BY THE HERMIT: BELIEF SYSTEM, BASIS FOR DECISIONS
UPRIGHT: Independence. Survival. Doing your best. Being the best. Success. Life rooted in physical/material well-being. **INVERTED:** Too focused on the Physical Plane, even fearful. Primary motive is physical survival, perhaps at any cost, as in a nation's over-armament. Drive for material success may be solely to satisfy the lower ego.

10 GOVERNED BY THE WHEEL OF FORTUNE: CENTRAL MESSAGE, THEME OF READING
UPRIGHT: Material/physical success in the offing. Enjoy. A new beginning, or successful completion with great satisfaction, on the Physical/material Plane, (Health, diet, exercise, work, home, lifestyle, etc.) Realize and accept the strength of your position. Important to begin, or finish, on time. **INVERTED:** A delay on a major new project necessary; be patient. Or, difficulty with completion to standards. The type or level of success will be less than expected. Prepare/accept. Or, success surpassing expectations presents its own set of problems.

11 GOVERNED BY JUSTICE: STATE/CONTENT OF MIND, PLANS
UPRIGHT: Planning a new start, new venture, or completing an old one. Cashing in your chips, liquefying assets, mobilizing resources for a new phase. Content with your physical/material situation. Physical/material plans are solid. *INVERTED:* Procrastinating a new beginning, or delaying a completion. Check timing. Could be starting too soon, or finishing too late. Not content with basics of situation. Possible flaw in material/physical plans.

12 GOVERNED BY THE HANGED MAN: STATE OF EMOTIONS, SUBCONSCIOUS
UPRIGHT: Yearning for a new beginning or a successful completion in the Physical Plane. Enjoyment of, or desire for, good fortune, good health, physical prowess. *INVERTED:* Present physical situation, plans or outcomes, may be offering some distress to the heart.

13 GOVERNED BY DEATH: PHYSICAL SITUATION, HARD REALITY
UPRIGHT: Success, good health, rewards, at hand. Major departure, new beginning at hand. *INVERTED:* Less success, less good health, less rewards, than you would like. New beginning on hold, perhaps blocked. Or, success, etc. could so far exceed expectations as to bring its own circumstances to handle.

14 GOVERNED BY TEMPERANCE: EMOTIONAL TEST, NEAR FUTURE
UPRIGHT: Pressure of success, effect on relationships and/or creativity. Pressure/effect of new start. Desire for truth and deeper understanding of material world. Environmentalism asserts itself. *INVERTED:* How to handle frustrations with material Plane, or difficulties with new beginnings? Careful not to make your creative, emotional standards unrealistically high, or your material appetite too large. Also, don't compromise your standards either.

15 GOVERNED BY THE DEVIL: TEMPTATION/CHALLENGE, FEARS, NEAR FUTURE
UPRIGHT: Excitement, lure of a new venture. Test of your resolve. Drawn to material/physical perfection. *INVERTED:* Overly ambitious (money, body, beauty...). Fear of new venture, of success. Problem of things never being good enough. Difficulty/fear of getting started. Also, difficulty with completion, especially to a standard, most likely your own. Unreasonable fear of the earth plane, of the environment, nature, animals, elementals, rudimentary spirits. Fear of fear.

16 GOVERNED BY THE TOWER: NEXT LESSON, GRACE OF GOD
UPRIGHT: Much as with interpretations for position 10, but in the near future. This information will help you with implementing the healthy challenges discovered in position 15. Knowing your Material Plane will be graced is to allow your attentions to focus on the other planes. *INVERTED:* Much as with interpretations for position 10, but in the near future.

17 GOVERNED BY THE STAR: ASPIRATIONS OF EGO, GOALS, MAXIMUM EXPECTATIONS
UPRIGHT: Material and/or physical success is your aim, whether your goal is athletics or business. You have great confidence, and expect to do very well in what you attempt. Here is the drive of the inventor, the desire to be first as well as best, to propose solutions to elusive problems. *INVERTED:* Desire to be first and best may make it hard to be part of the team, and to be less than the leader. Here would be the lack of confidence, with little motivation to be first or best. At the extreme, this might even be the desire to never be first, to in fact lose.

18 GOVERNED BY THE MOON: ASPIRATIONS OF HEART, COMPASSION
UPRIGHT: High level of appreciation for the finest aspects of the Material/physical Plane, a true realization of the goodness in everything. A desire to have abundance in order to share with others. *INVERTED:* May get lost in the deliciousness of material life, in the ecstasy of the divinity in everything. Or the reverse, a difficulty appreciating enough of the material/physical side of life...an improper application of asceticism for example...or a misunderstanding of the healthy duality of spiritual/material. Even misguided radical environmentalism fits here.

19 GOVERNED BY THE SUN: MATERIAL FULFILLMENT/ EVALUATION
UPRIGHT: Great achievement and sense of completion in Material/physical Plane, with good potential for more to come from these assets. Here is a healthy material legacy for the next generation. *INVERTED:* Achievement and estate may be enormous, suggesting that much attention be paid to its direction. Last wishes may not be adequately arranged. Or, material/physical achievements may be less than expected, though not lacking in any real sense.

20 GOVERNED BY JUDGEMENT: HEART'S FULFILLMENT/ EVALUATION
UPRIGHT: The physical aspects of all relationships, the effects of your loves and creations, are as you would have them in your final stage of life. *INVERTED:* At one extreme, these relationships are the picture of ideal harmony, as with three or four generations of one family, or any harmonious commune, living happily and productively under one roof. At the other extreme, one or more important links are missing from an otherwise perfect ending.

21 GOVERNED BY THE WORLD: EGO'S FULFILLMENT/ EVALUATION
UPRIGHT: The degree of material/physical success is the major contributor to the sense of legacy, of having done well. Much will survive of your efforts in this lifetime. *INVERTED:* Your achievement(s) may be legendary, ranking with others whose works have changed the course of the world. Or, whatever your achievements, your appraisal of them may be conservative compare to that of others.

22/0 GOVERNED BY THE FOOL: SOUL'S FULFILLMENT/ EVALUATION
UPRIGHT: Material perfection. Ultimate performance on the Physical Plane. *INVERTED:* Same as upright, but perhaps somewhat more, or less, than Karmic Contract called for.

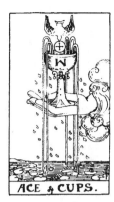

ACE OF CUPS.

ACE OF CUPS

UPRIGHT: Here are the beginnings of things emotional and creative. Also, the ultimate and successful completion of emotional and/or creative matters to the highest standards. Emotional fulfillment, perfection, blessings. Here is receptivity. The opening of the heart chakra. Also can be the opening of the genital or the solar plexus chakras. Here is fertility, as sexual/emotional potential, applying to relationships and to creative projects. May be a proposal of love, or of marriage, for here is the offering of oneself to another. It is also the offering of oneself to the world through one's talents and energies. Baptism and anointing. As symbol of the Holy Grail, or the Holy Spirit, here is God's message delivered straight to the heart. God's grace. Emotional, creative nourishment, a boost. Cleansing. Healing. Happiness with relationships and self-expression. **INVERTED:** Difficulties with beginnings or completions on the Emotional Plane. Blockages of the heart, genital, or solar plexus chakras. But there may also be too much of an opening or a problem with timing.

In This Spread Position...Interpret the Ace Of Cups Meanings to Include:

1 GOVERNED BY THE MAGICIAN: PHYSICAL GIVENS, OUT OF THE FATHER
UPRIGHT: Instinctively sensitive to the affairs of the material world, to the physical body, to the requirements for survival. Here is the physically attractive, the sensuous. The ability to generate a great deal of energy. Material drive will protect, even increase, emotional well-being. A strong, yet gentle hand. **INVERTED:** Difficulty from being too sensitive, too emotional. Or, perhaps not sensitive enough or at the right times.

2 GOVERNED BY THE HIGH PRIESTESS: EMOTIONAL GIVENS, OUT OF THE MOTHER
UPRIGHT: A delicate, yet strong sensitivity to the world of the emotions, of creativity. Emotionally blessed—there will be little difficulty in staying centered emotionally, in remaining dedicated to your loves/talents. Here is the quintessential attractive person, due primarily to the balance of give and take on the Emotional Plane, the full, flowing heart. **INVERTED:** Emotionally so open that you are receiving and processing some things meant for others. May have difficulty with letting go.

3 GOVERNED BY THE EMPRESS: MENTAL GIVENS, INTELLECTUAL PREDISPOSITION
UPRIGHT: An emotional thinker, gut instincts ever assertive into the rational process. Mind suited for work of the Emotional Plane, for highly creative projects (i.e., poet, novelist, choreographer, counselor). Think here of the oracle at Delphi. **INVERTED:** Subject to being misled, to listening to inappropriate messengers. Bad channeling. Subversion of the astral plane. May have too much of the emotional imposing on the mental.

4 GOVERNED BY THE EMPEROR: SPIRITUAL GIVENS, LIFE PURPOSE
UPRIGHT: Initiation and achievement on the Emotional Plane, therefore relationships and/or creative endeavors, will predominate. It falls to you to find original expression for your feelings and perhaps to assist others likewise, although a highly public life is not necessary with this card. However, what comes from you in this lifetime may eventually affect many. **INVERTED:** Creative drive, feelings may be so profound that acceptance and expression are difficult. This includes the "problem" of being too attractive—to people, to information, etc.

5 GOVERNED BY THE HIEROPHANT: SYSTEMS BORN INTO, SOCIETAL INFLUENCE
UPRIGHT: Healthy early environment, full of supportive relationships and conducive to creativity. **INVERTED:** Surroundings may be so strong as to be overwhelming, stifling rather than encouraging, depending on the status/strength of the young ego. For some reason, advantages of early influences not taken fully.

6 GOVERNED BY THE LOVERS: EMOTIONAL TAPES, BASIS FOR RELATING/CREATING
UPRIGHT: The love of loving, of nurturing, of caring, of creating—all as facets of the desire to give of oneself. Infusion at an early age with spirit of universal love. Here one wants to be a "source." **INVERTED:** Innocence, leading to a falling in love that is not advantageous. Possibly overly affected by the ideal of universal love, or by some form of external input, less appropriate to this Karmic Contract. Caution: The love of giving must be balanced with the love of receiving. Examine motivations for wanting to be a "source."

7 GOVERNED BY THE CHARIOT: PHYSICAL RESOURCES, MEANS TO ACHIEVE
UPRIGHT: A baptism. A re-birthing. A cleansing. A "walk-in"—an acceptance of the spirit of a guide, or a strong aspect of the self from a past life, fully appropriate to this life path. Physical/material achievement based on emotional/creative resources. Brilliant originality in practical affairs along with proper motives. Nothing done at the expense of others, rather with full consideration of others and of nature. **INVERTED:** Difficulty moving forward, a block with an emotional or creative beginning or completion. Physical matters have been too subordinated to the emotional. Check suitability of all inner influence, such as from guides, past lives, readings, and the like.

8 GOVERNED BY STRENGTH: EMOTIONAL RESOURCES, ENERGY
UPRIGHT: You bring a full heart into all you do. Emotional maturity and understanding of people and relationships are your bedrock. There is boundless energy for interactions with others and for use in fueling your creative endeavors. You are able to initiate while others stand back. **INVERTED:** A lack of energy, or misapplied energy in relationships or creativity. A problem with initiating, of asserting, of taking advantage of things appropriate for your path. Check for a balance of give/take; there may have been too much giving and not enough taking...or vice versa.

9 GOVERNED BY THE HERMIT: BELIEF SYSTEM, BASIS FOR DECISIONS
UPRIGHT: Love, emotional fulfillment, feelings are the crux of your philosophy. All of the positive aspects of the concept of universal love permeate your thinking. Your approach to matters is gentle and well meaning. You lead, as well as follow, with your heart. **INVERTED:** A misunderstanding and/or misapplication of the principles underlying universal love. Perhaps infatuated with picturesque ideals, false heavens, non-existent nirvanas. Or, the reverse, a lack of confidence in the aspect of love and harmony as part of the whole, may be reflected in your ability to generate such love and harmony yourself. The former leads to a sense of false security or feeling over-protected, while the latter to feeling ever-vulnerable.

10 GOVERNED BY THE WHEEL OF FORTUNE : CENTRAL MESSAGE, THEME OF READING
UPRIGHT: This is a time of emotional blessings, gifts from others, cleansing, healing, invigoration. A new emotional beginning. A successful conclusion to an emotional issue or creative project of long standing. *INVERSION:* Allow for time to take its course with emotional matters, for the energy you require to build up. This suggests the need for patience if you have been trying to push an issue. On the other hand, if you have been laid back, or far too passive, the suggestion could be the opposite, and you may need to move more quickly and aggressively. Give where love is needed. Take where love is offered.

11 GOVERNED BY JUSTICE: STATE/CONTENT OF MIND, PLANS
UPRIGHT: You are clear, fresh, rejuvenated, and confident with the possibility of a new start. Here are plans for a creative project, the possibilities of a new relationship, as the mind dedicates itself to matters at the emotional level. The mind is in love, kindly disposed to self and others. Universal love permeates your immediate plans, your approach to things. *INVERTED:* You may be concerned with, or actually causing, a delay with a relationship or your creative potential. How do you begin? A review and clarification of motives may be at root.

12 GOVERNED BY THE HANGED MAN: STATE OF EMOTIONS, SUBCONSCIOUS
UPRIGHT: Wide, clear opening of the Heart, the Solar Plexus, and/or the Genital Chakras. Emotional balance and creative purity par excellence. *INVERTED:* There may be too much activity in one or all of these aforementioned chakras, and there may be some discomfort, pain, or the sweet pain of too much pleasure. Or the discomfort may come from these chakras being too closed rather than too open.

13 GOVERNED BY DEATH: PHYSICAL SITUATION, HARD REALITY
UPRIGHT: Emotional/ creative abundance. Highly energized situation. Beginning of a new love or project, or the carrying of it to a supreme level. *INVERTED:* Energy in situation may be too great or inappropriate. Difficulty with the beginning of an emotional/creative matter. Perhaps just short of an emotional expectation.

14 GOVERNED BY TEMPERANCE: EMOTIONAL TEST, NEAR FUTURE
UPRIGHT: Emotional well-being. Sense of belonging, of being in the right place at the right time. Major relationships intact and rewarding. Creativity and energy levels at a peak. *INVERTED:* Flood of emotions. Your evaluation of your relationships, or of your creativity, may be at odds with that of others. Be fair with yourself and others.

15 GOVERNED BY THE DEVIL: TEMPTATION/CHALLENGE, FEARS, NEAR FUTURE
UPRIGHT: The mind must accept emotional fulfillment. Or, it's a matter of taking up the challenge of a new love. *INVERTED:* Guard against a fear of love, of happiness. Learn here to accept what is at hand.

16 GOVERNED BY THE TOWER: NEXT LESSON, GRACE OF GOD
UPRIGHT: Breath of fresh air. New emotions, new opportunities. A sense of being loved, of being able to love. *INVERTED:* You will be either pushed forward at a faster pace, or held back at a slower pace, in your Emotional Plane, as is necessary to compensate for your behavior in the near future, you may say in the next year.

17 GOVERNED BY THE STAR: ASPIRATIONS OF EGO, GOALS, MAXIMUM EXPECTATIONS
UPRIGHT: Emotional fulfillment is your goal. You want to be a source for others, to nurture and heal wherever possible. *INVERTED:* May have the ability to start new emotionally as your goal. This isn't improper, but you need to project beyond this for your maximum expectations. Examine your motives in wanting to help or heal others. Subconsciously, you may see this as one way to prove you are more powerful, more evolved than those who need your help.

18 GOVERNED BY THE MOON: ASPIRATIONS OF HEART, COMPASSION
UPRIGHT: A genuine, selfless desire to be intimately involved with the lives and needs of others. An ability to give and receive at one and the same time, thereby avoiding the pitfalls of pity and guilt. Actions grow directly from the innate understanding of the interdependence of all of God's creation. The ability to love the whole yet not to be dissolved into it. *INVERTED:* Difficulty separating the needs of self and others. A sacrificing of self for others where unnecessary or inappropriate.

19 GOVERNED BY THE SUN: MATERIAL FULFILLMENT/ EVALUATION
UPRIGHT: A fresh vitality awaits you as you advance in years. Sensuality, sexuality actually increase with time. Originality and creativity do not peak until the very last as well. *INVERTED:* You may be overdoing it in the emotional arena. Or, you may actually be capable of more than you give yourself credit for.

20 GOVERNED BY JUDGEMENT: HEART'S FULFILLMENT/EVALUATION
UPRIGHT: This is the A+ report card as the heart's grade for performance in the Emotional Plane. Relationships have been full and productive. No forgiveness of self or others is necessary. There is no hint of guilt. *INVERTED:* All of the above is still true, but perhaps with a grade of A- .

21 GOVERNED BY THE WORLD: EGO'S FULFILLMENT /EVALUATION
UPRIGHT: The mind is pleased with the choice of lifework and the richness of your relationships. You have reached the pinnacle of achievement in using your creative talents. You have had a major impact on your fellow man, on your environment, and equally important you have been impacted profoundly by them as well. *INVERTED:* All of the above is still true, but perhaps with a grade of A- .

22/0 GOVERNED BY THE FOOL: SOUL'S FULFILLMENT/EVALUATION
UPRIGHT: The ability to master the need for balancing Giving and Receiving in the lifetime is achieved. The soul's epitaph will read, "This was a life marked by its vibrancy, by its ability to openly and fearlessly interact with others and with nature. Here was a soul who knew what it was to love unconditionally."

ACE OF SWORDS

ACE OF SWORDS

UPRIGHT: Here are the beginnings, or the successful completion, of mental matters to the highest standards. New concepts, proposals. Intellectual fulfillment, perfection, blessings. Awards for mental achievement. Clarity of thought. Highly analytical. Rational. Self-assured. Origins of philosophies, systems of belief, ethics, and morality, hence justice, law and order. Excellent communication, administration, and teaching/learning skills. The opening and development of the Throat Chakra. This is the sword of Gabriel, the shaft of light which illuminates the mind and aligns the seven chakras with words of truth. This communication is visible, conscious, and delivered through external means. Reliable mind, truth, useable information.
INVERTED: There may be too much or too little of the principles mentioned above. For example: Too much or too little knowledge, truth. Unabashed honesty at unnecessary moment on one extreme, versus outright lies when truth is crucial. There may be difficulty with the early stages of an idea or plan, or in formulating goals. Or, there may be trouble with completion. The confusion of too many ideas, or the indecision of too few. Mental talents, like everything else, must fit the situation. Examine the circumstances as to whether you are too strong or too weak for the situation at hand. Innocence and naivete vs. conscious distortion.

In This Spread Position...Interpret the Ace Of Swords Meanings to Include:

1 GOVERNED BY THE MAGICIAN: PHYSICAL GIVENS, OUT OF THE FATHER
UPRIGHT: Mental acumen and assertive spirit through the father. Active and forthright in the physical plane. A self starter. A doer. Strong, clear body language. Will be drawn to mental interests and professions, and have excellent communication and teaching skills in them. Disciplined, efficient in physical/material matters. **INVERTED:** May be prone to acting before thinking. Or, may tend to over think when time for action has come. Overly critical in physical/material matters. Over-disciplined, or under-disciplined.

2 GOVERNED BY THE HIGH PRIESTESS: EMOTIONAL GIVENS, OUT OF THE MOTHER
UPRIGHT: Mental acumen and assertive spirit through the mother. Active, forthright, forceful, and deeply motivated in the emotional plane. Emotionally and creatively assertive, capable of self-control and management. Personal life may be dominated by your higher than average intelligence and talents. **INVERTED:** May be either too demanding, or not demanding enough, of your relationships, or of yourself. You must work to use your more than adequate intelligence appropriately to support, not to dominate, your emotional life and your talents.

3 GOVERNED BY THE EMPRESS: MENTAL GIVENS, INTELLECTUAL PREDISPOSITION
UPRIGHT: Here are mental blessings par excellence. Exceptional intelligence. Ability to analyze, rationalize, investigate, communicate, learn, teach, at the highest levels. **INVERTED:** How to integrate your extraordinary mind into the fullness of your personality, to balance mind with body and heart, will mark your lifetime.

4 GOVERNED BY THE EMPEROR: SPIRITUAL GIVENS, LIFE PURPOSE
UPRIGHT: Yours is to transmit from above to below, the role of the scribe, prophet, communicator. Your life purpose will seem to be that of observer as you allow yourself and your energy to help get the message across to your fellow man. **INVERTED:** There are many lessons for you in learning how to perform this function well. While getting the message may come fairly easy, getting it across may prove to be the real task.

5 GOVERNED BY THE HIEROPHANT: SYSTEMS BORN INTO, SOCIETAL INFLUENCE
UPRIGHT: Your early environment was highly ordered and efficient. Communication was paramount and learning was highly valued. **INVERTED:** Too much order, too much discipline. Efficiency valued more as an end than a means. Communication and learning in and of themselves rather than as bearers of knowledge of lessons to be learned. Or, there may have been a lack of these things.

6 GOVERNED BY THE LOVERS: EMOTIONAL TAPES, BASIS FOR RELATING/CREATING
UPRIGHT: Your first love belongs to the mental level, not the emotional. A passion for knowledge, order, and discipline, seeing things work well. You enjoy communicating in all its forms - talking, writing, computers, et al. Facilitating the exchange of ideas propels you. Your personal loves and family life must satisfy these criteria. **INVERTED:** Too much mind in your emotional tapes, the love for order and discipline may be inordinate.

7 GOVERNED BY THE CHARIOT: PHYSICAL RESOURCES, MEANS TO ACHIEVE
UPRIGHT: Originality, appropriateness of ideas. Profound knowledge of the body, finances, business, the workings of nature, and such. Good education, communication, organizational skills. Mental leadership. **INVERTED:** Shore up your abilities in the aforementioned to secure your base or operations and to maximize the present potential.

8 GOVERNED BY STRENGTH: EMOTIONAL RESOURCES, ENERGY
UPRIGHT: Assertive personality, confidence, consistency, efficiency, are the centerpieces attracting others to you. Your apparent knowledge of love and emotional issues and your calm under fire have been enviable. Excellent judge of people, and good at validating information received instinctively and intuitively. **INVERTED:** May actually be irrational in emotional affairs by being too rational? Mind may have had a tendency to throw emotional timing off. Chakras may be seriously misaligned, leaving you inconsistent from situation to situation.

9 GOVERNED BY THE HERMIT: BELIEF SYSTEM, BASIS FOR DECISIONS
UPRIGHT: Reason is all. For you everything is rationally knowable. Power of intellect. Driven by the knowledge of the known, the outer world of facts, of science, of mathematics, and in all means of recording and sharing what is known. A profound sense of history and of the future. **INVERTED:** Reason may be carried to an extreme, becoming a false god itself in an unwillingness or an inability to see the spiritual level above mind. The logic underlying your beliefs may be faulty or incomplete. Open yourself to observation and criticism for checks and balances.

10 GOVERNED BY THE WHEEL OF FORTUNE: CENTRAL MESSAGE, THEME OF READING
UPRIGHT: Be assertive. Communicate now what you already know or have planned. Use the kundalini energy from your healthy alignment of opened chakras. Intuition is vivid and reliable. Guides may be very obvious or even visible. **INVERTED:** Listen to what others may be telling you. Prepare for major message, for

alignment of chakras must occur now for work ahead. Check immediate environment now for message already visible but not yet discovered or internalized. May need to subordinate yourself more in present situation.

11 GOVERNED BY JUSTICE: STATE/CONTENT OF MIND, PLANS

UPRIGHT: Present idea is on target. Confidence is appropriate. New input is reliable. Accept responsibility. You are moving correctly and timely in accordance with your beliefs and they are centered with universal truth. ***INVERTED:*** While you may be on target, adjustments for timing, or to incorporate the ideas, even the leadership, of others may be necessary. Question of originality; be careful of plagiarism, distortion of truth. Check new information; may be incomplete or inaccurate.

12 GOVERNED BY THE HANGED MAN: STATE OF EMOTIONS, SUBCONSCIOUS

UPRIGHT: Heart, subconscious, gut feelings strong and sure on the reliability of present situation or question at hand. Deep inside, you are confident and want to act. Idea developing in back of your mind, put forward by your heart. Instincts are accurate. ***INVERTED:*** Gut feeling, subconscious may be either overly optimistic or unreasonably pessimistic. Instincts are either unreliable now, or they are so certain, that they have taken over and you are virtually on automatic.

13 GOVERNED BY DEATH: PHYSICAL SITUATION, HARD REALITY

UPRIGHT: Body very healthy in support of clear thinking. Timing good for major step forward with plans. Order and discipline prevail. Major completion/ new beginning involving mental disciplines in your Physical Plane. Beginning yoga, meditation, new education, new schedule, new careers related to the Suit of Swords are examples. Healthy criticism. discernment in effect. ***INVERTED:*** Either too tight or too loose. Too much or too little criticism. Difficulty beginning or ending project. Straighten up, stiffen your backbone, fly right, then get on with the program.

14 GOVERNED BY TEMPERANCE: EMOTIONAL TEST, NEAR FUTURE

UPRIGHT: Impact of mental clarity, new ideas, or realization of long held goal on the Emotional Plane affecting relationships and/or creativity. A breakthrough in understanding your emotions. Clarity and order prevail as light is shed on previously dark corners. ***INVERTED:*** New ideas, realizations may be incomplete, or even faulty. Thoughts may be divisive of relationships, or corrosive of creativity. You may have more information than is necessary or appropriate for the situation at hand.

15 GOVERNED BY THE DEVIL: TEMPTATION/CHALLENGE, FEARS, NEAR FUTURE

UPRIGHT: Lower and higher mind meet, as ego comes to grips with Ego. You are pulled to higher sources of knowledge. Ending of old, beginning of new, mental endeavors. Universal truth asserts itself on your personal path. as you see more clearly than ever before, using the sword to lift the veil. ***INVERTED:*** Fear intrudes as you realize, through what you have already learned, the immensity of what still lies ahead. Severe distortion of information can throw you off track. You may lack confidence, or you may be foolishly overconfident.

16 GOVERNED BY THE TOWER: NEXT LESSON, GRACE OF GOD

UPRIGHT: A mental breakthrough lies ahead, within a year at the most. Bring divergent thoughts under one roof. Organize for better control and more efficient output. ***INVERTED:*** Allow new input to challenge your complacency. Routines must be examined and altered. You may have things backwards, looking through the wrong end of the telescope. More may have been revealed than you would like; nevertheless use your internal Chairman of the Board, the big Ego, to mandate to all of your elementals just what needs to be done, and will be done, starting now.

17 GOVERNED BY THE STAR: ASPIRATIONS OF THE EGO, GOALS, MAXIMUM EXPECTATIONS

UPRIGHT: Highly important that you succeed, be first, the originator, and if at all possible best. You set difficult goals, but never doubt you can achieve them. Mental achievement is top priority, not that you want to beat others, just that you enjoy the thrill of innovation and must perform to the maximum. You want what only knowledge brings. ***INVERTED:*** You enjoy defeating someone else as much as winning yourself. You may want the power that knowledge brings for less than the noblest reasons. Inordinate fear, or its complete lack, may be distorting your goals.

18 GOVERNED BY THE MOON: ASPIRATION OF THE HEART, COMPASSION

UPRIGHT: Heart enlists the mind as champion of the good fight to secure justice for all. The desire is to communicate well with others in order to be at one with them, to understand, to empathize. Your motivation may well be to initiate new, better ways of intercommunication and understanding. ***INVERTED:*** Distortion of means to justify ends. A willingness to force, or sacrifice, one thing for another. Problem of the mental assessment distorting an emotional truth.

19 GOVERNED BY THE SUN: MATERIAL FULFILLMENT/EVALUATION

UPRIGHT: Mind serves you well throughout life, being major contributor to your physical success and well being. Very much in control even as you reach old age, being active, alert, and ever innovative. ***INVERTED:*** Careful not to abuse your knowledge and position as you get older. Let others share your status; delegating authority to go with responsibility is a sure way.

20 GOVERNED BY JUDGEMENT: HEART'S FULFILLMENT/ EVALUATION

UPRIGHT: Lifetime clear and consistent in emotional affairs, always having worked at letting others know how you felt. It was easy to initiate and facilitate contacts. ***INVERTED:*** Could have done better at listening and/or communicating. May have kidded yourself or even deliberately distorted issues. You must determine how much of this may have been naivete.

21 GOVERNED BY THE WORLD: EGO'S FULFILLMENT/EVALUATION

UPRIGHT: The Ego is content that the mind has served you well, bringing maximum efficiency and achievement. The mental legacy is great. There is complete awareness of how well your personal philosophy has served you. There is great intellectual understanding of the spiritual. ***INVERTED:*** All of the above may be true, but to a lesser extent. There is an awareness of your having drawn up shy of your potential. Or, you may have succeeded beyond your wildest dreams and therein have derived paradoxically some difficulties.

22/0 GOVERNED BY THE FOOL: SOUL'S FULFILLMENT/EVALUATION

UPRIGHT: The Soul is content that the mind has maximized its potential, satisfying the Karmic Contract in full. The next lifetime will most likely begin and work entirely on the spiritual plane as servant/guide to assist others with their paths. ***INVERTED:*** The same as above, but to a lesser extent. The soul may be somewhat less thrilled with your performance than your mind, or even your heart.

ACE OF WANDS

ACE OF WANDS

UPRIGHT: Here are spiritual roots and beginnings. Also, the successful completion of spiritual matters to the highest standards. Commencement/completion of a spiritual path or project. This is spiritual independence, a true centering on the being within. From here your karmic purposes can unfold gently and completely. This is acceptance of initiateship, your vow to take a vow. Awakening/Rebirth. Highly intuitive. Apparent good luck, as you achieve major goals with ease. This can also show the opening and development of the Third Eye. Here is the staff of the shepherd, the golden thread linking the crown chakra with the clouds, the magician's wand for facilitating as above so below, the antenna for receiving God's messages of your lessons to be learned.
INVERTED: All of the above may be true, but to a lesser extent. You may be on the verge of a spiritual breakthrough, but there is a block of some sort. You may very much be a medium through which a great deal is being accomplished. This wand/channel between you and the firmament may be too efficient and thereby picking up more than is appropriate. Or, it may be inefficient and not picking up all that is meant for you. For these inefficiencies to be taking place, there will be obvious difficulties at the lower levels bringing this about, for you are meant to be fully efficient and receiving everything you need to know to be completely successful on your path.

In This Spread Position...Interpret the Ace Of Wands Meanings to Include:

1 GOVERNED BY THE MAGICIAN: PHYSICAL GIVENS, OUT OF THE FATHER
UPRIGHT: Highest regard for the physical body as a temple, and for the spirituality inherent in all things material. At one with nature. Bringing God down to earth, especially the masculine side of the Godhead. Hearing the spiritual directly through the material world. **INVERTED:** May literally worship the body, something material, or the Physical Plane in general. Physical life very much in tune with spirituality, but with a strong tendency toward the passive, toward observation, listening to your environment.

2 GOVERNED BY THE HIGH PRIESTESS: EMOTIONAL GIVENS, OUT OF THE MOTHER
UPRIGHT: Highest regard for the emotions, for relationships, and the divine gift of your talents. Bringing God down to earth, especially the feminine side of the Godhead. The positive aspect of what we call negative, the passive, i.e., its beneficial qualities. Hearing the spiritual through the emotional world. **INVERTED:** May literally worship your talents, or loved one(s). May literally worship your gifts, or relationship(s), or the Emotional Plane in general. Emotional life very much in tune with spirituality, but with a strong tendency toward the passive, letting others take the lead, learning from participation/observation.

3 GOVERNED BY THE EMPRESS: MENTAL GIVENS, INTELLECTUAL PREDISPOSITION
UPRIGHT: A Platonic, Hermetic, Gnostic thinker. Highly intuitive mind concerned with "as above, so below." Excellent listener. May formally pursue study of universal themes, spirituality, philosophy, or the like. Accuracy, clarity. Originality. Excellent theorist. **INVERTED:** Perhaps idealistic in the extreme, enjoying the world of theories to the world of reality—a profile suited to the researcher or hard core academic.

4 GOVERNED BY THE EMPEROR: SPIRITUAL GIVENS, LIFE PURPOSE
UPRIGHT: A lifetime of service is the essence of your Karmic Contract. Yours is the ability to cope with major upheavals with relative ease, in order to make most of your energy available to help others in their times of trial. There is an easy flow to your nature as you even out the peaks and valleys of everyday life. Source of new message, prophetic. A spiritual livelihood. **INVERTED:** Much of this path will be in how you maintain your balance without an air of detachment, or even frivolity. Your living must derive from the path itself, in extreme cases even if it means passing the plate.

5 GOVERNED BY THE HIEROPHANT: SYSTEMS BORN INTO, SOCIETAL INFLUENCE
UPRIGHT: Vibrant, natural spirituality in early surroundings. Truth was practiced, not merely theorized or taught. This was "do as I do," not "do as I say do." **INVERTED:** Spiritual character of everyday life was pervasive, possibly even isolated, to maintain purity of practice, devotion.

6 GOVERNED BY THE LOVERS: EMOTIONAL TAPES, BASIS FOR RELATING/CARING
UPRIGHT: This is not just the love of God, but an infatuation with the ability to communicate intimately with the Divine. The mark of the poet/prophet. A healthy respect/love for your own core of creativity. Realization of the path as very real, perhaps through an early religious experience; an initiate at an early age. **INVERTED:** Dedication to the Divine may be extreme and so dictate every facet of adult life. Or, may be stuck with the symbology of a profound revelation, rather than getting on with the lesson itself.

7 GOVERNED BY THE CHARIOT: PHYSICAL RESOURCES, MEANS TO ACHIEVE
UPRIGHT: Strong foundation much in the sense of the marsh reed, which, though it blows easily in the wind, nevertheless remains strong, useful for many purposes. Although perhaps not physically apparent, your resources are inexhaustible due to the depth and breadth of awareness, rooted in your becoming an Initiate. **INVERTED:** Some difficulty in starting deliberate work on your path, in implementing the messages you've received. Or, the reverse, that you began in earnest and perhaps too quickly, too forcefully. Listen carefully for updates, elucidation of the original inspiration.

8 GOVERNED BY STRENGTH: EMOTIONAL RESOURCES, ENERGY
UPRIGHT: Your awareness of your spiritual path is your strength. People benefit from the messages you've received just by knowing you. Creative juices are flowing. Your desires and motivations are perfect for your path. **INVERTED:** Your emotional path depends now on your ability to consciously commit to disciplines of spiritual study and observation. There has been some delay in accepting the challenge of serious commitment.

9 GOVERNED BY THE HERMIT: BELIEF SYSTEM, BASIS FOR DECISIONS
UPRIGHT: Your personal philosophy is on target and of maximum effectiveness in bringing you to full realization of your life purpose. Your center has aligned with universal truth. **INVERTED:** While the aforementioned is true, there may be some difficulty in others getting the picture that you see. Or, there may be difficulty in formulating the messages reaching you and generating appropriate action.

10 GOVERNED BY THE WHEEL OF FORTUNE: CENTRAL MESSAGE, THEME OF READING
UPRIGHT: Blessings abound. A spiritual rebirthing is in progress. Begin now to actively integrate spirituality into your daily routine. Enrich all that you do by paying greater attention to the wonder, the lessons, inherent in the simplest of tasks and activities. **INVERTED:** Be patient with yourself,

with the beginnings of earnest endeavors, with the start of the new you. Allow yourself to be used as a guardian angel for someone else; may require you to speak or act out of character.

11 GOVERNED BY JUSTICE: STATE/CONTENT OF MIND, PLANS
UPRIGHT: You are at peak of conscious integration of your intuition, filled with messages that you understand well and are ready to use. You are very pleased with your status, your progress to this point and with your potential. Yet, it is time for a major new step forward, integrating conscious pathwork in every aspect of your life. Intellect reinvigorated, mental rebirthing. *INVERTED:* Some discomfort, impatience with progress, with an inexplicable delay. Receiving messages, but not fully understood.

12 GOVERNED BY THE HANGED MAN: STATE OF EMOTIONS, SUB-CONSCIOUS
UPRIGHT: You are at the peak of heart awareness, of the accuracy of your gut instincts, of the positive effect of your subconscious. Dream interpretation will be very accurate and helpful. All sub-conscious activity, inner resources will be very strong and amazingly similar in clarity and subject matter and content to your conscious daily activities. An infusion of the holy spirit. *INVERTED:* The aforementioned has been taking place, but the heart is yet to be fully moved.

13 GOVERNED BY DEATH: PHYSICAL SITUATION, HARD REALITY
UPRIGHT: You are feeling effects of blessing and renewal throughout your body. The physical changes may be very noticeable, and yet in actuality nothing may have altered. Things may be the same, yet entirely different. However, the new mood is most likely to eventually, if not immediately, generate considerable change in your Physical/material Plane. *INVERTED:* A delay in actual physical/material change. Or, the effects of renewal may be astounding, causing a domino effect throughout this plane.

14 GOVERNED BY TEMPERANCE: EMOTIONAL TEST, NEAR FUTURE
UPRIGHT: Impact of spiritual blessings and change on your relationships, on your creativity, extension of self. *INVERTED:* Impact may be profound; may affect others around you as much or more than yourself. Your blessings may have been a conduit for those of others as well.

15 GOVERNED BY THE DEVIL: TEMPTATION/CHALLENGE, FEARS, NEAR FUTURE
UPRIGHT: Impact of spiritual awareness on mental affairs. Awakening. Lifting of the veil. Opening of the Third Eye. Challenge to accommodate higher truth, authenticity. *INVERTED:* On one extreme, not opening fully to what has already been realized. On the other, an acceptance through abstraction as a means to avoid true openness and the change it should bring. Going through the motions.

16 GOVERNED BY THE TOWER: NEXT LESSON, GRACE OF GOD
UPRIGHT: A major gate awaits you, not later than a year from now. Get as much old business taken care of as possible, in preparation for a new turn on your path. *INVERTED:* This fork in your path may close many aspects of your past. There may be more unfinished business than you like as you interpret much as lost opportunities. You will be helped to realize otherwise.

17 GOVERNED BY THE STAR: ASPIRATIONS OF EGO, GOALS, MAXIMUM EXPECTATIONS
UPRIGHT: Your goal is to be a true seeker, a serious Initiate, to hear and obey the word of God. This is the goal of self-realization in its finest sense, as the soul seeks to balance the inner and outer aspects of God. *INVERTED:* The goal of seeker may be confused or ignoble, the lower ego seeking to be the source, the oracle, rather than to hear it and become part of the process of revelation. At the extreme, there can even be a conscious effort to block revelation or to distort the message.

18 GOVERNED BY THE MOON: ASPIRATIONS OF HEART, COMPASSION
UPRIGHT: Your desire is to be able to hear, and to share, what has been revealed to you— in all your relationships, in all self-expression through the talents that God has given you. *INVERTED:* There can be a jealousy in the approach to the Divine, of wanting to feel what others do not feel, rather than a sharing and participation. Here too can be the inappropriate desire to disappear into the One, rather than to identify with and bear witness to it in our separateness for the benefit of this world and all in it.

19 GOVERNED BY THE SUN: MATERIAL FULFILLMENT/EVALUATION
UPRIGHT: A serenely happy and purposeful finale awaits you. Your centered awareness and efficiency in learning the lesson of your Karmic Contract has rendered you alert, physically strong, and exceptionally attractive. Many people will seek you out. You should either make your living in overt spiritual endeavors or, at the least, spirituality will pervade all your enterprises. *INVERTED:* There may be a tendency to enjoy all too privately your serenity. The lifetime has been too good to leave unfinished business or quit just before the finish line.

20 GOVERNED BY JUDGEMENT: HEART'S FULFILLMENT/EVALUATION
UPRIGHT: Love of God has permeated all relationships and creative work. The quality here is as high as it gets, for all the efficiency in receiving from the divine has been matched by an equal efficiency in giving back to the divine as well. This is a dedicated heart. *INVERTED:* There is an imbalance in what has been received and what has been given. There may be the tendency to over-identify with the source of the love and creative energy.

21 GOVERNED BY THE WORLD: EGO'S FULFILLMENT/EVALUATION
UPRIGHT: There is a legacy of inspired work, teachings in the mystic sense, of knowledge beyond knowledge. The ego is fully aware that it has fulfilled the karmic purpose of this lifetime. *INVERTED:* There may be a sense of incompletion, perhaps justified, perhaps not. This sense of less than perfection may derive from a mis-application of the mind to future karmic purpose in the next lifetime rather than what was actually achieved in fulfillment of this Karmic Contract.

22 GOVERNED BY THE FOOL: SOUL'S FULFILLMENT/EVALUATION
UPRIGHT: The soul celebrates the successful completion of all aspects of the Karmic Contract with ruffles and flourishes. *INVERTED:* The core of the karmic purpose has been achieved, but perhaps without the flourishes.

TWO OF PENTACLES

UPRIGHT: Here is the entrance of "other" at the physical level. The dual aspect of the number two in the Physical/material Plane of the Pentacles gives us first—the recognition of choice, of alternatives, then second— the action in relation to that choice. The search here is for means of growth in terms of physical health and security, work advancement, financial reliability. Evaluation is in terms of physical skills and prowess and contribution to well-being. Sizing up, enjoying the competition, be it business or sports. Probing. Detection. Extroverted, touch-oriented. Hands-on. Active/decisive. Tests of strength, reliability. Ambition. This is the stirring of responsibility in the hunter to provide for the tribe. Good neighbor. Business, material negotiations. Joining. Here even may be the physical aspects of the sex act without the emotional, mental, or spiritual components. Gentlemanly, ladylike. Dexterity, Agility. Flexibility. Physically active. **INVERTED:** Difficulties with physical choices or competitive situations. Enjoining the battle, as opposed to seeking a solution. Confrontation replaces competition. Your winning requires someone else lose, or vice versa. Physical impotence, a lack of means, of choice in the matter. Too good a neighbor on one extreme, or not at all a good neighbor on the other. Intrusive, nosy. Rude. Clumsy. Physically less active, indecisive.

In This Spread Position...Interpret the Two Of Pentacles Meanings to Include:

1 GOVERNED BY THE MAGICIAN: PHYSICAL GIVENS, OUT OF THE FATHER
UPRIGHT: Generator of physical alternatives and selection in the Physical/material Plane. Excellent teammate, business partner. Highly competitive, yet fair. Keen awareness of opposition. Good instincts for survival. Dedicated to physical improvement, material advancement. **INVERTED:** Competition everything, an end in itself. May be some masochism or sadism here, over enjoying of the defeat/victory. Machismo.

2 GOVERNED BY THE HIGH PRIESTESS: EMOTIONAL GIVENS. OUT OF THE MOTHER
UPRIGHT: Generator of physical alternatives and selection in the Emotional/creative Plane. Genteel confidant. Creative partner. Pragmatic with emotional issues. Businesslike with creative careers. Combination of athletics and arts is likely, such as dance or gymnastics. **INVERTED:** Physical abilities/disabilities may flavor the lessons of the Emotional Plane. You present a formidable challenge to admirers. On the other hand, your physical package may be less refined and disarming in a completely opposite manner. At the extreme, you could be very difficult to deal with.

3 GOVERNED BY THE EMPRESS: MENTAL GIVENS, INTELLECTUAL PREDISPOSITION
UPRIGHT: Mind weighs all sides of a problem, much as a laboratory scientist or a private investigator. Pragmatic thinker. A hands-on deal maker. Prefer development rather than theorizing from scratch. Good at grass roots operations. **INVERTED:** So capable of managing things, you can manipulate them if desired. Conversely, your mind might simply be uninterested or irresponsible when dealing with the Physical Plane.

4 GOVERNED BY THE EMPEROR: SPIRITUAL GIVENS, LIFE PURPOSE
UPRIGHT: You must foster progress in the affairs of the Physical/material Plane, i.e. health, physical security, work. Your talent in defining choices in these areas will help many people. Whether nutritionist, gym instructor, scientist, or investment broker, you frame options that make decisive growth possible. **INVERTED:** On one extreme, you could be fanatical in these areas and generate problems. Or, you could be remiss about establishing and promoting yourself up to your potential and generate difficulties of an entirely different kind.

5 GOVERNED BY THE HIEROPHANT: SYSTEMS BORN INTO, SOCIETAL INFLUENCE
UPRIGHT: Healthy choice of activities, with good examples set by others. Energetic, not dull. Touch-oriented, open. Good interchange with community. Family productive, finances fluid. **INVERTED:** Not enough activity to generate an ideal set of alternatives, or role models. Perhaps not open, not interactive, not touch-oriented. Maybe shut off from community. Erratic family finances.

6 GOVERNED BY THE LOVERS: EMOTIONAL TAPES, BASIS FOR RELATING/CREATING
UPRIGHT: Passion here is for balance, physical/material balance. To always be alert, on your feet ready to go at a minute's notice to grab the next hook, to be ready when opportunity knocks. To always have what you need, in personal health and resources to manage successfully the next step. To be productive, capable of taking in raw material and turning out a finished product for a profit. **INVERTED:** Desire here is to manipulate the Physical/material Plane rather than to work with it to foster harmony.

7 GOVERNED BY THE CHARIOT: PHYSICAL RESOURCES, MEANS TO ACHIEVE
UPRIGHT: Ability to manage time/materials and keep many balls in the air serves you well. Your combination of physical gifts and ambition is unbeatable. Even when you lose, you don't lose. At times what you do seems like magic to others. You have generated much good will. Good instinctive decisions. **INVERTED:** Not realizing your capacity in the above mentioned has weakened your position. Do not let doubt drain your momentum. Be decisive, act in a timely manner. Do not wait for perfection. Each action can correct/improve the preceding.

8 GOVERNED BY STRENGTH: EMOTIONAL RESOURCES, ENERGY
UPRIGHT: You are in demand as you energize those around you. The speed and efficiency with which you operate generates confidence. Your physical strength and reliability augment your inner core of true strength. You can bring things together to achieve larger ends than would be possible alone. **INVERTED:** Perhaps physical prowess, dexterity, drive have not been your strong point. Until these can be worked on and improved, lean on your present strengths, or if the situation calls for it, realize that you must lean on someone else with these qualities for now.

9 GOVERNED BY THE HERMIT: BELIEF SYSTEM, BASIS FOR DECISIONS
UPRIGHT: The well known "God helps those who help themselves" applies here. This belief structure, while giving thanks for what it already has, is indefatigably working to secure a better material future. It enjoys the idea of work toward reward, and thrives on physical exercise and activity. **INVERTED:** At one extreme, this type believes that one does not, or should not, have to work. They mistakenly believe in a garden of Eden that required no work and in Heavens and Nirvanas that will be paradises of leisure. At the other extreme, this type mistakenly believes that we have to work, but as a result of falling from Eden, as a punishment.

10 GOVERNED BY THE WHEEL OF FORTUNE: CENTRAL MESSAGE, THEME OF READING
UPRIGHT: Accept the challenge. Move outward, forward to add to and strengthen your present position. Increase is possible now but only if you consider

some new options as variations, improvements on what exists now. This is not a major change, rather a continuation with modifications. ***INVERTED:*** Timing is the issue here. To move forward now will require an unnecessary struggle. Better to wait and review possibilities, work on preparations for confrontation as a contingency. Let time be your friend.

11 GOVERNED BY JUSTICE: STATE/CONTENT OF MIND, PLANS
UPRIGHT: You are considering options, in physical/material matters. Or, review of options has already generated a plan. Examine other positions in the spread to see where this idea has come from and to assure its validity for your karmic purposes. ***INVERTED:*** You have not been able to generate or decide among options. Perhaps you do not want movement or merger, or any additional contact at the moment, preferring the status quo. Or, you could have even generated a plan beyond your expectations or needs which is assuming a life of its own.

12 GOVERNED BY THE HANGED MAN: STATE OF EMOTIONS, SUBCONSCIOUS
UPRIGHT: Heart considering material/physical options, ambitious to enrich relationships or to advance a creative project. To enlarge what already exists as opposed to something altogether new. One possibility is the the physical pleasure of sex. Another is the special bond of friendship developed through common effort on a difficult project. ***INVERTED:*** The attempt to achieve growth emotionally through something that is predominantly physical is producing some discomfort, even heartache here. Or, the heart is not enthusiastic about a physical/material option.

13 GOVERNED BY DEATH: PHYSICAL SITUATION, HARD REALITY
UPRIGHT: Whether still considering options or having taken decisive steps, you are enjoying the interaction with new factors/players in one or more aspects of your Physical Plane, i.e. your health, security, work, or finances. Your agreement to get on with it, or to get it on, will be highly productive. ***INVERTED:*** Vacillation, reversal, disorganization. Any or all of these may mark the present or near future situation. The present situation is not productive.

14 GOVERNED BY TEMPERANCE: EMOTIONAL TEST, NEAR FUTURE
UPRIGHT: Here is the impact of physical/material choice/alternatives on the Emotional Plane, on relationships and your creative thrust. ***INVERTED:*** Effect on the emotions of ignoring physical/material alternatives. Sluggishness in any of the Physical Plane activities has a direct cause/effect relationship with the Emotional Plane. You cannot be successful in your relationships or creative work without healthy movement, progress physically.

15 GOVERNED BY THE DEVIL: TEMPTATION/CHALLENGE, FEARS, NEAR FUTURE
UPRIGHT: Physical harmony of opposites takes precedence. Interest in the new, the different, is stirring the pot. An intellectual interest in new physical/material things, i.e. a new diet, a new profession, changing gymnasiums or starting jogging, your first investment in the stock market. ***INVERTED:*** Fear of the opposition, of the physically different, of taking the next physical step, of changing routine. At the extreme, this will be an unwillingness to change anything of consequence in your physical plane.

16 GOVERNED BY THE TOWER: NEXT LESSON, GRACE OF GOD
UPRIGHT: You will find yourself more agile, more ambitious, more flexible than you ever imagined possible. Here is the street juggler mainstreaming in your life path. Look closely at the three cards which follow, at Stage 6 in your reading. All this comes with these newfound talents and extroverted courage. ***INVERTED:*** Use this rebirthing of your innate gifts to balance, to manage your affairs with subtlety for maximum effect in your environment.

17 GOVERNED BY THE STAR: ASPIRATIONS OF EGO, GOALS, MAXIMUM EXPECTATIONS
UPRIGHT: To be physically effective, capable of manipulating to positive effect the Material Plane. To be able to assemble one's own capabilities and unite them with another for greater effect. To dance the dance of hard reality with a light foot. To be the good neighbor. To win and be gracious in victory. ***INVERTED:*** To be a manipulator, in the extreme a con man, to know the opponent well, to gain the unfair advantage, as opposed to a genuine interest in them. To play only to make another lose.

18 GOVERNED BY THE MOON: ASPIRATIONS OF HEART, COMPASSION
UPRIGHT: To recognize potential pairings in the Physical Plane and help them materialize. To be effective, meaningful in the most basic of senses. Heart's compulsion to identify suitable additions to your present core of being and unite with them. ***INVERTED:*** There may be an over enthusiasm for alternatives, or a desire for alternatives in themselves as opposed to fresh additions to what you already are.

19 GOVERNED BY THE SUN: MATERIAL FULFILLMENT/EVALUATION
UPRIGHT: Active and capable of playing the game until the very end. There is no hint of slowing down, much less any infirmity here. You remain productive throughout your lifetime. Confidence and courage to experiment with new activities prevails. ***INVERTED:*** On the one hand, you may try to overplay, to do much more than is necessary, as if to prove that you still can. On the other hand, you may slow down much more than you need to, or than is appropriate for your Karmic Contract, because you think that is what older people should do.

20 GOVERNED BY JUDGEMENT: HEART'S FULFILLMENT/EVALUATION
UPRIGHT: Your remaining vibrant and active throughout your life has enabled you to profit from all your relationships and they from you. The Emotional Plane has profited from your pragmatic, hard-working sensibility. ***INVERTED:*** You may have been, or some may have felt you to have been, too assertive, too competitive, too intrusive. Work now to integrate the lessons presented in this reading to avoid these conclusions. Examine your actions, they may be inappropriate applications of rather proper motivations. Don't allow yourself to be misunderstood.

21 GOVERNED BY THE WORLD: EGO'S FULFILLMENT/EVALUATION
UPRIGHT: You have been not only a self-starter and tireless worker, but a catalyst in the affairs of others. Others will remember you as the perfect partner, the ideal teammate, and the formidable opponent. Whether your expertise was in business, health, athletics, or another of the many disciplines of the Physical/material Plane, your mark was in your youthful vigor and freshness. ***INVERTED:*** You may not grade yourself as highly as others will, but this tendency to underrate yourself exists now and can be corrected.

22 GOVERNED BY THE FOOL: SOUL'S FULFILLMENT/EVALUATION
UPRIGHT: Ambition has served you well in this lifetime. Both personal and universal goals have been satisfied thanks to your untiring body and healthy approach to life. Your inborn instincts for survival have blended well with daily intuition to give you an exciting and rich experience, benefiting all who knew you as well. ***INVERTED:*** The aforementioned is the direction in which you are headed and the realization of your potential. Listen now to the messages that will help you get there.

TWO OF CUPS

UPRIGHT: Here is the entrance of "other" at the emotional level. The dual aspect of the number two in the emotional plane of the Cups gives us first the recognition of choice, of alternatives, then second it gives the action in relation to that choice. So it is we see Sex, Passion, Love, Proposals but also Engagement, Marriage and Partnership. Harmony of opposites. One-to-one relationships. Reconciliation. Cooperation. The willingness, the ability, to experience give and take. Consideration of extensions of the self. In the creative process, here is the recognition of the talent as an aspect of the self, yet something bigger than the self as well, and from which a relationship will develop just as one person with another. **INVERTED:** Difficulty with either recognition of an emotional choice, or with identifying and partnering with that choice to make a fertile relationship. At the extreme there may be blockage preventing a beneficial merger, hindering a creative process, or slowing the development of a talent. Divorce. Or, the blockage of divorce in a relationship detracting from rather than adding to your emotional energy and creative resources. Infertility, sexual or creative. Or, there may be an inappropriate forcing of a talent or relationship. Marriage of convenience. Bigamy.

In This Spread Position...Interpret the Two Of Cups Meanings to Include:

1 GOVERNED BY THE MAGICIAN: PHYSICAL GIVENS, OUT OF THE FATHER
UPRIGHT: Generator of emotional/creative alternatives in the physical/material plane; also the merging of those alternatives. A deal maker. Excellent at one-on-one, be it romance, conversation, business, or games. A good mate. Seeker of appropriate challenge, opportunity. Good with healthy compromise, cooperation, in physical matters. **INVERTED:** Perhaps too good a mate, making too many deals with too many people. (Extreme examples include the bigamist and the con man.) Or, the opposite of not being that good a mate.

2 GOVERNED BY THE HIGH PRIESTESS: EMOTIONAL GIVENS, OUT OF THE MOTHER
UPRIGHT: Generator of emotional/creative alternatives; also the merging of those alternatives. A matchmaker. Born to be a good mate and an excellent lover. Longevity in relationships aided by creativity, loyalty, and devotion. Innate understanding of give and take at the emotional level. **INVERTED:** Could generate more than enough alternatives making choices difficult. May be a life requiring a number of one-on-one relationships, as opposed to one life-long mate. A matchbreaker. Either give or take may be predominant instinct, requiring balance through lessons in life. One-on-one relationships present a challenge.

3 GOVERNED BY THE EMPRESS: MENTAL GIVENS, INTELLECTUAL PREDISPOSITION
UPRIGHT: Mind understands innately the nature of relationships and merger, and is at home in the world of challenge and compromise, of give and take. Mind set to maximize the effectiveness of love, marriage, and commitment to an "other." Knowledgable about relationships and the creative process, with an ability to write, to act, to teach in these areas. This could well be the mark of the poet, the songwriter. **INVERTED:** Complete innocence, naivete in one-on-one relationships, from onset through commitment. The mind may be given partial blinders as regards relationships and the creative process in order to maximize the role of the so-called right brain in these matters. Such is the life, for example, of the gut-reactive artist. Predisposed to being totally emersed in marriage, or, to being single for life.

4 GOVERNED BY THE EMPEROR: SPIRITUAL GIVENS, LIFE PURPOSE
UPRIGHT: Life's lessons will filter through the lens of emotional and creative choice, and commitment. Personal expansion through partnering and/or development of your special gifts must take precedence in all that you do. **INVERTED:** The above requirements may be very strong. Or, the karmic purpose will be to sort through the difficulties of emotional/creative choice and dedication. Assist in keeping love bonds strong and productive rather than destructive.

5 GOVERNED BY THE HIEROPHANT: SYSTEMS BORN INTO, SOCIETAL INFLUENCE
UPRIGHT: Healthy observation of affection between adults. Learned the importance of closeness, of caring and touching. Talents of individuals in such an environment were nurtured and encouraged. **INVERTED:** An inappropriate amount or type of affection on display as the norm. Or, a lack of healthy interaction, even puritanical restrictions. Creativity may have been neglected or discouraged. One-on-one relationships seen as counterproductive, limiting rather than expansive.

6 GOVERNED BY THE LOVERS: EMOTIONAL TAPES, BASIS FOR RELATING/CREATING
UPRIGHT: True love, romance, life parnership/marriage are the driving images of your emotions. Nothing is more important to your heart. This is the program for your subconscious. **INVERTED:** At the extreme, these images may be too ideal of too fixed. Or, they may be faulty in some other regard, including being dominant yet weak models on which to build.

7 GOVERNED BY THE CHARIOT: PHYSICAL RESOURCES, MEANS TO ACHIEVE
UPRIGHT: Your marriage may be a true partnership; you may even be in business together. Your ability one-on-one is your strongest asset, the kingpin in what you are building. Healthy understanding of compromise in material matters. **INVERTED:** Too much or too little of the above. For example: A divorce or problems in marriage may be undermining your health or career. Or, the opposite, too much attention and time involvement in your marriage or love partner may be hurting your work. An unhealthy pairing.

8 GOVERNED BY STRENGTH: EMOTIONAL RESOURCES, ENERGY
UPRIGHT: Your marriage, one-one-one relationships energize and motivate you. Your expertise at give and take make you invincible. **INVERTED:** Perhaps you enjoy the problems of love to generate the pleasure or making up. Or, your relationships or creative endeavors drain, rather than energize, you as they should. Give and take may be in proper amounts, but not in proper phase.

9 GOVERNED BY THE HERMIT: BELIEF SYSTEM, BASIS FOR DECISIONS
UPRIGHT: Life to you is a dance that we must attend and enjoy, and for maximum pleasure, indeed to achieve our true purpose, we must seek out and find the mate fate is impatient to deliver to us. We must learn to love our opposite. **INVERTED:** In merging with your opposite, you may have compromised too much, or too little for the purposes you think you are attending to. Or, you may object to the idea of the dance and in particular the idea of one fated partner all together.

10 GOVERNED BY THE WHEEL OF FORTUNE : CENTRAL MESSAGE, THEME OF READING
UPRIGHT: Time for selection and commitment. Harmony of opposites. Emotional choice is at hand. Act now in support of your most important relationship.
INVERTED: Permanence or condition of major relationship may be changing, may even need to change, or..it may be too strong and actually interfering with some other aspect which needs attention. You cannot live for a relationship alone, at the expense of all other people or issues.

11 GOVERNED BY JUSTICE: STATE/CONTENT OF MIND, PLANS
UPRIGHT: Sexual union. Engagement, Marriage on your mind. Either the search for the right candidate or formalizing of your relationship if already found. Evaluating what you are giving up for what you are getting; what you are leaving behind and what is ahead. *INVERTED:* Realize ineffectiveness, or over effectiveness, of your love match. Separation or divorce may be planned. Reconciliation under consideration if there has already been separation. May be putting much too much emphasis on your partnership, taking time and energy properly spent on additional things. Or, it could be the opposite of not enough emphasis. Could be against the idea of union altogether and strategizing how to avoid it.

12 GOVERNED BY THE HANGED MAN: STATE OF EMOTIONS, SUBCONSCIOUS
UPRIGHT: In your heart you desire to find your true love. If already found, to cement the bond between you. This can range from the desire for sex the first time together to wanting to get married. *INVERTED:* Much of the above interpretation for position 11 translates from the realm of the mind to the heart here. There may be a broken heart, or a foolishly infatuated one in the wrong situation.

13 GOVERNED BY DEATH: PHYSICAL SITUATION, HARD REALITY
UPRIGHT: Sexual relationship of importance. Serious courtship and/or action undertaken to bring about plans for engagement or marriage in the present or near future. *INVERTED:* On the one hand, going overboard on courtship or marriage. On the other hand, not doing enough of the right things. And possibly, ending of any of the above, including divorce. Relationship not working in its present form, or because of incorrect match.

14 GOVERNED BY TEMPERANCE: EMOTIONAL TEST, NEAR FUTURE
UPRIGHT: Here is the impact on the heart of formalizing your deepest felt relationship on that relationship itself and that of all your other relationships, as well as your creative processes. Here is the impact of difficulties with, or the ending of, your most heartfelt love. Remember that this love may not be another person; it may well be a special talent you are meant to foster. It can be anything from any of the four Planes. *INVERTED:* The impact may be from too much or too little in the above. This includes ending a relationship.

15 GOVERNED BY THE DEVIL: TEMPTATION/CHALLENGE, FEARS, NEAR FUTURE
UPRIGHT: Sexual, emotional harmony of opposites takes precedence in the mental arena. Strong recognition, formalization of relationship necessary before beliefs, long-term plans can go further. *INVERTED:* If married, for example, you must either take your present relationship much further than heretofore, in a new direction...or, you must back away from it altogether. You might fear formal commitment, or one-on-one altogether. Or, you might like the outer formality of marriage all too much, as a cover or protection, without inner commitment.

16 GOVERNED BY THE TOWER: NEXT LESSON, GRACE OF GOD
UPRIGHT: Ready or not, here comes the relationship you have been programming for. Marriage, in whatever form appropriate for you, will be the appropriate move by this time next year at the latest. *INVERTED:* Radical change in, or the ending of, a formal relationship will be best if you want to honor your beliefs and realize your goals. Careful here; the divorce in question may be the one you have with an internal creative program that is not your main talent.

17 GOVERNED BY THE STAR: ASPIRATIONS OF THE EGO, GOALS, MAXIMUM EXPECTATIONS
UPRIGHT: Your master plan is centered around achieving a bedrock relationship on which to build. You see it as both the means and the ends of what you wish to achieve, to leave behind. To bring hearts together intellectually. *INVERTED:* You may be placing an inordinate burden on what such a relationship can provide. Particularly inappropriate would be the goal of using an apparent alliance of the heart to advance yourself materially or politically.

18 GOVERNED BY THE MOON: ASPIRATIONS OF THE HEART, COMPASSION
UPRIGHT: The heart is intent on achieving the ideal relationship, but not in a selfish sense, in the proper sense that mating with a true, intended karmic partner, provides the soul with a micro laboratory for reflecting the macro world of universal love. Such mating magnifies your ability to enjoin the game of give and take, thereby enlarging the emotional pie. *INVERTED*: A misunderstanding of soul mates and the demands and responsibilities of such intense and selfless love.

19 GOVERNED BY THE SUN: MATERIAL FULFILLMENT/EVALUATION
UPRIGHT: True partner/marriage late in life. Reconciliation if previously estranged. Easy, rewarding give and take with important people of your life. May well consider your partner in love/marriage as your greatest physical achievement. *INVERTED:* Possible estrangement or divorce late in life. Too much, or too little, credit placed on the impact of emotional partnership in life. Relationships may be hard to handle, or not given enough physical attention, enough time.

20 GOVERNED BY JUDGEMENT: HEART'S FULFILLMENT/EVALUATION
UPRIGHT: Partner/marriage the key to resolution of, and to lessons learned from, all relationships, and the lynch pin in creativity. This was the source of your drive and energy. *INVERTED:* Late in life you may be still learning these lessons, working with forgiveness of yourself and others in your principal relationship(s). Harmony with opposites still not achieved; prejudice may still intrude.

21 GOVERNED BY THE WORLD: EGO'S FULFILLMENT/EVALUATION
UPRIGHT: Emotional pairing, ability in intimate relationships, be they sexual or platonic, is the hallmark of your mental achievement and your legacy. *INVERTED:* Could make your mark as the nemesis, the thorn in the side, of cooperation, compromise, and emotional harmony. Perhaps a reputation for nipping the bud of creativity. Or, you may be almost too good at matchmaking.

22/0 GOVERNED BY THE FOOL: SOUL'S FULFILLMENT/EVALUTAION
UPRIGHT: Achievement of a productive coupling, a marriage of happy souls. A successful search for a love outside of yourself to stir the creative juices and enlarge the soul. A life of dedicated service in the cause of harmony of opposites . *INVERTED:* In order to achieve the desired ends of the above, listen intently to the lessons advanced in the reading.

TWO OF SWORDS

UPRIGHT: Here is the entrance of "other" at the mental level; the Antithesis to the Thesis of the Ace of Swords. The dual aspect of the number two in the Mental Plane of the Swords gives us first the recognition of an alternative, then second it gives the action in relation to that choice—decision. Devil's advocacy, the desire and ability to identify and understand the other side. Arbitration, debate. Defining position/opposition. Objectivity. A second opinion. Reviews/critiques. Negotiation. Compromise. Truce. Compatibility. Contracts. Tact, diplomacy. To agree, to unite mentally. **INVERTED:** To divide mentally. Any of the above mentioned in too great or too little amounts. Either of the extremes in these matters will block mental resolution and progress. Mental impasse, indecision. Mind may be unclear for one reason or another, including the intrusion of the lower emotions. Argumentative. Problem with investigative process, with definition of alternatives, over or under the mark. Overly cautious or the opposite, careless. Looking at wrong thing. The agreement/compromise may not be a good one. Being totally for or against the other position. Opinionated, prejudiced, non-objective. Adoption of other view in violation of previous personal/group beliefs (i.e. traitor). Prosecution. To disagree, to divide mentally. To distort, to bring confusion. Vacillation.

In This Spread Position...Interpret the Two Of Swords Meanings to Include:

1 GOVERNED BY THE MAGICIAN: PHYSICAL GIVENS, OUT OF THE FATHER
UPRIGHT: Generator, identifier of mental alternatives in the Physical/material Plane. Deal maker. Peacemaker. Business, military strategist. **INVERTED:** You may be tempted to look for, or sympathize with, the other view more than necessary. Or, the reverse, you may not consider the other side often enough. Also, you may be either exceptionally good at making deals, or, this may not be one of your stronger points. If exceptionally good, you must work not to take advantage of your opponents.

2 GOVERNED BY THE HIGH PRIESTESS: EMOTIONAL GIVENS, OUT OF THE MOTHER
UPRIGHT: Generator, identifier of mental alternatives in the Emotional/creative Plane. Innate ability to arbitrate emotional matters, to see the pros and the cons of relationships. Ability to distance oneself from the heat of the matter, to be truly objective. **INVERTED:** There could be a tendency to meddle in the personal affairs of your partners or in the affairs of other relationships. Or, the opposite, that you will tend to sweep even the obvious under the rug.

3 GOVERNED BY THE EMPRESS: MENTAL GIVENS, INTELLECTUAL PREDISPOSITION
UPRIGHT: The mind's role is to divide in order to understand, whereas the emotion's role is to unite. Your mind is dedicated to the principal of "divide in order to unite." Good powers of observation, discernment. Knack for negotiation. Mentally adventurous. Healthy curiosity. The natural born critic. **INVERTED:** Overly cautious in mental matters on the one hand; careless on the other. Penchant for turning over too many stones, or, not turning over enough. Skepticism and doubt. Mind may be blindfolded in relation to certain things to focus those lessons onto the other planes. Argumentative.

4 GOVERNED BY THE EMPEROR: SPIRITUAL GIVENS, LIFE PURPOSE
UPRIGHT: Life's lessons will filter through the lens of mental choice and commitment, defining choice and facilitating commitment. Personal expansion will principally involve mergers and partnerships on the Mental Plane. **INVERTED:** Objectivity, mental fairness, open-mindedness may be the contents of your crucible. These have been hard for you in the past.

5 GOVERNED BY THE HIEROPHANT: SYSTEMS BORN INTO, SOCIETAL INFLUENCE
UPRIGHT: A world of open-minded intellectual curiosity. Healthy entertainment of alternative viewpoints and positive debate. Mother/Father, or other principal actors in your environment, from highly different backgrounds, ideologies. **INVERTED:** A "grass is greener on the other side of the fence" attitude may have existed. A contentious setting. Beliefs locked and fostering pre-judgement. Self-righteousness..

6 GOVERNED BY THE LOVERS: EMOTIONAL TAPES, BASIS FOR RELATING/CREATING
UPRIGHT: Passion for the open forum, the consideration/inclusion of all views, the democracy of the mind. Thirst for positive debate. **INVERTED:** At one extreme, an envy of the "other" viewpoint, even another entirely different culture; at the other extreme, a bias toward the position of "self" even to the rejection, suppression of another person or culture. Love of one's own ideas above and to the exclusion of all others.

7 GOVERNED BY THE CHARIOT: PHYSICAL RESOURCES, MEANS TO ACHIEVE
UPRIGHT: Healthy agreements, liaisons, contracts. Knack for knowing your opponent. Ability to negotiate, to find the desirable compromise. **INVERTED:** May either be bogged down with agreements and conditions and knowing the opposition, or, you may not be sufficient in these matters. Inability to compromise versus the pitfall of over-compromise.

8 GOVERNED BY STRENGTH: EMOTIONAL RESOURCES, ENERGY
UPRIGHT: You draw great strength from your ability to project into the mind of your object of attention. It magnifies your personal, in some cases romantic, relationships. Once there, you feel their position as your own. (This may end up in the Moon.) This mental objectivity stiffens your emotional resolve and clarifies your motives. **INVERTED:** You don't want to be more preoccupied with the position of "other" at the expense of understanding "self." And certainly, you are not made stronger if you wish to understand the "other" in order to bend it to your desires.

9 GOVERNED BY THE HERMIT: BELIEF SYSTEM, BASIS FOR DECISIONS
UPRIGHT: Life is a scavenger hunt for the bits and pieces of universal truth permeating our world. Ours is but to find and acknowledge. Here we believe in the continuing process of identifying and uniting, bit by bit. Here, put into action, is the philosopher Heraclitus' observation that we cannot step into the same river twice. **INVERTED:** At one extreme, we are over concerned with finding the "other" pieces and neglect our own. At the other, we are much too concerned with our pieces and neglect the "other's." Here there is little confidence in compromise. When there is interest at all in the "other" it will be some variety of identify and conquer.

10 GOVERNED BY THE WHEEL OF FORTUNE: CENTRAL MESSAGE, THEME OF READING
UPRIGHT: Identify and understand the other side. Mental opportunity. All is ready, decide. Agreement is at hand. **INVERTED:** Be neither too cautious or

careless in the arrangements at hand. There is good reason for another look at the question. There may be neither enough information at hand, nor the correct information. Be thorough in getting all the facts. Do not ignore the input, overtures of others. This is a time to disagree if you have the slightest hesitation.

11 GOVERNED BY JUSTICE: STATE/CONTENT OF MIND, PLANS

UPRIGHT: Dissatisfaction with the status quo; clarifying alternatives. Mental engagement. Agreement with a proposal. See necessity of moving beyond present viewpoint, of the potential of integrating the ideas of an "other." Contract negotiations/signing. *INVERTED:* Either disagreement, or over agreement. Mental avoidance. Inability to define choices, or if choices clear, then inability to make a decision. Preference for the status quo, even though you know it isn't working. Possibly too bound up with formal agreements, or the reverse, need more structure, reliability than now exists.

12 GOVERNED BY THE HANGED MAN: STATE OF EMOTIONS, SUBCONSCIOUS

UPRIGHT: Heart open to other views, ideologies. More so from your gut or your subconscious than your mind. Feeling, empathizing with the "other," in some cases an adversary. *INVERTED:* At the extreme, on the one hand we see the feeling for the opposition make us leave our base of operation all together - the dilemma of the traitor, the double spy for example. On the other hand is the callous non-feeling for the position of the opposition.

13 GOVERNED BY DEATH: PHYSICAL SITUATION, HARD REALITY

UPRIGHT: The items described in positions 10, 11, and 12 are in the Physical Plane now or in the near future. Your future is unfolding through this mental clarification. *INVERTED:* Important to review the reversed interpretations for the cards in positions 10, 11, and 12, in order to free the Physical Plane from the grips of the mind.

14 GOVERNED BY TEMPERANCE: EMOTIONAL TEST, NEAR FUTURE

UPRIGHT: Impact of mental alternatives/agreement on the Emotional Plane, on relationships and your creative thrust. *INVERTED:* Effect on the emotions of ignoring mental alternatives. It isn't uncommon for our consideration of the "other" mentally to be taken as a flirtation, an emotional involvement, and be difficult for our personal partners to accommodate. Many men's preoccupation with sports as source of aggravation for their mates is a simple example, as is many women's preoccupation with talking with their friends aggravating to their mates.

15 GOVERNED BY THE DEVIL: TEMPTATION/CHALLENGE, FEARS, NEAR FUTURE

UPRIGHT: Mental harmony of opposites takes precedence. Interest in others' ideas. Critique for improvement purposes. Important to see and internalize the good aspects of the opposition for our purposes. A shoring up of the gaps in our ideology, in our plans, of integrating the shadow side. Refining your position. *INVERTED:* Doubt where unnecessary, unproductive. Fomenting chaos. Criticism for destructive purposes, over-critical. Ignoring alternatives. Beware of bias, self-righteousness, hard-headedness. Fear of new ideas. Mental complacency.

16 GOVERNED BY THE TOWER: NEXT LESSON, GRACE OF GOD

UPRIGHT: The other side asserts itself, alternatives become patently clear where they may have been hard to determine. A breakthrough in negotiations. Healthy compromise. *INVERTED:* This breakthrough to a new position may be very hard work on both sides, perhaps requiring considerable accommodation by one or both parties, but it will come. Conversely, it could be much easier than anyone might expect, producing surprising results.

17 GOVERNED BY THE STAR: ASPIRATIONS OF EGO, GOALS, MAXIMUM EXPECTATIONS

UPRIGHT: To always seek a better answer. A healthy discontent with the status quo. Here is the eternal child with her eternal question, "Why?" To bring minds together, mental partnership. To increase order, discipline in the world. *INVERTED:* An unhealthy discontent with the status quo. Change merely for change's sake, suggesting there is no position on which to build, or that there is complete rejection of the present belief system. Look closely at the card in position 9. A penchant for confusion rather than clarity. Discipline as means of control.

18 GOVERNED BY THE MOON: ASPIRATIONS OF HEART, COMPASSION

UPRIGHT: To be the peacemaker. To bring minds together with the practice of love. Literally to engage minds. Perhaps this is Star Trek's "mind-meld of Dr. Spock." *INVERTED:* An inappropriate desire to read others' minds. The mistaken desire to be on the other side of the veil, or worse to be the other side.

19 GOVERNED BY THE SUN: MATERIAL FULFILLMENT/EVALUATION

UPRIGHT: Major mental breakthroughs late in life. Lasting, functional appreciation of the need to stay fresh with new ideas even in your sunset years. The secret of the fountain of youth is to drink change with enthusiasm. A healthy break with tradition. *INVERTED:* Too much change for change sake often being careless, or the opposite of being overly cautious and not changing when it was prudent. An unhealthy break with tradition, or an extrapolation of an old tradition to new extremes.

20 GOVERNED BY JUDGEMENT: HEART'S FULFILLMENT/EVALUATION

UPRIGHT: The ability to see the view of the "other" has enriched your creative path and all of your relationships. The thrill of converting a onetime adversary to a friend, a loved one is indescribable. It encourages us to make peace with our polar inner opposite—for a man his inner female; for a woman her inner male. *INVERTED:* The heart has tasted and yet not served up this feast of mental merging.

21 GOVERNED BY THE WORLD: EGO'S FULFILLMENT/EVALUATION

UPRIGHT: Your mental legacy is in the nature of the healthy critique, of being discriminating without being incriminating, of judging without prejudice, of defining the opposition without opposing, of compromising without being compromised, of actually being able to improve on an original. *INVERTED:* There may well have been some difficulty with the aforementioned, or you may have perfected these matters to a fine art.

22/0 GOVERNED BY THE FOOL: SOUL'S FULFILLMENT/EVALUATION

UPRIGHT: Here is a soul that was fully responsive to life, accepting new lessons, integrating them into the old, in the everchanging partnership of ideas that transforms the world, the universe instant by instant. *INVERTED:* The lessons brought through the other positions in this reading will allow you to inscribe the above mentioned as your true epitaph.

TWO OF WANDS

UPRIGHT: Here is spiritual curiosity, wonder leading to choice, choice leading to more wonder. Alternatives for growth, a selection of potentialities, the entrance of "other" at the intuitive level. The dual aspect of the number two in the Spiritual Plane of the Wands gives us first—recognition of choice, of alternatives, then second—it gives the action in relation to that choice. Here is quality discernment. The world is calling you, infusing a spirit of adventure to see firsthand what wonders await. The potential for true growth, real opportunity. Having realized the physical reality of the spiritual path, you have been offered and have accepted the mantel of initiate. Through this door you will never return. As indicator of your initiation, the Ace of Wands is your vow to take a vow, dedicating yourself to the path. The Two of Wands is the vow itself, through which you become a groom/bride of the divine. Just as you must "mate" on the Physical, Emotional, and Mental levels, so must you choose and "mate" on the Spiritual level as well. Oaths. Pledges. **INVERTED:** There may be difficulty in taking this step, in understanding its implications, in choosing the correct discipline for yourself. There may be many choices competing for your dedication, or it may be hard clarifying a choice already made. Some of what beckons you must be regarded with care, much as with the calls of sirens at sea. Pursue your visions with a discerning eye, ever cautious that the discernment dual not deteriorate into discrimination.

In This Spread Position...Interpret the Two Of Wands Meanings to Include:

1 GOVERNED BY THE MAGICIAN: PHYSICAL GIVENS, OUT OF THE FATHER
UPRIGHT: Generator of spiritual/intuitive alternatives in the Physical/material Plane; also the merging of those alternatives. Excellent traveling companion. Highest standards in one-on-one negotiations, in competition. Keen spiritual awareness in the material world. Reliable instincts. Body chooses wisely. Dedication to God through the father. **INVERTED:** Less than perfect traveling companion. May be tested often whether you can take the high road. Use your intuitive abilities for the mutual advantage of yourself and others for win/win solutions rather than win/lose.

2 GOVERNED BY THE HIGH PRIESTESS: EMOTIONAL GIVENS, OUT OF THE MOTHER
UPRIGHT: Generator of spiritual/intuitive alternatives in the Emotional/creative Plane; also the merging of those alternatives. Companion with whom people can share their deepest, most heartfelt secrets. Highest standards of fidelity—a perfect mate, friend. You bring the noblest motivations to your creativity. Heart is dedicated to healthy choices, and you have the ability to choose well. Dedication to God through the mother. **INVERTED:** Either too good for your own good in these matters, or you may feel that you do not meet your own standards.

3 GOVERNED BY THE EMPRESS: MENTAL GIVENS, INTELLECTUAL PREDISPOSITION
UPRIGHT: The mind understands innately the balance between the Will of God and the Will of Man, the marriage of the outer and inner aspects of the Divine. You will be actively a student and teacher of the architecture of spirituality, of metaphysics. A mind is married to God. **INVERTED:** The life path may be intensely spiritually intellectual, and take harsh ascetic alternatives. Or, it may be the complete opposite wherein the inner path is devoted but not obvious to an outside observer.

4 GOVERNED BY THE EMPEROR: SPIRITUAL GIVENS, LIFE PURPOSE
UPRIGHT: Lifetime will involve a conscious selection from spiritual path alternatives, with the ability to help others travel with and behind you as your movements will be open and obvious, although they may be subtle. Your disciplines and observations in which you participate with the Divine will most likely be shared by others. **INVERTED:** On one extreme, this path will be very public and derive its tests of steadfastness and accuracy from those pressures. On the other extreme, there will be a necessity for a more private, perhaps lonely, path.

5 GOVERNED BY THE HIEROPHANT: SYSTEMS BORN INTO, SOCIETAL INFLUENCE
UPRIGHT: This early environment was a fertile field for self-discovery at an early age. Your awareness, not of religion, but of the true spirituality, the relationship of self to the Divine, of the inner to the outer God may have actually begun in childhood in this setting before puberty . **INVERTED:** In some cases, this suggests that one is swept up in the swirl of spiritual exercises of others, of elders, while being relatively oblivious ourselves. In other cases, this may suggest an inappropriateness of this form of seeking, of this path, for the readee.

6 GOVERNED BY STRENGTH: EMOTIONAL TAPES, BASIS FOR RELATING/CREATING
UPRIGHT: Passion here is for the path itself with its myriad choices, for what the journey brings the moment it is engaged—a passion that surpasses all other loves. But, this love does not crowd out other loves. It requires the opposite, a multi-faceted experience of personal and universal love. **INVERTED:** Passion for path misleads some to reject an inclusive emotional approach. Another extreme is excess of passion for the path itself, evinced in excessive ritual or asceticism. Sometimes this passion is a rejection of a given path with which they have had an unpleasant contact.

7 GOVERNED BY THE CHARIOT: PHYSICAL RESOURCES, MEANS TO ACHIEVE
UPRIGHT: Your ability to see the gates open, and chose the correct one, makes for efficient worldly progress. Your sensitivity to your Karmic Contract brings you the supplies needed to build your material world. Spiritual commitment has enhanced your material progress. **INVERTED:** There is still some confusion as to what you have committed to. Impact of spiritual commitments not fully taken advantage of. Clarify your spiritual marriage before laying more bricks. Some problem with the mechanics, the physical observations, rituals, and such related to your path.

8 GOVERNED BY STRENGTH: EMOTIONAL RESOURCES, ENERGY
UPRIGHT: You are fully motivated by your higher emotions and spiritual goals. Energy will be available for anything you need to do. Your powers of discernment and correct decision making have secured you a host of productive relationships on which you can rely. You are well-balanced in giving and taking. **INVERTED:** Harness this energy. Let it remain passive, to be drawn upon as needed by projects coordinated by higher mind rather than initiated in the lower emotions.

9 GOVERNED BY THE HERMIT: BELIEF SYSTEM, BASIS FOR DECISIONS
UPRIGHT: Identify your source and make it your goal, in effect observing a marriage between beginning and end. You believe in the grandest adventure of all, the supreme merger of self and "other," the observation and then dissolution of duality at the spiritual level. You believe in the sanctity of the initiate's vow in this process as the key to its success. This is your objective awareness of the steps taken by your soul. **INVERTED:** This "seriousness" must never become an end in itself. The process should not distort the path. In some cases, this will be a rejection of the principal of the path, but in such a way that that rejection itself becomes the belief system on which the readee is building.

10 GOVERNED BY THE WHEEL OF FORTUNE: CENTRAL MESSAGE, THEME OF READING

UPRIGHT: Yield to your sense of wonder and spiritual alternatives will become very clear. The disciplines, forms of practice and observation, are presenting themselves for review. Your guides will speak very clearly now. Take an oath. ***INVERTED:*** If this fork in your path seems radical, take the time you need and avail yourself of offered guidance to integrate the necessary changes into your habits. If, on the other hand, this fork is very subtle, do not misinterpret the subtlety for less importance. Minor adjustments are sometimes much harder to achieve than major ones.

11 GOVERNED BY JUSTICE: STATE/CONTENT OF MIND, PLANS

UPRIGHT: The mind begins to recognize itself in the "other." A conscious decision to seek further knowledge, a hunger for the wisdom that comes with closer union with God, the very same wisdom that requires a deeper understanding of self. This choice places spiritual matters at the pragmatic forefront of your mental processes and shapes all decisions from this point on. Raising the standards of your priorities to the highest levels. ***INVERTED:*** This conscious decision has not been made in its final form. Perhaps it is even being delayed for some reason.

12 GOVERNED BY THE HANGED MAN: STATE OF EMOTIONS, SUBCONSCIOUS

UPRIGHT: The heart begins to recognize itself in the "other." This is where the "self" falls in love with the "Self." Your greatest desire now is to taste the thrill of the journey. ***INVERTED:*** On the one hand, subconsciously you may want this to take place, but it simply hasn't kicked in yet. On the other hand, it may have kicked in and taken over. The heart must use this feeling, not lose itself in it.

13 GOVERNED BY DEATH: PHYSICAL SITUATION, HARD REALITY

UPRIGHT: Content as you are with the now, nevertheless you approach every moment as an opportunity not to be missed. The promises being made now are promises made to yourself, but they may take the form of pledges to anyone/anything you admire. ***INVERTED:*** The quality of your discernment is in question. The disciplines appealing to you may be false mirrors, and you may be dedicating yourself to someone else's path, not yours. Inability to make a pledge, or breaking one already made. Also, this can be the keeping of an improper or outdated oath.

14 GOVERNED BY TEMPERANCE: EMOTIONAL TEST, NEAR FUTURE

UPRIGHT: As you move toward the center in your Spiritual Plane, your relationships and creative activities in your Emotional Plane will be pulled into line as well. While all of this centering is positive, it generates change which must be accommodated. ***INVERTED:*** The number and/or intensity of these types of changes may be considerable.

15 GOVERNED BY THE DEVIL: TEMPTATION/CHALLENGE, FEARS, NEAR FUTURE

UPRIGHT: You are pulled toward your true destiny by your Karmic Contract. This next year you must make major commitments to honor and reclaim as an adult that sense of mystery and awe that was natural in you as a child. ***INVERTED:*** Work hard to overcome your apprehension of taking the wrong step, of making the wrong pledge. You are signing up for the pleasure of the voyage, not its destination.

16 GOVERNED BY THE TOWER: NEXT LESSON, GRACE OF GOD

UPRIGHT: You have completed your novitiate and will be exposed to deeper lessons; greater demands will be made. Remember you have signed up for greater knowledge/responsibility. You are expanding through the magic of identification. A spiritual engagement/marriage. ***INVERTED:*** You should remain with your present group a while longer. Either you are not yet ready for your intended projects, or they are not yet ready for you. Listen closely for verification as to whether you are aspiring to the right disciplines, the correct path for you. A spiritual separation.

17 GOVERNED BY THE STAR: ASPIRATIONS OF EGO, GOALS, MAXIMUM EXPECTATIONS

UPRIGHT: To be able to hear and respond to the call. To be drawn to a worthy cause and truly dedicated to its success. To be a resolute seeker, a full-time, perhaps professional seeker—of knowledge, of wisdom. To be a spiritual partner. ***INVERTED:*** There are aspects of this goal which can be clarified and improved upon. Remember that progress at the spiritual level requires commensurate dedication and attention to detail at the mental, emotional and physical levels.

18 GOVERNED BY THE MOON: ASPIRATIONS OF HEART, COMPASSION

UPRIGHT: To become immersed in the spiritual expansion process, wherein the sum does truly exceed the total of its parts. To be a devoted seeker of the higher lessons of love. To help spread the unity of love inherent in spiritual wisdom. To fall in love, to unite spiritually. To help others to take this important step on their path. ***INVERTED:*** Remember that this is part of the means, not the end in itself.

19 GOVERNED BY THE SUN: MATERIAL FULFILLMENT/EVALUATION

UPRIGHT: Full embracement of the physical reality of the spiritual path permeates your material achievements. This is called by some "witnessing," by others, "walking your talk." In personal one-on-one relationships there is the unmistakable sense of rightness and depth of shared experience. ***INVERTED:*** None of your satisfaction with having broken through into this level of awareness should allow discernment to deteriorate into discrimination, i.e. feelings of superiority. In some cases this may indicate the rejection, or break of a spiritual union.

20 GOVERNED BY JUDGEMENT: HEART'S FULFILLMENT/EVALUATION

UPRIGHT: Heart is pleased with the maturity and depth of its personal relationships. There has been a wealth of respect paid by you and to you as you have been acutely aware of the lessons to be learned from all contacts. You are anxious to continue your lessons with your loved ones and guides in the next incarnation. ***INVERTED:*** Do not allow yourself to be either too pleased, or too disappointed, with the pledge phase of your path. Be neither in awe nor arrogant. And do your best to avoid envy and jealousy, of your fellow travelers, and certainly of the Divine.

21 GOVERNED BY THE WORLD: EGO'S FULFILLMENT/EVALUATION

UPRIGHT: Your mental legacy may be in helping define spiritual options, not only for yourself, but for others. This is not the initial conscious awareness of the hard reality of the path, rather the ability to navigate surely and safely, to identify the forks and to choose appropriately. ***INVERTED:*** Your contribution in these matters may be outstanding. Or, you may feel that you could have done much better.

22/0 GOVERNED BY THE FOOL: SOUL'S FULFILLMENT/EVALUATION

UPRIGHT: Here is a soul that was capable of infusing quality of choice down through the Mental, Emotional, and Physical Planes maintaining control over partnerships and mergers in service of its true goal, its spiritual marriage with God. ***INVERTED:*** The lessons detailed in the other positions of this reading will help you inscribe these words on your headstone.

THREE OF PENTACLES

UPRIGHT: Here are the fruits of your physical/material choices, and the resulting growth. The resolution, expression, and creation from the physical thesis/antithesis of the Ace and Two of Pentacles. Productive labor. Healthy progress. Craftsmanship. Correct, quality workmanship. Dedicated student/apprentice in a quality program with good guidance. A working, hands-on knowledge of things physical/material. The application/blending of mind with the physical. Practicality.
INVERTED: Perhaps the category of work is wrong. Lack of direction, wrong direction. Productivity is blocked, or below an acceptable level. The student/apprentice may not be doing as well learning the trade as he might. Supervision may be too harsh, or lacking altogether. There may be some sort of subversion of a productive process. On the one hand, there may be physical inertia, laziness. On the other hand, there may be an over enthusiasm or too much work taking place. In the latter, the amount of work being done exceeds what is proper or necessary for the desired end product—the mark of a workaholic fits in here.

In This Spread Position...Interpret the Three Of Pentacles Meanings to Include:

1 GOVERNED BY THE MAGICIAN: PHYSICAL GIVENS, OUT OF THE FATHER
UPRIGHT: Craftsmanship, inherited skills, livelihood through your father. Early recognition/dedication to your craft, from woodworking to architecture, from massage to medicine. Your profession should be a lifelong one around which everything revolves. You do best with your body, your hands (your feet and head if you are a socker player). *INVERTED:* You may be better than, or not as good as, your father or the family tradition. Or, you may depart from the pattern in some way, minor or major. If this is so, it will still be built on, or against, this tradition.

2 GOVERNED BY THE HIGH PRIESTESS: EMOTIONAL GIVENS, OUT OF THE MOTHER
UPRIGHT: Craftsmanship, inherited skill, livelihood through your mother's lineage. Early recognition and dedication of time and practice to your choice of activity/work. Skill will be more in the arts than crafts as such. This card here can be the mark of the prodigy. Music, dance, theater, painting, sculpture are possibilities. *INVERTED:* You may be better than, or not as good as, your mother or the family tradition. Or, you may be meant to depart from the pattern in some way, minor or major. If this is so, it will nevertheless still be built on, or against, this tradition.

3 GOVERNED BY THE EMPRESS: MENTAL GIVENS, INTELLECTUAL PREDISPOSITION
UPRIGHT: Mental skills dedicated to work with crafts and physical arts and sciences. Mental mastery, leadership, administration, business affairs, in your creative community, your field of crafts/arts. Intellectually at the top of leadership and achievement in these disciplines, with the content and quality of your work making its own philosophical commentary. *INVERTED:* The mental, ideological aspect may be a distortion of the work itself, or get in the way of the work. The reverse could also be true with the mental, ideological content not getting its just due.

4 GOVERNED BY THE EMPEROR: SPIRITUAL GIVENS, LIFE PURPOSE
UPRIGHT: Your art— the output of your handiwork, the beauty that flows from the movement, the use of your body, the mystery you unlock from the inert materials of the world—is carried to such a high level as to bear witness to the hard reality of the spiritual realm, of the certain existence of God. *INVERTED:* There will be parallel developments/effects in this lifetime directly as a result of the power this talent possesses. The work will predominate.

5 GOVERNED BY THE HIEROPHANT: SYSTEMS BORN INTO, SOCIETAL INFLUENCE
UPRIGHT: Early environment centered around the work; in some cases the family business. The larger community itself may be involved in the art/craft, as was true with early American Shaker furniture. The protestant work ethic applies here too, where work as a good in itself lies at the root of decisions/activities. *INVERTED:* On one extreme, there could have been too much emphasis on work and control. On the other extreme, there could have been the complete opposite with a more Dionysian, free spirit, antithesis to a work ethic—a community devoted to pleasure.

6 GOVERNED BY THE LOVERS: EMOTIONAL TAPES, BASIS FOR RELATING/CREATING
UPRIGHT: Passion for an art/craft, even a material, i.e. a sculptor's love for stone, a weaver's love for cloth, the farmer's love of the soil. This will most likely be your livelihood, but it may make do as your hobby. Relationships and activities will be subordinated to this love for your work. *INVERTED:* In one extreme, this passion may be excessive. Without balancing with other input/activity to some degree, the work itself will suffer by losing its relevance and vitality. In the other extreme, the passion is not sufficiently honored and not for appropriate reasons.

7 GOVERNED BY THE CHARIOT: PHYSICAL RESOURCES, MEANS TO ACHIEVE
UPRIGHT: Your ability to extract a finished product from something entirely raw. Your art, your craft itself. You, once you turned on and applied yourself to the task. Independence. Resourcefulness. The survivor's instinct and talent to shape his environment to his support rather than his demise. *INVERTED:* It's hard to imagine how one can be too resourceful, too independent, but that can be what is implied here. Or, that you have much more of these qualities than you have used thus far.

8 GOVERNED BY STRENGTH: EMOTIONAL RESOURCES, ENERGY
UPRIGHT: By putting yourself into the creative equation, you become part of a conduit of energy from the divine to the material, and from the material back to the divine. You make yourself instrumental in the give and take pulse of the universe. For all the energy this requires of you, it is replaced and then some. The creative ecstasy is in a class by itself. Just like sex or an ineffable moment of revelation, you have to be there. *INVERTED:* If your processes are the right ones for you, they will be energizing, not draining. One does not need to suffer to be creative.

9 GOVERNED BY THE HERMIT: BELIEF SYSTEM, BASIS FOR DECISIONS
UPRIGHT: Any job worth doing is worth doing well. Complete dedication to your work with complete confidence that all else flows from that. This has been the credo of western civilization—the idea of progress, which lies at the root of the concept of democracy. *INVERTED:* The belief in growth and productivity at any cost is an extreme. Conversely, an anti-growth policy is the opposite extreme here. Between these two extremes lies the contemporary problem of how to handle the world's economy without destroying the earth and her resources in the process.

10 GOVERNED BY THE WHEEL OF FORTUNE: CENTRAL MESSAGE, THEME OF READING
UPRIGHT: Healthy progress/growth presents itself. Produce now. You are awakening to the work that is your craft. Raise your will to the potential that will be released when you truly apply yourself. Now is the time for you to take charge of your affairs. The energy you invest will be rewarded. *INVERTED:* On the one extreme, the production/progress will be more than expected and a problem to deal with in itself. On the other extreme, production/progress will be less than expected. Or, hold up production for the moment. Check materials, production process, and such.

11 GOVERNED BY JUSTICE: STATE/CONTENT OF MIND, PLANS
UPRIGHT: You are planning now for growth in your Physical/material Plane, i.e. health, business, et al. Perhaps taking a much more personal interest in your business or personal affairs, i.e. how to improve the quality/quantity. *INVERTED:* Perhaps over doing the thinking in these matters. On the other hand you may not be planning enough, or about the correct things.

12 GOVERNED BY THE HANGED MAN: STATE OF EMOTIONS, SUBCONSCIOUS
UPRIGHT: While you may not be talking openly about your health, work, or security, internally this is your concern. Your gut feels it and will push for mental accommodation. *INVERTED:* The discomfort here may be severe, with vivid, assertive dreams possible. Or, the opposite can be true, that the gut feeling is not correct and that your fears are unjustified. The subject stills needs to reach the light, the attention of mind but not for accommodation, for clarification.

13 GOVERNED BY DEATH: PHYSICAL SITUATION, HARD REALITY
UPRIGHT: You are immersed in increase in your Physical/material Plane—matters of work, diet, exercise, finances, or such. You may take this as a status report that things are as they should be. You are doing your work, your exercise, things going well. *INVERTED:* Read the above mentioned general interpretations for the inverted position of this card. Something is affecting your productivity adversely.

14 GOVERNED BY TEMPERANCE: EMOTIONAL TEST, NEAR FUTURE
UPRIGHT: Your feelings will center optimistically around physical/material progress. Your activities in work, diet, exercise, finances or such, on your relationships, your personal life and/or creative endeavors will be very positive. *INVERTED:* Question of proper progress/conduct in physical/material matters will be of concern. The effect of your physical/material activities is positive but so profound as to require accommodation. On other hand, the effect may be potentially harmful and will have to be handled deftly.

15 GOVERNED BY THE DEVIL: TEMPTATION/CHALLENGE, FEARS, NEAR FUTURE
UPRIGHT: You will be tested in matters of business, health, et al. There is nothing to fear here. These are challenges to bring you further toward you goal (see card in position 17). *INVERTED:* On the one hand, you may have worries in these matters, but these problems will be more in your head than in reality. On the other hand, you may be too carefree and not paying enough concern to these matters. You may not be meeting the challenges.

16 GOVERNED BY THE TOWER: NEXT MESSAGE, GRACE OF GOD
UPRIGHT: Your safety net, the grace on which you can depend this next year, involves resolution, healthy growth in your Physical/material Plane. The card preceding (position 15) and the card following (position 17) help define this message. *INVERTED:* On the one hand, the matters of the Physical Plane, i.e. business, health, et al are doing so well as to free your attention for the other Planes (Emotional, Mental, Spiritual). On the other hand, problems with the Physical Plane will rivet your attention there, for positive work that needs to be done.

17 GOVERNED BY THE STAR: ASPIRATIONS OF EGO, GOALS, MAXIMUM EXPECTATIONS
UPRIGHT: To be productive, efficient in what you do so that there is a healthy surplus. To make the material pie grow. Physical, athletic growth. Financial growth. *INVERTED:* Productivity and growth for their own sakes, rather than as means to more integrated ends. This is related but not the same as greed, power, or the sin of pride. It is an over extrapolation of the positive aspect of growth. On the other hand, the goal could be the opposite...anti-growth, or reduction.

18 GOVERNED BY THE MOON: ASPIRATIONS OF HEART, COMPASSION
UPRIGHT: A heart-felt desire to be so efficient at fulfilling your needs as to have a surplus available for the use of others. This is a desire to raise the living standards of all fellow humans, indeed creatures. This is related the Buddhist concept of Boddhitsatvas, and the belief that no soul can pass out of the cycle of reincarnation until all souls have completed their lessons. We must help each other until we can all enter the pearly gates together. *INVERTED:* As noble as this goal sounds, like all other principles it can be ruined by the extremes of too much or too little.

19 GOVERNED BY THE SUN: MATERIAL FULFILLMENT/EVALUATION
UPRIGHT: You will be pleased with the level of work and/or physical activity into your senior years. No hint of retirement here. *INVERTED:* Retirement is possible, and in some cases there will be a resistance to the idea. In other cases, there will be the desire but the inability. There is a slowing of productivity, perhaps an inability to continue the craft. In other cases, you may insist on continuing but with a diminishing effect on the work.

20 GOVERNED BY JUDGEMENT: HEART'S FULFILLMENT/EVALUATION
UPRIGHT: Your ability to generate material needs and comfort was the centerpiece of your success with people, both family and society in general. Your generosity without attachment was endearing to all who knew you. *INVERTED:* Begin now to assure that your ability to produce your brand of prosperity or growth works for those around you as well. Ask them.

21 GOVERNED BY THE WORLD: EGO'S FULFILLMENT/EVALUATION
UPRIGHT: You are most satisfied with your having produced the work you set out to give the world. Your handiwork is in evidence everywhere and many people benefit from the fruits of your labors. *INVERTED:* Perhaps you did not achieve the goal you set for yourself, or maybe that is only your perception. You may have far exceeded your expectations. In some cases, this will be much like the work of the artist which reached its critical and financial zenith long after the artist's passing.

22/0 GOVERNED BY THE FOOL: SOUL'S FULFILLMENT/EVALUATION
UPRIGHT: Here was "a work," a prodigious effort. The soul itself is amazed at how much it has achieved in the material world. Its path is highly visible by the tracks it left behind, and in so many front yards. *INVERTED:* Examine the lessons of the other positions of this reading to better assure this result to your Karmic Contract; there is no doubt that your physical efforts can and will affect them. Make the effect as grand and beneficial as possible.

THREE OF CUPS

UPRIGHT: The dual aspect of the number three in the Emotional Plane of the Cups gives us first the ends, the results of our alliances established in the Two of Cups, then second it shows the means by which we hope to create the tranquility of a security/foundation as symbolized in the Four of Cups. Here are the fruits of your emotional choices and decisions. Emotional/creative life flourishes. Love of what love can bring. Joy. Pregnancy. Children/ Happy Issue. Creative Issue. Projects of love. Love growing/expanding. Commitment. Sociability. Opening up emotionally. Continuing to open up emotionally, but still predominantly one-on-one, yet not necessarily limited to your mate or romantic/sexual partner. The results of love, affection, and sex. The effect of the mind on the emotions pushes you forward to experience, to feel more, in a completely positive sense. **INVERTED:** A hedonistic lifestyle. An emotional or creative block. Problems with what has issued from your emotions or creative projects. The proper function of the mind to push you forward emotionally, to tempt you if you will, will be a force to be reconned with. An unwanted pregnancy/child. Not wanting what love can bring...Infertility...Abortion. Even having/wanting the pain that can come with love, i.e. unrequited love, grief, sadness.

In This Spread Position...Interpret the Three Of Cups Meanings to Include:

1 GOVERNED BY THE MAGICIAN: PHYSICAL GIVENS, OUT OF THE FATHER
UPRIGHT: Here is the open, affectionate energy of the masculine. Assertive creative energy will permeate all physical/material affairs. There will be intimacy, extroversion in all pragmatic affairs. A healthy respect for this plane that nevertheless demands enjoyment, a direct sensation/experience. At times it may be hard to separate pleasure from work. Most likely to want a family, to be a parent. **INVERTED:** On the one hand, all of the upright interpretations apply but in a more subdued manner. On the other hand, the interpretations will be stronger. You must be disciplined and harness the ego of the emotions in physical/material matters.

2 GOVERNED BY THE HIGH PRIESTESS: EMOTIONAL GIVENS, OUT OF THE MOTHER
UPRIGHT: Here is the open, affectionate energy of the feminine. Assertive creative energy will permeate all emotional/creative affairs. There will be intimacy, extroversion in all emotional/creative matters. Most relationships will tend to be emotionally close; many will be overtly affectionate. Relationships will be most important to your path. Most likely to want a family, to be a parent. **INVERTED:** On the one hand, all of the upright interpretations apply but in a more subdued manner. On the other hand, the interpretations will be stronger. You must be disciplined and harness the ego of the emotions in emotional/creative matters.

3 GOVERNED BY THE EMPRESS: MENTAL GIVENS, INTELLECTUAL PREDISPOSITION
UPRIGHT: Oriented to matters of the heart, to expression of feelings. Like with the Two of Cups this can be the mark of the poet or songwriter, but it is also the storyteller for children, the mind that wishes to take the innocent heart forward. Here is the home of many myths. This intellect is open, fluid, expansive. There is commitment to the family, to children, to the products of fruitful relationships. **INVERTED:** This mind could move so deeply into the worlds of myth, of children, of creative process that it may have trouble keeping its objectivity. Or, this mind may not accept fully enough the reality of these things and the need to move in these right-brain worlds. Mind may be disinclined toward children.

4 GOVERNED BY THE EMPEROR: SOUL GIVENS, LIFE PURPOSE
UPRIGHT: This is a path of emotional responsibility, family in its most obvious guise. But, this responsibility can take many forms. Here the path is one of intimacy and involvement, an intertwining of paths that produces additional paths. **INVERTED:** This can indicate the uniqueness of the path in fulfilling this archteype of karmic purpose. The definition of "family" or "happy issue" may be unconventional, including the paradoxical combination of a hedonistic, yet familial lifestyle as the productive fruit. This life may require not having biological offspring.

5 GOVERNED BY THE HIEROPHANT: SYSTEMS BORN INTO, SOCIETAL INFLUENCE
UPRIGHT: In this home or social setting the children, or the creative issue, were given predominance. **INVERTED:** In this early environment children, or creative issue, may disproportionately have been given too much, or too little, attention/importance.

6 GOVERNED BY THE LOVERS: EMOTIONAL TAPES, BASIS FOR RELATING/CREATING
UPRIGHT: The ideal of children, of creative issue, of generating something new and vital in partnership with an other/others, speaks loudest to your heart. **INVERTED:** This ideal may be in some extreme form, either of wanting to produce in quantity, or of not wanting to produce at all.

7 GOVERNED BY THE CHARIOT: PHYSICAL RESOURCES, MEANS TO ACHIEVE
UPRIGHT: Your greatest physical/material resources come from what you have produced from your emotional/creative partnerships. In one most obvious sense this is from one's children, in the physcial/material assistance they offer. But it can also be from the jewel produced in a creative partnership, such as a stage play. **INVERTED:** This suggests that the aforementioned are your best assests and means of support, but that some aspect of them can be improved to strengthen your foundation before proceeding.

8 GOVERNED BY STRENGTH: EMOTIONAL RESOURCES, ENERGY
UPRIGHT: Energy for your activities comes directly back from the energy you have given others. Your productive issue—children, relationships, creative output—has generated a field from which you draw enormous sustenance. But your greatest strength comes from your heart's wisdom to avoid the pitfalls of over attachment, encouraging you and your loved ones to keep your hearts open to growth, expanding the circle of friendship and love. **INVERTED:** Do not allow either extreme here to weaken you. Neither be so attached that you cannot seek or allow others into your inner circle, nor so extroverted and open that you do not foster special attention to those closest to you.

9 GOVERNED BY THE HERMIT: BELIEF SYSTEM, BASIS FOR DECISIONS
UPRIGHT: Everything for you keys around love—emotional growth, freedom of expression and experience, and all that issues from that. You believe that it is your natural state to be happy and productive. No one would ever have to make you work, as long as it is sensible work that will truly benefit you or others. Your work will grow from your heart. **INVERTED:** In the extremes, these keys may be exaggerated making you either driven by your passions to work furiously at your beliefs, or the opposite of being rather lackadasical relying on love to provide/conquer all.

10 GOVERNED BY THE WHEEL OF FORTUNE: CENTRAL MESSAGE, THEME OF READING
UPRIGHT: Expect the joyful fruits of your labor. This is a time when you should want to produce, to seek and enjoy evidence of your heart's enterprises.

Something new is being created. There is joyful birth here. **INVERTED:** There may be a delay, adjust your expectations. Or, the product of your labor may be other than anticipated, possibly much more or much less.

11 GOVERNED BY JUSTICE: STATE/CONTENT OF MIND, PLANS

UPRIGHT: You are thinking about fruition, expression, creation. You are planning for expansion in your Emotional Plane, out of the relationship(s) you have already established, or out of the creative groundwork you have already laid. As with the germination of an idea, here is the seed of emotional growth planted first in the mind. **INVERTED:** You may want to delay or stop any emotional new seed at this point. But the opposite could also be true; you may be planning for growth in degrees or ways that are excessive. You cannot force joy, or sadness; they are the results of intricate, long-term interactions.

12 GOVERNED BY THE HANGED MAN: STATE OF EMOTIONS, SUBCONSCIOUS

UPRIGHT: You may not be consciously thinking about the matters mentioned above in position 11, but these are the concerns of your heart and of your subconscious mind. Here is the seed of emotional growth rooted in the heart. **INVERTED:** Either the heart is passionately obsessed with this potential for emotional growth, or it desires the reverse. It may want to maintain the status quo for the moment, or in extremes, it may actually want a reversal or diminution of the emotional package. The heart may want to simplify its world.

13 GOVERNED BY DEATH: PHYSICAL SITUATION, HARD REALITY

UPRIGHT: Review the general meanings, as one or more of these aspects of emotional fruition and growth are present in your world now, or they will be in the near future. This should be a time of fullness and excitement as you are filled with the energy of new life, new possibilities. You are able to witness and enjoy the results of your love and creativity, perhaps the birth of a child or project. **INVERTED:** Neither let too much joy distort the moment of fruition, nor too much sadness a moment of disappointment.

14 GOVERNED BY TEMPERANCE: EMOTIONAL TEST

UPRIGHT: The heart reacts as relationships respond to the growth in your emotional world. You become bigger in the coming year with desirable additions/extensions in your Emotional Plane. **INVERTED:** Do not try to cast too many characters in your play, or try to throw too many clay pots on your wheel. Or, the opposite extreme, do not hold back and limit yourself unnecessarily.

15 GOVERNED BY THE DEVIL: TEMPTATION/CHALLENGE, FEARS

UPRIGHT: The love of truth and the urge for understanding push you forward into new emotional, creative dimensions. Here is the impact of the products of your fertility on your Mental Plane. What you have been doing based on your emotions must now pass the test of mind. **INVERTED:** You may have fears related to your projections from love, or you may be completely lacking in even reasonable concerns in these matters.

16 GOVERNED BY THE TOWER: NEXT LESSON, GRACE OF GOD

UPRIGHT: Healthy issue in your Emotional Plane, the next step in your expression/experience of love. This could have come earlier, but it is appropriate here. This may be the child you have been waiting for. **INVERTED:** This is what you must accept in your emotional/creative affairs by the end of this next year, as purposeful and good in your Karmic Contract. It will be much more, or much less than your heart had hoped for. Possibly, you will be infused with the urge to loosen up and expand, or you will be encouraged to cut back and accept a slower pace for a time.

17 GOVERNED BY THE STAR: ASPIRATIONS OF EGO, GOALS, MAXIMUM EXPECTATIONS

UPRIGHT: The aim here is for longevity through progeny or creative issue, i.e. someone, or something, to carry on the family name. To be known for what comes from your closest loves, relationships. All this to be accompanied by a healthy sense of contribution to a continuum, not just historical extension of the ego. **INVERTED:** The same goals as above, but with far too much emphasis on "my" children, or "my" work. This is a subversion of past and future generations to your needs in the present. In some instances, the opposite will be the case, with a goal to reproduce, to create, not for the self but out of a sense of duty.

18 GOVERNED BY THE MOON: ASPIRATIONS OF HEART, COMPASSION

UPRIGHT: The heart wishes to be able to create for the joy, the wonder of participating in the cosmic dance of life. To experience the feeling of being instrumental in bringing life, a new creation, to this earth. To be a feeling, contributing player in the eternal cycle of creativity. **INVERTED:** One pitfall here is the trap of needing too much the feeling of "I made this," or "this is mine." A rarer distortion of this archetype is the goal that rejects this process of new life and continuity.

19 GOVERNED BY THE SUN: MATERIAL FULFILLMENT/EVALUATION

UPRIGHT: Energetic participation, fertility, are with you throughout this lifetime. Extroversion marks your senior years. Children/grandchildren, or other youth, animals, even others of your own generation benefit from your time and energy. **INVERTED:** Your later years may be more subdued with a quieter, more reclusive environment and lifestyle. Creativity here would be inward rather than outward. But as with all inverted cards, the complete opposite may be the case with you possibly being even more active than in your youth.

20 GOVERNED BY JUDGEMENT: HEART'S FULFILLMENT/EVALUATION

UPRIGHT: Your heart's desire to bring new being into the world is your pleasure, with healthy interaction with all that has come from you. As life ends your surroundings are pregnant with possibilities because of your ability to love, to create, to give and take, and your having fostered that ability. **INVERTED:** Do everything in your power to see your understanding of love and creativity passed on to your loved ones, to your fellow man, but then you must rest and let free will have its rein. Otherwise you only exaccerbate the problem.

21 GOVERNED BY THE WORLD: EGO'S FULFILLMENT/EVALUATION

UPRIGHT: You have successfully balanced the needs of past and future generations while not neglecting your own. Whether through your progeny or your creative legacies you have projected yourself through the veil into the timeless side of reality. Congratulations are in order for this most difficult balancing act of past/present/future. **INVERTED:** The lessons presented in the other positions of this reading are aimed in part at helping you achieve this balance, rather than continue a path that will allow one or more of the generations to subvert the other(s).

22/0 GOVERNED BY THE FOOL: SOUL'S FULFILLMENT/EVALUATION

UPRIGHT: The Karmic Contract to be an active and willing participant, open to the joys and responsibility of love and the creative process has been well fulfilled. **INVERTED:** The soul will be much happier with what was created in this lifetime than in the motivations behind those creations. Look at the lessons of the other positions in this reading for guidance in raising these motivations.

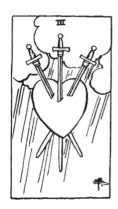

THREE OF SWORDS

UPRIGHT: The dual aspect of the number three here in Swords gives us first the ends/results of arbitration and agreements from the Two of Swords, then second the means by which we can achieve the meditative/secure foundation symbolized in the Four of Swords. Mental resolution and clarity emerging from the influence of the lower emotions. This card does not damage or limit the heart, rather it represents the wise mind that springs from the strength of a loving, pure heart. The elemental heart is harnessed in order to use its energy for: Self-expression. Ambition. Productivity. Efficiency. Organization. Progression. Articulation. Communication. Literacy. Wit. Extroversion. Expression. Enthusiasm. Directness. Publicity. Commitment. Thrust. Decisiveness (here the Synthesis, after the Thesis/Antithesis of the Ace and Two of Swords). Pragmatism. Rationality. Factuality. **INVERTED:** Some difficulty in integrating lower emotions into requirements of mind. Or, mind may not be integrating/using heart energy properly. Difficulty with self-expression, or expressing too much. Too secretive, too gossipy. Illiterate, or too literate. On one extreme, anger/loss of control; on the other extreme, placid to a fault. Misunderstanding and misuse of mind in relation to heart. Introverted, or too extroverted. Shy. Taciturn, or too verbose.

In This Spread Position...Interpret the Three Of Swords Meanings to Include:

1 GOVERNED BY THE MAGICIAN: PHYSICAL GIVENS, OUT OF THE FATHER
UPRIGHT: Your physical/material affairs are marked by clarity of expression and drive. Good advisor in matters of the earth plane. An excellent scientist, researcher would have this card, for the ability to objectively observe the physical world and articulate the practical results of their experiments. **INVERTED:** Expression, enthusiasm may not be your strong points in this plane, You will prefer the immediate results of hands-on activities to thinking, May react very quickly, or very slowly.

2 GOVERNED BY THE HIGH PRIESTESS: EMOTIONAL GIVENS, OUT OF THE MOTHER
UPRIGHT: Your emotional/creative affairs are marked by clarity of expression and drive. Good advisor in matters of romance/relationships, as well as the fields of the Emotional/creative Plane. An excellent drama critic, art teacher, choreographer would have this card, for the ability to coolly dip their toes into the hot maelstrom of creative juices. **INVERTED:** Your emotions are less objective, more passionate. And while all of the above still apply, you are a more fiery participant in these affairs, with decisions coming more quickly and from the gut more than the head.

3 GOVERNED BY THE EMPRESS: MENTAL GIVENS, INTELLECTUAL PREDISPOSITION
UPRIGHT: As you always consider all sides before deciding, you can express yourself fully and follow through with authority, efficiency, and attention to detail. No one doubts how you come to your conclusions, or why. Emotional noise does not confuse you. Ideal for management. **INVERTED:** On one extreme, this is efficiency, decisiveness, and communication to a fault, bringing discomfort to others who have to follow in your trail of dust. On the other extreme, decisions and accuracy come more slowly, especially if you are guided too much by emotions.

4 GOVERNED BY THE THE EMPEROR: SPIRITUAL GIVENS, LIFE PURPOSE
UPRIGHT: You are a warrior for clarity of purpose and efficiency of execution. To be able to listen and learn, to talk and to teach. Determination here leads to organization and preparedness. **INVERTED:** Your temptation will be to rush your programs. Remember to be patient while synthesis is evolving. Work to develop consensus even though you are confident with your evaluation and want to get on with things.

5 GOVERNED BY THE HIEROPHANT: SYSTEMS BORN INTO, SOCIETAL INFLUENCE
UPRIGHT: The early environment was open and direct, with everyone knowing where they stood. Intellectually progressive, encouraging, highly animated, vibrant. Healthy parental aspirations for your future. **INVERTED:** Early environment too open, or too closed. Difficulty knowing which end was up. Too progressive, or too backward. Dull, or overly animated. Low expectations, or unreasonably high expectations for you.

6 GOVERNED BY THE LOVERS: EMOTIONAL TAPES, BASIS FOR RELATING/CREATING
UPRIGHT: Passion for the advancement of knowledge, the progress of mind. You honor the assertiveness of your mind in all your relationships and creative affairs. You are able to express your emotions mentally as well as your ideas. The heart is in love with the mind's ability to express itself in terms that please the heart. This is the mark of the poet/playwright and every facet of drama, advertising, publicity. Especially original and creative in mental fields. **INVERTED:** The passions of the heart must never yield entirely to the mind. The path is love, not an exercise.

7 GOVERNED BY THE CHARIOT: PHYSICAL RESOURCES, MEANS TO ACHIEVE
UPRIGHT: Great clarity, organization, and communication in your physical world. Personal/business regimens are efficient, geared for quick response; hence your good logistics and mobility when needed. **INVERTED:** Do not let your penchant for organization become an end in itself. Neither go to the opposite extreme of not having the organization and clarity you might need for contingencies as well as for daily physical needs.

8 GOVERNED BY STRENGTH: EMOTIONAL RESOURCES, ENERGY
UPRIGHT: Great clarity, organization, and communication in your emotional world. Relationships/creative affairs are efficient. You can rally the people and energy you need to support your heart's master plan. **INVERTED:** Do not let your penchant for organization become an end in itself. Neither go to the opposite extreme of not having the organization and clarity you might need for contingencies as well as for daily emotional needs.

9 GOVERNED BY THE HERMIT: BELIEF SYSTEM, BASIS FOR DECISIONS
UPRIGHT: You believe the ability to listen and learn (to take in), and to talk and teach (to give out), is the key to progress on the path. Knowing that knowledge is properly sought for greater responsibility, not power, you are the eternal student sharing all he knows at each stage. **INVERTED:** Good communication must be your means, not your end. Remember that all thought is revealed to you, not created by you.

10 GOVERNED BY THE WHEEL OF FORTUNE: CENTRAL MESSAGE, THEME OF READING
UPRIGHT: You will have the clarity and sense of purpose you need to commit yourself to timely tasks. See the organization around you in nature and realize that very same administration is in you. Move forward now with confidence to secure the mental foundation that awaits. **INVERTED:** Be patient, your mind is waiting for the energy the heart must give it to move forward. That process is evident in this reading.

11 GOVERNED BY JUSTICE: STATE/CONTENT OF MIND, PLANS
UPRIGHT: There is considerable activity mentally, a programming to carry out your beliefs in learning/teaching. Out of much consideration of the works of others, and of merging their thoughts with yours, now comes the reward of new thoughts that seem oddly yours. You are deciding where you want to go with these mental children, these new thoughts of yours. *INVERTED:* Here you may be either too forward, or too backward. And while there may be hesitation from lack of confidence, you might well be avoiding the discipline and work required.

12 GOVERNED BY THE HANGED MAN: STATE OF EMOTIONS, SUBCONSCIOUS
UPRIGHT: There is considerable activity emotionally, a pleasant unrest in the heart to be actively emersed in the swirl of ideas in your head, to give them greater life, greater physicality. Here is the heart's decision to be a player on the world stage. *INVERTED:* Distortion of the above includes a heart that is too emersed in the swirl of the mind, refusing to come out into the physical world, or a heart that refuses to fund the energy necessary for such mental projects.

13 GOVERNED BY DEATH: PHYSICAL SITUATION, HARD REALITY
UPRIGHT: The projections of your mind are the center of your actions. A time for self-expression and influence on your environment and those around you, ranging from informal conversations to taking to the stage, the page, or the podium. You are putting your best foot forward. A time of organizing for maximum effectiveness. *INVERTED:* Be sure that it is your best foot that you put forward. When cleaning house, do not throw the baby out with the bath water.

14 GOVERNED BY TEMPERANCE: EMOTIONAL TEST
UPRIGHT: As your intellectual acumen increases and it becomes more and more evident in how you express yourself, it ripples through your relationships and creative activities. In the near future, three months to a year, this effect will be particularly strong. Enjoy your expanded personality and look forward to where it is taking you. *INVERTED:* Your mental growth is positive and proper for your path, but it doesn't have to be aggressive or subdued to avoid conflict.

15 GOVERNED BY THE DEVIL: TEMPTATION/CHALLENGE, FEARS
UPRIGHT: You must face how to handle your mental growth, how to extract your position and self-expression from what has influenced you thus far. Apprehension here comes from the fact that this is a cutting of the intellectual umbilical cord as you launch into the unknown of your own ideas. But just as you did not lose your mother when you separated from her at birth, neither will you be alone in this process. You do not need to wait for further information or advice. *INVERTED:* While you certainly need not fear this extroversion of your personality and goals, you should not race ahead expecting the waters to part as the world falls at your feet. You must be convincing at each step.

16 GOVERNED BY THE TOWER: NEXT MESSAGE, GRACE OF GOD
UPRIGHT: Here is the wise mind springing forth from the loving, pure heart. This marks the beginning of a productive period of self-assertion, building on a solid base of discerning knowledge. You are energized and ready to make yourself seen and heard, with a mind directed to the noblest of causes. *INVERTED:* You will need to be patient, as your mind waits for the energy the heart must give it to move forward. That process is taking place. The lessons presented in this reading are aimed at helping that happen now. The knowledge you will have acquired outpaces temporarily the heart's motivation to use it to maximum effect.

17 GOVERNED BY THE STAR: ASPIRATIONS OF EGO, GOALS, MAXIMUM EXPECTATIONS
UPRIGHT: Your goal is to be capable of digesting, understanding, organizing, and communicating as much as you can in the shortest amount of time possible. To use the heart's desires effectively. *INVERTED:* This goal can be lofty, with teaching and sharing your knowledge as the end purpose of the hours of assimilation and study, but it can also be debased into a self-serving exercise of the lower ego caught up in the sheer capacity of the intellect.

18 GOVERNED BY THE MOON: ASPIRATIONS OF HEART, COMPASSION
UPRIGHT: The heart wishes to provide the mind with the energy and motivation it needs to reach higher and higher levels of knowledge and understanding. You will see that wisdom comes from the mutual effort of the heart to satisfy the will of mind, and the mind to satisfy the desire of the heart. *INVERTED:* The heart, just as the mind, is capable of erring. It must not provide the mind with more energy than it needs, and certainly it must renege if the mind's projects are improper. But the heart can err in favoring it's own projects at the expense of worthwhile mental endeavors.

19 GOVERNED BY THE SUN: MATERIAL FULFILLMENT/EVALUATION
UPRIGHT: A strong, clear mind very much active and in control of your affairs. An important contributor in the daily affairs of society. You continue to grow and produce throughout this lifetime. *INVERTED:* Study the general interpretations (inverted) for the Three of Swords to assure that you are not headed in any of these directions.

20 GOVERNED BY JUDGEMENT: HEART'S FULFILLMENT/EVALUATION
UPRIGHT: The heart is pleased with the work the mind has done in integrating the inner needs into the programs of the ego. As a result your creative potential has been maximized along with the interaction in all major relationships. *INVERTED:* Look at the interpretations of this reading with the upright meaning in mind to move more efficiently in this direction. Do not neglect the mental component in your relationships and creative thrust. The heart must feed the mind.

21 GOVERNED BY THE WORLD: EGO'S FULFILLMENT/EVALUATION
UPRIGHT: You know that you have managed your mental affairs well, taking full advantage of opportunities to learn and yet pausing to teach as well. You have laid a solid foundation for yourself and your heirs. Founders of schools leave this mark. *INVERTED:* Look at the interpretations of this reading with the upright meaning in mind to move more efficiently in this direction. Neither neglect the role of mind to be a voice for your emotions, nor let the emotions make so much noise that the mind is distracted from its duties .

22/0 GOVERNED BY THE FOOL: SOUL'S FULFILLMENT/EVALUATION
UPRIGHT: This soul has proven well the positive role of ambition, to improve the human condition at each and every step, by listening to and drawing upon the heart, yet strengthening the heart in turn by expanding its influence. *INVERTED:* To achieve the desired ends spoken above, listen with a seeking heart to the lessons outlined in the interpretations of the other positions in this reading.

THREE OF WANDS

UPRIGHT: Here is spiritual purpose moving with the will of a dedicated, efficient mind behind it. Intuitive decisions have been made, and the wheels are in motion. This is fruition and extension of past discoveries rather than a launch into the totally new. There is optimism, a "knowing that you know" kind of confidence that feeds your commitment to serious work. There is an objective awareness of your Karmic Contract and enthusiastic agreement to carry it out to the letter. Dedication. Visionary insight joins the clarity of mind, enabling you to be meticulous, accurate, painstaking as you organize in the Spiritual/intuitive Plane and prepare toward your foundation. Now there is power and strength and wisdom enough for major achievements. One eye on the past, the other on the future as you walk the balance beam of life. **INVERTED:** There can be flaws that interfere with the above, keeping dramatic progress on the path just out of reach. On the other hand, the desired qualities for this stage may be present in abundance, but for some reason, the project at hand is off target. Check, possibly right project, wrong motivation. Or, right motivation, wrong project. Guard against over optimism, and spiritual vanity, as you would against pessimism. Guard against complacency as you would against a nomadic restlessness forever more and more.

In This Spread Position...Interpret the Three Of Wands Meanings to Include:

1 GOVERNED BY THE MAGICIAN: PHYSICAL GIVENS, OUT OF THE FATHER
UPRIGHT: The affairs of the Physical/material Plane, health, home, work are of utmost importance to you, as you see them as part and parcel of your spiritual growth, not as something separate and alien. Look for your spiritual quest to determine your travels and quests in the physical world. Perhaps Marco Polo, or the Knights Templar. **INVERTED:** The merging of "higher" and "lower" paths must not be allowed to blur the healthy distinction of the spiritual and physical to be enjoyed in any incarnation. Guard against spiritual nomadism as well as complacency and smugness.

2 GOVERNED BY THE HIGH PRIESTESS: EMOTIONAL GIVENS, OUT OF THE MOTHER
UPRIGHT: The affairs of the Emotional/creative Plane, relationships and expression of your talents, are of utmost importance, for you see them as one with your spiritual growth, not as something to be watched and subdued. Your spiritual quest will determine your selection of experiences on the emotional path. Perhaps Lancelot, or Michelangelo. **INVERTED:** The merging of "higher" and "lower" paths must not be allowed to blur the healthy distinction of the spiritual and emotional to be enjoyed in any incarnation. Guard against spiritual isolation and asceticism.

3 GOVERNED BY THE EMPRESS: MENTAL GIVENS, INTELLECTUAL PREDISPOSITION
UPRIGHT: The business of the Mental Plane, the ability of mind to improve the overall condition of the self (and eventually others), is of utmost importance to you. For you, mental progress is one with spiritual progress, and not something to be feared and tamed. Look for your spiritual quest to set the agenda for your intellect. Perhaps Galileo, or Shakespeare. **INVERTED:** The merging of "higher" and "lower" paths must not be allowed to blur the healthy distinction between mind and spirit to be enjoyed in any incarnation. Guard against self-righteousness and presumption.

4 GOVERNED BY THE EMPEROR: SPIRITUAL GIVENS, LIFE PURPOSE
UPRIGHT: This lifetime is marked by activity and preparation. There is a pleasant restlessness, a balance of contentment with what you already have in your spiritual portfolio and of dissatisfaction with the status quo, a hunger for the effect of the unknown. **INVERTED:** You may be required to use your energies more in shoring up the existing portfolio which may try your patience, or you may be required to spend your time almost entirely in projections into new discoveries which may test your continuity with the past.

5 GOVERNED BY THE HIEROPHANT: SYSTEMS BORN INTO, SOCIETAL INFLUENCE
UPRIGHT: A respect for tradition tinged with a fascination with the new, the yet to be known, marks this early environment. Myths and fairy tales are passed on in such an atmosphere. A sense of responsibility for continuity, but with the past, present, and the future having their distinct responsibilities. A respect for the fact that the future is rooted in the past. **INVERTED:** Some distortion of continuity existed. An insistence on either the past, the present, or the future, with a neglect of the importance of the others, prevailed. Commonly, this is an insistence on tradition at the cost of new needs.

6 GOVERNED BY THE LOVERS: EMOTIONAL TAPES, BASIS FOR RELATING/CREATING
UPRIGHT: This passion is for the sensation of the journey itself, between departure and arrival. Here is the excitement of movement, once choice has been made...until time for the next choice. This interim carries its own special sensations. There is a sense of rightness about past events tinged with the mystery of future events, but both are overwhelmed by the liberty of the moment at hand. **INVERTED:** The pitfall here is like that in position 5 above. Do not misunderstand the meaning of "living in the present." The eternal now which passes drop by drop with our help contains all of our past and all of our future.

7 GOVERNED BY THE CHARIOT: PHYSICAL RESOURCES, MEANS TO ACHIEVE
UPRIGHT: You tend to be in the right place at the right time. Some call this lucky, but it is because you pay close attention to your Physical/ material Plane. You do this, not out of fear of things going wrong, but because you are happier when things go right. You are a contingency planner, with an excellent early warning system based on your ability to see the big picture, and in detail. **INVERTED:** At one extreme, this may have the discomfort of predestination, of knowing in advance. Another extreme, you may enjoy too much this penchant for knowing.

8 GOVERNED BY STRENGTH: EMOTIONAL RESOURCES, ENERGY
UPRIGHT: While your passion is for the journey itself, your strength in personal relationships and the source of your creativity comes from your heart's span of concern from your port of departure to port of destination. You honor your past lives and your genetic heritage in your spiritual observations, knowing full well that everything living in you today will travel with you into tomorrow. **INVERTED:** To be strong with full energy for this path, do not get lost in past lives, heritage, or guides. They are all alive in and through you, not vice versa.

9 GOVERNED BY THE HERMIT: BELIEF SYSTEM, BASIS FOR DECISIONS
UPRIGHT: As with the passion of the heart, the mind believes in the journey and so will always be prepared, able to carry everything of value with it, on its back so to speak. The nomadic arab, as well as the ancient tribes of Israel, are examples of entire peoples operating from this basic tenet. **INVERTED:** This willingness, preparedness to move when and wherever necessary to learn one's lessons can degenerate into the purposeless wanderer. This can show a distaste for organization, and lack of understanding and respect for continuity.

10 GOVERNED BY THE WHEEL OF FORTUNE: CENTRAL MESSAGE, THEME OF READING
UPRIGHT: This is the time when you can build a bridge between the past and the future. You are in the vanguard and should look within and ahead now rather than behind for answers. Others will need to look to you, even as you continue to learn now from your guides, from the path itself. **INVERTED:** There is still work to be done studying the past, before you can integrate the old fully into the needs of today and tomorrow.

11 GOVERNED BY JUSTICE: STATE/CONTENT OF MIND, PLANS
UPRIGHT: You have decided that you are ready to assume more independence, to speak your mind as you organize and re-organize for greater effectiveness. You have discovered things you know others need to know as well, and at the same time, you are beginning to be original in your thinking and want to share these thoughts as well. **INVERTED:** Some problems with the above. Are you correct in your interpretations of past work? Is your work ready? Are you properly organized?

12 GOVERNED BY THE HANGED MAN: STATE OF EMOTIONS, SUBCONSCIOUS
UPRIGHT: Your heart longs for the new experience of the fork in the path you have taken. It will provide the desire and the energy if the will decides this is the right time for you to be more independent and assertive. **INVERTED:** For one reason or another, the heart may be hesitant to support the will in this regard. Considerable sacrifice of one thing for the other may be involved. Conversely, the heart may be pushing for action through the subconscious, perhaps against a resistant will.

13 GOVERNED BY DEATH: PHYSICAL SITUATION, HARD REALITY
UPRIGHT: You have begun, or will begin in the near future, an ambitious expansion of your activities toward your goals. This action brings much more interaction with others. As Sherlock Holmes would have said, "The game is afoot." Your mental/spiritual affairs have taken center stage. **INVERTED:** Check the scope and/or the timing of your program, also the mechanics and physical resources.

14 GOVERNED BY TEMPERANCE: EMOTIONAL TEST
UPRIGHT: Considerable time and energy will be devoted to the administration and execution of your program/journey. Resources previously allotted elsewhere will be diverted to these new channels. This will be your heart's priority in the near future. **INVERTED:** The heart may have a different priority or timing than you have programmed, a test of will and desire.

15 GOVERNED BY THE DEVIL: TEMPTATION/CHALLENGE, FEARS
UPRIGHT: This is the complimentary test to that shown in position 14 above. Here we see that it is the will that is the wind in your sails. The excitement and promise that this holds out for you is generating your plans at this time. Perhaps you have seen the travel agent, even bought the ticket already. **INVERTED:** There may be doubts holding you back, but face all these fears squarely. What appears to be left behind now, will be with you in spirit on your journey and with you physically in your destination.

16 GOVERNED BY THE TOWER: NEXT LESSON, GRACE OF GOD
UPRIGHT: Better for you to have organized and launched your own voyage, but here it is ready or not. It was imminent. Now it is here. Bon Voyage! Once underway you will have trouble realizing what all the hesitation was about. **INVERTED:** This is a matter of the degree of efficiency with which this takes place, of how much luggage gets left behind, and how far you have to jump to catch the boarding ramp as it was being raised.

17 GOVERNED BY THE STAR: ASPIRATIONS OF EGO, GOALS, MAXIMUM EXPECTATIONS
UPRIGHT: Your goal deals with the mental aspects of things spiritual. You may aspire to a certain level of understanding with which you will be content for this lifetime. You will push no further except to communicate what you have learned more and more efficiently. This is the mark of the true teacher, also the perfectionist. In metaphysical terms this is a function of a gatekeeper, to stay behind for awhile and show others the way when they are ready. **INVERTED:** This may not be the right goal for you; perhaps you should continue on your own.

18 GOVERNED BY THE MOON: ASPIRATIONS OF HEART, COMPASSION
UPRIGHT: You want to be so efficient with your life path, that you have energy left over to help others with their lessons. You are ready for this gate in this lifetime and it is a highly significant one. This surplus energy will make you glow, attracting others for whom your excess can provide the extra push they need. This process is at the root of the ability to heal. **INVERTED:** Clarify your desire to be strong in this plane. Examine your motives for wanting to help others learn, for wanting to be a healer.

19 GOVERNED BY THE SUN: MATERIAL FULFILLMENT/EVALUATION
UPRIGHT: Your body serves you well throughout this lifetime, supporting your tireless projects. You observe with good practices in this plane the core of your spiritual knowledge. You practice your faith by integrating it into your daily regimen, perhaps even your work. You walk your talk. **INVERTED:** You may be headed toward too much or too little of the above in your present practices. The rest of the reading should provide strong clues.

20 GOVERNED BY JUDGEMENT: HEART'S FULFILLMENT/EVALUATION
UPRIGHT: Your relationships and creative projects have integrated well into your spiritual program. The four planes are well on their way to moving in unison. The efficiency of give and take has blessed you with an enviable harmony in your Emotional Plane. **INVERTED:** Look at your present handling of your spiritual drive in relation to those around you, in relation to your creativity. Perhaps there is an imbalance here that can be easily corrected.

21 GOVERNED BY THE WORLD: EGO'S FULFILLMENT/EVALUATION
UPRIGHT: You have collected the spiritual materials from which your port of embarkation, as well as your ocean worthy ship, can be built. With this hard work of your mind, coming to grips with the rudiments of the ethereal, your foundation for future work will be laid. If others can understand what you have tried to explain, they can travel with you. That is your legacy. **INVERTED:** Build what is necessary for this stage. The temptation will be to do either too much or too little. Also, it must not be your intention to take others with you, but simply to share what you have learned.

22/0 GOVERNED BY THE FOOL: SOUL'S FULFILLMENT/EVALUATION
UPRIGHT: Here was a worthy traveler, a spiritual adventurer with a healthy appetite, yet never in a hurry or too voracious to share his meal. **INVERTED:** The lessons detailed in the other positions in this reading will help you be this worthy traveler.

FOUR OF PENTACLES

UPRIGHT: Physical foundation and stability. Here is a reaping of the rewards for having become well centered physically/materially. This can be the completion of a significant physical phase, with the security of your accomplishments to back you up. This is establishment in its most colloquial sense. Finance Institutions. Insurance. Fixated on the present physical situation. Physical confidence. Excellent physique. Physical and fiscal balance. Physical and fiscal security. Achievement of good health/wealth. Civilization. Dependability/reliability. Physical/material control. Military/Police. ***INVERTED:*** The contentment of the moment may lead to an important oversight. Can also show greed and other forms of physical insecurity not justified by the circumstances—miserliness out of fear that you will not have enough for yourself. Refusal to use money/resources by hanging onto it all will eventually lead to ruin, just as a body not used atrophies. An acquisitiveness in order to impress rather than for true personal appreciation. An undesirable turn on the physical path. Abuse of physical power and/or position. Also, literally physical abuse.

In This Spread Position...Interpret the Four Of Pentacles Meanings to Include:

1 GOVERNED BY THE MAGICIAN: PHYSICAL GIVENS, OUT OF THE FATHER
UPRIGHT: You began life with a physical/material foundation from your father's line that some do not achieve in a lifetime. It is for you to use this blessing to maximum advantage in the execution of your Karmic Contract. This suggests that others will depend on you. You may well be part of the continuity of a financial legacy, a family, an industry, a company, the health care professions. You are highly responsible in this plane. ***INVERTED:*** This substantial financial/material continuum may have ended with your father. If so, with you begins a new ball game.

2 GOVERNED BY THE HIGH PRIESTESS: EMOTIONAL GIVENS, OUT OF THE MOTHER
UPRIGHT: You began life with a physical/material foundation from your mother's line that some do not achieve in a lifetime. It is for you to use this blessing to maximum advantage in the execution of your Karmic Contract. This suggests that others will depend on you. You may well be part of the continuity of a financial legacy, a family, an industry, a company, the health care professions. You are highly responsible in this plane. ***INVERTED:*** This substantial financial/material continuum may have ended with your mother. If so, with you begins a new ball game.

3 GOVERNED BY THE EMPRESS: MENTAL GIVENS, INTELLECTUAL PREDISPOSITION
UPRIGHT: Your mind has a natural affinity for the affairs of the Physical/material Plane. While such things may be difficult or uninteresting to many others, you find them easy and highly interesting, more like play than work. You may in fact turn your mind itself into a business. ***INVERTED:*** In the extreme, you may not enjoy the mental aspects of the material world. Or, you may find that you enjoy it all too much.

4 GOVERNED BY THE EMPEROR: SPIRITUAL GIVENS, LIFE PURPOSE
UPRIGHT: The buck stops here, literally. Additionally, we must say that the buck starts here. You must deal with the pragmatic world, with responsibility for the provision (i.e., beginning or continuing) of a solid physical and/or financial base. You are a strong link in the chain of civilization. You are an investor, a physical resource for others. The financial philosopher. The wise doctor. ***INVERTED:*** It could fall to you to deal with the more uncivilized aspects of human occupation of planet Earth; or, to bring mankind to substantially greater heights with giant steps forward. Physical demands on you may be great as many will call on you.

5 GOVERNED BY THE HIEROPHANT: SYSTEMS BORN INTO, SOCIETAL INFLUENCE
UPRIGHT: Your early years were secure, protected, with your needs being well taken care of. Also, availability of good food, good exercise giving you a head start in developing healthy habits. Household ordered and efficient. ***INVERTED:*** On one extreme, there may have been an insecure, unprotected early environment with needs not being provided for. On the other extreme, too much may have been taken care of with you not developing enough self-reliance skills early on. Also on this extreme, there can be a distortion of the order and discipline, up to and including physical abuse.

6 GOVERNED BY THE LOVERS: EMOTIONAL TAPES, BASIS FOR RELATING/CREATING
UPRIGHT: Physical security and its offshoots (i.e., health, wealth, status, safety, independence...) are the roots from which you are growing your relationships and your creative trees. ***INVERTED:*** A passion for power and control. At one extreme, you may find yourself uncomfortable with anyone other than people of means, and with physical situations that take place in anything short of luxury. Or, an offshoot of the same extreme, comfortable only with healthy people. Another extreme is more the reverse—with physical security et al being anathema to you. Your passion in this case will be toward the opposite, toward the less affluent, or even the destitute. Here also, is a passion for the unhealthy, a love of weakness.

7 GOVERNED BY THE CHARIOT: PHYSICAL RESOURCES, MEANS TO ACHIEVE
UPRIGHT: Your greatest physical resources are just that, your physical resources. You are most fortunate to have the health and/or the wealth you need to support your projects. ***INVERTED:*** You may have so much more than you need in resources that it becomes a problem of its own. However, the interpretation for the opposite extreme is that you do not have the physical/material resources you need for the project at hand.

8 GOVERNED BY STRENGTH: EMOTIONAL RESOURCES, ENERGY
UPRIGHT: Your physical and/or fiscal confidence has infused your emotional plane, mixing well into all your relationships and creative projects. They are inseparable, perhaps indistinguishable. ***INVERTED:*** This physical/fiscal well-being and confidence may be dominating and in a way distorting, even poisoning your intended progress in the Emotional Plane.

9 GOVERNED BY THE HERMIT: BELIEF SYSTEM, BASIS FOR DECISIONS
UPRIGHT: A faith in the fundamental principles of economics in the broadest sense, in the understanding of resources and how to use them to productive ends. How to manage increase, to create growth for its most basic of purposes...survival. From Adam Smith to Carl Marx, from laissez-faire to socialism, the full range applies here. This is Politics. In a separate but equally valid vein is faith in the status of the body, in health itself. ***INVERTED:*** There are many distortions in the extremes of this archetype, from the health fanatic to the political boss gone power mad, to the financial wizard who mistakenly lives in a world of abstract figures instead of people.

10 GOVERNED BY THE WHEEL OF FORTUNE: CENTRAL MESSAGE, THEME OF READING
UPRIGHT: Your physical/material foundation is secure and reliable. You are covered for your needs in the present and near future. ***INVERTED:*** Use your financial resources positively. On one extreme, do not try to keep everything for yourself; on the other extreme, do not think you have to invest in everything and everybody. A change in, or information about, the condition of your physical foundation. Whether it is financial, or health, or another of the possibilities presented above in the general interpretations, will be clear when viewed with all of the other cards in the reading, particularly the other cards in the positions of the present and near future, positions 11, 12, and 13.

11 GOVERNED BY JUSTICE: STATE/CONTENT OF MIND, PLANS
UPRIGHT: You are at work planning now on the affairs of your Physical Plane, on how to shore up, to manage, to improve your condition. ***INVERTED:*** Concerned with one or more of the aspects of your physical/material welfare. Either something has happened already that you wish to correct or you are making contingency plans because you are worried something might happen.

12 GOVERNED BY THE HANGED MAN: STATE OF EMOTIONS, SUBCONSCIOUS
UPRIGHT: Most important to your heart at the moment is your stability in the Physical/material Plane. The feeling is positive, not a worry. But accept openly that your situation, be it health or wealth, is at the top of your want list. ***INVERTED:*** Perhaps there have been dreams or daydreams raising some difficulties in these areas. This feeling you have may only be in your subconscious now. This reading is to help bring it up into the light of day. There could be emotional abuse through physical means.

13 GOVERNED BY DEATH: PHYSICAL SITUATION, HARD REALITY
UPRIGHT: It should come as no surprise to you that you are doing pretty well. Let this card here serve as a major focal point to reference, while interpreting all of the other positions. ***INVERTED:*** Conversely, this suggests that you are doing either outrageously well, or that there have been some difficulties.

14 GOVERNED BY TEMPERANCE: EMOTIONAL TEST
UPRIGHT: Here is the impact of success and abundance on your Emotional Plane. Prepare for the effect on your relationships. Backing will be available for your creative projects. Review this card's general meanings, for this can be where your heart is headed. ***INVERTED:*** Be wary that you do not let distortions or problems with the Physical Plane adversely affect your relationships/creativity. If your physical/material well-being has been at the center of your desires, you may find this changing in the near future. Expected financial backing may not materialize.

15 GOVERNED BY THE DEVIL: TEMPTATION/CHALLENGE, FEARS
UPRIGHT: Your mind will be focused on your physical/material foundation in the near future. This could be a time for investment, rethinking, taking stock. ***INVERTED:*** You may be diverted from questions about your health, finances, and such. You may decide that your physical affairs are not as they should be and plan to make major changes. They could prove to be far better, or far worse, than you thought.

16 GOVERNED BY THE TOWER: NEXT LESSON, GRACE OF GOD
UPRIGHT: Rest assured that your physical foundation will be healthy and secure by this time next year. How you achieve this may have some variations, but you are intended to know your situation will be solid. This spiritual insurance is intended to offer you peace of mind to contend with other matters in very much the same sense as a physical insurance policy does. ***INVERTED:*** Neither squander your resources unnecessarily, nor refuse to invest in what is prudent.

17 GOVERNED BY THE STAR: ASPIRATIONS OF EGO, GOALS, MAXIMUM EXPECTATIONS
UPRIGHT: To be physically developed and strong. To be financially independent and secure, well-positioned. These are your mental targets. You expect to do very well, surpassing all your personal material needs by a substantial margin. ***INVERTED:*** On the one hand, you may expect to do exceptionally well materially, even beyond your needs, perhaps with avarice and a thirst for power over others. Conversely, your expectations may be very low, or your goal may be not to succeed physical/materially, at least not from a secure base. You may be a wildcatter. The possibility of failure excites you.

18 GOVERNED BY THE MOON: ASPIRATIONS OF HEART, COMPASSION
UPRIGHT: You aspire to be healthy and strong, well-positioned and equipped, in order to bring about projects that will help others. ***INVERTED:*** Consider your motives. Do you want money and/or a strong body for the position and power it will give you over others, rather than for others? Does your heart want more than its fair share? Do you simply love what money can buy?

19 GOVERNED BY THE SUN: MATERIAL FULFILLMENT/EVALUATION
UPRIGHT: Your physical plane ends with you secure and healthy and in control of your surroundings. You will leave behind a most reliable foundation for your heirs to build on. ***INVERTED:*** One extreme here is the obvious one that we all fear—that we will not be secure or healthy in our advancing years. But the other extreme, while hard to imagine in the negative is just as hard on the path, i.e. of being overly secure or healthy, or trying to be so. You must use all your resources, including your body, in order to preserve them. They cannot be saved by saving them.

20 GOVERNED BY JUDGEMENT: HEART'S FULFILLMENT/EVALUATION
UPRIGHT: Your emotional harvest is the rich interaction made possible in all of your relationships through your enterprise and encouragement, or how well all your relationships have supported your endeavors. ***INVERTED:*** Work now to avoid adverse effects that physical abundance can have on the Emotional Plane. Money and physical ability must be used with sensitivity and not for domination or control. Do not let appreciation of your own body or property be all that your heart can deliver to your soul on your passing.

21 GOVERNED BY THE WORLD: EGO'S FULFILLMENT/EVALUATION
UPRIGHT: Your mental harvest is the wealth of practical achievement your mind has brought forth. This was no theoretical head trip. You have brought material increase and/or improved health and longevity to your fellow travelers with your disciplined hard work. ***INVERTED:*** Work now to assure that your material legacy will be appropriate to your mental objectives.

22/0 GOVERNED BY THE FOOL: SOUL'S FULFILLMENT/EVALUATION
UPRIGHT: What a foundation you have laid. You have understood and handled successfully the difficulties of the most material of the planes, the physical. With great respect for your God given body and with sensitive use of the earth's resources you have established the rock on which you can build in the next lifetime. ***INVERTED:*** Let the cards in this reading help you build a firm foundation.

FOUR OF CUPS

UPRIGHT: The Emotional Plane is centered and you are serene in the knowledge of your emotional blessings. Here is an emotional/creative plateau that will serve as your foundation. Emotional stability and confidence. Healthy acceptance/love of self. Amiability. Primary relationships under control and supportive of your desires/needs. You know the love you need will always be there. Managing talents well. Friendliness. Faithfulness. Loyalty. Trustworthiness, as well as trust. Respect. This is the Buddha and his bodhi tree. Peace of heart. **INVERTED:** Uncentered emotionally. Unappreciative of your blessings, of your present emotional lot in life. Here can be apathy, complacency. Moodiness. Over-satiation. Too much self-love (narcissism, vanity) or too little (self-deprecation). Overly submissive, or overly dominant; at the extremes, sadomasochism. Jealousy. Possessiveness. Infidelity. Sycophancy. Disrespect. Looking at the wrong things. There are emotional possibilities, offerings, that you are unaware of, even in the subconscious. These can be in the nature of a "chance of a lifetime" opportunity.

In This Spread Position...Interpret the Four Of Cups Meanings to Include:

1 GOVERNED BY THE MAGICIAN: PHYSICAL GIVENS, OUT OF THE FATHER
UPRIGHT: Life began with an emotional/creative foundation from your father's line. Use this blessing to maximum advantage in the execution of your Karmic Contract. You are to continue a creative legacy. There is security in dealing with people in physical/material matters. You are comfortable with your body and could easily be a nudist. Professions requiring physical openness and/or contact come easily. **INVERTED:** You may feel too secure/comfortable in business and finance, and/or dealing with the physical body, or you may find it a difficulty. You may be loyal or trusting to the extreme, or you may lack those virtues, in physical/material matters.

2 GOVERNED BY THE HIGH PRIESTESS: EMOTIONAL GIVENS, OUT OF THE MOTHER
UPRIGHT: Life began with an emotional/creative foundation from your mother's line. Use this blessing to maximum advantage in the execution of your Karmic Contract. You are to continue a creative legacy. You possess the qualities of the ideal, the true friend or mate. You are comfortable with yourself and so find it easy to be comfortable with others, as they are with you. **INVERTED:** This substantial emotional/creative continuum may have ended with your mother. If so, with you begins a new ball game. Read the list of qualities in the general meanings above, especially inverted. If any of these strike a familiar chord, remember that these are your givens to help, not to limit or punish you.

3 GOVERNED BY THE EMPRESS: MENTAL GIVENS, INTELLECTUAL PREDISPOSITION
UPRIGHT: Your mind is calmed with the waters of well-tempered emotions. You should rarely lose your temper. Prone to high self-esteem, especially with regard to your talents and your abilities with people. **INVERTED:** In your mental predisposition you may have too much or too little of one or more of the characteristics mentioned above in the general meanings, (inverted). Remember that it is a given, and if properly understood you will be able to use it to your advantage.

4 GOVERNED BY THE EMPEROR: SPIRITUAL GIVENS, LIFE PURPOSE
UPRIGHT: Your Karmic Contract is to establish and nourish a stable foundation for your relationships and creative enterprises. **INVERTED:** While there are many distortions—too much or too little—of this archetype, usually there is one which will be dominant. If none of the characteristics listed in general meanings (inverted), jumps out at you, the twenty-one other cards in the reading will help.

5 GOVERNED BY THE HIEROPHANT: SYSTEMS BORN INTO, SOCIETAL INFLUENCE
UPRIGHT: The early environment was an emotional haven that instilled a sense of belonging and confidence. Much of the lesson on balancing individual needs with that of the family, the group, was taught here. **INVERTED:** The early influence may not have been very stable. In one extreme, it would have been undisciplined, either the adults themselves or their lack of discipline of their children. In the other extreme, it would have been overdisciplined and there may have been abuse. This interpretation addresses how it was, not how you perceived it to be.

6 GOVERNED BY THE LOVERS: EMOTIONAL TAPES, BASIS FOR RELATING/CREATING
UPRIGHT: You want emotional security, the backup of energy from successful relationships and proven talents. Does a white house with a white picket fence come to mind? You like being liked. **INVERTED:** Your passion may be more toward the extremes of this card, in a desire for too much or too little emotional stability. We cannot succeed wanting to be totally captive or totally free. And we cannot be happy wanting more, or less, than the share our soul requires. The misplaced passions possible here are numerous, but a few of the most frequent ones are: narcissism, dominance/control, submissiveness with a hoped for protector over you. The need to be liked too dominant, or missing altogether.

7 GOVERNED BY THE CHARIOT: PHYSICAL RESOURCES, MEANS TO ACHIEVE
UPRIGHT: Your self-appreciation anchors you in the sea of material life, much as a buoy in a busy harbor. You always know who and where you are. The stability of your emotional life allows you all the energy and attention you need for physical/material affairs **INVERTED:** Too much stability may tend to turn you inward, and at the extremes be dominated by fears of something happening to change it all. Too little stability may drain you of energy and assets you need in the Physical/material Plane, ranging from your own health to your business.

8 GOVERNED BY STRENGTH: EMOTIONAL RESOURCES, ENERGY
UPRIGHT: Your ability to control the flux of energy in and out of the Emotional Plane is enviable. You derive immense pleasure and strength from your relationships and talents and can in turn put more energy back into emotional affairs and creative drive. **INVERTED:** A problem with your emotional foundation has been sapping your strength and will continue to do so unless resolved.

9 GOVERNED BY THE HERMIT: BELIEF SYSTEM, BASIS FOR DECISIONS
UPRIGHT: You believe in yourself—your abilities with people, and in your talents. And you believe in the major people that surround you, your principle relationships, and that the love you need will always be there. **INVERTED:** You may want to believe in yourself, in things like trust, loyalty, fidelity, but just do not have that faith yet. Or, your belief may be a non-belief in these same things, leaving you cynical, sardonic. Work to prevent this from descending into an amoral code of behavior.

10 GOVERNED BY THE WHEEL OF FORTUNE: CENTRAL MESSAGE, THEME OF READING

UPRIGHT: Time for emotional confidence. Believe in the love that is yours for the having. Your foundation is in place if you will but center yourself upon it and use it. Trust in your own abilities as they are already developed, as well as their potential. Rest assured of the loyalty of those on whom you depend. *INVERTED:* There is an imbalance in this archetype of emotional/creative foundation. There could be a shake up in your inner circle of family/friends. The problem could well be within you however. Review the general meanings (inverted) of the Four of Cups letting the other cards in the reading speak, amplifying this central message.

11 GOVERNED BY JUSTICE: STATE/CONTENT OF MIND, PLANS

UPRIGHT: You are taking charge of your personal affairs and talents, for you are confident now and plan to take advantage of the moment. Your emotional confidence is reinforcing and charging your confidence in mental affairs. *INVERTED:* Your excess of emotional/creative control, or the lack of it, may be causing parallel difficulties in your mental affairs. Lack of confidence here is at the root of all the possible culprits which include: jealousy/possessiveness, mental abuse, sadomasochism, infidelity.

12 GOVERNED BY THE HANGED MAN: STATE OF EMOTIONS, SUBCONSCIOUS

UPRIGHT: Your heart is aware of your disarming effect on those nearest you, of the fact that people simply like you and love you. There is a healthy awareness that there is more for the having, for you, and for your loved ones through you. Your heart feels the positive characteristics of this archetype of emotional security. *INVERTED:* Your subconscious may be distorting this archetype. A major purpose of this reading will be to bring these unhealthy extremes into the light. Be certain there is no emotional abuse.

13 GOVERNED BY DEATH: PHYSICAL SITUATION, HARD REALITY

UPRIGHT: The Physical Plane is infused with the positive energy of your emotional well-being, helping you seize your brass rings. There is mutual support/respect in your inner circle. *INVERTED:* On the one hand, you may be missing an opportunity if you do not become more aware. On the other hand, you should not pretend to see an opportunity where there is none. The discipline here may have become physical abuse.

14 GOVERNED BY TEMPERANCE: EMOTIONAL TEST

UPRIGHT: The restless serenity of the Buddha under the bodhi tree comes in your near future. Your emotional stability is a foundation, and a foundation is to built upon. What do you do with this foundation once it is yours? How will it transform your relationships and your creative enterprise? *INVERTED:* Neither be too serene, nor too restless. This archetype is yours for the having in the near future if you can withstand the test of one or more of the distortions, the nest of the worms (jealousy, vanity et al.). Remember, no one can stop you from loving yourself or from loving others.

15 GOVERNED BY THE DEVIL: TEMPTATION/CHALLENGE, FEARS

UPRIGHT: As the restless serenity of the Buddha under the bodhi tree symbolized a test for the heart, so does it as well for the mind. With peace of heart the mind can leap forward toward its goals without emotional distraction. *INVERTED:* On the one hand, do not be lulled into mental complacency because your emotional house is so comfortable. On the other hand, if it isn't all that comfortable, do not use that as an excuse to falter in your mental obligations. Be neither submissive, nor dominant, and yet be both.

16 GOVERNED BY THE TOWER: NEXT LESSON, GRACE OF GOD

UPRIGHT: Sit under a tree. Root yourself to the ground and look to the sky. Stiffen your backbone and allow the sword of Gabriel to fill you with light even as you rest before raising your emotional house. Your emotional foundation, the gate of stability through which you must pass in order to mingle and mix safely and successfully with many more of your brethren is yours within this next year. *INVERTED:* While for some this gate will cause but a small ripple in their personal relationships or their creative pursuits, for others the ripple will be more like a wave, for a few perhaps a tidal wave. But for all, the effects are beneficial.

17 GOVERNED BY THE STAR: ASPIRATIONS OF EGO, GOALS, MAXIMUM EXPECTATIONS

UPRIGHT: To be emotionally and creatively developed, strong. To be emotionally independent and secure, well-positioned. These are your mental targets. You expect to do well, surpassing all your emotional/creative needs by a substantial margin. *INVERTED:* On the one hand, you may expect to do exceptionally well emotionally/creatively, even beyond your needs, perhaps coveting what is not intended for you. You may wish to control people through the Emotional/sexual Plane. Conversely, you may have very low expectations in these matters.

18 GOVERNED BY THE MOON: ASPIRATIONS OF HEART, COMPASSION

UPRIGHT: While this card deals with an emotional foundation rooted in self-love, in this position you see its future significance to your path. For without this acceptance of self, you would find it next to impossible to love others and you would make it very difficult to impossible for others to love you. Here the heart is declaring its recognition of the Divine within, its devotion to the Divine self. *INVERTED:* The distortions of self-love fill the pages of mythology and the classics.

19 GOVERNED BY THE SUN: MATERIAL FULFILLMENT/EVALUATION

UPRIGHT: In your later years, you will be blessed with having your family and friends near you or capable of easy and frequent travel to be together. *INVERTED:* Your inner circle may be either all too close or much to far away to suit you.

20 GOVERNED BY JUDGEMENT: HEART'S FULFILLMENT/EVALUATION

UPRIGHT: You have been efficient in this, the Emotional Plane. You have many strong relationships in your family and extended family. There is no pressure at the end to make up for lost time. *INVERTED:* More people could have been included in your inner circle of friends and family. Begin with the information in this reading to open yourself to others who deserve your friendship and will enrich your life.

21 GOVERNED BY THE WORLD: EGO'S FULFILLMENT/EVALUATION

UPRIGHT: With the discipline, order, and dedication of your mind, you have prepared the way for a group of people, through their bonding, to achieve much more than they could have alone. The productivity of this band of merry men extends beyond your passing. *INVERTED:* Work now to secure the potential of your family and extended family. Do not let the distortions of this archetype drive your group apart.

22/0 GOVERNED BY THE FOOL: SOUL'S FULFILLMENT/EVALUATION

UPRIGHT: When all is said and done, you will have balanced the serenity of emotional well-being with the restlessness necessary to move the heart forward, using the emotional and creative security as a base to widen the circle of harmony to include others, as many others as possible with time. *INVERTED:* The reading brings twenty-one clues to help you achieve the above.

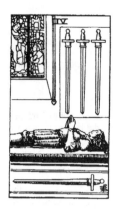

FOUR OF SWORDS

UPRIGHT: Here is meditative composure, a well-centered mentality. A mental plateau. Mental stability, reliability. A centering of thoughts before going on, mental foundation. An introspective turn of the mind, but not in the sense of The Hermit. This is a break in the "affairs of the day," so that you may soon return refreshed and ready to "do battle" again. Here is the completion of mental projects, graduations/certifications. A laying of mental foundations. Introspection. Strong sense of identity, self-worth. Planning. Fundamental understanding. Pragmatic mind. Rationality. Practicality. Facts. Objectivity. Order. A need for cleanliness. Discipline. Obedience. Law. Control. Civility/Civilization. Dignity. Self-confidence. Competency. Patience. ***INVERTED:*** There may be difficulty in this centering process, such as not being able to discern just where your progress to date has brought you, or simply indulging in too much thinking/introspection. Desiring too much mental abundance, mental greed. Intellectual complacency, also insecurity. Do not try to over protect your mind or your ideas for they will wither and disappear as though they never existed. Misuse of order, discipline, authority, control, cleanliness, et al.

In This Spread Position...Interpret the Four Of Swords Meanings to Include:

1 GOVERNED BY THE MAGICIAN: PHYSICAL GIVENS, OUT OF THE FATHER
UPRIGHT: The affairs of the Physical/material Plane will be marked by a sense of calm, of control. Actions will be well thought out and timely executed. You should be able to rest virtually at will, even able to refresh yourself with short time outs. You would do well as a follower of Raja or Gnani Yoga, as well as Zen, Taoist, or Confucian philosophy. ***INVERTED:*** Except for formal periods of sleep, you may be much too active for stationery reflection, preferring to take your meditation on the run. Your relaxation may come more through non-mental disciplines, such as exercise or sports.

2 GOVERNED BY THE HIGH PRIESTESS: EMOTIONAL GIVENS, OUT OF THE MOTHER
UPRIGHT: The affairs of the Emotional/creative Plane will be marked by a sense of calm, of control. Hatha or Tantra yoga may well be an appropriate practice here. Relationships and creative projects will be well thought out and controlled. ***INVERTED:*** Your relationships and creative affairs may keep you on the run. Or, you may have such a strong will to keep this plane calm and under control that you dampen your potential here unless you are careful.

3 GOVERNED BY THE EMPRESS: MENTAL GIVENS, INTELLECTUAL PREDISPOSITION
UPRIGHT: The affairs of the Mental Plane will be marked by a sense of calm, of control. You are virtually unshakable and have a very high tolerance for stress. An extraordinarily disciplined mind. A large and accessible memory. Strong sense of identity, self-worth. ***INVERTED:*** On the one extreme, you appear so calm as to make others uncomfortable. You have little need for much activity to keep yourself productively occupied. On the other extreme, you are not very calm and may be easily distracted.

4 GOVERNED BY THE EMPEROR: SPIRITUAL GIVENS, LIFE PURPOSE
UPRIGHT: This is a lifetime dedicated to the establishment of mental order, the necessary stability and foundation for serious intellectual work. A very strong, healthy sense of self characterizes this path. Fields requiring law, order, discipline, objectivity are favored. ***INVERTED:*** It could fall to you to deal with the more severe distortions of this archetype, with disorder, lack of discipline, criminality, for example.

5 GOVERNED BY THE HIEROPHANT: SYSTEMS BORN INTO, SOCIETAL INFLUENCE
UPRIGHT: A healthy sense of order and discipline prevailed so that more could be accomplished by everyone. Mental projects were encouraged. ***INVERTED:*** Even this ideal can be perverted—in the extremes where there is too much organization and intellectual push, or its antithesis of too much confusion. Dictatorship, abuse of authority on one radical extreme; anarchy and chaos on the other, either of which destroys the healthy heart.

6 GOVERNED BY THE LOVERS: EMOTIONAL TAPES, BASIS FOR RELATING/CREATING
UPRIGHT: Your passion is to be in control of your emotions, and to be cool and steadfast under fire. One who can package and present the emotions. ***INVERTED:*** There may be a tendency to hold in too much; or you may tend too let too much out. The passion for control and discipline can be distorted in numerous ways. Sexually, it can show up in sadomasochistic preferences, with you continually looking for someone to dominate or who easily dominates you.

7 GOVERNED BY THE CHARIOT: PHYSICAL RESOURCES, MEANS TO ACHIEVE
UPRIGHT: The ability to find what you want on a moments notice, to mobilize people and material quickly when necessary. Here is the ideal community leader during the crisis of a natural disaster. You never give up no matter how tired or how hopeless a situation may look. ***INVERTED:*** In one extreme, not knowing when to quit can lessen your future potential. In the other extreme, you can work mentally toward realizing that you have more physical endurance than you think.

8 GOVERNED BY STRENGTH: EMOTIONAL RESOURCES, ENERGY
UPRIGHT: Your forthrightness and dedication endear your friends. They are comforted and encouraged in their own lives by the way you direct your affairs. In one respect, this can be seen as tough love. This is the temperament required of a Mother Superior in a convent or girl's boarding school. ***INVERTED:*** Perhaps your exterior is where you are softest and your interior is where the mettle is. Whichever, these still must maintain a balanced role with each other for maximum effectiveness.

9 GOVERNED BY THE HERMIT: BELIEF SYSTEMS, BASIS FOR DECISIONS
UPRIGHT: Cleanliness is next to godliness. Order is the mathematical magic of a balanced universe and so it must be the basis of everything in your world. ***INVERTED:*** At one extreme, we have something a psychoanalyst might call anal-retentive, wherein there is a mania about cleanliness and everything being in its exact place all the time. At the other extreme, the belief system will be based on a complete lack of appreciation for order, with more appreciation for chaos.

10 GOVERNED BY THE WHEEL OF FORTUNE: CENTRAL MESSAGE, THEME OF READING
UPRIGHT: Be confident. You have done your homework and are mentally well prepared. Be composed, meditate, and continue to establish greater order, discipline, and accuracy. ***INVERTED:*** There is an imbalance in this archetype for mental stability and foundation which the cards in the next three positions,

11,12, and 13 will help to define. For example: There may be a potential difficulty with the law. Or, simply that you are not yet prepared. Or, you are misunderstanding, misusing the principles of order and discipline.

11 GOVERNED BY JUSTICE: STATE/CONTENT OF MIND, PLANS
UPRIGHT: You are confident, calm knowing you are ready. You are composed, well-centered in your thoughts. Your approach is valid. ***INVERTED:*** On one extreme, you are not calm because you know you are not ready. On the other extreme, you are much too calm under the mistaken idea that you are more than ready.

12 GOVERNED BY THE HANGED MAN: STATE OF EMOTIONS, SUBCONSCIOUS
UPRIGHT: In your gut, your subconscious, you feel on top of things, or at least that you have your Emotional Plane and creative energy under control. To have this card here instead of position 11 as described above suggests that your conscious mind may not have this same opinion, or that you may not be as organized in your Mental Plane. In other words, to outward appearances you may look scattered, but actually be quite together underneath. ***INVERTED:*** The reverse of the above may apply. Your gut, subconscious says you are not as on top of things as you might think.

13 GOVERNED BY DEATH: PHYSICAL SITUATION, HARD REALITY
UPRIGHT: The mind is very much in charge, and to your advantage. This could be a time of physical rest, a retreat to take stock. You are in a waiting mode, a period for patience. ***INVERTED:*** Your mind is too much in charge, or too little. If too much, there may be serious abuse of control, at the extreme causing physical damage to property or harm to others. There may be an inappropriate slacking off under the guise of rest and retrenchment. You are contemplating your navel.

14 GOVERNED BY TEMPERANCE: EMOTIONAL TEST
UPRIGHT: As you center in your mental affairs, your self-assured calm, may stir some waters. For, as you center you actually present a different facade to onlookers. This could be disconcerting to your mate, or to some of your inner circle. What happens as a desire for order and control hits the Emotional Plane? ***INVERTED:*** What happens if you are inordinately authoritative or on a tear for cleanliness? Here is the effect of too much or too little order from your mental house.

15 GOVERNED BY THE DEVIL: TEMPTATION/CHALLENGE, FEARS
UPRIGHT: You are being pulled toward the mental plateau that will serve as your foundation for the rest of your life. The most obvious symbol of this is a graduation. Go willingly, if not enthusiastically. ***INVERTED:*** Do not succumb to the extreme distortions of this archetype. Begin now to keep your eye on a valid goal and be certain you do not use inappropriate means to reach those ends.

16 GOVERNED BY THE TOWER: NEXT LESSON, GRACE OF GOD
UPRIGHT: You will be assured, beyond a shadow of a doubt that your mind is serving you well, that you are centered and working toward the right goals. You will be empowered to act decisively and to great effect with all the authority you need to accomplish your goals. ***INVERTED:*** One or more of the imbalances of this archetype will fall away as if by magic.

17 GOVERNED BY THE STAR: ASPIRATIONS OF EGO, GOALS, MAXIMUM EXPECTATIONS
UPRIGHT: You might aspire to prominence and control over your life, like that of an established author with a relative degree of periodic public exposure, or perhaps to the ivory tower existence of a contemplative monk or theologian. But whichever path you choose, you certainly aspire to control over your daily affairs and maybe those of your closest compadres. ***INVERTED:*** Do not aspire to a life of idealism and escapism, nor to one of regimented self-imprisonment, nor to improper control of anything or anyone.

18 GOVERNED BY THE MOON: ASPIRATIONS OF HEART, COMPASSION
UPRIGHT: The order and discipline aspired to here is a desire to emulate the divine order to bring about the hermetic dictum "as above, so below." ***INVERTED:*** The tightrope that must be walked here is to want to emulate the divine order, not to be it. Otherwise, you will be laying the subconscious groundwork for certain misery via self-righteousness and odious piety.

19 GOVERNED BY THE SUN: MATERIAL FULFILLMENT/EVALUATION
UPRIGHT: One might say that things end for you picture perfect. Your physical environment bespeaks the order that prevails in your mind. ***INVERTED:*** At one extreme, you, your business, and your surroundings will appear very uncomfortable because of their over organization and imposing order. At the other extreme, things may appear uncomfortable due to a very real lack of order.

20 GOVERNED BY JUDGEMENT: HEART'S FULFILLMENT/EVALUATION
UPRIGHT: Relationships have been handled in such a way as to please any guide to manners and ethics. But there may or may not have been any large degree of warmth involved. But all emotional contracts have been honored. The letter of the law has been honored but perhaps out of a sense of duty, or because it simply was the law, rather than out of love. ***INVERTED:*** Work now to be sure that you do not use the heart to control, particularly the most important people in your life. The ability to control should not be your main desire.

21 GOVERNED BY THE WORLD: EGO'S FULFILLMENT/EVALUATION
UPRIGHT: The mind is at rest as you finish up the affairs of this incarnation. This lifetime was a laboratory of efficiency. You have honored your beliefs while integrating the thoughts of others. ***INVERTED:*** Work now to be sure that the mind is not serving itself at the cost of the other planes, nor is it at odds with the overall Karmic Contract.

22/0 GOVERNED BY THE FOOL: SOUL'S FULFILLMENT/EVALUATION
UPRIGHT: Confidence in your mind's ability to carry the day for your heart. A trust in your rational ability to pull yourself up out of your elemental roots and present your enlightened being to a patiently waiting God. The belief that with the power of your mind you can and will prevail. ***INVERTED:*** You must be on guard against the extremes here. Be neither arrogant as to the mind's capacity, nor naive.

FOUR OF WANDS

UPRIGHT: You are an initiate enjoying the comfort of being spiritually centered on your path, secure in the knowledge of accomplishments satisfying the Karmic Contract. Spiritual foundation for future work in this incarnation. Your course has been established and proven. Feedback is excellent. Your position feels strong and correct. Strong value system in place. There is justifiable celebration. Here are religious and spiritual holidays, mystagogia. Fellowship. There is thanksgiving for what you have received and will receive. Practicing your faith. Utilizing, integrating ritual into daily life. Here is the time for counting your blessings. Profound honesty in all relationships. The balance and harmony indicated by the Four of Wands suggests that the lower three levels (Mental, Emotional, and Physical) are balanced as well. Spiritual self-confidence, dedication, order, control, discipline. Confirmation. A theology. **INVERTED:** Here is a lack of pause, of respect, and of understanding in correct measure for your status/progress, for you are too caught up in the physical, emotional, mental aspects of the moment. Not properly observing, celebrating, giving thanks. An inadequate performance, according to the responsibilities of your spiritual position. Inadequate/improper use of spiritual position and/or knowledge. Spiritual complacency, selfishness, vanity, greed.

In This Spread Position...Interpret the Four Of Wands Meanings to Include:

1 GOVERNED BY THE MAGICIAN: PHYSICAL GIVENS, OUT OF THE FATHER
UPRIGHT: The affairs of the Physical Plane are marked by a sensitivity to values much higher than the instincts for protection and survival. While you may not be a priest in this lifetime, your level of devotion and integration of spirit into the Material Plane have ordained you nevertheless. Your work will be richly inspired. **INVERTED:** In time your observation of divine law may lead you to extreme, perhaps rare, forms of devotion.

2 GOVERNED BY THE HIGH PRIESTESS: EMOTIONAL GIVENS, OUT OF THE MOTHER
UPRIGHT: The affairs of the Emotional Plane are marked by a sensitivity to values much higher than the desire for procreation and extension via creativity. This spiritual foundation offers a base for receiving profound inspiration to inform your talents and give them expression, and it lays a ground for your network of relationships to fertilize. You are demonstrative in all your relationships. **INVERTED:** You are capable of exceptional works of great beauty, some of which will be your relationships themselves. The depth and range of your emotional perception will be a challenge.

3 GOVERNED BY THE EMPRESS: MENTAL GIVENS, INTELLECTUAL PREDISPOSITION
UPRIGHT: The affairs of the Mental Plane are marked by a sensitivity to values much higher than the drive for continuity through the legacy of your intellectual achievements. You will be well informed principally because you will always be listening. There is a pleasant seriousness in your ambition to be of value. **INVERTED:** You will enjoy the intricacies of spiritual observation with an attention for detail matched by few. The depth and range of your mental perception will be a challenge.

4 GOVERNED BY THE EMPEROR: SPIRITUAL GIVENS, LIFE PURPOSE
UPRIGHT: Your life is to be a celebration, an observation of perennial wisdom. There is a lightness to you even at your most serious moments of which there are many. For you are a most serious person, tenaciously efficient, yet so obviously effective to everyone's benefit as to draw no criticism. Quite the contrary, you are sought out for that quality and for your natural ability to teach by example. **INVERTED:** As people profit by being near you, it may be difficult to guard the time you need for yourself. Ritual and observation may become forces to be reckoned with.

5 GOVERNED BY THE HIEROPHANT: SYSTEMS BORN INTO, SOCIETAL INFLUENCE
UPRIGHT: The spiritual practices observed in your early environment may or may not have been of an organized religious nature. But they were truly spiritual in a meaningful way. There was great awareness and there was ritual observation. Daily practice here was a healthy blueprint for living. **INVERTED:** What you saw was not necessarily what you got. There may have been empty observations, even hypocrisy. Discipline may have been forced as a misunderstanding/misapplication of spiritual order.

6 GOVERNED BY THE LOVERS: EMOTIONAL TAPES, BASIS FOR RELATING/CREATING
UPRIGHT: Your passion is for faith itself. The excitement of interacting with the rituals and observations energizes you. And yet, it is the underlying security and stability of the state of believing that means the most. **INVERTED:** You may be drawn to the abstract trappings of faith more than to the underlying truths and the demands they make on your soul. Ritual, spiritual practice can easily deteriorate into self-serving, empty operations. They are not ends in themselves.

7 GOVERNED BY THE CHARIOT: PHYSICAL RESOURCES, MEANS TO ACHIEVE
UPRIGHT: Within your spiritual home, there lies your main assets and your base of operations. Whether you need extra muscle or money, you know you can count on the material resources that come with your spiritual path. **INVERTED:** Neither become overly dependent on these resources in your spiritual community, nor be remiss in not taking advantage of them when you need them.

8 GOVERNED BY STRENGTH: EMOTIONAL RESOURCES, ENERGY
UPRIGHT: Your relationships and creative projects are based on the soundest principles and will withstand the tests of time. Your strength lies in the degree to which faith and spirituality are integrated into your emotional life. You are living love. **INVERTED:** Your Emotional Plane is vibrant because it is rooted in spirit. Do not try to put that foundation on top of your emotional affairs; it will smother rather than support them.

9 GOVERNED BY THE HERMIT: BELIEF SYSTEM, BASIS FOR DECISIONS
UPRIGHT: Your personal beliefs have found a home, a group or ideology of common ground and you subscribe to the need for, and benefits of, fellowship. You accede to the wisdom of giving thanks for what has already been received, and of invoking help in what yet remains a need. **INVERTED:** You do not ascribe to the need for spiritual observation, alone or with a group. You are stoic, living fully in the outer sensorial world, giving little credence to spirituality or any concept of God. But to have this card here suggests that your belief is in fact a "non-belief."

10 GOVERNED BY THE WHEEL OF FORTUNE: CENTRAL MESSAGE, THEME OF READING
UPRIGHT: The spiritual home you have been preparing is ready. This is a foundation you can rely on for the rest of your life. It represents a body of lessons opening a major gate on your path. The garden in which you now stand will grow and prosper forever, for it is an outer courtyard to the garden of Eden.

Celebration is in the air. *INVERTED:* On one extreme, do not be negligent in your observations. Your spiritual meditation and rituals are very important, especially at this time. On the other extreme, do not overfill your life with unnecessary, or empty formalities.

11 GOVERNED BY JUSTICE: STATE/CONTENT OF MIND
UPRIGHT: You know that you are well-positioned and confident now that everything seems to add up. Everything seems right. A celebration or special ceremony is being considered. *INVERTED:* You know that something just doesn't quite fit with everything else. Or, the fact that everything appears to be perfect is what troubles you. You may be questioning your alignment with others in spiritual matters. One possible dilemma: Have you joined the right group? Is it you or the group?

12 GOVERNED BY THE HANGED MAN: STATE OF EMOTIONS, SUBCONSCIOUS
UPRIGHT: Relationships and creative projects are in fundamental agreement and in support of your spiritual path. This is a time of great joy as your heart celebrates your coming of spiritual age. In formal religions this is the age of confirmation, usually coinciding with the onset of puberty, the coming alive of your sexuality. Here is celebration of your coming alive spiritually. *INVERTED:* The heart is confused, for it is not rejoicing when in fact it should be.

13 GOVERNED BY DEATH: PHYSICAL SITUATION, HARD REALITY
UPRIGHT: You are doing the right work/activities in your Physical/material Plane. It's quite possible that this work and activity is taking on more and more of an overt spiritual nature. A ceremony or its equivalent occupies the stage now or in the near future. There is hard evidence, a witnessing of the progress that has been made on the path. These are timely observations of the cycles of life. Thanksgiving and/or invocation are in progress. *INVERTED:* There may be too much or too little celebration, observation, ritual. You may be trying to convert unnecessarily your entire Physical Plane into the spiritual, even to make your living on line in spiritual endeavors. Remember that everything contains the spiritual.

14 GOVERNED BY TEMPERANCE: EMOTIONAL TEST
UPRIGHT: You will be integrating more and more your Spiritual and Emotional Planes as you try to include others into the joy of what you have discovered. You will be creative in how you express, how you witness your faith, initiating new practices while honoring old. *INVERTED:* How do your practices affect your relationships and vice versa. Spiritual integrity can create enormous pressures on families and groups. Practices must not be imposed on those not ready or willing.

15 GOVERNED BY THE DEVIL: TEMPTATION/CHALLENGE, FEARS
UPRIGHT: Armed with our spiritual diploma and backed by the foundation of our fellowship, we can be dangerous to ourselves and our brethren. Enjoy your moment of exhilaration at what you know you have achieved but also know that the path is much, much longer. *INVERTED:* There may well be growing pains within you, or within your fellowship. Guard against the pitfalls of spiritual vanity. Neither be complacent with your spiritual status, turning your back on further growth while presuming you hold the truth everyone else should observe, nor rush too quickly ahead of your foundation into new and unchartered waters without your spiritual lifeline.

16 GOVERNED BY THE TOWER: NEXT LESSON, GRACE OF GOD
UPRIGHT: Confirmation awaits you, within this next year. There will be many signs to inform and assure you as the myriad pieces you have assembled fall into place. Once imprinted with this picture, your spiritual foundation is secure. From here on life will be both easier and more difficult. Easier, because you will be armed with understanding and learn your lessons at the higher levels where there is little or no pain and negativity. More difficult, because you will be a brighter light drawing more responsibility since you are equipped to handle it. *INVERTED:* Grace will intervene to help center this archetype.

17 GOVERNED BY THE STAR: ASPIRATIONS OF EGO, GOALS, MAXIMUM EXPECTATIONS
UPRIGHT: You expect to reach a level of holistic awareness, a spiritually reliable mental foundation, a theology. By extension, to establish a fellowship, school, or church, which will mark that level of mental realization for you and enable you to teach it to others. *INVERTED:* Be certain that in your goal you think of yourself as a medium for transmitting and observing universal truth and not as the source of those truths and all will be well.

18 GOVERNED BY THE MOON: ASPIRATIONS OF HEART, COMPASSION
UPRIGHT: Your heart wants nothing less than to participate in, to bring about, a valid fellowship, a working church, a mutual foundation on which you and others like you can dance, arm in arm, to the tune of the gods. *INVERTED:* Be certain that this desire has no escapist elements in it, for in the long run this must be a universal fellowship that you aspire to.

19 GOVERNED BY THE SUN: MATERIAL FULFILLMENT/EVALUATION
UPRIGHT: When all is said and done you will have integrated your Material and Spiritual Planes very well. The probability is high that you have made your living walking your talk. You practice your faith to the end. *INVERTED:* You certainly do not have to quit your job and join a group of missionaries or enter a convent, but begin now to integrate your present level of spiritual awareness into your daily regimen so that you can achieve integration of the Material and Spiritual Planes in this lifetime.

20 GOVERNED BY JUDGEMENT: HEART'S FULFILLMENT/EVALUATION
UPRIGHT: Your heart rejoices at the degree to which your Emotional Plane has succeeded. You have been able to share openly and fully your level of spiritual awareness with many friends, especially your closest loved ones. Your motivations have been noble, generating work that has reached deep into the hearts of many. *INVERTED:* Some of your loved ones will not be able to share your open heart and level of participation in divine truth. Or, it may be the other way around. Let your heart purify your motives and your Emotional Plane will thrive.

21 GOVERNED BY THE WORLD: EGO'S FULFILLMENT/EVALUATION
UPRIGHT: Your mind is content, knowing as it does, that you have reached the outer courtyard to the garden of Eden. While God is by definition ineffable, our path requires us to listen to the muses for as much of God's message as our hearts can contain and our minds comprehend. This ego is justifiably proud in having done just that. *INVERTED:* Work now so that you do not have to feign pride at what you did not achieve.

22/0 GOVERNED BY THE FOOL: SOUL'S FULFILLMENT/EVALUATION
UPRIGHT: You achieved balance in all four levels (Physical, Emotional, Mental, and Spiritual), and did your very best to implement the hermetic dictum, "as above, so below." With this card you leave this lifetime with fully packed bags for your next incarnation. You are ready. *INVERTED:* You are intended to acquire the lessons of this archetype in this lifetime. This reading offers guidance in that direction.

FIVE OF PENTACLES

UPRIGHT: Here is the paradox of freedom and uncertainty, a multiplicity of choice at the physical/material level, in matters of health, work, transportation, finance—things that constitute hard reality. The dilemma: How to preserve the order and discipline from the foundation of the Four of Pentacles while moving forward? This card represents that movement but the activity in this phase is within a limited range, while there is pause for reparation. The Five of Pentacles takes stock of your physical world before committing. Which among the good choices is yours? Here are things like: flexibility, versatility, patience, relaxation (no need for movement/action), curiosity, carefreeness, independence. But there is inherent restlessness in this stasis, a positive instability that will eventually necessitate change. This is a time for repairing the nets so that you will be ready when the fish come. The self is adjusting to an increased demand on the soul, to give priority to others as well as self, primarily family and friends. The ambivalence of all the Fives is seen in the fact that the number five derives either from the combination of 2 and 3 (the duality of emotional/mental), or the combination of 1 and 4 (the duality of physical/spiritual). Here the effect of the latter predominates in the Suit of Pentacles. **INVERTED:** Not utilizing the positive potential of a period of rest. Also, too much movement when stillness is required. Restlessness itself, hastiness, carelessness/recklessness. Looking at physical losses instead of gains—this is an effect of mind on the Physical Plane. On the negative side of this coin are things like: apathy, ambivalence, laziness, stagnancy, and the plethora of problems that can derive from lack of movement. When money doesn't move the economy falters, personal finances suffer. When you do not exercise your muscles, they atrophy. If you don't move the proper foods through your body, your health suffers.

In This Spread Position...Interpret the Five Of Pentacles Meanings to Include:

1 GOVERNED BY THE MAGICIAN: PHYSICAL GIVENS, OUT OF THE FATHER
UPRIGHT: Your casual handling of the affairs of the Physical/material Plane may run counter to the grain, but they suit you. You aren't necessarily a gambler, but you are more than willing to take your chances. Here is the peculiar confidence of a carefree adventurer, one willing to roll with the punches. **INVERTED:** Be prepared, for you may infuriate many who are much more conventional in their habits.

2 GOVERNED BY THE HIGH PRIESTESS: EMOTIONAL GIVENS, OUT OF THE MOTHER
UPRIGHT: You will not require many of the physical trappings that most people like to have with their relationships, or with their creative endeavors. Nor will you need physical proximity. You could well live apart from your loved ones for lengths of time. **INVERTED:** Your lack of attachment and freedom of movement is not the norm and you must find people who understand and accept this quality in you.

3 GOVERNED BY THE EMPRESS: MENTAL GIVENS, INTELLECTUAL PREDISPOSITION
UPRIGHT: Here is the student to drive teachers crazy. While you may stay occupied, it is rarely with the teacher's assignments. You occupy you own world, but it is very real, not fantasy. Your mind prefers to ponder the possibilities of the Physical/material Plane. You are intensely hobby oriented. **INVERTED:** Your sense of timing and reaction will leave others bewildered. Others ideas may disappear into you like Brer Rabbit's fist into the tar baby.

4 GOVERNED BY THE EMPEROR: SPIRITUAL GIVENS, LIFE PURPOSE
UPRIGHT: It is especially hard to ask the Spiritual Plane to be patient, for the soul is ever so hungry to be reunited. But patience is the byword for this lifetime. Many of the qualities contemporary society does not value will be the hallmark of your path. Remember, in the right context, the ability to take it easy is a virtue of the highest order. Rest assured that this would not be your Karmic Path if your bases were not to be covered while you are taking a break. **INVERTED:** You may be asked to help many others with this path.

5 GOVERNED BY THE HIEROPHANT: SYSTEMS BORN INTO, SOCIETAL INFLUENCE
UPRIGHT: A healthy sense of freedom energized by a wide range of options. Unfettered by your early environment. **INVERTED:** Too much freedom and uncertainty here would have brought mistakes, inefficiency, and the resulting loss in physical/material affairs—health, finances, et al. Too little freedom, limiting the ability to take advantage of opportunities, would have brought deficiency and loss as well. In such cases, hardship would have been the norm.

6 GOVERNED BY THE LOVERS; EMOTIONAL TAPES, BASIS FOR RELATING/CREATING
UPRIGHT: You love your physical freedom, and your relationships, be they friend or lover, will have to give you a wide berth. This is not to say they you cannot be both an excellent friend and a good lover, but your ground rules will have to be accepted. **INVERTED:** Being in virtual bondage as if owned is one far extreme here; it's opposite is irresponsible, non-committal freedom. Either present great difficulties.

7 GOVERNED BY THE CHARIOT: PHYSICAL RESOURCES, MEANS TO ACHIEVE
UPRIGHT: You are similar to the cat who can always land on her feet. You are resourceful in the hardest of circumstances, your instincts for survival close to that of an animal. Your physical/material demands are not that great. But like the tortoise and the hare, you, the tortoise, always get where you want to go, frequently before the other guy. **INVERTED:** Physical assets may not exist or be liquid enough if a project is the question. Your needs may outreach your means. Physically, you may not be up to the task of the moment.

8 GOVERNED BY STRENGTH: EMOTIONAL RESOURCES, ENERGY
UPRIGHT: You are low-keyed and do not waste energy. You are like an engine with a smooth idle. This controlled temperament enables you to roll with the punches and move on. While you can be knocked down, you can never be counted out. **INVERTED:** The extremes of this archetype which may give you the most trouble are: On the one hand, you are too low keyed, or too fixed in your ways, letting opportunities pass. On the other hand, you are unable to rest and regroup, and much too free and unreliable, chasing opportunities away.

9 GOVERNED BY THE HERMIT: BELIEF SYSTEM, BASIS FOR DECISIONS
UPRIGHT: What you count most important is physical freedom, liberty, and choice. But, here also is the belief in material moderation, placing minimum demands on nature to supply our needs. An environmentalist, consumer advocate, or political activist fits here. **INVERTED:** At one extreme, this is the anarchist, the radical individualist who ideally would place himself in a cabin in the wilderness. At another extreme, this ideal reduces everyone to a common denominator resembling the extreme side of socialism/communism. At even another extreme is radical environmentalism.

10 GOVERNED BY THE WHEEL OF FORTUNE: CENTRAL MESSAGE, THEME OF READING
UPRIGHT: The lack of movement, of apparent growth at the physical level, be it the progress of a body-building program, or of increase in finances, is

appropriate for the moment. All of the fives, but especially the Five of Pentacles, tell us that our souls are waiting for things to line up, to catch up with each other. Gates must be constructed for us to move through. *INVERTED:* Improvement, increase in efficiency, progress must come from a shoring up of the existing situation.

11 GOVERNED BY JUSTICE: STATE/CONTENT OF MIND, PLANS

UPRIGHT: The mind is centered on the interim in your physical world allowing a reprieve. Rest and relaxation may be on the schedule. You may be occupied with mental pastimes. *INVERTED:* On one extreme, your stasis at the physical level is the number one priority, for the imbalances are hurting. On the other extreme, your mind is on other matters—neither on the problems at hand, nor engaged in positive refueling for another day.

12 GOVERNED BY THE HANGED MAN: STATE OF EMOTIONS, SUBCONSCIOUS

UPRIGHT: The heart is helping you find happiness, whatever your circumstances— to enjoy leisure if that is your good fortune, to be able to find the silver lining in your physical troubles if that is your present lot. It offers no explanations, no excuses, just love. This is Tiny Tim's ability to love Scrooge. *INVERTED:* On the one hand, this heart is indifferent to the problems of the physical plane. On the other hand, you could be exacerbating the problem with overreaction and misplaced sentiment.

13 GOVERNED BY DEATH: PHYSICAL SITUATION, HARD REALITY

UPRIGHT: Time out. Vacation. Rest and Relaxation. Do the things you could not otherwise if you were in your normal routine. *INVERTED:* One possibility is that hard lessons on your path have stopped you so that you can focus your attention and redirect your activities. These can include financial or health problems. Another result of imbalance here is the lack of choice, of freedom. Another is the reverse, to be to free, unattached and out of the system altogether. This complete freedom is total uncertainty, cut off from motivation and direction. Surely you are not slacking off.

14 GOVERNED BY TEMPERANCE: EMOTIONAL TEST

UPRIGHT: Here is the impact of the pause in your physical routine, of your new, if temporary, freedom in your emotional house. *INVERTED:* Here is the impact of stasis, whether by external means or through your inaction/misaction, on your relationships and your creative work.

15 GOVERNED BY THE DEVIL: TEMPTATION/CHALLENGE, FEARS

UPRIGHT: There is an appropriate lull in your affairs this year. Your mind needs the rest. *INVERTED:* Because you are not confident that the physical/material tunnel your are in has a light at the end of it, you are hurting your ability to find that light. But your inability to see the light is only because the tunnel has a curve in it. You must move into and through the tunnel enough to pass the blind curve.

16 GOVERNED BY THE TOWER: NEXT LESSON, GRACE OF GOD

UPRIGHT: There will be a plateau in your Physical Plane to enable you to catch your breath. In this interim there are numerous tumblers that will be aligning to open your next gate. Use your time productively and the interim will be short and pleasant. *INVERTED:* At least one, and maybe more, of your most troublesome imbalances in this archetype will be righted for you.

17 GOVERNED BY THE STAR: ASPIRATIONS OF THE EGO, GOALS, MAXIMUM EXPECTATIONS

UPRIGHT: To enjoy the productive harmony that comes from freedom balanced with constraint in the material plane. To enjoy the simple, unfettered life. To integrate the laws of nature into your life and accept all of God's package of free will with enthusiasm. *INVERTED:* A distortion here is to have the goal of avoiding physical uncertainty, to be sure and secure with absolute predictability. Another distortion is the misunderstanding of freedom and free will, which does not understand that they too can become prisons if abused.

18 GOVERNED BY THE MOON: ASPIRATIONS OF THE HEART, COMPASSION

UPRIGHT: To be capable of empathizing and joining with others as they learn and recuperate in their periods of rest. To have the courage to seek freedom, accepting uncertainty as a blessing. Here you aspire to identify with what man has experienced and endured. You wish for full empathy for what has been. *INVERTED:* You need to raise others to the joy of understanding in all things, rather than to over empathize and fall into their suffering with them.

19 GOVERNED BY THE SUN: MATERIAL FULFILLMENT/EVALUATION

UPRIGHT: While your schedule may not be busy and your range of activity small, your freedom to maximize your material pleasures is great. You are more than content at how you have managed your health and your resources. You have harmonized with your environment. *INVERTED:* Begin now to look for the advantages in your present material circumstances so that you can claim the above as your fulfillment.

20 GOVERNED BY JUDGEMENT: HEART'S FULFILLMENT/EVALUATION

UPRIGHT: The qualities of patience, flexibility, versatility, are clues to the success of this heart, as it taught itself and its loved ones to meet the challenge of freedom and uncertainty. *INVERTED:* Pursue the challenge of choice with a dedicated heart lest you be disappointed even in the midst of health and wealth.

21 GOVERNED BY THE WORLD: EGO'S FULFILLMENT/EVALUATION

UPRIGHT: You have not attacked the vicissitudes of fate, understanding the delicate weave life must make of God's will and man's will. *INVERTED:* Perhaps you are falling prey to one or the other extreme here. On the one hand, deferring too much to fate and not asserting your will to make the best of the hand you were dealt. Or, on the other hand, rejecting fate and insisting your will be done, swimming upstream like the salmon all the way.

22/0 GOVERNED BY THE FOOL: SOUL'S FULFILLMENT/EVALUATION

UPRIGHT: Your soul has been wise, as if privy to the master timekeeper's watch, for you were able to use your waiting days productively as you and your fellow group travelers caught up with each other. Your patience in physical/material affairs saved many a day. *INVERTED:* You must learn from every experience.

FIVE OF CUPS

UPRIGHT: Here is the paradox of freedom and uncertainty, a multiplicity of choice at the emotional/creative level. The dilemma: How to preserve the order and discipline from the foundation of the Four of Cups while moving forward? This card represents that movement but the activity in this phase is within a limited range, while there is pause for reparation by the heart. But this card does not represent movement. On the contrary, it represents a lack of movement, a pause. There may be activity but it is circular, investigative, short-ranged. The Five of Cups is testing the waters of your emotional world determining where and how to enhance it. With the Fives there is the beginning of the need for priorities to grow into the extensions of self, into family and close friends. On the positive side of this coin are things like: An easy going, light-hearted nature, agreeability, adaptability, openness, multi-faceted personality, refreshing presence, emotional independence, unfettered creative originality. Sadness, disappointment, frustration, guilt/shame/conscience, hesitation, when appropriate. The positive effect of a brainstorming mind on the emotions. The ambivalence of all the Fives is seen in the fact that the number five derives either from the combination of 2 and 3 (the duality of emotional/mental), or the combination of 1 and 4 (the duality of physical/spiritual). Here the effect of the former predominates in the Suit of Cups. **INVERTED:** On the negative side of this coin are things like: Careless. Inconsiderate of others' feelings. Frivolous behavior. Emotional immaturity. Ineptitude. Wasting of creative potential. Unharnessed energy. Looking at emotional/creative losses instead of gains, this glass is always seen as half empty rather than half full. Sadness, disappointment, frustration, guilt/shame, hesitation, when inappropriate. Difficulty letting go, attachment. Problems of the disoriented, unsureness of the mind affecting the Emotional Plane.

In This Spread Position...Interpret the Five Of Cups Meanings to Include:

1 GOVERNED BY THE MAGICIAN: PHYSICAL GIVENS, OUT OF THE FATHER
UPRIGHT: You are in no hurry, be it business or pleasure, You should have no trouble with blood pressure. While your cool head and calm under fire suit you well for competition, do not join any track teams. **INVERTED:** You may drive associates, who want to move faster, up the wall. Those who know you realize that you get there eventually, and usually on time.

2 GOVERNED BY THE HIGH PRIESTESS: EMOTIONAL GIVENS, OUT OF THE MOTHER
UPRIGHT: Your devil may care, equivocal attitude in matters of the emotions and creativity, a Bohemian attitude to some, is outside the norm but not for one on your path. As with the Physical Plane above, you are willing to take your chances. Is there any other way? Are you Don Juan or Don Juanita? **INVERTED:** Be assured, for all the problems that this given can lead you to, it is correct for you.

3 GOVERNED BY THE EMPRESS: MENTAL GIVENS, INTELLECTUAL PREDISPOSITION
UPRIGHT: You bring a full range of emotions to the Mental Plane, giving you refreshing objectivity regardless of the subject matter. Your free-ranging mind may have trouble staying on the subject. But with your patience and tenacity you can work on a project forever, even if you leave it and come back to it many times. **INVERTED:** You can be easily distracted, and by people and things far outside the field of concern.

4 GOVERNED BY THE EMPEROR: SPIRITUAL GIVENS, LIFE PURPOSE
UPRIGHT: Emotional freedom and choice lead the charge in this brigade. Uncertainty is accepted in the bargain. You will champion people's, even animal's rights across the board. You may choose the creative arts as your choice of weapon, to get your point across. **INVERTED:** Although you guard your independence of lifestyle, preferring to go your own way, you may find yourself in frequent diversions fighting for the same lifestyle for others. An ironic twist for your Karmic Contract.

5 GOVERNED BY THE HIEROPHANT: SYSTEMS BORN INTO, SOCIETAL INFLUENCE
UPRIGHT: This was an environment capable of responding equally to times of joy and times of sadness. Tears were shed in both. **INVERTED:** Emotions in this setting were not so much unpredictable as they were inappropriate, and/or extreme for the circumstances. Inexplicable mood swings, unnecessary guilt/shame may have been the norm.

6 GOVERNED BY THE LOVERS: EMOTIONAL TAPES, BASIS FOR RELATING/CREATING
UPRIGHT: You love your freedom, and being able to choose. You thrive on the uncertainty of life. And so your relationships, be they friend or lover, will have to give you a wide berth. This is not to say that you cannot be both an excellent friend and a good lover, but your ground rules will have to be accepted. **INVERTED:** Neither be wooed into giving up your freedom completely, much less enjoying restriction or imprisonment, nor be so footless and fancy free that you miss the lessons of this archetype altogether.

7 GOVERNED BY THE CHARIOT: PHYSICAL RESOURCES. MEANS TO ACHIEVE
UPRIGHT: Your physical/material base of operations is varied and decentralized, giving you a great deal of flexibility. Problems in one area are easily compensated for by strengths in other areas. **INVERTED:** Be sure that your support systems are not too diverse or too scattered, and that you have the means to coordinate and draw on them all efficiently. Guard against fragmentation and duplicity.

8 GOVERNED BY STRENGTH: EMOTIONAL RESOURCES, ENERGY
UPRIGHT: You are a breath of fresh air in the lives of your loved ones and friends. And you breathe freshness into the creative process with your ability to be both inside and outside a project at the same time. You have not allowed others to tap into your energy and drain you surreptitiously. **INVERTED:** You don't want to be so much fresh air that you blow people away. Remember to change gears when you enter others' arenas. Too much wind will also blow out the flame of love.

9 GOVERNED BY THE HERMIT: BELIEF SYSTEM, BASIS FOR DECISIONS
UPRIGHT: You believe in freedom or expression in creativity and love. As simple as it sounds, it is among the most complicated concepts to grasp, much less to live by. Both the word love and the word free are big, covering a multitude of meanings. Put them together and the meanings multiply. But, in fact, this is a metaphysical archetype that must be learned by us all eventually. Relationships must balance attachment and non-attachment, in which all parties are therefore loving and loved, and free as well as committed. **INVERTED:** Your belief in freedom for the Emotional/creative Plane, in free love, is distorted, too little or too much.

10 GOVERNED BY THE WHEEL OF FORTUNE: CENTRAL MESSAGE, THEME OF READING
UPRIGHT: With all of the Fives in the Minor Arcana Pips, our souls are seen to be in a holding pattern as energies and entities catch up to one another. With

the Five of Cups we feel this most in our relationships, with people, or to aspects of our own talents. But along with the uncertainties comes great freedom and time. Use them well. *INVERTED:* One or more of the distortions of this archetype will be centered now.

11 GOVERNED BY JUSTICE: STATE/CONTENT OF MIND

UPRIGHT: You are approaching this emotional interim well, going over your relationships and/or your creative interests doing some spring-cleaning before moving on. You are enjoying your sense of freedom and are looking backward now only so you can go forward. *INVERTED:* In one extreme, you are so oriented to your freedom and the future that you may be leaving something important behind. In the opposite extreme, you are not as free as you should be, preferring to look backward, hanging onto issues that are truly finished except in your mind. Any of the distortions could creep in here, i.e. guilt, frustration, depression.

12 GOVERNED BY THE HANGED MAN: STATE OF EMOTIONS, SUBCONSCIOUS

UPRIGHT: The heart is waiting. It knows it must move on but the time is not right. The urge is to enjoy the freedom, the range of choices. Time here is best spent on self-improvement, personal projects, or in light friendships. *INVERTED:* The heart is impatient to realize its desires. Be cautious here neither to rekindle issues left in the past, nor to try and jump start situations that are not for you. In one extreme, this can be enormous heartache. In the opposite extreme, a more callous heart feels little at the loss of something or someone valuable.

13 GOVERNED BY DEATH: PHYSICAL SITUATION, HARD REALITY

UPRIGHT: Physical or material projects for which you care a great deal are stagnant, maybe even ending, or already finished. Personal creative projects or businesses, athletic endeavors, a competition—these are what can suffer in such times. You are dealing with these issues well. In one sense, there is even relief to be free of these "loves." *INVERTED:* At this point you may be feeling one of two extremes: First, that you are profoundly affected and having trouble adjusting to the glitch in your Physical Plane. Second, that you are unaffected, even glib, and not taking appropriate stock of what has happened.

14 GOVERNED BY TEMPERANCE: EMOTIONAL TEST

UPRIGHT: In the near future you will be given the opportunity to take five in your emotional/creative affairs, Here is the breathing room your have needed. Others may not be as thrilled as you are with these new circumstances, with your use of your time. *INVERTED:* You may not see this emotional/creative breather is such a positive light. If there is heartache here, it may be over the loss of something you never really had. There is also the possibility, in the opposite vein, that you have lost something of value and are oblivious to it.

15 GOVERNED BY THE DEVIL: TEMPTATION/CHALLENGE, FEARS

UPRIGHT: In this next three months to a year at the latest, your emotional/creative obligations will be in balance and you will be completely free to establish a whole new range of relationships and/or create fresh from your talent pool. *INVERTED:* What now? The question may strike fear in your heart but this is the time for rethinking your emotional/creative world. Get over yourself, and over others if need be, to get on with things.

16 GOVERNED BY THE TOWER: NEXT LESSON, GRACE OF GOD

UPRIGHT: The emotional and creative corner that you will be turning by this time next year, is a broad and gradual one. Just keep your hands on the wheel and your foot on the gas and you will make it to the straight-away again. Remind yourself that a straight road without a curve is boring. *INVERTED:* One or more of the distortions of this archetype will be aligned with grace in order for you to maximize the lessons in Stage Six: Higher Emotions.

17 GOVERNED BY THE STAR: ASPIRATIONS OF EGO, GOALS, MAXIMUM EXPECTATIONS

UPRIGHT: Gilligan's Island might have suited you, except that you are serious about this idea of freedom and the wherewithal to enjoy it. You are determined to express yourself as you see fit in emotional and creative affairs. *INVERTED:* You may aspire to that part of the lifestyles of the rich and famous that allows them control of their time and the ability to implement their beliefs. Rich and famous are incidental to you. If necessary, okay, but they would only be means to an end.

18 GOVERNED BY THE MOON: ASPIRATIONS OF HEART, COMPASSION

UPRIGHT: Your heart's desire to prove its contents to one and all sets the stage for some grand performances. They should all be well attended. No one need ever doubt what you are thinking or feeling as you will be wearing your heart on your sleeve. *INVERTED:* Yours is a fiercely independent path and you must be cognizant that you cut a wide swath through many others' lives. Guard against an air of emotional haughtiness as a distortion of your innate courage in this Plane.

19 GOVERNED BY THE SUN: PHYSICAL FULFILLMENT/EVALUATION

UPRIGHT: While others, most of us in fact, will accept some infringements on our range of activities, building our own compounds of limitation as we age, your path remains fresh and full of options to the end. *INVERTED:* At one extreme of this archetype, you do accept, or place on yourself, severe limitations on who you see and what you do in emotional creative affairs. At the other extreme, you seem to be overdoing your independence for unhealthy reasons.

20 GOVERNED BY JUDGEMENT: HEART'S FULFILLMENT/EVALUATION

UPRIGHT: For those of us who could not do this well it seems next to impossible—a full lifetime on an emotional path of preparation. The heart has studied self-love and universal love, from the middle, as detached as is possible from within an incarnated body, as objectively as is possible for the heart, for this is a talent of the mind. *INVERTED:* The correct bias here for the Five of Cups is toward healthy self-love, not universal love, but be certain that you are not going overboard.

21 GOVERNED BY THE WORLD: EGO'S FULFILLMENT/EVALUATION

UPRIGHT: Intellectually you have contributed to this archetype, helping others to get the message of this card. Your credo has been that we all must be able to express ourselves freely, fully, and honestly, otherwise, we are living on a foundation that is like a stacked house of cards that can fall with the slightest breeze. That credo has been realized in your own life and advanced in others. *INVERTED:* Retrace the interpretations of cards in this row for special guidance toward achieving this karmic report card on your Mental Plane.

22/0 GOVERNED BY THE FOOL: SOUL'S FULFILLMENT EVALUATION

UPRIGHT: In this lifetime you have been an efficiency expert at gleaning the meaning from a full range of emotions. You have been able to look through the facade in disappointing times and see the core of God's will and grace in all circumstances. You have been happy when appropriate and you have been sad when appropriate. *INVERTED:* To have this archetype as your epitaph is within your grasp if you look harder at disappointments for their silver lining.

FIVE OF SWORDS

UPRIGHT: Here is the paradox of freedom and uncertainty, a multiplicity of choice at the mental level. The dilemma: How to preserve the order and discipline from the foundation of the Four of Swords while moving forward? This card represents that movement but the activity in this phase is within a limited range, while there is pause for reparation. Activity is local, circular, repetitive rather than linear, yet it is progressive. The Five of Swords is rummaging the file cabinet of the mind, investigating, reviewing, evaluating, prioritizing. Picking up the pieces you want, discarding the dross. Looking for potential problems, but only to ferret them out, not to be negative. Here, as with all the Fives, the self begins to become a larger self with priorities that include the extended family of loved ones and close friends. A time for detailed planning. Contemplation. Thoughts, communication flow freely. Positive critique. Collecting information, old and new. Experimentation with ideas. This can be continuing education, but only to flesh out your existing fields of knowledge, nothing drastically new. Mental patience. Appropriate worry, sadness, disappointment, guilt/shame. In this military camp the general is getting ready to win his next engagement. The ambivalence of all the Fives is seen in the fact that the number five derives either from the combination of 2 and 3 (the duality of emotional/mental), or the combination of 1 and 4 (the duality of physical/spiritual). Here the effect of the former predominates in the suit of swords. *INVERTED:* Too much/too little mental freedom/uncertainty, too many or too few choices. As mind looks at itself ineffectively, it will either tend to be passive and lax, or it will be over enthusiastic and cause havoc. Criticism of self/others can be harsh and inaccurate. A sharp tongue. A sense of mental loss rather than gain. Anger. Confusion, Argument. Covering things up. Impulsive. Impatient. Hasty. Nervous. Stubborn. Complacent. Inappropriate worry, sadness, depression, disappointment, guilt/shame. In this military camp the general is concentrating more on his plan of retreat.

In This Spread Position...Interpret the Five Of Swords Meanings to Include:

1 GOVERNED BY THE MAGICIAN: PHYSICAL GIVENS, OUT OF THE FATHER
UPRIGHT: For someone who may not be covering a lot of turf, you are one of the busiest people around. You bring a free-thinking, broad ranging mind to the affairs of the Physical/material Plane. You are the perfect candidate for the planning committee, practically guaranteeing single-handedly that the dance will be a huge success. *INVERTED:* You may do much more work behind the scenes than is necessary.

2 GOVERNED BY THE HIGH PRIESTESS: EMOTIONAL GIVENS, OUT OF THE MOTHER
UPRIGHT: The Emotional/creative Plane is a giant laboratory to you, where the unfettered mind is invited in to do its thing. Here things are meant to be examined, played with, pushed and pulled, exercised, certainly used to the nth degree. The heart is happiest when the mind is stirring things up. You will always analyze your emotional and creative affairs. Your mind and heart are good partners. This archetype serves well the writer of children's stories and tales of adventure, as well as the inventor of games. *INVERTED:* At times you may wish your mind would go and play elsewhere than in your Emotional Plane.

3 GOVERNED BY THE EMPRESS: MENTAL GIVENS, INTELLECTUAL PREDISPOSITION
UPRIGHT: Just tell a mind to relax, to cool it, and stand back for the blast. For it is the job of the mind to push, to take us forward whether by temptation or by goal. Your mental path may appear overly calm and laid back to most people. But underneath it all, you are busy dotting the "I's" and crossing the "T's" doing your homework. *INVERTED:* This is a hard given to swallow, for at times you may even doubt whether you are using your mind efficiently. This can mark the earnest, hardworking student, with or without the degrees.

4 GOVERNED BY THE EMPEROR: SPIRITUAL GIVENS, LIFE PURPOSE
UPRIGHT: While others may be involved in unproductive play, or bogged down in monotonous routine, you are skipping delightfully down the middle of them both, serious about your leisure and lighthearted about your work. You must make all the minutes count. Centered so thoroughly in the now, what many others overlook, your keen eye picks up with ease. You are a master at choosing, at selection. A keen judge of character. *INVERTED:* With your gifts you will be called upon to fill in where there are gaps, where bridges need to be built and missing links filled.

5 GOVERNED BY THE HIEROPHANT: SYSTEMS BORN INTO, SOCIETAL INFLUENCE
UPRIGHT: This was a serious, and yet not so serious environment, your early years. There was an abundance of information bandied about freely, perhaps a bit like being born into a debating society. All ideas were given a chance, and no stones were left unturned. Civilized, Cultured. Literate. *INVERTED:* The atmosphere may have seemed somewhat rudderless, full of activity but to what avail? Or, the climate may have been argumentative and opinionated, with little freedom of thought encouraged. Too much or too little culture, civility.

6 GOVERNED BY THE LOVERS: EMOTIONAL TAPES, BASIS FOR RELATING/CREATING
UPRIGHT: Your passion for mental exchange, conversation, debate, critique leads you by the nose. Your fascination with language and communication serves you well in your relationships and hopefully this talent is being used professionally. This archetype serves well the newspaper reporter. God bless your supportive mate and family. *INVERTED:* Your passion may be for the heat of the argument, or simply to possess large quantities of information for your own satisfaction, to be clever for the sake of being clever.

7 GOVERNED BY THE CHARIOT: PHYSICAL RESOURCES. MEANS TO ACHIEVE
UPRIGHT: Your file cabinet or its equivalent is what you rely on to make your living. There is always an idea, a solution in your bag. You can jettison a losing position quickly in favor of a better solution. Your quickness of mind enables you to keep many irons in the fire. This archetype serves well the researcher/experimenter. *INVERTED:* You can be too quick to shift positions. Review the general meanings (inverted) above for the distortions such as restlessness, inconsistency, a sharp tongue, may have weakened your foundation.

8 GOVERNED BY STRENGTH: EMOTIONAL RESOURCES, ENERGY
UPRIGHT: Your ability to parry and thrust, quickness of foot as well as mind have enabled you to keep a stable of reliable relationships ongoing. You are a valuable and highly desirable ally. You are robust and ready at all times. *INVERTED:* Sometimes you may need all your energy to keep things untangled. Your agility can be self-defeating on occasion. You waste energy unnecessarily. Sometimes you seem to be competing with yourself.

9 GOVERNED BY THE HERMIT: BELIEF SYSTEM, BASIS FOR DECISIONS
UPRIGHT: Ideas must be stirred to keep them alive. If not a gypsy in your heart, you are one in your mind. For you may not require freedom to roam physically, even emotionally, but you will always reserve the privilege to travel with your mind, and yes, to change your mind. One or your mottos is "Give a

person the information and let them make up their own mind." You are Socrates at the core. ***INVERTED:*** At some point you must begin to weigh various viewpoints and then some become more equal than others.

10 GOVERNED BY THE WHEEL OF FORTUNE: CENTRAL MESSAGE, THEME OF READING
UPRIGHT: It may be a mental holiday, but you had better take your homework along. A time for editing. How to make the past relevant to the future? For now, forget the long-range plan. Use one interim plan after another. Concentrate on the short term. ***INVERTED:*** Avoid all the distortions of this archetype by keeping them in mind. Be decisive in small steps, with things over which you have control and can be certain. Then expand.

11 GOVERNED BY JUSTICE: STATE/CONTENT OF MIND
UPRIGHT: The mind thinks of itself here - how to improve, to better satisfy its goals. With what does it want to spend its time? Brainstorming an idea or project without a pressing deadline. Mental leisure is at the top of your agenda. ***INVERTED:*** Meaning here is similar to interpretations for the Fve of Cups except the question is about ideas, goals, not emotions. In one extreme, you are so oriented to your freedom of expression and the future that you may be leaving something important behind. In the opposite extreme, you are not as free as you should be, preferring to look backward, hanging onto old issues or ideas that are truly finished except in your mind.

12 GOVERNED BY THE HANGED MAN: STATE OF EMOTIONS, SUBCONSCIOUS
UPRIGHT: The mind swirling in the Emotional Plane. Heart's priority is on your mental situation, concerned about your progress toward goals of the ego. ***INVERTED:*** Depression. Disappointment. On one hand, this heart is indifferent to the problems of the Mental Plane. On the other hand, you could be exacerbating the problem with overreaction and misplaced sentiment.

13 GOVERNED BY DEATH: PHYSICAL SITUATION, HARD REALITY
UPRIGHT: Mental projects for which you care a great deal are stagnant, maybe even ending, or already finished. Research, re-education, journals/histories/autobiographies, critiques, debates - these are what can suffer in such times. You are dealing with these issues well. In some cases, you may actually be relieved to be free of these projects. ***INVERTED:*** At this point you may be feeling one of two extremes: First, that you are profoundly affected and having trouble adjusting to the mental glitches in your Physical Plane. Second, that you are unaffected, even glib, and not taking appropriate stock of what has happened.

14 GOVERNED BY TEMPERANCE: EMOTIONAL TEST
UPRIGHT: You are to be given breathing room in your mental affairs in the near future. Those normally around you may not be as pleased with your new circumstances as you are, but the pause is what you need to shore up these relationships. The resulting adjustments will bring improvements. ***INVERTED:*** Your heart may not know how to react to this mental respite. In many respects it puts more of a spotlight on the Emotional Plane to take the lead, at least for a while.

15 GOVERNED BY THE DEVIL: TEMPTATION/CHALLENGE, FEARS
UPRIGHT: The advantage of a pause will give you time to beat the bushes and shake out the cobwebs before pushing on toward your main goals. ***INVERTED:*** As the mind whirls about here and there picking up bits and pieces, it must be clear on where everything comes from and give credit where credit is due.

16 GOVERNED BY THE TOWER: NEXT LESSON, GRACE OF GOD
UPRIGHT: You will be given the break, the freedom you need to reorder your thoughts, to pick up the loose ends. Any ideas inappropriate to your karmic path will no longer imprison you as you see them in a new light given this additional time. ***INVERTED:*** With freedom can come the crushing weight of uncertainty and heavy burdens on free will, but grace here spares you this sort of agony to give you a healthy push into Stage Six: Higher Emotions.

17 GOVERNED BY THE STAR: ASPIRATIONS OF EGO, GOALS, MAXIMUM EXPECTATIONS
UPRIGHT: You want always to be able to be honest about what you think and to be able to express those thoughts openly. To be able to study what man has accomplished and to understand how he did it. It is more important to you to understand than to do, than to be original. For you, it is more important to be thorough. ***INVERTED:*** At this time even your goals may all seem more immediate. At an extreme, this is a lack of, or ambiguity in, personal ambition.

18 GOVERNED BY THE MOON: ASPIRATIONS OF HEART, COMPASSION
UPRIGHT: Here the heart is drawn toward the nobility of free will and the role of mind in directing it. The sentiments felt toward the founding fathers of the United States of America and the documents written by them convey this sort of aspiration. ***INVERTED:*** At an extreme, the heart can fall into the trap of crediting man with being the source of free will rather than the recipient of it.

19 GOVERNED BY THE SUN: PHYSICAL FULFILLMENT/EVALUATION
UPRIGHT: Busy with details to the very end, no delegator you. You like the hands on approach and it is not likely you will turn the reins over to anyone else, not even your mate. You will leave behind a tidy ship. You may well have been an avid collector, especially of things with a mental twist to them, the most obvious of which is books. ***INVERTED:*** Staying involved is one thing; trying to do everything is another. Things may be in disarray and need someone, if not you, to tidy up your affairs a bit.

20 GOVERNED BY JUDGEMENT: HEART'S FULFILLMENT/EVALUATION
UPRIGHT: The heart is relieved that it was able to carry the heavier emotions well in appropriate situations. Worry, sadness, and the like were reserved for the right moments and not lingered upon. You made your energy, especially via your mind, available when it was needed in worthwhile situations. Your relationships, as well as your creative interests, thrived on healthy mental interaction. ***INVERTED:*** Work now to see that those contests of intellect are productive and not ego exercises or primers of passion.

21 GOVERNED BY THE WORLD: EGO'S FULFILLMENT/EVALUATION
UPRIGHT: You have been instrumental in preservation and conservation in the mental arena. Contributions to history, biography, library science, fields like anthropology, fill your scrapbook of achievements. You have clarified, filled in gaps, and elaborated, thus leaving a comprehensive, reliable base that the next generation can use with confidence. ***INVERTED:*** As long as you can be fulfilled handling and expounding upon other people's information, albeit creatively, you will be very successful and happy.

22/0 GOVERNED BY THE FOOL: SOUL'S FULFILLMENT EVALUATION
UPRIGHT: Here is a soul that not only knew how to weather a storm, but how to harness one as well. And frequently the storm was actually a deceptive calm. But yours was a disciplined, investigative mind even in the most deceptive of circumstances. ***INVERTED:*** Work always to be part of the solution, not part of the problem.

FIVE OF WANDS

UPRIGHT: Here is the paradox of freedom and uncertainty, a multiplicity of choice at the spiritual level, as you have moved on from the foundation of the Four of Wands, yet not far enough to know your ultimate direction. This card represents that movement but a movement of non-movement, a pause yet an active pause. Paradox begins to play a bigger role on your path. Whereas, with the Four of Wands you felt you had a reasonable grasp of the situation, here you feel humbled by the magnitude of the potential and tasks at hand and to come. It is similar to the comedown you feel when you graduate from high school and first set foot on a university campus. Here is where you test your wings to see if you are ready to fly. There is unlimited freedom to choose, and therein lies the nature of the new struggle. In a sense you must defend your belief structures to date, even against yourself, as you dredge it all up for review. Validation of principles. Spiritual options. A possible or likely reordering of priorities. The struggle to rationalize the intuitive. As the self expands, it is struggling to include others, principally very close loved ones and friends, before it can enter more universal waters. The ambivalence of all the Fives is seen in the fact that the number five derives either from the combination of 2 and 3 (the duality of emotional/mental, or the combination of 1 and 4 (the duality of physical/spiritual). Here the effect of the latter predominates in the Suit of Wands. **INVERTED:** As with all the Fives the mind is a strong influence, and here its negative effects include: attachment to old forms with an attendant defensiveness to new input; a temptation to overrationalize the issues. Spiritual recklessness, carelessness, restlessness. Non-conformity to your correct spiritual group, guides—the reluctant student. Moral dilemmas. Amorality. Difficulty with challenges of the path. On the one hand spiritual apathy, on the other unnecessary spiritual forays.

In This Spread Position...Interpret the Five Of Wands Meanings to Include:

1 GOVERNED BY THE MAGICIAN: PHYSICAL GIVENS, OUT OF THE FATHER
UPRIGHT: This plane will see a lot of activity as you may try your hand at a number of sports/recreational activities, a variety of work alternatives, even a wide assortment of food diets, health regimens, and/or changes of style and appearance. **INVERTED:** There is consistency in all of this variety from your privileged perspective, but others may be less sure.

2 GOVERNED BY THE HIGH PRIESTESS: EMOTIONAL GIVENS, OUT OF THE MOTHER
UPRIGHT: This plane will see a lot of activity as you seek out people and situations to test your hypotheses. Your creative interests may run a wide gamut before you are done. You will make a fascinating partner but you will be a challenge to live with. **INVERTED:** Even though you are well gifted in all that you try, you may tire easily and prefer to move on from talent to talent. At times it will seem as though you are trying to listen to all of the muses at once.

3 GOVERNED BY THE EMPRESS: MENTAL GIVENS, INTELLECTUAL PREDISPOSITION
UPRIGHT: Your mind is dedicated to making sense of spiritual wonder and being able to hang on to your explanation long enough to work up a good defense for it. Most of the defenses you prepare will be defeated sooner or later by yourself, although others will get their chances as well. **INVERTED:** Wands tend to put one into the tendency toward idealism, but you require the real world of hard interaction, preferably mental, and try to avoid ivory towers as much as possible.

4 GOVERNED BY THE EMPEROR: SPIRITUAL GIVENS, LIFE PURPOSE
UPRIGHT: Everything in this lifetime will go towards discovering, then clarifying your spiritual position. You enjoy the challenge of defending your faith, because you always discover new weaknesses in your argument, and retire to your theological den to make the needed repairs. **INVERTED:** You may find yourself part of a group of individuals, all doing the same as you, somewhat like a rogue batch of monks traveling the Himalayan passes together.

5 GOVERNED BY THE HIEROPHANT: SYSTEMS BORN INTO, SOCIETAL INFLUENCE
UPRIGHT: Your early home may have been the scene of many a lively discussion, of high and lofty things of course. Your family's position relative to the larger community would have been much like that described for you in the first four positions, your Karmic Contract. **INVERTED:** This archetype could have been distorted to basic spiritual inconsistency in one extreme, to amorality in another.

6 GOVERNED BY THE LOVERS: EMOTIONAL TAPES, BASIS FOR RELATING/CREATING
UPRIGHT: The young student who chooses the spiritual path early and embarks on a lifetime commitment of study and service fits here. The passion is for the spiritual foray, the struggle to find and reveal the truth, the truth that makes us free from the struggle, as the Christ promised. **INVERTED:** Passion here can be for the struggle, not for the path itself, and you can come to enjoy the combat too much for your or anyone else's good. In another look at this distortion, here can be a form of avoidance at getting on with the responsibilities that come with the maturity of choice. Once we choose one thing, we have not chosen all those other alternatives and must leave them behind, devoting our energies to the one rather than the many.

7 GOVERNED BY THE CHARIOT: PHYSICAL RESOURCES. MEANS TO ACHIEVE
UPRIGHT: You could probably talk your way into or out of just about any situation. For just as the snake charmer actually controls the cobra with subtle rhythms, so can you charm your audience when you need to. This is your art. You may or may not have many assets, but you certainly can get what you need when you need it. **INVERTED:** You may try to rely too much on your ability to charm simply because you are so good at it and it generally works.

8 GOVERNED BY STRENGTH: EMOTIONAL RESOURCES, ENERGY
UPRIGHT: The more you are challenged, the more energized you become, like one of the Three Musketeers. Nothing like a good logjam to make you roll up your sleeves. But with each skirmish you learn and become just that much stronger for the next battle. **INVERTED:** A weakness perhaps: To be led around by the nose of the irresistibility of anyone who says "no" to you. An extreme here, is to require the threat of defeat to become energized. A profound weakness since the path requires we find our strength within, not without.

9 GOVERNED BY THE HERMIT: BELIEF SYSTEM, BASIS FOR DECISIONS
UPRIGHT: You believe in the need to believe. You believe that there is something to believe in. But you are still working on the details. You are a spiritual rowdy, a Knight Templar, a crusader. You can fight for the cause without being quite sure what the cause is. **INVERTED:** There is always morality here, but it can shift quickly and at the extreme, it can change shape to fit the cause.

10 GOVERNED BY THE WHEEL OF FORTUNE: CENTRAL MESSAGE, THEME OF READING
UPRIGHT: Here comes the tete-a-tete you have been waiting for. And the timing is right for you. Take good notes for your position as such is not the winner. The contest is a draw. The winner is the one who takes something from everyone who participates and generates the solution. *INVERTED:* Your position going in may lose, but you can come out the winner anyway, by what you learn, by the terms negotiated in the peace treaty.

11 GOVERNED BY JUSTICE: STATE/CONTENT OF MIND
UPRIGHT: It is up in the air, and where it shall land nobody knows. Even the metaphors are mixed. But you helped toss "it." Another healthy round of spiritual options, but these are all on the table, in the light of day, an intellectual game of "I'll show you mine if you show me yours." *INVERTED:* On one extreme, you are not as willing a participant in this round of wand beating. On another, you are looking for an opportunity to test your ideas, at this point to no avail. No contest.

12 GOVERNED BY THE HANGED MAN: STATE OF EMOTIONS, SUBCONSCIOUS
UPRIGHT: The heart is enjoying the freedom, the multiple interchanges and variety of energies of a changing cast of characters, as it knows the time is not right, or spiritual commitment is still forming. The pieces with which it must merge are evolving also. *INVERTED:* Even without a spiritual resolution this is serious business and the heart should not be too light. Being too serious too soon would be an error in the opposite extreme.

13 GOVERNED BY DEATH: PHYSICAL SITUATION, HARD REALITY
UPRIGHT: Spiritual projects to which you have been committed are not moving at this time, or perhaps they may not have materialized as planned. *INVERTED:* On one extreme, this is not stalled, but finished, and you should turn your attention elsewhere rather than pouring more resources into what now belongs to the past. The other extreme shows your project moving but with much resistance and/or competition.

14 GOVERNED BY TEMPERANCE: EMOTIONAL TEST
UPRIGHT: The near future sees you able to slow down in your spiritual affairs, to enjoy where you are for awhile. Others around you, especially your antagonists and fellow players may not be happy with your new schedule. Patience, they will wait. They need you as much as you need them. *INVERTED:* This may be a forced break that you are left with, rather than one chosen. One or more of your key spiritual playmates has taken a short respite for some reason or other.

15 GOVERNED BY THE DEVIL: TEMPTATION/CHALLENGE, FEARS
UPRIGHT: Delays may present themselves as moral dilemmas. Let this push you to higher standards. Doing good must be hard, right? Wrong! *INVERTED:* You may fear whether you can be good enough as your mind comes down on the side that sees how difficult a challenge true comprehension and authentic expression can be. But rest assured, there is another side where these will come to you with ease. Let the pendulum of your mind complete its swing through the difficult side.

16 GOVERNED BY THE TOWER: NEXT LESSON, GRACE OF GOD
UPRIGHT: The gift here is time, a freedom from the need to make major choices at the moment. But use the interim from pressure to reorder your priorities. That, however, does call for many smaller decisions. *INVERTED:* A spiritual housecleaning to clear away loose ends, clean out the cobwebs, to order your notes, put old and tired theories to rest once and for all. You can no longer carry the extra luggage of outworn clothes just to make yourself feel like you have a great wardrobe.

17 GOVERNED BY THE STAR: ASPIRATIONS OF EGO, GOALS, MAXIMUM EXPECTATIONS
UPRIGHT: More than spiritual resolution and absolutism, you aspire to the excitement of the crusade itself. You are tireless in your ongoing pursuit, looking everywhere you can comprehend, listening anywhere bright opinions are voiced, and talking whenever someone worthy will listen. *INVERTED:* You may enjoy the struggle too much itself, becoming like the crusader who was gone so long from home that he lost touch of what he was fighting for. There may be the willingness to fight for society, but an unwillingness to actually join it yourself, to give up the necessary freedom. Another distortion here is the reverse, to want to avoid the conflict at all costs, an unwillingness to witness any of the pain.

18 GOVERNED BY THE MOON: ASPIRATIONS OF HEART, COMPASSION
UPRIGHT: Here, your heart's passion must widen to include the breadth of God's will without putting out the heroic flame of your own free will. *INVERTED:* The heart struggles here, for it wants so much to be one with universal love, and yet it yearns to be the free and independent spirit as well. It will not be resolved that easily for that is the paradox of the path itself. Much of what the heart provides energy and motivation to fight for are things from which it wishes to keep its own distance.

19 GOVERNED BY THE SUN: PHYSICAL FULFILLMENT/EVALUATION
UPRIGHT: Fiercely strong and plucky, capable of mixing it up and making things happen all the way through. No one may really know much about the real you, especially your physical and material affairs. If you don't leave a well-documented will, they will never know. *INVERTED:* Perhaps you didn't need to fight as much as you did, but then you really would not have had it any other way.

20 GOVERNED BY JUDGEMENT: HEART'S FULFILLMENT/EVALUATION
UPRIGHT: Even those closest to you will know that they have not been with the whole you, for much of you was in the heavens even while here on earth. *INVERTED:* Much of the work in the major relationships of this lifetime may be left to the very end. It is much harder that way, but then perhaps it is your way. Creative messages may be tangled, incomplete.

21 GOVERNED BY THE WORLD: EGO'S FULFILLMENT/EVALUATION
UPRIGHT: You did what you had to do. Yours was a mission meant only for you and you accepted it. You have worked hard to leave a good and accurate record so that others will not have to go through all that you did. *INVERTED:* You may still be defining just what that mission was, even as it is finished.

22/0 GOVERNED BY THE FOOL: SOUL'S FULFILLMENT EVALUATION
UPRIGHT: A worthy adversary they will say. And that you were. The gentleman soldier. A battle to the end, but an end without a kill. Champion of individuality and freedom. *INVERTED:* The interpretations of this reading will help you to learn the lessons of this archetype.

SIX OF PENTACLES

UPRIGHT: Here are the emotions at work in the Physical/material Plane, as duty and service make themselves felt, as you begin to see others as extensions of the self. Here the hermetic dictum "as above, so below" begins to take physical effect and assert itself to become reality. You become physically demonstrative, openly appreciative, interactive, as dependable for others as you have become for yourself. Giving and receiving. Material generosity. Presents/gifts. Charity, philanthropy. Physical favors and volunteering. Giving from the six level is rarely anonymous and family will always come before close friends, close friends before community, local community before state, state before country, country before world, and then lastly universal, metaphysical good. After all, this is pragmatic philanthropy. Paying of dues/fees/taxes for the collective good. Paying your way and then some. Sacrifice. Accepted obligation, duty. The ability to accept, to receive from others, to give thanks. We are as obliged to accept for our needs as we are to share from our abundance. Physical recognition. **INVERTED:** The above qualities may be distorted—giving too much or too little...or receiving too much or too little. Things like: Bribery, use of favors for expected gain. Generosity to a fault. One cannot give beyond one's means, however noble the motivation. We can share only what we have. Beyond that we are obligating someone else's resources without their permission. Lower emotions clouding the physical.

In This Spread Position...Interpret the Six Of Pentacles Meanings to Include:

1 GOVERNED BY THE MAGICIAN: PHYSICAL GIVENS, OUT OF THE FATHER
UPRIGHT: What lucky family and friends you have, for you will have the physical means, the emotional leanings, and the mental will to see their needs met as you would your own, for at this stage on your path you consider their needs as yours. In your family and immediate circle there is communal sharing of property and concern for each other's health and well-being reminiscent of tribal cultures, and in Europe in the higher aspects of feudal culture. A responsibility for one's own. **INVERTED:** This may be of strategic importance to you in your physical/material affairs, as you develop your independent path within such a structure of interdependence.

2 GOVERNED BY THE HIGH PRIESTESS: EMOTIONAL GIVENS, OUT OF THE MOTHER
UPRIGHT: Here is the physical and financial support of family for creative endeavors and help in bringing to fruition one's dreams. That which you love becomes that which your family loves. They are there by your side, most likely literally. In turn, you will foster the same with your progeny. **INVERTED:** At the extreme, imagine the advantages and disadvantages that accrue to one of Queen Elizabeth II of England's children as a result of the blessing of being born into the House of Windsor.

3 GOVERNED BY THE EMPRESS: MENTAL GIVENS, INTELLECTUAL PREDISPOSITION
UPRIGHT: As with the emotional plane, here the mind will be supported with its opinions and its projects, whether they match those of the family or not. The physical and emotional ties that bind with this card transcend any mere differences of ideology! You will be predisposed to do the same in your own turn, for whatever your philosophy you will find a way to weave this characteristic into it. **INVERTED:** You may require considerable financial/material assistance with your Mental Plane, i.e. your education and the implementation of your projects, the reaching of your goals.

4 GOVERNED BY THE EMPEROR: SPIRITUAL GIVENS, LIFE PURPOSE
UPRIGHT: The progress made in your Material Plane will allow you to practice the lessons of generosity. And while you may be fortunate enough to be a patron of society as well, your major efforts will be in supporting and encouraging your loved ones and closest friends as an extended family. **INVERTED:** Your generosity may assume an air of duty and obligation with a number of demands placed on you to test your capacity.

5 GOVERNED BY THE HIEROPHANT: SYSTEMS BORN INTO, SOCIETAL INFLUENCE
UPRIGHT: The Rockefeller family serves here as an example on a grand scale. Philanthropy is a large part of this legacy, but as witnessed by the sons, and sons of sons, who are today's beneficiaries of the original accumulation of one man's path, the family and its extensions have come first. **INVERTED:** The distortions of this archetype include: being given more than you need, being too dependent. There may also have been enormous obligations and duties binding this sort of environment together.

6 GOVERNED BY THE LOVERS: EMOTIONAL TAPES, BASIS FOR RELATING/CREATING
UPRIGHT: One can imagine this passion as being one similar to Mother Theresa's, except that she has already included the family of man as her personal family. This is the passion that drives the devoted matriarch or patriarch of an established family, or the hard working mother that comes home and cooks for a large family and then volunteers to cook for the church bazaar on Saturday. **INVERTED:** It is hard to imagine these admirable qualities being distorted. But, again remember that metaphysical law demands a balance, and we must accept as much as we give. At the opposite extreme, distortion brings us a person who will prefer accepting to the extreme, and thus distort their soul's need for independence.

7 GOVERNED BY THE CHARIOT: PHYSICAL RESOURCES. MEANS TO ACHIEVE
UPRIGHT: Your having participated in the lessons of give and take have prepared you for the unpredictable in your physical/material plane. You and your extended family can move as a unit in time of trouble to meet any foe, rise above any disaster. Your financial and/or material reserves are plentiful and deep. **INVERTED:** Your material reserves may not be what you think they are. You may not be able to call in your chips.

8 GOVERNED BY STRENGTH: EMOTIONAL RESOURCES, ENERGY
UPRIGHT: Your have learned many lessons of caring and being cared for and these have made your heart strong and ready for the unexpected in your Emotional/creative Plane. You and your loved ones can rely on each other for physical and material assistance without fail in times of emotional crisis. Your energy reserves are ready and willing on a moment's notice. **INVERTED:** Your reserves may not be what you think they are. Others may not be as committed as you are. This is not to say that you have not done your part, but try to assess your situation realistically.

9 GOVERNED BY THE HERMIT: BELIEF SYSTEM, BASIS FOR DECISIONS
UPRIGHT: As a belief system, this could well have served as the basis of the oligarchies, in the feudal systems that pervaded in Europe in the middle ages. There are many facets to this complicated way of life, but at root is the belief that as one rises to the eminence and rewards justified by one's station and lot in life, that one accepts the responsibilities as well as the goodies that go with the territory. **INVERTED:** In this, as in many a system, it is usually the desire to be the guy at the very top, but not always. Motives as well as belief are especially important here. Check closely your cards in the positions of the Emotional Plane to be sure that you are on the right track.

10 GOVERNED BY THE WHEEL OF FORTUNE: CENTRAL MESSAGE, THEME OF READING

UPRIGHT: Balanced giving and/or receiving in your Physical/material Plane are most important now. Your circumstances probably make it fairly obvious which you need to consider most. If not, the reading is dedicated to this subject and will shed the necessary light that you need. *INVERTED:* There has been a serious imbalance here and it is urgent that it be corrected now. Review the general meanings (inverted) for the Six of pentacles for guidance if necessary.

11 GOVERNED BY JUSTICE: STATE/CONTENT OF MIND

UPRIGHT: You are already aware that you are in an expansion of your abilities, your concerns in your Physical/material Plane. Whether you have been doing well yourself and will now be able to help others, or you have decided to accept help from others, you will have advanced the cause of your material path. *INVERTED:* Perhaps you have decided in these matters, but not correctly, Think through carefully your income and your expenses, i.e. how/where it comes in, and how/where it goes out. A plan for bribery or extortion would show here.

12 GOVERNED BY THE HANGED MAN: STATE OF EMOTIONS, SUBCONSCIOUS

UPRIGHT: Your heart has accepted a commitment, and the fact that this card is here rather than in position 11 suggests that perhaps it is only the subconscious and not the conscious mind that has this view of the situation. If your mind eventually agrees, then you will accept this burden or this gift, whichever the case may be. *INVERTED:* Your heart may be distorting the matter in either of the extremes. On the one hand, you may be considering doing far too much. On the other hand, you may be refusing an offer more correctly accepted.

13 GOVERNED BY DEATH: PHYSICAL SITUATION, HARD REALITY

UPRIGHT: Money or material assistance is flowing in or out of your coffers. And this exchange is proper for the giver and the receiver. *INVERTED:* This exchange is not the best thing for one or both parties, the giver and the receiver. For example: The receiver may be worthy, but you are extending beyond your means, or it would be better if they were aided by someone else. Or, it is fully within your means and it would please you greatly to help this person or group, but this particular assistance, the timing, and/or you as the source is incorrect.

14 GOVERNED BY TEMPERANCE: EMOTIONAL TEST

UPRIGHT: A material exchange is in the near future. More than the actual benefits or outfall in the material level will be the effects on your relationships or creative affairs. *INVERTED:* There will be a significant effect in your emotional house from a material exchange. The effect could be a structural realignment of relationships.

15 GOVERNED BY THE DEVIL: TEMPTATION/CHALLENGE, FEARS

UPRIGHT: A material exchange is in the near future. The major impact of this transaction will be in your Mental Plane. For example, if this is financial backing for schooling or a project toward your goals. *INVERTED:* This could be your not getting the backing you were looking forward to. Or, in the opposite mode, getting backing when you should not have, for instance to go to the wrong school and take the wrong degree.

16 GOVERNED BY THE TOWER: NEXT LESSON, GRACE OF GOD

UPRIGHT: A situation requiring balanced giving and/or receiving will arise and be most important in the near future, not longer than a year from now. Your circumstances should make it clear which is the case. If not, the reading will shed the necessary light that you need. *INVERTED:* There has been a serious imbalance here and it is urgent that it be corrected. Review the inverted general meanings for guidance if necessary.

17 GOVERNED BY THE STAR: ASPIRATIONS OF EGO, GOALS, MAXIMUM EXPECTATIONS

UPRIGHT: Your master plan is to be so well-established that you can respond not only to any of your needs, but to those of your family and extended family. You accept willingly, enthusiastically the responsibilities that go with such expectations. *INVERTED:* This archetype can distort into the twists of power that are possible if others not just rely on you, but come to absolutely depend on you, for their welfare. An example of a serious distortion is that of the Godfather complex, the personality of the Mafia Don in organized crime.

18 GOVERNED BY THE MOON: ASPIRATIONS OF HEART, COMPASSION

UPRIGHT: Your heart's fondest dream is to be able to help your loved ones to realize their dreams. For you, the desires of your extended family have become your desires. *INVERTED:* Carried to an extreme, you can want to live vicariously through the dreams, the achievements of your children or a best friend you admire too much. Remember the aspect of distortion in this archetype that leads us to neglect our own situation.

19 GOVERNED BY THE SUN: PHYSICAL FULFILLMENT/EVALUATION

UPRIGHT: Many would envy such an end to their Material Plane, fully capable in health and resources to help those who need them most, those with whom their karmic path is physically woven. A positive twist on this is, of course, to end with all that you need provided by others. Either is appropriate progress for the Material Plane of a given Karmic Contract. *INVERTED:* Presently, your course may not take you to either of the above and yet, with proper foresight and attention to your lessons, the above will be your material report card for this lifetime.

20 GOVERNED BY JUDGEMENT: HEART'S FULFILLMENT/EVALUATION

UPRIGHT: Your heart is well satisfied to have negotiated the difficult path of having material and emotional affairs closely intertwined with your dearest loved ones. *INVERTED:* Some of our worst qualities as humans come out in our relationships with the people we are closest to, especially when our material and physical lives are practically one. To surmount these potential difficulties is a large part of your emotional Karmic Contract.

21 GOVERNED BY THE WORLD: EGO'S FULFILLMENT/EVALUATION

UPRIGHT: Your ego is justifiably satisfied that you have left a mental legacy capable of administrating your affairs and the affairs of your extended family. In modern society we can even consider some corporations and privately owned businesses (other than just family operations), as examples of the extended family. *INVERTED:* You may be headed for some disappointment in your mental legacy for your extended family, but this card here suggests that it is correctable.

22/0 GOVERNED BY THE FOOL: SOUL'S FULFILLMENT EVALUATION

UPRIGHT: The soul has fulfilled its Karmic Contract of achieving sufficient expansion and externalization with the attendant acceptance of duty and obligation in the Physical/material Plane. *INVERTED:* Give where and when it is appropriate, receive where and when it is appropriate, and you will increase your efficiency with this archetype and reach this goal.

SIX OF CUPS

UPRIGHT: Here are the feelings of love and respect, caring involvement in the emotional and creative affairs of those closest to you, especially the family. But the level of the Sixes teaches the necessity for expansion beyond the self, not only into our blood relatives, but into the broader range of an extended family with which we can share the close emotions formerly reserved only for our bloodline. Good memories of the sort only intimacy, interdependence and time well spent can bring. Emotional and creative generosity, self-sacrifice. Sincerity. Good manners. Charm. Compliments, sincere flattery. Sympathy/empathy. Work, professions relying on these qualities. Emotional recognition. *INVERTED:* Nostalgia to a fault. Sentimentality. Too much family/friends. You cannot extend for the sake of extending, rushing into or pushing relationships with people not suited for, or appropriate to, your path. Just as we are not meant to bed with, or mate with, everyone we meet, neither are we to bond with just anyone. Many tests of give and take reciprocity are required. Courtship applies to the Six of Cups as well as to the Two of Cups. One caution is against the improper notion that being a blood relative is automatic entitlement to privileges not earned. All relationships must establish their mutual bonds of love and respect by their actions, not by their birth, and in the case of marriages not by fact of law. Bad memories. Too emotional for the given circumstances. Insincere flattery.

In This Spread Position...Interpret the Six Of Cups Meanings to Include:

1 GOVERNED BY THE MAGICIAN: PHYSICAL GIVENS, OUT OF THE FATHER
UPRIGHT: You were born into an extended family that will flavor the affairs of your Physical/material Plane. A family business may or may not be your path, but if its your karma to be president of a corporation, it will be of one like those in Japan, with mutual caring up and down the ladder of responsibility. *INVERTED:* Emotions of the type that bind families closely together will flavor the karmic purpose of this plane and present unique challenges that will make you physically and materially stronger.

2 GOVERNED BY THE HIGH PRIESTESS: EMOTIONAL GIVENS, OUT OF THE MOTHER
UPRIGHT: You were born into an extended family that will flavor the affairs of your Emotional/creative Plane. It is likely there will be a strong hierarchy involved with ritual observations like the return to the senior member's house for special occasions and holidays. There will be ties with layers of interconnections, some formal, others informal, that will be honored and observed in matters of romance, marriage, friendships, careers, and creative interests. You can count on a great deal of emotional backing. *INVERTED:* This network of inter-caring could be wieldy.

3 GOVERNED BY THE EMPRESS: MENTAL GIVENS, INTELLECTUAL PREDISPOSITION
UPRIGHT: There will certainly be a great deal of support from loved ones for your mental projects, for your beliefs and your goals. And in turn, perhaps not surprisingly, much of your intellect and creative enterprise may be involved with your loved ones, and if not actually your family/extended family, then with the concept. A writer whose subject matter is romance, or children, or even housekeeping tips would fit here.
INVERTED: Family matters may be so strong as to offer a challenge to your mental independence.

4 GOVERNED BY THE EMPEROR: SPIRITUAL GIVENS, LIFE PURPOSE
UPRIGHT: The progress made in your Emotional Plane will allow you to practice the lessons of emotional generosity. The people closest to you will be the primary beneficiaries. *INVERTED:* The emotional/creative demands made upon you may be great, but nothing so great as to interfere with completion of your karmic purpose. Just the opposite, all difficulties will support your purpose.

5 GOVERNED BY THE HIEROPHANT: SYSTEMS BORN INTO, SOCIETAL INFLUENCE
UPRIGHT: This early environment was loving and supportive, as you were encouraged to develop your gifts as part of the family store of talent. You were given a healthy amount of attention in balance with the rest of the family. *INVERTED:* In your early years the adults supervising you may have given either too much or too little love/attention. At one extreme is the orphan who lacks direct and deep caring on a personal basis, as one not fortunate enough to have been adopted. At the other extreme is the child who is inordinately made to feel that they are the center of the world, with child's play taking precedent over adult activities. Also, the overabundance of family ties and observances. Suffocating love.

6 GOVERNED BY THE LOVERS: EMOTIONAL TAPES, BASIS FOR RELATING/CREATING
UPRIGHT: You desire most of all to have the energy and emotional means to provide love and care to those most important to you. While this sounds like good old-fashioned mothering, here the difference is this love and care you desire is a step removed from the ego. These people do not have to be your children, or your family. For example: This could be the motivation that leads a person to become director of a shelter for abused women and children. *INVERTED:* This person requires the immersion in a thick family atmosphere with rich interdependence.

7 GOVERNED BY THE CHARIOT: PHYSICAL RESOURCES. MEANS TO ACHIEVE
UPRIGHT: Your having participated in the lessons of emotional/creative give and take have prepared you for the unpredictable in your Physical/material Plane. You and your extended family will cover each other's bases in time of need. Your reserves include the time and energy available in your family storehouse; there may or may not be money or material assets for you to draw on. *INVERTED:* Your reserves may not be what you think they are. You may not be able to call in your chips.

8 GOVERNED BY STRENGTH: EMOTIONAL RESOURCES, ENERGY
UPRIGHT: Your attention to the lessons of sincere involvement with those you love, and who love you, have made your heart strong and ready for the unexpected in your Emotional/creative Plane. You and your extended family can rely on each other to be there helping heal in times of emotional crisis. Your energy reserves are ready and willing on a moment's notice. *INVERTED:* Your reserves may not be what you think they are. Others may not be as committed as you are. This is not to say that you have not done your part, but try to assess your situation realistically.

9 GOVERNED BY THE HERMIT: BELIEF SYSTEM, BASIS FOR DECISIONS
UPRIGHT: For you , the root of your life lies in the need to be caring for others, the need to be fundamentally involved with family and community. Here is the type of person who becomes a church deacon, a boy scout leader, a hospital volunteer. *INVERTED:* This can be a misunderstanding of the values of family, with too much or too little emphasis, or a host of distortions in between. An attempt to force this archetype into the model of the nuclear family is one distortion all too common.

10 GOVERNED BY THE WHEEL OF FORTUNE: CENTRAL MESSAGE, THEME OF READING
UPRIGHT: Balanced giving and/or receiving in your Emotional/creative Plane are most important now. Your circumstances probably make it fairly obvious which you need to consider most. If not, the reading is dedicated to this subject and will shed the necessary light that you need. ***INVERTED:*** There has been a serious imbalance here and it is urgent that it be corrected now. Review the general meanings (inverted) of the Six of Cups for guidance if necessary.

11 GOVERNED BY JUSTICE: STATE/CONTENT OF MIND
UPRIGHT: You are already aware that you are in an expansion of your capacity for loving care, for healing, and all the affairs of the Emotional/creative Plane. Whether you have been helping others, or have accepted help from others, you will have advanced the cause of your emotional path. You are mentally on top of these emotional matters. ***INVERTED:*** Perhaps you have decided something in these matters, but not correctly. Think through carefully who is doing what for whom. Are the energies flowing in the right direction?

12 GOVERNED BY THE HANGED MAN: STATE OF EMOTIONS, SUBCONSCIOUS
UPRIGHT: You are warmed by the glow of healthy love that surrounds you and to which you contribute your fair share. The feelings here are open and sincere. You are becoming one with these people and your commitment will be lasting. They are to be a part of you now. ***INVERTED:*** The family or extended family may be wrecking havoc. Insincerity. Taking advantage.

13 GOVERNED BY DEATH: PHYSICAL SITUATION, HARD REALITY
UPRIGHT: Emotional contributions to the physical situation bring about a marked improvement. This can range from something as light-hearted as your brightening up a social occasion to your making someone feel better. ***INVERTED:*** At one extreme, there is insincere or rude behavior with a negative effect on the audience. At the other extreme, the emotional outpouring is so genuine and strong that it can surpass making someone's mood improve, it can help facilitate a cure in someone very ill. This is the healing power of the touch of love.

14 GOVERNED BY TEMPERANCE: EMOTIONAL TEST
UPRIGHT: In the near future there is an act, or a wave, of emotional generosity that reverberates through your life and/or the lives of your loved ones. ***INVERTED:*** This emotional exchange will be more than the doctor ordered. Perhaps embarrassing, perhaps infuriating.

15 GOVERNED BY THE DEVIL: TEMPTATION/CHALLENGE, FEARS
UPRIGHT: There will be a new level of familial interaction and caring that you must integrate into your personal activities and goals. ***INVERTED:*** There will be concern about the nature and benefit of relationships with your loved ones. Honesty and sincerity may cut through some of your weaker ties.

16 GOVERNED BY THE TOWER: NEXT LESSON, GRACE OF GOD
UPRIGHT: A situation requiring balanced giving and/or receiving in your Emotional/creative Plane will arise and be most important in the near future, not longer than a year from now. Your circumstances should make it clear which is the case. If not, the reading will shed the necessary light that you need. ***INVERTED:*** There has been a serious imbalance here and it is urgent that it be corrected. Review the inverted general meanings for guidance if necessary. Be honest with yourself and sincere with others.

17 GOVERNED BY THE STAR: ASPIRATIONS OF EGO, GOALS, MAXIMUM EXPECTATIONS
UPRIGHT: Your mental goal is to be able to focus and direct your energies as part of a larger, interactive whole, working symbiotically toward the same ends, ends which never could have been reached separately. Green Peace is such an organization; its officers and members would share this archetype. ***INVERTED:*** The type of emotional bonding that you project as the centerpiece of your mental goal will not stand up to the weight that you expect it to carry.

18 GOVERNED BY THE MOON: ASPIRATIONS OF HEART, COMPASSION
UPRIGHT: You heart's master plan is for you to be an integral part of a group of interdependent people who love and care for one another in such a way as to bring about an increase of emotional energy and well-being in a family or community. ***INVERTED:*** The desire to be a positive addition of love and healing is tainted. Check your motivations to see if another, subconscious desire is in actuality the overriding desire, such as for the security of being in such a group. Also, the attempt to control others through love, or even your ability to heal, to keep others healthy.

19 GOVERNED BY THE SUN: PHYSICAL FULFILLMENT/EVALUATION
UPRIGHT: You are among the fortunate who have many loved ones to cherish and on whom you too can rely as you complete this journey. ***INVERTED:*** Work now to insure sincerity and mutual respect between your loved ones so that you may turn this card upright.

20 GOVERNED BY JUDGEMENT: HEART'S FULFILLMENT/EVALUATION
UPRIGHT: You have enriched the lives of those closest to you, and they you. These bonds have been strong and productive. ***INVERTED:*** The present line-up of closest associates may not be the healthiest for you and/or for them.

21 GOVERNED BY THE WORLD: EGO'S FULFILLMENT/EVALUATION
UPRIGHT: You are pleased that your mental goals have been achieved while honoring and fostering the needs in your emotional house. ***INVERTED:*** Less than happy memories from your earliest years, of the actions of others, or from your own adulthood and own actions, may mar the mind's finale, overriding all other achievements.

22/0 GOVERNED BY THE FOOL: SOUL'S FULFILLMENT EVALUATION
UPRIGHT: Your time has been well spent, bringing an increase of energy and pleasure to those who knew you best and were fortunate to spend enough time with you. ***INVERTED:*** Let this reading speak to you so that you may move one step closer to this epitaph. Review the inverted general meanings of this card and see if any chords are struck.

SIX OF SWORDS

UPRIGHT: Here are the emotions at work in the Mental Plane, as duty and obligation make service a more attractive as well as necessary adjunct to the ego's programs. With the expansive lessons of the sixes, your mind begins to know that the boundaries of self do not stop at the surface of your skin and your goals begin to take on the air of the extended self. Helping others, with mental generosity, is seen as the way of helping self, as your personal goals become more and more integrated with those of others. Even independent thought has an inclusive element of the immediate other, of the thoughts of those most important to you. The necessity of balancing give and take mentally is dealt with. Responsibility is accepted willingly as you become as reliable to others as you were to yourself at the level of the Fours. Service as work/profession appears here. Here is the application of mind to longer, more complex tasks, many of which are worthwhile causes. Advancement and promotion of ideas is increasingly important as progress comes principally through mental effort. Your heart is energizing and pushing your mind, supporting your projects. Motivation is high as mental goals are raised. Mental obligations and duties present themselves as laboratories for you to learn in. Protective mind in a positive sense. Consideration. Mental recognition. **INVERTED:** Distortions of either too much or too little in the above archetype. Mental retreat. Procrastination. Deterrence from projects at hand. Interference of emotions in mental work. Defensive, neurotic mind.

In This Spread Position...Interpret the Six Of Swords Meanings to Include:

1 GOVERNED BY THE MAGICIAN: PHYSICAL GIVENS, OUT OF THE FATHER
UPRIGHT: The family of thought into which you have been born may well provide your means of livelihood, even as it determines all other aspects of your Physical/material Plane. Much of your time will be spent in front of groups speaking, advising, and listening to them as well. **INVERTED:** This promises to be a relatively public life, even perhaps your personal life will be open to view by many.

2 GOVERNED BY THE HIGH PRIESTESS: EMOTIONAL GIVENS, OUT OF THE MOTHER
UPRIGHT: You have the talent to communicate what you feel as part of the package of information you receive and are meant to share. The theater is in your blood and you may well teach or direct in drama. **INVERTED:** Keeping your personal emotional life separate, yet together with this talent for expression, will be a good high wire act.

3 GOVERNED BY THE EMPRESS: MENTAL GIVENS, INTELLECTUAL PREDISPOSITION
UPRIGHT: You have been born into a well-developed family of thought. Your group karma will be of exceptional importance even in the early stages of independent ego development. Many will have said that you were born a wise, conscientious man. You are considerate as you "considerate." **INVERTED:** The pitfall here is to be too serious for one's own good. While a great deal may depend on you, not everything does. Remember to let others have the floor every now and then.

4 GOVERNED BY THE EMPEROR: SPIRITUAL GIVENS, LIFE PURPOSE
UPRIGHT: The progress made in your Mental Plane will allow you to practice the lessons of mental generosity and inclusion. The people closest to you will be the primary beneficiaries. Where you go, so goes your entire extended family. **INVERTED:** The mental demands made upon you may be great, but nothing so great as to interfere with completion of your karmic purpose. Just the opposite, all difficulties will support your purpose.

5 GOVERNED BY THE HIEROPHANT: SYSTEMS BORN INTO, SOCIETAL INFLUENCE
UPRIGHT: You were expected to listen, but also to participate with your own contributions at an early age. You were not separated from the adults. The issues of the day were prominent at the dinner table. Responsibilities were shared as everyone pulled together. **INVERTED:** At one extreme, there may have been little time for childhood games and pastimes.

6 GOVERNED BY THE LOVERS: EMOTIONAL TAPES, BASIS FOR RELATING/CREATING
UPRIGHT: A strong blend of mind and heart here can generate a passion that harnesses the talents of a communicative and dedicated mind to worthwhile causes. But also here is a love for what the group mind can achieve. Together these desires are the fuel that motivates great leaders. **INVERTED:** A personal life with personal romance and delicious moments of privacy may suffer under the extreme distortions of this archetype.

7 GOVERNED BY THE CHARIOT: PHYSICAL RESOURCES. MEANS TO ACHIEVE
UPRIGHT: Whether by the content of what you say or by the magic of your voice, you are able to muster the resources you need when you need them. Because you have accepted responsibility for others and been there when they needed advice, physical/material help will be there should you need it. **INVERTED:** Your ability to charm with your mind may come up short in the Physical Plane, or you may be too effective for your own good at times.

8 GOVERNED BY STRENGTH: EMOTIONAL RESOURCES, ENERGY
UPRIGHT: Your ability to consider a multitude of facts involving many different people to reach consensus has endeared you to your circle of loved ones. The strength derives from the wide base you are able to lay down before taking action. Your emotional table has very strong legs. **INVERTED:** The process of consensus that you have tried to bring about is not as efficient as you need it to be.

9 GOVERNED BY THE HERMIT: BELIEF SYSTEM, BASIS FOR DECISIONS
UPRIGHT: You believe that we take it all with us, at least the content of our minds. Actually, you know that the metaphysics of that statement is true; we take the lessons of everything we have accumulated, at each of the four levels, with us through all future incarnations. Our caravan does indeed grow as we trek across the desert from oasis to oasis, from experience to experience, from revelation to revelation. You know that true growth comes only through acceptance of greater and then greater responsibility. **INVERTED:** You may honestly believe that you make the trip alone. If so you may perfect an unusually bizarre strain of selfishness.

10 GOVERNED BY THE WHEEL OF FORTUNE: CENTRAL MESSAGE, THEME OF READING
UPRIGHT: At this time you must open to accept a greater range of responsibility for the administration of others' affairs as well as your own. Your intellect is needed by those close to you. **INVERTED:** If you have been avoiding or diverting duties that rightfully fall to you, you should act quickly and decisively to put things in order.

11 GOVERNED BY JUSTICE: STATE/CONTENT OF MIND

UPRIGHT: You are aware that you have a greater scope now, and if the canvas of your mind is not yet larger, you have already purchased more oils in expectation of doing a bigger painting. People may be knocking on your door, ideas demanding attention. ***INVERTED:*** You may know that you will in turn be left behind if you leave the wrong things or wrong people behind now, and yet you procrastinate.

12 GOVERNED BY THE HANGED MAN: STATE OF EMOTIONS, SUBCONSCIOUS

UPRIGHT: The heart has already committed to a much broader frame which the mind must react to. The extended family exerts enormous pull on you to join in. Your role awaits you. ***INVERTED:*** The heart is delaying for much of what is taking place is primarily in the realm of mind, and it knows that your Emotional Plane will never be the same again, having to grow with your mind. The heart struggles to mature.

13 GOVERNED BY DEATH: PHYSICAL SITUATION, HARD REALITY

UPRIGHT: Moving day, theoretically for your mind, but the mental expansion may have indeed necessitated a physical change. If not actually changing homes or offices, the physical "moving" may be in the furniture and equipment which facilitates your mental work. Rearrangement or integration of new gear, new technology are possible. ***INVERTED:*** Perhaps the above changes are necessary, even planned, but somehow blocked at this time.

14 GOVERNED BY TEMPERANCE: EMOTIONAL TEST

UPRIGHT: Mental expansion in new, larger areas with a larger cast of characters ripples through your personal life. There are changes in the value and hierarchy of opinion at home, at work, or between home and work. ***INVERTED:*** Either there will be virtually no effects, or the effects will be great and require much orf your attention.

15 GOVERNED BY THE DEVIL: TEMPTATION/CHALLENGE, FEARS

UPRIGHT: Deal head on with hesitation to mix your thoughts with the thoughts of others. Your ideas will not only survive, but thrive. ***INVERTED:*** On the one extreme, there will be a fear of others with similar, yet different ideas than yours. On the other extreme, there will be a strong urge to run roughshod over the similar, yet different ideas of your comrades.

16 GOVERNED BY THE TOWER: NEXT LESSON, GRACE OF GOD

UPRIGHT: Should you have missed the opportunities and lessons such as mentioned in position 14 and 15 just above, grace will provide them before this time next year. ***INVERTED:*** Even God's grace can taste like a mother's dose of medicine given for our own good. How this medicine tastes is up to you.

17 GOVERNED BY THE STAR: ASPIRATIONS OF EGO, GOALS, MAXIMUM EXPECTATIONS

UPRIGHT: Your mind aspires to the growth of knowledge, of intellect in order to increase the common good, to serve to your extended family. Here is the administrator/educator in institutions such as church affiliated schools, or schools with family or group patronage. This goal is the advancement of a way of thinking belonging to many. ***INVERTED:*** This may be the advancement of one group's thinking, perhaps even a majority, but at the expense of another smaller, or less powerful group.

18 GOVERNED BY THE MOON: ASPIRATIONS OF HEART, COMPASSION

UPRIGHT: The heart's desire is to be one with a group sharing a common ideology or goal. ***INVERTED:*** If you have to retreat from your mental position to become a part of this group, be certain you gain more than you lose in the process.

19 GOVERNED BY THE SUN: PHYSICAL FULFILLMENT/EVALUATION

UPRIGHT: You successfully integrated the independent program of the ego self with that of your extended family. As this lifetime ends you will be traveling with many like-minded souls. ***INVERTED:*** Much needs to be done to bring about this physical/material report card. Study the interpretations of this row carefully for guidance.

20 GOVERNED BY JUDGEMENT: HEART'S FULFILLMENT/EVALUATION

UPRIGHT: The mind served the heart well, with the harmonious and productive integration of ideas into your lifestyle and relationships, and those of your closest loved ones. Obligations here were never obligations. Group creativity here was prodigious. ***INVERTED:*** While duty may have been observed and obligations met, you may not have reached the magic point where your heart has chosen them of its own volition.

21 GOVERNED BY THE WORLD: EGO'S FULFILLMENT/EVALUATION

UPRIGHT: With obligation as the bait your soul used to pull your mind forward, you properly cast your mental net outward, working with others to catch as much of universal truth as the fishing season of this lifetime would allow. ***INVERTED:*** Work harder to see that as many as possible of your group are knowledgeable.

22/0 GOVERNED BY THE FOOL: SOUL'S FULFILLMENT/EVALUATION

UPRIGHT: This soul correctly discerned the positive function of obligation, of duty, as the way your soul could inform you of the collective, group karmic purposes awaiting on your path, to not only compliment but help fulfill your individual purpose. ***INVERTED:*** Look for the responsibilities that do not chafe at the bit and you will have found the appropriate obligations to fulfill your karmic purpose.

SIX OF WANDS

UPRIGHT: Here are spiritual movement and externalization. A sense of mission. As with the other Sixes there is a noticeable shift of emphasis from the self as a very independent self, albeit on the spiritual path, to a sense of self that fundamentally includes others, and is included by others. Your individual path recognizes its parallel group path. Two-way communication is vital, as you balance spiritual give and take. Helen Keller, blind and deaf from the age of two, by overcoming her disabilities, was able to convey to us how truly alone we are when we cannot share our thoughts or feelings. Your ability to share is intrinsic to your knowledge of God. Ironically, you can come to know God more quickly with a sense of the other, through the other, than through the self. The information you need for your path will come more quickly now as you have access to the additional sources of others with which you have joined. Evidence of progress is seen in the appreciation by others, and the effects of your good example and teaching. Further evidence is offered by: Spiritual recognition. Moral victories. Promotions. Rewards. Credit for something done right. There is a need to pause for recognition and to accept energy from others, or to offer recognition and energy to others. Goals and progress are validated. **INVERTED:** Blame for something done wrong. Difficulty with pride and the dangers of success. Need to guard against self-righteousness. Here, in a distortion of this archetype, is the missionary going forth to convert an indigenous people whose native religion is purer than the missionary's. As we stretch our spiritual muscle and extend into larger and larger worlds of awareness, we are meant to seek others, those of related paths with similar karmic purpose, but to do so all we need do is witness our beliefs and we will be mutually attractive to our kindred spirits. There is never a need to convert.

In This Spread Position...Interpret the Six Of Wands Meanings to Include:

1 GOVERNED BY THE MAGICIAN: PHYSICAL GIVENS, OUT OF THE FATHER
UPRIGHT: The Physical/material Plane will yield in every case to the expansive nature of this spiritual path. Since the majority of your waking hours, not to mention your dreams, will be occupied with the objectives of your Spiritual Plane, it is likely that you will make your living giving witness to and advancing your beliefs. **INVERTED:** Remember to balance the Physical Plane with equal doses from the Mental and Emotional planes as well as the Spiritual. The balance will help you to keep your Physical Plane just that, physical.

2 GOVERNED BY THE HIGH PRIESTESS: EMOTIONAL GIVENS, OUT OF THE MOTHER
UPRIGHT: The Emotional/creative Plane will yield in every case to the expansive nature of this spiritual path. Your relationships will be very much in tune with your spiritual nature and goals. Your talents will first be devoted to helping you reach your extended family, then to expressing and celebrating with them the joy of your discoveries. **INVERTED:** Remember to balance the Emotional Plane with equal doses from the Mental and Physical planes as well as the Spiritual. The balance will help you to keep your Emotional Plane just that, emotional.

3 GOVERNED BY THE EMPRESS: MENTAL GIVENS, INTELLECTUAL PREDISPOSITION
UPRIGHT: The Mental Plane will yield in every case to the expansive nature of this spiritual path. It will be the eyes and ears, and the voice of your progress. Here is the scribe who packs his slate into his camel's saddlebags and moves with his tribe to witness first hand, and thus accurately chronicle, their discoveries for history's sake. This scribe cannot tell only what he is told, or what he sees; it must be what he himself feels in common with his people. **INVERTED:** Remember to balance the Mental Plane with equal doses from the Physical and Emotional planes as well as the Spiritual. The balance will help you to keep your Mental Plane just that, mental.

4 GOVERNED BY THE EMPEROR: SPIRITUAL GIVENS, LIFE PURPOSE
UPRIGHT: The internal pressure to move forward from your relatively comfortable spiritual base and find new blood to mix with yours will make an adventurer of you in this lifetime. Here is the spiritual hunter, backed by his tribe, in search of validation, vindication, yet deep in his soul ready for the jolt of meeting with the expected unexpected. **INVERTED:** Be ready, for it is you who are most likely to be converted in this lifetime.

5 GOVERNED BY THE HIEROPHANT: SYSTEMS BORN INTO, SOCIETAL INFLUENCE
UPRIGHT: Spiritually vibrant, on the move, alert, pleasantly aggressive were the adults around you in your early years, as they sought to include others in their circle. In such circumstances, you would have been expected to both follow the lead of your superiors and to move forward on your own to even greater heights. **INVERTED:** The delicate balance between towing the line and asserting your independence may have proved somewhat difficult.

6 GOVERNED BY THE LOVERS: EMOTIONAL TAPES, BASIS FOR RELATING/CREATING
UPRIGHT: Your passion requires you to share even as you search, for you require the energy of the feedback and recognition that comes with the interaction of fellow seekers. You wish to know intimately the character of your search even if it is impossible to know more than a hint of the ineffable nature of your destination. **INVERTED:** To lust after the path as a mission to be fulfilled, with conquests to be made, is a path with many forks that lead to dead ends.

7 GOVERNED BY THE CHARIOT: PHYSICAL RESOURCES. MEANS TO ACHIEVE
UPRIGHT: You are never alone. In any situation in your Physical/material Plane whatever happens to you is felt and shared by your spiritual companions, much as two identical twins are able to respond to each other's needs instantaneously. **INVERTED:** As others in your extended spiritual family can and will respond to your crises, so too are you called upon to assist them.

8 GOVERNED BY STRENGTH: EMOTIONAL RESOURCES, ENERGY
UPRIGHT: You are never alone. In any situation in your Emotional/creative Plane whatever happens to you is felt and shared by your spiritual companions, much as two identical twins are able to respond to each other's needs instantaneously. **INVERTED:** As others in your extended spiritual family can and will respond to your crises, so too are you called upon to assist them.

9 GOVERNED BY THE HERMIT: BELIEF SYSTEM, BASIS FOR DECISIONS
UPRIGHT: You are guided by your confidence in your fellowship, the common bond of belief that binds and liberates at the same time. **INVERTED:** Your belief and confidence in membership may smack of elitism. Whenever a circle is drawn and you step inside, you must be especially careful how you then relate to what is on the outside. This is the same problem whether the distinction is made in hierarchies within the group, or between your group and others. It is the same problem whether you are priest or member of a religion, an adherent to fellowships of the Great White Brotherhood, or a fraternity member on a college campus.

10 GOVERNED BY THE WHEEL OF FORTUNE: CENTRAL MESSAGE, THEME OF READING
UPRIGHT: This is a time when you should fill with the assurance that you are moving well on your path. But as a runner in a marathon may pause only to grab for the refreshing cup as he continues on, so this is the nature of this realization. Progress at the other three levels, the Physical, Emotional, and Mental Planes offer much more tangible feedback of our progress. Physical success can bring money, emotional success the new love, and mental success the Pulitzer Prize, while spiritual success must be felt, acknowledged, and rewarded all within ourselves. *INVERTED:* You are probably not feeling the degree to which you have advanced and this reading is meant to reassure you. Persevere.

11 GOVERNED BY JUSTICE: STATE/CONTENT OF MIND
UPRIGHT: Plans are in the air for a campaign, as you have decided to turn up the volume, to increase the watts of power and reach out to a larger audience. *INVERTED:* Be reminded that you must listen to a wider audience as you increase your activity and scope.

12 GOVERNED BY THE HANGED MAN: STATE OF EMOTIONS, SUBCONSCIOUS
UPRIGHT: Perhaps your heart has plans of which you are not yet aware. It may wish for closer ties, much more interaction, with many more people than your extended self now embraces. *INVERTED:* At one extreme, the heart is not into this campaign, not yet willing to give up the intimacy of the existing inner circle, the present family. At the other extreme, the heart is much too hungry for new blood to flow through the collective veins of your extended family.

13 GOVERNED BY DEATH: PHYSICAL SITUATION, HARD REALITY
UPRIGHT: You are on the road to bigger and better things, asking for much more growth, which means more knowledge...which means more power....which means more responsibility. *INVERTED:* Your campaign for bigger and better is blocked, or lacks the proper logistics. At one extreme, this is the wrong campaign, at the wrong time, in the wrong place,

14 GOVERNED BY TEMPERANCE: EMOTIONAL TEST
UPRIGHT: Growth and expansion at the level of the Sixes is difficult on existing relationships, on partners and closest loved ones, but the Six of Wands is especially trying. We all must pass out through this gate of our home city of comfort surrounded by known loved ones, and go out into the countryside and expand our spiritual trade routes. Soon it will be your turn. *INVERTED:* With this test we are meant to carry all of our loved ones with us fully in our hearts, leaving nothing behind. This path is to add to, not to replace.

15 GOVERNED BY THE DEVIL: TEMPTATION/CHALLENGE, FEARS
UPRIGHT: There is excitement at the expectation of challenge as you prepare to submit your faith to the test in a greater arena. But for now you are to muster all the members of your clan and assure yourselves of your position and provisions for the campaign ahead. *INVERTED:* Do not let fear paralyze you into non-action. Expose and promote your beliefs and they will propel you forward.

16 GOVERNED BY THE TOWER: NEXT LESSON, GRACE OF GOD
UPRIGHT: Control your timing. Do not be pushed too fast, or held back too long. Major movement should begin not later than this time next year. *INVERTED:* Grace will help you find the courage.

17 GOVERNED BY THE STAR: ASPIRATIONS OF EGO, GOALS, MAXIMUM EXPECTATIONS
UPRIGHT: You aspire to be part of an established, growing spiritual presence and movement. All the better if you can be a significant contributor to its success. Even better if you could be its leader. What a coup should you turn out to be its founder. *INVERTED:* Your major goal should not be the ego satisfaction you get from this spiritual enterprise, or for the potential of its power.

18 GOVERNED BY THE MOON: ASPIRATIONS OF HEART, COMPASSION
UPRIGHT: The heart desires this archetype of devotion to and with others in common cause, because it is a correct step up the ladder to universal common cause. We must learn to live with and love ourselves first, then our mates and children, our families, and then step by step we must learn to live with and love many others until we can love all. *INVERTED:* Here the proper balance should center around the extended family, not just your bloodline, and not the entire world.

19 GOVERNED BY THE SUN: PHYSICAL FULFILLMENT/EVALUATION
UPRIGHT: You have good physical evidence of your spiritual progress. There are hard assets to support the future work of your family. *INVERTED:* Bring yourself down out of the heavens to attend more to the complementary work which must support you here in the Physical Plane.

20 GOVERNED BY JUDGEMENT: HEART'S FULFILLMENT/EVALUATION
UPRIGHT: There is great love and harmony in your extended family like you cherish in your bloodline. The heart of your group has beat as one. *INVERTED:* All that you can do to achieve this archetype here is to do your part. Neither hold back too much within your family core, neglecting greater emotional responsibilities, nor extend too far into the ideal of universal love and neglect both your core and your extended family.

21 GOVERNED BY THE WORLD: EGO'S FULFILLMENT/EVALUATION
UPRIGHT: There has been evidence of your spiritual progress here in the Mental Plane. Recognition has been significant suggesting there is a body of work, fruits of your mental labors, which you are leaving behind. *INVERTED:* While the above mentioned may be true, you may still be somewhat disappointed in yourself, having had much higher expectations of yourself than others.

22/0 GOVERNED BY THE FOOL: SOUL'S FULFILLMENT/EVALUATION
UPRIGHT: Acceptance of appropriate responsibilities here was so efficient there seemed to be little or no distinction between obligation to self in fulfillment of your Karmic Contract and in carrying out duties toward your group. Personal and group karma merged smoothly in this lifetime. *INVERTED:* Use this reading as an opportunity to reach this objective of harmony between individual and group karma, to keep one or the other from dominating.

SEVEN OF PENTACLES

UPRIGHT: With the Sevens, the second cycle (4 thru 7) wherein the individual has begun to include others as extensions of the self draws to a close ushering in the last and highest of the three cycles in the Minor Arcana (7 thru 10). These Sevens mark new cycles and directions based on previous achievements, such as the harvest which must save part of the crop for seeding next year's planting, as opposed to the totally new beginnings of the Aces. Here are the material results of hard physical work and the shifting from one aspect of a task to another, as in from farming to harvesting/storage. Also a shift from one job to another within a company or a given field. There is abundant supply, enough for reserves. Ample food supply. Inventory, taking stock of material worth. Savings. Investments/stocks. Good results of a fund drive. A healthy budget for the next phase. Harnessing of, yet harmony with, nature. A ripeness, maturity. Preparedness. An advanced level of establishment, cycles of security over a number of years, in some cases generations. Physically and materially worldly, experienced. Here is the professional, one who knows the ins and outs of their livelihood, and has become inseparable from it. Gourmet, the expert with food— preparation, service, and enjoyment in eating. Aspects of real property, real estate. A good season in business, especially retail. A significant stature has been achieved at this point. Aristocratic in all the good senses of the term. **INVERTED:** A lack of resources, perhaps in spite of good efforts. A poor harvest. The next phase may require a tightening of the belt, budgeting, rationing. Delay or blockage with a new cycle. Immaturity in a physical/material matter. A lack of physical readiness for the next phase. Inexperienced, unworldly. Ineptness with food. Insensitivity to the material world, to nature as well as to man's inventiveness. A rift with nature. On the one hand, man attempting too much control over, or disrespect for, nature. On the other hand, a natural disaster destroying man's property. Also, man coveting another man's possessions and even theft, the harvesting of another man's crop.

In This Spread Position...Interpret the Seven Of Pentacles Meanings to Include:

1 GOVERNED BY THE MAGICIAN: PHYSICAL GIVENS, OUT OF THE FATHER
UPRIGHT: The symbology of this archetype suggests the carrying on of a family business or tradition, as in a fourth generation farmer. Broader interpretation suggests a harmony with the Physical/material Plane inherited along with considerable assets and some responsibility to preserve, protect and extend into future generations. **INVERTED:** Achieving your own physical/material mark in the world, within a strong field of inheritance, will appear easier to the observer, who naturally envies you, than it does to you.

2 GOVERNED BY THE HIGH PRIESTESS: EMOTIONAL GIVENS, OUT OF THE MOTHER
UPRIGHT: All of the above interpretation for the position of the Magician may apply here as well, with the distinction that the inheritance and tradition derives from the line of the mother. Also, the harvest and new planting here might suggest a related but different creative career to that of our mother, or her line. You are mature in emotional and creative affairs. **INVERTED:** Achieving your own emotional/creative mark in the world, within a strong field of inheritance, will appear easier to the observer, who naturally envies you, than it does to you.

3 GOVERNED BY THE EMPRESS: MENTAL GIVENS, INTELLECTUAL PREDISPOSITION
UPRIGHT: You will be well-educated and very knowledgeable, sophisticated in worldly matters, applying mind to pragmatic affairs which may range from business to politics, from health to athletics. This archetype here suggests the ability to begin a new and significant branch of study in an existing field. **INVERTED:** As with the previous two positions, this card here suggests others may see your path to intellectual prominence as being much easier than it actually is. Your facility makes it look easy.

4 GOVERNED BY THE EMPEROR: SPIRITUAL GIVENS, LIFE PURPOSE
UPRIGHT: Your path will bear the mark of the aristocrat, with all the advantages and responsibilities accruing thereto. Part of your arsenal is your distinguished bearing, broadcasting your level of knowledge and achievement in pragmatic affairs, affecting the lives of many. **INVERTED:** In your line, it has fallen to your generation to make something new of the seeds you were given. You may not even get to plant the same crop, or use the same field. You must continue the old while initiating the new.

5 GOVERNED BY THE HIEROPHANT: SYSTEMS BORN INTO, SOCIETAL INFLUENCE
UPRIGHT: Your early environment was rich in all the things you need to carry out your karmic purpose. Your surroundings themselves were your primary education. There was a way of living here, a way of looking at the world. There was an appetite for life balanced by a profound respect for it as well. **INVERTED:** The generation preceding you may have made errors in their harvest, in the handling of their legacy. Too much of the harvest may have been consumed leaving few seeds to plant for the next season.

6 GOVERNED BY THE LOVERS: EMOTIONAL TAPES, BASIS FOR RELATING/CREATING
UPRIGHT: Your passion lies in the handling of the harvest. Here also are the tapes for the consummate professional. The gourmet chef fits here, as does the organic farmer, or an investment banker. The deft handling of resources to bring about increase and pleasure is the common denominator. **INVERTED:** Too much in this archetype can lead to avarice, gluttony, and the like. Little appreciation for the next generation. You may lust after what belongs to others.

7 GOVERNED BY THE CHARIOT: PHYSICAL RESOURCES. MEANS TO ACHIEVE
UPRIGHT: Your physical resources are just that, your physical resources. You may draw at will on the reserves amassed through your past efficiencies. You have been in harmony with your environment. **INVERTED:** You may have miscalculated and do not have what you think you have, or what you need, for the project at hand. There may be resources, but they are not yours. There could have even been theft here. You may have killed the golden goose.

8 GOVERNED BY STRENGTH: EMOTIONAL RESOURCES, ENERGY
UPRIGHT: Abundance and good health go a long way to shoring up your energy reserves. The harder you work the more energy you have. Your enterprises make it possible for loved ones to be together, to work together, and support each other. But above all, you draw great pleasure and energy from your harmony with nature itself. **INVERTED:** Allow flexibility in your Emotional/creative Plane. You do not have to hold it together. Others must provide their own energy. Likewise, do not rely on the energy resources of others. Only so much pleasure can be properly derived from the property of others.

9 GOVERNED BY THE HERMIT: BELIEF SYSTEM, BASIS FOR DECISIONS
UPRIGHT: You are a do-it-yourselfer that realizes he cannot do it alone. You believe in yourself as a strategic link in what has to be done. Your beliefs are rooted in historical fact, in precedent laced with innovation. There is an ease in your bearing that comes from your comfort with your place in the scheme of

things. Here is the humorist/philosopher Will Rogers. ***INVERTED:*** Here could be a misconception of your place as inheritor of a good physical/material package. Be neither smug in assuming the efforts of the past as yours, nor intimidated and self-effacing; assume your proper place and take proper credit.

10 GOVERNED BY THE WHEEL OF FORTUNE: CENTRAL MESSAGE, THEME OF READING
UPRIGHT: Prepare for the harvest time, or for the new planting, as this represents the cusp of reinvigoration. Summon the maturity of your wealth of experience, for this is a turning point, a new direction for the course you have already begun. Collect the assets that are yours, claiming all debts that are due. An increase in material appetite is appropriate, albeit with greater selectivity. ***INVERTED:*** Do not try to rely on any resources that are not yours. Curb your appetite.

11 GOVERNED BY JUSTICE: STATE/CONTENT OF MIND
UPRIGHT: Taking stock of the harvest and/or making plans for the next major turning point in your Physical/material Plane. You are confident that you have the resources you need. ***INVERTED:*** Perhaps you do not feel prepared for the next move. You may be eyeing resources that are not yours.

12 GOVERNED BY THE HANGED MAN: STATE OF EMOTIONS, SUBCONSCIOUS
UPRIGHT: There is a warmth, a sense of satisfaction at a job well done, enriched by the security your past efforts have afforded. There is also the excitement of anticipation of the next phase of growth. ***INVERTED:*** Whether the harvest was in fact good or it failed, the sense here is not satisfaction. The reaction could be straight forward disappointment, or it could be facetious celebration.

13 GOVERNED BY DEATH: PHYSICAL SITUATION, HARD REALITY
UPRIGHT: You are selling some of your old stock to invest in new issues, or in order to collect capitol for investing in some other new venture. Taking energy accrued in the past and putting it to work for the future. A shift in jobs within the same company or field. ***INVERTED:*** The extreme that would be feared here most would be the loss due to bad investment. But the other extreme has its potential drawbacks—The harvest here might have been inordinately large, such as over-promotion above the level of competency at this time.

14 GOVERNED BY TEMPERANCE: EMOTIONAL TEST
UPRIGHT: When the silos are full again in the near future, you will have the dynamics of change at work in your Emotional Pane, impacting relationships and/or creative affairs. ***INVERTED:*** Likewise, if the silos are overflowing, or if the harvest was unsuccessful, there are emotional ramifications.

15 GOVERNED BY THE DEVIL: TEMPTATION/CHALLENGE, FEARS
UPRIGHT: What to do? How to collect wisely? How to spend wisely? The responsibility for investing wisely the results of your's and others' past labors. ***INVERTED:*** Responsibility for material affairs can degenerate into fear of severe loss, and at this level more than its ramifications to your personal safety and security, is the potential effect on many others.

16 GOVERNED BY THE TOWER: NEXT LESSON, GRACE OF GOD
UPRIGHT: Begin now to prepare for the shift from past to future that marks the selection of the next major fork on your path. Your physical environment, any of the major elements of your Physical/material Plane, especially livelihood, may be involved. ***INVERTED:*** The fork presented within this next year will have drawbacks that you must seriously consider.

17 GOVERNED BY THE STAR: ASPIRATIONS OF EGO, GOALS, MAXIMUM EXPECTATIONS
UPRIGHT: It is strategic that you maximize the material legacy you were handed, in terms of healthy self-achievement. ***INVERTED:*** You may feel you are in competition with your legacy. At the extreme, you will be driven to surpass it. Even more destructive, you may seek to destroy it if you cannot best it.

18 GOVERNED BY THE MOON: ASPIRATIONS OF HEART, COMPASSION
UPRIGHT: Your heart aspires to maximize the material legacy you were handed, but in terms of the continuity between generations, to do your part to see that the members of your extended family, and the social network you move in, benefit from your actions. ***INVERTED:*** You may be too fond of the outer aspects of the material as opposed to the well-being of your legacy.

19 GOVERNED BY THE SUN: PHYSICAL FULFILLMENT/EVALUATION
UPRIGHT: You complete life with all the material needs of you and your extended family well-provided for. Your affairs are in order and you have made plans for smooth continuity once you are gone. You have respected and worked well with the earth plane. ***INVERTED:*** Look to the lessons of this reading to help you leave your Physical/material Plane in good order.

20 GOVERNED BY JUDGEMENT: HEART'S FULFILLMENT/EVALUATION
UPRIGHT: As you were loved and cared for by your family, so have you fulfilled your responsibilities to yours. Love has extended beyond the limits of humans to include the greater scope of God's creation, to plants and animals, to the earth itself. ***INVERTED:*** Work now to see that your emotional affairs are not evaluated in material terms. Pay closer attention to the earth and all it contains, not solely to the affairs of man.

21 GOVERNED BY THE WORLD: EGO'S FULFILLMENT/EVALUATION
UPRIGHT: Here is the positive side of pride, justified by having done well with the care of what was entrusted to you. There is a rich sense of self-accomplishment within the overall legacy of continuity. ***INVERTED:*** In the one extreme, you may feel you have not fulfilled your responsibilities to the care and increase of your inheritance. In the other extreme, you may be taking far more credit that you deserve and playing with the sin of pride.

22/0 GOVERNED BY THE FOOL: SOUL'S FULFILLMENT/EVALUATION
UPRIGHT: Yours was an abundant spirit capable of enjoying the material magnificence Mother Earth is so capable of providing. and yet you replenished her stocks many fold through your wisdom and sensitivity. ***INVERTED:*** Use the lessons learned with this reading as part of your pledge to work toward this epitaph.

SEVEN OF CUPS

UPRIGHT: As with the other Sevens, the Seven of Cups marks the closing of the second cycle (4 thru 7) wherein the individual has begun to include others as extensions of the self, and ushers in the last and highest of the three cycles in the Minor Arcana (7 thru 10). As the self approaches the ideal of universal love it must somehow accomodate the world as extension of the self. Here is a taking stock, a look at the material interface, a harvesting at the emotional level, and then a reinvestment in the emotional future. As such you must open up to take a good look at your emotional storage bins. In the process, not only do you survey your progress to date, but in a sense you open up Pandora's Box. It is a test for all relationships and for any creative affairs. Its function is not to destroy what we already have, rather to expand and enrich as we move out into, and eventually through, our extended family in the lessons of the higher Cups. If our existing relationships are not up to facilitating this enrichment, we may be asked to leave them behind and should we not do so, they will wither and fall away of their own accord, for rest assured everyone's emotional karma demands growth and inclusion, not exclusion. The result is a barrage of new opportunities, and you are becoming fully aware of them. Here are the positive aspects of fantasy, of myth. **INVERTED:** A lack of emotional resources in spite of good efforts. A poor emotional harvest, resulting either from personal error or through natural disaster. There may be a shortage of energy and emotional stock for your next phase. A delay or block with a new emotional cycle. Here you may see problems that come with some of the contents of Pandora's box. Of particular note are the difficulties of emotional greed and an overly strong sexual appetite. There may be escapism into your fantasies, trying to live mythology, emotional confusion, difficulty in choosing/defining your emotional path. You may envy another's relationships, not being satisfied with what you have, coveting another's partner. Immaturity in emotional/creative matters. A lack of proper emotional and/or sexual experience. A disrespect for the affairs of this plane.

In This Spread Position...Interpret the Seven Of Cups Meanings to Include:

1 GOVERNED BY THE MAGICIAN: PHYSICAL GIVENS, OUT OF THE FATHER
UPRIGHT: The rich emotional estate that you have inherited will flavor all of your physical/material affairs. How you make your living, your leisure activities, the atmosphere in your home, your eating habits, will all be infused with your wealth of natural talent. **INVERTED:** This strong aesthetic underpinning will be very demanding on your surroundings.

2 GOVERNED BY THE HIGH PRIESTESS: EMOTIONAL GIVENS, OUT OF THE MOTHER
UPRIGHT: The rich emotional estate that you have inherited will flavor all of your emotional/creative affairs. Highly romantic, you will need a high level of performance in your relationships and your creative projects. **INVERTED:** It goes without saying that you will most likely never be completely satisfied as you aspire to perfection. You will however reach heights of satisfaction others only dream about.

3 GOVERNED BY THE EMPRESS: MENTAL GIVENS, INTELLECTUAL PREDISPOSITION
UPRIGHT: You will be highly emotional and creative in your Mental Plane, being much more intuitive than rational. You may well be part of an emotional/mental artistic legacy. **INVERTED:** While you certainly will have no shortage of ideas, you may want to have others around to help you organize them. You may not have, or want to take, the time.

4 GOVERNED BY THE EMPEROR: SPIRITUAL GIVENS, LIFE PURPOSE
UPRIGHT: Your life will be the stuff myths are made of. Everything that happens will carry emotional weight that others will find fascinating and want to measure for themselves. You cannot help but be visible and set an example of how life is meant to be experienced. **INVERTED:** You are certainly ready for this archetype as your principal card of karmic purpose, otherwise you would not be given it. Nevertheless, as when one's intention is to walk on hot coals, one must remain focused and disciplined and all will go well.

5 GOVERNED BY THE HIEROPHANT: SYSTEMS BORN INTO, SOCIETAL INFLUENCE
UPRIGHT: This early environment may well have been theatrical, either in its broadest sense or literally. But while there was most likely a wide range of emotional and creative expression to draw upon, this was a most mature emotional background, as being born into the family of the Barrymores. **INVERTED:** It may have been challenging to look for role models in a constantly changing scenario, especially if there was a shortage of emotional maturity.

6 GOVERNED BY THE LOVERS: EMOTIONAL TAPES, BASIS FOR RELATING/CREATING
UPRIGHT: Two actresses will anchor our wide span of the positive side here. First, Katherine Hepburn whose range of emotional awareness and experience challenges the limits of human understanding and yet with a personal life centering on few partners, principally one, Spencer Tracy whom she never married. Second, Elizabeth Taylor, whose range is also challenging to mere mortals and with a personal life splashed with many true loves whom she married. **INVERTED:** The passion here is a rejection of the fuller experience of emotions, which at its extreme might resemble the Victorian attitude.

7 GOVERNED BY THE CHARIOT: PHYSICAL RESOURCES, MEANS TO ACHIEVE
UPRIGHT: Your base may appear solid and indeed it may be as reliable as granite, but its pieces are highly energized and mobile. Its strength is in the number of pieces and the quickness with which you can cover your bases. Your physical strength is your physical involvement in numerous arenas. **INVERTED:** Your resources are only as reliable as the energy you have had to sustain them, and you may end up having to rob Peter to pay Paul. Every facet of your life may seem to be in motion. As long as you can keep juggling, nothing will fall.

8 GOVERNED BY STRENGTH: EMOTIONAL RESOURCES, ENERGY
UPRIGHT: You have laid much of the groundwork proper for later stages of life, but correctly, and will now be able to integrate more personal and intimate relationships into that framework. **INVERTED:** You have been extroverted and tried to do much of the expansive emotional work before you laid the emotional/creative groundwork that the expansion phase is meant to serve.

9 GOVERNED BY THE HERMIT: BELIEF SYSTEM, BASIS FOR DECISIONS
UPRIGHT: Your motto might well be the advice that Auntie Mame gives to her nephew. "Live, live, live; life is a banquet, Patrick, and most poor suckers are starving to death." **INVERTED:** If you go intimately into the things you choose to experience and learn all they have to offer through full participation with your heart, then you are on your way to becoming a Zen master. If you try to devour things from the outside to put experiential notches on your life belt, then odds are you will need a Zen master.

10 GOVERNED BY THE WHEEL OF FORTUNE: CENTRAL MESSAGE, THEME OF READING
UPRIGHT: Now is the correct time to try many new things. Save for the encouragement of this reading, you would most likely turn down some extraordinary opportunities. These are not things you have done much of before. *INVERTED:* Get ready, things may get a little bumpy for there are many things coming across your path that you have little experience with. Some are right for you, others not, so pick with care. The rest of the reading will help you prepare.

11 GOVERNED BY JUSTICE: STATE/CONTENT OF MIND
UPRIGHT: Is your bed covered with travel brochures? Making a list, checking it twice? To say that you have plans is an understatement. *INVERTED:* What an appetite! The problem may be that you have many plans rather than a plan. You may just be spinning mental wheels.

12 GOVERNED BY THE HANGED MAN: STATE OF EMOTIONS, SUBCONSCIOUS
UPRIGHT: There is great satisfaction with your emotional and creative affairs as they have been fruitful for you. Your heart wishes to bring a wealth of new energy into that circle, and to be even more fruitful, as it anticipates the next level of growth on your path. *INVERTED:* Check the motivations here, for what is appropriate should be good for the emotional package at hand, for you and your extended family, not just you alone. Your heart may be confused with unexpected, and possibly mysterious, opportunities.

13 GOVERNED BY DEATH: PHYSICAL SITUATION, HARD REALITY
UPRIGHT: Your physical body and/or your material world is undergoing a range of experiences perhaps more varied and powerful than anything yet to cross your path. Enjoy, it's all delicious and just what the doctor ordered. *INVERTED:* Life may feel a little bit like a grade B hollywood movie. Most of these opportunities are not for you. But take notes, it will make interesting reading in your autobiography, that you had these chances and turned them down.

14 GOVERNED BY TEMPERANCE: EMOTIONAL TEST
UPRIGHT: In the near future your emotional/creative palate will be full with the rewards of the past as you reap an emotional harvest. How do you reinvest? Which energies do you use and which do you conserve? Here you heart must review the many possibilities for the future. In what do you plant your emotional seeds for the new season? *INVERTED:* At one extreme too many things, inner and outer will vie for your attention. Much of it is undesirable confusion. In such a period of sensory overload, it is best when unsure of any offer, to turn it down. There are no opportunities offered in such a climate that you cannot live without. At the other extreme, there will be a dearth of harvest and/or opportunity. This too will pass, and do not accept or force any situations out of boredom or impatience.

15 GOVERNED BY THE DEVIL: TEMPTATION/CHALLENGE, FEARS
UPRIGHT: This will be a time when the creative juices will flow with little or no encouragement. Your sensitivity will be at a peak, your mind abuzz with possibilities. Serious decisions will be made to successfully transform your Emotional/creative Plane into a broader, more productive use of your full potential. *INVERTED:* As with this card in the Temperance position cited above, there can be too much/too little and caution should be exercised.

16 GOVERNED BY THE TOWER: NEXT LESSON, GRACE OF GOD
UPRIGHT: Begin now to prepare for the third and highest level of your emotional path. Whereas in the first level (Cups 1 thru 4) self was concerned with the individual, and in the second level (Cups 4 thru 7) self grew into concern of others as extensions of itself, here in the third level (Cups 7-10) the self is growing into concern with the world as extension of self as it approaches universal love. *INVERTED:* This reinvestment in your emotional/creative future will be made more difficult by either of the extremes—too many choices, or too few choices. Be patient. And do not throw the baby out with the bath water.

17 GOVERNED BY THE STAR: ASPIRATIONS OF EGO, GOALS, MAXIMUM EXPECTATIONS
UPRIGHT: Here is a worldly appetite, as the mind wants to be on intimate terms with everything, building on the past but ever reaching into the future for more understanding through sensory experience and its subsequent expression. *INVERTED:* The goal here is simply to consume. There is little understanding or respect for the proper role of emotions, of desire, to raise up, not to tear down.

18 GOVERNED BY THE MOON: ASPIRATIONS OF HEART, COMPASSION
UPRIGHT: Here is a worldly heart, drawn properly toward the goal of universal love, but with the lessons of self, and extensions of self, safely tucked into its sensory belt. The appetite is healthy, guided by this secure and wise heart. *INVERTED:* The goal here is simply to feel, to experience, without proper frames of reference or sense of continuity.

19 GOVERNED BY THE SUN: PHYSICAL FULFILLMENT/EVALUATION
UPRIGHT: At the end of this road is a material world rich in sensory pleasures, all proper for your karmic path. You will be the envy of many a younger person, but most likely people have always envied your joie de vivre. *INVERTED:* Maybe you did not overdo it all of your life, but you are certainly giving it a run for the money on the tail end.

20 GOVERNED BY JUDGEMENT: HEART'S FULFILLMENT/EVALUATION
UPRIGHT: The wheels of your relationships and creative affairs were greased by the facility with which you generated and handled emotional opportunities. With this much extroversion and honest expression there was little room for misunderstanding and guilt. *INVERTED:* This wonderful archetype will be your heart's fulfillment if you can just manage the proper balance.

21 GOVERNED BY THE WORLD: EGO'S FULFILLMENT/EVALUATION
UPRIGHT: The fertility of your imagination and the ability of your mind to harness it into highly productive channels enabled you to be creative beyond expectations. Through your example many others with less courage will be able to romp vicariously through some of the more extraordinary possibilities our wonderful planet affords. *INVERTED:* Achieve the balance in this plane and your mind will have achieved its goal of experiencing life to the fullest.

22/0 GOVERNED BY THE FOOL: SOUL'S FULFILLMENT/EVALUATION
UPRIGHT: You have selected wisely your food from your emotional harvest, for yourself and your loved ones, and set a proper stage for those that follow in your example. *INVERTED:* Study the lessons of this reading to improve your efficiency in realizing the full potential of this archetype.

SEVEN OF SWORDS

UPRIGHT: As with the other Sevens, the Seven of Swords marks the closing of the second cycle (4 thru 7) wherein the individual has begun to include others as extensions of the self, and ushers in the last and highest of the three cycles in the Minor Arcana (7 thru 10). Here is the higher physical aspect of mind, its dedication and application in the hard realities of the world, but with the goal of proving to itself the existence of God in everything, to rationalize faith through the actual experience of divinity in the physical world. This is a time for mental harvesting, for analysis/measuring of progress in preparation for the next round of thought, decision, and action. A bit of a perfectionist. Here is the informed, the qualified, the certified, the approved, the accepted. Education, particularly advanced education, schooling with a definitive purpose. Investigation and research. Observation/recording. Calculation. Measuring. Comparison. Speaking out, advancing your opinions. Physically carrying out mental projects. Materializing ideas into mechanics. Moving information. News. Communication. Publishing. Writing. Editing. Computers. Storage of information—libraries, archives, computer banks. **INVERTED:** Inefficient editing of our mental track record—cutting out too much, or leaving too much in. Perfectionist to a fault.There may be plagiarism, professional jealousy, extreme exaggeration or lying. Improper application of the intellect in general. Also, hiding your thoughts from others.

In This Spread Position...Interpret the Seven Of Swords Meanings to Include:

1 GOVERNED BY THE MAGICIAN: PHYSICAL GIVENS, OUT OF THE FATHER
UPRIGHT: The rich mental estate that you have inherited will flavor all of your physical/material affairs. The thirst for more and more information will lead you into thoughtful activities, both for work and play. Thinking is your game, as you work to honor the best of the past while seeking an innovative future. **INVERTED:** To be both traditional and innovative in your physical/material affairs will be a challenge.

2 GOVERNED BY THE HIGH PRIESTESS: EMOTIONAL GIVENS, OUT OF THE MOTHER
UPRIGHT: The rich mental estate that you have inherited will flavor all of your emotional/creative affairs. Your appetite for knowledge will flavor your search for companionship and your expression of love and beauty. You will seek ways to use the best of romantic and creative traditions, but only to reinforce and invigorate ever new experience and expression. **INVERTED:** To be both traditional and innovative in your emotional/creative affairs will be a challenge.

3 GOVERNED BY THE EMPRESS: MENTAL GIVENS, INTELLECTUAL PREDISPOSITION
UPRIGHT: The power of your mind and its ability to bridge past with future sets your intellectual course. Yours is a rich blend of the Physical and Mental Planes, as you harness the mind to problems with practical solutions. You will never stop your studies. **INVERTED:** As you walk the line between past and future great care must be taken to know the difference. Claim only what is yours.

4 GOVERNED BY THE EMPEROR: SPIRITUAL GIVENS, LIFE PURPOSE
UPRIGHT: The mind is enlisted in the highest uses of intellect, in learning and communicating the lessons which transform the lowly ego into the higher self which is identifying with the world/universe. This is the procession of self to Self. **INVERTED:** There is much hard study and dedication required here but no more than your soul is capable of embracing with enthusiasm.

5 GOVERNED BY THE HIEROPHANT: SYSTEMS BORN INTO, SOCIETAL INFLUENCE
UPRIGHT: Although probably not steeped in fixed mental attitudes and practices, there was keen awareness of history. You were encouraged to reach out with your mind and encompass all that you could handle. **INVERTED:** One distortion involves considerable confusion over correctness, accuracy, reliability of knowledge. Another distortion sees the readee as having great pressure placed on him to study and succeed mentally.

6 GOVERNED BY THE LOVERS: EMOTIONAL TAPES, BASIS FOR RELATING/CREATING
UPRIGHT: Here is the passion of the intellectual, the love of books, of study and knowledge, and in contemporary times the computer whiz with an enormous appetite for information. **INVERTED:** Knowledge for knowledge's sake has many wrong forks which will take you far from you soul's true goals. This love, like all others, must be a means to an end....which then becomes a means....and so on.

7 GOVERNED BY THE CHARIOT: PHYSICAL RESOURCES. MEANS TO ACHIEVE
UPRIGHT: The information, the knowledge you hold in store, is your greatest asset, and much of it goes with you wherever you go. If all else were stripped from you, you could rebuild from this kernel. **INVERTED:** Check all of your information vaults to be certain this commodity is secure from any man made or natural disaster.

8 GOVERNED BY STRENGTH: EMOTIONAL RESOURCES, ENERGY
UPRIGHT: Your circle of knowledge is entwined with your circle of friends and family. It is the heart and soul of your creative output. This sharing of like minds is energy that you can draw on as well as contribute to, helping you balance give and take and stay emotionally centered and strong. **INVERTED:** Keep this circle open and fluid to allow ever new energy and to assure revitalization.

9 GOVERNED BY THE HERMIT: BELIEF SYSTEM, BASIS FOR DECISIONS
UPRIGHT: This is a faith in knowledge, that our future is nothing less than the sum of what we learn and how we use it. And while it certainly does not preclude a belief in a hierarchy of knowledge that takes us step by step to God via a Jacob's ladder of lessons learned, it is much more Aristotelian than it is Platonic, saying only that greater knowledge is for the good. **INVERTED:** This suggests just what the upright card avoids, that our path is of this world, more scientific than spiritual, and that it is the power of man's mind that holds the key. It does not require a god as source of man's accomplishments.

10 GOVERNED BY THE WHEEL OF FORTUNE: CENTRAL MESSAGE, THEME OF READING
UPRIGHT: Better clean out those files, it is mental moving day. Save only what is necessary for a valid reference for future projects. Also, purge the memory of unneeded trivia. Review procedures, study/work habits. The mind has serious work to do. **INVERTED:** Be certain that the mind is properly engaged. Is your information correct? Allocate credit where credit is due.

11 GOVERNED BY JUSTICE: STATE/CONTENT OF MIND
UPRIGHT: The Mental Plane shifts gears. Plans now involve hard data, depth of evaluation. You are stepping forward with your agenda. And while speaking

out is always a feature of the higher swords, this feels more like speech writing than speech making. ***INVERTED:*** There may be mental retreat, a regrouping. You may be aware of some inaccuracy or untruth.

12 GOVERNED BY THE HANGED MAN: STATE OF EMOTIONS, SUBCONSCIOUS
UPRIGHT: The heart gives thanks for what the mind has accomplished, yet yearns for a new cycle of learning and mental involvement. It is hungry for the environment of the inner courtyard leading to the garden of Eden, where the fragrance of wisdom fills the air and stirs the senses with an almost unbearable sweetness. ***INVERTED:*** The process of thanksgiving must be complete before any new invocation can be heard.

13 GOVERNED BY DEATH: PHYSICAL SITUATION, HARD REALITY
UPRIGHT: Here are the physical/material ramifications of your mental harvest and new planting season to come. New work or relocation may be in the offing to accommodate this major shift. ***INVERTED:*** Such changes to work or residence, if proper, will seem obvious and need not be forced. Do not play with information or its sources to support predeterminations. Let the information speak for itself.

14 GOVERNED BY TEMPERANCE: EMOTIONAL TEST
UPRIGHT: As the mind seeks higher and higher truth, all that has gone before must pass through these new tests, this new gate of authenticity. What was once satisfactory at a lower level may no longer suffice. But everything that was part of our true path will pass through the gate leading to the inner courtyard. ***INVERTED:*** Your penchant for truth must be handled delicately, not like a mace to punish others for their lack of comprehension or inauthenticity.

15 GOVERNED BY THE DEVIL: TEMPTATION/CHALLENGE, FEARS
UPRIGHT: Here the passion for knowledge and the passion for truth should be one and the same in order to progress rapidly and safely. You will accept the challenge of your intellect. ***INVERTED:*** In one extreme there can be fear of knowledge itself, a sensing of what you would rather not believe, in every day affairs, or in the headier realms of metaphysical reality where knowledge make you face the work of your Karmic Contract.

16 GOVERNED BY THE TOWER: NEXT LESSON, GRACE OF GOD
UPRIGHT: This is a time for validation, for you must build now on what you believe to be the truth, as you must now work to contribute to that truth. As you increase your ability to focus and you see in minute detail the wonders around you, your mind will easily support the projects your heart is pulling you towards. ***INVERTED:*** This may be a major fork wherein you choose consciously a lesser fork than would take you more directly to your life purpose.

17 GOVERNED BY THE STAR: ASPIRATIONS OF EGO, GOALS, MAXIMUM EXPECTATIONS
UPRIGHT: Among the more noble goals of this archetype is the will to be of value in the preservation of man's accomplishments, and to facilitate access to, and use of, records so that future efforts do not have to reinvent the wheel. To use your mental gifts to the greatest extent possible for increasing the total extent of man's knowledge. ***INVERTED:*** In one extreme there is a desire for information as power without enough corresponding responsibility, such as a ruthless newspaper publisher, or a J. Edgar Hoover at the head of the Federal Bureau of Investigation.

18 GOVERNED BY THE MOON: ASPIRATIONS OF HEART, COMPASSION
UPRIGHT: This heart is aware that without the power of the mind, the ability to know God is limited. The greatest gift to man is this extra dimension of understanding. And so, here the heart aspires to share in the mind's journey and it's discoveries. ***INVERTED:*** The pitfall here is the adoration of the mental process itself rather than what it reveals.

19 GOVERNED BY THE SUN: PHYSICAL FULFILLMENT/EVALUATION
UPRIGHT: You could well end this lifetime on the verge of another major project or mental breakthrough. You will be innovative and active with an eye toward the future. You will never think of yourself as old, being very comfortable at any age. ***INVERTED:*** Make sure you install safeguards of objectivity as you age so that you do not slip into bias or inaccuracy, and certainly you want to end with honesty and dignity.

20 GOVERNED BY JUDGEMENT: HEART'S FULFILLMENT/EVALUATION
UPRIGHT: Your emotional path is judged to be successful as a family of thought carried in common by your extended family, shoring up and amplifying all of your relationships and creative projects, setting the stage for the next generation to continue. ***INVERTED:*** Some of your extended family may choose paths different from yours.

21 GOVERNED BY THE WORLD: EGO'S FULFILLMENT/EVALUATION
UPRIGHT: The mind has successfully navigated the waters of the lower ego self and its extension to include others and set itself directly on course to embrace universal mind. You are an active student to the end. ***INVERTED:*** Never let your mind isolate itself, and when it does focus, as it must in proper phase, on the inner self, make sure that it looks to the self with the self, to the inner God.

22/0 GOVERNED BY THE FOOL: SOUL'S FULFILLMENT/EVALUATION
UPRIGHT: This soul has mastered the link between past and present, ending the second cycle of the Minor Arcana by successfully including the other and establishing a healthy extended family, and beginning with similar aptitude the beginning of the third cycle which must extend the self even further with the inclusion of more of the world/universe. ***INVERTED:*** Use the opportunity of this reading to meditate on the ideal of this archetype as your life's fulfillment.

SEVEN OF WANDS

UPRIGHT: As with the other Sevens, the Seven of Wands marks the closing of the second cycle (4 thru 7) wherein the individual has begun to include others as extensions of the self, and ushers in the last and highest of the three cycles in the Minor Arcana (7 thru 10) during which the distinction between self will and the will of God diminishes, then disappears. Here then in the Seven of Wands is the higher physical aspect of the Spiritual Plane. The foundation is laid for the integration of the body, the heart, and the mind with the spiritual. They must perfect the art of remaining separate while becoming one. Paradoxes begin to play strongly with the level of the Sevens, particularly in the Suit of Wands. Here you are enlightened enough to function as one with the environment, i.e., with everything else, as duality merges into the one. The paradox is that this state of enlightenment has set you apart from others not yet at that stage. The test is to not let enlightenment separate you from those less enlightened; it must make you less separate. Here faith has crystallized into its mature form for this incarnation, but its defense against other forms is still necessary, for it is mature but not complete. Your belief system is put to the test by physical realities. Taking a stand. Strong character and integrity. There is major new input on the spiritual level. Unsolicited advice may appear. Here, the disciplines of Zen and Hatha Yoga are seen working. There are physical things which must be considered in order to advance further. The lessons of this card are to correct any flaws in your belief systems which could prevent proper development/advancement. Resolve. Conviction. Here is the warrior, certainly spiritual, but otherwise as well, for this is an archetype of the defender. You cannot fight for one minute unless you are fighting for something you believe in. **INVERTED:** Paranoia. Unnecessary precaution or hesitation. Lack of sufficient conviction in professed beliefs. Cowardice.

In This Spread Position...Interpret the Seven Of Wands Meanings to Include:

1 GOVERNED BY THE MAGICIAN: PHYSICAL GIVENS, OUT OF THE FATHER
UPRIGHT: The rich spiritual estate that you have inherited will flavor all of your physical/material affairs. Your profound awareness of the higher aspects of man will mark the activities of this plane. You will bear earnest witness to what you have discovered in your work and your play. You will walk your talk, and talk your walk. **INVERTED:** To live with the conscious awareness of the Divine permeating your Physical Plane will be new and challenging in itself. You cannot turn off the voice of God, and yet you must live and work with others who do not hear and see as you do.

2 GOVERNED BY THE HIGH PRIESTESS: EMOTIONAL GIVENS, OUT OF THE MOTHER
UPRIGHT: The rich spiritual estate that you have inherited will flavor all of your emotional/creative affairs. Your keen insight into the higher aspects of man will mark your relationships and your creative endeavors as you bear witness to what you have learned. Much time is given to the use of creative talents in the outer courtyard leading to the garden of Eden. **INVERTED:** You bring to all relationships and creative tasks a conscious awareness of the Divine permeating your Emotional Plane. This will be new and challenging in itself. You cannot turn off the voice of God, and yet you must live and work with others who do not hear and see as you do.

3 GOVERNED BY THE EMPRESS: MENTAL GIVENS, INTELLECTUAL PREDISPOSITION
UPRIGHT: The rich spiritual estate that you have inherited will flavor all of mental affairs. Your knowledge of the higher aspects of man will set the agenda for the conduct of this plane. The mind is totally committed to gnosis. **INVERTED:** You bring to all intellectual endeavors a conscious awareness of the Divine permeating your Mental Plane. The new challenge here lies in the permanence of that shift in awareness. You hear God's voice in everything, everywhere.

4 GOVERNED BY THE EMPEROR: SPIRITUAL GIVENS, LIFE PURPOSE
UPRIGHT: The Initiate has reached and will enter the gate to the inner courtyard leading to the garden of Eden. The feeling bears some resemblance to reaching puberty; an innocence is lost but more is gained. **INVERTED:** This lifetime represents a major jump in responsibility for the knowledge you are about to receive on this leg of your journey, but you are ready.

5 GOVERNED BY THE HIEROPHANT: SYSTEMS BORN INTO, SOCIETAL INFLUENCE
UPRIGHT: Already here in the early environment there is a sense of the torch being passed. Things may have been somewhat lively as the system surrounding you defended itself from time to time, if not continuously. But there was an underlying strength of convictions. **INVERTED:** While a strong spiritual ambiance may have been present, it was not strong in its convictions, or convincing in its tactics.

6 GOVERNED BY THE LOVERS: EMOTIONAL TAPES, BASIS FOR RELATING/CREATING
UPRIGHT: There is some of St. Joan of Arc here, in the passion for the battle itself. Where would faith be without its defenders, its Knights Templar, its holy warriors. The act of defense frames the boundaries of the faith. **INVERTED:** While this archetype recognizes that the love here includes, by necessity of this path a taste for blood to pique one's courage, a pitfall here would be in losing sight of the faith, the cause behind the fight. At an extreme, this readee would love the fight purely for itself.

7 GOVERNED BY THE CHARIOT: PHYSICAL RESOURCES. MEANS TO ACHIEVE
UPRIGHT: Your clarity of purpose and resolve can always be relied upon. With your eye clearly on your goals, you simply will not give up. And while you know your position at all times, likewise you know the positions of your adversaries. **INVERTED:** Shore up any cracks in your purpose and resolve before committing to any new campaigns. You may have manpower and material, but your validity and/or your resolve is questionable.

8 GOVERNED BY STRENGTH: EMOTIONAL RESOURCES, ENERGY
UPRIGHT: Because of your having taken a stand exposing your views, you have drawn others of like mind and spirit to you. You will never be alone as there are others equally committed. Passion stands behind conviction. **INVERTED:** Exposing too much or too little will keep you at less than your peak strength. Too much, will diminish the number of allies who will see eye to eye enough to stand with you. Too little, will not send a strong enough signal to attract enough allies.

9 GOVERNED BY THE HERMIT: BELIEF SYSTEM, BASIS FOR DECISIONS
UPRIGHT: You believe simply that one must believe, and that in fact everyone does believe in something, even if that something is a non-belief. Every mental process, every decision hinges on the belief system in effect at that moment. For some, seeing is believing. For you, believing is seeing. **INVERTED:** There could be a tendency to try and freeze your beliefs at a certain point. Beliefs must remain dynamic to stay valid. Otherwise, they distort and decay into dogma.

10 GOVERNED BY THE WHEEL OF FORTUNE: CENTRAL MESSAGE, THEME OF READING
UPRIGHT: You are being filled with a sense of purpose, as you identify more and more clearly the meaning of spirituality in your life, in the daily function of your Mental, Emotional, and Physical Planes. *INVERTED:* While decisions and action will come easily, so does reaction. But now that you know what your ground is, you can stand and defend it. You may be bombarded with unsolicited advice.

11 GOVERNED BY JUSTICE: STATE/CONTENT OF MIND
UPRIGHT: The clearer your mind becomes, the more defined your position. You are aware that you have drawn your spiritual line in the sand. *INVERTED:* Rather than taking up a position for something, you may be setting yourself up against something. Work toward the positive, not against the negative. You will draw more than enough adversaries to keep you busy.

12 GOVERNED BY THE HANGED MAN: STATE OF EMOTIONS, SUBCONSCIOUS
UPRIGHT: You are empowered by your excitement at having discovered your center, your way of linking the past with the future, your place in the present. *INVERTED:* Now that you are discovering your spiritual muscle, you have the urge to exercise it. This suggests that you may not be concerned enough with where and why you display your new strength.

13 GOVERNED BY DEATH: PHYSICAL SITUATION, HARD REALITY
UPRIGHT: Here is the proof that spirituality is a contact sport. You are up to your neck in witnessing, in physically implementing your beliefs. Integration of spirituality into the physical daily regimen is taking place. This is the early appearance of Zen, wherein everything done is infused with an awareness of its importance in the overall scheme of things, nothing is unimportant and so is done with care. Also, the early appearance of Hatha Yoga and other body-work/body movement systems which reflect this same depth of awareness of God in the body and nature. *INVERTED:* At one extreme, there may be a serious contest, a battle to defend your position, your beliefs. At the other extreme, you may not be standing up for them at all. Here the Physical/material Plane is not seen with enough reverence.

14 GOVERNED BY TEMPERANCE: EMOTIONAL TEST
UPRIGHT: As you discover what is truly important to you and begin to move and act with conviction, you will be rocking the boat of your present establishment of relationships and the conduct of your creative affairs. Oddly enough, your expansion of appreciation in the Mental and Physical Planes may prove bothersome to many, threatening to others. *INVERTED:* Look for what you love, not for what you detest.

15 GOVERNED BY THE DEVIL: TEMPTATION/CHALLENGE, FEARS
UPRIGHT: There are many versions of Satan's fall from grace as the result of his refusal to bow down before God's new creation, man, so too are we tempted not to bow before our fellow man. The lesson here is that we must bow down before one another as recognition of the divinity that resides within everything. *INVERTED:* At one extreme, a refusal to see the value in another man's proposition, and to yield to it is a refusal of God's command as surely as Satan's misunderstanding and subsequent disobedience.

16 GOVERNED BY THE TOWER: NEXT LESSON, GRACE OF GOD
UPRIGHT: Your next lesson requires you to integrate your lofty ideals in very pragmatic ways. Your spirituality must be worn on your sleeve, not in loud, garish colors, but in sensitive and sensible observation in daily habits. *INVERTED:* Do not become so preoccupied with defending your present position that you stop growing.

17 GOVERNED BY THE STAR: ASPIRATIONS OF EGO, GOALS, MAXIMUM EXPECTATIONS
UPRIGHT: This goal may come more in the guise of a vow, a pledge to oneself and to others to walk with one foot in heaven and the other on earth, as seen by the wearing of one delicate shoe and one heavy boot. Which is to trod the path above, and which below? Which the more difficult? *INVERTED:* Here, the goal is to see the spreading of one's belief , and to be part and parcel of its foundation. Here, the split between physical and spiritual is real and abused.

18 GOVERNED BY THE MOON: ASPIRATIONS OF HEART, COMPASSION
UPRIGHT: To fall in love with love, not war. To see the victory of your cause as a means to peace and goodwill. *INVERTED:* To see the victory of your cause, but with scant consideration for the loser.

19 GOVERNED BY THE SUN: PHYSICAL FULFILLMENT/EVALUATION
UPRIGHT: You have fought for and won the tests of your beliefs in the hard reality of the Physical/material Plane. *INVERTED:* The spiritual may have been misunderstood and misapplied against the innate beauty of the physical.

20 GOVERNED BY JUDGEMENT: HEART'S FULFILLMENT/EVALUATION
UPRIGHT: The strength of your resolve has brought you and your extended family to the level where emotions blend with spirituality. The battles that you have fought together have only enriched your relationships and the ability to enjoy one another. You will live on in the hearts of many. *INVERTED:* Do not let misunderstanding and misapplication of the spiritual create tensions and lessen the pleasure that is appropriate for the Emotional Plane.

21 GOVERNED BY THE WORLD: EGO'S FULFILLMENT/EVALUATION
UPRIGHT: Whether actually part of the foundation of a new or revitalized ideology or religion, you are content in the knowledge that you have seen the light and helped many others to see that same light. You will live on in the minds of those who have walked with you, more in the legacy of your actions themselves than in words. *INVERTED:* Work now to strengthen your resolve so that you have few regrets over improper or inadequate actions.

22/0 GOVERNED BY THE FOOL: SOUL'S FULFILLMENT/EVALUATION
UPRIGHT: You have been able to integrate the duality of physical/spiritual without sacrificing one to the other. You have been an eager Zen archer, selecting and placing your arrows with great accuracy. All that you accomplished on each of the four planes (Physical, Emotional, Mental, and Spiritual) is secure and will stand the test of time, for your achievements were rooted in the timeless. *INVERTED:* Work now to purge the spiritual bully from your path and achieve the full potential of this archetype.

EIGHT OF PENTACLES

UPRIGHT: Here is the effect of the highest order of emotions on the Physical Plane, wherein the physical aspires to the spiritual, as indeed the spiritual has aspired to the physical through your incarnation.There is increase in productivity with the joy of proper work. Your physical/material foundation itself moves forward. Pleasure in material things in a very positive sense, as you begin to truly see and experience the pulse of God in nature and all things material, organic and inorganic. Your environmental support systems are in place and working—you efficiently identify with them as they are literally extensions of your self. Great enjoyment of physical exertion, whether work or leisure—an avid sports fan as well as active player. Physical prowess. Dedicated, mature worker. Good use of power and resources. Thoroughness. Precision. The physical level produces quality and quantity that surpasses individual needs, surpasses extended family needs, offering the excess of its efficiency to the greater good of all who require it. This is the efficient use of material resources and manpower to the aggrandizement of both. Less makes more. Here the total exceeds the sum of its parts. Teamwork, physically coordinated with others as group output, takes priority. Networking. Lower and higher reality combine here to great effect. Eight is the combination of 1 and 7 (two levels of the Physical Plane), of 2 and 6 (two levels of the Emotional Plane), 3 and 5 (two levels of the Mental Plane), and of 4 and 4 (the addition of the lower level of the Spiritual Plane to itself). Most important to the Eight of Pentacles is the addition of 1 and 7, for it is the equal accommodation of these that sets the stage for this card. Recognition and honoring of the physical origin (the father) which is a looking backward to the past (1), together with the honoring of the product of the father (the son), which in turn is the father and likewise becomes the new physical origin with an eye to the future (7). The energy of the Major Arcana archetypes of Magician (1) and the Chariot (7) combine giving an air of magic to the efficient and prodigious output now possible. **INVERTED:** There may be distortion of the above, too little or too much of these principles. For instance: You may be too attached to your work, or to exercise. Production of more than can be used or stored efficiently, and without waste. Over-reliance on teamwork, networking. On the one hand, a lack of professionalism, even clumsiness. On the other hand, a fanatic perfectionist, meticulous to a fault.

In This Spread Position...Interpret the Eight Of Pentacles Meanings to Include:

1 GOVERNED BY THE MAGICIAN: PHYSICAL GIVENS, OUT OF THE FATHER
UPRIGHT: Yours may be considered the Midas touch, for you succeed in all that you do in this plane. You begin with the lower lessons of the Physical/material Plane behind you so that you can lead by example, stimulating others to achieve the same order and contribute to abundance. **INVERTED:** You will be very, very busy, some might say preoccupied.

2 GOVERNED BY THE HIGH PRIESTESS: EMOTIONAL GIVENS, OUT OF THE MOTHER
UPRIGHT: There will be much for you to enjoy in the wealth of talent and productivity surrounding you. **INVERTED:** This level of emotional maturity may be demanding on others if they want to relate to you. "Things" come first, but not in a negative sense. The emotions will however be in service to the physical.

3 GOVERNED BY THE EMPRESS: MENTAL GIVENS, INTELLECTUAL PREDISPOSITION
UPRIGHT: You are naturally disposed to an understanding of the Physical/material Plane—the body, the earth and its raw materials, finances, and construction for example. Your mind will be drawn to problems in these areas. There is an appreciation for the material world, the positive effect of man on his environment that will underline all your relationships and creative endeavors. **INVERTED:** Problem solving—How to advance technology so that man is advancing God's cause not harming it, is an example of the weight to which your intellect must be tested.

4 GOVERNED BY THE EMPEROR: SPIRITUAL GIVENS, LIFE PURPOSE
UPRIGHT: Master craftsman. The ability to harness the energy of love and understanding and use it in the material world. To achieve the paradox of using something and instead of depletion there is increase.Your ordered personal world will help bring order to the world at large. Seeing the handiwork of such a gifted man reinforces our closeness to God, for we know then that we are indeed seeing God. **INVERTED:** You will work intimately with the products of this good earth, and with much efficiency and productivity. You may or may not enjoy, or even care to enjoy, conventional material comforts. Your work and your products are your reward, not money.

5 GOVERNED BY THE HIEROPHANT: SYSTEMS BORN INTO, SOCIETAL INFLUENCE
UPRIGHT: From parents who might have been co-founders of Findhorn or Greenpeace, to a father who spearheaded a large organic farm, to a mother manufacturing environmentally sensitive cosmetics—these are examples of the sort of adults who influenced you early on. **INVERTED:** All work, no matter how sensitive and valid, is neglectful of other priorities. On another extreme however, is the climate in which work was not valued. Or, where the profit, not the work, was of primary importance with little respect for the material or nature.

6 GOVERNED BY THE LOVERS: EMOTIONAL TAPES, BASIS FOR RELATING/CREATING
UPRIGHT: Your love will be to see the effect you can have on a raw process, the ability to bring order and refinement to something that leaves it more beautiful and valid in every sense. To be the missing link that makes something work. **INVERTED:** The passion for work, or for appreciation of material things may be excessive. This is not materialism in its negative contemporary, shop until you drop, sense. Rather, simply an overinvolvement with the beauty of a given material or category of object, like wood or Ming dynasty vases.

7 GOVERNED BY THE CHARIOT: PHYSICAL RESOURCES. MEANS TO ACHIEVE
UPRIGHT: You could be dropped in the middle of nowhere and in three hours have the natives organized and producing a product that would turn a third world backwater into a thriving member of the international economy. Resourcefulness. Reserves. **INVERTED:** You may not be giving enough attention to your resources and what is left behind once you use them up. You may have produced or stored far more than you need.

8 GOVERNED BY STRENGTH: EMOTIONAL RESOURCES, ENERGY
UPRIGHT: Your ability to get along with others, to work well with them, blends your Emotional and Physical Planes in a very healthy way. It is said that the family that plays together, stays together. Well, it may be even more true that the family that works together, stays together. And in this case, we may not be talking just family or extended family, but the larger community as a whole. **INVERTED:** The Emotional Plane must be multi-dimensional. All relationships and creative activity should not be centered around or dependent on the work or craft.

9 GOVERNED BY THE HERMIT: BELIEF SYSTEM, BASIS FOR DECISIONS
UPRIGHT: This is not only a "can do," but a "better do, do better," the buck stops here kind of philosophy. This is a man who knows we fell into the garden

of Eden, not out of it, and is intent on being as good a caretaker/gardener as he can manage. He takes everything that is, as exactly that. "This is it," as Alan Watts liked to say. If there is a disaster, you begin by picking up the pieces, not by wondering "why me?". **INVERTED:** At one extreme is the negative attitude that nothing one does matters. This is a horrid distortion of a belief that it is all God's will, so why bother. At the other extreme is the attitude that it is all up to me, a distortion in the other direction that believes it is all Man's will.

10 GOVERNED BY THE WHEEL OF FORTUNE: CENTRAL MESSAGE, THEME OF READING
UPRIGHT: Now is the opportunity to make concrete headway. Here is work that you love and do well. This is the color of your parachute. Get the team ready. **INVERTED:** More work and more perfection is not the answer. And, by the way, you do not have to do everything. Some things are better left undone.

11 GOVERNED BY JUSTICE: STATE/CONTENT OF MIND
UPRIGHT: You feel prepared, content that you are doing all that you can do to bring the present situation to its right conclusion. **INVERTED:** On one extreme, you think that you have done all that you can do and that it may not be enough; what have the others done? Another extreme is that you are not content with your work, either the quality, the quantity, or both.

12 GOVERNED BY THE HANGED MAN: STATE OF EMOTIONS, SUBCONSCIOUS
UPRIGHT: You are very caught up in the work at hand, the activity at the physical/material level. When you are in your studio, you are in your heaven. **INVERTED:** For you, what you are doing is solving everyone's problem, not just yours. But look around, is it really? Your work may be so introspective and sheltered that it is losing the very validity that you cherish. Have all the right people been involved? Or, too many?

13 GOVERNED BY DEATH: PHYSICAL SITUATION, HARD REALITY
UPRIGHT: The production line is running. Get the boxes ready; it is time to package and deliver. Now you can see what all the talking has been about. Here is the latest model, the newest creation. **INVERTED:** The output may not be going according to plan, or desire. Could the plans and the production be going too well? Will the process stop when you want it to?

14 GOVERNED BY TEMPERANCE: EMOTIONAL TEST
UPRIGHT: With your involvement with your projects and your success, you must work even harder at how you interface with your loved ones and co-workers. For as much as they share your dreams and back you, they cannot know all that you know, and feel all that you feel. **INVERTED:** On the one hand, you may be much too engrossed in your work or physical activity. On the other hand, you may have difficulty keeping up your level of energy and desire to pursue your work or physical interests.

15 GOVERNED BY THE DEVIL: TEMPTATION/CHALLENGE, FEARS
UPRIGHT: Your integration of spirit into your work produces amazing results, perhaps more amazing to others than to you. **INVERTED:** Your success may be somewhat daunting to others, even to yourself in some respects. Another extreme is that your intellectual interest in your work, your physical activities, or in material matters is on the wane.

16 GOVERNED BY THE TOWER: NEXT LESSON, GRACE OF GOD
UPRIGHT: This is the mark of the professional, not the amateur or the apprentice. People will look to you for the best in your field of expertise. If you have been awaiting accreditation or licensing, it will be yours not later than this time next year. For others already in gear, this will be a time to put your best foot forward. Your work will be right on target. **INVERTED:** This suggests that you may be attempting the wrong thing, or too much of a good thing. On the one hand, your product may be the wrong product or not good enough for the situation. On the other hand, it may be too good and therefore inappropriate.

17 GOVERNED BY THE STAR: ASPIRATIONS OF EGO, GOALS, MAXIMUM EXPECTATIONS
UPRIGHT: Your goal is to be the best at what you do, and you expect nothing less from yourself. And if possible, you want to be able to extract the same high level of performance from many others as well. **INVERTED:** To be of quality, in and of itself, is more important than what you would be doing. A painful twist here is to want to be the best but to not believe in your ability to get there.

18 GOVERNED BY THE MOON: ASPIRATIONS OF HEART, COMPASSION
UPRIGHT: You want to be successful so that not only are your needs well met, but your extremes of quality and quantity allow others to benefit from and enjoy what you enjoy. In more esoteric terms, you aspire to help others reach the same degree of pleasure as you when you smell the roses. **INVERTED:** This aspiration leans too far toward the enjoyment of the ends of the process rather than the pleasure of the process itself.

19 GOVERNED BY THE SUN: PHYSICAL FULFILLMENT/EVALUATION
UPRIGHT: Everything in the Physical/material Plane that you have achieved is up and running smoothly even as you end this leg of your journey. The suggestion is that you never quit, working like Picasso to the very end. **INVERTED:** In one extreme, for one reason or another, you may try to work too much in your later years, much more than is necessary or suitable for your own ends. You would be working for the wrong reasons. But another extreme has you stopping your productivity before necessary.

20 GOVERNED BY JUDGEMENT: HEART'S FULFILLMENT/EVALUATION
UPRIGHT: There is great pleasure between you and all of your extended family at what has been accomplished. Your feelings for one another cannot be divorced from what you have achieved together. **INVERTED:** Disappointment with the work itself, or at your own or others' performance, may shadow an otherwise happy ending. Study the principles of this archetype and this reading to head off that disappointment.

21 GOVERNED BY THE WORLD: EGO'S FULFILLMENT/EVALUATION
UPRIGHT: The ego is swelled with proper pride for you have helped to bring abundance and beauty into this world. **INVERTED:** Neither be too proud, detracting from the proper applause that is yours, nor apply harsher standards to yourself and thus disappoint God.

22/0 GOVERNED BY THE FOOL: SOUL'S FULFILLMENT/EVALUATION
UPRIGHT: You have walked the path of beauty possible only with eyes that see the Divine inside everything physical. Filled with the knowledge that the higher physical is our goal, it being one with the spiritual, you have contributed to the increase that is God's desire. **INVERTED:** This card is your potential in this lifetime.

EIGHT OF CUPS

UPRIGHT: Here are mature emotions, secured with the lessons of love without improper attachment, and capable of seeing beyond immediate surroundings. Your heart is opening wider, getting larger as your love expands beyond the immediate circle of mate, family, and close friends into a more universal love. This is the heart's parallel growth to the ego, which has begun to integrate with universal mind at this level of the Eights. Emotional drive here comes, not from dissatisfaction with what you already have, but because your emotional world is growing, your emotional pie is actually getting bigger. Magically, everyone already in your life will still get the same size piece of pie, even as your time is prorated for others. Much of the biblical parable of the prodigal son is here. Emotional quests/crusades. Creative productivity/expansion. A blending of the masculine and feminine energy. Emotional efficiency creates an abundance of reliable interactivity—emotional stockpiling. The emotional foundation, the package itself is on the move. As with the Eight of Pentacles, the combinations of 1 and 7, 2 and 6, 3 and 5, as well as 4 and 4, are all number pairs operating in the Eights, but principally here is the effect of the two levels from the Emotional Plane, 2 and 6. It is the tension between these two, and the lessons learned in accommodating both, that set the stage for the highest emotional lessons of the eight. Love of self and love of other must balance, as they move toward becoming one and the same. Extroversion and inclusion. Enrichment and enhancement. Emotional focus. Involvement. Exuberance. Incentive. Altruism. Bounty. **INVERTED:** Distortions in the extreme include: Prodigality and gluttony vs. emotional starvation and denial. Lecherous and bothersome vs. inattentive. Emotional/sexual excess vs. emotional/sexual apathy. Promiscuity/cheating. Emotional recklessness. Sexual addictions. Imposition. Insistence on giving where it is not needed or not wanted.

In This Spread Position...Interpret the Eight Of Cups Meanings to Include:

1 GOVERNED BY THE MAGICIAN: PHYSICAL GIVENS, OUT OF THE FATHER
UPRIGHT: A healthy emotional appetite energizes your physical/material world leading you into activities that enrich life's possibilities for yourself and others. Your home and your work will be as open and inclusive as you can manage, and as mobile. **INVERTED:** This degree of extroversion, as you try to include everyone in your affairs, will present challenges to your loved ones, your business associates, just about everybody but you.

2 GOVERNED BY THE HIGH PRIESTESS: EMOTIONAL GIVENS, OUT OF THE MOTHER
UPRIGHT: A healthy emotional appetite energizes your emotional/creative world leading you into relationships and creative projects that seek a profusion of delight, a rejoicing that allows your heart's blood to flow freely and deeply. **INVERTED:** You may find it difficult trying to move your emotional foundation around with you. Your family may not like trailers as much as you do.

3 GOVERNED BY THE EMPRESS: MENTAL GIVENS, INTELLECTUAL PREDISPOSITION
UPRIGHT: Your expansive emotional nature infuses your mind with the challenge to match its courageous search for God's playhouse on earth, and to make sure it is large enough to accommodate everybody. **INVERTED:** This is serious business to your mind, but it may look frivolous to others. Part of your job is to make sure that you are not misunderstood, for this archetype is one everyone must learn eventually.

4 GOVERNED BY THE EMPEROR: SPIRITUAL GIVENS, LIFE PURPOSE
UPRIGHT: This is the magic path of the unbounded yet faithful heart, which will successfully balance the purity and power of personal romantic love and its extension into family with an equal and complementary love for mankind and all creation. Power to heal through love and intensity of involvement. Emotional focus/mastery create abundance of love and energy. **INVERTED:** The phrase "common love" suggests the difficulties of this path—for in seeking what is common to all of creation, temptations to and accusations of debasement may be all too "common."

5 GOVERNED BY THE HIEROPHANT: SYSTEMS BORN INTO, SOCIETAL INFLUENCE
UPRIGHT: Very often, the lessons of jealousy, patience, envy, independence, and the like are on the childhood plate of those born into an environment of this archetype, for here you are expected early on to share the parents and other adults you love and depend on most. **INVERTED:** Here, the lack of parental or family type love and contact may have been extreme, and perhaps the reasons for their absence were less than noble. Reliance on others or on yourself was your alternative, and your training ground.

6 GOVERNED BY THE LOVERS: EMOTIONAL TAPES, BASIS FOR RELATING/CREATING
UPRIGHT: Anyone who marries this archetype has all of the lessons mentioned above in position 5 and then some. For here is a person who is compelled by the grace of God to help foster universal love. This is the calling of John the Baptist, of Christ, and the mission of the Apostles. Even though the Apostles were commissioned to teach, theirs was nevertheless the path toward universality. **INVERTED:** In one extreme, this person may decide not to marry, because the pull to universality is simply too strong and demanding, to ask someone else to share.

7 GOVERNED BY THE CHARIOT: PHYSICAL RESOURCES, MEANS TO ACHIEVE
UPRIGHT: You can find a needle in a haystack, and find energy when and where you need it, for you can extract joy from the least likely of circumstances, pleasure from sources of pain. And, you can move mountains. **INVERTED:** If you are too active and keep too many irons in the fire, you run the risk of not being where you need to be on occasion, or of being short on the energy you need to move that mountain.

8 GOVERNED BY STRENGTH: EMOTIONAL RESOURCES, ENERGY
UPRIGHT: You balance give and take so well that you can literally rob Peter to pay Paul. Your most intimate relationships are so valid and secure that they energize you for your expeditions. Likewise, your discoveries and newfound relationships energize you for your inner circle, family, and mate. **INVERTED:** You may be robbing Peter to pay Paul and not getting the money back in Peter's bank account fast enough.

9 GOVERNED BY THE HERMIT: BELIEF SYSTEM, BASIS FOR DECISIONS
UPRIGHT: Yours is the philosophy of the epicurean, in the most positive sense. The emphasis here, as opposed to that of the Seven of Cups, is on people and creative experience, not on food and other material things. You believe simply that to know God we need to experience the full nature and extent of his territory. There is nothing lascivious here. For you, this belief is tantamount to experiencing the truth. Nothing less is acceptable. In fact, to attempt otherwise is to waste time, for this is the path we all must come back to sooner or later. **INVERTED:** The extreme (too much) of this archetype is what gives hedonism it's bad press. The extreme (too little) is the confused state of mind that permeated the Victorian era.

10 GOVERNED BY THE WHEEL OF FORTUNE: CENTRAL MESSAGE, THEME OF READING

UPRIGHT: Your emotional house is in order, your creative energy in good supply, and you can explore the corners of your heart for new possibilities. Your emotional pie is going to grow, unless you subvert it. ***INVERTED:*** This is not a time to pursue this archetype. The effect of misapplication of this principle may already be influencing events. Let the reading guide you.

11 GOVERNED BY JUSTICE: STATE/CONTENT OF MIND

UPRIGHT: There is confidence here, even exuberance. Good taste is at work. You are reviewing a situation ripe with possibilities, pushing your mind out as an advanced scout. You have added some new plays to your playbook. Now to wait for the game. ***INVERTED:*** In one extreme, there is some distaste here for the misuse of the sensible.

12 GOVERNED BY THE HANGED MAN: STATE OF EMOTIONS, SUBCONSCIOUS

UPRIGHT: One of the most difficult principles to understand and follow is the lesson of non-attachment. Even the teachings of Jesus on these matters has been distorted in the New Testament, suggesting that his followers were told to turn their backs on their families. What is meant here is that we must not limit ourselves to our families, to our extensions of ourselves, anymore than we can limit ourselves to a love of self. In order to honor the self, our path requires that we extend outward as much as we can, requiring what has been called non-attachment. This heart appears poised to seek and to offer more love. ***INVERTED:*** This heart is troubled with this archetype. Most likely it can explain why.

13 GOVERNED BY DEATH: PHYSICAL SITUATION, HARD REALITY

UPRIGHT: Emotional/creative enterprise is underway. A profusion of possibility is in the air. You are influential now, and should have things your way. ***INVERTED:*** Your desire to move into new areas may be meeting with some difficulty. You may have already moved into territory that is causing trouble. This archetype is not being handled correctly by you, or by someone affecting you. Back off. Too much, too soon.

14 GOVERNED BY TEMPERANCE: EMOTIONAL TEST

UPRIGHT: Time for major expansion in your Emotional/creative Plane in the near future, and the pull you are feeling is symbolized by the positive effect of the moon. The lure of the unknown as part of the grand design to stir us to seek more experience of the one. To know, normally a mental term, is used in the Bible to suggest carnal knowledge of another and so correctly connotes the participation of our emotional/sexual and creative natures in bringing us knowledge of God. ***INVERTED:*** You must deal with a distortion of this archetype in the near future, affecting you and/or your loved ones. An over-compassionate nature may cause you some pain through confusion.

15 GOVERNED BY THE DEVIL: TEMPTATION/CHALLENGE, FEARS

UPRIGHT: You will be presented the challenge to enrich your emotional/creative house with new energy. ***INVERTED:*** It concerns you that you do not feel the same toward everyone. Be patient with yourself as you try to approach this goal, but realize that just as you develop the ability to love even your enemies, you must and will have a hierarchy of those who mean the most to you, even within universal love. We must love all equally, just some more equally than others. Another paradox.

16 GOVERNED BY THE TOWER: NEXT LESSON, GRACE OF GOD

UPRIGHT: The breadth and depth of your life will expand by this time next year in such a way as to amaze you, even though you have set the appropriate wheels in motion yourself. It may take your breath away like the heart's gasp on first seeing the magnificence of the Grand Canyon, or the tree lined Champs-Elysee lit up with thousands of tiny lights at Christmas. ***INVERTED:*** Grace will offer you the chance to learn the shadow side of this archetype with little or no pain.

17 GOVERNED BY THE STAR: ASPIRATIONS OF EGO, GOALS, MAXIMUM EXPECTATIONS

UPRIGHT: This archetype is formidable as a primary goal because the pitfalls are many and deep, but nevertheless it is proper, and one we all must accept sooner or later to reach the end of the path. The suggestion here is that the proper path must include many stops for savoring the scenery, and it must include many "day trips" off to the side. The proper path then is not narrow but wide with purposeful meandering. ***INVERTED:*** This goal smacks of prodigality, a taking of far too many side trips without serious purpose.

18 GOVERNED BY THE MOON: ASPIRATIONS OF HEART, COMPASSION

UPRIGHT: This is the compassionate heart that yearns for the most contact and interaction that a heart can stand without breaking. Here may have been the heart's aspiration for Dr. Livingston. His desire was not to convert the African people he encountered, but simply to encounter them. ***INVERTED:*** Remember the balance of give and take. Even the most profound desire to give and be of service is ignoble if the underlying motivation is your soul's need to give rather than a genuine response to someone else's need to receive. Round pegs must find round holes.

19 GOVERNED BY THE SUN: PHYSICAL FULFILLMENT/EVALUATION

UPRIGHT: Yours will be an active environment, full of energetic people spanning a range of generations, with a paradoxical maturity in the younger folk and a surprising youthfulness in the older folk. ***INVERTED:*** If you do not force things and try to do too much, that is the extraordinary, you will be pleased at the wide range of activities and social mobility you have even in your oldest years.

20 GOVERNED BY JUDGEMENT: HEART'S FULFILLMENT/EVALUATION

UPRIGHT: You and your loved ones, perhaps even your entire community, have been emotionally and creatively adventurous and so rewarded with a range of experience which most people cannot even conceive. Your relationships have been strengthened by the maturity and wisdom that exposure to such diversity inevitably brings. ***INVERTED:*** Remember that to fulfill the lesson of this archetype successfully you must be able to travel your path with all your emotional levels intact. Nothing is sacrificed if done properly.

21 GOVERNED BY THE WORLD: EGO'S FULFILLMENT/EVALUATION

UPRIGHT: Marco Polo must have felt this archetype at the end of his life, having enriched first the Orient with his knowledge of the West, and then in turn enriching his fellow citizens of Venice in the West with what he had learned from his years in China. This is the mark of the mental bee pollinating human flowers. ***INVERTED:*** As with the heart's fulfillment above, this lesson must be learned without sacrificing the intricate emotional staircase we have climbed. You must travel this route with all of your emotional luggage intact.

22/0 GOVERNED BY THE FOOL: SOUL'S FULFILLMENT/EVALUATION

UPRIGHT: Here is emotional bounty achieved by a courageous heart that followed the sirens of its own guiding soul to stretch for the fullest expression of creativity and love a human can muster, and to submit to the maximum acceptance of devotion that is our birthright. ***INVERTED:*** Follow the signs and this will be the mark of this lifetime.

EIGHT OF SWORDS

UPRIGHT: Here the objective, conscious mind reaches the limits of the lower ego, which under the impact and pull of higher emotions and compassion, realizes that to achieve even its most personal and self-oriented goals, it must advance to a more mature Ego, paradoxically an even bigger ego than the lower ego, which encompasses more of the universal mind. The mind has heretofore opened to include extensions of the personal self with a mate and children, or their equivalent, and later to a widening circle of close friends. Now the circle must widen further. This brings its own variety of new challenges as you are presented with increased demands from your mental Karmic Contract. Your first reaction is to close your eyes to the magnitude of the task. It can be quite a shock, like that moment as a teenager when it dawns on us that we are going to have to work, to take care of ourselves and eventually others, rather than the other way around. Greater responsibility. The mind's role in organizing is challenged by the higher order of consciousness realized as the higher emotions' compassion and universal love bring new sensations, new data that defy rationalization. And yet, to rationalize this new process is precisely what the mind must do. With this greater ability to see the extent of order in the above, so grows the ability to see the extent of disorder in the below. Here is the effect at the level of the Eights of the combination of the lower mental levels, 3 and 5. The three's creative fruition and self-assured expression, in which the lower ego is pulsing with its potential, must pair with the five's maturing process of uncertainty and freedom that undergirds free will. **INVERTED:** There may be an attempt to force this new level of revelation and awareness of emotional instincts and their accompanying spiritual realities into existing mental molds, into the world of the lower ego. If so, philosophical dead ends and frustration may result. The lower ego may rebel, not wanting to accept its inevitable conversion. The onset of doubts about your ability to accept more responsibility. Are you working in the right arena, on the right projects?

In This Spread Position...Interpret the Eight Of Swords Meanings to Include:

1 GOVERNED BY THE MAGICIAN: PHYSICAL GIVENS, OUT OF THE FATHER
UPRIGHT: A healthy mental appetite dominates your Physical/material Plane, leading you into sophisticated, discriminating avenues whether at work or at home, in business or at leisure as you look for better and better ways of doing things. There is a need to be highly effective. Good taste predominates. **INVERTED:** Some will say you are a difficult person to live with.

2 GOVERNED BY THE HIGH PRIESTESS: EMOTIONAL GIVENS, OUT OF THE MOTHER
UPRIGHT: A healthy mental appetite dominates your Emotional/creative Plane, giving an intellectual tone to both your relationships and your talents. Your heart has a strong partnership with your mind. Creative projects will be conceived on a grand scale. **INVERTED:** While you will not necessarily be an intellectual snob, you will prefer spending time with people who challenge your mind.

3 GOVERNED BY THE EMPRESS: MENTAL GIVENS, INTELLECTUAL PREDISPOSITION
UPRIGHT: Your mind has reached the level of sophistication wherein the lower ego is being successfully harnessed, guaranteeing enough discipline for you to begin the demanding intellectual task of satisfying your personal goals, the goals of your extended family, and the more universal goals of society at large, as if they were one and the same. **INVERTED:** You may burn your fair share of midnight oil.

4 GOVERNED BY THE EMPEROR: SPIRITUAL GIVENS, LIFE PURPOSE
UPRIGHT: Here is the mental crusade that is launched by the mature mind, the higher mind, which in order to be unbounded in its pursuit of universal knowledge, must bind and control to its proper limits the more limited capacity of the lower mind/ego. The paradox—In order to be unlimited the mind must be limited. **INVERTED:** Some refer to this process, begun in the Suit of Swords at the 7 and running through the 10, as "the dark night of the soul." Others call it "the death of the ego." It is but the metamorphosis of the small, personal, caterpillar ego changing into the grand butterfly Ego that will grow to encompass Universal Mind.

5 GOVERNED BY THE HIEROPHANT: SYSTEMS BORN INTO, SOCIETAL INFLUENCE
UPRIGHT: This is a very heady atmosphere to be born into, challenging, exciting. But just when you may have wanted someone to play with you, they were preoccupied with a book, or solving some problem, and that is if they were at home. But you were resourceful; besides, you had some pretty exciting "play" activities yourself. **INVERTED:** The mental waters here may have been too deep for the swimmers with a great deal of unnecessary thrashing about.

6 GOVERNED BY THE LOVERS: EMOTIONAL TAPES, BASIS FOR RELATING/CREATING
UPRIGHT: The passion here is for the product of mind, for some, almost a love of mind itself, a desire by mind to know mind, wherein it could then duplicate itself, multiply its contents, and through such increase make its excess of knowledge available to others. To be so good at learning that there is both something to teach and the time to teach it. **INVERTED:** This passion is the trap of mind itself. A selfish, possessive attitude toward knowledge and the gifts of mind. It must be overturned or in time there will be little or nothing for anyone to steal.

7 GOVERNED BY THE CHARIOT: PHYSICAL RESOURCES. MEANS TO ACHIEVE
UPRIGHT: Ideas which are both solid, having proved themselves in the practical arena, and ideas which are fluid and changing in search of other ideas to mix with—such is your greatest material asset. And while this may be your mind itself, it is likely that these ideas have materialized into your surroundings. But physical as they may be, they are your ideas. **INVERTED:** Be cautious of the lower ego. Your ideas may not be big enough by themselves for where you want and need to go next.

8 GOVERNED BY STRENGTH: EMOTIONAL RESOURCES, ENERGY
UPRIGHT: You have a healthy combination of hubris and humility, the confidence of your lower ego proud of its achievements, and the wisdom of your higher Ego which seeks after that which it knows it cannot fully know. This endears you to everyone you meet, for you embody the essence of their own dilemma with this duality, and so openly. **INVERTED:** Oddly enough, if these are balanced at too early a stage we may seem to stagnate. Nothing like a healthy dose of one or the other at the appropriate moment to energize the situation.

9 GOVERNED BY THE HERMIT: BELIEF SYSTEM, BASIS FOR DECISIONS
UPRIGHT: You believe in everything and nothing. And your belief serves you well. At the time that calls for action, you have all you require to make a good decision. However, in the interim you are troubled by what you do not know and seek deeper understanding. **INVERTED:** At times it must be difficult, for you believe in yourself, in many others whom you have come to respect, and in what you have come to understand of universal truth.

10 GOVERNED BY THE WHEEL OF FORTUNE: CENTRAL MESSAGE, THEME OF READING
UPRIGHT: You may be deprived of complete understanding of the immediate situation, but only so that you may look for the greater meaning that lies beneath the obvious. Wear your blinders with conviction, letting others who offer lead you. You are far from lost and seek a direction that ordinary sight cannot provide. **INVERTED:** You are trying to see everything with your eyes. Surely you know that is not possible.

11 GOVERNED BY JUSTICE: STATE/CONTENT OF MIND
UPRIGHT: You do not have a clue as to how to reconcile all of the input in the present situation. But somewhere in between what you think, what your friends and advisors think, and your hunches about what the hierarchy has to say about the matter, therein lies the answer. Productive confusion. **INVERTED:** One or the other inputs to the matter at hand has not been reconciled and indecision prevails. At its worst this distortion depresses the mind, making it less and less capable, more dependent on the heart and of course grace. At the extreme, rational ability is severely handicapped. A first step up out of the trap is to go with any of the options, anything but indecision. You can correct your course later, after you are out of the pit.

12 GOVERNED BY THE HANGED MAN: STATE OF EMOTIONS, SUBCONSCIOUS
UPRIGHT: The heart sympathizes with the mind's dilemma, and is doing all that it can to meet the challenge of satisfying all facets of ego pulling the diverse views together. **INVERTED:** The heart may be over sympathetic and therefore not do as well as it might to help the situation. On the other hand, the heart may be entirely unsympathetic and initiate a program of its own to resolve the situation.

13 GOVERNED BY DEATH: PHYSICAL SITUATION, HARD REALITY
UPRIGHT: Mental enterprise is underway. The possibilities are limitless and there is great chance of success as you have utilized many levels of input in addition to your own. Many people look to you with confidence. **INVERTED:** Either things may have started a bit prematurely, or there is some delay waiting for more input.

14 GOVERNED BY TEMPERANCE: EMOTIONAL TEST
UPRIGHT: Your involvement with many others in mental matters creates new dimensions in your emotional house for your relationships and your creative projects. Your intellectual progress in the near future is startling to those around you, perhaps to yourself as well. **INVERTED:** It becomes harder and harder, as you work closely with others of like goals and ideologies, to keep all your lessons in their proper places.

15 GOVERNED BY THE DEVIL: TEMPTATION/CHALLENGE, FEARS
UPRIGHT: As the identity of the lower self sees its place in the universal mind and feels its thoughts merging with the one, the ego looks for ways in which it can survive and die at the same time. This is not an identity crisis if all goes well, rather it is an identity opportunity. **INVERTED:** This is an identity crisis derived from the above process not going well. On one extreme, the identity aligns much too closely with the universal mind losing its individuality. On the other extreme, the identity balks and does anything it can to avoid alignment.

16 GOVERNED BY THE TOWER: NEXT LESSON, GRACE OF GOD
UPRIGHT: This dark night/light morning of the soul, the death of the ego and birth of the Ego, will reach its peak not later than this time next year, but can be as soon as tomorrow, or today. **INVERTED:** Initially, you may not be enthused about the identity that emerges, missing a bit too much the old you. But rest assured this is the real you. Imagine the butterfly preferring its caterpillar body. While it is proper to miss your caterpillar stage, after all it was you, it is not proper to want to return to it.

17 GOVERNED BY THE STAR: ASPIRATIONS OF EGO, GOALS, MAXIMUM EXPECTATIONS
UPRIGHT: As the Initiate looks forward to the ceremony in which he is led step by step through rituals which embody and transmit by their very structure the inner language which must be learned, so you anticipate eagerly knowledge of the world within the world, and the world without the world. **INVERTED:** Here is the longing for the secrets of knowledge without the commensurate longing for the secrets of responsibility.

18 GOVERNED BY THE MOON: ASPIRATIONS OF HEART, COMPASSION
UPRIGHT: Here the heart aspires to the responsibility of the path and it will ask the mind to gather the needed knowledge only in order to fulfill its responsibilities. **INVERTED:** In one extreme, the desire is for too much responsibility, presuming much too much of God's responsibility for the self, even the enlightened Self.

19 GOVERNED BY THE SUN: PHYSICAL FULFILLMENT/EVALUATION
UPRIGHT: Such a mind is positioned well between the world of man and the world of the gods. It wears a blindfold in each in order to see into the other. You have been able to see and plan well and continue to do so helping many others into your senior years. **INVERTED:** Do not try to achieve order so much that you miss the point and create chaos instead.

20 GOVERNED BY JUDGEMENT: HEART'S FULFILLMENT/EVALUATION
UPRIGHT: Your intellectual prowess has been the centerpiece of your Emotional as well as Mental Plane. But ideas and ideologies proved to be healthy medicine for your relationships and your creative affairs. **INVERTED:** Use your mind correctly and it will be the glue that holds your emotional world together.

21 GOVERNED BY THE WORLD: EGO'S FULFILLMENT/EVALUATION
UPRIGHT: You have been brilliant, some will say too brilliant. But you have often been first to push your mind into corners where others were afraid to even follow. But in so doing you have added the buoyancy of higher, more integrated mind while preserving the weight of lower, more separated mind. **INVERTED:** Work now to assure that neither aspect of mind, lower or higher is neglected.

22/0 GOVERNED BY THE FOOL: SOUL'S FULFILLMENT/EVALUATION
UPRIGHT: Your circle has widened to include an enormous range of people and ideas in this lifetime and you have achieved your place securely with all your mental luggage intact ready for the next lesson. The personality has found its place and it fits above and below. **INVERTED:** There is much in this reading to help you achieve this archetype.

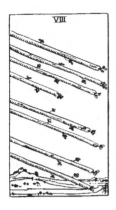

EIGHT OF WANDS

UPRIGHT: Here is a level of emotional drive and commitment to matters spiritual. The love of God moves you, as the higher emotions put you to work for the Spiritual Plane. Major creative/spiritual breakthroughs are possible. Rapid growth. High level of energy and strong sense of purpose. Your course is well plotted and you busy yourself now implementing it. Spiritual activities increase as devotion and ritual assume greater significance and take up more time and space in your regimen. Your spiritual foundation is on the move, agile and light on its feet. The same penchant for order that ran through the level of Fours is at work here, only more so, but there is little pause for order in and of itself. Here, order is the expected norm and is maintained per diem ingrained into your habits. No pauses are necessary to put things in order. Eight is the combination of 4 and 4, the addition of the lower level of the Spiritual Plane to itself. The power residing in the eights derives from the double foundation of the two 4's—one foot walks on the foundation above in spirit, the other foot walks on the foundation below on earth. This power is especially formidable in the Suit of Wands, where the Eight acts as receiver from above, transmitter to below. The means for expressing these messages permeate the world of the artist, the writer, the sage/teacher, and the gifted channel/medium. The energy of Tantra Yoga contributes here. Inner, spiritual communication.
INVERTED: Here are the problems of the extremes in these matters. A major temptation is to move too fast. But to try and move too slowly will not work either. Delays at the spiritual level, especially as high as the work going on with the Eights, is like letting a rubber band be drawn tighter as the lead end moves on; eventually the tail end must be let loose and will spring forward to join the lead end in one great snap to make up for the lost time. The backlash can hurt.

In This Spread Position...Interpret the Eight Of Wands Meanings to Include:

1 GOVERNED BY THE MAGICIAN: PHYSICAL GIVENS, OUT OF THE FATHER
UPRIGHT: Stability and yet movement, along with many other paradoxes will run through your Physical/material Plane in this lifetime as the need for spiritual order asserts itself. In many respects your work and your leisure activities will appear very conventional, but just beneath the surface, and not hiding, is a secure and flowering spirituality. **INVERTED:** At this point you are living your beliefs and your material path will of course follow the spiritual path already being followed.

2 GOVERNED BY THE HIGH PRIESTESS: EMOTIONAL GIVENS, OUT OF THE MOTHER
UPRIGHT: Stability and yet movement, along with many other paradoxes will run through your Emotional/creative Plane in this lifetime as the need for spiritual order asserts itself. Your relationships and your creative affairs will be expressions of the thin line separating the higher emotions and the spiritual. **INVERTED:** Your beliefs permeate your Emotional Plane and your relationships and creativity will follow the higher laws of compassion and altruism.

3 GOVERNED BY THE EMPRESS: MENTAL GIVENS, INTELLECTUAL PREDISPOSITION
UPRIGHT: Stability and yet movement, along with many other paradoxes will run through your Mental Plane in this lifetime as the need for spiritual order asserts itself. Your education and mental prowess are dedicated to the serious investigation of reality and experience. **INVERTED:** No stones will be left unturned by this mind in its quest for big answers to big questions.

4 GOVERNED BY THE EMPEROR: SPIRITUAL GIVENS, LIFE PURPOSE
UPRIGHT: Although you do not have to be a vagabond, a spiritual traveler you will be. In conscious thought, in daydreams, in meditative trance, in the dreams of deep sleep, in astral travel, you will roam the ether following your quest to know more of your God. And you will return home time and time again to share your latest discoveries with those who choose to tune into your channel. **INVERTED:** Even though you may never leave home, the life of the spiritual gypsy will take your soul where it needs to go. Keep your spiritual bags packed. Being a messenger is not easy; remember that he is the one who frequently catches the worst of it.

5 GOVERNED BY THE HIEROPHANT: SYSTEMS BORN INTO, SOCIETAL INFLUENCE
UPRIGHT: This team was up and running when your soul asked/was asked to join. A very stimulating setting full of meaningful activity. Things were done carefully, deliberately, respectfully, with great attention to detail. Aesthetics and art were important but as an ancillary to the whole approach to living, not as an end in themselves, even in the cases where art was the means of livelihood. **INVERTED:** This team was up and running but in circles much of the time.

6 GOVERNED BY THE LOVERS: EMOTIONAL TAPES, BASIS FOR RELATING/CREATING
UPRIGHT: The deep appreciation of things in the now, of beauty intrinsic in nature and man, is paralleled by a desire to see the beauty of the unseen. This is the desire to see God that infuses all great artists' work. This emotional path is highly sensual. **INVERTED:** The depth of feeling here may be compassionate yet private, shying away from physical contact, preferring to look inward.

7 GOVERNED BY THE CHARIOT: PHYSICAL RESOURCES. MEANS TO ACHIEVE
UPRIGHT: Although your surroundings and personal habits are relaxed and natural, they are nevertheless very organized and that is one of your strongest points. You may have considerable belongings, but everything you have is working and in regular use, be they an old reference book or a cooking utensil you collected on your last trip. **INVERTED:** The upright interpretation just cited is what you have tried to achieve, but to date you cannot operate as efficiently, as responsively as you would like.

8 GOVERNED BY STRENGTH: EMOTIONAL RESOURCES, ENERGY
UPRIGHT: Although you are most likely to have many people close to you, your strength comes primarily from the position you are in, poised between the foundations of upper and lower. It is of course reinforced by people and the processes to which you lend your gifts. You are your art and to all who enjoy your art goes just that little bit of you. **INVERTED:** You cannot lose this position, but you can abuse it, or let it lie fallow.

9 GOVERNED BY THE HERMIT: BELIEF SYSTEM, BASIS FOR DECISIONS
UPRIGHT: Not to make light of this belief for it is a most valuable one, but the phrase recalls the oath of the Boy Scouts of America. It is "be prepared." It is your watchword. To balance between the inner and outer aspects of God, between Man's will and God's will, is to be ever ready when called on to receive, or to give. **INVERTED:** Pride may enter into this archetype in the over-enjoyment of the centrality and significance of your position.

10 GOVERNED BY THE WHEEL OF FORTUNE: CENTRAL MESSAGE, THEME OF READING
UPRIGHT: Listen and you will hear with your heart the ever soft whispers from the ether reaches of our space and time blowing through the trees (the wands) in the inner courtyard of the garden of Eden. *INVERTED:* What you hear may be more for others than for yourself.

11 GOVERNED BY JUSTICE: STATE/CONTENT OF MIND
UPRIGHT: You are very aware of the richness of possibility around you. There is an abundance of information, possibly an abundance of sources. *INVERTED:* You are not pleased with the intensity that is imposing itself on you. You may question the validity of the information and/or the sources you have been receiving. At a very distorted extreme, you may be aware that you are passing poor information.

12 GOVERNED BY THE HANGED MAN: STATE OF EMOTIONS, SUBCONSCIOUS
UPRIGHT: Inspiration has struck and with a mighty hammer. There may be more information than you think you can handle. You are in the midst of that wonderful moment of original creativity when the sheer magnificence of what you have just been handed humbles you to acknowledge a source outside and above you, but at the same time you also are intensely aware that it is indeed you as well operating as creator. *INVERTED:* Your heart may struggle with giving, or accepting, credit where it is due.

13 GOVERNED BY DEATH: PHYSICAL SITUATION, HARD REALITY
UPRIGHT: You are moved, perhaps not with a moving van, but nevertheless moved. And too, everything probably has remained the same here in the Physical/material Plane, at least for now. Spiritual change inevitably brings change to all the planes. Sometimes the change is subtle, sometimes not. *INVERTED:* Awareness seems to be outpacing action. Your foundation may be too heavy and unable to respond.

14 GOVERNED BY TEMPERANCE: EMOTIONAL TEST
UPRIGHT: Strong demands are being placed on your emotional house, for sincere commitment to the highest of standards by you and all those around you sharing this path. *INVERTED:* Slow things down a little bit. This will give time for the sincere yet slower members of your group to catch up. Also this will give those less sincere the opportunity to lose patience and drop out of their own accord.

15 GOVERNED BY THE DEVIL: TEMPTATION/CHALLENGE, FEARS
UPRIGHT: In the near future you will be washed with a wave of confidence to urge you forward. Your mental projects will be clear and move much more easily afterwards. *INVERTED:* This is a wave of doubt to make you reconsider and rework mental projects that are not yet up to your full potential.

16 GOVERNED BY THE TOWER: NEXT LESSON, GRACE OF GOD
UPRIGHT: The order and organization that you need to move forward will be easy to achieve. Your heart will provide all the energy you need. *INVERTED:* The mobile organization that will support your goals may require considerable reorganization. It will be easier than it looks.

17 GOVERNED BY THE STAR: ASPIRATIONS OF EGO, GOALS, MAXIMUM EXPECTATIONS
UPRIGHT: This is an ambitious spiritual, intellectual appetite wanting nothing less than a working understanding of man's best thinking to date in spiritual/religious matters. It is the goal of a formal theologian. But there are surprisingly many who share this appetite. In its most noble forms the aspirant seeks the knowledge in order to increase the understanding of others. *INVERTED:* Here is the less noble form in which the aspirer is mainly intellectually curious for himself, and maybe not even an aware initiate seeking gnosis.

18 GOVERNED BY THE MOON: ASPIRATIONS OF HEART, COMPASSION
UPRIGHT: This is the courageous heart that wants nothing less than to be in the center of the action at the crossroads, staring the fates in the face, feeling the full force of the contesting wills of men and gods. It wants to feel, full out with no protection. And it is prepared to successfully do just that because it cannot expect any other to do what it would not. And if it would not, and another would not, and another, then creation would cease. *INVERTED:* This is a more foolish heart for it not only lacks the courage but is not even seeking it, preferring to find a shortcut to glory.

19 GOVERNED BY THE SUN: PHYSICAL FULFILLMENT/EVALUATION
UPRIGHT: There is an ageless quality for you in this plane. When your time comes you will simply leave, no sickness, no pain. You have lived as physical a life as anyone, but almost as if in a protective bubble, working mainly in the Spiritual, not Physical Plane. *INVERTED:* In order to fulfill this archetype you cannot neglect the day to day business of the Physical Plane.

20 GOVERNED BY JUDGEMENT: HEART'S FULFILLMENT/EVALUATION
UPRIGHT: There is a timeless quality for you in this plane. You have keyed into such fundamental energies that you already sense the essence of continuity in all of your relationships, and the evolution of your creative talents before, during, and eventually after. *INVERTED:* In order to fulfill this archetype you cannot neglect the day to day affairs of the Emotional Plane.

21 GOVERNED BY THE WORLD: EGO'S FULFILLMENT/EVALUATION
UPRIGHT: To be intellectually aware, and capable of expressing, the hearts highest callings—that will be your justifiable claim. This is the mark of a poetic mind able to approach the ineffable in its understanding of our miraculous world. *INVERTED:* In order to fulfill this archetype you cannot neglect the day to day affairs of the Mental Plane.

22/0 GOVERNED BY THE FOOL: SOUL'S FULFILLMENT/EVALUATION
UPRIGHT: The mark of the oracle/priest, blessed with equal ability to tell his fellow man what the gods are having for dinner tonight, while also telling the gods what he and his fellow man would like to see on their table tomorrow. *INVERTED:* With your gifts you will have much help in achieving this archetype.

NINE OF PENTACLES

UPRIGHT: The Nines are the effect of the highest mental order on the four planes, here in the Suit of Pentacles on the Physical/material Plane. You will work hard to satisfy the goals of your mind as it stretches to accommodate the universal mind. In so doing mind insists that the planes align themselves, first within themselves and then with each other. There is security of position and the ability to appreciate the benefits of good health and/or material success. If you so desire, a life of active leisure is possible, as your personal garden of Eden is all around you. Physical well-being is protected by the power of your mind, and that power is available to help others. Physical healing is possible here as an adjunct of your ability to achieve and maintain order in your Physical Plane. The conventional avenues of medicine are more common here—doctors, nurses—but non-allopathic, holistic, and other alternative health care apply as well. There is good integration of your physical needs with the environment (on all levels: mineral, plant, animal, and other people). There is great appreciation of nature; your actions can benefit and bring increase in the world system. This is the princess in her garden and the horticulturist in his. Here is physical evidence of the work of the intellect in the form of knowledge storage, i.e., books and libraries. **INVERTED:** Various forms of improper understanding/use of this level of comfort, such as allowing yourself to become overly dependent on others, even to the extreme of becoming a "kept person." There can be improper use of intelligence and knowledge of nature, leading to a decrease in the world system. Here we find smug, complacent, lazy behavior.

In This Spread Position...Interpret the Nine Of Pentacles Meanings to Include:

1 GOVERNED BY THE MAGICIAN: PHYSICAL GIVENS, OUT OF THE FATHER
UPRIGHT: The suggestion of an inheritance is strong, through your father's line. Your Physical Plane will be secure, encompassing health and financial matters, allowing much of your attention to go toward lessons in the other three Planes—Emotional, Mental, and Spiritual. **INVERTED:** There may be an inheritance or financial security of large proportions setting up a background for all your lessons.

2 GOVERNED BY THE HIGH PRIESTESS: EMOTIONAL GIVENS, OUT OF THE MOTHER
UPRIGHT: The suggestion of an inheritance is strong, through your mother's line. Your material security will set the stage, and perhaps direct the play, in your relationships and your creative endeavors. **INVERTED:** You will be learning that financial security offers its own set of challenges, different but no less difficult in this Emotional Plane.

3 GOVERNED BY THE EMPRESS: MENTAL GIVENS, INTELLECTUAL PREDISPOSITION
UPRIGHT: Your mental gifts will be used to maintain the garden of sustenance that secures you and all that you love. You will be motivated to see that the garden grows to support many more people than at your birth. You will work to make the system we know as civilization work. **INVERTED:** You will be involved in major rethinking and changes to the way we do things at the most basic levels, i.e., how we care for ourselves and each other and live as long and productively as possible.

4 GOVERNED BY THE EMPEROR: SPIRITUAL GIVENS, LIFE PURPOSE
UPRIGHT: The highest application of mind to practical purposes, generating greater efficiency and comfort in life for self and others. The ability to match people and their environments—the mark of the designer, in particular the industrial designer, the civil engineer, and the architect. The humanitarian scientist, the grass roots politician, the pragmatic inventor all make an appearance here. **INVERTED:** In order for mind to achieve the proper goals of this lifetime, you may have to rely on others for support.

5 GOVERNED BY THE HIEROPHANT: SYSTEMS BORN INTO, SOCIETAL INFLUENCE
UPRIGHT: For many this is the ideal of a head start program in the early environment, as this archetype represents us surrounded by everything that we need to support us in our karmic purpose. And while we know that all the cards upright in all the positions have centered value for our relative needs, this card in this position still evokes a special sense of blessing. **INVERTED:** At one extreme, there was so much support available that the test will be in how you manage not to be overly dependent on your roots. At the other extreme, there was not much support available and perhaps even more difficult in that it seemed to be there but just out of reach.

6 GOVERNED BY THE LOVERS: EMOTIONAL TAPES, BASIS FOR RELATING/CREATING
UPRIGHT: The legend of Johnny Appleseed in a love affair with trees. St. Francis of Assissi in his love for animals. The passion here is for the garden that is the earth itself, for a true garden is that which sustains us to be ourselves. **INVERTED:** The garden is complete only with the people that occupy it. Love of nature, of the environment which supports us, cannot be divorced from love of ourselves and our fellow man.

7 GOVERNED BY THE CHARIOT: PHYSICAL RESOURCES. MEANS TO ACHIEVE
UPRIGHT: You have all the physical resources you need to achieve anything you want to do. **INVERTED:** At the one extreme, your challenge is in which resources to access and for what purposes, for there is an abundance far beyond your requirements. At the other extreme, what you need is not readily available. There may be resources aplenty, but not for your project.

8 GOVERNED BY STRENGTH: EMOTIONAL RESOURCES, ENERGY
UPRIGHT: You derive energy directly from your surroundings, the more natural the better. But your warm environment and your ease in entertaining bring many to your door who want to share in your experience. **INVERTED:** On the one hand, you may be so absorbed with and into your garden that you are distant and hard for people to reach. On the other hand, you may be at odds with your garden, if indeed you are in it, and so lack the nourishment/replenishment that is needed.

9 GOVERNED BY THE HERMIT: BELIEF SYSTEM, BASIS FOR DECISIONS
UPRIGHT: You have come to understand that we must be centered physically within ourselves and within our environment, that the Physical Plane is the foundation on which this incarnation stands, literally. For you, body and nature are metaphors you can use to translate and learn the lessons of the Emotional, Mental, and Spiritual planes in addition to the Physical. To be well centered in the physical is to be centered on all levels. **INVERTED:** The limitation here is the overemphasis of the physical as though it were the all. This is not centering in the physical. Centering is inclusive of the other planes, not exclusive.

10 GOVERNED BY THE WHEEL OF FORTUNE: CENTRAL MESSAGE, THEME OF READING

UPRIGHT: Look around. Things should be turning out the way you would have them. But maybe you have not realized it yet. *INVERTED:* On the one hand, things may be so good as to entrap you. On the other hand, you may be trying to kid yourself into thinking you are in a supportive situation and you are not.

11 GOVERNED BY JUSTICE: STATE/CONTENT OF MIND

UPRIGHT: You are very aware that you have everything you need at hand to complete your master plan. It really is up to you. There are no excuses now. You have all the pieces and need only to assemble the puzzle. *INVERTED:* In one extreme, you know you have too much support for your needs, or too much of the wrong stuff. In the other extreme, you know you do not have what you need.

12 GOVERNED BY THE HANGED MAN: STATE OF EMOTIONS, SUBCONSCIOUS

UPRIGHT: You are energized by your fortunate circumstances and wish only to share your experiences and your pleasure with others. *INVERTED:* On the one hand, you may be all too comfortable and inert in your setting, neglecting your Karmic Contract. On the other hand, you may be sad at the lack of proper fit between you and your circumstances.

13 GOVERNED BY DEATH: PHYSICAL SITUATION, HARD REALITY

UPRIGHT: One certainly hopes that you are enjoying the blessings of such bounty for your karmic purpose. *INVERTED:* The situation you are in is not healthy. On one extreme, you are withering from lack of water. On the other extreme, you are drowning from too much of it.

14 GOVERNED BY TEMPERANCE: EMOTIONAL TEST

UPRIGHT: What seems so perfect for you, may or may not be for others. *INVERTED:* What is so right for your basic needs, may provide an ironic test for your creative endeavors. A starving artist you are not, at least not physically. But your physical situation may be far from what you need to bring you into the proper arenas for your emotional and creative purposes.

15 GOVERNED BY THE DEVIL: TEMPTATION/CHALLENGE, FEARS

UPRIGHT: Your challenge is to use your resources as just that, resources to produce more, rather than to luxuriate in and consume irresponsibly. It is a blessing to have all that you need to survive and be comfortable in the process, for it allots you the time others less fortunate do not have. *INVERTED:* You may fear your ability to achieve on your own.

16 GOVERNED BY THE TOWER: NEXT LESSON, GRACE OF GOD

UPRIGHT: This archetype addresses the eternal question whether man is innately lazy or industrious. Would we be working if we had not been thrown out of the garden of Eden? The presumption in perennial philosophy and thus in the Tarot is that of course we are naturally industrious, ever seeking the productive fulfillment of our karmic purpose. Tend to the needs of your garden. Maintenance will preserve and magnify the beauty of what you already have. *INVERTED:* The old adage, "necessity is the mother of invention," suggests one difficulty shown by this archetype. Namely, the temptation that if we don't have to we won't. Do not let that happen with you. It also suggests the very positive function of necessity.

17 GOVERNED BY THE STAR: ASPIRATIONS OF EGO, GOALS, MAXIMUM EXPECTATIONS

UPRIGHT: From wanting the house of your dreams, on the edge of a pine forest, on a cliff overlooking the Pacific ocean...to the goal of providing affordable housing for fellow citizens less fortunate, is a wide span of healthy aspirations fitting here. From the more personal to the more universal, depending on the level of the question. *INVERTED:* The details behind your goals and the motivations may distort them and hinder rather than advance your path. For instance, your house should not desecrate the forest or the cliff, nor dump waste into the ocean.

18 GOVERNED BY THE MOON: ASPIRATIONS OF HEART, COMPASSION

UPRIGHT: The heart may have a specific hope that drives a cause, such as saving the rain forests of the Amazon. This heart cannot desire anything for itself that it sees as harmful to another. As a result it will lean toward doctrines of non-violence like that of ahimsa in the Buddhist, Hindu, and Jainist religions, and toward a vegetarian diet. *INVERTED:* At an extreme, this can deteriorate into an improper understanding of the material and a rejection of things physical.

19 GOVERNED BY THE SUN: PHYSICAL FULFILLMENT/EVALUATION

UPRIGHT: You will complete this journey in the comfort of your garden with a gazebo tailored to your needs. What you have achieved has been in harmony with nature and the rights and needs of your fellow man. *INVERTED:* With the proper weeding and good drainage you will achieve this archetype.

20 GOVERNED BY JUDGEMENT: HEART'S FULFILLMENT/EVALUATION

UPRIGHT: There certainly should be enough for everyone in your extended family to enjoy to their heart's desire, and enough time together to share a wealth of experiences. *INVERTED:* Continue to offer/accept generosity where it is proper and you will enjoy the lessons of this card.

21 GOVERNED BY THE WORLD: EGO'S FULFILLMENT/EVALUATION

UPRIGHT: Your physical legacy is a tribute to the beauty inherent in the mind. The architecture of your achievements will bring pleasure to those privileged to walk its halls and stroll its paths. *INVERTED:* Be clear in your motives and steadfast in your goals.

22/0 GOVERNED BY THE FOOL: SOUL'S FULFILLMENT EVALUATION

UPRIGHT: You have tended well the needs of the garden entrusted to you in this lifetime. *INVERTED:* This is your karmic fulfillment if you can do the necessary maintenance.

NINE OF CUPS

UPRIGHT: Here is the impact of higher mind on the Emotional Plane. With the resulting increase in emotional and creative awareness there is great comfort and joy with yourself and life in general. You have good emotional support systems in place giving you emotional security and restorative power. Abundance of energy. Desires are being fulfilled. You are deeply compassionate and creative, as you are in touch, in tune. An artistic or poetic lifestyle of the highest order. Interest and work in the arts, theater, music. Sensitivity. Dramatic personality. You may wear your heart on your sleeve. Benevolent power. Restorative power. **INVERTED:** You may be overdoing it emotionally. The emotions may have become ends in themselves, goaded on by the ego. Everything exaggerated for effect. Sensitivity to a fault; your feel everything, pain is everywhere. You could be thriving on the pain itself, rather than recognizing pain as the initial part of the positive lesson to be learned. A person stuck here may never get beyond the pain—a nasty form of addiction.

In This Spread Position...Interpret the Nine Of Cups Meanings to Include:

1 GOVERNED BY THE MAGICIAN: PHYSICAL GIVENS, OUT OF THE FATHER
UPRIGHT: With such creative juices flowing in your veins, your Physical/material Plane will benefit from an astute aesthetic sense. If your business sense is half that of your emotional sensitivity, then you will be one of those fortunate enough to make money while making beauty. **INVERTED:** You will enjoy so much what you are doing you may forget why you are doing it.

2 GOVERNED BY THE HIGH PRIESTESS: EMOTIONAL GIVENS, OUT OF THE MOTHER
UPRIGHT: You are the type of person everyone wants to know. Full of energy and the life of the party. In the old Hollywood movie, you are the one sitting at the piano with a room full of attentive people hanging on your every note. **INVERTED:** Some people will wonder how you can sustain your joviality and your pace. Others will be green with envy. You should be too busy to notice either.

3 GOVERNED BY THE EMPRESS: MENTAL GIVENS, INTELLECTUAL PREDISPOSITION
UPRIGHT: A mind with enough good energy to run hundreds of worthwhile projects at the same time. This mind can sustain family needs, society benefits, and not neglect personal creativity. This is the artistic temperament found sitting in the back corner of a cafe bar turning out a sketch or the world's next great novel. **INVERTED:** You may rarely be alone, even when you are thinking.

4 GOVERNED BY THE EMPEROR: SPIRITUAL GIVENS, LIFE PURPOSE
UPRIGHT: You are meant to enjoy life with the wide range of sensitivities you have been blessed with. Yours is the art of living. Your learning is hands on, experiential, and your teaching is by example and the content of your creative projects. **INVERTED:** There may be times when your depth of sensitivity may be almost too much, too sweet, but those moments carry lessons meant specifically for you.

5 GOVERNED BY THE HIEROPHANT: SYSTEMS BORN INTO, SOCIETAL INFLUENCE
UPRIGHT: This could be the archetype for the childhood of Geraldine Chaplin, daughter of Charlie, or of Isabella Rossalini, daughter of Ingrid Bergman. Or, it could be the youth born into a large, loving family with many brothers and sisters all interacting to support one another and to achieve. For this early environment will have been flowing with expression of feelings for one another and for getting the most out of life. **INVERTED:** Creativity and love make interesting chemistry but the emotional frustration in balancing family and personal affairs can mar an otherwise supportive environment. The family of Michael Jackson struggles with this archetype, because of both the intense family chemistry/love and the obvious depth of talent.

6 GOVERNED BY THE LOVERS: EMOTIONAL TAPES, BASIS FOR RELATING/CREATING
UPRIGHT: You are in love with the possibilities that love has for bringing and keeping people together, its positive binding attributes. Identification of commonalities. Family, profession, nationality, are a few of the ways you may choose to package your emotional identity. **INVERTED:** One distortion here takes you to the extreme that is motivated by a distaste and avoidance for too much bonding/binding, preferring a much freer course. At the other extreme, the liking for familial or creative interrelationship and ties may be much too strong. Function outside of the group in such cases will be difficult to impossible.

7 GOVERNED BY THE CHARIOT: PHYSICAL RESOURCES. MEANS TO ACHIEVE
UPRIGHT: The depth of your creative resources are with you wherever you go. And nothing can take them away from you. These talents can be applied in a wide range of pragmatic applications as necessary so you are secure in any set of circumstances. **INVERTED:** You may have constructed an ivory tower for personal enjoyment of your emotional/creative wealth and not have applied your gifts much toward pragmatic reward.

8 GOVERNED BY STRENGTH: EMOTIONAL RESOURCES, ENERGY
UPRIGHT: The depth and range of your Emotional Plane, extending your heart in an infinity of directions has paradoxically enabled you to be most independent when necessary, for even alone you are in contact with the network of sensitivity you have nurtured. **INVERTED:** Your strength may lie in the support you can muster, but it is a weakness in that without that support you may falter.

9 GOVERNED BY THE HERMIT: BELIEF SYSTEM, BASIS FOR DECISIONS
UPRIGHT: Here is tremendous faith in what the heart can achieve with the power of higher mind along for direction. This is a highly disciplined approach whether involved with the compassionate enterprise of directing a large humanitarian relief organization, or with matriarchal management of a large extended family, or with the administrative control over one's own personal creative enterprise. **INVERTED:** The emotional enterprise is what must lead in this belief system. The mind in this case should be the support team.

10 GOVERNED BY THE WHEEL OF FORTUNE: CENTRAL MESSAGE, THEME OF READING
UPRIGHT: The emotional backing, all the energy you will need, is coming your way. What is now available to you is the result of your past work in your Emotional Plane, with relationships and/or your creative projects. You may relax and simply enjoy the moment. **INVERTED:** At one extreme, you may be somewhat overwhelmed at your emotional good fortune. At the other extreme, you may be somewhat disappointed.

11 GOVERNED BY JUSTICE: STATE/CONTENT OF MIND

UPRIGHT: You are fully aware of your good fortune with emotional matters. Intellectual satisfaction with product or conduct of relationships, family, extended family, projects of compassion. Or, mental satisfaction with the progress of creative endeavors. *INVERTED:* The mind may be overwhelmed with the results in your Emotional Plane, either for the good, or the bad.

12 GOVERNED BY THE HANGED MAN: STATE OF EMOTIONS, SUBCONSCIOUS

UPRIGHT: A time of great joy, rejoicing, at the good results in your interrelationships with the people you hold close in your heart. Anyone in your sphere of influence is also benefiting at this time. The emotional reward may be at the successful accomplishment of creative goals. *INVERTED:* This suggests tears, either of joy so great as to bring you to your knees, or of profound sadness and disappointment.

13 GOVERNED BY DEATH: PHYSICAL SITUATION, HARD REALITY

UPRIGHT: You are strong now and others can lean on you for support. This could well be a time for feasting, as all the senses are in full play wanting to enjoy the luxury of the moment. *INVERTED:* You may be much too full emotionally to be truly strong. Do not take in too much before you balance with some giving. In the other extreme, you may not be strong enough at the moment for the emotional demands that are being place on you. You need to refill your cup some before you can offer more drink to others.

14 GOVERNED BY TEMPERANCE: EMOTIONAL TEST

UPRIGHT: Can you handle emotional success? In large quantities? The near future sees you under the most fortunate of circumstances in your emotional and creative affairs. *INVERTED:* Prepare for the extremes in your Emotional Plane. There may be disappointment. Or, there could be a large demand on your energy, on your creative resources.

15 GOVERNED BY THE DEVIL: TEMPTATION/CHALLENGE, FEARS

UPRIGHT: The ego will be most satisfied with the possibilities in your emotional world. It almost looks too good to be true. *INVERTED:* At one extreme is that nasty fear of things actually going too well. The other extreme is the more easy to understand fear of failure in either relationships or creative matters.

16 GOVERNED BY THE TOWER: NEXT LESSON, GRACE OF GOD

UPRIGHT: You are to be rewarded with a rush of energy, of backing beyond your expectations. This is all energy you will need to complete your projects and meet the demands others will place on you. *INVERTED:* The emotional demands placed on you will be substantial, but not beyond your ability to cope. At another extreme, the emotional attention showered on you will be taxing.

17 GOVERNED BY THE STAR: ASPIRATIONS OF EGO, GOALS, MAXIMUM EXPECTATIONS

UPRIGHT: You are keenly aware of your gifts and wish to see them fully expressed and enjoyed by many others. This is a plan to participate fully in the game of life, and to win. *INVERTED:* This can be the goal of creative success but with much too much ego, enough to smother the talent itself. Wanting the attention for the abstract self more than for proper respect of the creativity you possess.

18 GOVERNED BY THE MOON: ASPIRATIONS OF HEART, COMPASSION

UPRIGHT: For some, this aspiration will be to enjoy the rewards of family life and extended family to the very maximum, even taking that to an art form. For others, this aspiration will be more altruistic and require the feedback of involvement with many people in a much more public life of service to others. *INVERTED:* This archetype can distort into a need for the satisfaction received from your involvement that takes on more importance than the objects of your attention. In the extreme, the love here is no longer for others, but for your feelings alone. They are merely a means to your end.

19 GOVERNED BY THE SUN: PHYSICAL FULFILLMENT/EVALUATION

UPRIGHT: Even if you retire from business life, your days will be full of people and your favorite pastimes. You are someone who knows how to make life interesting and that will only increase as you get older and have more and more experiences to share. *INVERTED:* Do not let distorted sentimentality place unreasonable demands on you as you age. Maintain your same pace and your same attitudes. They will serve you well all the way through.

20 GOVERNED BY JUDGEMENT: HEART'S FULFILLMENT/EVALUATION

UPRIGHT: Life may well have been a circus, but you have enjoyed all the acts. In fact, you have been in most of them. You have been intimate and open with the important people in your life and you have worked out your karmic purposes together as you went along. There is good mutual affection and understanding. *INVERTED:* There are many players in your game, but at times some of them seem to be using another set of rules. Stick to the rules of the game and your heart will be well content.

21 GOVERNED BY THE WORLD: EGO'S FULFILLMENT/EVALUATION

UPRIGHT: This is a creative path that lives to see and enjoy its appreciation in the critical arena, perhaps in the financial arena as well. *INVERTED:* Remember to work for yourself, and your work itself. Critics can, unfortunately, be a big thorn in your side, but they cannot harm the quality of the work itself unless you let them affect you negatively. Use the public arena as the feedback you need to objectively evaluate yourself and improve toward this archetype.

22/0 GOVERNED BY THE FOOL: SOUL'S FULFILLMENT/EVALUATION

UPRIGHT: Here is a soul who understands the true nature of power, the possibilities derived from an earnest mind harnessed to a pure heart. The energy that accrues when the team of mind/heart looks for and finds reciprocity, where give and take whirl about, turning arenas of creative interaction into generators of even greater possibilities. Mutual responsibility is the mother of power. *INVERTED:* Let this reading help you towards this archetype.

NINE OF SWORDS

UPRIGHT: Here the higher mind takes aim at its own plane. Mind is now keenly aware of self, and of the magnitude of what it has asked to be privy. It has asked for, and been given access to, a level of knowledge which has a commensurate level of responsibility that now demands the letter of the law. This is the Faustian bargain stripped of its melodrama and subterfusion. Quite simply, the more you know, the more you owe. And paradoxically, the more you know, the more you know do not know (and that you will never know). The only game over which mind can exercise free will is in how well it exercises its duties as the caretaker of what it knows. That is a matter of wisdom, the mastery of the management of knowledge. For knowledge and responsibility are Siamese twins. One cannot live without the other, for they share one heart. One cannot carry out responsibility without the knowledge to do so, and one cannot be truly knowledgeable without responsibility, because responsibility is inherent in every piece of information. Responsibility is natural, unless it is selectively blotted out by the mind, skillfully separated by the surgical scalpel of potentially errant free will. You take a hard look at objective progress, as your goals demand that they be attempted in earnest, if not met. But this mind is not interested in any excuses, from you or anybody else. This is a "pass in review" for what you have achieved, in some cases an actual list-making exercise. Raja Yoga makes a contribution here. Deep conscious thinking and non-thinking, meditation. The ink is drying on your philosophy and goals for this lifetime. Here is the impact of idealism, and you will be tough on yourself. This is the archetype of major decisions, decisions which select a major fork on your path. On these decisions you must build. They are one-way gates through which you will never pass again. You may see here the theoretician, mathematician, psychologist, philosopher, or scientist. **INVERTED:** Too much or too little of this archetype. You are being too hard on yourself, too idealistic. Over-working. Thinking too much. The mind and its store of information can be either a prison, or what liberates us from prison.

In This Spread Position...Interpret the Nine Of Swords Meanings to Include:

1 GOVERNED BY THE MAGICIAN: PHYSICAL GIVENS, OUT OF THE FATHER
UPRIGHT: No one can know much more about the affairs of the Physical/material Plane than you do. Informed, articulate, attentive, concerned. You are the dream on anyone's Board of Directors. People know that where you are concerned, nothing will go unnoticed. **INVERTED:** Do not bury yourself in stacks of paper on your desk. Too many facts and you will not be able to see the forest for the trees.

2 GOVERNED BY THE HIGH PRIESTESS: EMOTIONAL GIVENS, OUT OF THE MOTHER
UPRIGHT: Here is an archetype of the psychiatrist/psychologist and all those with intricate knowledge of the inner workings of the emotional plane and the subconscious. **INVERTED:** You will be very serious about these matters but so much the better to make you a good writer or the like using the power of the mind to unravel and explain the secrets of the heart.

3 GOVERNED BY THE EMPRESS: MENTAL GIVENS, INTELLECTUAL PREDISPOSITION
UPRIGHT: You are a repository of much knowledge, and manage information well. Your opinions are of great value. A judge would be lucky to have such an archetype here; most do not. **INVERTED:** You are naturally prone to accept responsibility in any set of circumstances. Do not step on others' toes in the process. Others have their responsibilities too.

4 GOVERNED BY THE EMPEROR: SPIRITUAL GIVENS, LIFE PURPOSE
UPRIGHT: This is a path of wisdom with nobility of purpose. Here you become a master of the management of knowledge. As you approach universal mind you are becoming more aware of the darkest dark as well as the lightest light. A pervasive, though not unpleasant, sense of urgency is present. **INVERTED:** As knowledge at this level increases, each increment of growth brings noticeable increments of greater responsibility. The easy path is the one in which the responsibility is as eagerly sought and welcomed as the knowledge.

5 GOVERNED BY THE HIEROPHANT: SYSTEMS BORN INTO, SOCIETAL INFLUENCE
UPRIGHT: Your earliest living environment may have been as much a school as it was a home, for it was full of knowledge. **INVERTED:** There may have been an abundance of information, but with a surprising lack of real understanding. Discipline and pressure to achieve may have been excessive. You may not have been afforded much time for true childhood, being thrust into adult responsibilities very early.

6 GOVERNED BY THE LOVERS: EMOTIONAL TAPES, BASIS FOR RELATING/CREATING
UPRIGHT: This is a very prodigious archetype for early emotional tapes. This is the higher mind impressing the heart with its knowledge of the situations that need attention in the world. This young heart not only accepted the challenge to do something about improving the world, it made that challenge its number one priority, its passion. **INVERTED:** Even with the nobility of such an altruistic passion as yours, you are not relieved of the responsibility of fulfilling what we call the "lower" emotions—to love, possibly to mate, to experience sensual pleasure, to enjoy family and friends and simple humor. These are called lower only in that they usually come first, not that they are any the less important.

7 GOVERNED BY THE CHARIOT: PHYSICAL RESOURCES, MEANS TO ACHIEVE
UPRIGHT: You know the names of all the plants in the inner courtyard, and you know which are life giving and which are poison. Armed as you are with an encyclopedia of helpful tidbits, you can bring formidable intelligence to any problem put on your table. **INVERTED:** Too much, or too little, information/thinking. Also the likelihood that you are too intent on the information itself instead of what it is to be used for.

8 GOVERNED BY STRENGTH: EMOTIONAL RESOURCES, ENERGY
UPRIGHT: Your depth of knowledge and accuracy has been important to many besides yourself, and your mind has been dedicated to the affairs of the Emotional Plane insuring you a network of like-hearted souls working together toward common goals. Your mind has given your heart conviction to add to its instinctive faith. **INVERTED:** The heart is stronger if it neither depends on too much mental corroboration or too little. Heart faith/love must be neither completely blind to mind, nor blinded by it.

9 GOVERNED BY THE HERMIT: BELIEF SYSTEM, BASIS FOR DECISIONS
UPRIGHT: Here, one's confidence is placed in man's ability to know. And, while at the level of the Suit of Swords there may still be no commitment to an actual faith in God, in the physical reality of the spiritual in and of itself as something above mind and body, the intellect is on a path that will take it there eventually. This is the path to gnosis. **INVERTED:** At one extreme, this is such profound belief in mind, in knowledge itself, that it sees nothing else at the top but mind and so leads to agnosticism or atheism.

10 GOVERNED BY THE WHEEL OF FORTUNE: CENTRAL MESSAGE, THEME OF READING
UPRIGHT: The mind is making a list, so you might as well get out a pencil and write it down. This is a time for turning up the volume. There is a considerable amount of information, perhaps from a number of sources, all vying for your attention. *INVERTED:* While the number of options may be confusing, be flattered, then do your review and make your cuts. Some will make the team, others will not.

11 GOVERNED BY JUSTICE: STATE/CONTENT OF MIND
UPRIGHT: You are intensely aware of more than you might care to know, but you also know that you asked for it. Now comes the task of making sense of everything, and in terms of your spiritual path it means literally that...making sense of everything. There is pressure here, but in the sense of exciting challenge. *INVERTED:* This may feel more like the pressure of what to do next. The mind may have overestimated its role in this matter. Give the other levels equal time and your headache should go away.

12 GOVERNED BY THE HANGED MAN: STATE OF EMOTIONS, SUBCONSCIOUS
UPRIGHT: The world of your heart is responding to a growing list of concerns presented to it by mind. For, as the mind expands, so does the heart have a blessed opportunity for new relationships and creative expression. This is a time of positive challenge for your heart. *INVERTED:* In a distortion of this archetype, in one extreme the heart may be overwhelmed and saddened by its new awareness. Some hearts may be initially less than enthusiastic about what the mind has presented, balking at responsibility and heightened compassion.

13 GOVERNED BY DEATH: PHYSICAL SITUATION, HARD REALITY
UPRIGHT: The buck stops here. Here is the "pass in review" of all that you have done. There is a wealth of material for consideration, but this is just as you would have it. You may be in a phase of deep contemplation. *INVERTED:* You may be having trouble getting things to add up these days.

14 GOVERNED BY TEMPERANCE: EMOTIONAL TEST
UPRIGHT: The higher mind brings greater awareness and with your increased scope of concerns, a testing and realignment for your Emotional Plane. *INVERTED:* Make no major changes in your emotional house while your mind is overloaded or confused. This card can show one as being overly idealistic and impatient in the drive toward truth. Be gentle with loved ones especially, but go easy in your day to day encounters as well.

15 GOVERNED BY THE DEVIL: TEMPTATION/CHALLENGE, FEARS
UPRIGHT: The mind and its store of information can be either a prison, or what liberates you from prison. *INVERTED:* The temptation out of fear to bury your head in the sand, to avoid the information as if your not knowing will make a problem go away. In more esoteric terms, some will argue that the quest can be fulfilled on what they call faith alone. It cannot. That faith alone is actually seeded with doubt, with the fear that if it sought an answer, it may either not get one or get one it did not like.

16 GOVERNED BY THE TOWER: NEXT LESSON, GRACE OF GOD
UPRIGHT: Let the higher Ego come into full play. It is proper for you to be feeling accomplished, on target, wise, and a host of other good emotions about yourself. This is not the sin of pride. This is simply the healthy pride of the Ego acknowledging its knowledge. As the self becomes more worldly, literally approaching the World archetype at the end of the Mental Plane, it must feel larger. *INVERTED:* Be on your guard as you experience this archetype in the near future, against both the sin of pride and the opposite extreme—denial of self-knowledge.

17 GOVERNED BY THE STAR: ASPIRATIONS OF EGO, GOALS, MAXIMUM EXPECTATIONS
UPRIGHT: This is the proper goal, the aspiration to gnosis that brings true faith. Only by knowing is the link between the inner and outer aspects of God established and healthy two-way communication able to materialize "as above, so below." *INVERTED:* The proper goal of gnosis is an acceptance of the process toward ever increasing wisdom, not a belief in a fixed pinnacle of wisdom-reality waiting as an apple to be plucked.

18 GOVERNED BY THE MOON: ASPIRATIONS OF HEART, COMPASSION
UPRIGHT: Here the heart desires to bring together knowledge and responsibility. It offers energy and support to the quest of mind so that in turn the mind can guide the full and caring heart toward worthy compassionate ends. Here the heart itself seeks wisdom, gnosis. *INVERTED:* In one extreme, the heart is far too fond of the ability of mind and will not be an adequate check. In the other extreme, the heart lacks enough respect for the mind and will be more likely to be foolish.

19 GOVERNED BY THE SUN: PHYSICAL FULFILLMENT/EVALUATION
UPRIGHT: The Physical/material Plane has served well the projects of higher mind, and vice versa. You will be sitting in the midst of your achievements.You will be mentally alert and active into your later years. *INVERTED:* This archetype is achievable if you heed the lessons of your karmic purpose.

20 GOVERNED BY JUDGEMENT: HEART'S FULFILLMENT/EVALUATION
UPRIGHT: The wedding of heart and mind has produced abundant evidence in the sophistication of your relationships and the intellectual impact of your creative projects. A writer of great passion would have this archetype. *INVERTED:* This is an ambitious archetype, but yours for the having with perseverance.

21 GOVERNED BY THE WORLD: EGO'S FULFILLMENT/EVALUATION
UPRIGHT: What a thrill for the mind to achieve this in a lifetime. To have submitted the mind of the ego to the full investigation of itself. You no longer have any secrets to hide from yourself. This is a precondition of true gnosis, in which higher mind performs the same operation on itself. *INVERTED:* The pain that can come with this level of mental intensity compares directly to the ache of our muscles after strenuous physical labor, and with the ache of our heart as it stretches to accommodate more and more. This is the pain of growth, of true faith.

22/0 GOVERNED BY THE FOOL: SOUL'S FULFILLMENT/EVALUATION
UPRIGHT: This path has been relatively easy, even though much has happened and many lessons have been learned, because responsibility has been sought and accepted with as much eagerness as knowledge. *INVERTED:* In death, the darkest of the dark, is to be found the lightest of the light. The path of the former can contain formidable pain. The path of the latter is the path of wisdom and need contain no pain.

NINE OF WANDS

UPRIGHT: With the impact of the hard work of higher mind, the mental and spiritual are in productive working agreement. There is a solid philosophy in place, as you begin to experientially know spiritual truths at the intellectual level. Mind has established a level of truth for the self which echoes universal truth. When someone approaches you they cannot help but sense the degree to which your center is aligned with the center of the all. This gives you an air of authority that predisposes people to submit to you rather than to challenge you. There is good communication between your Spiritual and Mental Planes. This is knowing God intellectually. A mark of a theologian. The impact of grace on a well-trained mind. On target with the Karmic Contract. The eastern discipline of Gnani Yoga (knowledge as the path leading to enlightenment) shows its influence here. Strength in reserve. You have a firm foundation and backup resources, at all four levels, (physical, emotional, mental, and spiritual). Perhaps hidden resources are available, even some heretofore unknown to you. Depth. You may have much more depth than you are aware of. True determination, due to your identification with your beliefs. Identification with a core of established beliefs, such as a church or spiritual/intellectual group. **INVERTED:** You are weighted down by the structure of your belief and support systems. You are too idealistic. The extensions of self at this point may have made you too heavy. This may show the impact of a top-heavy, overly bureaucratic, spiritual organization. The image of an overweight monk comes to mind. This could show spiritual smugness, complacency. Spiritual conceit. In a sense, this is quitting before you get to the end of the path, because it feels so good in this place that you do not want to leave. Also spiritual fatigue.

In This Spread Position...Interpret the Nine Of Wands Meanings to Include:

1 GOVERNED BY THE MAGICIAN: PHYSICAL GIVENS, OUT OF THE FATHER
UPRIGHT: Spirituality will permeate, and be very visible, in your Physical/material Plane. If you do not make your living outwardly with spiritual enterprise, it will somehow still occupy the majority of your time. **INVERTED:** Being dedicated to God, if not actually a man of God, carries obvious challenges to the conduct of physical and material affairs.

2 GOVERNED BY THE HIGH PRIESTESS: EMOTIONAL GIVENS, OUT OF THE MOTHER
UPRIGHT: Spirituality will permeate, and be very visible, in your Emotional/creative Plane. Those closest to you, your mate, and close friends will share in your level and means of experience. **INVERTED:** You will not have to reject people in this plane; they will deflect from you of their own accord if they do not feel attracted to the truth that you have seen and now give witness.

3 GOVERNED BY THE EMPRESS: MENTAL GIVENS, INTELLECTUAL PREDISPOSITION
UPRIGHT: Spirituality will permeate, and be very visible, in your Mental Plane. The mind at this level will be in complete service to gnosis. **INVERTED:** Your aura of knowledgeable authority will automatically turn many away from you, but that is as intended and you will not be offended.

4 GOVERNED BY THE EMPEROR: SPIRITUAL GIVENS, LIFE PURPOSE
UPRIGHT: The integration of spirituality into all of your lower levels is not so much a requirement at this point as it is simply a matter of fact. Spiritual exercise and ritual is for you a way of life. Spiritual progress at this point is very much the summation, the cap of the progress at the physical, emotional, and mental levels. **INVERTED:** The majority of your lessons for this lifetime will lie in how well you are able to help others reach your level of understanding, rather than in advancing yourself. You will be blessed with contentment at your level, and well you should be content.

5 GOVERNED BY THE HIEROPHANT: SYSTEMS BORN INTO, SOCIETAL INFLUENCE
UPRIGHT: This was a household/community that radiated its obvious intimacy with profound truths. Learning was most important here; one was expected to walk one's talk. This archetype in one positive extreme includes environments like the monastic communities that preserved civilization as well as religion in the Middle Ages. **INVERTED:** Here we could have the likes of groups/communities that ran into some difficulties in spite of good knowledge and good intentions, i.e., Gurdjieff's followers especially during the later years after he closed the Prieure outside Paris in 1933 until he died in 1949, or the confusion and eventual break-up of the Order of the Golden Dawn in England in the very beginning of the twentieth century.

6 GOVERNED BY THE LOVERS: EMOTIONAL TAPES, BASIS FOR RELATING/CREATING
UPRIGHT: Here is a fondness for spiritual stability, establishment, identification of a core of beliefs that inspire and wrap you in a blanket of truth on which you can rely. **INVERTED:** To give oneself over to an ideology of spirituality at an early age may circumvent other necessary emotional development of a more personal and family nature. For a few paths this may be the appropriate karmic path. For most it is not.

7 GOVERNED BY THE CHARIOT: PHYSICAL RESOURCES. MEANS TO ACHIEVE
UPRIGHT: These spiritual wands will provide more than enough timber for the spokes of your chariot, taking you everywhere you need to go in good time. Your foundation is most firm, as the monasteries were able to physically withstand the ravages of the Middle Ages as well as the intellectual and spiritual destitution. **INVERTED:** The proper spiritual path should not diminish or create hardship in your Physical/material Plane.

8 GOVERNED BY STRENGTH: EMOTIONAL RESOURCES, ENERGY
UPRIGHT: The spiritual truths that have centered you will have aligned you with many kindred spirits. This is an emotional family of love as well as an intellectual family of thought. **INVERTED:** True strength lies in the change which you undergo personally enabling you to withstand many a difficulty on your own, as opposed to an over reliance on your group for support.

9 GOVERNED BY THE HERMIT: BELIEF SYSTEM, BASIS FOR DECISIONS
UPRIGHT: The core of your belief is an elaborate, yet simple, system of rational understanding of the nature of spirituality, a mental fix on that which cannot be fixed. **INVERTED:** Healthy belief, while generating confidence capable of guiding you toward the fulfillment of your Karmic Contract, must always be kept alive with the shadow of positive doubt—the ever questioning purification process that raises man and keeps him aloft. The trick here, as everywhere with duality traps along our path, is to have neither too much doubt so as to destroy belief altogether, nor too little doubt wherein the belief stagnates and eventually putrefies, destroying itself.

10 GOVERNED BY THE WHEEL OF FORTUNE: CENTRAL MESSAGE, THEME OF READING
UPRIGHT: The spiritual system which you have worked to understand and bring on line in your life, perhaps even the community of like-minded souls, is at hand. Your position is most secure as you need only bear witness to your beliefs and others will accept and follow. *INVERTED:* You can lighten up for awhile; let someone else take the point position.

11 GOVERNED BY JUSTICE: STATE/CONTENT OF MIND
UPRIGHT: It must be an exciting time for you, to have reached the level of assurance that is yours for the keeping. But the excitement is tempered by awe. *INVERTED:* Rather than excitement, there may be the weight of the moment, and an unwieldiness until such time as your legs get strong enough for the increased load. You may literally feel heavy.

12 GOVERNED BY THE HANGED MAN: STATE OF EMOTIONS, SUBCONSCIOUS
UPRIGHT: The heart is greatly pleased because it too, like the mind, is privy to so much more and is filling with universal spirit. *INVERTED:* This heart is overwhelmed by the immensity of universal need uncovered by higher mind and put on its doorstep. It needs time to adjust.

13 GOVERNED BY DEATH: PHYSICAL SITUATION, HARD REALITY
UPRIGHT: It may be time for you to deliver an important message, to bring your spiritual expertise on line for effect in the Physical Plane. The delivery of the "I Have A Dream" speech of Martin Luther King, Jr. on the mall in Washington, D.C. was such a message on a grand scale. *INVERTED:* You may be taking an important stand, important for what it symbolizes for many others and for the converts it will make.

14 GOVERNED BY TEMPERANCE: EMOTIONAL TEST
UPRIGHT: If a major spiritual breakthrough has come to you, or to someone near you, you know the profound effect it has on others. The moment of enlightenment throws a wide beam of light hitting all nearby. And while understanding may not come with the wash of light, a warm glow of well-being is experienced, and everyone, not just the central character, is affected. *INVERTED:* Some of those around you may not understand, and if they are not ready and able to integrate your experience, they may react negatively, and in the extreme, no longer wishing to continue their contact with you.

15 GOVERNED BY THE DEVIL: TEMPTATION/CHALLENGE, FEARS
UPRIGHT: The major mental test here is in maintaining your momentum on the path. You have achieved so much already and are in great demand to share and to teach what you have experienced first hand, that it is all too easy to stop and bask in the glory of your present position. *INVERTED:* In one extreme, this resembles the plight of a fallen angel—so very near to God, that there is a vast amount of power residing in one's wisdom, and without availing oneself of the same amount of responsibility, big mistakes can be made. In the other extreme, fear and doubt can strike at any level, and there can be tremendous fear at such dizzying heights.

16 GOVERNED BY THE TOWER: NEXT LESSON, GRACE OF GOD
UPRIGHT: Here is the impact of grace on a well-trained mind. Any difficulties you might have had functioning well at this level of heightened spirituality will not accrue at this time for there are things for you to do. You will be very much the guardian angel to the lessons of others in the near future, not later than this time next year. *INVERTED:* Your lesson will be in how well you can reach down and pull others up to the level you have achieved. This is your karmic purpose kicking in big time.

17 GOVERNED BY THE STAR: ASPIRATIONS OF EGO, GOALS, MAXIMUM EXPECTATIONS
UPRIGHT: There is open acknowledgement of your goal of gnosis. There is a desire for knowledge for all the right reasons. What's more, you believe that you will reach a major plateau of understanding in this lifetime, for already your goal is merging into the process itself as you move closer to self-mastery. *INVERTED:* There is more intellectuality than spirituality in this aspiration. Best you try some major doses of responsibility to be better assured you can handle the power that will come with this expanded awareness.

18 GOVERNED BY THE MOON: ASPIRATIONS OF HEART, COMPASSION
UPRIGHT: This heart is aware of both sides of the coin of universal love/gnosis, all of the beautiful wonders of understanding and all of the pain of misunderstanding. Nevertheless, it wishes to commit itself to the fullest with hopes that its offer will be accepted. *INVERTED:* This heart has volunteered for the front lines, without the full understanding and therefore not for the right reasons. But, that is not to say that it will not do a good job if enlisted.

19 GOVERNED BY THE SUN: PHYSICAL FULFILLMENT/EVALUATION
UPRIGHT: This soul has been actively pursuing the force of truth where it is most difficult, the Physical/material Plane. Much good has been done through your hands on efforts to bring the above to the below. *INVERTED:* Continue to work hard and this archetype will be your achievement in the material world.

20 GOVERNED BY JUDGEMENT: HEART'S FULFILLMENT/EVALUATION
UPRIGHT: Your efforts to see universal principles pulsing through human veins have been richly rewarded. Your presence has brought a rare quality to the relationships of those fortunate to live, work , and play with you. Your principal means of teaching the truths you had come to know was by example, by the way you treated everyone. Yours was the Golden Rule. *INVERTED:* You have a heart that can lead you to this fulfillment.

21 GOVERNED BY THE WORLD: EGO'S FULFILLMENT/EVALUATION
UPRIGHT: For as much as one can say gnosis is achieved, it can be said here of you. Your legacy is great, for it is everything that you touched, everyone that you knew. And though there is likely much physical evidence to record your work in this lifetime, the unwritten, non-physical record in the effect you have had on others will be your greater gift. *INVERTED:* Your mind was born to this superb archetype. Give it full rein and it will take you to this fulfillment.

22/0 GOVERNED BY THE FOOL: SOUL'S FULFILLMENT/EVALUATION
UPRIGHT: Here is the sense of spiritual accomplishment that words are hard pressed to express. But, this is where you are headed, with your track record for so efficiently internalizing your lessons, that you are given over to helping others more with theirs. *INVERTED:* Remember, the more you know, the more you know you do not know.

TEN OF PENTACLES

UPRIGHT: Here is completion of a major physical/material cycle, with outcomes as you would have them, successful by the applicable standards of measurement. Established success, with visible benefits of your excess carried over for the material benefit of others, as in one generation of a family to the next. Material legacies. Family affairs in business. Lasting security. The results of your material success are strategically important to others. Abundance. Endurance. Maturity. Physical longevity. An ultimate extension of self, in the Physical Plane. In story books, in mythology, here is the fairy tale ending of "and they lived happily ever after," which basically meant that all of the main characters got exactly what they wanted. These tales have become classics because they relate the metaphysical truth that we are all meant to have exactly what we need (if not want). The only thing which prevents us from reaching all of our karmic goals is ourselves, in our inability to learn our lessons efficiently. **INVERTED:** Difficulties deriving from bountiful blessings here, either from physical prowess/beauty or from material possessions. Problems with inheritances or legacies appear here. Lack of true appreciation for the magnitude of the material blessings. Improper/inadequate use of wealth. Fortune atrophying, need to invest. There is no concern or factoring in here of how many carcasses were strewn along the way to achieve such material success. At one extreme, this can even be the mafia godfather kind of ending, in which one's own family ends up well off and very secure, but nothing is said of the families of others. In another example, the sacking of towns in the Crusades may have ended with the placement of one's self and one's men in the castle built with the hard and just labor of an enemy of the Christian god.

In This Spread Position...Interpret the Ten Of Pentacles Meanings to Include:

1 GOVERNED BY THE MAGICIAN: PHYSICAL GIVENS, OUT OF THE FATHER
UPRIGHT: A substantial physical/material legacy of the father's line, from the good genetic package of a strong and handsome body to financial wealth. Continuance of a family way is suggested as opposed to any new sharp diversions. With such material well-being as a given, one possibility is that most of your lessons may be in the upper three planes. However, the path may involve your ability to maximize the good gifts you were given. **INVERTED:** Some of your lessons could deal with how you manage the material package you came in with, with many good challenges to your talents. This applies to physical as well as financial prowess. There may have been cracks in this material foundation.

2 GOVERNED BY THE HIGH PRIESTESS: EMOTIONAL GIVENS, OUT OF THE MOTHER
UPRIGHT: This shows a more than ample physical/material legacy of the mother's line, with an eye to seeing it all continue virtually intact through your efforts. Whom you marry is most important such a scenario, for as you were important to your parents' legacy, so too are your children of importance to you. The majority of your relationships of consequence will be important to this family equation. Your creative gifts as well. **INVERTED:** Some of your emotional/creative lessons could involve the handling of this material package from birth. There may have been cracks in this material foundation.

3 GOVERNED BY THE EMPRESS: MENTAL GIVENS, INTELLECTUAL PREDISPOSITION
UPRIGHT: Your mental gifts are predisposed with a natural talent for the world of finance and trade. Accounting and mathematics should come easy and be appealing, as well as mechanics and physics. Here also is profound, innate knowledge of the body and its workings, a suggestion of the sort of mind given to Leonardo da Vinci. You will be well-educated, well-trained, but not necessarily all with formal schooling. **INVERTED:** You will be a very busy person, and when you sleep, your mind will not.

4 GOVERNED BY THE EMPEROR: SPIRITUAL GIVENS, LIFE PURPOSE
UPRIGHT: Yours is a path that must accommodate physical and material beauty and abundance. To those on the outside looking in at your obvious material well-being, it may seem as though you have been given an easy route, but your lessons will be tailored to this path, not theirs. **INVERTED:** A gentle reminder: This path, for all its obvious advantages, has no more and no less than any other, given your complete Karmic Contract. It may fall to you to hold an aging system together.

5 GOVERNED BY THE HIEROPHANT: SYSTEMS BORN INTO, SOCIETAL INFLUENCE
UPRIGHT: Your early childhood provided well for your physical/material needs. Your family/extended family may have been very large. It was a fertile foundation for you to be rooted in. Maturity. Reliability. Endurance. **INVERTED:** There may have been health and wealth, but there may have been problems in that set of circumstances. The youngest in a long line of an aging family system.

6 GOVERNED BY THE LOVERS: EMOTIONAL TAPES, BASIS FOR RELATING/CREATING
UPRIGHT: Here is the dream of a little girl to be the princess living in the moated castle with her loving king/father and queen/mother with all the securities and benefits that go with the package, so secure that the dream has an extended ending in which she has become the queen with her own daughter/princess. **INVERTED:** The things that can go wrong with such a dream are the stuff of fairy tales. At one extreme, there is the obvious problem of over idealism and unreasonable expectations. At the other extreme, there is the little girl with no dream, with no vision that anything approaching such well-being and happiness is remotely possible.

7 GOVERNED BY THE CHARIOT: PHYSICAL RESOURCES. MEANS TO ACHIEVE
UPRIGHT: Here is a man with an army and the war chest to pay them. This is what most of us would like to think of as our resources. **INVERTED:** Generally, there has been much in the way of physical and material resources, but there may be a hitch somewhere. Maybe it is time to review the troops, inspect the warehouse. Or, the resources you have are not well-suited for the situation at hand.

8 GOVERNED BY STRENGTH: EMOTIONAL RESOURCES, ENERGY
UPRIGHT: The material well-being has gone a long way to shoring up your family and loved ones. Many of you may be working, even living together or near one another. You can physically depend on one another in emotional crises. **INVERTED:** What should be your strength—your family and close friends—may not be.

9 GOVERNED BY THE HERMIT: BELIEF SYSTEM, BASIS FOR DECISIONS
UPRIGHT: The ultimate pragmatist, from the scientist and physicist to the farmer and dairyman, from the weatherman to the geneticist, here are men who believe in physical law and man's ability to control nature for the betterment of all. In its most positive sense this includes the contemporary environmentalist. **INVERTED:** In one extreme, we have a mentality so confident in man and fixated on his wants/needs, that it really wants to dominate nature rather than to

seek a place within a harmonious, living Gaia Earth. At an extreme of the extreme, we could see our geneticist character trying to arrange it so that man would live forever in his present body, even if everything else on earth was converted or destroyed in the process. At the other extreme we might have an environmentalist so distrustful of man's intentions that he would become a terrorist of the worst order deeming man as a species unfit to share the planet with the rest of creation.

10 GOVERNED BY THE WHEEL OF FORTUNE: CENTRAL MESSAGE, THEME OF READING
UPRIGHT: Physical/material blessings are at hand for you and yours. The longer-term security you have been seeking is coming to pass. ***INVERTED:*** There may be a need for a second line of defense in your material world. Contingencies should be readied. The other extreme suggests an unexpected boon such as inheriting a house or substantial estate.

11 GOVERNED BY JUSTICE: STATE/CONTENT OF MIND
UPRIGHT: You are currently working on longer-term personal/family finances. ***INVERTED:*** There may not be as much material support from or for your family as you were counting on. Or, you may be planning a major reworking of finances.

12 GOVERNED BY THE HANGED MAN: STATE OF EMOTIONS, SUBCONSCIOUS
UPRIGHT: The heart's feelings are centered around the material aspects of the family, possibly of all the creative energy that pours from the homestead itself. These feelings may be in the form of an unspoken wish for the warmth and good times to continue indefinitely. ***INVERTED:*** In one extreme, there is concern for family well-being.

13 GOVERNED BY DEATH: PHYSICAL SITUATION, HARD REALITY
UPRIGHT: Open up the banquet hall and let the feast begin. There is material abundance available that is more than most achieve in a lifetime. But it is here; it is now. ***INVERTED:*** On the one hand, what you have achieved is shocking by its excess. On the other hand, what you have achieved has fallen short of the mark.

14 GOVERNED BY TEMPERANCE: EMOTIONAL TEST
UPRIGHT: Whether through inheritance or through self-achievement, much has come your way, and its effects will have to be dealt with in all of your relationships, at home, work, and play. Quite simply, money changes people. Here too, the effect would be one of profound physical improvement to you personally, in physique or cosmetically. ***INVERTED:*** Actions, reactions may be in the extreme.

15 GOVERNED BY THE DEVIL: TEMPTATION/CHALLENGE, FEARS
UPRIGHT: There is a possibility of using or becoming part of a family venture, or the family itself as a venture. A large medical opportunity appears here as well. There could be a genuine need for you to step in and save or preserve the enterprise/estate. ***INVERTED:*** Might you be scuttling your own expectations? Could this be fear of wealth, of being and looking successful? Can you handle it? Will it change your beliefs?

16 GOVERNED BY THE TOWER: NEXT LESSON, GRACE OF GOD
UPRIGHT: Material opportunities appear to challenge existing goals and expectations. ***INVERTED:*** It will be a whole new world you are looking at. At one extreme, cracks in the financial foundation or the area of health care, that require immediate attention. At the other extreme, expansion and success to be coped with.

17 GOVERNED BY THE STAR: ASPIRATIONS OF EGO, GOALS, MAXIMUM EXPECTATIONS
UPRIGHT: If you could you would mastermind the total material success of your entire sphere of responsibility. Certainly yourself, then your family, extended family, and....ultimately everything and everyone. You plan to succeed on a grand scale. You expect to be an expert of the first magnitude in the financial arena, or with medicine or physical fitness. ***INVERTED:*** Your goal may be more for money or fame than in the great contribution you could make.

18 GOVERNED BY THE MOON: ASPIRATIONS OF HEART, COMPASSION
UPRIGHT: The heart wishes to be surrounded by familiar places and things, and to have loved ones near. But the radius of its familiarity may be quite large. It cares intensely about the basic stability of the environment and for an end to world hunger. ***INVERTED:*** This heart cares for these same things, but they may be much more personal than universal at this reading.

19 GOVERNED BY THE SUN: PHYSICAL FULFILLMENT/EVALUATION
UPRIGHT: Here is fruition of all seeds planted. Would that all men could end their days at the exact level of health and wealth appropriate for their karmic purpose. You have done well for yourself and your loved ones. ***INVERTED:*** Be attentive to your lessons and this will be yours.

20 GOVERNED BY JUDGEMENT: HEART'S FULFILLMENT/EVALUATION
UPRIGHT: The hard realities of the material world have been kind to your heart and its concerns. The settings for your talents and your relationships have been ideal giving the lessons of the Emotional /creative Plane a friendly playing field. ***INVERTED:*** Maintain a healthy give and take in all of your relationships and this archetype will be yours.

21 GOVERNED BY THE WORLD: EGO'S FULFILLMENT/EVALUATION
UPRIGHT: The mind has no doubts about how well it has done because of all the evidence bouncing around in your Material Plane. Your work has improved the quality of life for many and you have been recognized for your contributions, reputationally and financially. ***INVERTED:*** Perhaps your achievements have been more personal and family oriented than universal, but they have been immensely successful.

22/0 GOVERNED BY THE FOOL: SOUL'S FULFILLMENT/EVALUATION
UPRIGHT: Here is a lasting legacy of your depth of understanding of Mother Earth and all her occupants. You have helped to build an earthly Eden of material lushness capable of quality sustenance of life. ***INVERTED:*** The lessons of this reading are aimed at reinforcing this archetype for you.

TEN OF CUPS

UPRIGHT: Here is the completion of a major emotional/creative cycle, with outcomes as you would have them. This is the effect on the Emotional/creative Plane of having centered spiritually. Here are the highest possible emotional achievements. Emotional longevity. You are emotionally secure, comfortable with your relationships, your progeny, and your self (both inner and outer). You have good emotional support systems in place and functioning. Emotional stability. Life is rich with sensations, meaning, and social interaction. You are as important to others as they are to you. This is the ultimate extension of self, in the Emotional/creative Plane. In terms of emotional/creative continuity and longevity, this can be the base, the encouragement to help you succeed. **INVERTED:** There can be serious problems with your emotional "families." They may be strong, but they may not be correct or productive. A family or group may be smothering, or in other ways taking advantage. The emotions of the group may be healthy within the group but may be too self-serving in the bigger picture.

In This Spread Position...Interpret the Ten Of Cups Meanings to Include:

1 GOVERNED BY THE MAGICIAN: PHYSICAL GIVENS, OUT OF THE FATHER
UPRIGHT: The Physical/material Plane will be awash with your creative energy and strong sense of family values. Your work, your activities will be oriented to the subjects of the Emotional/creative Plane. **INVERTED:** Nepotism will flavor your business affairs, and if the business is large enough and successful enough there may be three or four generations involved at the same time, offering a unique set of challenges both within the family itself and to the family from outside.

2 GOVERNED BY THE HIGH PRIESTESS: EMOTIONAL GIVENS, OUT OF THE MOTHER
UPRIGHT: You are the continuation of an emotional dynasty. You were blessed to begin your life with many of the lessons of the Emotional/creative Plane already in you as a fait accompli. In one instance, this is the mark of a child prodigy with an amazing talent, most visible in the gifted young musician. Also, a family line that has perfected the gift of loving care that holds generations of members together in a functional sharing unit. **INVERTED:** The challenges of such a strong family, or such a strong talent are worth it, considering the the rewards.

3 GOVERNED BY THE EMPRESS: MENTAL GIVENS, INTELLECTUAL PREDISPOSITION
UPRIGHT: Here the mind is set to engage the world of the emotions and creative enterprise as though it already possessed a Ph.D. on the subject. The world of the arts has more appeal here, with literature and music topping the list, but also in fields dealing with relationships, such as psychiatry and the myriad forms of counseling. **INVERTED:** The intricacies of human emotions and creativity, the heights as well as the depths may challenge this mind.

4 GOVERNED BY THE EMPEROR: SPIRITUAL GIVENS, LIFE PURPOSE
UPRIGHT: The archetype of success and happiness as the crowning glory of lessons well-learned in the emotional/creative arena—this is your karmic purpose. Not so much to achieve it, as to live with it and share its lessons with others in all that you do. It will permeate your activities. **INVERTED:** This calls on you to help others achieve this archetype, whether in your own family or in society at large, while hanging on to the principles of love you have already digested.

5 GOVERNED BY THE HIEROPHANT: SYSTEMS BORN INTO, SOCIETAL INFLUENCE
UPRIGHT: This was a mansion of love, of caring interdependence and support moving in every direction and in many layers. If this setting could be given to every child on the front end of life, we would have gone a long way to solving most of the world's problems. **INVERTED:** As with all good things, they can be good to a fault. Imagine too much family love, caring. It happens, creating over dependence, and setting up a need to rebel to assert freedom. At the other extreme, there may have been a potential of this archetype for you, but for some reason it escaped you in particular. One example: A family that functioned well through three children, then shortly after the fourth came divorce.

6 GOVERNED BY THE LOVERS: EMOTIONAL TAPES, BASIS FOR RELATING/CREATING
UPRIGHT: With the ideal of love as your main tapes, this will guide you in your passions and in your creative searches. This is one of the archetypes most advantageous here. Your approach to matters in this plane will be well-disposed to balancing personal and universal love, passion and compassion. **INVERTED:** At one extreme, the promise of love as the solution, the panacea of all the world's problems is somewhat distorted, most likely over-idealized. Some facet of your emotional package—your marriage, your family, your creative project—may be seen too much as an end rather than a means and part of a much larger continuum. In another extreme, the ideal of universal love and its perfection may be hindering you on the more personal level.

7 GOVERNED BY THE CHARIOT: PHYSICAL RESOURCES. MEANS TO ACHIEVE
UPRIGHT: This is similar to the interpretation that follows for this card in position 8 below, except that the emotional bonding and love makes material resources available. Most obvious is manpower. People are there when you need them. **INVERTED:** You may be too dependent on others, or they on you, strapping you for resources at this time.

8 GOVERNED BY STRENGTH: EMOTIONAL RESOURCES, ENERGY
UPRIGHT: With the archetype of family love, of universal love for your emotional resources, you should be a pillar of strength on which many others can depend. For you now, in your turn, can make available all that has been made available to you. The lessons of give and take here are perfectly balanced. In the act of giving, you are receiving at the same time, and in the act of receiving, you are giving at the same time. No debts are incurred. That is emotional/creative efficiency! **INVERTED:** Either dependency of you on the family, or the family on you may have left you less energy than you need.

9 GOVERNED BY THE HERMIT: BELIEF SYSTEM, BASIS FOR DECISIONS
UPRIGHT: "I believe in love; I believe in you." The words of that song sing your tune, except that those words "love" and "you" can be very big concepts in your mind. The song, "People from the broadway show "Funny Girl" that helped launch Barbra Streisand's career also puts your philosophy in a nut shell. "People who need people are the luckiest people in the world." **INVERTED:** Here as always, remember balance is what makes all the archetypes work for you rather than against.

10 GOVERNED BY THE WHEEL OF FORTUNE: CENTRAL MESSAGE, THEME OF READING
UPRIGHT: An emotional/creative jackpot is at hand. This will put things in your emotional house right where you want them. Now if you can just package the feeling. *INVERTED:* This may be more than you have expected. Or, it may be less than you had hoped for, or with a twist of some kind.

11 GOVERNED BY JUSTICE: STATE/CONTENT OF MIND
UPRIGHT: The business of your Emotional Plane is uppermost in your mind, and well it should be from the looks of things. Whether by luck or hard work the present good conditions in your relationships and/or creative endeavors are set to last a long time. *INVERTED:* You may be over or under evaluating the moment. A break in the emotional long-run may be contemplated. You may be sensing the end of a major cycle with many factors completely out of your control.

12 GOVERNED BY THE HANGED MAN: STATE OF EMOTIONS, SUBCONSCIOUS
UPRIGHT: This is the feeling we like to imagine as prevalent in holiday celebrations with families, or in successful opening nights after years of creative preparation. This is emotional/creative reward time. *INVERTED:* The reward, the celebration may be almost too grand for your heart to stand and it may be bursting with joy. The opposite extreme here may be disappointment, that the expected, the deserved, did not materialize.

13 GOVERNED BY DEATH: PHYSICAL SITUATION, HARD REALITY
UPRIGHT: The impact of such emotional and creative abundance on the Physical/material Plane is most welcome. These accomplishments are getting down where you can really enjoy them. This could be the emotional ebullience as the direct result of great financial or athletic news, even of great news about health. The positive effect of the energy being released here is enormous, and it will propel you into the next year with a head start. *INVERTED:* The events affecting your emotional/creative house may have overshot the mark, or fallen short.

14 GOVERNED BY TEMPERANCE: EMOTIONAL TEST
UPRIGHT: You may achieve your major emotional goals for this lifetime much earlier than expected, even in the near future. Success has its own brand of challenge, that your heart will experience as it projects toward even greater possibilities. *INVERTED:* The early achievement of a lifetime goal for your heart may stretch relationships and creativity in ways not anticipated. Likewise, for the disappointment of seeing a long-term goal disappear into impossibility. There may be a lack of support here for your emotional/creative goals.

15 GOVERNED BY THE DEVIL: TEMPTATION/CHALLENGE, FEARS
UPRIGHT: Here may be the sense of accomplishment that broadens when others are involved with us in our goals. When you succeed, so do many others. On the positive, this is encouragement that cannot be bought; it must be earned and it is invaluable. *INVERTED:* You may actually fear the forces operating within the structure of family, or in a creative legacy bound up with your strong talent. This is the onus of responsibility not to disappoint others, much more than a concern for self. There may be a lack of encouragement here, particularly for mental work.

16 GOVERNED BY THE TOWER: NEXT LESSON, GRACE OF GOD
UPRIGHT: The degree of harmony and success in your Emotional/creative Plane that you achieve not later than this time next year may catch you somewhat off guard. *INVERTED:* The emotional goals toward which you have been working will take on a new light. There are new factors which will change the chemistry of this plane.

17 GOVERNED BY THE STAR: ASPIRATIONS OF EGO, GOALS, MAXIMUM EXPECTATIONS
UPRIGHT: Take the philosophy of this card, expressed in the position of the Hermit (9) and project it into the future and you have the key to your aspirations. You are thorough in making long-term arrangements for family and/or career. Love as both cause and effect is your goal. This archetype here also expands to a more universal scale of planning for the world community as you would for yourself. *INVERTED:* On the one extreme, the noble goal of trying to achieve a true "family of man." On the other extreme, you might be myopically concerned with only the affairs and well-being of your immediate family.

18 GOVERNED BY THE MOON: ASPIRATIONS OF HEART, COMPASSION
UPRIGHT: Here is the heart's desire for all of the possible combinations of love in a reciprocity of give and take that would restore the emotional Eden to Earth. Take here the Royal Court of the Minor Arcana as prototype for the perfect family, on a personal or universal scale: Father—King of Pentacles; Mother—Queen of Cups; Son—Knight of Swords; Daughter—Page of Wands. These principles combine for the ideal of this archetype as the earthly realization of love/universal love. *INVERTED:* The emotional principles of this card, however noble, must be balanced with the principles of the Tens from the other three planes.

19 GOVERNED BY THE SUN: PHYSICAL FULFILLMENT/EVALUATION
UPRIGHT: Much of your material legacy is your family and/or the effect of your creative genius here in the Physical Plane. You will be surrounded by the fruits of your Emotional Plane as you grow older. In a sense, every day will be like Thanksgiving Day. *INVERTED:* This archetype is proper for you in this lifetime, but there is work to be done to achieve it.

20 GOVERNED BY JUDGEMENT: HEART'S FULFILLMENT/EVALUATION
UPRIGHT: This is the Minor Arcana card which most closely echoes the Major Arcana card, Judgement, which influences this position, for each represents the ultimate fulfillment of the Emotional Plane. Well done! *INVERTED:* What activity there was in your Emotional Plane, and with such a huge cast. This archetype will be your emotional report card if you continue to sign up for the courses and do all your homework assignments.

21 GOVERNED BY THE WORLD: EGO'S FULFILLMENT/EVALUATION
UPRIGHT: Your dedication to increasing the amount and effect of love ranges from the personal harmony of family to the ideal of world peace. The dove could be your symbol; "Let there be peace on earth and let it begin with me," your motto. There is a deep warmth to your feeling of success, for the mind's success is that of the heart. *INVERTED:* So much to do, and plenty of time. Study this archetype and let it pull you toward your mental goals.

22/0 GOVERNED BY THE FOOL: SOUL'S FULFILLMENT/EVALUATION
UPRIGHT: This is a soul whose ability to love spread out in all directions stopping at no artificial boundaries and accepting no limitations. *INVERTED:* Those whose paths cross yours as you work toward this archetype will consider themselves fortunate.

TEN OF SWORDS

UPRIGHT: Here is the completion of a major mental cycle, with outcomes as you would have them. The imagery of this card can easily confuse, often mislead. The mind succeeds by doing just that, succeeding itself. The old self is truly dead, killed by your own thoughts; long live the new Self. Here you see the death of the little ego self, and its rebirthing as a new revitalized greater Self. But this is the ultimate extension of the original self, albeit transformed, in the Mental Plane. The power of the spirit, the bigger Ego, the true Self, has killed the conscious mind's ability to control you. From now on, the intuitive spirit will have greater control. Here then is major philosophical change. In a less dramatic sense, the mind has matured and will always function, together with the intuitive, as an ever present factor in all matters of the intellect. In another analogy, the original self was none other than a hodgepodge of many little selves, each vying for the supremacy of its program. With the awakening/arrival of the higher Self, you now function as Chairman of the Board over the ever present, but subordinated little ego selves, and can finally make some real progress. This now is true intellectual freedom, yet with a strong commitment guided by free will. The soul is free but it is choosing in its best interests. Here too is mental longevity. ***INVERTED:*** Here are mental conclusions that are not correct in the given situation, and the struggle of the ego continues against the input of the intuitive/spiritual. At an extreme, the ego can be very much out of control and causing damage to yourself and others. Mental immaturity. Old-fashioned, raw egotism. Little or no mental longevity, lack of identification with universal mind.

In This Spread Position...Interpret the Ten Of Swords Meanings to Include:

1 GOVERNED BY THE MAGICIAN: PHYSICAL GIVENS, OUT OF THE FATHER
UPRIGHT: The activity of mind is paramount and highly evident in your Physical/material Plane. Your intellectual interests may parallel those of your father. The mind is consciously intent on the higher purposes of man and your work choice will reflect your seriousness. ***INVERTED:*** Others may not be as intent on the "whys" of things, and while you are not necessarily heavy or pressing with your penchant for philosophy, more than likely quite humorous, it will nevertheless cause some to shy away.

2 GOVERNED BY THE HIGH PRIESTESS: EMOTIONAL GIVENS, OUT OF THE MOTHER
UPRIGHT: The activity of mind is paramount and highly evident in your Emotional/creative Plane. Your intellectual interests may parallel those of your mother. As you apply higher mind to the affairs of this plane, all relationships will effectively carry much spiritual significance making off the cuff sex or sentimentality out of the question. Also, it will raise your creative work to the level of significant spiritual commentary. ***INVERTED:*** You are in earnest about everything that occurs in this plane and must remember that many people will not take things with as much seriousness and meaning as you do.

3 GOVERNED BY THE EMPRESS: MENTAL GIVENS, INTELLECTUAL PREDISPOSITION
UPRIGHT: For you in this lifetime, the major battles of the little egos are over before they even begin. This is not to say that there will not be occasional, or even frequent skirmishes. But, the Mental Plane will be allowed to work with singularity of purpose and dedication as a highly efficient part of universal mind. ***INVERTED:*** This is not to say that the mind is free from concern with the realm of lower mind and the pragmatic reality of everyday life. Just the reverse. The everyday must be faced squarely and pulled to the level of higher mind. Put the other way around, the higher mind must infuse the sensate planes with principle.

4 GOVERNED BY THE EMPEROR: SPIRITUAL GIVENS, LIFE PURPOSE
UPRIGHT: Self-mastery. "Yea, though I walk through the valley of the shadow of death, I will fear no evil: for thou art with me; thy rod and thy staff they comfort me." This fourth verse of the 23rd Psalm is the beautiful state of conscious confidence in God that the mind reaches with the Ten of Swords. And what follows is the lessons of the Suit of Wands..."thy rod and thy staff they comfort me." ***INVERTED:*** You must solidify your control over the lower selves in this lifetime.

5 GOVERNED BY THE HIEROPHANT: SYSTEMS BORN INTO, SOCIETAL INFLUENCE
UPRIGHT: The intellectual power of this early environment is its strongest feature. There was a strong commitment here for man to strive for the very best he could achieve. Part and parcel of that was the necessity to try and understand as much of the "why" of things as possible. ***INVERTED:*** The intellectual intensity may have been harsh, with a drive for knowledge not properly connected to the "why" that leads to an exploration of the spiritual nature of man above the mental level, part and yet apart from man himself. Some very notable people who set the stage for the spiritual rebirth of consciousness in what is called the New Age had this limitation, including Abraham Maslow and Carl Jung.

6 GOVERNED BY THE LOVERS: EMOTIONAL TAPES, BASIS FOR RELATING/CREATING
UPRIGHT: The passionate side of self-mastery, is the extraordinary feeling of self-love made possible by the ability of mind to acknowledge the God within, which is at one and the same time the absolute love of God, the God without. To have this guiding your early emotional tapes is fortunate indeed. ***INVERTED:*** Balancing the inner and outer aspects of God are especially important on this path. One extreme leads to separation, the other to over-identification.

7 GOVERNED BY THE CHARIOT: PHYSICAL RESOURCES. MEANS TO ACHIEVE
UPRIGHT: Your greatest physical asset is your mind. It is the bedrock of all your achievements in the hard reality of life in the physical/material realm. ***INVERTED:*** You may be relying on some aspect of your intellectual armament that it is not well-suited for. Either the prospect you are involved with is not the best for you, or the prospect may be correct but you need to pull in additional mental guns.

8 GOVERNED BY STRENGTH: EMOTIONAL RESOURCES, ENERGY
UPRIGHT: The understanding that your mind has of the emotions gives you great advantage in your relationships and creative affairs, both in the ability to manage, and in the ability to extract, great significance and depth of appreciation. ***INVERTED:*** The struggle to identify the true Self and therefore the path to the truth, the true God, must not be allowed to diminish the important role of the emotions which must not be subverted, or progress of both heart and mind will suffer.

9 GOVERNED BY THE HERMIT: BELIEF SYSTEM, BASIS FOR DECISIONS
UPRIGHT: God is dead. Long live God. Man is dead. Long live man. Herein lies the power that is Christianity, for both God and man die and are reborn. Its power derives from the metaphysical truth to which it bears witness. Everything is born so that it may die. Everything dies so that it may be born. ***INVERTED:*** Nietzsche's "God is Dead" is a distorted projection of the belief that man is dead (or rather dies) onto the concept of God . It is a belief in half the process. Much of Judaism is stuck here; this is what Jesus, and his brother James after him, were trying to resolve.

10 GOVERNED BY THE WHEEL OF FORTUNE: CENTRAL MESSAGE, THEME OF READING
UPRIGHT: As Herod says to the accused Jesus, "Die you innocent bastard, die." It is important to note that what dies here is innocence, not guilt. There is no real punishment being administered in the conversion of the conglomeration of little selves called the ego into the uplifted Self. Rather, this is reward for achieving the level of knowledge which opens the door to initiation, the beginning in earnest and complete conscious awareness of the lessons of the spiritual level. *INVERTED:* The catharsis from mental to spiritual is in progress. What pain there may be is yours, yours alone; enjoy it now as it will pass and you will forever miss it, for it is sweet pain indeed. This is the pain of separateness which you are leaving behind. By going easy on others, you will be going easier on yourself.

11 GOVERNED BY JUSTICE: STATE/CONTENT OF MIND
UPRIGHT: You are very aware of the transformation through which you are going. You may even be dealing with this subject of the dark night of the soul for someone else or for purposes of study. *INVERTED:* Too much or too little conscious attention has been paid to the subject of transformation. Try and get a grip on what all the knowledge you have been given is for.

12 GOVERNED BY THE HANGED MAN: STATE OF EMOTIONS, SUBCONSCIOUS
UPRIGHT: The heart, and therefore your subconscious, are immersed in the catharsis of the ego into greater awareness. This increase in knowledge and the greater acceptance of responsibility is enriching the contents of your emotional world, your relationships and your creative endeavors. *INVERTED:* Difficulties with too much or too little of this archetype may be painful and trying on your relationships. Or, it may be affecting your energy and ability to create.

13 GOVERNED BY DEATH: PHYSICAL SITUATION, HARD REALITY
UPRIGHT: Say goodbye to the old you, hello to the new, for this is a moment of profound change. And while this is a transformation centered on the cusp between the mental and the spiritual, there will be profound physical changes as well. While you are intellectually more heavy, having acquired much knowledge and accepted much responsibility, paradoxically you will be much lighter, in spirit. You may appear both older and younger at the same time—older because your wisdom shows through, and younger because of your buoyancy. *INVERTED:* Because this transformation at the upper levels does have physical repercussions, your body may have some difficulty assimilating the changes. But rest assured that these are growing pains much like those experienced as a teenager and the discomfort will pass. Exercise and bodywork are especially important at this time.

14 GOVERNED BY TEMPERANCE: EMOTIONAL TEST
UPRIGHT: Those less secure in their relationships with you may feel they are losing you. But if anything is lost, it will not be because of anything you do or say. *INVERTED:* Yes, you are a pretty smart cookie, but how are you using it in your relationships? How are you using your talents?

15 GOVERNED BY THE DEVIL: TEMPTATION/CHALLENGE, FEARS
UPRIGHT: That wonderful moment lies in the near future, when you will have assimilated enough knowledge and assumed enough of its related responsibilities to be thrust onto the higher path to wisdom. You are smart, you know it, but you will not blow it. *INVERTED:* This archetype in this position may just be what the word temptation was coined for. You have achieved such a mass of knowledge and have been so successful in the use of your willpower that you may be on the threshold of thinking that the power of mind is all you need, and since you have that.....

16 GOVERNED BY THE TOWER: NEXT LESSON, GRACE OF GOD
UPRIGHT: Your transition to higher mind in preparation for the robes of the initiate is very smooth. *INVERTED:* There may be some rough spots in your transition but they will be met by you confidently and with dispatch for you are being called forward and must be ready.

17 GOVERNED BY THE STAR: ASPIRATIONS OF EGO, GOALS, MAXIMUM EXPECTATIONS
UPRIGHT: To some you must appear to be very singular in purpose, dedicated to a cause, for this is mind on course for mind. As narrow as that may sound, it is proper and very efficient. *INVERTED:* This goal is singular in purpose, to a fault, for it is the ego in search of simple self-satisfaction. This is the desire for knowledge in order to control one's destiny.

18 GOVERNED BY THE MOON: ASPIRATIONS OF HEART, COMPASSION
UPRIGHT: Instinctively the heart realizes that without this mental transformation, it will never evolve from passion to compassion, from self to universal love and so it aspires to this archetype of self-mastery. This is the strength of heart that makes it possible to withstand the pain of the cross of the transfiguration. *INVERTED:* This heart aspires to the resurrection, but not the crucifixion.

19 GOVERNED BY THE SUN: PHYSICAL FULFILLMENT/EVALUATION
UPRIGHT: There will be a definite air of finality as you finish out your Physical/material Plane. You will have everything in order and leave explicit instructions for when you are gone. *INVERTED:* Work now toward the upright interpretation, otherwise you will be leaving behind quite a mess for others to deal with.

20 GOVERNED BY JUDGEMENT: HEART'S FULFILLMENT/EVALUATION
UPRIGHT: What mourning and what joy there will be on your passing. Your loved ones will share your transition and though they will miss you terribly, they will be excited at your prospects. *INVERTED:* Let everyone share your path and your creativity now as you work toward this fulfillment.

21 GOVERNED BY THE WORLD: EGO'S FULFILLMENT/EVALUATION
UPRIGHT: This is the archetype that best fulfills the potential of the mental path. No one could have done better than you have done. *INVERTED:* If your mind gets in the way of itself, let your heart do its natural task of steering the ship from below when the helmsman is otherwise preoccupied.

22/0 GOVERNED BY THE FOOL: SOUL'S FULFILLMENT/EVALUATION
UPRIGHT: This has been the path of intelligence that leads to wisdom. Here is the nobility of mind for which God created man. Here is the knowledge of how to bring God to earth. *INVERTED:* Use the lessons of this reading to shed light on your path to this archetype.

TEN OF WANDS

UPRIGHT: This is the completion of a major spiritual cycle, with outcomes as God would have them. It is the ultimate extension of the self, in the Spiritual Plane. This God, however, is the merging of the god within (self-will/ man's will) with the god without (God's will). The imagery of this card suggests hard work and so correctly communicates the paradox of spiritual fulfillment as more work, more responsibility, not less. And so it is that our path leads ever to more work, but we are ever more capable of handling it. Things get both harder and easier. And how fitting, for everything at this level is a duality, a paradox. The suggestion is very clearly that completion of one major cycle is indeed merely preparation for the next, even greater task. But the meaning here is a knowing relationship with the Divine, a hands-on working knowledge of the endless cycle of paradoxes underlying ultimate truths. This is the soul in control. A spiritual master in the making, for not only do we have the wisdom which is the ability to manage knowledge, there is the Wisdom which is the ability to manage spirit. Spiritual longevity, individual spirit identified with universal spirit. A dedicated life. "To whom much is given, much is required." Wisdom. **INVERTED:** There may be an overly long pause at this level, a hesitation to go on with the next task. Spiritual egotism. Presumption of a high order. Spiritual abuse, negligence. Spiritual vertigo. The symbol of Fascist Italy was a bundle of rods tightly tied together, suggesting that the Italian State had combined and coordinated the force of all its elements. Here is power without the commensurate level of responsibility.

In This Spread Position...Interpret the Ten Of Wands Meanings to Include:

1 GOVERNED BY THE MAGICIAN: PHYSICAL GIVENS, OUT OF THE FATHER
UPRIGHT: The affairs of the Physical/material Plane are virtually the affairs of the Spiritual Plane. Witnessing almost seems too tame a word for the degree to which this soul will act out all that it knows and to which it is dedicated. Every minute of every day will be a ritual of observation of the truths now embodied in every molecule of your body. **INVERTED:** While such a path offers itself to any situation that calls on it, nothing will be beyond your means.

2 GOVERNED BY THE HIGH PRIESTESS: EMOTIONAL GIVENS, OUT OF THE MOTHER
UPRIGHT: The affairs of the Emotional/creative Plane are virtually the affairs of the Spiritual Plane. Every relationship and all your creative gifts will be dedicated to expressing the possibilities that await the pure and dedicated heart. **INVERTED:** Much will be asked of such a path, for through your very involvement situations can be improved. Yours is a healing presence.

3 GOVERNED BY THE EMPRESS: MENTAL GIVENS, INTELLECTUAL PREDISPOSITION
UPRIGHT: The affairs of the Mental Plane are virtually the affairs of the Spiritual Plane. Knowledge here is in service to universal mind and there is no sense of sacrifice as self-will is in harmony with God's will. **INVERTED:** This mind will be asked to teach, to share what it understands with as many people as will listen.

4 GOVERNED BY THE EMPEROR: SPIRITUAL GIVENS, LIFE PURPOSE
UPRIGHT: Much of your energy in this incarnation will be lent to others, to help them with their lessons. To do this, you will be side by side with them experiencing the same thoughts, the same feelings, but with your understanding you will lend that extra advantage to help them along. This is to be an arm of God's grace. **INVERTED:** Your lessons are in how to be a good guardian angel. You must learn how to polish the apple, not how to be an apple polisher.

5 GOVERNED BY THE HIEROPHANT: SYSTEMS BORN INTO, SOCIETAL INFLUENCE
UPRIGHT: Spirituality, not religion, was the mark of this early environment. Principle, understanding, balance, dedication, all these and more were the norm. Here was a nest from which a prize swan could emerge with full spread wings ready to fly. **INVERTED:** The adults in this environment were much advanced but they may have had difficulty even at such heights. Spiritual vertigo, egotism perhaps.

6 GOVERNED BY THE LOVERS: EMOTIONAL TAPES, BASIS FOR RELATING/CREATING
UPRIGHT: The passion here at such a young age is hard to imagine for it is so filled with spiritual fervor—a depth of love that usually requires years of study and experience—but the love of God which strikes every mortal heart every second of every day can be returned by any of us, even at such an early stage. This passion is purely and simply love of the spirit that infills man, love of God. **INVERTED:** This love of Godly spirit, however noble, must not be in lieu of worldly love or it is not Godly spirit. Even the recluse, the monk, the ascetic, to be on the proper path, must love the world and all its material wonders and be intimately and intricately involved with its progress.

7 GOVERNED BY THE CHARIOT: PHYSICAL RESOURCES. MEANS TO ACHIEVE
UPRIGHT: To others, your resources may seem as magic for what you need is always at hand when you need it. It may not, however, be there the day before. For this path never asks for more than it needs, allowing the world resources to be allocated when and where the need is greatest. It has no need for stockpiling against the advent of disaster. **INVERTED:** There may be the temptation to perform magic, thereby distorting the spiritually equitable distribution of material resources.

8 GOVERNED BY STRENGTH: EMOTIONAL RESOURCES, ENERGY
UPRIGHT: There can be no greater strength than this archetype provides. It is the key to power and in its healthy state, balanced between self-will and the will of God, it can provide the energy to feed any emotional or creative need. **INVERTED:** This energy can be strong but short-lived, and it can be misdirected.

9 GOVERNED BY THE HERMIT: BELIEF SYSTEM, BASIS FOR DECISIONS
UPRIGHT: This is a belief in belief itself. This is the self that believes in God, and the God that believes in the Self. This is self believing in self, God believing in God. This is the head that believes in the tail of the ouroborus; the tail in the head. This is the yin that believes in the yang; the yang in the yin. This is the above that believes in the below; the below in the above. This is the inner that knows the outer, the outer that knows the inner. **INVERTED:** Here is the mind that knows all of the above, and yet there is still something...

10 GOVERNED BY THE WHEEL OF FORTUNE: CENTRAL MESSAGE, THEME OF READING
UPRIGHT: This is the work for which you were born. Accomplish well what is on your table now and more will be given to you, and more, and more.
INVERTED: What you have presumed was your work is the work of another.

11 GOVERNED BY JUSTICE: STATE/CONTENT OF MIND

UPRIGHT: You are aware of the importance of this time and of what you are doing. It is both difficult and yet easy, for it is right and it feels right. *INVERTED:* The present work situation does not add up for you. Your evaluation may be correct; this may not be the correct work. Or, this may be the correct work and it is your evaluation, your attitude that is in error.

12 GOVERNED BY THE HANGED MAN: STATE OF EMOTIONS, SUBCONSCIOUS

UPRIGHT: Here is energy and motivation of the highest order for the worthwhile purposes at hand. *INVERTED:* Your heart is having difficulty offering up the energy, the motivation you need if you are to meet this task. At another extreme, your heart may be offering too much energy for the situation, or energy for the wrong situation.

13 GOVERNED BY DEATH: PHYSICAL SITUATION, HARD REALITY

UPRIGHT: If everything seems to be happening at once, that's because it is. It may be a very simple event in itself, involving just yourself or you and a few close to you, but there may be far-reaching implications. But, it also may be a truly grand affair, creating quite a stir for others as well as yourself. You may be very instrumental in bringing this event of consequence about. *INVERTED:* There may be considerable abuse of power taking place here.

14 GOVERNED BY TEMPERANCE: EMOTIONAL TEST

UPRIGHT: In the near future as your heart commits to higher goals, there will be adjustments for you and those nearest you. *INVERTED:* The demands of higher responsibility may be hard for you to accept this next year, but the choice is yours. You may not get much help from others.

15 GOVERNED BY THE DEVIL: TEMPTATION/CHALLENGE, FEARS

UPRIGHT: This next year your mind will grow by leaps and bounds as you learn your lessons at a dizzying pace. But your appetite will be for no more than you can handle well. You will feel the insurge of power. *INVERTED:* This interim may be a little frustrating as you will feel you are ready for more responsibility, but you must handle what is in front of you before asking for more.

16 GOVERNED BY THE TOWER: NEXT LESSON, GRACE OF GOD

UPRIGHT: You can safely accept greater responsibility for your willingness and ability to learn has made you much stronger. *INVERTED:* It is easy to get confused even at this level, for with greater knowledge comes greater temptation, greater power. Be cautious of the trap of accepting only one-half of the inner/outer duality/reality of God. Neither assume the identity of God via the godness in you, nor disappear in the God outside of you losing the identity which is the purpose of your incarnation.

17 GOVERNED BY THE STAR: ASPIRATIONS OF EGO, GOALS, MAXIMUM EXPECTATIONS

UPRIGHT: You aspire to nothing less than wisdom. This is not a wish for knowledge, or power, but the open-eyed desire to assume your correct place in the caravan on the path. You wish to have the presence of mind and wherewithal to follow the tracks of those ahead of you, and to have like presence of mind and means to leave tracks for those that follow you. *INVERTED:* You may have one, but not both, of these presences of mind. The truly foolish mind thinks that the caravan has already arrived. With nothing of concern ahead and nothing behind, to this mind there is only now and this is not the eternal now of the Buddhist which includes a full future and a full past; it is a very small, non-inclusive now even though it tries to fill that now with everything but time.

18 GOVERNED BY THE MOON: ASPIRATIONS OF HEART, COMPASSION

UPRIGHT: The heart too can aspire to wisdom and here it does just that. For it aches to join those in the front of the caravan just as it aches for those behind to join with it. *INVERTED:* The foolish heart, like the foolish mind, can decide to live only in the now of indulgence and manipulation.

19 GOVERNED BY THE SUN: PHYSICAL FULFILLMENT/EVALUATION

UPRIGHT: The material fullness of this lifetime vibrated with the awareness of God's essence in everything. Great attention has been given to all that you possess. Just as your possessions have cared for you, so have you cared for all that you possess. You have owned nothing as everything was there of its own free will. *INVERTED:* Continue to work on your garden of Eden.

20 GOVERNED BY JUDGEMENT: HEART'S FULFILLMENT/EVALUATION

UPRIGHT: The emotional richness of your path will bear witness to your eagerness to feel and express God in all your relationships and talents. *INVERTED:* Your heart, unfettered, will carry you to this ideal.

21 GOVERNED BY THE WORLD: EGO'S FULFILLMENT/EVALUATION

UPRIGHT: Oh, what work your mind has been able to direct, to accomplish so much and yet with such a delicate touch, like the gifted gardener who can nurture everything to glorious maturity with no trace of human hand. *INVERTED:* Balance knowledge with responsibility and the wisdom of the gardener will be yours.

22/0 GOVERNED BY THE FOOL: SOUL'S FULFILLMENT/EVALUATION

UPRIGHT: The dedicated life fulfilled. From whom much was required, much was given. *INVERTED:* Let the lessons of this card pull you home.

KING of PENTACLES.

KING OF PENTACLES (EARTH/EARTH)

UPRIGHT: Mature male of marriageable age. Physical type: Dark hair with dark complexion and dark eyes. Also, black hair with very fair complexion and light blue, green or violet eyes. Personality type: Dependable. Resourceful. Can-doer. Watchful. Good instincts. Good physical leader. Great endurance. Ruled by the drive of necessity. Father/provider. Maintaining security of family or group. Practical. Generous. Good manager. Eye for finance. Builder. Architect. Athlete. Farmer. Retailer. Physical health care. Doctor, Nurse. Bodywork. Think here of King Arthur. **INVERTED:** A distortion of the above characteristics, either to a greater or lesser degree, with the derivative problems. For example: A propensity toward ill health. Recurring material/financial problems. A preoccupation with physical appearances, or with material or health matters, i.e., a conspicuous consumer, a man controlled by his possessions, or a hypochondriac. Avoidance of responsibilities versus worrying too much about security. **Note:** *Remember that the Courts are personifications which carry lessons to be learned, just as any of the Pips or Majors. First, they may represent characteristics of yourself. Second, they may represent people in this incarnation with you (past, present, or future). Third, they may represent people or guides not in the Earth plane with you at this time, including: yourself in past lives, others from this life passed on, others from past lifetimes, and any number of guides in the hierarchy between the Earth plane and God.*

In This Spread Position...Interpret the King Of Pentacles Meanings to Include:

1 GOVERNED BY THE MAGICIAN: PHYSICAL GIVENS, OUT OF THE FATHER
UPRIGHT: Born into the influence of the king of kings, the King of Pentacles with all the attendant acceptance of responsibility thereto, especially in the Physical/material Plane. To have this here suggests that your father's line may be one of great productivity, perhaps in a given field of expertise now handed to you. **INVERTED**: Work hard to avoid letting your position separate you from those very people who depend on you so much.

2 GOVERNED BY THE HIGH PRIESTESS: EMOTIONAL GIVENS, OUT OF THE MOTHER
UPRIGHT: Position of responsibility and leadership, capable of doing anything for the security and success of the affairs of this plane. Your mother may have come from a long line of farmers or businessmen or the like. You will have the heart of business and pragmatic affairs and it will serve your creative enterprise well, such as in the fashion industry, or in show business. Family, romance, business, and social life may be hard to keep separate. **INVERTED:** Some will say you sacrifice your personal life for work. Prove them wrong.

3 GOVERNED BY THE EMPRESS: MENTAL GIVENS, INTELLECTUAL PREDISPOSITION
UPRIGHT: Mixing a strong mind and a strong body is not a bad way to begin. A football coach or quarterback need these. Ultimate responsibility in the Mental Plane suggests the work of finance ministers in government, or treasurers of corporations, and investment counselors on Wall Street. **INVERTED:** There could be a tendency to use most of your attributes that make you a good father here in the mental arena and neglect your family. Guard against the mental becoming a slave to the physical/material.

4 GOVERNED BY THE EMPEROR: SPIRITUAL GIVENS, LIFE PURPOSE
UPRIGHT: Many will depend on you for their basic needs and security, possibly their livelihood, even their lives. This harks back to the lord of the manor/castle whose extended family lived literally under his wing. Our Chief Executive Officers, leaders of industry, and heads of family businesses are contemporary society's closest equivalents. **INVERTED:** You may be one of those called upon to carry an extra heavy load.

5 GOVERNED BY THE HIEROPHANT: SYSTEMS BORN INTO, SOCIETAL INFLUENCE
UPRIGHT: Here is the providing father as symbol of your early environment. Your father, or another prominent male figure, set the tone for the security and welfare that was yours. On Thanksgiving day at your house Dad carved the turkey, and the ham, and perhaps the roast as well. **INVERTED:** At one extreme, you may have had more father figures than you would have liked. At the other extreme, the most lasting effect on you was the fact that there was no one to fill this role, at least not well.

6 GOVERNED BY THE LOVERS: EMOTIONAL TAPES, BASIS FOR RELATING/CREATING
UPRIGHT: Your earliest tapes of imprint are of this providing father figure, perhaps your own father. But it could be of an older family figure such as a grandfather, or of course someone outside the family, perhaps someone famous whom you came to admire. **INVERTED:** Distorted, this otherwise very healthy archetype can become a block instead of a blueprint/foundation for love and creativity. At one extreme, the figure is idolized and idealized and real life will find it hard to compete. At the other extreme, the figure is loathed and by extension either all men or all of certain types of men are not to be loved/trusted.

7 GOVERNED BY THE CHARIOT: PHYSICAL RESOURCES. MEANS TO ACHIEVE
UPRIGHT: You have someone—a family member, a partner, an angel—that you can fall back on. Being part of a family business, or an extended family working together fill this bill nicely. **INVERTED:** At one extreme, this suggests that the aforementioned may have been your safety net, but that it is not as strong for you at this time. At the other extreme, there may be too much support that you have relied on too heavily for your own independent development.

8 GOVERNED BY STRENGTH: EMOTIONAL RESOURCES, ENERGY
UPRIGHT: This king personifies your strength, and whether this is your own character or that of another, you are fortunate that your emotions are shored up with responsibility and pragmatic interdependence. The family you have, the friends you make along the way, should be with you to the end. **INVERTED:** At one extreme, you have been able to lean too heavily on this king for your physical and material needs, and it will only slow your independent growth in the Emotional Plane. At the other extreme, you feel less than complete because this piece is missing or not functioning as it should be. This can be disappointed love.

9 GOVERNED BY THE HERMIT: BELIEF SYSTEM, BASIS FOR DECISIONS
UPRIGHT: You could write the handbook for fatherhood, at the least the part about bringing home the bacon and paying for the kids to go to college. This is acceptance of responsibility; the buck stops as well as starts here. And it is the thinking rooted in provision of safety and security from which the principles of sound government and organized societies arise. **INVERTED:** At one extreme, as with any inverted Court card in this position, this can suggest a dependence on another person's philosophy rather than having developed your own. At another extreme, this can be a rather narrow interpretation of authority—right or wrong....do as I say do.

10 GOVERNED BY THE WHEEL OF FORTUNE: CENTRAL MESSAGE, THEME OF READING
UPRIGHT: Think well on this card for he is coming to you in one guise or another. For there is order to be put in your physical/material house, to take charge and make things right. More leadership and control is needed here. **INVERTED:** Of course, you need to heed the King of Pentacles for your own benefit, but there are others who depend on you to take hold and take charge, and to produce.

11 GOVERNED BY JUSTICE: STATE/CONTENT OF MIND
UPRIGHT: The mind is on the king. He may represent a plan underway to assume responsibility, take charge, or he may be the key player in the present game underfoot. **INVERTED:** You may think adversely about this king, or he about you. As an aspect of yourself, you may be thinking of getting out from under a responsibility.

12 GOVERNED BY THE HANGED MAN: STATE OF EMOTIONS, SUBCONSCIOUS
UPRIGHT: The heart is on the king. He may be an object of your affection, or the centerpiece of a creative project underway. Your heart is accepting a great amount of responsibility. **INVERTED:** Your heart may be involved with this king, but rather not be. Or, the opposite, this can be the symbol of your heart's sadness over this person.

13 GOVERNED BY DEATH: PHYSICAL SITUATION, HARD REALITY
UPRIGHT: You are very much in control, centered in your affairs with an eye on all the details. The lord of the manor is in, and he is in his throne room. This suggests that things are much to your liking and for all the duties and work involved, being king is nice at the moment. **INVERTED:** The king may be thrown for a loop. But it appears to be more personal than directed at your holdings or family, your responsibilities. Other possibilities are the extremes of either having taken on too much responsibility for the moment, or not enough.

14 GOVERNED BY TEMPERANCE: EMOTIONAL TEST
UPRIGHT: King on the emotional horizon in the near future. This brings much more authority and security into your love life, maybe even your creative life. You may have to make some minor adjustments in some areas, as kings like to be well-accommodated. **INVERTED:** If this is someone already in your life, there will be emotions to deal with here. The kind and depth will depend on who says no to whom.

15 GOVERNED BY THE DEVIL: TEMPTATION/CHALLENGE, FEARS
UPRIGHT: King on the mental horizon in the near future. You may be setting up a new situation with yourself as head. The mind is dedicated to pragmatic affairs, determined that this project or business will succeed. **INVERTED:** If this represents someone already in your life, this may show a turn of mind between you. You may be setting yourself up with too much to do. Avoid taking on too much responsibility, especially without commensurate authority.

16 GOVERNED BY THE TOWER: NEXT LESSON, GRACE OF GOD
UPRIGHT: Here is the support, the energy and resources that you need to secure your Physical/material Plane, and it may well come in the physical personage of the King of Pentacles. It may however, be the access to what he represents. Necessity has proved to be the father of invention in this case. **INVERTED:** Much of this blessing will be passed through you to others.

17 GOVERNED BY THE STAR: ASPIRATIONS OF EGO, GOALS, MAXIMUM EXPECTATIONS
UPRIGHT: So you want to be Chairman of the Board. The goal here is not power, but the sense of accomplishment in taking on a big job and doing it well, and in doing something that will make good work for many others as well. **INVERTED:** This mental goal could be to have nothing less than this King of Pentacles. You may not love him, but you will have him.

18 GOVERNED BY THE MOON: ASPIRATIONS OF HEART, COMPASSION
UPRIGHT: This is the heart in its ambitious nature, for it wants to be in the position of being able to provide for the welfare of many others. **INVERTED:** You may actually be programming to fall in love and be loved by this King of Pentacles. But there is a distortion of the upright meaning which is to enjoy the position in which others depend on you. Others get helped but you get the extra kick of pleasure.

19 GOVERNED BY THE SUN: PHYSICAL FULFILLMENT/EVALUATION
UPRIGHT: Whether this is the man of your dreams, or the man with his dreams fulfilled at the end of the Physical Plane, could you ask for more? The suggestion is one of an ongoing productive life until the end. **INVERTED:** Let the King of Pentacles help you to your physical fulfillment.

20 GOVERNED BY JUDGEMENT: HEART'S FULFILLMENT/EVALUATION
UPRIGHT: The King of Pentacles here can suggest that the love of this person was the centerpiece and the fulfillment of your life. Also, however, it can be the wonderful satisfaction of having been able to provide for and maintain an extended family comfortably, and to enjoy their company to the very last. **INVERTED:** Let the King of Pentacles help you to your heart's fulfillment.

21 GOVERNED BY THE WORLD: EGO'S FULFILLMENT/EVALUATION
UPRIGHT: Here the very mechanics of business and work and your great ability at it can be the satisfaction that carries you highest. You have enjoyed the responsibilities that you have accepted, for they have been welcome causes to this wonderful effect of success. **INVERTED:** Let the King of Pentacles help you to your ego's fulfillment.

22/0 GOVERNED BY THE FOOL: SOUL'S FULFILLMENT/EVALUATION
UPRIGHT: This king deserves his position for he carried his load high and far without one word of complaint. **INVERTED:** Let the King of Pentacles help you to your soul's fulfillment.

KING of CUPS.

KING OF CUPS (EARTH/WATER)

UPRIGHT: Mature male of marriageable age. Physical type: Light brown to sandy-blond hair and medium complexion, sometimes olive, with brown, blue or gray-blue eyes. Personality type: Emotional. Sensitive. Creative. Dedicated. Motivated. Sensual/sexy. Tender. Soothing. Loving father. Ruled by the drive of necessity. Involved with family/friends/fellow workers. Frequently the heart of the group. Confident. Involved in the Arts. Artist. Designer. Decorator. Leader/volunteer. Healer by example and by touch. Salesman. Counselor/advisor. Sailor. Think here of the Egyptian pharoah, Akhenaten (14th cent.B.C.), whose faith was love, centered on the one god, Aten. ***INVERTED:*** A distortion of the above characteristics, either to a greater or lesser degree, with the derivative problems. For example: A man uneasy with emotional issues. Uncaring. At one extreme, under-emotional; at the other, over-emotional. ***Note:*** *Remember that the Courts are personifications which carry lessons to be learned, just as any of the Pips or Majors. First, they may represent characteristics of yourself. Second, they may represent people in this incarnation with you (past, present, or future). Third, they may represent people or guides not in the Earth plane with you at this time, including: yourself in past lives, others from this life passed on, others from past lifetimes, and any number of guides in the hierarchy between the Earth plane and God.*

In This Spread Position...Interpret the King Of Cups Meanings to Include:

1 GOVERNED BY THE MAGICIAN: PHYSICAL GIVENS, OUT OF THE FATHER
UPRIGHT: Here the Physical/material Plane will be sheltered by the king's tender love and care. Responsibility, in providing the necessities of life for self and loved ones, will be administered with a gentle hands-on touch. There is a strong creativity here that will flavor choice of profession and leisure activities. Aesthetics will be important to your personal appearance and to surroundings. ***INVERTED:*** Your surroundings and activities are attractive and many will want to enjoy the products of your labors.

2 GOVERNED BY THE HIGH PRIESTESS: EMOTIONAL GIVENS, OUT OF THE MOTHER
UPRIGHT: Here, a blend of kingly strength with the softness of the Cups sets the tone for your Emotional Plane. You will have many people in your life, and most will look to you as the leader. You are well-disposed to do well in combinations of business and creative work, actually being the sort who could be a self-managing artist. ***INVERTED:*** People will be drawn to you for both your strength and your gentleness, but they may get confused about which works where and when, as you might yourself.

3 GOVERNED BY THE EMPRESS: MENTAL GIVENS, INTELLECTUAL PREDISPOSITION
UPRIGHT: A blend of authority and sensitivity sets this mind for tasks as diverse as museum director, hospital administrator, social worker, school principal, zookeeper, the Peace Corps, or ship's captain. Ever capable of using the information at hand, but always open to last minute suggestion. ***INVERTED:*** Your openness and close working relationships may mislead some into neglecting your authority, mistaking your consideration for weakness.

4 GOVERNED BY THE EMPEROR: SPIRITUAL GIVENS, LIFE PURPOSE
UPRIGHT: You will be looked to for your authority and position, but more so for your compassionate use of your position. If falls to you to show that people may need leaders and organization to avoid chaos and work efficiently, but they do not need anyone to make them work, or do anything for that matter. You seek to motivate by example. ***INVERTED:*** How you balance your kingly qualities with your emotional sensitivity may be the test of this lifetime.

5 GOVERNED BY THE HIEROPHANT: SYSTEMS BORN INTO, SOCIETAL INFLUENCE
UPRIGHT: Here is the loving father as symbol of your early environment. Your father, or another prominent figure, set the tone for the closeness and warmth that was yours. At your house, Dad was always around when you needed him and his knee was your favorite seat. ***INVERTED:*** At one extreme there could have been too much attention, but at the other extreme, there may have been little of this masculine caring, or this figure may not have been present.

6 GOVERNED BY THE LOVERS: EMOTIONAL TAPES, BASIS FOR RELATING/CREATING
UPRIGHT: Your earliest tapes of imprint are of this loving father figure, perhaps your own father. But it could be of an older family figure such as a grandfather, or of course someone outside of the family, perhaps someone famous whom you came to admire. ***INVERTED:*** Distorted, this otherwise very healthy archetype can become a block instead of a blueprint/foundation for love and creativity. At one extreme, the figure is idolized and idealized and real life will find it hard to compete. At the other extreme, the figure is loathed and by extension either all men or all of certain types of men are not to be loved/trusted.

7 GOVERNED BY THE CHARIOT: PHYSICAL RESOURCES. MEANS TO ACHIEVE
UPRIGHT: You have someone—a family member, a partner, an angel—that you can fall back on. But more than financial or physical help, this is the strong shoulder to cry on, the caring ear that can listen to your problems. This man can help heal your wounds. ***INVERTED:*** At one extreme, this suggests that the aforementioned may have been your safety net, but that it is not as strong for you at this time. At the other extreme, there may be too much support that you have relied on too heavily for your own independent development.

8 GOVERNED BY STRENGTH: EMOTIONAL RESOURCES, ENERGY
UPRIGHT: This king personifies your strength, and whether this is your own character or that of another, you are fortunate that your emotions are shored up with the healing power of love in your heart that generates your dedication to your friends and family. ***INVERTED:*** At one extreme, you have been able to lean too heavily on this king for your physical and material needs, and it will only slow your independent growth in the Emotional Plane. At the other extreme, you feel less than complete because this piece is missing or not functioning as it should be. This can be disappointed love.

9 GOVERNED BY THE HERMIT: BELIEF SYSTEM, BASIS FOR DECISIONS
UPRIGHT: Your philosophy is love 'em and keep on lovin' 'em. As romantic as you are, you are also a loyalist. Feelings come first and then if necessary you will find the words to fit them. Your ideology follows your heart. But your cup is the cup of Bacchus and you will always be open and expressive. For you, life should be, and is, a pleasure. ***INVERTED:*** At one extreme, this life might be a party, too much of a party. The tender love and care here might be too tender and too loving. At another extreme, this life may not know how to party, how to integrate pleasure into the responsibility of family and work.

10 GOVERNED BY THE WHEEL OF FORTUNE: CENTRAL MESSAGE, THEME OF READING
UPRIGHT: Think well on this card for he is coming to you in one guise or another. For there is order to be put in your emotional/creative house, to take

charge and make things right. More leadership and control is needed here. ***INVERTED:*** Of course, you need to heed the King of Cups for your own benefit, but there are others who depend on you for your soothing, healing presence.

11 GOVERNED BY JUSTICE: STATE/CONTENT OF MIND
UPRIGHT: The mind is on this king of the emotions. He may be a key player in the game on your table. You are being both authoritative and considerate in this matter. ***INVERTED:*** You may think adversely about this king, or he about you. There may be a tug of war between responsibility and your lust for life.

12 GOVERNED BY THE HANGED MAN: STATE OF EMOTIONS, SUBCONSCIOUS
UPRIGHT: The heart is on this king of the emotions. He may be an object of your affection, or the centerpiece of a creative project underway. ***INVERTED:*** Your heart may be involved with this king, but rather not be. Or, the opposite, this can be the symbol of your heart's sadness over this person. At another extreme, you may be enjoying yourself a little too much for your situation.

13 GOVERNED BY DEATH: PHYSICAL SITUATION, HARD REALITY
UPRIGHT: This king may be on your doorstep. He brings the possibilities of good times and rejoicing as he shows you how to do your chores and have fun at the same time. ***INVERTED:*** At one extreme, there may be a strong influence, a person, who can easily persuade you to go into too deep water. At the other extreme, this person who charms you may be working absolute wonders healing your physical and material woes.

14 GOVERNED BY TEMPERANCE: EMOTIONAL TEST
UPRIGHT: Here comes a mature masculine influence in your near future, and of course it may be delivered in person. As a result you will be more focused and purposeful in your emotional affairs and your creative projects can flourish with such motivation and encouragement behind them. ***INVERTED:*** If the king is someone in your life already, this can show a problem. At one extreme, there is such a showering of affection that it can create difficulties, a smothering effect. At the other extreme, there is a lack of caring attention to support your needs.

15 GOVERNED BY THE DEVIL: TEMPTATION/CHALLENGE, FEARS
UPRIGHT: Here on the mental horizon in the near future comes power with a heart. This can be the partner you have needed to help your realize your goals. For with the intellect here are the personality and people skills to work miracles. ***INVERTED:*** At one extreme, the charming character here can distort into the charlatan. At the other extreme, the messenger can succeed all too well leaving the message in the shadows.

16 GOVERNED BY THE TOWER: NEXT LESSON, GRACE OF GOD
UPRIGHT: Here is the support, the energy and resources that you need to secure your Emotional/creative Plane, and it may well come in the physical personage of the King of Cups. It may however, be the access to what he represents. You must be able to wear both masks of the theater in the Emotional Plane—the smile and the frown. ***INVERTED:*** Much of this blessing will be passed through you to others.

17 GOVERNED BY THE STAR: ASPIRATIONS OF EGO, GOALS, MAXIMUM EXPECTATIONS
UPRIGHT: Here is the goal to be the loving father/leader. You want to be effective, but you want also be loved in return by your people. ***INVERTED:*** The primary fault here is to want to be loved more than to be effective.

18 GOVERNED BY THE MOON: ASPIRATIONS OF HEART, COMPASSION
UPRIGHT: Here the goal of the heart is the same as the mind—to be the caring, nurturing father. But here the scope is a little broader and more compassionate and without the reciprocal love of your people you would cease to exist, the king would die. ***INVERTED:*** Here the goal can become so passionate in the extreme as to distort the roles of all the characters and become an orgy of confusion.

19 GOVERNED BY THE SUN: PHYSICAL FULFILLMENT/EVALUATION
UPRIGHT: Whether the gentle man has just reentered your life or is the symbol of its full tour, it bodes well that your establishment is both solid and soft. ***INVERTED:*** Let the King of Cups help you to your physical fulfillment.

20 GOVERNED BY JUDGEMENT: HEART'S FULFILLMENT/EVALUATION
UPRIGHT: The King of Cups here can suggest that the life of this person was the centerpiece and the fulfillment of your life. Also, however, it can be the satisfaction of how well you balanced control and caring and so have no judgement issues to face at the last. ***INVERTED:*** Let the King of Cups help you to your heart's fulfillment.

21 GOVERNED BY THE WORLD: EGO'S FULFILLMENT/EVALUATION
UPRIGHT: You have nursed your mental projects as you have your children and they show the results of your tender love and care. You have been a gentle king even in this the most harsh of the planes, that of the mind. ***INVERTED:*** Let the King of Cups help you to your ego's fulfillment.

22/0 GOVERNED BY THE FOOL: SOUL'S FULFILLMENT/EVALUATION
UPRIGHT: Let it be said of this king that it was impossible to tell where he ended and his kingdom began. ***INVERTED:*** Let the King of Cups help you to your soul's fulfillment.

KING OF SWORDS (EARTH / AIR)

UPRIGHT: Mature male of marriageable age. Physical type: Blond to light blond hair and fair complexion with blue, blue-gray, or greenish-brown eyes. Personality type: Mental. Assertive. Perfectionist. Defender/protector. Philosophical. Studious. Alert. Direct. A knowledgeable leader. Tactician. Soldier. Father of ideas and ideals. Good planner. Ruled by the drive of necessity. Pilot. Teacher. Mentor. Researcher. Highly informed. Courageous. Think here of Alexander the Great (356-323 B.C.), or of Charlemagne (742-814 A.D.). ***INVERTED:*** A distortion of the above characteristics, either to a greater or lesser degree, with the derivative problems. For example: At one extreme, an overly aggressive man, self-righteous or egomaniacal; at the other extreme, a weak, unassertive type, with a lack of self-esteem. Too studious versus lazy intellect. Fastidious organizer/perfectionist versus the sloppy non-organizer. Non-stop talker versus the silent type. Someone who never listens versus the nosy eavesdropper. Bad planner versus the over planner, the worrier. ***Note:*** *Remember that the Courts are personifications which carry lessons to be learned, just as any of the Pips or Majors. First, they may represent characteristics of yourself. Second, they may represent people in this incarnation with you (past, present, or future). Third, they may represent people or guides not in the Earth plane with you at this time, including: yourself in past lives, others from this life passed on, others from past lifetimes, and any number of guides in the hierarchy between the Earth plane and God.*

In This Spread Position...Interpret the King Of Swords Meanings to Include:

1 GOVERNED BY THE MAGICIAN: PHYSICAL GIVENS, OUT OF THE FATHER
UPRIGHT: Here the Physical/material Plane is protected, not in the sense of provider or nurturer, but literally of defending loved ones and property. You have come from a lineage of great strength with the knowledge and physical ability to back up what you believe in and value. ***INVERTED:*** You will command great respect wherever you go. Those who may fear you do so because of their own motives, for you are not threatening, using your power to conquer only in defense.

2 GOVERNED BY THE HIGH PRIESTESS: EMOTIONAL GIVENS, OUT OF THE MOTHER
UPRIGHT: This king brings clarity, decisiveness, and means to carry out your emotional goals, much as Joan of Arc was able to do for her passions with sword in early 15th century France. Loyalties run deep in this path. Your creative talent is backed by a drive that will see it expressed one way or another. ***INVERTED:*** Anyone who is foolish enough to slight you, your loved ones, or your loved projects does so clearly at their own peril.

3 GOVERNED BY THE EMPRESS: MENTAL GIVENS, INTELLECTUAL PREDISPOSITION
UPRIGHT: You are infused with the discipline of the head master in your intellectual and practical affairs. A career in education, the military, or the government is an excellent way to use this karmic gift. For you are a harmonious blend of mentor, advisor, manager, and defender. ***INVERTED:*** Your beliefs are clear in your mind as well as your heart and you know how to defend them when they are being threatened.

4 GOVERNED BY THE EMPEROR: SPIRITUAL GIVENS, LIFE PURPOSE
UPRIGHT: Defender to be sure, but also you are strategically involved in the determination of the value of things, in helping decide what is to be protected and worth saving, not just for now but for posterity. ***INVERTED:*** Much of what you will be called upon to save will belong to many others.

5 GOVERNED BY THE HIEROPHANT: SYSTEMS BORN INTO, SOCIETAL INFLUENCE
UPRIGHT: The male point of view predominated. Perhaps born into a military family or to parents who are teachers or public servants. This was a disciplined and ordered atmosphere and you were expected and encouraged to do your very best. ***INVERTED:*** At one extreme, this may have been overly harsh and dogmatic, with more than enough rules to go around. At the other extreme, where you might have expected direction and advice there was very little.

6 GOVERNED BY THE LOVERS: EMOTIONAL TAPES, BASIS FOR RELATING/CREATING
UPRIGHT: Your earliest tapes of imprint are of this protective and knowledgeable father figure, perhaps your own father. But it could be of an older family figure such as a grandfather, or of course someone outside the family, perhaps someone famous whom you came to admire. ***INVERTED:*** Distorted, this otherwise very healthy archetype can become a block instead of a blueprint/foundation for love and creativity. At one extreme, the figure is idolized and idealized and real life will find it hard to compete. At the other extreme, the figure is loathed and by extension either all men or all of certain types of men are not to be loved/trusted.

7 GOVERNED BY THE CHARIOT: PHYSICAL RESOURCES. MEANS TO ACHIEVE
UPRIGHT: You have someone, a family member, a partner, an angel, that you can fall back on. And this shoulder is one who can help you think your way out of a problem as well as fight your way out. ***INVERTED:*** At one extreme, this suggests that the aforementioned may have been your safety net, but that it is not as strong for you at this time. At the other extreme, there may be too much support that you have relied on too heavily for your own independent development.

8 GOVERNED BY STRENGTH: EMOTIONAL RESOURCES, ENERGY
UPRIGHT: This king personifies your strength, and whether this is your own character or that of another, you are fortunate that your emotions are shored up with a bright and dedicated mind, clear on its goals and its loyalties. ***INVERTED:*** At one extreme, you have been able to lean too heavily on this king for your physical and material needs, and it will only slow your independent growth in the Emotional Plane. At the other extreme, you feel less than complete because this piece is missing or not functioning as it should be. This can be disappointed love.

9 GOVERNED BY THE HERMIT: BELIEF SYSTEM, BASIS FOR DECISIONS
UPRIGHT: This is the philosophy of the empire builder, of Alexander the Great, or of Julius Caesar—he tactical military genius, wizard of cultural politics, master of logistics, and governor general. And too, this is Confucianism, the belief in the right and the responsibility of the knowledgeable to administer the needs of society. ***INVERTED:*** At one extreme, this is the despot, who not only knows what is best for everybody, but powerful and willful enough to see that others agree. At the other extreme, this is the anarchist or the freedom fighter who cannot govern once the battle is won.

10 GOVERNED BY THE WHEEL OF FORTUNE: CENTRAL MESSAGE, THEME OF READING
UPRIGHT: Think well on this card for he is coming to you in one guise or another. For there is order to be put in your mental house, to take charge and make things right. More leadership and control is needed here. ***INVERTED:*** Of course, you need to heed the King of Swords for your own benefit, but there are others who depend on you for your intelligence and courage.

11 GOVERNED BY JUSTICE: STATE/CONTENT OF MIND

UPRIGHT: The King of Swords is what you are thinking of at present, either in his person or what he represents. You are taking a stand, having staked out your position. This is your mind at its best, highly rational and well-centered. **INVERTED:** You may think adversely about this king, or he about you. You may believe that aggression is possible.

12 GOVERNED BY THE HANGED MAN: STATE OF EMOTIONS, SUBCONSCIOUS

UPRIGHT: The heart is on this king of the mind. He may be an object of your affection, or the centerpiece of a creative project underway. **INVERTED:** Your heart may be involved with this king, but rather not be. Or, the opposite, this can be the symbol of your heart's sadness over this person. Someone may have been far too assertive or aggressive for this situation.

13 GOVERNED BY DEATH: PHYSICAL SITUATION, HARD REALITY

UPRIGHT: Perhaps the king has been invited to dinner, or to join you at work. Whatever, things are very much in control in your Physical/material Plane. This bodes well for the continued advancement of your ideas and goals. You are ready for action. **INVERTED:** At one extreme, you may have received poor advice or help in your material affairs, or with health. At another extreme, you may be under someone's influence or control that is not in your best interests.

14 GOVERNED BY TEMPERANCE: EMOTIONAL TEST

UPRIGHT: Here comes a mature masculine influence in your near future, and of course it may be delivered in person. As a result you will be more focused and purposeful in your emotional affairs and your creative projects can flourish with such intelligent supervision and assertiveness. **INVERTED:** If this is someone already in your life, this may test your love. At one extreme, this can be too much imposition on you from outside, stifling your individuality and preferences, whether or not the intentions were good.

15 GOVERNED BY THE DEVIL: TEMPTATION/CHALLENGE, FEARS

UPRIGHT: Here on the mental horizon in the near future comes power with a mind to direct it. This can be someone, a confidant with whom you can work toward your goals. Now is the time to assert the leadership and authority to get things done the way you think best. **INVERTED:** If this is someone already in your life, this may show a turn of mind between you. At one extreme, there is too much authority and power.

16 GOVERNED BY THE TOWER: NEXT LESSON, GRACE OF GOD

UPRIGHT: Here is the support, the energy and resources that you need to secure your Mental Plane, and it may well come in the physical personage of the King of Swords. It may, however, be the access to what he represents. Now is the time; you must pull Excalibur from the rock, let it teach you and you will use it well. **INVERTED:** Much of this blessing will be passed through you to others.

17 GOVERNED BY THE STAR: ASPIRATIONS OF EGO, GOALS, MAXIMUM EXPECTATIONS

UPRIGHT: The goal here is to be a father of ideas, to secure the environment from which a well-ordered and dedicated society can mature and flourish. To have knowledge in order to raise the level of civilization. **INVERTED:** The goal should not be to have knowledge in order to control.

18 GOVERNED BY THE MOON: ASPIRATIONS OF HEART, COMPASSION

UPRIGHT: Here the heart of the mentor beats, hoping to influence the improvement of man's condition by sharing all it knows with as many students as will seek it out. **INVERTED:** At an extreme, this can be the pitfall of enjoying too much the feeling of superiority by position of one's knowledge, and the knowledge of one's position.

19 GOVERNED BY THE SUN: PHYSICAL FULFILLMENT/EVALUATION

UPRIGHT: Whether this strong and knowledgeable man has just entered or reentered your life, or is the symbol of its full tour, it bodes well that your material world shows the results of your enterprise and tenacity. **INVERTED:** Let the King of Swords help you to your physical fulfillment.

20 GOVERNED BY JUDGEMENT: HEART'S FULFILLMENT/EVALUATION

UPRIGHT: The King of Swords here can suggest that the life of this person was the centerpiece and the fulfillment of your life. Also, however, it can be the satisfaction of a well-ordered emotional house in which much was accomplished and appreciated by your entire cast of characters. **INVERTED:** Let the King of Swords help you to your heart's fulfillment.

21 GOVERNED BY THE WORLD: EGO'S FULFILLMENT/EVALUATION

UPRIGHT: The Chairman of the Board is pleased because everything got done on time and in good form. **INVERTED:** Let the King of Swords help you to your ego's fulfillment.

22/0 GOVERNED BY THE FOOL: SOUL'S FULFILLMENT/EVALUATION

UPRIGHT: All the right battles have been engaged and won. Territory therefore has been consolidated and efficient administration is in place. **INVERTED:** Let the King of Swords help you to your soul's fulfillment.

KING of WANDS

KING OF WANDS (EARTH/FIRE)

UPRIGHT: Mature male of marriageable age. Physical type: Red to reddish-blond or reddish-brown hair, and fair or freckled complexion with green or blue eyes. Personality type: Intuitive. Spiritual. Vibrant. Fiery. Introspective. Humorous. Father of beliefs. Benevolent. Dedicated. Spiritual advisor. Clergyman. Mystic. Metaphysician. Natural leader. Ruled by the drive of necessity. Think here of the biblical King Saul or King David. *INVERTED:* A distortion of the above characteristics, either to a greater or lesser degree, with the derivative problems. For example: An uncentered man, out of touch, erratic and misguided, with distorted beliefs. No belief in the spiritual level, versus someone addicted to the spiritual. *Note: Remember that the Courts are personifications which carry lessons to be learned, just as any of the Pips or Majors. First, they may represent characteristics of yourself. Second, they may represent people in this incarnation with you (past, present, or future). Third, they may represent people or guides not in the Earth plane with you at this time, including: yourself in past lives, others from this life passed on, others from past lifetimes, and any number of guides in the hierarchy between the Earth plane and God.*

In This Spread Position...Interpret the King Of Wands Meanings to Include:

1 GOVERNED BY THE MAGICIAN: PHYSICAL GIVENS, OUT OF THE FATHER
UPRIGHT: The everyday affairs of your Physical/material Plane will be intricately intertwined with the spiritual business that man must attend to as he goes about his business and pleasure. Your line through your father has accepted much responsibility for administering God's will on earth. *INVERTED:* The father of beliefs must sometimes make decisions which cannot be fully understood by all who are under his care, and can expect some difficulty in getting compliance.

2 GOVERNED BY THE HIGH PRIESTESS: EMOTIONAL GIVENS, OUT OF THE MOTHER
UPRIGHT: Your Emotional Plane will feel the pull of spiritual responsibility. Your heart will demand that your relationships meet the highest standards. You will find that your creative talents will be producing works that embody and convey the essence of the spiritual path, trying to reproduce something of the music of the spheres on your earthly instrument. *INVERTED:* You exude a spiritual energy of openness and closeness that some will mistake for sexuality.

3 GOVERNED BY THE EMPRESS: MENTAL GIVENS, INTELLECTUAL PREDISPOSITION
UPRIGHT: Here is mind sharp and alert, reading all the signs to better interpret the way. Truth is pursued tirelessly and codified for greater understanding by self and others. *INVERTED:* While you are comfortable with others irregardless of their spiritual station, some others will be uncomfortable with you because of yours.

4 GOVERNED BY THE EMPEROR: SPIRITUAL GIVENS, LIFE PURPOSE
UPRIGHT: Yours is a call to leadership of the highest order, to lead others on the path to greater understanding of the spirit. *INVERTED:* Though you are versed with the words, willing in the heart, and capable in body, it will take all these and more to keep the caravan on the right road.

5 GOVERNED BY THE HIEROPHANT: SYSTEMS BORN INTO, SOCIETAL INFLUENCE
UPRIGHT: Your early environment was dominated by a male perspective, albeit an enlightened and spiritual one. This includes almost the entire Western religious and philosophical viewpoint. Although formal religion may not have played a part, there were proper observances of the relationship to the higher order and a spiritual discipline was prevalent. *INVERTED:* At one extreme, a relatively narrow perspective of spirituality and observance may have dominated these early years, creating rejection rather than acceptance.

6 GOVERNED BY THE LOVERS: EMOTIONAL TAPES, BASIS FOR RELATING/CREATING
UPRIGHT: Your earliest tapes of imprint are of this spiritual figure of authority, perhaps your own father. But it could be of an older family figure such as a grandfather, or of course someone outside the family, perhaps someone famous whom you came to admire. *INVERTED:* Distorted, this otherwise very healthy archetype can become a block instead of a blueprint/foundation for love and creativity. At one extreme, the figure is idolized and idealized and real life will find it hard to compete. At the other extreme, the figure is loathed and by extension either all men or all of certain types of men are not to be loved/trusted.

7 GOVERNED BY THE CHARIOT: PHYSICAL RESOURCES. MEANS TO ACHIEVE
UPRIGHT: You have someone—a family, a partner, an angel—that you can fall back on. And this shoulder is one who can show you the greater scope in which your difficulties are resolved as lessons learned. With him by your side no problem will be too great to handle. *INVERTED:* At one extreme, this suggests that the aforementioned may have been your safety net, but that it is not as strong for you at this time. At the other extreme, there may be too much support that you have relied on too heavily for your own independent development.

8 GOVERNED BY STRENGTH: EMOTIONAL RESOURCES, ENERGY
UPRIGHT: This king personifies your strength, and whether this is your own character or that of another, you are fortunate that your emotions are shored up with this instinctive wisdom from your Spiritual Plane intent on seeing you get full pleasure from your loving heart. *INVERTED:* At one extreme, you have been able to lean too heavily on this king for your physical and material needs, and it will only slow your independent growth in the Emotional Plane. At the other extreme, you feel less than complete because this piece is missing or not functioning as it should be. This can be disappointed love.

9 GOVERNED BY THE HERMIT: BELIEF SYSTEM, BASIS FOR DECISIONS
UPRIGHT: Here is the wisdom of Solomon, for you make every human effort to bring to the affairs of men the intelligence that keeps order in the heavens. But this wisdom accepts that man, divinely inspired, is crucial in maintaining this order. Here in the Minor Arcana is the purest energy of the divine right of kings. *INVERTED:* At one extreme, is the divinely inspired soul, which however well intended, attempts too much, accepting and thereby presuming much of God's responsibility/authority. At another extreme, is the man in a position of spiritual leadership who simply presumes too much without good intentions.

10 GOVERNED BY THE WHEEL OF FORTUNE: CENTRAL MESSAGE, THEME OF READING
UPRIGHT: Think well on this card for he is coming to you in one guise or another. For there is order to be put in your spiritual house, to take charge and

make things right. More leadership and control is needed here. ***INVERTED:*** Of course, you need to heed the King of Wands for your own benefit, but there are others who depend on you for your spiritual knowledge.

11 GOVERNED BY JUSTICE: STATE/CONTENT OF MIND
UPRIGHT: The King of Wands occupies your thoughts, either in his person or his characteristics. Clarification of spiritual issues, of messages that affect those who listen to you, is the issue, of formal procedures in spiritual business—this is the nature of your mental moment. ***INVERTED:*** You may think adversely about this king, or he about you. A subversion of the spiritual dogma or message is possible.

12 GOVERNED BY THE HANGED MAN: STATE OF EMOTIONS, SUBCONSCIOUS
UPRIGHT: The King of Wands fills your heart. It may be his person that attracts and occupies you, or his lessons may be part of a creative project on your drawing board. ***INVERTED:*** Your heart may be involved with this king, but rather not be. Or, the opposite, this can be the symbol of your heart's sadness over this person. Spiritual betrayal by one's teacher/mentor can appear here.

13 GOVERNED BY DEATH: PHYSICAL SITUATION, HARD REALITY
UPRIGHT: This king is already in your house of physical/material affairs. Things may be glowing with his presence. Sometimes guardian angels can be very physical. ***INVERTED:*** As good and wonderful for others as this person may be, he seems to be adversely affecting your day to day reality. There are mismatches of all kinds on all levels.

14 GOVERNED BY TEMPERANCE: EMOTIONAL TEST
UPRIGHT: As the mature man with the fiery spirit comes into your Emotional Plane in the near future, you have an opportunity to open up your heart to greater mysteries of appreciation as your emotional vision is enhanced manyfold. ***INVERTED:*** At one extreme, if this is someone already in your life, this may be a test of that relationship. At another extreme, this may represent a disappointment at the formal structure or presentation of a spiritual way.

15 GOVERNED BY THE DEVIL: TEMPTATION/CHALLENGE, FEARS
UPRIGHT: In the near future the mind will be focused on this king or his lessons. Your mind is coming to accept the role of spiritual leadership that lies in its path. ***INVERTED:*** If this is already someone in your life, this may show a turn of mind between you.

16 GOVERNED BY THE TOWER: NEXT LESSON, GRACE OF GOD
UPRIGHT: It is time for you to pick up the wand. You must trust yourself eventually; why not now? This is your next lesson, none other. ***INVERTED:*** Consider carefully accepting this mantle of spiritual leadership for your fellow travelers need you especially at this time.

17 GOVERNED BY THE STAR: ASPIRATIONS OF EGO, GOALS, MAXIMUM EXPECTATIONS
UPRIGHT: This king will try, as did David and Saul before him, to make the lives of those who depend on him much better because he existed. This leader is usually chosen, not self-appointed. ***INVERTED:*** There is a spiritual point of view, which heartedly endorsed by this king, is then presumed to be the best course for all to take, with little enough feedback accepted.

18 GOVERNED BY THE MOON: ASPIRATIONS OF HEART, COMPASSION
UPRIGHT: Here beats the heart of a true spiritual leader, keeping time with the heartbeats of his followers. This leader is the outgrowth of the aspirations of his people. There is benevolence here without condescension. ***INVERTED:*** At one extreme, this king can fall prey to the adoration of his followers, allowing and even encouraging the love that belongs to God to stop at his feet.

19 GOVERNED BY THE SUN: PHYSICAL FULFILLMENT/EVALUATION
UPRIGHT: This can suggest the appearance or reappearance of this fiery personality in the flesh, or the magic of his character. Whichever, you can be content in your well-centered world with all the right things to occupy your time. ***INVERTED:*** Let the King of Wands help you to your physical fulfillment.

20 GOVERNED BY JUDGEMENT: HEART'S FULFILLMENT/EVALUATION
UPRIGHT: The King of Wands here can suggest that the life of this person was the centerpiece and the fulfillment of your life. Also, however, it can be the satisfaction of a spiritually motivated emotional house which achieved love on the purest and most meaningful levels. ***INVERTED:*** Let the King of Wands help you to your heart's fulfillment.

21 GOVERNED BY THE WORLD: EGO'S FULFILLMENT/EVALUATION
UPRIGHT: You have proven mind to be the key to true understanding when backed up by a pure and devoted heart. ***INVERTED:*** Let the King of Wands help you to your ego's fulfillment.

22/0 GOVERNED BY THE FOOL: SOUL'S FULFILLMENT/EVALUATION
UPRIGHT: Your leadership has been exemplary. To lead by divine right is also to lead at the will of the people. ***INVERTED:*** Let the King of Wands help you to your soul's fulfillment.

QUEEN OF PENTACLES

QUEEN OF PENTACLES (WATER/EARTH)

UPRIGHT: Mature female of marriageable age. Physical type: Dark hair with dark complexion and dark eyes. Also, black hair with very fair complexion and light blue, green, or violet eyes. Personality type: Dependable. Resourceful. Can-doer. Watchful. Generous. Good instincts. Good physical leader. Great endurance. Ruled by the drive of the heart. Mother/provider. Mother Earth. Naturalist. Concern for physical health and the safety of the family. Nourishment. Food preparer/dietician. Hygienist. Physical health care. Doctor. Nurse. Bodywork. Athlete. Gardener. Businesswoman. Retailer. Accountant. Channel for practical information. **INVERTED:** A distortion of the above characteristics, either to a greater or lesser degree, with the derivative problems. For example: Irresponsible versus doting. Disregard for nature versus extreme interest in and identity with environmental factors. Abuse of material items. Bad money manager. Recurrent health problems versus the health fanatic. **Note:** *Remember that the Courts are personifications which carry lessons to be learned, just as any of the Pips or Majors. First, they may represent characteristics of yourself. Second, they may represent people in this incarnation with you (past, present, or future). Third, they may represent people or guides not in the Earth plane with you at this time, including: yourself in past lives, others from this life passed on, others from past lifetimes, and any number of guides in the hierarchy between the Earth plane and God.*

In This Spread Position...Interpret the Queen Of Pentacles Meanings to Include:

1 GOVERNED BY THE MAGICIAN: PHYSICAL GIVENS, OUT OF THE FATHER
UPRIGHT: Your Physical/material Plane will be guided by a sensitivity to things of the Earth, nature and all her offspring. Many of the secrets of good health are revealed in you. This Queen well symbolizes the dual role that the working mother in contemporary society must fill—that of nurturer, but also that of provider. This is the same duality which for the working father was the reverse, that of provider, but also that of nurturer. **INVERTED:** Blending the feminine and masculine here may be a challenge.

2 GOVERNED BY THE HIGH PRIESTESS: EMOTIONAL GIVENS, OUT OF THE MOTHER
UPRIGHT: Your Emotional/creative Plane will show a bias to things natural, i.e., down to earth people, living plants, cotton and silk clothing, wood, organic foods and vegetarianism. You are touch oriented and your relationships will be literally close. Your physical talents help you immensely in this plane. Your creative talents are well-suited to handwork and crafts. **INVERTED:** Some may be put off by your level of independence and forthrightness.

3 GOVERNED BY THE EMPRESS: MENTAL GIVENS, INTELLECTUAL PREDISPOSITION
UPRIGHT: Your Mental Plane will be both pragmatic and humane. Productivity is important, but people and the natural order of things comes first. Your preferred subject matter is things of the Earth plane, concerning yourself with ways to make things more abundant, more comfortable for people. **INVERTED:** You will not always have to have a conscious reason for doing something, as you have a good working relationship with elemental, instinctive sources.

4 GOVERNED BY THE EMPEROR: SPIRITUAL GIVENS, LIFE PURPOSE
UPRIGHT: Here is the goddess of agriculture, the likes of the Greek Demeter, and in the Minor Arcana the closest archetype to the concept of Gaia, the living Earth. This is the energy that runs through this lifetime for you and will see you working steadily for as much and as long as it takes to get things done. You are keenly sensitive to the rhythms of nature, that things must be done in their season and on time or there will be no harvest. **INVERTED:** Many will look to you, as those who wait to see which fork the hostess picks up first.

5 GOVERNED BY THE HIEROPHANT: SYSTEMS BORN INTO, SOCIETAL INFLUENCE
UPRIGHT: Born into a farm community, or into a setting where homecooked meals were interspersed with homebaked goodies. Pets allowed, and in the house to boot. Exposure and immersion in a setting governed by natural processes so that you were able to observe many basic laws at work first hand. **INVERTED:** At one extreme, this archetype distorts to things too natural, to a lack of civilized organization, and a tendency towards turning the clock back.

6 GOVERNED BY THE LOVERS: EMOTIONAL TAPES, BASIS FOR RELATING/CREATING
UPRIGHT: Here is the sort of passion that might fill the heart of a young rural girl or boy in the Future Farmers of America, with a prize winning lamb in the county fair, or of the city boy or girl with a prize winning experiment at the science fair. Here is a love for how things live and work. This may also be a mother figure, real or idealized. **INVERTED:** A mother figure may be distorted, even rejected. Also, at an extreme, this archetype can become an obsession with nature and/or science.

7 GOVERNED BY THE CHARIOT: PHYSICAL RESOURCES. MEANS TO ACHIEVE
UPRIGHT: This may be a family member or other person on whom you can fall back. It can also suggest that you have very basic, healthy processes and instincts that serve you well. You are in harmony with your surroundings and should have many a safe harbor if you need it. **INVERTED:** You may not have that person you have always counted on before to help in this situation. At another extreme, you have been less than efficient in your relationship to your environment.

8 GOVERNED BY STRENGTH: EMOTIONAL RESOURCES, ENERGY
UPRIGHT: This queen personifies your strength. She may represent your own character or that of another. Whichever, you have ended up with her qualities of security and endurance in your relationships and your creative endeavors, because you have kept things simple and direct, reducing confusion to a bare minimum. **INVERTED:** This can suggest that there has been too much work and pragmatism, lack of comforts, for the heart to find room for its activities. This can be a disappointed love.

9 GOVERNED BY THE HERMIT: BELIEF SYSTEM, BASIS FOR DECISIONS
UPRIGHT: Here is the Law of Parsimony, the principle of conservation, whereby everything that exists must be respected and if used for the benefit of something else, it is to be used sparingly, and efficiently, with a minimum of energy and maximum of output for a given input. This is the invention of agriculture in response to these principles, wherein one conserves and preserves, extending the past into the future. It is the origin and root of domesticity. **INVERTED:** At one extreme, there is more of the hunter/gatherer here than the farmer, with a mentality, however, of little attention to conservation and efficiency, little thought to tomorrow, and hence less appreciation for the present. This can be a rejection of civilization and what it stands for.

10 GOVERNED BY THE WHEEL OF FORTUNE: CENTRAL MESSAGE, THEME OF READING
UPRIGHT: Think well on this card for she is coming to you in one guise or another. As a guide and source of inspiration, she is directing your attention to

your physical/material house, that you may increase the efficiency there. ***INVERTED:*** This suggests that you are needed to help another or others with their physical/material house, especially diet, exercise and health matters, and/or environmental concerns.

11 GOVERNED BY JUSTICE: STATE/CONTENT OF MIND
UPRIGHT: Your mind is on this queen. She may represent a rise in consciousness for the Physical Plane and its programs, such as environmental awareness or concern for health, diet, exercise. ***INVERTED:*** You may think adversely about this queen, or she about you. As an aspect of yourself, you may be avoiding thinking about the appropriateness and efficiency of your actions in physical/material matters.

12 GOVERNED BY THE HANGED MAN: STATE OF EMOTIONS, SUBCONSCIOUS
UPRIGHT: Your heart is on this queen. She may be an object of your affection, or the centerpiece of a creative project underway. Her programs may dominate your feelings. ***INVERTED:*** Your heart may be involved with the queen, but rather not be. Or, the opposite, this can be the symbol of your heart's sadness over this person.

13 GOVERNED BY DEATH: PHYSICAL SITUATION, HARD REALITY
UPRIGHT: The queen is in your house. This archetype can make a house a home full of health and vitality, and good things to eat, for of all the queens she is the better cook. ***INVERTED:*** There may be disharmony between this archetype and your Physical/material Plane. The atmosphere will be less than pleasant until it is satisfied.

14 GOVERNED BY TEMPERANCE: EMOTIONAL TEST
UPRIGHT: This queen is on your emotional horizon in the near future. If she is not presenting herself in person, then earthly matters are pulling at your heart. How are you and your extended family of loved ones relating to your surroundings, to nature? ***INVERTED:*** If this is someone already in your life there are emotions to deal with here, as one or the other of you turn away.

15 GOVERNED BY THE DEVIL: TEMPTATION/CHALLENGE, FEARS
UPRIGHT: This queen is on your mental horizon in the near future. If she is not presenting herself in person, then the archetype is demanding attention to her programs. It is important to the realization of your goals that you integrate more of her principles into your work. ***INVERTED:*** If this represents someone already in your life, this may show a turn of mind between you. There may be a tendency to fear the forces of nature, that shows up in a propensity for too much civilization, too much technology in your solutions.

16 GOVERNED BY THE TOWER: NEXT LESSON, GRACE OF GOD
UPRIGHT: Here is the support, the energy and resources that you need to enhance your Physical/material Plane, and it may well come in the physical personage of the Queen of Pentacles. It may however, be the access to what she represents. Here are resources and replenishment for your basic needs. ***INVERTED:*** Much of this blessing will be passed through you to others.

17 GOVERNED BY THE STAR: ASPIRATIONS OF EGO, GOALS, MAXIMUM EXPECTATIONS
UPRIGHT: You want to extract as much of the Earth's treasures as man requires for his needs, but in a way that brings increase in return to the Earth itself. For you, if done properly, both nature and man (as a subset of nature) will increase together. ***INVERTED:*** At one extreme, this is to think of man in his/her dominion over nature and all its contents. A misunderstanding of civilization.

18 GOVERNED BY THE MOON: ASPIRATIONS OF HEART, COMPASSION
UPRIGHT: You want to be instrumental in making the Earth a true garden of Eden, with nature and man supporting each other in complete harmony as is meant to be. This is a marvelous blend of active and passive, for you actively pursue finding your natural position in the scheme of things. ***INVERTED:*** A desire for the unnatural, as Demeter had to pursue her daughter Persephone after her abduction into the underworld by Pluto.

19 GOVERNED BY THE SUN: PHYSICAL FULFILLMENT/EVALUATION
UPRIGHT: This queen is the pot of gold at the end of your rainbow, be she a person or the symbol of your material well-being. You are able to enjoy the rewards of your work in comfort. ***INVERTED:*** Let the Queen of Pentacles help you to your physical fulfillment.

20 GOVERNED BY JUDGEMENT: HEART'S FULFILLMENT/EVALUATION
UPRIGHT: The queen here can suggest that the love of this person was the centerpiece and the fulfillment of your life. She symbolizes the depth of physical comfort and pleasure afforded you by your family and friends. ***INVERTED:*** Let the Queen of Pentacles help you to your heart's fulfillment.

21 GOVERNED BY THE WORLD: EGO'S FULFILLMENT/EVALUATION
UPRIGHT: You have done much to secure the healthy relationship between man and the environment. Another related legacy is the advancement of natural health care as opposed to conventional allopathic medicine. ***INVERTED:*** Let the Queen of Pentacles help you to your ego's fulfillment.

22/0 GOVERNED BY THE FOOL: SOUL'S FULFILLMENT/EVALUATION
UPRIGHT: Like Alice, you too have seen your Wonderland, but yours was on this side of the mirror. ***INVERTED:*** Let the Queen of Pentacles help you to your soul's fulfillment.

QUEEN of CUPS.

QUEEN OF CUPS (WATER/WATER)

UPRIGHT: Mature female of marriageable age. Physical type: Light brown to sandy-blonde hair and medium complexion, sometimes olive, with brown, blue or gray-blue eyes. Personality type: Emotional. Sensitive. creative. Dedicated. Motivated. Sensual. Tender. Soothing. Loving mother. Ruled by the drive of the heart. Involved with family, friends, fellow workers. Frequently the center of the group. Confident. Involved in the Arts. Leader/volunteer. Healer by example. Nurturer. Channel for love. Creative. Psychic abilities. Enchantress. Nurse for emotional wounds. Extroverted saleslady. Product representative. Artist. Designer. Decorator. Counselor. ***INVERTED:*** A distortion of the above characteristics, either to a greater or lesser degree, with the derivative problems. For example: Unnurturing, neglectful, unloving. Cool personality. Also, smothering love, overattachment, oversentimental. Creative block. Siren. Incorrect development/use of psychic abilities. ***Note:*** *Remember that the Courts are personifications which carry lessons to be learned, just as any of the Pips or Majors. First, they may represent characteristics of yourself. Second, they may represent people in this incarnation with you (past, present, or future). Third, they may represent people or guides not in the Earth plane with you at this time, including: yourself in past lives, others from this life passed on, others from past lifetimes, and any number of guides in the hierarchy between the Earth plane and God.*

In This Spread Position...Interpret the Queen Of Cups Meanings to Include:

1 GOVERNED BY THE MAGICIAN: PHYSICAL GIVENS, OUT OF THE FATHER
UPRIGHT: Your Physical/material Plane will be highly sensual with an insistence on beauty and aesthetics in everything around you. There will be an intimacy in the affairs of this plane as you prefer direct involvement and personal experience. ***INVERTED:*** Some may accuse you of only liking what is beautiful to the eye, but you can prove them wrong by seeking the potential for love in all things, the inner beauty.

2 GOVERNED BY THE HIGH PRIESTESS: EMOTIONAL GIVENS, OUT OF THE MOTHER
UPRIGHT: Your Pmotional/creative Plane will be open and loving, enabling many others to share your appreciation for life. You will have deep resources of energy for your creative projects as your potential for love grows and grows. ***INVERTED:*** Some will accuse you of being too generous with your affections, but only because they are not as open as you.

3 GOVERNED BY THE EMPRESS: MENTAL GIVENS, INTELLECTUAL PREDISPOSITION
UPRIGHT: Your Mental Plane will be dedicated to many of the causes of the heart. Here is the frame of mind for the leader/volunteer, the psychic/author, and the mother turned humorist/writer. It also suggests an informal and soft tone in intellectual matters. ***INVERTED:*** Some will find the subjectivity of your approach hard to work with.

4 GOVERNED BY THE EMPEROR: SPIRITUAL GIVENS, LIFE PURPOSE
UPRIGHT: You will be the source of love and inspiration to many. Through you they will learn to see the beauty that caring attention can extract from the mundane. ***INVERTED:*** You may be asked to teach love and beauty in some difficult classrooms to some very needy students.

5 GOVERNED BY THE HIEROPHANT: SYSTEMS BORN INTO, SOCIETAL INFLUENCE
UPRIGHT: This early environment will have felt very matriarchal. Most likely, children and their related needs were the top priority. ***INVERTED:*** At one extreme, mothering may have been too strong, with an exceptionally short apron string and undo fears. At the other extreme, mothering may have been too weak, with lack of supervision and little concern for health and safety.

6 GOVERNED BY THE LOVERS: EMOTIONAL TAPES, BASIS FOR RELATING/CREATING
UPRIGHT: The ideal of motherhood is strongest with this archetype, and for this child playing with dolls may have been serious business. This may also be a mother figure, real or idealized. ***INVERTED:*** A mother figure may be distorted, even rejected. Also, at an extreme, this archetype can have a idealized vision, or a negative vision, of motherhood flavoring the emotions in the present.

7 GOVERNED BY THE CHARIOT: PHYSICAL RESOURCES. MEANS TO ACHIEVE
UPRIGHT: This may be a family member or other person on whom you can fall back. This also suggests that you have a vast network of caring friends and associates that are there if you need them. ***INVERTED:*** You may not have that person you have always counted on before to help in this situation. At another extreme, you have been less than efficient in your relationship to your environment.

8 GOVERNED BY STRENGTH: EMOTIONAL RESOURCES, ENERGY
UPRIGHT: This queen personifies your strength. She may represent your own character or that of another. Whichever, much of your strength is inherent in the fact that others need you to be strong for them. Your strength is that you cannot afford to be weak. More than that, it is your desire to be able to help others that keeps you vibrant and ready. ***INVERTED:*** Perhaps even you can have limits to how much you can give, in a given period of time. Figure out how you can refuel, for you must receive equally in some form or another, the same amount of energy that you put out. This can be a disappointed love.

9 GOVERNED BY THE HERMIT: BELIEF SYSTEM, BASIS FOR DECISIONS
UPRIGHT: Here is a fundamental belief in the power of love, with a good measure of that being physical, practical, hands-on attention. For instance, this includes a belief in the therapeutic effect of touch, the healing presence. And turned slightly to another of its facets, this is the belief in beauty itself as a conjunction of love and order. ***INVERTED:*** At one extreme, this can be the belief in the power of love to manipulate or control, as in the domineering mother.

10 GOVERNED BY THE WHEEL OF FORTUNE: CENTRAL MESSAGE, THEME OF READING
UPRIGHT: Think well on this card for she is coming to you in one guise or another. As a guide and source of inspiration, she is directing your attention to your emotional/creative house, that you may increase the efficiency there. ***INVERTED:*** This suggests that you are needed to help another or others with their emotional/creative house, to improve the flow of energy and allow more contact and pleasure.

11 GOVERNED BY JUSTICE: STATE/CONTENT OF MIND
UPRIGHT: Your mind is on this queen. You may be preparing to make a very generous offer. Or, you may be planning something very amorous. ***INVERTED:*** You may think adversely about this queen, or she about you. You may be planning to seduce someone with your winsome charm.

12 GOVERNED BY THE HANGED MAN: STATE OF EMOTIONS, SUBCONSCIOUS

UPRIGHT: Your heart is on this queen, and how appropriate, for she is the queen of hearts. She may be the object of your affection, or the centerpiece of a creative project underway. Her programs dominate your feelings. *INVERTED:* Your heart may be involved with the queen, but rather not be. Or, the opposite, this can be the symbol of your heart's sadness over this person.

13 GOVERNED BY DEATH: PHYSICAL SITUATION, HARD REALITY

UPRIGHT: The queen is making herself at home in your physical/material house. This should be quite nice to watch as everything takes on the special glow from her reflection. Your material affairs are being nourished and should produce new growth. *INVERTED:* You may be under the serious influence, even seduction, of this lady.

14 GOVERNED BY TEMPERANCE: EMOTIONAL TEST

UPRIGHT: This queen is on your emotional horizon in the near future. If she is not presenting herself in person, then emotional or creative matters are pulling at your heart. Your heart is accepting greater responsibility. *INVERTED:* If this is someone already in your life, there are emotions to deal with here as one or the other of you turn away.

15 GOVERNED BY THE DEVIL: TEMPTATION/CHALLENGE, FEARS

UPRIGHT: This queen is on your mental horizon in the near future. If she is not presenting herself in person, then the archetype is demanding attention to her programs. It is important to the realization of your goals that you integrate more of her principles into your work. *INVERTED:* If this represents someone already in your life, this may show a turn of mind between you. You may fear the power and responsibility of love, either in a romantic situation or the responsibility of mothering, of caring intensely after others.

16 GOVERNED BY THE TOWER: NEXT LESSON, GRACE OF GOD

UPRIGHT: Here is the support, the energy and resources that you need to enhance your Emotional/creative Plane, and it may well come in the physical personage of the Queen of Cups. It may however, be access to what she represents. She brings a soothing and healing balm with her. *INVERTED:* Much of this blessing will be passed through you to others.

17 GOVERNED BY THE STAR: ASPIRATIONS OF EGO, GOALS, MAXIMUM EXPECTATIONS

UPRIGHT: Short of being able to "mother" the world yourself, you will work to see that the ideals and nurturing principles of motherhood are upheld in our institutions, from schools to government. *INVERTED:* At one extreme, this can distort into the problems of over-socialization and the welfare state, undermining independence and ultimately spiritual growth.

18 GOVERNED BY THE MOON: ASPIRATIONS OF HEART, COMPASSION

UPRIGHT: As with the aspirations of mind above, short of being able to "mother" the world yourself, you will work to see that everyone has the benefits of this absolutely essential exposure to elementary love, for this is the front line of God's love, the extended hand to guide the way ultimately to universal love. *INVERTED:* At one extreme, there will be an attempt to be and do all this mothering beyond reason. This can easily be the pitfall of attachment.

19 GOVERNED BY THE SUN: PHYSICAL FULFILLMENT/EVALUATION

UPRIGHT: With this queen at the end of your Physical Plane, your life is a living valentine. Your entire environment could be a healing center run on the energy of love. There may be a great deal of water to keep you company. *INVERTED:* Let the Queen of Cups help you to your physical fulfillment.

20 GOVERNED BY JUDGEMENT: HEART'S FULFILLMENT/EVALUATION

UPRIGHT: The queen here can suggest that the love of this person was the centerpiece and the fulfillment of your life. She symbolizes the depth of emotional reward that your relationships and creative talents have brought you. Your arms have comforted and healed many. *INVERTED:* Let the Queen of Cups help you to your heart's fulfillment.

21 GOVERNED BY THE WORLD: EGO'S FULFILLMENT/EVALUATION

UPRIGHT: You have brought the healing power of love into the domain of mind, explaining much that was heretofore unexplained. *INVERTED:* Let the Queen of Cups help you to your ego's fulfillment.

22/0 GOVERNED BY THE FOOL: SOUL'S FULFILLMENT/EVALUATION

UPRIGHT: You have drunk liberally from the cup of life, but left it full to the brim for those who follow. *INVERTED:* Let the Queen of Cups help you to your soul's fulfillment.

QUEEN of SWORDS.

QUEEN OF SWORDS (WATER/AIR)

UPRIGHT: Mature female of marriageable age. Physical type: Blonde to light blonde hair and fair complexion with blue, blue-gray or greenish-brown eyes. Personality type: Mental. Assertive. Perfectionist. Protective, ambitious mother. Mother of solutions. Philosophical. Studious. Alert. Direct. Good director and planner. A knowledgeable leader. Tactician. Fighter. Mother of ideas and ideals. Ruled by the drive of the heart. Pilot. Teacher. Professor. Principal. Librarian. Historian. Mentor. Researcher. Highly informed. Good communicator. Mother of technology, of invention. Channel for thought. Here is the source of the will to achieve, to maximize the potential of the self. **INVERTED:** A distortion of the above characteristics, either to a greater or lesser degree, with the derivative problems. For example: An aggressive woman versus unrealized potential. A mother too busy for her family versus the mother who is always there, looking over your shoulder. Bad planner versus the over planner. Idealist to a fault. **Note:** *Remember that the Courts are personifications which carry lessons to be learned, just as any of the Pips or Majors. First, they may represent characteristics of yourself. Second, they may represent people in this incarnation with you (past, present, or future). Third, they may represent people or guides not in the Earth plane with you at this time, including: yourself in past lives, others from this life passed on, others from past lifetimes, and any number of guides in the hierarchy between the Earth plane and God.*

In This Spread Position...Interpret the Queen Of Swords Meanings to Include:

1 GOVERNED BY THE MAGICIAN: PHYSICAL GIVENS, OUT OF THE FATHER
UPRIGHT: Your Physical/material Plane will be a careful blend of mind and heart like that of the administrative and organizing half of motherhood that balances the nurturer. Home and work will bear the mark of an efficient planner and things will always be in their assigned place. **INVERTED:** Some may have a little trouble relaxing in environments that you find absolutely perfect.

2 GOVERNED BY THE HIGH PRIESTESS: EMOTIONAL GIVENS, OUT OF THE MOTHER
UPRIGHT: In your Emotional/creative Plane you will be independent by nature and not easily committed, but very loyal to those who have won your love and trust. You are very energetic and highly motivated in those relationships and creative endeavors that appeal to your heart. Your emotions are focused and you are always in charge of them, never the other way around. **INVERTED:** Some may feel slighted that they did not make the cut into your inner circle.

3 GOVERNED BY THE EMPRESS: MENTAL GIVENS, INTELLECTUAL PREDISPOSITION
UPRIGHT: In your Mental Plane there will be great clarity and decisiveness, but always with an open mind. There is a fierce determination here for seeing worthwhile causes through to completion, with a combination of iron will and caring heart. You may well make your living as some sort of educator. In groups you are frequently the source of ideas. **INVERTED:** Some might find you somewhat unyielding once you have identified a goal.

4 GOVERNED BY THE EMPEROR: SPIRITUAL GIVENS, LIFE PURPOSE
UPRIGHT: Here the intellect is applied to nurturing and caring. Here is society's librarian who is guardian of our collective knowledge, our recorded history. This is the spirit that modern society is witnessing at the turn of the twenty-first century, the spirit that asserts equal priority of the feminine principle. This is the warrior female whose causes are passions worth fighting to the death for. Joan of Arc lives in this archetype. **INVERTED:** You will be called on to be the champion for many who need your courage.

5 GOVERNED BY THE HIEROPHANT: SYSTEMS BORN INTO, SOCIETAL INFLUENCE
UPRIGHT: Discipline and order may have been more obvious than tender,. love, and care, yet this was a safe and encouraging environment in which your best interests were of importance. **INVERTED:** At one extreme, there may have been more discipline than necessary and you may have been pushed to excel. In some cases there may have been little obvious love, and for some even abuse may have been the norm.

6 GOVERNED BY THE LOVERS: EMOTIONAL TAPES, BASIS FOR RELATING/CREATING
UPRIGHT: Here is the passion for knowledge, for gnosis, an early understanding of the central importance of learning which enables us to be fully human and to realize and maximize our potential. Here is the source of mental will which merges with emotional desire to move us upward. This is ambition in a young heart. **INVERTED:** At one extreme, you may be driven to achieve, to establish control over your affairs, and if needed, the affairs of others.

7 GOVERNED BY THE CHARIOT: PHYSICAL RESOURCES. MEANS TO ACHIEVE
UPRIGHT: This may be someone, perhaps a family member on whom you can fall back. The advice you receive here is most important. This could also suggest that your own independence is your greatest asset. You react quickly, stepping into the breach of any problem to nip it in the bud. **INVERTED:** At one extreme, you may try to be much more independent than is necessary or wise.

8 GOVERNED BY STRENGTH: EMOTIONAL RESOURCES, ENERGY
UPRIGHT: You are stronger than most because you have the objectivity that many lack in matters emotional. No one who knows you would even consider taking advantage of you. Your relationships and creative projects work because they are so soundly rooted in reality. **INVERTED:** At one extreme, you may be so overtly strong that you are ironically making yourself weaker in this plane by denying yourself some healthy situations. Too much independence perhaps. This can be a disappointed love.

9 GOVERNED BY THE HERMIT: BELIEF SYSTEM, BASIS FOR DECISIONS
UPRIGHT: A clean mind for you is a pure heart as well, and you will work to make everything fit into place in your ideology. Here is faith in man's mind, in his inventive nature and capacity. You seek to understand history, your present surroundings, and the future. This is the belief in Sophia, wisdom as the path. This is the root of Gnosticism, the movement with the power of mind toward the center of all that is, which is a female divinity, nameless and unknowable, prior to creation and the male creator god of the western Judaeo-Christian tradition. **INVERTED:** The pitfall here is like that of many mental systems, that belief can all too easily become dogma, and be used to justify actions.

10 GOVERNED BY THE WHEEL OF FORTUNE: CENTRAL MESSAGE, THEME OF READING
UPRIGHT: Think well on this card for she is coming to you in one guise or another. As a guide and source of inspiration, she is directing your attention to your mental house, that you may increase the efficiency there. **INVERTED:** This suggests that you are needed to help another or others with their mental house, to improve communication and bring order.

11 GOVERNED BY JUSTICE: STATE/CONTENT OF MIND

UPRIGHT: Much of this queen's energy is in the Major Arcana card Justice, which governs this very position in the spread. Your thoughts are very much on the entire process of centering, of balancing forces, and of mental projects. You may, of course, be thinking of this queen personified. *INVERTED:* You may think adversely about this queen, or she about you. As an aspect of yourself, you may be avoiding thinking about your mental affairs.

12 GOVERNED BY THE HANGED MAN: STATE OF EMOTIONS, SUBCONSCIOUS

UPRIGHT: Perhaps your heart is on this queen. She may be an object of your affection, or the centerpiece of a creative project underway. Her programs may dominate your feelings. *INVERTED:* Your heart may be involved with the queen, but rather not be. Or, the opposite, this can be the symbol of your heart's sadness over this person.

13 GOVERNED BY DEATH: PHYSICAL SITUATION, HARD REALITY

UPRIGHT: This queen is in your house. This archetype will bring authority and direction to your material affairs. She may give everyone a list of things to do. *INVERTED:* Just who does this queen think she is anyway? The problem here may be in how to get her out of your house while you still can.

14 GOVERNED BY TEMPERANCE: EMOTIONAL TEST

UPRIGHT: This queen is in your emotional house in the near future. If she is not presenting herself in person, then mental matters are pulling at your heart. Another possibility is that you are to be much more alert and responsible in your emotional and creative affairs. *INVERTED:* If this is someone already in your life, there are emotions to deal with here as one or the other of you turn away.

15 GOVERNED BY THE DEVIL: TEMPTATION/CHALLENGE, FEARS

UPRIGHT: This queen is on your mental horizon in the near future. If she is not presenting herself in person, then the archetype is demanding attention to her programs. It is important to the realization of your goals that you integrate more of her principles into your work. *INVERTED:* If this represents someone already in your life, this may show a turn of mind between you. There may some fear of authority. Or, there may be abuse of authority.

16 GOVERNED BY THE TOWER: NEXT LESSON, GRACE OF GOD

UPRIGHT: Here is the support, the energy and resources that you need to enhance your Mental Plane, and it may well come in the physical personage of the Queen of Swords. It may however, be the access to what she represents. She brings the knowledge and courage you need to formulate and advance your goals. *INVERTED:* Much of this blessing will be passed through you to others.

17 GOVERNED BY THE STAR: ASPIRATIONS OF EGO, GOALS, MAXIMUM EXPECTATIONS

UPRIGHT: This is the goal to have the knowledge that provides an overview, an ability to administer, to manage the affairs of man that advance what we have come to know as civilization. The more specialized mind may aspire to invent something that will improve the quality of life. *INVERTED:* Distortions of the ego may desire all of the aforementioned, but with much more personal gain in mind.

18 GOVERNED BY THE MOON: ASPIRATIONS OF HEART, COMPASSION

UPRIGHT: This heart aspires to knowledge and the civilized state it fosters as the means to greater love and understanding between men, and between man and nature. It not only adheres to the saying that a mind is a terrible thing to waste, but it knows that our potential for sin lies not in failing to achieve, but in not trying to the best of our ability. *INVERTED:* At one extreme, this hunger for knowledge can distort and destroy rather than foster love.

19 GOVERNED BY THE SUN: PHYSICAL FULFILLMENT/EVALUATION

UPRIGHT: Everywhere in your surroundings is evidence of your inventiveness, and an appropriateness and sense of belonging in your material comforts. The efficiency expert has left her mark. *INVERTED:* Let the Queen of Swords help you to your physical fulfillment.

20 GOVERNED BY JUDGEMENT: HEART'S FULFILLMENT/EVALUATION

UPRIGHT: The queen here can suggest that the love of this person was the centerpiece and the fulfillment of your life. She symbolizes the depth of mental reward that your relationships and creative talents have brought you. Your words have comforted and healed many. *INVERTED:* Let the Queen of Swords help you to your heart's fulfillment.

21 GOVERNED BY THE WORLD: EGO'S FULFILLMENT/EVALUATION

UPRIGHT: Your mind has been sharp and effective, but with such a delicate and human touch. There is a physical record to this legacy, so that others may build on what you have accomplished. *INVERTED:* Let the Queen of Swords help you to your ego's fulfillment.

22/0 GOVERNED BY THE FOOL: SOUL'S FULFILLMENT/EVALUATION

UPRIGHT: In discovering more of your own and thus man's capacity for growth, you have come to know a bigger and better God. *INVERTED:* Let the Queen of Swords help you to your soul's fulfillment.

QUEEN OF WANDS (WATER/FIRE)

UPRIGHT: Mature female of marriageable age. Physical type: Red to reddish-blonde or reddish-brown hair and fair or freckled complexion with green or blue eyes. Personality type: Intuitive. Spiritual. Vibrant. Fiery. Introspective. Humorous. Mother of beliefs. Benevolent. Dedicated. Philosophical guide. Spiritual advisor. Spiritual nurse. Mystic. Metaphysician. Natural leader by example. Ruled by the drive of the heart. Channel for divine insight. Inner confidence. Spiritual energy/drive. Here are Hildegard of Bingen, 12th century mystic in the school of Western thought, and Anandamayi Ma, contemporary Indian mast/god-intoxicate, in the school of Eastern thought. **INVERTED:** A distortion of the above characteristics, either to a greater or lesser degree, with the derivative problems. For example: A fire and brimstone personality. Out of touch with reality. Undeveloped spirituality. **Note:** *Remember that the Courts are personifications which carry lessons to be learned, just as any of the Pips or Majors. First, they may represent characteristics of yourself. Second, they may represent people in this incarnation with you (past, present, or future). Third, they may represent people or guides not in the Earth plane with you at this time, including: yourself in past lives, others from this life passed on, others from past lifetimes, and any number of guides in the hierarchy between the Earth plane and God.*

In This Spread Position...Interpret the Queen Of Wands Meanings to Include:

1 GOVERNED BY THE MAGICIAN: PHYSICAL GIVENS, OUT OF THE FATHER
UPRIGHT: Your day to day affairs in the Physical/material Plane will be very much determined by your willingness and desire to serve at the direction of spiritual guides in all matters. Here sensitivity to messages is extreme and the body responds virtually automatically to divine will. This is divine will at work in the front lines, such as with Mother Theresa in India. **INVERTED:** Evidence of divine presence in a person can be either reassuring or discomforting to witnesses.

2 GOVERNED BY THE HIGH PRIESTESS: EMOTIONAL GIVENS, OUT OF THE MOTHER
UPRIGHT: Your day to day affairs in the Emotional/creative Plane will be very much determined by your willingness and desire to serve at the direction of spiritual guides in all matters. Here your sensitivity keeps you so centered in receiving your messages that your relationships will be caught up in the same wave of inspiration with you. Everything that you do with others and to express your reactions through your talents will bear witness to your experience of spiritual reality. **INVERTED:** The difficulty here is to see and use this spiritual awareness in the real world.

3 GOVERNED BY THE EMPRESS: MENTAL GIVENS, INTELLECTUAL PREDISPOSITION
UPRIGHT: This may be where Hildegard of Bingen best belongs, for the continuing inspiration she shares through her literary record of her experiences in letters, songs, and sermons. Such is the nature of this path—to give to others evidence of the lessons you have received through divine inspiration. **INVERTED:** The test here is to continue to share, to teach, whether or not there are many who will listen, much less understand.

4 GOVERNED BY THE EMPEROR: SPIRITUAL GIVENS, LIFE PURPOSE
UPRIGHT: Yours is to bear witness to everything you experience, sharing your entire life at all of its levels and in so doing motivate others to do likewise. This is to show the correctness of things in your actions so that others may follow. **INVERTED:** In the extreme, this can be a lifetime given over entirely to getting more of God's message into the Earth plane. It can be much more difficult for those around you than for you who understand what is taking place.

5 GOVERNED BY THE HIEROPHANT: SYSTEMS BORN INTO, SOCIETAL INFLUENCE
UPRIGHT: Your early environment was dominated by a female perspective, albeit an enlightened and spiritual one. This is much more likely to have been the Eastern religious and philosophical viewpoint. Although formal religion may not have played a part, there were proper observances of man's relationship to the higher order and a spiritual discipline was prevalent. **INVERTED:** At one extreme, a relatively narrow perspective of spirituality and observance may have dominated these early years, creating rejection rather than acceptance.

6 GOVERNED BY THE LOVERS: EMOTIONAL TAPES, BASIS FOR RELATING/CREATING
UPRIGHT: Your earliest tapes of imprint are of this spiritual figure of authority, perhaps your own mother. But it could be of an older family figure such as a grandmother, or of course someone outside the family, perhaps someone famous whom you came to admire. **INVERTED:** Distorted, this otherwise very healthy archetype can become a block instead of a blueprint/foundation for love and creativity. At one extreme, the figure is idolized and idealized and real life will find it hard to compete. At the other extreme, the figure is loathed and by extension either all women or all of certain types of women are not to be loved/trusted.

7 GOVERNED BY THE CHARIOT: PHYSICAL RESOURCES. MEANS TO ACHIEVE
UPRIGHT: This may be someone, perhaps a family member on whom you can fall back. The accuracy of your information and its relevance to the future are decided advantages to doing the right thing at the right time. **INVERTED:** The people, or the guides, on whom you have relied are not available/reliable in the present situation.

8 GOVERNED BY STRENGTH: EMOTIONAL RESOURCES, ENERGY
UPRIGHT: You are stronger than most because of the purity of your motives. As you have tried to align your personal goals with more universal purposes, you carry an inner confidence in the inevitability of your success. Right will out. The love and backing of this queen in a person may be the source of your strength. **INVERTED:** This can be a disappointed love that has weakened you for the moment.

9 GOVERNED BY THE HERMIT: BELIEF SYSTEM, BASIS FOR DECISIONS
UPRIGHT: Here is a healthy balance of belief and confidence in the lessons of the worlds of physics and metaphysics, as this queen is the mother of beliefs. Belief, inspiration is taken into your body and nurtured so that it can emerge as enriched belief in all that you say and do. You breathe in the word of God so that it can take form in and through you. **INVERTED:** Just as with children, beliefs must be let loose to mature on their own. You cannot possess your beliefs anymore than you can possess your children.

10 GOVERNED BY THE WHEEL OF FORTUNE: CENTRAL MESSAGE, THEME OF READING
UPRIGHT: Think well on this card for she is coming to you in one guise or another. As a guide and source of inspiration, she is directing your attention

directly to your spiritual house, that you may increase the efficiency there. ***INVERTED:*** This suggests that you are needed to help another or others with their spiritual house.

11 GOVERNED BY JUSTICE: STATE/CONTENT OF MIND

UPRIGHT: The Queen of Wands occupies your thoughts, either in her person or her characteristics. The soothing effect of this passive centering is the enviable state of many meditations. From here much can be accomplished. ***INVERTED:*** You may think adversely about this queen, or she about you. Confusion, or subversion of a message may be taking place.

12 GOVERNED BY THE HANGED MAN: STATE OF EMOTIONS, SUBCONSCIOUS

UPRIGHT: The Queen of Wands fills your heart. She may be the centerpiece of your affection, or the centerpiece of a creative project underway. Her programs may dominate your feelings. ***INVERTED:*** Your heart may be involved with the queen, but rather not be. Or, the opposite, this can be the symbol of your heart's sadness over this person.

13 GOVERNED BY DEATH: PHYSICAL SITUATION, HARD REALITY

UPRIGHT: The queen is in your house. Her energy should bathe everything in a warm glow. The healing here transcends the physical, as it is a centering of all four levels that is taking place. ***INVERTED:*** There is little that can cause more trouble than intercepting someone else's message and working with it like it was your own.

14 GOVERNED BY TEMPERANCE: EMOTIONAL TEST

UPRIGHT: This queen is on your emotional horizon in the near future. If she is not presenting herself in person, then spiritual matters are pulling at your heart. The message content of your creative work may be raised. Your relationships may take on a deeper significance. ***INVERTED:*** If this is someone already in your life, there are emotions to deal with here as one or the other of you turn away.

15 GOVERNED BY THE DEVIL: TEMPTATION/CHALLENGE, FEARS

UPRIGHT: This queen is on your mental horizon in the near future. If she is not presenting herself in person, then the archetype is demanding attention to her programs. It is important to the realization of your goals that you integrate more of her principles into your work. ***INVERTED:*** If this represents someone already in your life, this may show a turn of mind between you. There may be a lack of confidence derivative from a fear of the unknown, or of listening to inaccurate or inappropriate sources.

16 GOVERNED BY THE TOWER: NEXT LESSON, GRACE OF GOD

UPRIGHT: Here is the support, the energy, and resources that you need to enhance your Spiritual Plane, and it may well come in the physical personage of the Queen of Wands. It may however, be the access to what she represents. ***INVERTED:*** Much of this blessing will be passed through you to others.

17 GOVERNED BY THE STAR: ASPIRATIONS OF EGO, GOALS, MAXIMUM EXPECTATIONS

UPRIGHT: Your goal is to see the institutions of society—schools, churches, governments— reflect as closely as possible the laws of the universe that we call truths, discovering these truths just as individuals must do. You must try, like Pythagoras, or Lao-Tsu, to ennoble society by enlightening man. ***INVERTED:*** This delicate task can distort into attempts to lead the horse to water and then force him to drink. All spiritual growth is voluntary, as God's gift of free will to man. Ironically, it is a fixed requirement that such growth is voluntary.

18 GOVERNED BY THE MOON: ASPIRATIONS OF HEART, COMPASSION

UPRIGHT: As a mother would want to suckle and nourish her child in physical growth, so does this queen wish to suckle and nourish her dependents in spiritual growth. Her goal is our complete well-being, not just physical. ***INVERTED:*** Just as the mother may offer her tit but the child must suckle, so too the spiritual mother can only offer. You cannot aspire that others follow you, only that they seek their true path.

19 GOVERNED BY THE SUN: PHYSICAL FULFILLMENT/EVALUATION

UPRIGHT: This can suggest the appearance or reappearance of this fiery personality in the flesh or the magic of her character. Whichever, your material world serves you well as the foundation for your spiritual quest. ***INVERTED:*** Let the Queen of Wands help you to your physical fulfillment.

20 GOVERNED BY JUDGEMENT: HEART'S FULFILLMENT/EVALUATION

UPRIGHT: The Queen of Wands here can suggest that the life of this person was the centerpiece and the fulfillment of your life. Also, however, it can symbolize your having succeeded in nourishing your dependents with meaningful spirituality. ***INVERTED:*** Let the Queen of Wands help you to your heart's fulfillment.

21 GOVERNED BY THE WORLD: EGO'S FULFILLMENT/EVALUATION

UPRIGHT: You are content that the mind has been applied to noble enterprises and patterns have been established that will continue after you are gone. ***INVERTED:*** Let the Queen of Wands help you to your ego's fulfillment.

22/0 GOVERNED BY THE FOOL: SOUL'S FULFILLMENT/EVALUATION

UPRIGHT: Yours has been a liberated soul that shackled itself to the will of God. ***INVERTED:*** Let the Queen of Wands help you to your soul's fulfillment.

KNIGHT OF PENTACLES

KNIGHT OF PENTACLES (AIR/EARTH)

UPRIGHT: Unmarried young adults, age 12 and up, of both sexes. Physical type: Dark hair with dark complexion and dark eyes. Also, black hair with very fair complexion and light blue, green or violet eyes. Personality type: Dependable. Resourceful. Can-doer. Watchful. Good instincts. Good physical leader. Ruled by the drive for expansion. Good brother/sister loyalty. Protective. Sense of duty, loyalty. Service to leader, then to cause. Practical. Physically active. Athletic. Outdoor and nature activities. Physical movement. Physical change agent. Trade representative. Salesman. Repairman. This Knight represents the mental, expansive side of things physical. As such, it shows physical training and craft apprenticeship, physical growth and physical additions. New resources. New capital. In romantic situations knights can represent someone considerably younger than you. Look to the Order of the Knights Templar (1118—1313 A.D.) for a wealth of examples to the meaning of this archetype. *INVERTED:* A distortion of the above characteristics, either to a greater or lesser degree, with the derivative problems. For example: Unathletic versus overathletic. Lazy versus hyperactive. Poor worker. Impractical. Careless versus overly exacting. *Note: Remember that the Courts are personifications which carry lessons to be learned, just as any of the Pips or Majors. First, they may represent characteristics of yourself. Second, they may represent people in this incarnation with you (past, present, or future). Third, they may represent people or guides not in the Earth plane with you at this time, including: yourself in past lives, others from this life passed on, others from past lifetimes, and any number of guides in the hierarchy between the Earth plane and God.*

In This Spread Position...Interpret the Knight Of Pentacles Meanings to Include:

1 GOVERNED BY THE MAGICIAN: PHYSICAL GIVENS, OUT OF THE FATHER
UPRIGHT: Here a blend of dependability with youthful vigor set the stage for the activities of the Physical/mental Plane in this lifetime. There is an athletic tone to all that you do here, and much of what you do will be out of doors. You will be the physical agent through which many people get things done. *INVERTED:* Some may find you a little rough around the edges but that comes not from a lack of manners but from your forthright manner and the quickness of your moves. Little time will be wasted in your world.

2 GOVERNED BY THE HIGH PRIESTESS: EMOTIONAL GIVENS, OUT OF THE MOTHER
UPRIGHT: Here that wonderful blend of dependability and youthful vigor enable you to blaze trails that many want to follow. You are literally a breath of fresh air to many. Relationships and creative endeavors will favor activities and interests in the Physical Plane. *INVERTED:* Those who do not prefer activity and challenge will find you less than charming, but no one will ever accuse you of being boring. Many will envy you from a safe distance.

3 GOVERNED BY THE EMPRESS: MENTAL GIVENS, INTELLECTUAL PREDISPOSITION
UPRIGHT: The mind will give priority to innovation in physical and material matters. Even as an adult, the mind will be adventurous in its manner, as well as in its preference of subject matter. Here we find the explorer, anthropologist, field scientist and the like. *INVERTED:* There will always be a tug of war between the adult and the child in you, but responsibility always wins out in the long-run.

4 GOVERNED BY THE EMPEROR: SPIRITUAL GIVENS, LIFE PURPOSE
UPRIGHT: All knights serve a higher master in this world, independent of their spiritual leanings. As such your purpose will be seen in the context of an older person's or group's purpose. *INVERTED:* The main difficulty for knights comes during their youth, when they need to learn to serve themselves well, becoming strong and self-reliant before dedicating themselves to their cause.

5 GOVERNED BY THE HIEROPHANT: SYSTEMS BORN INTO, SOCIETAL INFLUENCE
UPRIGHT: You may have had great freedom and spent the majority of your time among your young peers rather than in the company of adults. You may have gone to a boarding school. Otherwise, the adults themselves in your early environment were youthful and active beyond the norm. There is even the hint of a gypsy atmosphere for some. *INVERTED:* At one extreme, you were left far too much to your own devises, and as a result may have been learning many things the hard way.

6 GOVERNED BY THE LOVERS: EMOTIONAL TAPES, BASIS FOR RELATING/CREATING
UPRIGHT: Any of the knights may represent the ideal of a strong hero on a horse that fills our storybooks, but this knight represents the hero who is not only warm and likeable, but comes complete with a bag of tricks and talents that can save us. It recalls the American Indian riding bareback, or the cowboy/cowgirl who becomes one with his/her horse. *INVERTED:* As with the kings, this archetype can become distorted and block, rather than foster, love and creativity. At one extreme, the figure is idolized and idealized and real life will find it hard to compete. At the other extreme, the figure is loathed and by extension either all youth or all of certain types of youth are not to be loved/trusted.

7 GOVERNED BY THE CHARIOT: PHYSICAL RESOURCES. MEANS TO ACHIEVE
UPRIGHT: In some cases this can be a young person on whom you must rely. But for most, this will be your very own energy and resourcefulness that is your strongest asset. Someone working and putting themselves through school serves this archetype. But many carry this same energy and esprit de corps through their entire lifetime. You are on your way. *INVERTED:* This suggests that the youthful posture here may be less than beneficial, perhaps even irresponsible.

8 GOVERNED BY STRENGTH: EMOTIONAL RESOURCES, ENERGY
UPRIGHT: Your depth of understanding of physical/material things, from the human body to mother nature herself, together with your robust manner, make you very attractive and you have had no lack of friends or lovers. All this has instilled you with a well-deserved sense of confidence. *INVERTED:* At one extreme, this archetype can distort into roguish behavior that is endearing to almost no one. Younger people are able to get away with a lot more of this bravado than mature adults.

9 GOVERNED BY THE HERMIT: BELIEF SYSTEM, BASIS FOR DECISIONS
UPRIGHT: This is the belief in the hero/heroine storyline. Here is confidence in the idea that given enough courage, enough time, and enough dogged determination (here of the kind that usually only comes with the naivete of youth), victory will eventually be ours. That folks, is Hollywood faith. A bit of it beats in all our hearts. Here, it is a credo. *INVERTED:* As valuable a philosophy as this is at its metaphysical core of half faith in self and half faith in God, in its distorted form this can be a dangerous approach to the world.

10 GOVERNED BY THE WHEEL OF FORTUNE: CENTRAL MESSAGE, THEME OF READING
UPRIGHT: Think well on this card for it is coming to you in one form or another. This is the extra manpower, the added energy, the new resources, the

movement that you have needed. This increases your flexibility and your security. ***INVERTED:*** You are the agent through which this knight can deliver his/her gifts.

11 GOVERNED BY JUSTICE: STATE/CONTENT OF MIND

UPRIGHT: You are focused on the new knight that will make your days brighter. Here you see the means to reinvigorated goals. This can even be a plan to invest. ***INVERTED:*** You may think adversely about this knight or he/she about you.

12 GOVERNED BY THE HANGED MAN: STATE OF EMOTIONS, SUBCONSCIOUS

UPRIGHT: Your heart is on the knight. He/she may be an object of your affection, or the centerpiece of a creative project underway. ***INVERTED:*** Your heart may be involved with this knight, but rather not be. Or, the opposite, this can be the symbol of your heart's sadness over this person.

13 GOVERNED BY DEATH: PHYSICAL SITUATION, HARD REALITY

UPRIGHT: The knight is in your physical house. You may have accepted your son/daughter, or another, as a new member in your business. This is a sign of movement and so relocation of some sort may be afoot. With new investment comes change. ***INVERTED:*** At one extreme, too much youth, inexperience, irresponsibility may mark your present situation. At another extreme, you may lack the youth, the energy, the investment that you need at this time.

14 GOVERNED BY TEMPERANCE: EMOTIONAL TEST

UPRIGHT: As the cards have been known to say, "there is a tall, dark, handsome, young man" in your future. Your emotional affairs will be charged with new energy and the status quo will be history. Another interpretation has your heart excited about a new financial prospect, perhaps in support of a creative project. ***INVERTED:*** At one extreme, you are going overboard with your emotions here. At another extreme, there is disappointment.

15 GOVERNED BY THE DEVIL: TEMPTATION/CHALLENGE, FEARS

UPRIGHT: This can be thoughts about a young man or woman—a child, a friend, or a lover—but in the Mental Plane rather than the heart, as in concern for their schooling, or their finances. You may be considering a new health regimen or reviewing ways to get your finances moving. ***INVERTED:*** Thoughts may have become concerns which have become fears.

16 GOVERNED BY THE TOWER: NEXT LESSON, GRACE OF GOD

UPRIGHT: Here is the support, the energy and resources that you need to invigorate your Physical/material Plane, and it may well come in the physical personage of the Knight of Pentacles. It may however, be the access to what he/she represents. ***INVERTED:*** Much of this blessing will be passed through you to others.

17 GOVERNED BY THE STAR: ASPIRATIONS OF EGO, GOALS, MAXIMUM EXPECTATIONS

UPRIGHT: Knights above all else need to be needed. The goal is to make things happen. Stasis is the enemy. Service here will be to other men and their institutions as with soldiers and the military, craft apprenticeship and unions, young farmers and the land/community. ***INVERTED:*** In time, service must be to the principles behind institutions rather than the men who run them, and eventually to spirit not matter. At one extreme, a mistake here is to seek change for change sake in a restlessness that finds little peace. This is the cowboy seen riding out of town at the end of every movie.

18 GOVERNED BY THE MOON: ASPIRATIONS OF HEART, COMPASSION

UPRIGHT: This is the desire of the knight who would protect the weak and defenseless, whomever and wherever they might be. There is deep felt principle at work here, related to the most noble of spiritual goals—universal love. This is the protective mandate in the chivalric orders of medieval society, the birth of romanticism and individual rights as we aspire to them in modern society. ***INVERTED:*** Even this noble goal can be distorted. We must work so that others rise to be able to defend themselves. Certainly, we must not come to enjoy their dependence on us.

19 GOVERNED BY THE SUN: PHYSICAL FULFILLMENT/EVALUATION

UPRIGHT: You are able to serve and defend to the end. This suggests a great deal of flexibility and mobility in later years. ***INVERTED:*** Let the Knight of Pentacles help you to your physical fulfillment.

20 GOVERNED BY JUDGEMENT: HEART'S FULFILLMENT/EVALUATION

UPRIGHT: The Knight of Pentacles here can suggest that the love of this person was the centerpiece and the fulfillment of your life. Love of duty as extending love and protection normally reserved for family into the larger realm of humanity. ***INVERTED:*** Let the Knight of Pentacles help you to your heart's fulfillment.

21 GOVERNED BY THE WORLD: EGO'S FULFILLMENT/EVALUATION

UPRIGHT: From the establishment of a new trading system on the stock exchange, to the formulation of battle plans by the military tactician, such is the span of the interests and abilities of this mind. Somehow society itself is younger, invigorated for your having served this lifetime. ***INVERTED:*** Let the Knight of Pentacles help you to your ego's fulfillment.

22/0 GOVERNED BY THE FOOL: SOUL'S FULFILLMENT/EVALUATION

UPRIGHT: Ever the apprentice, yet capable of the finest workmanship; ever the youth and yet always accepting more responsibility—this soul blended the vitality of a youthful body with the sensibility of a wise old mind. ***INVERTED:*** Let the Knight of Pentacles help you to your soul's fulfillment.

KNIGHT OF CUPS.

KNIGHT OF CUPS (AIR/WATER)

UPRIGHT: Unmarried young adults, age 12 and up, of both sexes. Physical type: Light brown to sandy-blonde hair and medium complexion, sometimes olive, with brown, blue, or gray-blue eyes. Personality type: Emotional. Sensitive. Creative. Dedicated. Motivated. Sensual. Tender. A loving person. Ruled by the drive for expansion. Close ties with family and friends. Defender of heart, honor. Frequently the heart of the group. Leader/volunteer. The Arts. Emotional change agent. Nurturing agent. An emotional investment. This Knight represents the mental, expansive side of things emotional. As such, it shows the emotional learning and growth. The Novice. Can represent the younger lover of an older partner, or someone taken under the wing of an emotional advisor. Innocence maturing. Student of romance. Sacrificing for someone/something else. Here are both Romeo and Juliet. Here is Lancelot. Here is Prince Charming. Here are the medieval Knights Hospitalier. ***INVERTED:*** A distortion of the above characteristics, either to a greater or lesser degree, with the derivative problems. For example: Slow emotional growth versus developing too fast. Missing emotional opportunities versus overindulgence. Too sensitive versus insensitive. Creative block. Unmotivated. Inconsiderate versus caring to an extreme. Too cool versus too hot. Taking too much energy from the group versus giving them too much. ***Note:*** *Remember that the Courts are personifications which carry lessons to be learned, just as any of the Pips or Majors. First, they may represent characteristics of yourself. Second, they may represent people in this incarnation with you (past, present, or future). Third, they may represent people or guides not in the Earth plane with you at this time, including: yourself in past lives, others from this life passed on, others from past lifetimes, and any number of guides in the hierarchy between the Earth plane and God.*

In This Spread Position...Interpret the Knight Of Cups Meanings to Include:

1 GOVERNED BY THE MAGICIAN: PHYSICAL GIVENS, OUT OF THE FATHER
UPRIGHT: The energy of love and devotion, dedication to loved ones and to the realization of creative talents will flavor the activities of the Physical/material Plane. You may be the emotional agent through which many people get things done. Businesses related to the senses, to romance and pleasure are favored, i.e., manufacture of perfumes, the fashion industry, advertising. ***INVERTED:*** There may be some difficulty in understanding the thin line here between business and pleasure, the public and the personal.

2 GOVERNED BY THE HIGH PRIESTESS: EMOTIONAL GIVENS, OUT OF THE MOTHER
UPRIGHT: You will find yourself the catalyst in many an equation. You bring life and movement where it is needed. Your innocence and willingness to lend yourself wholeheartedly to the causes of your heart make you a lover in the deepest, classical sense. You hold nothing back. ***INVERTED:*** Some will try to stop time to keep you as you are, but you must use the power of love to promote change and growth.

3 GOVERNED BY THE EMPRESS: MENTAL GIVENS, INTELLECTUAL PREDISPOSITION
UPRIGHT: Your mind is devoted to devotion itself. Here is the appreciation of the power of individual love and its movement to the forefront of thinking with the likes of medieval chivalry, humanism, and the enlightenment. Language here is more poetry than prose. ***INVERTED:*** There can be confusion between the specific and the general, with a tendency to get lost in the individual, losing sight of the group.

4 GOVERNED BY THE EMPEROR: SPIRITUAL GIVENS, LIFE PURPOSE
UPRIGHT: The allegiance of this knight will always be to the heart, as Lancelot was led by his to follow Gwenivere rather than his vows to King Arthur. There is great nobility and power in this ability of the human heart to love so deeply that it will offer all to its cause, even against insurmountable odds. ***INVERTED:*** Here is a curious blend of the active and passive principle, for in loving you are passively surrendering yourself to that love, and yet once committed, you are active in defending your love to the end if necessary. Here both passive and active are maximized giving it the power to create legends.

5 GOVERNED BY THE HIEROPHANT: SYSTEMS BORN INTO, SOCIETAL INFLUENCE
UPRIGHT: You may have been born to very young parents; certainly, they were young in heart. Here touching and affection were open and frequent. Expression of feelings was encouraged and the arts were an integral part of your environment and activities. ***INVERTED:*** At one extreme, the adults in this setting were immature and possibly still much more interested in their personal relationship and pleasure, than in family.

6 GOVERNED BY THE LOVERS: EMOTIONAL TAPES, BASIS FOR RELATING/CREATING
UPRIGHT: The ideal of the lover, either as yourself, or for yourself. ***INVERTED:*** As in the story Elvira Madigan, where the young circus girl falls madly in love with the calvary soldier and they run off to be together in their bliss, only to learn tragically in a double suicide of despair, that you cannot get very far with a frozen concept of idealized love divorced from all the varied currents of life weaving through it, frequently against it, ironically keeping it alive.

7 GOVERNED BY THE CHARIOT: PHYSICAL RESOURCES, MEANS TO ACHIEVE
UPRIGHT: In some cases this can be a young person on whom you must rely. Otherwise, this is your own creative energy and intimate contact with the people and things you love. You are one with your surroundings, sensitive to the most subtle of changes and have usually reacted before others have even been aware. This is the mark of a good fencer. ***INVERTED:*** If this is a person, they may not be backing you up at this time. Otherwise, you may be too involved with your objects of love and unable to move freely and quickly to meet new demands.

8 GOVERNED BY STRENGTH: EMOTIONAL RESOURCES, ENERGY
UPRIGHT: You may be drawing strength from someone this knight represents. The knight is both committed to his/her loves and yet has the drive to push that love to new heights, to use it rather than lose it. This balance of being able to appreciate, to even lose oneself in the moment and yet maintain a presence of mind, is the strength of centered emotions, a very Zen-like posture from which much can be accomplished. ***INVERTED:*** A disappointment in love may have weakened you temporarily.

9 GOVERNED BY THE HERMIT: BELIEF SYSTEM, BASIS FOR DECISIONS
UPRIGHT: Love conquers all. Without love there is nothing. The power of love to change the world. Add to all these generalities your confidence in your own prowess and ability to make things happen with the force of your love and you have an emotionally based belief system of love that parallels the spirituality of faith. In a sense we can say that love is to the worldly what faith is to the otherworldly. ***INVERTED:*** All of the aforementioned about love is metaphysical truth if the love is open-ended and inclusive of universal love. Otherwise, it is sugar candy.

10 GOVERNED BY THE WHEEL OF FORTUNE: CENTRAL MESSAGE, THEME OF READING
UPRIGHT: Think well on this card for it is coming to you in one form or another. This is the extra manpower, the added energy, the new resources, the movement that you have needed. This increases your sensitivity to who and what is important, and your ability to express your feelings. *INVERTED:* You are the agent through which this knight can deliver his/her gifts.

11 GOVERNED BY JUSTICE: STATE/CONTENT OF MIND
UPRIGHT: This knight has your attention, either in person or influence. New emotional factors, new input is anticipated to change the status quo. This can be a bright new idea in the subject matter related to the Emotional/creative Plane, a highly creative or sense oriented business. An emotional investment. *INVERTED:* You may think adversely about this knight or he/she about you.

12 GOVERNED BY THE HANGED MAN: STATE OF EMOTIONS, SUBCONSCIOUS
UPRIGHT: Your heart is on this knight. He/she may be an object of your affection, or the centerpiece of a creative project underway. *INVERTED:* Your heart may be involved with this knight, but rather not be. Or, the opposite, this can be the symbol of your heart's sadness over this person.

13 GOVERNED BY DEATH: PHYSICAL SITUATION, HARD REALITY
UPRIGHT: The knight is in your physical house. There is sensitivity here as your Material Plane takes on a delicacy and attention to the emotional ramifications to things physical. A new creative project may be emerging. *INVERTED:* There may be a temporary block in your material affairs stemming from the emotional. Also, physical matters may have adversely affected the Emotional/creative Plane.

14 GOVERNED BY THE TEMPERANCE: EMOTIONAL TEST
UPRIGHT: The Knight of Cups may be arriving in person in the near future. The energy of this archetype is refreshing and meant to generate movement here, from personal love to creative projects. *INVERTED:* At one extreme, there may be a retreat by you or the knight.

15 GOVERNED BY THE DEVIL: TEMPTATION/CHALLENGE, FEARS
UPRIGHT: Your mind may be on this knight in the near future. This may be the birth of a project whose energy and/or subject matter is rooted in the Emotional Plane. The emotions are at work to stimulate and support the mind. Poetry, romance novels, storybooks, childcare, couple and family counseling, are just a few of the areas of interest. *INVERTED:* The emotions here may be working against the mental program, ranging from the effect an emotional problem has on the efficiency of the mind, to a lack of enthusiasm for the mind's goals.

16 GOVERNED BY THE TOWER: NEXT LESSON, GRACE OF GOD
UPRIGHT: Here is the support, the energy and resources that you need to invigorate your Emotional/creative Plane, and it may well come in the physical personage of the Knight of Cups. It may, however, be the access to what he/she represents. *INVERTED:* Much of this blessing will be passed through you to others.

17 GOVERNED BY THE STAR: ASPIRATIONS OF EGO, GOALS, MAXIMUM EXPECTATIONS
UPRIGHT: Knights above all else need to be needed, and especially in this case to be loved. But in order to feel love and to maintain the sensations it generates, there has to be movement, a delicate friction, a controlled nuclear reaction of sorts. Service here will be to others, but to the objects of one's affections rather than the more abstract service to a leader or an ideology. *INVERTED:* The goal cannot be to become another, or to possess another, or to freeze time in any way, or the love will evaporate like the mirage of a desert oasis.

18 GOVERNED BY THE MOON: ASPIRATIONS OF HEART, COMPASSION
UPRIGHT: This is the desire of the knight who would protect the object of affection at all costs. He/she aspires to true love that brings a sweetness bordering on pain, the worldly equivalent of divine intoxication. *INVERTED:* In its proper balance this intensity of personal love for another is the mirror image of the love that enlightenment affords the self of the Divine. Distorted, this intensity seeks no further than mundane earthly pleasure, and soon dies under its own weight of self-indulgence.

19 GOVERNED BY THE SUN: PHYSICAL FULFILLMENT/EVALUATION
UPRIGHT: Lover to the very last. You are surrounded by the objects of your affection. *INVERTED:* Let the Knight of Cups help you to the physical fulfillment.

20 GOVERNED BY JUDGEMENT: HEART'S FULFILLMENT/EVALUATION
UPRIGHT: The Knight of Cups here can suggest that the love of this person was the centerpiece and the fulfillment of your life. Your capacity for love and your open display of your innermost feelings has cleared your path of the misunderstandings that can cloud emotional fulfillment. *INVERTED:* Let the Knight of Cups help you to the heart's fulfillment.

21 GOVERNED BY THE WORLD: EGO'S FULFILLMENT/EVALUATION
UPRIGHT: Relevant, vibrant, probing—there were no dusty corners in this mind. You have ridden your loves to their logical conclusions. *INVERTED:* Let the Knight of Cups help you to the ego's fulfillment.

22/0 GOVERNED BY THE FOOL: SOUL'S FULFILLMENT/EVALUATION
UPRIGHT: Ah, sweet prince, how many are the happier for your having graced their lives. You have been the cup of wine that complimented many a feast. *INVERTED:* Let the Knight of Cups help you to the soul's fulfillment.

KNIGHT of SWORDS.

KNIGHT OF SWORDS (AIR/AIR)

UPRIGHT: Unmarried young adults, age 12 and up, of both sexes. Physical type: Light brown to sandy-blonde hair and medium complexion, sometimes olive, with brown, blue, or gray-blue eyes. Personality type: Mental. Assertive. Perfectionist. Protective. Philosophical. Studious. Alert. Direct. Knowledgeable leader. Change agent for ideas and ideals. Ruled by the drive for expansion. Missionary for ideologies and the mental work of religious expansion. Ambassador. Action-oriented. New methods. Mental investment. Investigative. Law enforcing. Mental recreation. Gambling/risk taking. Curious. Highly informed. Cutting edge technology. This Knight is the expansive side of things mental and represents formal education/training. Also, defender of ideologies, student of philosophy. **INVERTED:** A distortion of the above characteristics, either to a greater or lesser degree, with the derivative problems. For example: Illogical thinker versus overly rational, analytical thinker. Protective to a fault. Unnecessarily aggressive, passive to a fault. Mentally stagnant. Overly nervous. **Note:** *Remember that the Courts are personifications which carry lessons to be learned, just as any of the Pips or Majors. First, they may represent characteristics of yourself. Second, they may represent people in this incarnation with you (past, present, or future). Third, they may represent people or guides not in the Earth plane with you at this time, including: yourself in past lives, others from this life passed on, others from past lifetimes, and any number of guides in the hierarchy between the Earth plane and God.*

In This Spread Position...Interpret the Knight Of Swords Meanings to Include:

1 GOVERNED BY THE MAGICIAN: PHYSICAL GIVENS, OUT OF THE FATHER
UPRIGHT: There will be little waste in time or material in your Physical Plane. Everything will have its place and its purpose. At one time or another, everything will be put to use, very little or nothing being purely for show. You may be the mental agent through which others get things done. Here is the aggressive drive of the athlete to win. Business interests include: Information handling/computers, writing, agent/representation, marketing, investigation, law enforcement. **INVERTED:** You will be "too much" for some folks, i.e., your being so up on the latest and greatest will not excite everyone, particularly those who prior to meeting you thought they were the cat's meow.

2 GOVERNED BY THE HIGH PRIESTESS: EMOTIONAL GIVENS, OUT OF THE MOTHER
UPRIGHT: For you, the subconscious is a short stopover on the way to full expression. Creative talents, especially in the knight's fields of special interest (like those listed in general meanings and in spread position 1 above) will thrive with the enthusiasm and will power of this active mind to steer them. Your heart is predisposed to a fondness of things mental. **INVERTED:** Anyone who wants to have a relationship with you had better like excitement and staying on the go, for this heart likes to beat fast.

3 GOVERNED BY THE EMPRESS: MENTAL GIVENS, INTELLECTUAL PREDISPOSITION
UPRIGHT: Here is a mind blessed with an automatic cobweb remover. Dust is not given the chance to settle. Here is the scalpel that the mind can use, even on mind itself as necessary, to probe the darkness, to expand the territory of man's knowledge. Here, the answer to each question will be, very clearly, the next question. **INVERTED:** As with the young child with the never ending question, Why?, you may annoy your fair share of people.

4 GOVERNED BY THE EMPEROR: SPIRITUAL GIVENS, LIFE PURPOSE
UPRIGHT: Between being the defender of ideologies which already exist, and being the change agent for new ideas and ideals, you promise to be a very busy person. **INVERTED:** The knights are born to service but you will be needed to pick up where many others have left off.

5 GOVERNED BY THE HIEROPHANT: SYSTEMS BORN INTO, SOCIETAL INFLUENCE
UPRIGHT: It is as though you were born into a library on wheels. The environment was information rich and committed to bringing about change, such as in a missionary school. Schools such as the Montessori method or that of Rudolf Steiner, magnet schools and head start programs of the public school system, that challenge the young mind to reach for the stars, these are examples of the atmosphere in which you cut your mental teeth. **INVERTED:** At one extreme, some attempts to push the mind forward and better equip it for the tasks ahead can paradoxically be very narrow and limiting if burdened with too much ideology as opposed to methodology.

6 GOVERNED BY THE LOVERS: EMOTIONAL TAPES, BASIS FOR RELATING/CREATING
UPRIGHT: Your knight on a white horse may have won the spelling bee or been the debating team captain. But this hero is not lacking in courage for his/her motivation comes from the core of belief, and is the stuff revolutionary leaders are made of, a combination of mental wizardry of the football quarterback and the right guard. **INVERTED:** As with the kings, this archetype can become distorted and block rather than foster love and creativity. At one extreme, the figure is idolized and idealized and real life will find it hard to compete. At the other extreme, the figure is loathed and by extension either all youth or all of certain types of youth are not to be loved/trusted.

7 GOVERNED BY THE CHARIOT: PHYSICAL RESOURCES. MEANS TO ACHIEVE
UPRIGHT: In some cases this can be a young person on whom you must rely. Otherwise, this is your own mental energy and your ability to position yourself ideally in physical/material matters. This is the mark of a good tactician, a knowledgeable leader. You operate with the latest information and technology. Your factories will never be outdated any more than you will. **INVERTED:** If this is a person, they may not be backing you up at this time. At one extreme, you may be overdoing it at having the latest and greatest, throwing much of the baby out with the bathwater.

8 GOVERNED BY STRENGTH: EMOTIONAL RESOURCES, ENERGY
UPRIGHT: You may be drawing strength from someone this knight represents. Otherwise, this is your ability to run with the times, staying forever youthful as you become older and wiser. Your relationships span from young to old as do your interests in both the latest music and the classics. You may appear either young or mature, or both, depending on your circumstances. **INVERTED:** At one extreme, this ability to be both young and old is more like the exterior capacity of the chameleon to change colors rather than an integral, deep rooted reflection of a wide range of interests and knowledge.

9 GOVERNED BY THE HERMIT: BELIEF SYSTEM, BASIS FOR DECISIONS
UPRIGHT: Knowledge conquers all. Here is faith in science, in the modern method of analysis and deduction, in all its best aspects. For this knight is the strongest symbol of the drive to knowledge and its eventual management (wisdom) that is our path, our reason for being. It is the inescapable drive to gnosis.

INVERTED: As this archetype distorts we see many of the contemporary problems confronting science and technology, the mistakes that can be made by an arrogant, overly aggressive mind.

10 GOVERNED BY THE WHEEL OF FORTUNE: CENTRAL MESSAGE, THEME OF READING

UPRIGHT: Think well on this card for it is coming to you in one form or another. This is the extra manpower, the added energy, the new resources, the movement that you have needed. This increases your store of knowledge and your ability to retrieve and use it. ***INVERTED:*** You are the agent through which this knight can deliver his/her gifts.

11 GOVERNED BY JUSTICE: STATE/CONTENT OF MIND

UPRIGHT: This knight has your attention, either in person or influence. New mental factors, new input is anticipated to change the status quo. You may be asserting your position, making your thoughts known. ***INVERTED:*** You may think adversely about this knight or he/she about you.

12 GOVERNED BY THE HANGED MAN: STATE OF EMOTIONS, SUBCONSCIOUS

UPRIGHT: Your heart is on this knight. He/she may be an object of your affection, or the centerpiece of a creative project underway. ***INVERTED:*** Your heart may be involved with this knight but rather not be. Or, the opposite, this can be the symbol of your heart's sadness over this person.

13 GOVERNED BY DEATH: PHYSICAL SITUATION, HARD REALITY

UPRIGHT: The knight is in your physical house. You should be able to feel the winds of mental change. There may be calculated risks being undertaken. Anything not set in concrete may be moved, and those things that are set in concrete may get left behind. ***INVERTED:*** There may be a temporary block in your material affairs stemming from the mental. Also, physical matters may have adversely affected the Mental Plane.

14 GOVERNED BY TEMPERANCE: EMOTIONAL TEST

UPRIGHT: The Knight of Swords may be arriving in person in the near future. Whether felt as a refreshing breeze or more like a hurricane, this is a positive wind breathing new life into your emotional/creative affairs. Openness and extroversion will prevail. ***INVERTED:*** At one extreme, there may be a retreat by you or the knight.

15 GOVERNED BY THE DEVIL: TEMPTATION/CHALLENGE, FEARS

UPRIGHT: Your mind will be on this knight in the near future. This may be the birth of a mental project. New knowledge is to be acquired. ***INVERTED:*** There may be fear of new information, of what it may reveal in and of itself, or of what it may do to your cherished picture of reality.

16 GOVERNED BY THE TOWER: NEXT LESSON, GRACE OF GOD

UPRIGHT: Here is the support, the energy and resources that you need to invigorate your Mental Plane, and it may well come in the physical personage of the Knight of Swords. It may, however, be the access to what he/she represents. ***INVERTED:*** Much of this blessing will be passed through you to others.

17 GOVERNED BY THE STAR: ASPIRATIONS OF EGO, GOALS, MAXIMUM EXPECTATIONS

UPRIGHT: Knights above all else need to be needed. The goal is to make things happen, or at the very least to be there when they happen. Stasis is the enemy. You aspire to be this knight who rides in at the last minute, after surmounting all the ordeals put in his/her way, with the answer to the king's question. ***INVERTED:*** The answer to the question must be sought in order to achieve a noble purpose, not for the satisfaction of having been clever enough to retrieve it.

18 GOVERNED BY THE MOON: ASPIRATIONS OF HEART, COMPASSION

UPRIGHT: You must bring back to your people the key, the holy Grail, that will open the gate to the inner courtyard. But this is not to simply gain entrance for self. This is as to part the Red Sea so that your entire people may follow you. ***INVERTED:*** One distortion would be to do this for self alone, or for self and a few close loved ones.

19 GOVERNED BY THE SUN: PHYSICAL FULFILLMENT/EVALUATION

UPRIGHT: Warrior to the last. All your resources remain on active alert like those of a national guard unit, ready if needed. ***INVERTED:*** Let the Knight of Swords help you to the physical fulfillment.

20 GOVERNED BY JUDGEMENT: HEART'S FULFILLMENT/EVALUATION

UPRIGHT: The Knight of Swords here can suggest that the love of this person was the centerpiece and the fulfillment of your life. Love of knowledge and its pursuit have led you to all the objects of your affection and held you together. ***INVERTED:*** Let the Knight of Swords help you to the heart's fulfillment.

21 GOVERNED BY THE WORLD: EGO'S FULFILLMENT/EVALUATION

UPRIGHT: The eternal student, knowledgeable enough to be sincerely humbled at the magnitude of what remains yet unknown. ***INVERTED:*** Let the Knight of Swords help you to the ego's fulfillment.

22/0 GOVERNED BY THE FOOL: SOUL'S FULFILLMENT/EVALUATION

UPRIGHT: You have joined the fraternity of mental adventurers on which the known world depends for its very existence. ***INVERTED:*** Let the Knight of Swords help you to the soul's fulfillment.

KNIGHT OF WANDS (AIR/FIRE)

UPRIGHT: Unmarried young adults, age 12 and up, of both sexes. Physical type: Red to reddish-blonde or reddish-brown hair and fair or freckled complexion with green or blue eyes. Personality type: Intuitive. Spiritual. Vibrant. Fiery. Introspective. Humorous. Defender of beliefs. Benevolent. Dedicated. Natural leader. Student of religion and metaphysics. Ruled by the drive for expansion. This Knight is the expansive side of things spiritual and represents spiritual enlightenment and growth. Intellectual growth. New world views. Intuitive action. An initiate. A disciple. **INVERTED:** A distortion of the above characteristics, either to a greater or lesser degree, with the derivative problems. For example: Obvious brilliance unfilled. Confusion. Possible philosophical/spiritual overload. A fundamental developmental block. ***Note:*** *Remember that the Courts are personifications which carry lessons to be learned, just as any of the Pips or Majors. First, they may represent characteristics of yourself. Second, they may represent people in this incarnation with you (past, present, or future). Third, they may represent people or guides not in the Earth plane with you at this time, including: yourself in past lives, others from this life passed on. others from past lifetimes, and any number of guides in the hierarchy between the Earth plane and God.*

In This Spread Position...Interpret the Knight Of Wands Meanings to Include:

1 GOVERNED BY THE MAGICIAN: PHYSICAL GIVENS, OUT OF THE FATHER
UPRIGHT: The Physical/material Plane itself may seem totally dedicated to spiritual enlightenment and growth. Enterprise here is attuned to higher purpose and to helping foster greater understanding. Here is the effect of the aggressive drive of the seeker. The urge to learn and teach manifests in institutions as a way of life, such as monasteries, religious retreats, holistic treatment centers, seminaries, and the like. **INVERTED:** Some will be unable to reconcile your spirituality and your success in the material realm.

2 GOVERNED BY THE HIGH PRIESTESS: EMOTIONAL GIVENS, OUT OF THE MOTHER
UPRIGHT: Your Emotional/creative Plane will seem completely dedicated to spiritual enlightenment and growth. Every relationship and every talent will be experienced through the filter of this archetype. **INVERTED:** You are attractive and desirable and many will seek you out for reasons not attuned to your path.

3 GOVERNED BY THE EMPRESS: MENTAL GIVENS, INTELLECTUAL PREDISPOSITION
UPRIGHT: This is the path of one given to aggressive study at the highest levels. You have the capacity for learning the subtleties of the path that escape many ardent Initiates. You will be the retriever of pieces of insight needed by others. **INVERTED:** You must avoid the attempts of others to elevate you too high, to give you too much responsibility thereby restricting your knightly function of change agent/retriever and student.

4 GOVERNED BY THE EMPEROR: SPIRITUAL GIVENS, LIFE PURPOSE
UPRIGHT: Yours is a young soul for your group, but your group is of the elders. You must balance your role as defender of the faith with that of change agent for belief. As a student who must work to support his studies, you must be on call to fight the worthy battle, but never neglecting your responsibility to push that very same faith you defend to higher and higher ground with the power of gnosis. **INVERTED:** The call to defend may be heavy, but be confident your studies will not be sacrificed with this path.

5 GOVERNED BY THE HIEROPHANT: SYSTEMS BORN INTO, SOCIETAL INFLUENCE
UPRIGHT: You may have been given over to formal study of metaphysics and the like at an early age, as in some societies children are literally taken from their parental homes. One or both of your parents may have been given the duties of this knight as part of their Karmic Contract. **INVERTED:** At one extreme, this environment may have been too esoteric, with the adults not heeding their secular responsibilities.

6 GOVERNED BY THE LOVERS: EMOTIONAL TAPES, BASIS FOR RELATING/CREATING
UPRIGHT: Any of the knights may represent the ideal of a strong hero on a horse that fills our storybooks, but this knight represents the hero who can save our souls, the spiritual warrior who will storm into the temple and turn over the money tables, the believer who will allow herself to be eaten by lions in the arena for Caesar's pleasure rather than deny her God. **INVERTED:** As with the kings, this archetype can become distorted and block rather than foster love and creativity. At one extreme, the figure is idolized and idealized and real life will find it hard to compete. At the other extreme, the figure is loathed and by extension either all youth or all of certain types of youth are not to be loved/trusted.

7 GOVERNED BY THE CHARIOT: PHYSICAL RESOURCES. MEANS TO ACHIEVE
UPRIGHT: In some cases this can be a young person on whom you must rely. Otherwise, this is your own spiritual energy and your ability to position yourself well in spiritual matters. You seem to be doing the right things for the right reasons. Your material world is not cluttered with things that do not belong. **INVERTED:** If this is a person, they may not be backing you up at this time. At one extreme, you might be overzealous and missing the true inner mark while creating a great deal of smoke with your ritual observances.

8 GOVERNED BY STRENGTH: EMOTIONAL RESOURCES, ENERGY
UPRIGHT: You may be drawing strength from someone this knight represents. Otherwise, this is your ability to see the seriousness and the humor in the same situation, to enjoy the pleasure of spiritual and earthly pursuits as the singular pursuit they are. **INVERTED:** A disappointment in love related to this knight may have weakened you temporarily. Until you can see the earthly pleasure in the spiritual and the spiritual pleasure in the earthly you are not as strong as you could be.

9 GOVERNED BY THE HERMIT: BELIEF SYSTEM, BASIS FOR DECISIONS
UPRIGHT: Agape conquers all. This is no battle of good over evil. In fact, it is no battle at all. Rather, it is complete surrender by active will. It is will surrendering to Will. But make no mistake that here the belief is in the necessity to seek actively, to witness actively, and to defend actively when called upon to do so. **INVERTED:** Before you engage a battle, be it physical, emotional, or mental, you must assure yourself of its spiritual purpose—or failing to do so, turn away from the folly giving thanks for having been spared.

10 GOVERNED BY THE WHEEL OF FORTUNE: CENTRAL MESSAGE, THEME OF READING
UPRIGHT: Think well on this card for it is coming to you in one form or another. This is the extra manpower, the added energy, the new resources, the

movement that you have needed. This increases your spiritual knowledge and your ability to retrieve and use it. **_INVERTED:_** You are the agent through which this knight can deliver his/her gifts.

11 GOVERNED BY JUSTICE: STATE/CONTENT OF MIND
UPRIGHT: This knight has your attention, either in person or influence. Your mind is moving into new territory where it must catalog its discoveries for even further study. Your mind is well aware of your spiritual position and prepared to stand its ground. **_INVERTED:_** You may think adversely about this knight and he/she about you.

12 GOVERNED BY THE HANGED MAN: STATE OF EMOTIONS, SUBCONSCIOUS
UPRIGHT: Your heart is on this knight. He may be an object of your affection, or the centerpiece of a creative project underway. **_INVERTED:_** Your heart may be involved with this knight but rather not be. Or, the opposite, this can be the symbol of your heart's sadness over this person.

13 GOVERNED BY DEATH: PHYSICAL SITUATION, HARD REALITY
UPRIGHT: This knight is in your physical house. You are well-protected, centered as you are in your world, your very correct and appropriate world. But with the fort so well fortified, you may well consider another foray into the unknown. **_INVERTED:_** If this is a person in your environment, he/she may be throwing your affairs off center.

14 GOVERNED BY TEMPERANCE: EMOTIONAL TEST
UPRIGHT: The Knight of Wands may be arriving in person in the near future. There is a change in the emotional content of your beliefs, a deepening, and an even greater involvement. **_INVERTED:_** At one extreme, there may be a retreat by you or the knight.

15 GOVERNED BY THE DEVIL: TEMPTATION/CHALLENGE, FEARS
UPRIGHT: Your mind will be on this knight in the near future. This may be the birth of a spiritual project. New spiritual knowledge is to be acquired. **_INVERTED:_** There may be fear of new revelations and what they might do to disturb your comfort with your present beliefs.

16 GOVERNED BY THE TOWER: NEXT LESSON, GRACE OF GOD
UPRIGHT: Here is the support, the energy and resources that you need to invigorate your Mental Plane, and it may well come in the physical personage of the Knight of Wands. It may, however, be the access to what he/she represents. **_INVERTED:_** Much of this blessing will be passed through you to others.

17 GOVERNED BY THE STAR: ASPIRATIONS OF EGO, GOALS, MAXIMUM EXPECTATIONS
UPRIGHT: Knights above all else need to be needed. The aspiration of mind to be a spiritual warrior begins with a willingness to place yourself in the front lines to absorb the hardest shockwaves of revelation, to bravely stare into the face of Zeus using the mirror of your own soul's demands to satisfy pure spirit. It is the goal of this knight to fly as near as possible to the sun without suffering the fate of Icharus. The passive nature of the initial willingness is transcended and becomes an active seeking, a need. **_INVERTED:_** To aspire toward the one, and to aspire to be the one, are two very different things. To fly into the sun is to have the wax in our wings melt before we can get there, and so fall as did Icharus.

18 GOVERNED BY THE MOON: ASPIRATIONS OF HEART, COMPASSION
UPRIGHT: This is the heart's compliment to the mind's aspiration above. This is the desire that motivated Prometheus to steal fire from the gods and offer it as a gift to man. As the fall from the Eden in the Book of Genesis is our fall into knowledge, so the gift of Prometheus's fire is our fall into spirit, into our awareness of God, and our awareness in God. Without this inner spark of divinity, the recognition of our relationship to the gods, there would be no movement toward gnosis and the one. **_INVERTED:_** This goal can be distorted into an abstraction, a process that turns its back on the very world that carries all the lessons.

19 GOVERNED BY THE SUN: PHYSICAL FULFILLMENT/EVALUATION
UPRIGHT: Everything in your Physical/material Plane has been enlisted in the battles of this knight. It is difficult to tell where you end and your environment begins. **_INVERTED:_** Let the Knight of Wands help you to the physical fulfillment.

20 GOVERNED BY JUDGEMENT: HEART'S FULFILLMENT/EVALUATION
UPRIGHT: The Knight of Wands here can suggest that the love of this person was the centerpiece and the fulfillment of your life. Love of God, agape, and its pursuit have led you to all the objects of your affection and bound you together as one. **_INVERTED:_** Let the Knight of Wands help you to the heart's fulfillment.

21 GOVERNED BY THE WORLD: EGO'S FULFILLMENT/EVALUATION
UPRIGHT: Here we see the work of Thoth/Hermes/Mercury, messenger of the Gods, the retrieval and transcription of heavenly thought into digestible bits, has been done. **_INVERTED:_** Let the Knight of Wands help you to the ego's fulfillment.

22/0 GOVERNED BY THE FOOL: SOUL'S FULFILLMENT/EVALUATION
UPRIGHT: Both fierce and benevolent, strong yet gentle, wise yet simple, you have embodied a family of characteristics that can live side by side in only the most enlightened of souls. Thus, you have been able to bridge many a gap for your fellow seekers stalled at a spiritual ravine. **_INVERTED:_** Let the Knight of Wands help you to the soul's fulfillment.

PAGE OF PENTACLES

PAGE OF PENTACLES (FIRE/EARTH)

UPRIGHT: Children of both sexes under age 12, or prepubescent. Physical type: Dark hair with dark complexion and dark eyes. Also, black hair with fair complexion and light blue, green, or violet eyes. Personality type: Predictable (for a child). Physically resourceful. Physical means of discovery. Good instincts. Communication with earth spirits, Ruled by the drive for transformation. Physically playful and active. Playground of possibility. Physical innocence, purity. Appropriate naivete in physical/material things. Lack of experience. Lessons direct from sensory experience of physical world. Physical dependence on others. This Page of Pentacles is the transformation side of things physical and represents new physical opportunities, situations, events, and guides. Drive and the forces of change for the Pages are instinctive, passive, as the growth of a child is automatic, with eating and exercise as part of the divine pre-plan, as aging itself is unstoppable. Wonder at physical things. Eagerness. Enthusiasm. Amusement. Physical renewal. Physical news (Letters, events). Ponce de Leon's fountain of youth. There is of course will and desire here, but it is subtle compared to that of an adult. **INVERTED:** A distortion of the above characteristics, either to a greater or lesser degree, with the derivative problems. For example: Unpredictable. Not a self-starter. Not in touch with the body, the inner physical self. Could have basic physical deficiencies from birth. Out of phase with physical environment. Inability to see and seize physical opportunities. **Note:** *Remember that the Courts are personifications which carry lessons to be learned, just as any of the Pips or Majors. First, they may represent characteristics of yourself. Second, they may represent people in this incarnation with you (past, present, or future). Third, they may represent people or guides not in the Earth plane with you at this time, including: yourself in past lives, others from this life passed on, others from past lifetimes, and any number of guides in the hierarchy between the Earth plane and God.*

In This Spread Position...Interpret the Page Of Pentacles Meanings to Include:

1 GOVERNED BY THE MAGICIAN: PHYSICAL GIVENS, OUT OF THE FATHER
UPRIGHT: Many of the characteristics of the physical world of a child will flavor your Physical/material Plane. Everything is bigger than life and capable of inspiring awe. You appreciate things with a fresh perspective and eagerness. Your work may be related to children, as in making toys or running an amusement park. You may defer or depend on others for much of your physical security. The youthful energy of the child will always be visible in you, even as you age. **INVERTED:** To those jaded and weary of life, you are an enigma.

2 GOVERNED BY THE HIGH PRIESTESS: EMOTIONAL GIVENS, OUT OF THE MOTHER
UPRIGHT: Many of the characteristics of the physical world of a child will flavor your Emotional/creative Plane. You will be dependent on the closeness of others for your emotional security. You are well-equipped to work with children, especially with activities, games, or sports, as well as with health care. Your creative ideas and projects are delivered with the same simplicity and originality as a child's. **INVERTED:** Some may misinterpret your air of innocence for immaturity.

3 GOVERNED BY THE EMPRESS: MENTAL GIVENS, INTELLECTUAL PREDISPOSITION
UPRIGHT: Many of the characteristics of the physical world of a child will flavor your Mental Plane. You carry the natural curiosity of the child for animals and nature in the real world, for color and form in the abstract. Your mind will favor the totally new, the avant garde. This is a characteristic seen even in the old mind of a Nobel Prize winner. **INVERTED:** Some will think you are like Dorothy (of Kansas) or Alice (of Wonderland), living in a dream world, but one which you know to be the reality behind the illusion.

4 GOVERNED BY THE EMPEROR: SPIRITUAL GIVENS, LIFE PURPOSE
UPRIGHT: Yours is a world of constant discovery. As adults must allow the child to play (which is the rudiments of learning, i.e., learning how to learn), you must allow yourself to play at life, to enjoy fully the simplest of things. **INVERTED:** This is not to avoid responsibility or to literally remain a child, but to cherish these qualities in the face of those who would have you give them up.

5 GOVERNED BY THE HIEROPHANT: SYSTEMS BORN INTO, SOCIETAL INFLUENCE
UPRIGHT: In this early environment, the sense of wonder still thrived. Frequently, the world of the artisan, whose hands stay busy playing with materials to create new realities, carries this atmosphere. There were parents with a sense of adventure that put vacations on a par with work and adults whose work was also their play. **INVERTED:** At one extreme, here is play for play's sake with few lessons being learned and little personal progress. Play here was not in preparation for the adult world to come.

6 GOVERNED BY THE LOVERS: EMOTIONAL TAPES, BASIS FOR RELATING/CREATING
UPRIGHT: Here can be seen the love of the elementals of life, the elfin magic of the woods, the Fantasia of Walt Disney. Here is the simple love of God in nature. Nature itself becomes animated, then personified, then deified. This can also be the love of a child, or children. **INVERTED:** At an extreme, this distorts into the love of the wild, the untamed, and thus a rejection of the process of civilization, of growing up, of becoming fully human.

7 GOVERNED BY THE CHARIOT: PHYSICAL RESOURCES. MEANS TO ACHIEVE
UPRIGHT: You may have discovered the fountain of physical youth, or at the very least, of renewal. Of course, energy and enthusiasm are invaluable resources, but here, too, there seems an endless source of replenishment and in a mine that ever continues to reveal new veins. **INVERTED:** In a rare case, you might have become literally dependent on a young child for your support.

8 GOVERNED BY STRENGTH: EMOTIONAL RESOURCES, ENERGY
UPRIGHT: This fountain of yours brings emotional vitality along with physical renewal. Here the energy and enthusiasm has enabled you to maintain many relationships and to fuel your creative projects. Your apparent innocence and forthrightness serves you well here. But your greatest strength comes from your intimate contact with nature and her spirits. Your strength may derive directly from a youth this Page represents. **INVERTED:** All relationships must be give and take, and your intimacy with the Earth is no different. You must not allow your energies to be tapped without your approval or without replenishment, without repayment. Or, disappointment with this Page may have weakened you temporarily.

9 GOVERNED BY THE HERMIT: BELIEF SYSTEM, BASIS FOR DECISIONS
UPRIGHT: Here is faith in the fecundity of nature, the endless cycle of death and rebirth, in the immortality of the contents of the Physical Plane. You believe in change, thriving on its magic at work all around you. This is the belief of every parent in the value of investing in their progeny, in working to put everything

in the hands of the next generation. It is the pragmatic philosophy of "you can't take it with you" raised to a credo. ***INVERTED:*** At one extreme, you may acknowledge but resent this fact of life that nothing goes with you at the end, and work even harder to keep it all for yourself while you are alive. At another extreme, you so acknowledge this fact that it overwhelms you and you decide it isn't worth the effort if it's all for nothing. Some of these people abhor children.

10 GOVERNED BY THE WHEEL OF FORTUNE: CENTRAL MESSAGE, THEME OF READING

UPRIGHT: This child is coming to you in person or sending its lessons through other signs in the Physical Plane. Accept with open arms the changes to your physical/material house. Once welcomed there will be productive growth. ***INVERTED:*** You are the agent through which this Page can deliver his/her gifts.

11 GOVERNED BY JUSTICE: STATE/CONTENT OF MIND

UPRIGHT: This Page has your attention, either in person or influence. It has brought renewal and the potential for a whole renaissance of activity, a different phase to your material house. ***INVERTED:*** You may think adversely about this Page or he/she about you.

12 GOVERNED BY THE HANGED MAN: STATE OF EMOTIONS, SUBCONSCIOUS

UPRIGHT: Your heart is on this child. He/she may be the object of your love, or the centerpiece of a creative project underway. ***INVERTED:*** Your heart may be involved with this child, but rather not be. Or, the opposite, this can be the symbol of your heart's sadness over this child.

13 GOVERNED BY DEATH: PHYSICAL SITUATION, HARD REALITY

UPRIGHT: This child is in your physical house. Change has taken place and things will never be the same again; you must turn your enterprise to the future. ***INVERTED:*** You may reject this child or he/she may reject you.

14 GOVERNED BY TEMPERANCE: EMOTIONAL TEST

UPRIGHT: The Page of Pentacles may be arriving in person in the near future. Person or not, the influence here is to reinvigorate the heart with the utter innocence of youth and its raw potential for physical/material change. The heart slows down but enlarges. Enjoy the obvious, the natural things that are close at hand. ***INVERTED:*** At one extreme, there may be a retreat by you or by the Page.

15 GOVERNED BY THE DEVIL: TEMPTATION/CHALLENGE, FEARS

UPRIGHT: Your mind will be on this page in the near future. You are pulled more and more to nature and her ways as you listen to the spirits of the Earth. The mind is called on to invest in the future by embracing youth principles in the Physical/material Plane. ***INVERTED:*** You may fear this child or what he/she represents.

16 GOVERNED BY THE TOWER: NEXT LESSON, GRACE OF GOD

UPRIGHT: Here is the youth, the freshness and purity, the new resources you need for your program in the Physical/material Plane. It may well come in the personage of the Page of Pentacles. It may, however, be the access to what he/she represents.
INVERTED: Much of this blessing will be passed through you to others.

17 GOVERNED BY THE STAR: ASPIRATIONS OF EGO, GOALS, MAXIMUM EXPECTATIONS

UPRIGHT: While the goal of the path is to grow, which is made possible by time and therefore aging, we must also aspire to youth or movement of a sort in the opposite direction. With each successive generation, the older must observe the younger and so relive their own childhood, adding new levels of understanding to old lessons and including the past in the future. The healthy goal here is to aspire always to the new, and in this case it is predominantly the new in the Physical/material Plane, as the new is always the bearer of our next karmic lesson. ***INVERTED:*** At one extreme, this is a penchant for the new with little or no respect for the old, and ironically not for the new either.

18 GOVERNED BY THE MOON: ASPIRATIONS OF HEART, COMPASSION

UPRIGHT: This archetype suggests overtly the necessity of the heart to love and respect youth, but it also infers an equal love and respect for age. Our true path must be down the middle of this duality pair like that of all others. The Page of Pentacles reminds us that we must do this with all of physical creation, all of God's creatures, and all mankind. ***INVERTED:*** Disproportionate attention to either young or old, or a neglect of one for the other.

19 GOVERNED BY THE SUN: PHYSICAL FULFILLMENT/EVALUATION

UPRIGHT: It is as though your physical legacy is fulfilled before your eyes, for you are surrounded by the youthful vigor of new enterprise and growth. You may even be building a new house, a new office as you complete your tour here. ***INVERTED:*** Let the Page of Pentacles help you to the physical fulfillment.

20 GOVERNED BY JUDGEMENT: HEART'S FULFILLMENT/EVALUATION

UPRIGHT: The Page of Pentacles here can suggest that the love of this person was the centerpiece and the fulfillment of your life. Your heart can experience its legacy in the succession of relationships that surround you. ***INVERTED:*** Let the Page of Pentacles help you to the heart's fulfillment.

21 GOVERNED BY THE WORLD: EGO'S FULFILLMENT/EVALUATION

UPRIGHT: You may have saved your best for last, certainly your most innovative. You leave behind the groundwork for a new generation of thinking such as a new invention or patent for work in the Physical/material Plane. ***INVERTED:*** Let the Page of Pentacles help you to the ego's fulfillment.

22/0 GOVERNED BY THE FOOL: SOUL'S FULFILLMENT EVALUATION

UPRIGHT: You have understood that the process of becoming old is also the process of becoming young. ***INVERTED:*** Let the Page of Pentacles help you to the soul's fulfillment.

PAGE of CUPS.

PAGE OF CUPS (FIRE/WATER)

UPRIGHT: Children of both sexes under 12, or prepubescent. Physical type: Light brown to sand-blonde hair and medium complexion, sometimes olive, with brown, blue, or gray-blue eyes. Personality type: Emotional. Sensitive. Creative. Emotionally resourceful. Loyal. Tender. Affectionate. Emotionally dependent on others. Sentimental. Ruled by the drive for the transformation. Drive and the forces of change for the Pages are instinctive, passive, as the growth of a child is automatic, with eating and exercise as part of the divine pre-plan, as aging itself is unstoppable. Good emotional feel for things. Active subconscious. Wide range of emotions, exaggeration. Emotionally playful, light-hearted. Emotional innocence, purity. Appropriate naivete in emotional/creative affairs. Lack of emotional/sexual experience. This Page of Cups is the transformation side of things emotional and represents new emotional opportunities, situations, events, and guides. Learning lessons directly from emotional interaction. Emotional renewal. Emotional news (happenings with people). Here is the fountain of emotional youth which keeps our hearts from aging just as the fountain of influence under the Page of Pentacles serves to keep our bodies young. *INVERTED:* A distortion of the above characteristics, either to a greater or lesser degree, with the derivative problems. For example: Exaggerated emotional outbursts. Temperamental. Overly dependent. Generating too much emotional activity versus missing out on possibilities. *Note: Remember that the Courts are personifications which carry lessons to be learned, just as any of the Pips or Majors. First, they may represent characteristics of yourself. Second, they may represent people in this incarnation with you (past, present, or future). Third, they may represent people or guides not in the Earth plane with you at this time, including: yourself in past lives, others from this life passed on, others from past lifetimes, and any number of guides in the hierarchy between the Earth plane and God.*

In This Spread Position...Interpret the Page Of Cups Meanings to Include:

1 GOVERNED BY THE MAGICIAN: PHYSICAL GIVENS, OUT OF THE FATHER
UPRIGHT: Many of the characteristics of the emotional world of a child will flavor your Physical/material Plane. Reactions will be big in comparison to the event or stimulus. With exaggerated emotions underpinning this plane there will be a sense of drama in your demeanor and personal appearance, and in your environment. You will wear your heart on your sleeve. Your work may be related to children. *INVERTED:* People who know you less well may be caught off guard by your childlike candor and open affection.

2 GOVERNED BY THE HIGH PRIESTESS: EMOTIONAL GIVENS, OUT OF THE MOTHER
UPRIGHT: Many of the characteristics of the emotional world of a child will flavor your Emotional/creative Plane throughout life. You are emotionally dependent on others for security, but they do not have to be physically with you. You can work well with children, as they feel you are one of them, giving you the advantage of an insider in helping them with their problems. Your creativity carries the simplicity and directness of the child's heart. Here is the wellspring of the heart's fountain of youth. *INVERTED:* Some will mistake your open heart's willingness to trust for gullibility.

3 GOVERNED BY THE EMPRESS: MENTAL GIVENS, INTELLECTUAL PREDISPOSITION
UPRIGHT: You may not be able to think like a child, that is the province of the Page of Swords, but you are predisposed to understand their emotions. Many of the characteristics of the child's emotional world will flavor your Mental Plane, even becoming its preferred subject matter.You carry their natural curiosity about people and you are an avid people watcher dissecting every nuance of body language. Your mind will favor the new and unusual in emotional and creative affairs. This may lead you into avant garde art or literature, or better yet cartooning. *INVERTED:* You are very serious about what you do, but it may not seem like it to some.

4 GOVERNED BY THE EMPEROR: SPIRITUAL GIVENS, LIFE PURPOSE
UPRIGHT: Like the Page of Pentacles, yours is a world of constant discovery. But rather than focusing on nature and material things, you are collecting experiences, observing people and the things that happen between them and what they love, with the natural and undinted curiosity of a child. *INVERTED:* What you observe in this fashion, and what you learn about the art of learning, will benefit many others, as much or more than yourself.

5 GOVERNED BY THE HIEROPHANT: SYSTEMS BORN INTO, SOCIETAL INFLUENCE
UPRIGHT: This early environment was emotionally playful and light-hearted, innocent and pure. Children of actors may experience this sort of atmosphere. There were many social events and celebrations with many people coming and going for visits in between formal occasions. *INVERTED:* It is easy to cross over the line of sociability to frivolity, and at one extreme this can be the case here.

6 GOVERNED BY THE LOVERS: EMOTIONAL TAPES, BASIS FOR RELATING/CREATING
UPRIGHT: Here can be seen the love of the spirits than enliven the emotions, the water spirits. There is a love of God in the waters of the Earth, the passion of the mariner, or the olympic swimmer. And here, too, is a love of love itself, seen in the poet's verse, seen in the eyes of even the most experienced when they discover the heart of the matter, the love of God. This can also be the love of a child, or children. *INVERTED:* All passions can consume us if over indulged and this one is no different.

7 GOVERNED BY THE CHARIOT: PHYSICAL RESOURCES. MEANS TO ACHIEVE
UPRIGHT: Your facility with people and situations keeps a steady flow of new energy and manpower in your physical/material house. Much like a cat with nine lives, you can withstand a misfortune in one area because there is so much else going on, so much overlapping. *INVERTED:* In a rare case, you might have become literally dependent on a young child for your support.

8 GOVERNED BY STRENGTH: EMOTIONAL RESOURCES, ENERGY
UPRIGHT: Your emotional fountain of youth keeps you strong, lending you great resilience in your relationships and creative affairs. Here is emotional confidence that only a youthful heart can provide; hope springs eternal. But your greatest strength derives from the waters of the Earth and their spirits. Your strength may derive directly from a youth this Page represents. *INVERTED:* All relationships must be give and take and your intimacy with the waters of the Earth is no different. You must not allow your energies to be tapped without your approval or without replenishment, without repayment. Or, disappointment with this Page may have weakened you temporarily.

9 GOVERNED BY THE HERMIT: BELIEF SYSTEM, BASIS FOR DECISIONS
UPRIGHT: Here is faith in the productive capacity, the latent energy stored in the water of the emotions, in the immortality of the contents of the emotional

plane. Love is life; it both gives and maintains life. The capacity for love is boundless, and it cannot be diminished except by ourselves, for we can love another whether or not our love is returned. As with all the Pages, this is a belief in change, here especially emotional change. Love is the generator of change. And, whereas the Page of Pentacles is the acceptance of physical change—the changes of necessity imposed by nature—the Page of Cups is the acceptance of emotional change and introduces the element of humanity known as desire. ***INVERTED:*** If one is overwhelmed by the idea of change, then it can be hard to experience the joy of the now.

10 GOVERNED BY THE WHEEL OF FORTUNE: CENTRAL MESSAGE, THEME OF READING
UPRIGHT: This child is coming to you in person or sending its lessons through other signs in the Emotional Plane. Accept with open arms the changes that have come to your emotional/creative house. ***INVERTED:*** You are the agent through which this Page can deliver his/her gifts.

11 GOVERNED BY JUSTICE: STATE/CONTENT OF MIND
UPRIGHT: This Page has your attention, either in person or influence. It has brought renewal and the potential for a whole renaissance of activity, a different phase to your emotional/creative house. ***INVERTED:*** You may think adversely about this Page or he/she about you.

12 GOVERNED BY THE HANGED MAN: STATE OF EMOTIONS, SUBCONSCIOUS
UPRIGHT: Your heart is on this child. He/she may be the object of your love, or the centerpiece of a creative project underway. ***INVERTED:*** Your heart may be involved with this child, but rather not be. Or, the opposite, this can be the symbol of your heart's sadness over this child.

13 GOVERNED BY DEATH: PHYSICAL SITUATION, HARD REALITY
UPRIGHT: This youth is in your physical house. You are learning lessons directly from emotional interaction that will change your material affairs, even your attitude and approach to your health and physical appearance. ***INVERTED:*** You may reject this child or he/she you.

14 GOVERNED BY TEMPERANCE: EMOTIONAL TEST
UPRIGHT: The Page of Cups may be arriving in person in the near future. Person or not, the influence here is to reinvigorate the heart with the utter innocence of youth and its raw potential for emotional/creative change. There will be new dimensions opening in existing relationships and/or new relationships/creativity. ***INVERTED:*** At one extreme, there may be a retreat by you or by the Page.

15 GOVERNED BY THE DEVIL: TEMPTATION/CHALLENGE, FEARS
UPRIGHT: Your mind will be on this Page in the near future. You are pulled more and more to water and her ways as you listen to her spirits—the water sprites and undines—your guides. The mind is called on to invest in the future by embracing youth principles in the Emotional/creative Plane. ***INVERTED:*** You may fear this youth or what he/she represents.

16 GOVERNED BY THE TOWER: NEXT LESSON, GRACE OF GOD
UPRIGHT: Here is the youth, the freshness and purity, the new resources you need for your program in the Emotional/creative Plane. It may well come to you in the personage of the Page of Cups. It may, however, be the access to what he/she represents. ***INVERTED:*** Much of this blessing will be passed through you to others.

17 GOVERNED BY THE STAR: ASPIRATIONS OF EGO, GOALS, MAXIMUM EXPECTATIONS
UPRIGHT: While the goal of the path is to grow, which is made possible by time and therefore aging, we must also aspire to youth or movement of a sort in the opposite direction. With each successive generation, the older must observe the younger and so relive their own childhood, adding new levels of understanding to old lessons and including the past in the future. The healthy goal here is to aspire always to the new, and in this case it is predominantly the new in the Emotional/creative Plane, as the new is always the bearer of our next karmic lesson. ***INVERTED:*** At one extreme, this is a penchant for the new with little or no respect for the old, and ironically not for the new either.

18 GOVERNED BY THE MOON: ASPIRATIONS OF HEART, COMPASSION
UPRIGHT: This archetype suggests overtly the necessity of the heart to love and respect youth, but it also infers an equal love and respect for age. Our true path is down the middle of this duality pair like that of all others. The Page of Cups reminds us that we must look to both the innocent and the experienced in the ways of love, and allow the two to merge in our hearts. The Page of Cups also reminds us to look to the creatures living in the waters of the Earth. ***INVERTED:*** Disproportionate attention to either the young or old, or neglect of one for the other.

19 GOVERNED BY THE SUN: PHYSICAL FULFILLMENT/EVALUATION
UPRIGHT: You are surrounded physically by your emotional legacy, such as grandchildren or a host of new projects. ***INVERTED:*** Let the Page of Cups help you to the physical fulfillment.

20 GOVERNED BY JUDGEMENT: HEART'S FULFILLMENT/EVALUATION
UPRIGHT: The Page of Cups here can suggest that the love of this person was the centerpiece and the fulfillment of your life. Ever fresh, ever open to the new, your heart has been filled to the brim with new sensations to expand the definition of love. ***INVERTED:*** Let the Page of Cups help you to the heart's fulfillment.

21 GOVERNED BY THE WORLD: EGO'S FULFILLMENT/EVALUATION
UPRIGHT: The mind has been dedicated to this Page, and so to the ideal of ever new means to express new loves. You leave behind a record of a new way of loving. ***INVERTED:*** Let the Page of Cups help you to the ego's fulfillment.

22/0 GOVERNED BY THE FOOL: SOUL'S FULFILLMENT/EVALUATION
UPRIGHT: By following the path of the young heart you have enlarged your awareness of agape. ***INVERTED:*** Let the Page of Cups help you to the soul's fulfillment.

PAGE of SWORDS.

PAGE OF SWORDS (FIRE/AIR)

UPRIGHT: Children of both sexes under age 12, or prepubescent. Physical type: Blonde to light blonde hair and fair complexion with blue, blue-gray or greenish-brown eyes. Personality type: Mental. Assertive. Alert. Thoughtful. Impressionable. Investigative. Curious. Vigilant. Ruled by the drive for transformation. Drive and the forces of change for the Pages are instinctive, passive, as the growth of a child is automatic, with eating and exercise as part of the divine pre-plan, as aging itself is unstoppable. Insightful. Highly active consciousness. Probing. Mentally playful, Mental innocence, purity. Appropriate naivete in mental affairs. Lack of mental experience. This Page of Swords is the transformation side of things mental and represents new intellectual opportunities, situations, events, and guides. Learning lessons directly from mental interaction. Mental renewal. Mental news (radio, TV, conversations). Here is the fountain of mental youth which keeps our minds from aging just as the fountain of influence under the Page of Pentacles serves to keep our bodies young. **INVERTED:** A distortion of the above characteristics, either to a greater or lesser degree, with the derivative problems. For example: Overly curious versus apathetic. Mentally stagnant versus rambling inefficiency, with too much going on. Generating too many ideas but not enough follow-through. Inefficient in communications. ***Note:*** *Remember that the Courts are personifications which carry lessons to be learned, just as any of the Pips or Majors. First, they may represent characteristics of yourself. Second, they may represent people in this incarnation with you (past, present, or future). Third, they may represent people or guides not in the Earth plane with you at this time, including: yourself in past lives, others from this life passed on, others from past lifetimes, and any number of guides in the hierarchy between the Earth plane and God.*

In This Spread Position...Interpret the Page Of Swords Meanings to Include:

1 GOVERNED BY THE MAGICIAN: PHYSICAL GIVENS, OUT OF THE FATHER
UPRIGHT: Many of the characteristics of the mental world of a child will flavor your Physical/material Plane. Fantasy and imagination will play an important and positive role, as it does for the comedian/actor Robin Williams. Your livelihood may be related to children, especially educationally, as in books or schooling. **INVERTED:** You will be a constant source of amazement to your friends.

2 GOVERNED BY THE HIGH PRIESTESS: EMOTIONAL GIVENS, OUT OF THE MOTHER
UPRIGHT: Many of the characteristics of the mental world of a child will flavor your Emotional/creative Plane. You are mentally dependent on others for security, but they do not have to be physically near you. Here as well as in position 3, there is an ability to help children with their problems because you can think like they do. Creatively you have the advantage of an unspoiled, original imagination dedicated to bringing forth the new. **INVERTED:** You may frustrate those who want you to be serious, especially romantic partners because you always want to experiment and can find humor in any situation, and usually do.

3 GOVERNED BY THE EMPRESS: MENTAL GIVENS, INTELLECTUAL PREDISPOSITION
UPRIGHT: Many of the characteristics of the child's mental world will flavor this plane throughout life. You can think like a child and so make an excellent psychologist/counselor, and you will speak and write with their simplicity and directness. You are a natural at children's books, games, activities, Here is the wellspring of the mind's fountain of youth. You will always have the latest greatest on all the subjects of your interest. **INVERTED:** As you are so impressionable, many will try to impress you.

4 GOVERNED BY THE EMPEROR: SPIRITUAL GIVENS, LIFE PURPOSE
UPRIGHT: Like the Page of Pentacles, yours is a world of constant discovery. But you use principally your mind for your adventures and to collect your souvenirs. Whereas the Page of Pentacles turns his/her real world into a fantasy, you are capable of turning your fantasies into the real world. **INVERTED:** This is the mark of the dreamer, the daydreamer especially, so you may want to wear padded clothing for bumping into the odd telephone pole now and then.

5 GOVERNED BY THE HIEROPHANT: SYSTEMS BORN INTO, SOCIETAL INFLUENCE
UPRIGHT: Perhaps your early environment was like a testing laboratory for a consumer's advocacy magazine? Or, your house was built on a cushion of air? Light-hearted academia fits this profile as well, for here you were able to exercise your young mind freely and had plenty of resources to help you. **INVERTED:** At one extreme, everything was too fresh, with little or no anchor to tie the new to, like a room full of good references but with no filing system to retrieve any of it efficiently.

6 GOVERNED BY THE LOVERS: EMOTIONAL TAPES, BASIS FOR RELATING/CREATING
UPRIGHT: Here can be seen the love of the air spirits that enliven the mind, the fairies. This is a love of God in the winds and the heights of the Earth, the passion of the flyer and the mountain climber. Here, too, is the love of novelty, of revelation, seen in plan for a new invention, seen in the eyes of the most experienced when they discover the concept of the matter, the mind of God. **INVERTED:** All passions can consume us if over indulged and this one is no different.

7 GOVERNED BY THE CHARIOT: PHYSICAL RESOURCES. MEANS TO ACHIEVE
UPRIGHT: This is the advantage of the general who has the best reconnaissance team, the calvary officer with the best advance scout. Contemporary society is the age of information, and you have what you need at your fingertips. Collection and dissemination of information may be your business. **INVERTED:** Unless you are being paid to push information around, there may be too much here for your purposes. At the other extreme, there may be too little, or it may be dated.

8 GOVERNED BY STRENGTH: EMOTIONAL RESOURCES, ENERGY
UPRIGHT: Your mental fountain of youth keeps you strong as you maintain excellent communication between all the objects of your attention, both people and creative projects. Your greatest strength derives from the winds of the Earth and their spirits; the air talks to you. Your strength may derive directly from a youth this Page represents. **INVERTED:** All relationships must be give and take and your intimacy with the winds of the Earth is no different. You must not allow your energies to be tapped without your approval or without replenishment, without repayment. Or, disappointment with this Page may have weakened you temporarily.

9 GOVERNED BY THE HERMIT: BELIEF SYSTEM, BASIS FOR DECISIONS
UPRIGHT: Here is faith in the fertility, the patient potential waiting in the winds of the mind, in the immortality of the contents of the Mental Plane. Here is faith in mind as both plan and executor of life. As with all the Pages, this is a belief in change, here especially mental change. Mind is the management of

change; thus mental change is a change in the management of change. And, whereas the Page of Pentacles is the acceptance of physical change—the changes of necessity imposed by nature—the Page of Swords is the acceptance of mental change and introduces the element of humanity known as will. ***INVERTED:*** If one is overwhelmed by the idea of change, then it can be hard to experience the joy of the now.

10 GOVERNED BY THE WHEEL OF FORTUNE: CENTRAL MESSAGE, THEME OF READING
UPRIGHT: This child is coming to you in person or sending its lessons through other signs in the Mental Plane. Accept with open arms the changes that have come to your mental house. ***INVERTED:*** You are the agent through which the Page can deliver his/her gifts.

11 GOVERNED BY JUSTICE: STATE/CONTENT OF MIND
UPRIGHT: This Page has your attention, either in person or influence. It has brought renewal and the potential for a whole renaissance of activity, a different phase to your mental house. ***INVERTED:*** You may think adversely about this Page or he/she about you.

12 GOVERNED BY THE HANGED MAN: STATE OF EMOTIONS, SUBCONSCIOUS
UPRIGHT: Your heart is on this child. He/she may be the object of your love, or the centerpiece of a creative project underway. ***INVERTED:*** Your heart may be involved with this child, but rather not be. Or, the opposite, this can be the symbol of your heart's sadness over this child.

13 GOVERNED BY DEATH: PHYSICAL SITUATION, HARD REALITY
UPRIGHT: This youth is in your physical house. You are learning lessons directly from mental interaction that will change your material affairs, even your attitude and approach to your health and appearance. ***INVERTED:*** You may reject this child or he/she you.

14 GOVERNED BY TEMPERANCE: EMOTIONAL TEST
UPRIGHT: The Page of Swords may be arriving in person in the near future. Person or not, the influence here is to reinvigorate the heart with the mind's innocence and purity and draw support for mental change. This generates new possibilities in existing relationships and/or new relationships/creativity. ***INVERTED:*** At one extreme, there may be a retreat by you or by the Page.

15 GOVERNED BY THE DEVIL: TEMPTATION/CHALLENGE, FEARS
UPRIGHT: Your mind will be on this Page in the near future. You are pulled more and more to the element air and her ways as you listen to her spirits of the wind—the sylphs—your guides. The mind is called on to invest in the future by embracing youth principles in the Mental Plane. ***INVERTED:*** You may fear this youth or what he/she represents.

16 GOVERNED BY THE TOWER: NEXT LESSON, GRACE OF GOD
UPRIGHT: Here is the youth, the freshness and purity, the new resources you need for your program in the Mental Plane. It may well come to you in the personage of the Page of Cups. It may, however, be the access to what he/she represents. ***INVERTED:*** Much of this blessing will be passed through you to others.

17 GOVERNED BY THE STAR: ASPIRATIONS OF EGO, GOALS, MAXIMUM EXPECTATIONS
UPRIGHT: While the goal of the path is to grow, which is made possible by time and therefore aging, we must also aspire to youth or movement of a sort in the opposite direction. With each successive generation, the older must observe the younger and so relive their own childhood, adding new levels of understanding to old lessons and including the past in the future. The healthy goal here is to aspire always to the new, and in this case it is predominantly the new in the Mental Plane, as the new is always the bearer of our next karmic lesson. ***INVERTED:*** At one extreme, this is a penchant for the new with little or no respect for the old, and ironically not for the new either.

18 GOVERNED BY THE MOON: ASPIRATIONS OF HEART, COMPASSION
UPRIGHT: This archetype suggests overtly the necessity of the heart to love and respect youth, but it also infers an equal love and respect for age. Our true path is down the middle of this duality pair like that of all the others. The Page of Swords reminds us that we must look to history and the ways of elders and to the bright unburdened minds of youth, embracing both equally in our hearts. ***INVERTED:*** Disproportionate attention to either the young or old, or neglect of one for the other.

19 GOVERNED BY THE SUN: PHYSICAL FULFILLMENT/EVALUATION
UPRIGHT: You are surrounded by the material results of your invigorated and productive mind. The impact of your innovative mind is visible everywhere in your environment, and most likely that of many others as well. ***INVERTED:*** Let the Page of Swords help you to the physical fulfillment.

20 GOVERNED BY JUDGEMENT: HEART'S FULFILLMENT/EVALUATION
UPRIGHT: The Page of Swords here can suggest that the love of this person was the centerpiece and the fulfillment of your life. Your heart is most content lightened by its participation in the youthful, enlightening goals of your mind. ***INVERTED:*** Let the Page of Swords help you to the heart's fulfillment.

21 GOVERNED BY THE WORLD: EGO'S FULFILLMENT/EVALUATION
UPRIGHT: The mind has been dedicated to this Page, and so to the ideal of ever new means to express new thoughts. You leave behind a new way of thinking. ***INVERTED:*** Let the Page of Swords help you to the ego's fulfillment.

22/0 GOVERNED BY THE FOOL: SOUL'S FULFILLMENT/EVALUATION
UPRIGHT: You have used the playground of the mind as a means of grounding play. ***INVERTED:*** Let the Page of Swords help you to the soul's fulfillment.

PAGE OF WANDS (FIRE/FIRE)

UPRIGHT: Children of both sexes under age 12, or prepubescent. Physical type: Red to reddish-blonde or reddish-brown hair and fair or freckled complexion with green or blue eyes. Personality type: Highly intuitive. Very sensitive. Vibrant. Fiery. Introspective. Humorous. Sincere. Attentive. Uninhibited. A prodigy. Ruled by the drive for transformation. Drive and the forces of change for the Pages are instinctive, passive, as the growth of a child is automatic, with eating and exercise as part of the divine pre-plan, as aging itself is unstoppable. Superconsciousness. Spiritually playful. Spiritual innocence, purity. Appropriate naivete in spiritual affairs. This Page of Wands is the transformation side for things intuitive/spiritual and represents new opportunities, situations, events, and guides which bring us messages of exceptional insight and inspiration. Spiritual renewal. Spiritual news (insight, inspiration, guide's messages, synchronicity, serendipity). Here is the fountain of spiritual youth which keeps our souls vigorous in the Earth plane. **INVERTED:** A distortion of the above characteristics, whether to a greater or lesser degree, with the derivative problems. For example: Difficulty getting things going in intuitive/spiritual matters. Difficulty getting the message, recognizing guides, decoding events. A prodigy situation that is stagnant. Misapplied humor. Inhibited. Intemperate behavior. **Note:** *Remember that the Courts are personifications which carry lessons to be learned, just as any of the Pips or Majors. First, they may represent characteristics of yourself. Second, they may represent people in this incarnation with you (past, present, or future). Third, they may represent people or guides not in the Earth plane with you at this time, including: yourself in past lives, others from this life passed on, others from past lifetimes, and any number of guides in the hierarchy between the Earth plane and God.*

In This Spread Position...Interpret the Page Of Wands Meanings to Include:

1 GOVERNED BY THE MAGICIAN: PHYSICAL GIVENS, OUT OF THE FATHER
UPRIGHT: Many of the characteristics of the spiritual world of a child will flavor your Physical/material Plane. You can be comfortably alone in the midst of a crowd, for you carry your best friends with you everywhere. Your livelihood may be related to children, especially in religious and spiritual schooling/training. **INVERTED:** At one extreme, you may not ever work conventionally for a living.

2 GOVERNED BY THE HIGH PRIESTESS: EMOTIONAL GIVENS, OUT OF THE MOTHER
UPRIGHT: Many of the characteristics of the spiritual world of a child will flavor your Emotional/creative Plane. You will get along well with all age groups, but especially with children. Your interest in people goes deep into the whole person, even when your interest is intensely personal, even sexual. Your creativity is of unparalleled excellence, embodying as it does the energy of heaven. **INVERTED:** At one extreme, sex will be of little interest to you.

3 GOVERNED BY THE EMPRESS: MENTAL GIVENS, INTELLECTUAL PREDISPOSITION
UPRIGHT: Many of the characteristics of the child's spiritual world will flavor your Mental Plane, even becoming its preferred subject matter. Your mind will favor the subtleties of spirituality and will be meant to receive and relate the current revelations to guide today's society. You will teach all ages but when you teach adults you will teach them as little children, with great simplicity and clarity so that there is little room for confusion or loose interpretation. **INVERTED:** Because you carry the innocence and energy of a child, some will foolishly pay you little attention.

4 GOVERNED BY THE EMPEROR: SPIRITUAL GIVENS, LIFE PURPOSE
UPRIGHT: Like the other Pages, yours is a world of constant discovery. But your wonder embraces the fascinations of all three of their worlds, the material, emotional, and mental, and to that is added the wonder of continual spiritual revelation. **INVERTED:** What you observe and what you learn will be of benefit to many others as it is to yourself. This is the path of the wandering innocent who bears witness to what he has seen and heard in his travels.

5 GOVERNED BY THE HIEROPHANT: SYSTEMS BORN INTO, SOCIETAL INFLUENCE
UPRIGHT: An environment lacking in spiritual sophistication perhaps, i.e., little ritual or formal religion, but with a purity of purpose and strong ethical sense. One or more of the adults of authority here were highly attuned to their guides and very much on their karmic path. **INVERTED:** Spiritual discipline may have been erratic, or perhaps confusion with messages, disciplines. Many messages, little witnessing.

6 GOVERNED BY THE LOVERS: EMOTIONAL TAPES, BASIS FOR RELATING/CREATING
UPRIGHT: Here can be seen a love of the spirits that enliven spirit itself, that give it its name and identity. These are the energies, the guides from above which illuminate the pages of our Karmic Contract to remind us of our timely lessons. This passion is a love of God through his messengers, the archangels and the guides from our karmic lineage. **INVERTED:** All passions can consume us if overindulged and this one is no different. Our loves, at all levels and in all forms, are manifestations of an aspect of God and cannot be allowed to replace the One, the All. This is the lesson of the first commandment of the Bible, "Thou shalt have no other gods before me." (Exodus, 20:3)

7 GOVERNED BY THE CHARIOT: PHYSICAL RESOURCES. MEANS TO ACHIEVE
UPRIGHT: This is the advantage of insightful meditation, good prayer, spiritual divination, to bring us information that will help us in our physical lives. Your best resource is your access to the information you need for your health and business. **INVERTED:** In a rare case you may have become dependent on this youth for your support.

8 GOVERNED BY STRENGTH: EMOTIONAL RESOURCES, ENERGY
UPRIGHT: Your spiritual fountain of youth is your source of strength. In listening to and getting your messages at the spiritual level you remain centered and healthy. Your strength may derive directly from a youth this Page represents. **INVERTED:** All relationships must be give and take and your intimacy with your spiritual guides (spirits of fire) is no different. You must not allow your energies to be tapped without your approval or without replenishment, without repayment. Or, disappointment with this Page may have weakened you temporarily.

9 GOVERNED BY THE HERMIT: BELIEF SYSTEM, BASIS FOR DECISIONS
UPRIGHT: Here is faith in the energy that resides in the fires of the spirit, in the immortality of the contents of the Spiritual Plane. Here is faith in spirit, in the process of spirit communicating to man, of spirit manifesting in man when we tune in and witness. As with the other Pages, here too is belief in change, spiritual change, which is to say life eternal. And...whereas the Page of Pentacles is the acceptance of physical change (the changes of necessity imposed by nature), the Page of Cups is the acceptance of emotional change thereby introducing the human element of desire, the Page of Swords is the acceptance of mental change thereby introducing the human element of will...the Page of Wands is the acceptance of spiritual change and

introduces the element of humanity known as Self-Mastery. ***INVERTED:*** If one is overwhelmed by the idea of change, then it can be hard to experience the joy of the now.

10 GOVERNED BY THE WHEEL OF FORTUNE: CENTRAL MESSAGE, THEME OF READING

UPRIGHT: This child is coming to you in person or sending its lessons through other signs in the Spiritual Plane. Accept with open arms the changes that have come to your spiritual house. ***INVERTED:*** You are the agent through which the Page can deliver his/her gifts.

11 GOVERNED BY JUSTICE: STATE/CONTENT OF MIND

UPRIGHT: This Page has your attention, either in person or influence. It has brought renewal and the potential for a whole renaissance of activity, a different phase to your spiritual house. ***INVERTED:*** You may think adversely about this Page or he/she about you.

12 GOVERNED BY THE HANGED MAN: STATE OF EMOTIONS, SUBCONSCIOUS

UPRIGHT: Your heart is on this youth. He/she may be the object of your love, or the centerpiece of a creative project underway. ***INVERTED:*** Your heart may be involved with this child, but rather not be. Or, the opposite, this can be the symbol of your heart's sadness over this child.

13 GOVERNED BY DEATH: PHYSICAL SITUATION, HARD REALITY

UPRIGHT: This youth is in your physical house. You are learning directly from spiritual interaction what will change your material affairs, even your attitude and approach to your health and appearance. ***INVERTED:*** You may reject this child or he/she you.

14 GOVERNED BY TEMPERANCE: EMOTIONAL TEST

UPRIGHT: The Page of Wands may be arriving in person in the near future. Person or not, the influence here is to reinvigorate the heart with the innocence of spirit and draw support for spiritual change. This generates new possibilities in existing relationships and/or new relationships/creativity. ***INVERTED:*** At one extreme, there may be a retreat by you or by the Page.

15 GOVERNED BY THE DEVIL: TEMPTATION/CHALLENGE, FEARS

UPRIGHT: Your mind will be on this Page in the near future. You are pulled more and more into the element fire and her ways as you listen to her spirits—the salamanders—your guides. The mind is called on to invest in the future by embracing youth principles in the Spiritual Plane. ***INVERTED:*** You may fear this youth or what he/she represents.

16 GOVERNED BY THE TOWER: NEXT LESSON, GRACE OF GOD

UPRIGHT: Here is youth, the freshness and purity, the new resources you need for your program in the Mental Plane. It may well come to you in the personage of the Page of Wands. It may, however, be the access to what he/she represents. ***INVERTED:*** Much of this blessing will be passed through you to others.

17 GOVERNED BY THE STAR: ASPIRATIONS OF EGO, GOALS, MAXIMUM EXPECTATIONS

UPRIGHT: While the goal of the path is to grow, which is made possible by time and therefore aging, we must also aspire to youth or movement of a sort in the opposite direction. With each successive generation, the older must observe the younger and so relive their own childhood, adding new levels of understanding to old lessons and including the past in the future. The healthy goal here is to aspire always to the new, and in this case it is predominantly the new in the Spiritual Plane, as the new is always the bearer of our next karmic lesson. ***INVERTED:*** At one extreme, this is a penchant for the new with little or no respect for the old, and ironically not for the new either.

18 GOVERNED BY THE MOON: ASPIRATIONS OF HEART, COMPASSION

UPRIGHT: This archetype suggest overtly the necessity of the heart to love and respect youth, but it also infers an equal love and respect for age. Our true path is down the middle of this duality pair like that of all the others. The Page of Wands reminds us that we must listen to the instincts from below which is the wisdom instilled into us at our birth, and to the intuition from above which is the wisdom given to us each moment of our life, embracing both equally in our hearts. ***INVERTED:*** Disproportionate attention to either the instincts or the intuition, or neglect of one for the other.

19 GOVERNED BY THE SUN: PHYSICAL FULFILLMENT/EVALUATION

UPRIGHT: You are surrounded everywhere by the material results of your attention to the Spiritual Plane, and your successful balance of intuition and instinct. ***INVERTED:*** Let the Page of Wands help you to the physical fulfillment.

20 GOVERNED BY JUDGEMENT: HEART'S FULFILLMENT/EVALUATION

UPRIGHT: The Page of Wands here can suggest that the love of this person was the centerpiece and the fulfillment of your life. Your heart is full with the love of God and self, with self in God, and with God in self. ***INVERTED:*** Let the Page of Wands help you to the heart's fulfillment.

21 GOVERNED BY THE WORLD: EGO'S FULFILLMENT/EVALUATION

UPRIGHT: The mind has been dedicated to this Page, and so to the ideal of ever new revelations shared. You leave behind a new way of seeing and hearing God. ***INVERTED:*** Let the Page of Wands help you to the ego's fulfillment.

22/0 GOVERNED BY THE FOOL: SOUL'S FULFILLMENT/EVALUATION

UPRIGHT: Here is a man who could listen...and act out what he heard. ***INVERTED:*** Let the Page of Wands help you to the soul's fulfillment.

Chart 6
A SUMMARY OF MINOR ARCANA MEANINGS (PIPS)

ONEs (ACEs) BEGINNINGS UNITY/TOTALITY Physical	TWOs DUALITY/CHOICES COOPERATION Emotional	THREEs RESOLUTION/FRUI- TION/EXPRESSION Mental	FOURs FOUNDATION/STA- BILITY/RELIABILITY Spiritual	FIVEs UNCERTAIINTY/FREE- DOM/MULTIPLE CHOICE Mental	
1 Physical/Spiritual	**2 Emotional/Spiritual**	**3 Mental/Spiritual**	**4 Spiritual/Spiritual**	**5 Mental/Spiritual**	
- Spiritual beginnings - Spiritual fulfillment - Awakening/rebirth - Open'g Third Eye/ Crown Chakra - Highly intuitive - New beliefs/goals - An Initiate - Inspiration/insight - Apparent good luck - Happiness	- Spiritual & intuitive choices/uncertainty - Growth alternatives - Growth potential - Opportunity - Lure of adventure - Consideration - Receptiveness - Oaths, Vows, Pledges	- Optimism - Dedication - Intuitive decisions - Spiritual synthesis - Foresight, vision - Power/strength for major achievement	- Spiritual balance, foundation - Spiritual plateau - Reliable values, a working theology - Practising faith - Spiritual confidence - Celebration - Fellowship - Thanksgiving - Confirmation - Honesty	- Lack of spiritual movement. - Struggle with concepts - Freedom of Spirit - Moral dilemmas - Healthy conflict - Spiritual cptions - Competition - Asserting values - Testing waters	**WANDS** Spiritual
1 Physical/Mental	**2 Emotional/Mental**	**3 Mental/Mental**	**4 Spiritual/Mental**	**5 Mental/Mental**	
- Mental beginnings - Mental fulfillment - New concepts - Clarity of thought - Good teaching/ communication/ admin. skills - Opening of Throat Chakra - Mentally blessed - Root of Truth & Justice	- Mental choices - Negotiations, Arbitration, Debate, Compromise, Truce - Diplomacy, Tact - Contract - Devil's advocate - Critique, Review - Mental marriage - Objectivity	- Decisiveness - Directness - Mental clarity - Mind over emotions - Organization - Control - Efficiency - Factuality - Mental synthesis - Literacy/expression - Articulation, Wit - Enthusiasm	- Mental balance - Meditation - Mental plateau - Mental foundation - Graduation - Discipline - Self-esteem - Dignity - Competence - Patience - Mental confidence - Ment. institutions	- Lack of mental progression, resolution, yet wheels turning - Interim decisions - Prioritizing, Review - Investigation - Freedom of thought, options - Patience - Self-critical - Concern, worry	**SWORDS** Mental
1 Physical/Emotional	**2 Emotional/Emotional**	**3 Mental/Emotional**	**4 Spiritual/Emotional**	**5 Mental/Emotional**	
- Emotional beginning or fulfillment - Opening of Heart Chakra and/or Genital/ Solar Plexus - Proposal - Baptism - Great joy - Cleansing/healing - Fertility/receptivity	- Emotional/creative choices - Proposals - Passion/Sex, Love, & Marriage - Creative partner- ships, Harmony of opposites - Relationships, one to one - Reconciliation - Cooperation	- Pregnancy, Children - Happy issue - Results of love - Love expanding - Commitment - Emotional fruition - Creative outflow - Sociability - Joy	- Creative/emotional balance - Emotional founda- tion, stability - Emot. confidence - Emotional plateau - Faithful, Loyal - Creative balance - Healthy self-love - Amiability	- Lack of emotional/ creative movement - Emotional freedom, uncertainty - Adaptability - Heart options - Hard to let go - Sadness - Depression - Pessimism - Disappointment - Tolerance	**CUPS** Emotional
1 Physical/Physical	**2 Emotional/Physical**	**3 Mental/Physical**	**4 Spiritual/Physical**	**5 Mental/Physical**	
- Material beginnings - Material fulfillment - Good fortune - Good health - Material perfection - Physically blessed - New bus. ventures - New regimen/diet - Physical prowess - Material potential - Open'g 1st (Root) Chakra	- Physical/material choices - Bus. negotiations - Question re: Health, Security - Competition: i.e. Financial, Athletic - Tests of Strength, Reliability - Physical joining - Agility, Flexibility - Dexterity	- Productive labor - Craftsmanship - Apprenticeship - Working knowledge of physical plane - Physical therapy - Medicine & Health care - Practicality - Physical direction - Material synthesis - Athletic prowess	- Centered physically - Material foundation - Physical and Fiscal security - Institutions/Corp: Financial, Medical, Insurance - Civilization - Physical control, police, military - Dependability - Physical confidence	- Lack of movement, in Health, Finances - Physically idle - Restlessness - Hesitation - Independence - Phys. freedom, Uncertainty, Insecurity - Holding pattern	**PENTACLES** Physical

Note: See the individual definition sheets earlier in Chapter Seven for more detailed upright meanings and for inverted meanings.

Chart 6 (continued)
A SUMMARY OF MINOR ARCANA MEANINGS (PIPS)

	SIXs MOVEMENT/DUTY EXTERNALIZATION Emotional	SEVENs NEW BEGINNINGS/ DIRECTIONS Physical	EIGHTs INDUSTRY/ORDER INCENTIVE Emotional	NINEs REALIZATION SELFLESSNESS Mental	TENs COMPLETION PERFECTION Spiritual
WANDS Spiritual	**6 Emotional/Spiritual** - Spiritual recognition - Moral victory - Promotions/rewards - Goals, progress validated - Perseverance - Devotion, Resolve - Spiritual motivation - Progress w/Karma - Keeping/advancing the faith	**7 Physical/Spiritual** - Maturing process for faith - Spiritual harvest, Replanting - Taking a stand, Resolve - Defending beliefs - Zen, Hatha Yoga - Strong character, Integrity - Unsolicited advice	**8 Emotional/Spiritual** - Love of God motivates - Emotionally committed to Spiritual - Spirit takes wing - Creative/spiritual breakthrough - Spiritual power - Missionary zeal - Tantra Yoga	**9 Mental/Spiritual** - Solid philosophy - Personal truth aligned w/ universal - Knowing God intellectually - Theology - Purposeful life - On target w/Karma - Gnani Yoga - Hidden resources - Spiritual confidence - True teacher	**10 Spiritual/Spiritual** - Completion of Spiritual Cycle - Knowing God, Gnosis - Spirit in control - Spirituall Master - The dedicated life - Preparation for even greater work - Endurance, Longevity
SWORDS Mental	**6 Emotional/Mental** - Mental generosity - Responsibility - Promoting ideas - Advancing thought, Progress - Service as work - Emotions support mind - Conscientious - Considerate - Mental recognition	**7 Physical/Mental** - Mental harvest, Replanting - Mental bounty, numerous options - Perfectionist - Added Schooling, Training - Information storage/ transmittal, Media, Libraries, Computer - Materializing ideas - Measuring	**8 Emotional/Mental** - Maturing mind, Control of ego - Objective mind reaching limits - Open-minded, Broadminded - Perspective, Overview - Wealth of detailed information	**9 Mental/Mental** - You know what you don't know - Capping personal philosophy/beliefs - Major decisions - Raja Yoga - Deeply meditative - Idealistic - Theoretician/ Mathematician - Ultim. responsibility	**10 Spiritual/Mental** - Completion of Mental Cycle - Ego Death/Re-birth - Mind yields control to Spirit - Major change in philosophy/beliefs - Mind fully matures - Realization of Universal Mind
CUPS Emotional	**6 Emotional/Emotional** - Emotional generosity - Sincerity - Good manners - Sympathy/empathy - Emotional recognition - Nostalgia - Sentiment - Flattery, Charm - Extending family	**7 Physical/Emotional** - Emotional harvest, Replanting - Emotional bounty, numerous options - Heart's evaluation, storage - Pandora's Box, potentially - Emot. temptations	**8 Emotional/Emotional** - Maturing emotions - Emotional stockpiling - Emotional quest - Eagerness - Prodigal Son - Enrichment & Enhancement - Enlargement - Extroversion & Inclusion	**9 Mental/Emotional** - Contentment - Good emotional support systems - Benevolent, restorative power - Full of energy - Compassionate - Deeply creative, Sensitive - Poetic lifestyle - Theater/Arts/Music - In touch, in tune	**10 Spiritual/Emotional** - Completion of Emotional Cycle - Highest Emotional achievements - Realization of Universal Love - Emotional stability - Fullest enjoyment - Family events. - Life rich w/ meaning
PENTACLES Physical	**6 Emotional/Physical** - Material generosity - Charity - Physical/material favors, giving or receiving - Volunteering - Paying dues/fees - Sharing - Supporting self and others - Accepting obligations	**7 Physical/Physical** - Physical maturation - Harvest, Replanting - Abundant supply - Inventory, taking stock - Harnessing, yet harmony w/Nature - Savings, Stocks/ Investments - Well-positioned - Poised - Gourmet	**8 Emotional/Physical** - Appreciation of Physical/material - Love of work, quality results - Thoroughness, Precision/Efficiency - Physical prowess, Athleticism - Productivity/surplus - Proper use of power, resources - Teamwork/network	**9 Mental/Physical** - Appreciating good health, success - Personal Garden of Eden, healthy surroundings - Productive leisure - Fluent w/Nature - Effect of mind in physical healing - Evidence of mind in books, art, civilization	**10 Spiritual/Physical** - Completion of Physical Cycle - Material prosperity - Healthy family - Material/Financial Legacy - Ongoing security - Mat. achievements benefiting others

Chart 6A
A SUMMARY OF MINOR ARCANA MEANINGS (COURTS)

	PAGES (Spiritual) Children of both sexes under 12 Ruled by Transformative Drive	KNIGHTS (Mental) Teenagers & single young adults of both sexes Ruled by Expansive Drive	QUEENS (Emotional) Mature & married females Ruled by Drive of the Heart	KINGS (Physical) Mature & married males Ruled by Drive of Necessity
WANDS Spiritual/Intuition By Physical Type: These people will be of red or reddish-blonde hair with green, blue, blue-gray eyes. By Personality Type: These people will be active, keen, fiery & introspective.	**Page of Wands*** Spiritual/Spiritual • Combination of FIRE + FIRE • Spiritual guide • Spiritual news (insight, inspiration) • Highly intuitive, a prodigy • Messages from dreams • Uninhibited • Inner child • New faith	**Knight of Wands** Mental/Spiritual • Combination of AIR + FIRE • Defender of faith/beliefs • Philosophical shifts/ changes • Bringer of new insights/ world views • Disciple • Intuitive action	**Queen of Wands** Emotional/Spiritual • Combination of WATER + FIRE • Mother of Beliefs • Spiritual nurse • Female counselor • Inner confidence • Spiritual energy/drive • Female inspiration • Philosophical guide	**King of Wands** Physical/Spiritual • Combination of EARTH + FIRE • Father of beliefs • Benevolence • Advisor/counselor • Intuitive control • A divine leader
SWORDS Mental/Will/Action By Physical Type: These people will be of light blonde hair & fair skin with blue, blue-gray or greenish-brown eyes. By Personality Type: These people will be active, physically strong, direct & extroverted.	**Page of Swords** Spiritual/Mental • Combination of FIRE + AIR • Mental guide • Mental news (radio, TV, conversations) • Alertness, quickness • Thoughtful • Investigative, curious • Preparedness, vigilance • Intellectual • New knowledge	**Knight of Swords*** Mental/Mental • Combination of AIR + AIR • Defender of ideologies • Bringer of new ideas & methodologies • Intellectual growth • Student	**Queen of Swords** Emotional/Mental • Combination of WATER + AIR • Mother of solutions • Nurse of ideas • Channel of/for thought • Mental guide • Teaching, directing • Planning	**King of Swords** Physical/Mental • Combination of EARTH + AIR • Father of ideas • Defender • Confidant • Advisor • Mentor • Teacher • Manager • Knowledgeable leader
CUPS Emotional/Creativity By Physical Type: These people will be of light brown to dark brown hair with brown or gray-blue eyes. By Personality Type: These people will be sensitive, emotional, mood-swinging & dedicated when motivated.	**Page of Cups** Spiritual/Emotional • Combination of FIRE + WATER • Emotional guide • Emotional news (happenings with people) • Innocence, virginity • Temperamental, considerate • Sentimentality • New emotion	**Knight of Cups** Mental/Emotional • Combination of AIR + WATER • Defender of heart/honor • Novice • Lover (with older partner) (innocence maturing) • Sacrificing, expansive • Emotional change agent • Nurturing agent	**Queen of Cups*** Emotional/Emotional • Combination of WATER + WATER • Loving mother • Nurse of emotional wounds • Nurturing • Enchantress, muse • Psychic insights • Sensuality • Channel for love	**King of Cups** Physical/Emotional • Combination of EARTH + WATER • Loving father • Sensual • Tender • Bountiful • Soothing • Refreshing • Healer
PENTACLES Physical/Material By Physical Type: These people will be of dark hair & dark complexion (or extremely fair complexion) with dark brown, light blue, green or violet eyes. By Personality Type: These people are sturdy, reliable, hard-working & interesting can-doers.	**Page of Pentacles** Spiritual/Physical • Combination of FIRE + EARTH • Physical guide • Physical news (letters, events) • Physical opportunity • New material situation	**Knight of Pentacles** Mental/Physical • Combination of AIR + EARTH • Physical protector • Apprentice • Physical change agent • Actively involved with nature and/or the material/physical • Physical movement	**Queen of Pentacles** Emotional/Physical • Combination of WATER + EARTH • Providing mother • Nurse of physical wounds • Love of nature • Channel for practical info • Mother Earth • Endurance, security • Generosity	**King of Pentacles*** Physical/Physical • Combination of EARTH + EARTH • Providing father • Practical • Responsible • Financial source • Builder • Strong leader

Suit = Denominator   Court = Numerator   * = Royal Court

ENDNOTES

1. The Karmic Spread is excellent for showing where you are in your Minor Arcana progress.

2. The number 40 (Total number of Pips: 4 x 10): Forty appears repeatedly in mystical and scriptural literature as the metaphor for the trials that we must undertake 'below' in order to attain the 'above'. Numerologically, it reduces to 4, which is foundation, and further reduces (through addition of 1+2+3+4 = 10) to 1, which is source.

The number 16 (Total number of Courts: 4 x 4): The sixteen Courts establish the reality of the existence of each of the levels with the others, hence 4 x 4 = 16. This signifies the underlying interdependence of the family of man, externally with one another, and internally with each aspect of ourselves. Interestingly, 16 reduces to 7, the number of foundation moving through time, and the number of Stages we use in the Karmic Spread.

The number 10 (Number of Pips in each suit): Ten, the basis of our decimal number system, can be seen as emerging from a study of the Four Planes in the Minor Arcana, the four aspects of the self, and actually of everything in the material universe. When we look at the combinations possible for the Four Planes in a matrix with Four Planes, we get 10 non-redundant combinations:

1. Physical with Physical
2. Physical with Emotional
3. Physical with Mental
4. Physical with Spiritual
5. Emotional with Emotional
6. Emotional with Mental
7. Emotional with Spiritual
8. Mental with Mental
9. Mental with Spiritual
10. Spiritual with Spiritual

3. Iris Belhayes, *Spirit Guides* (San Diego, CA: ACS Publications, 1986). This is an excellent, easy-to-read, reference for information on the concept of spirit guides. Briefly, and for our purposes here in this book—to recognize and interpret guides in a reading, the author works with the belief that spirit guides serve as functional assistants to the Divine for getting us to recognize and accept the timely information we need to stay centered within and progress on our path, our evolution of consciousness. It is difficult for the conscious mind to deal directly with the huge oneness of the Divine, especially as regards pragmatic, day-to-day matters. The concept of spirit guides helps us break that hugeness down into a manageable, easy-to-relate-to friend, a friend in the Divine, as opposed to the Omnipotent One.

4. There are many good books on numerology, but I recommend: Matthew Oliver Goodwin, *Numerology: The Complete Guide, Vols. I & II* (North Hollywood, CA: Newcastle Publishing Co., 1981).

5. From Arthur M. Young, *The Geometry of Meaning* (San Francisco: Delacourte, Robert Briggs Assoc., 1976).

PART THREE

THE

READING

AND THE READER

CHAPTER NINE

The Reading

ATMOSPHERE AND CONTROL

The reading process consists of six principal factors, five objective:

    1. The Reader

    2. The Readee

    3. The Tarot Deck

    4. The Layout

    5. The Environment

and a subjective factor:

    6. The Provider.

First, there is the *reader,* the person laying out and interpreting the cards. Anyone can read the Tarot. All that is required are the physical abilities of sight and speech.[1]

Second, there is the *readee,* the person for whom the cards are being interpreted. (The term querent is most frequently used, but over the years I have found myself using the term readee, and it seems to work quite well.)

Third, there is the *Tarot deck* itself. There are many decks available commercially today and the choice of a deck is a highly personal matter. You should certainly study all the available information about the origins and characteristics of any decks that attract you, but in the final analysis, no one can tell you which deck will be the right one, or ones, for you. But I feel, however, that there is one condition that should be met by any deck you consider for reading the Tarot. It should be of what I call the "classic" type, one which has seventy-eight cards structured into a twenty-two-card Major Arcana and a fifty-six-card Minor Arcana—consisting of four Suits, each divided into ten numbered Pip cards and four Court cards. There are numerous other decks that have their own validity within their own systems of thought. You may be interested in having additional decks for reasons other than reading; i.e., for their beauty, historical value, or for a collection. But they cannot be used in a study of the classic Tarot, such as in this book, much the same as you could not use a Portugese dictionary to study German.

My deck of preference after many years is still the deck I first purchased, the Rider-Waite. Although I have collected and studied many other decks, it is still the deck I use most. I also use the Royal Fez Moroccan deck a great deal. It follows the Rider-Waite deck closely, but seems to be less emotional. The Rider-Waite has remained an extremely popular deck, partly because its Minor Arcana is fully illustrated in color. Many of the older decks do not have illustrations in the Pips. The Pips derive their meanings from the interface of the numerological significance of numbers 1 to 10 and the characteristics of the suits. Illustrations of the Pips seem to put unnecessary limitations on the meanings of these forty cards. It is one of my hopes that the analysis of the Minor Arcana in this book will free many people from a dependency on decks with illustrated Pips. This freedom should increase the ability to use, and therefore the popularity of, many of the very beautiful older decks.

The B.O.T.A. (Builders of the Adytum) deck, which is black and white, is a good one for studying the Karmic Tarot, as it is a classic seventy-eight card deck that follows the symbolism of the Rider-Waite deck in its Major Arcana and Minor Arcana Court cards, but does not have scenic illustrations for its 40 Pips. The Major Arcana and Court cards have black and white illustrations, allowing for personal color interpretations and study.

Fourth, there is the *layout*—the spread distribution of the cards. Besides the Karmic Spread, with its wide range of applications, there are many other existing spreads for various specific purposes, and there will be more invented in the future.[2] The fact that there are no other spreads presented in this book should not be interpreted to mean disapproval of other spreads. The selection of which spreads you use is much the same as the choice of the deck itself. However, there is no type of question that cannot be brought to the Karmic Spread. And unlike many others, the Karmic Spread gives you the ability to see time elements definitively.

Fifth, there is the *environment*—the atmosphere and conditions in which the reading is to take place. The Tarot can be approached at many levels but always it must be approached with respect. Under no circumstances should the Tarot be used frivolously. It is common for the Tarot to be used at carnivals, psychic fairs, charity fund-raisers, and the like. Although conditions are unpredictable and time is limited at such events, these are valid uses in that they can introduce the Tarot, and information through the Tarot, to people who might otherwise never be able to benefit from its therapeutic, healing qualities. However, it is important for the reader, even while maintaining a light, sociable demeanor, treat the reading seriously.

Generally, when it occurs to a potential readee that they want a Tarot reading, this is *indeed* the appropriate time for a message to come to them this way; they are predisposed to a suitable frame of mind and a positive attitude toward the Tarot.

It's a good idea whenever possible to set up an appointment for a reading in advance. This allows both reader and readee to get into the proper mindset. It will also encourage a setting with fewer distractions.

Occasionally, you will be presented with a potential readee who makes it clear one way or another that they are somewhat sceptical about the whole Tarot process.

Under no circumstances should you begin a reading while the atmosphere that exists amounts to a challenge for you to prove the validity of the Tarot. You must have the confidence of the readee before the spread is laid out. You must at least be dealing with an open mind. Otherwise, it will be impossible to do even an adequate, much less a truly satisfying, reading for such an individual, and you will only substantiate their original doubts.

A quick rereading of Chapter Two will help you see what can be said as a way of introducing the reading. By pointing out, in a simple and brief way, what the Tarot is and how it works, you can create a highly receptive attitude in the readee and increase the prospects of an exciting reading.

I approach the setting for my readings in much the same way as I would for meditating. You want all of your senses to be centered in the here and now of the reading setting. There are numerous subtle things that can support that end and they should be to your personal taste. Soft, neutral background music will help center the ears against outside interference. Scented candles or incense will add to the uniqueness of the moment. The reading table should be visually simple, allowing the cards to be the most striking and important items there.

The subjective factor, the *Provider*, is the Divine, the source of all information. In the reading process this becomes the intuition of the reader. "Indeed, the act of developing intuition, or telepathy, or revelation, is to feel inside our idiosyncrasies as they react to the person we are reading."[3]

The premise underlying all readings is that God wants each of us to have all the information we need to live happy, successful lives, to learn all our lessons, and to fulfill our Karmic Contract. The Tarot reading is one means of accessing this information.

The objective knowledge of the reader, i.e., the basic meanings of the seventy-eight cards and the basic meanings of positions of a given spread, are the "hooks" on which God can hang messages. He knows what knowledge is in the reader's head and can then supply the appropriate card in the appropriate slot to generate a given message. This is why it is valid for different readers to offer different meanings for the same card and/or position. In effect, Tarot is a language, but every reader speaks a different dialect known only to themselves and to God. Tarot functions much like our written/spoken languages. As individuals we learn a common alphabet and agree on common meanings for the combinations of our alphabet symbols into words so that we can communicate with each other and even publish dictionaries. But the fact that we must periodically update these dictionaries to include new words, and new meanings for old words, shows the living nature of language. The Tarot cards are the alphabet and words of a symbolic language and have strong archetypal meanings that have evolved over many years. Given spreads are like the sentence structures and grammar through which the cards can relate a meaning. But Tarot is also a living system. New meanings and interpretations for the cards are possible with every reading. They always derive from previous usage and meaning, but they can be very new as well. Such is the magic of language and symbols. Let this fact cause you excitement rather than frustration. Tarot is easily learned, but you never graduate.

THE READER AND THE READEE

The reader and readee should be facing each other across the table, never side by side, and preferably seated at the same height. If there must be a difference in height, the reader should be the higher. The cards should always be laid out by and facing the reader.

Shuffle the cards, making certain that their alignment in the pack, upright or inverted, is completely random. Interpretations vary for inverted and upright cards. I interpret cards as upright when they are facing the reader. Options for upright/inverted cards are explained below.

Whether the readee handles the cards is at the discretion of the reader and may vary with the situation and amount of time available. The majority of readers prefer to offer the cards to the readee at some point prior to laying the spread, with a request that the cards be cut and/or shuffled. I offer the cards three times in a row, asking that they be cut. I prefer not to have the readee shuffle them. I stress that the cards may be cut in any fashion and into as many stacks as the readee desires on each of the three offerings. You will develop a preference of your own on this facet of the reading, but whatever you do, keep this in mind: *The degree to which both the reader and readee focus on the moment at hand is the major factor underlying the potential success of the reading.* In case the readee has not sufficiently focused on what lies ahead, prior to this last moment before laying out the spread, offering the cards with a request for some action on their part will require them to consciously use of their mind in relation to the deck. This additional centering in the moment, however structured, guarantees at least some active participation by the readee.

What of the option by some readers not to offer the cards at any time? This seems to be related to the reason most readers will not allow other readers to use their decks. They simply do not want the confusion of other energies involved with their cards or to risk physical damage to them. While I agree with this regarding other readers, I do not agree as regards to the reader/readee relationship. First of all, by definition, in any given reading you want the energies and impressions of the readee. It is not the reader's reading, it is the readee's. Second, after every reading, the cards should be shuffled and handled in any way deemed necessary by the reader to neutralize the deck, and as the initial step in preparation for the next reading, before the cards are put away. This process should be adequate to offset any adverse effect of handling by the readee.

Whether to offer the cards seems also to be a choice of informality or formality. I prefer the active involvement of the readee in the entire process. Others may prefer more of a one-way process, with little active participation by the readee. However, under no circumstances should the cards be laid out by the readee. Their contact with the cards should be limited to the time prior to laying out the spread.

Tarot is excellent for telling us what our questions really are, even when our conscious minds are convinced otherwise. The readee should be given the opportunity to address the questions that motivated them to come for a reading. As the spread itself will either agree or address other questions, it is not a problem if the readee declines to ask any questions initially. It should be pointed out that the more the readee reacts to the reader's interpretations as the process unfolds, the greater the chances of receiving specific and detailed information. Remember that if the readee is actively involved, the reading will be full of life, rich in meaning, and of great value. If, on the other hand, the readee is only passively involved, the reading may be relatively meager in meaning and value.

The majority of my readings use more than one laying out of the cards. The Karmic Spread is excellent for defining the questions, and I allow the first layout to help me feel the parameters of the issue(s) at hand, to focus the reading, and to establish objective rapport with the readee. Subsequent layouts then simply follow through on the leads of the previous layout(s), allowing the information to become more and more specific. Always read the initial layout as a full-life spread. Then you can follow up with a layout using a contained time frame such as seven years, seven months, seven weeks, or even seven days. Even when you lay out the cards with a contained time frame in mind, there will always be an aspect of the full-life working behind the scenes as well. It is as though the reading is in layers.

It is important for reader and readee to note that the Tarot is not a decision-maker; it does not provide direct answers and does not, therefore, foretell a pre-ordained future. Reread the section, DIVINATION—WHAT IS; WHAT IT ISN'T at the end of Chapter Three. But here is the summation of that section: "When the present moment pulses between its extremes of infinitely small and infinitely large, the reading glimpses the future. But here again is the magic of paradox, for the future the reader sees is not a predestined fait accompli without free will. The future it sees is itself dependent on the present moment, on your free will and your sincere desire to maximize your life potential."

What the Tarot does, and does exceedingly well is tell you what your questions are, and what the options and potential consequences are for various possible conditions. It presents the relevant facts about the past, the conditions in the present, and the potential futures likely, given those past and present factors. The future is yours for the making, and with good information you increase your chances for the best of all possibilities to materialize.

What is even more amazing is the fact that the past is never over. You can, in fact, change the past by discovering new lessons never before realized. You can see the same old characters and events in new ways. Therefore the past is no more fixed than the future. Man is at the exact mid-point of what he sees as the past and the future, and he has the ability to determine it all.

THE USE OF A SIGNIFICATOR

Many spreads use what is known as a *Significator*. This is a card selected from the deck prior to laying out the cards and meant to represent the readee. This card is then laid down as the first card of the layout in the first position. Other cards are then laid upon it. The Karmic Spread does not use a Significator—I prefer to have the additional significance of the card or cards most exemplary of the readee free within the deck to fall on any of the positions.

It is relatively easy to select a Court card to represent the readee. Use the physical and personality characters of the Courts outlined in Chapter Eight for this process. Selection of a Major Arcana card is more difficult, but with repeated layouts for the readee, or if you know the person well enough, a Major Arcana card may also be apparent.

Certainly, when reading for yourself, one of the Major Arcana will assert itself as representing you in this lifetime. Additionally, you may come to recognize another of the Major Arcana as symbolizing your main work in this incarnation.

If, in the preliminary discussion with the readee, it has become obvious that information about one or more other people is expected to be included in the reading, you may also assign Minor Arcana cards to these people prior to the layout, much in the same manner as the selection of an appropriate card for the readee. This can be invaluable in determining the effect of existing versus new people in the readee's life.

IDENTIFYING GUIDES

Just as cards may be selected to represent people living on the earth plane with the readee now in order to identify them should they appear in a reading, it is also possible to select cards to represent people, or guides, who are on the other side of the veil. God is continuously trying to communicate everything you need to know to fulfill your life purpose. Everything you experience—every person, every billboard, every dream—is communicating part of God's message. To understand the totality of the Godhead is impossible, hence our concept of ineffability as experienced by mystics down through time. But man has the special ability to break down the messages from God into manageable pieces, and he tries to personify these messages as much as possible.

Imagine an inverted tree, trunk pointing upward toward the sky, branches down toward the ground. God, the One, is the trunk of the tree at the very top. Just below, the trunk divides into two branches, while below that each branch itself divides into two other branches. The process continues just like the TV commercial that says, "...and they told two people, and..." At the very bottom is an infinity of branches, each a bit of intelligence in the earth plane receiving part of God's message.

The channels or paths that information takes in reaching us are of many levels, some personified and others not—but all of them depend on the socio-cultural backgrounds from which we spring and on which we depend for our survival. Near the top, to someone who has been born into the Judaeo-Chrisitian tradition, are the Archangels, and to those in that tradition who have a more New Age or Theosophical orientation, there is the Great White Brotherhood. In Islam there are the ninety-nine names of God. In ancient Egypt and Greece there were pantheons of gods. And in Hinduism too, there is a pantheon of gods, each a facet of the Godhead to which believers can relate.

Further down our inverted tree are the biological families into which we have been born at one time or another, and even further down are the families in which we are now a structural part. And here we come to the root of religion in man, to the origins of animism, of ancestor worship and glorification of nature and nature-spirits. Early man instinctively recognized where he came from and what he was part of. This is the correct understanding of spiritualism, the proper communication with those who have passed on, but who even in their timeless home on the other side of the void are part of us. Even ourselves in past lives are available to help us receive our messages in this lifetime.

All of these levels are working to channel information from God to us. Meditating on which cards may represent any of these personifications can bring startling results.

READING FOR YOURSELF

In doing layouts for yourself, particularly in the beginning, remember that it is generally much harder to read your own cards than someone else's. Beginners tend to read predominantly for themselves and can easily be misled to believe that reading is too difficult; so the cards are put away forever. You will always want to read for yourself, but beginners should force themselves to read for others, even if they are not present (see below). If it is truly time for an aspiring reader to learn the Tarot, just as they were led to buy a deck of cards in the first place, so will they be presented with the opportunities to read. People, generally close friends or family, will ask for readings. The point here is not to refuse these requests. Again I stress that it will be much easier to read for others than for yourself.

READING FOR THE ABSENTEE READEE

Having the Readee present, face to face, is preferred, most obviously for the chance for repartee and observation. But it is also possible to do excellent readings with the readee absent. Although in the Karmic Spread a Significator is normally not used, here I recommend that a Significator be selected and placed above the entire spread (immediately above position 10). The selection of the Significator may be either from the Minor Arcana Courts or from the Major Arcana.

HOW TO LAY OUT THE CARDS

When the cards have been prepared and you are satisfied with all the conditions discussed above, the layout is begun. You should be holding a well-shuffled deck in which the cards are random—no prearranged order and no prearranged orientation. The cards should be held in one hand and dealt, one at a time, from the top of the deck with the other hand. (The cards should not be dealt from their storage box or from a stack sitting on the table.) As each of the cards is taken from the top of the deck, it is turned over and placed face up on the table, laid out according to the pattern of the Karmic Spread. Begin with position 1 and continue with positions 2, 3, 4 and so on, until all twenty-two cards are in place. The completed layout should be identical in form to the Karmic Spread as shown in Charts 1 and 1A. There are two basic ways of dealing cards to a face up position from a face down deck: the more common method is to rotate the card from top to bottom on its way from the deck to the table; the less common is to turn the card over from left to right. Either method is acceptable for getting the card to the table in a face up position, but they should not be interchanged in a given reading. Better yet, the reader should settle on one method and stick with it. The more common method of rotating top to bottom actually inverts the cards from their original orientation while face down in the deck. The left-to-right method does not.

HOW TO INTERPRET THE LAYOUT

Here are some suggestions for extracting meanings from any layout of cards in this twenty-two-card spread.

Begin by looking at the entire layout, first as a whole and then by scanning at random, allowing your eye to take in each card individually and in no particular order. Nothing should be said during this initial perusal. Simply allow the cards to register subconsciously before attempting any interpretation. Once you are satisfied that the cards are registering in your mind and that meanings are forthcoming, stop your scanning, close your eyes, and allow a few moments of invocative meditation. (This moment will eventually evolve into a very personal expression for each reader.)

Barring a rare probability, some or many of the twenty-two cards laid out will be inverted. Nothing negative should automatically be inferred from these inversions. Just remember that inverted cards can signify too much or too little of the principle in question when you begin to interpret each of them.

There is no particular order to interpreting the layout. The suggestions that follow should not be construed to indicate any sequence; they are simply a list of things you can generally look for.

1. Look at Position 10:

The card in this position (the spiritual level of the present moment) represents the intuitive message that is most important for the readee at this time. This is whatever has not been getting through to the readee's conscious reality, to the three aspects of the personality below the Spiritual, i.e., the Mental, Emotional, and Physical Planes. This card is the major clue to the reason the readee is having a Tarot reading at this time.

Also examine the three cards under position 10, i.e., cards in position 11 (Mental Plane), position 12 (Emotional Plane), and position 13 (Physical Plane). Together, these four cards comprise a profile of the present situation. Here will be all the major clues to the lessons the reading will be addressing.

2. Look at Positions 1 through 4:

These four cards constitute the Karmic Contract and will show the aspects of the soul's choices for this lifetime, with respect to the Physical, Emotional, Mental, and Spiritual Planes. The most strategic of these is position 4, the spiritual level. The card here reveals aspects of the principle purpose, the major lesson being learned in this lifetime. Cards in positions 1, 2, and 3 show the given situation at the time of birth for the Physical, Emotional, and Mental Planes. The interpretation of these cards sets the character and tone for analyzing progress in each of these three Planes through the seven Stages of the lifetime. In other words, all the cards that fall to the *right* of cards 1 through 4 must be read with these cards in mind. They are the base upon which the readee is experiencing life and learning the lessons of the four-fold path.

In addition, cards in positions 1 and 2 may be read as the effect of the readee's mother and father. Freudian psychology leans heavily on the types of information yielded by these two positions. But be careful not to interpret these as the readee's attitude toward, or relationship with, the parents. Proper meaning will be in terms of the major impact from the parents and clues to why the parents were selected by this incarnating soul.

3. Look at the Horizontal Rows:

The rows provide information about the journeys through each of the four Planes. Here is where the progress of the physical, emotional, mental, and spiritual journeys can be traced. (For a review of the detailed analysis of these journeys, see Chapter Six.) If there is a blockage, or particular difficulties on any of these Planes, it will be very apparent. The ability to identify and trace problems in these levels of the personality is one of the major advantages the Karmic Spread offers.

4. Look at the Vertical Columns:

The columns provide information about the seven major Stages of development: Stage Two (Early Childhood) and Stage Three (Recent Past) should be examined for things that remain unresolved, or in other words, for situations in the past that still contain major lessons for the readee. Look at vertical column of Stage Five for the Near Future, in particular, next year. (Remember that for greater time specificity, prior to laying any spread, you may set different time periods if they will better satisfy the readee's questions.) Position 16, the Spiritual Plane at Stage Five, will reveal the next most important intuitive guidance for the readee. Unless another time period has been established, this should be interpreted to be the spiritual safety net that lies at the end of the next year.

5. Look at Positions 19, 20, 21 and 22:

These cards represent the anticipated fulfillment of the four Planes. In one sense they can be interpreted as "report cards" on the progress that has been made (physically, emotionally, mentally and spiritually), given the readee's present course. The last card in the layout position 22, is the most significant. It is the culmination of the soul's purpose in this lifetime. It should be read as the soul's "report card" on itself. In other words, this is how well the readee will be seen, at the time of biological death, to have satisfied the Karmic Contract chosen at the time of birth. It is the summation of the effects of all the life experiences—past, present, and future—shown in all the preceding cards.

6. Positions 5 and 9:

These cards show the readee's basic belief systems and personal philosophy. Five reveals the belief systems the readee was born into and therefore the early constraints and conditioning of the environment. Nine reveals the philosophical stance the readee has developed as their own, and is their viewpoint and frame of reference coming into the present moment, up to the time of the present reading.

7. Position 6:

This card shows the earliest emotional impact on the readee and will frequently reveal unresolved emotional imprints during early childhood. You can call this your emotional "tapes." While the imprint we see here will be by definition emotional, that which leaves the imprint may be from one of the other Planes—it may be physical, mental, or spiritual.

8. Look at Positions 6 and 15:

These positions are governed respectively by The Lovers and The Devil. Here is the Birth of Duality (6) and the Death of Duality (15) within the lifetime. (Birth and Death themselves are the true birth and death of duality.) Here in position 6, the Birth of Duality, you see what has drawn the readee out of himself to value the world, to see what is important outside of, yet invaluable to, him. In position 15, Death of Duality, you see what is drawing the readee into the One, and paradoxically into his inner self, as a means of identifying and joining with the One. The sacrifice is one of transformation, not obliteration, of the ego.

9. Look at Positions 14 and 15:

These positions are governed by Temperance and the Devil. The card in position 14 suggests the *temperance* needed at the emotional level to enable the readee to hold back, whereas the card in position 15 shows the needed *temptation* at the mental level to push the readee forward. By balancing the two effects the readee can progress sensibly.

10. Look at Positions 11 and 12:

These positions are governed by Justice and The Hanged Man. I mention them, not in the sense of other positions, but because the center of the Spread lies between them. The center of the layout, of the reading, lies in a void, a space between the centered mind that is Justice and the centered heart that is The Hanged Man. To determine the readee's true center at the time of the reading, you must interpolate a meaning that is a blend of the two cards here. As God is in the void, so too are we.

11. Interpreting the Court Cards:

The Court cards may fall on any of the twenty-two positions, and the interpretation of that Court card (as defined in Chapter Eight) will be:

A. A real flesh-and-blood person interfacing with the readee;

B. A personality not incarnate on the Physical Plane, i.e., a spirit guide, deceased loved one, or any other entity between the readee on the Physical Plane and the level of the Divine;

C. Aspects of personality that refer to the readee rather than another being.

Remember that all cards, including Court cards representing personalities, embody messages about specific lessons being learned. You do not meet, dream about, or experience people in any manner except in their relationship to you on your path. In short, all people, all Court cards, are lessons.

12. A Note on Interpreting Major Arcana Cards:

Remember that the Major Arcana embody the most important principles, those categories of necessary education on the path, much as you might think of required courses of study in a university curriculum. Major Arcana are extremely powerful and significant when they fall on the position in the spread with which they are identified, and that they govern. When this occurs, you know that the readee is correctly centered on their Karmic Path at that point, maximizing the lessons of that card and that position. Chapter Seven provides detailed interpretations for these twenty-two cards.

13. Interpreting Multiples of a Given Category of a Pip or Court Card:

For example: What is the significance of receiving two, three, or four Aces or multiples of any other Pip cards? Or of two, three, or four Kings or multiples of any other Court cards?

While I make no special interpretation for multiples of only two of a given Pip or Court card, multiples of *three* begin to take on significance; it follows naturally that multiples of four are very important. Here again may be seen the importance of studying the characteristics of the basic four card-categories (the Planes, the Suits) to which each of the Pips and Court cards belong. Chapter Eight presents the meanings of the Aces through Tens for their numerological significance before going on to discuss the individual cards. The same is done for the Court cards in discussing Pages, Knights, Queens, and Kings as such. The Reader's familiarity with these categories will be invaluable in interpreting multiples.

Let's take the example of a given Karmic Spread layout that contains three 7's and four Knights (there are several possibilities for the distribution of these multiples, which must be considered separately):

A. They may be scattered throughout the spread in no significant pattern;

B. They may be in one of the horizontal rows (Planes);

C. They may be in one of the vertical columns (Stages).

Here are some possible interpretations: From your study of Chapter Eight and Chart 6, you know that 7's represent a plateau and new beginnings, and thus three 7's would be emphatic. If these were all in a vertical column, obviously that Stage would represent a significant new beginning on many levels. If these three 7's were all in a horizontal row, it would suggest that that Plane of the personality (whether Physical, Emotional, Mental or Spiritual) would be characterized by new beginnings and possible multiple levels of achievement. Also from Chapter Eight and from Chart 6A, you know that knights represent the drive for expansion, communication, new ideas, youthful expression. They also represent teenagers and young adults. Regardless of placement these may simply represent four specific young people in the readee's life. But we also must consider the placement for possible additional meanings. Multiple knights in a vertical row would signify abundant activity, expansion, etc., for that Stage in the readee's life. Multiple knights in a horizontal row would imply those knightly characteristics as dominating that Plane of the personality.

14. Last, Re-Read and Study the Definitions of the Spread Positions in Chapter Six:

These are summarized in Charts 4 and 4A. Resting within the definitions themselves are an unlimited number of patterns of interpretation not mentioned above. The origin and mechanics of the structure of the spread itself continuously offer up new possibilities. Here again, you will undoubtedly be blessed with personal insights that will enrich the use of the Karmic Spread.

ENDNOTES

1. More accurately, here I am saying that there needs to be an ability to know which cards have fallen and where in a given reading. Actually, a reader without sight can accept the assistance of a sighted person (who can even be the readee) for relaying the information on which cards have fallen where. As for lack of speech, the reader can write down the interpretations. The inability to see and interpret the colors is most likely offset by the extra sensitivity of the Third Eye in unsighted persons. Many people prefer to read with black and white decks, allowing the color impressions to be subjective rather than objective.

2. See: Doris Chase Doane and King Keyes, *Tarot-Card Spread Reader* (West Nyack, NY: Parker Publishing Co., 1967), and Sandor Konraad, *Classic Karmic Spreads* (Gloucester, MA: Para Research, Inc., 1985).

3. Pir Vilayat Inayat Khan, *The Message in Our Time* (San Francisco: Harper & Row, 1979).

CHAPTER TEN

The Reader

The previous chapter addressed the Tarot reading itself and the reader's role during it. This chapter offers suggestions and assistance for the reader outside of the reading process itself.

ORGANIZING A CONTINUING PROGRAM OF STUDY

Tarot is somewhat like a game of chess in that it's fairly easy to learn the rules of the game and actually begin playing, but one can spend a lifetime continuing to learn more about it. Tarot's basic "rules" are easily learned, but then the real fun begins.

The main object of these suggestions for further study is to deepen your understanding of the cards so you can be more specific about meanings time elements. You want more detail, not only in the "who, what, where, and why" but in the very elusive "when."

QUESTIONS INDEX

Create a *Questions Index*. Starting from scratch, with no previous Tarot books or references available, and, if possible, cleared from your mind, *prepare a list of questions you feel your Tarot system should be able to answer*. This is a wonderful exercise, particularly if done with an open mind, free from any thought or concern for the answers or for how they are arrived at. That part comes later. If this is done on index cards, they can later be shuffled around and organized into categories. At a certain point you will want to begin organizing your questions for easy reference. Your list will be a living list, always expanding as new thoughts arise.

Once you have your questions organized in a file system, at your leisure you can review them with this in mind: *Where in the Karmic Tarot system would I expect to find the answer to this question?* First, from which position(s) in the Karmic Spread can I best get a reading on this? Second, which of the Tarot cards can I expect to get information from? Note your conclusions on that question's index card. This can be done as a meditative or study activity. It is also a beautiful way to record significant discoveries of new meanings as you do actual readings (or shortly thereafter, while your memory is still fresh). With this system in place, when a question comes to mind, you can look up what previous answers have been provided, by which cards, and in what positions in the Karmic Spread.

The Questions Index is in a sense a mechanical memory device that can be referenced at will. Of equal or greater importance is the exercise of putting questions to the Tarot in an organized manner. This process is what reveals the underlying patterns at work and broadens the ability of the rational mind to handle the intuitive insights of future readings. It's like doing work at the ballet bar, so that your leg muscles will know what they can do when they are called upon during a performance.

THE 3432 SYSTEM

This is a system for defining interpretations using the Karmic Spread and recording them for future reference. It provides storage for the meanings of each of the seventy-eight cards in each of the twenty-two positions of the spread, much as I have for the Major Arcana in Chapter Seven, and the Minor Arcana in Chapter 8. Questions and answers discovered in the Questions Index system can be plugged into this system. While the Questions Index provides access from the viewpoint of the *question*, the 3432 *System* provides access from the viewpoint of the *card* that has fallen. The form you will need if you want to work with this system is shown as Chart 7.

The number 3,432 is derived from the fact that there are a total of 3,432 interpretations possible, because there are:

78 Cards x 22 Positions x 2 (card upright or inverted) = 3,432

Thus you see that the total number of possibilities is generated by the odds of any of the seventy-eight cards falling in any of twenty-two positions, and the card may fall either upright or inverted.

You will need seventy-eight copies of Chart 7, one for each of the cards. Assign a card to each one of these seventy-eight sheets and record the name of the card in the upper right-hand corner. I suggest you organize your sheets with the twenty-two Major Arcana first; then the Minor Arcana Pips; and then the Minor Arcana Court cards. Arrange the numbered Pips in a series of the four Aces, the four 2's, etc., as opposed to Ace, 2, 3, etc., of a given suit. It follows then that you arrange the Court cards in a series of the four Kings, the four Queens, the four Knights, and the four Pages. Within each of the Minor Arcana groupings of four, the order of the suits should be Pentacles, Cups, Swords, Wands.

The outline for your 3432 System should look like this:

MAJOR ARCANA
The Magician (1)
The High Priestess (2)
The Empress (3)
The Emperor (4)
The Hierophant (5)
The Lovers (6)
The Chariot (7)
Strength (8)
The Hermit (9)
Wheel of Fortune (10)
Justice (11)
The Hanged Man (12)
Death (13)
Temperance (14)
The Devil (15)
The Tower (16)
The Star (17)
The Moon (18)
The Sun (19)
Judgement (20)
The World (21)
The Fool (22/0)

MINOR ARCANA PIPS

Ace of Pentacles	Ace of Cups	Ace of Swords	Ace of Wands
Two of Pentacles	Two of Cups	Two of Swords	Two of Wands
Three of Pentacles	Three of Cups	Three of Swords	Three of Wands
Four of Pentacles	Four of Cups	Four of Swords	Four of Wands
Five of Pentacles	Five of Cups	Five of Swords	Five of Wands
Six of Pentacles	Six of Cups	Six of Swords	Six of Wands
Seven of Pentacles	Seven of Cups	Seven of Swords	Seven of Wands
Eight of Pentacles	Eight of Cups	Eight of Swords	Eight of Wands
Nine of Pentacles	Nine of Cups	Nine of Swords	Nine of Wands
Ten of Pentacles	Ten of Cups	Ten of Swords	Ten of Wands

MINOR ARCANA COURT CARDS

King of Pentacles	King of Cups	King of Swords	King of Wands
Queen of Pentacles	Queen of Cups	Queen of Swords	Queen of Wands
Knight of Pentacles	Knight of Cups	Knight of Swords	Knight of Wands
Page of Pentacles	Page of Cups	Page of Swords	Page of Wands

For easy reference, set the seventy-eight sheets into a loose-leaf binder and index the sections. Once your binder is established you will have a place to record the more outstanding interpretations from your readings. The 3432 System is an ongoing record.

GROUP SYSTEM

There are many groups that get together to study and meditate on given cards, particularly the Majors. This is an excellent way to broaden your knowledge. Group studies can include a more detailed study of the Minors as well. Brainstorming sessions built around the Questions Index and the 3432 System produce extraordinary results.

LESSONS TO BE LEARNED

In similar fashion to the Questions Index, let your mind run, discerning *Lessons to Be Learned* from the Tarot. Because Karmic Tarot sees your lifetime as a series of lessons to be learned, this exercise is an excellent way to identify and upgrade your level of achievement on your path.

Comparisons with the Classics

This is a follow-up to the *Lessons to Be Learned* exercise for avid readers, particularly of the classics—material that is full of legends and myths and archetypal symbology. Reviewing these with *Lessons to Be Learned* in mind offers a double reward. First, many of the fundamental lessons in the classics will be translated into your Tarot vocabulary, and your readings will be transformed. Second, the Tarot will give a new appreciation of the classics themselves, revealing aspects that have heretofore gone unnoticed.

Comparisons with Other Disciplines

Tarot is a spur to studying an unlimited number of other disciplines, particularly when viewed as an evolution of consciousness, a series of *Lessons to Be Learned*. Mathematics, logic, philosophy, psychology, religion, yoga, history, art, music, are only a few. The study of numerology, the origin and function of numbers and their evolution, is of special value and must become part of the study program for any serious student of the Tarot.

INVOCATION WITH THE KARMIC SPREAD

You can use the Tarot to clarify maximum expectations and goals, to register your vote with the universe. Here the intent is to be active, communicating your desires and will. Instead of doing a conventional reading here you will meditate on the entire deck and consciously select cards for each of the positions.

This is an invaluable tool in setting priorities and defining situations. This type of exercise should be done in the same vein as the proper use of creative visualization, power of positive thinking, affirmations and the like. You may wish to precede this layout with this invocation:

May this reading work to center me on my path and help achieve my Karmic Contract.

Chart 7
THE 3432 SYSTEM
A System for Learning and Recording the Meanings of All the Cards in All the Positions

KARMIC TAROT   CARD NAME/NUMBER_____

POSITION IN SPREAD	UPRIGHT	INVERTED
P P 1 MAGICIAN		
C P 2 PRIESTESS		
S P 3 EMPRESS		
W C/P P 4 EMPEROR		
S C 5 HIEROPHANT		
C C 6 LOVERS		
P S C 7 CHARIOT		
C S 8 STRENGTH		
S S 9 HERMIT		
W W S 10 WHEEL		
S W 11 JUSTICE		
C W W W 12 HANGED MAN		
P W S 13 DEATH		
C S 14 TEMPERANCE		
S S 15 DEVIL		
W C/S 16 TOWER		
S C 17 STAR		
C C 18 MOON		
P P/C 19 SUN		
C P 20 JUDGEMENT		
S P 21 WORLD		
W P 22 FOOL		

P = Pentacles   C = Cups   S = Swords   W = Wands

Note: Make 78 copies of this chart, one for each of the Tarot Cards. As you study and do readings you can make notes here for future reference. This will lead you to personal interpretations you can use in addition to those in Chapters Seven and Eight.

APPENDIX

Source Definitions for the Karmic Spread Positions and the Major Arcana

Here are the definitions of all twenty-two positions in the Karmic Spread, using the "Summary of Sources" categories for easy reference and study.

POSITION 1

Source 1A	Position 1 is number 1 in the series 1 to 22.
Source 1B	Position 1 is the first number 1 of the seven Stages series of 1 to 4.
Source 2	Major Arcana....The Magician.
Source 3	Consciousness Grid....Physical/Physical.
Source 4	Minor Arcana Grid....Pentacles/Pentacles.
Source 5	Elements Grid....Earth/Earth.
Source 6	Real-Time Factor....At Birth/ Monday/Third Month Past.
Source 7	Chakra....Root/Anal.
Source 8	Sense....Hearing.
Source 9	Color/Sound....Green/"C."
Source 10A	Major Arcana Journey....The Magician is the first stop on this journey.
Source 10B	Journey in the Planes....The Magician is the first stop on the progress through the Physical Plane.

POSITION 2

Source 1A	Position 2 is number 2 in the series 1 to 22.
Source 1B	Position 2 is the first number 2 of the seven Stages series of 1 to 4.

Source 2   Major Arcana....The High Priestess.
Source 3   Consciousness Grid....Emotional/Physical.
Source 4   Minor Arcana Grid....Cups/Pentacles.
Source 5   Elements Grid....Water/Earth.
Source 6   Real-Time Factor....At Birth/ Monday/Third Month Past.
Source 7   Chakra....Root/Anal.
Source 8   Sense....Hearing.
Source 9   Color/Sound....Green/"C."
Source 10A   Major Arcana Journey....The High Priestess is the second stop on the journey.
Source 10B   Journey in the Planes....The High Priestess is the first stop on the progress through the Emotional Plane.

POSITION 3

Source 1A   Position 3 is number 3 in the series 1 to 22.
Source 1B   Position 3 is the first number 3 of the seven Stages series of 1 to 4.
Source 2   Major Arcana....The Empress.
Source 3   Consciousness Grid....Mental/Physical.
Source 4   Minor Arcana Grid....Swords/Pentacles.
Source 5   Elements Grid....Air/Earth.
Source 6   Real-Time Factor....At Birth/ Monday/Third Month Past.
Source 7   Chakra....Root/Anal.
Source 8   Sense....Hearing.
Source 9   Color/Sound....Green/"C."
Source 10A   Major Arcana Journey....The Empress is the third stop on this journey.
Source 10B   Journey in the Planes....The Empress is the first stop on the progress through the Mental Plane.

POSITION 4

Source 1A   Position 4 is number 4 in the series 1 to 22.
Source 1B   Position 4 is the first number 4 and the second number 1 of the seven Stages series of 1 to 4.
Source 2   Major Arcana....The Emperor.
Source 3   Consciousness Grid....Spiritual/Physical, changing to Spiritual/Emotional.
Source 4   Minor Arcana Grid....Wands/Pentacles, changing to Wands/Emotional.
Source 5   Elements Grid....Fire/Earth, changing to Fire/Water.
Source 6   Real-Time Factor....At Birth/Monday/Third Month Past, changing to Early Childhood/Tuesday/Second Month Past.
Source 7   Chakra....Root/Anal, changing to Genital.
Source 8   Sense....Hearing, changing to Touch.
Source 9   Color/Sound....Green/"C," changing to Blue/"D."
Source 10A   Major Arcana Journey....The Emperor is the fourth stop on this journey.
Source 10B   Journey in the Planes....The Emperor is the first stop on the progress through the Spiritual Plane.

POSITION 5

Source 1A   Position 5 is number 5 in the series 1 to 22.
Source 1B   Position 5 is the second number 2 of the seven Stages series of 1 to 4.
Source 2   Major Arcana....The Hierophant.
Source 3   Consciousness Grid....Mental/Emotional.
Source 4   Minor Arcana Grid....Cups/Pentacles.
Source 5   Elements Grid....Water/Earth.
Source 6   Real-Time Factor....Early Childhood/ Tuesday/Second Month Past.
Source 7   Chakra....Genital.
Source 8   Sense....Touch.
Source 9   Color/Sound....Blue/"D."
Source 10A   Major Arcana Journey....The Hierophant is the fifth stop on this journey.
Source 10B   Journey in the Planes....The Hierophant is the second stop on the progress through the Mental Plane.

POSITION 6

Source 1A   Position 6 is number 6 in the series 1 to 22.
Source 1B   Position 6 is the second number 3 of the seven Stages series of 1 to 4.
Source 2   Major Arcana.... The Lovers.
Source 3   Consciousness Grid....Emotional/Emotional.
Source 4   Minor Arcana Grid....Cups/Cups.
Source 5   Elements Grid....Water/Water.
Source 6   Real-Time Factor....Early Childhood/Tuesday/Second Month Past.
Source 7   Chakra....Genital.
Source 8   Touch.
Source 9   Color/Sound....Blue/"D."
Source 10A   Major Arcana Journey....The Lovers is the sixth stop on this journey.
Source 10B   Journey in the Planes....The Lovers is the second stop on the progress through the Emotional Plane.

POSITION 7

Source 1A.   Position 7 is number 7 in the series 1 to 22.
Source 1B   Position 7 is the second number 4 and the third number 1 of of the seven Stages series of 1 to 4.
Source 2   Major Arcana....The Chariot.
Source 3   Consciousness Grid....Physical/Emotional, changing to Physical/Mental.
Source 4   Minor Arcana Grid....Pentacles/Cups, changing to Pentacles/Swords.
Source 5   Elements Grid....Earth/Water, changing to Earth/Air.
Source 6   Real-Time Factor....Early Childhood/Tuesday/Second Month Past, changing to Recent Past/ Wednesday/First Month Past.
Source 7   Chakra....Genital, changing to Solar Plexus.
Source 8   Sense....Touch, changing to Sight.
Source 9   Color/Sound....Blue/"D," changing to Yellow/"E".

Source 10A   Major Arcana Journey....The Chariot is the seventh stop on this journey.
Source 10B   Journey in the Planes....The Chariot is the second stop on the progress through the Physical Plane.

POSITION 8

Source 1A   Position 8 is number 8 in the series of 1 to 22.
Source 1B   Position 8 is the third number 2 of the seven Stages series of 1 to 4.
Source 2   Major Arcana....Strength.
Source 3   Consciousness Grid....Emotional/Mental.
Source 4   Minor Arcana Grid....Cups/Swords.
Source 5   Elements Grid....Water/Air.
Source 6   Real-Time Factor....Recent Past/ Wednesday/First Month Past.
Source 7   Chakra....Solar Plexus.
Source 8   Sense....Sight.
Source 9   Color/Sound....Yellow/"E."
Source 10A   Major Arcana Journey....Strength is the eighth stop on the journey.
Source 10B   Journey in the Planes....Strength is the third stop on the progress through the Emotional Plane.

POSITION 9

Source 1A   Position 9 is number 9 in the series of 1 to 22.
Source 1B   Position 9 is the third number 3 of the seven Stages series of 1 to 4.
Source 2   Major Arcana....The Hermit.
Source 3   Consciousness Grid....Mental/Mental.
Source 4   Minor Arcana Grid....Swords/Swords.
Source 5   Elements Grid....Air/Air
Source 6   Real-Time Factor....Recent Past/ Wednesday/First Month Past.
Source 7   Chakra....Solar Plexus.
Source 8   Sense....Sight.
Source 9   Color/Sound...."Yellow/"E."
Source 10A   Major Arcana Journey....The Hermit is the ninth stop on the journey
Source 10B   Journey in the Planes....The Hermit is the third stop on the progress through the Mental Plane.

POSITION 10

Source 1A   Position 10 is number 10 in the series of 1 to 22. It reduces to the number 1.
Source 1B   Position 10 is the third number 4 and the fourth number 1 of the seven Stages series of 1 to 4.
Source 2   Major Arcana....Wheel of Fortune.
Source 3   Consciousness Grid....Spiritual/Mental, changing to Spiritual/Spiritual.
Source 4   Minor Arcana Grid....Wands/Swords, changing to Wands/Wands.
Source 5   Elements Grid....Fire/Air, changing to Fire/Fire.
Source 6   Real Time Factor....Recent Past/ Wednesday/First Month Past, changing to Present/Thursday/Current Month.

Source 7   Chakra....Solar Plexus, changing to Heart.
Source 8   Sense....Sight, changing to Taste.
Source 9   Color/Sound....Yellow/"E," changing to Red/"F."
Source 10A   Major Arcana Journey....Wheel of Fortune is the tenth stop on the journey
Source 10B   Journey in the Planes....Wheel of Fortune is the second stop on the progress through the Spiritual Plane.

POSITION 11
Source 1A   Position 11 is number 11 in the series 1 to 22. It reduces to the number 2, but must also be considered for its value as an 11 as well.
Source 1B   Position 11 is the fourth number 2 of the seven Stages series of 1 to 4.
Source 2   Major Arcana....Justice.
Source 3   Consciousness Grid....Mental/Spiritual.
Source 4   Minor Arcana Grid....Swords/Wands.
Source 5   Elements Grid....Air/Fire.
Source 6   Real-Time Factor....Present/Thursday/Current Month.
Source 7   Chakra....Heart.
Source 8   Sense....Taste.
Source 9   Color/Sound....Red/"F."
Source 10A   Major Arcana Journey....Justice is the eleventh stop on the journey.
Source 10B   Journey in the Planes....Justice is the fourth stop on the progress through the Mental Plane.

POSITION 12
Source 1A   Position 12 is number 12 in the series 1 to 22. It reduces to the number 3.
Source 1B   Position 12 is the fourth number 3 of the seven Stages series of 1 to 4.
Source 2   Major Arcana....The Hanged Man.
Source 3   Consciousness Grid....Emotional/Spiritual.
Source 4   Minor Arcana Grid....Cups/Wands.
Source 5   Elements Grid....Water/Fire.
Source 6   Real Time Factor....Present/Thursday/Current Month.
Source 7   Chakra....Heart.
Source 8   Sense....Taste.
Source 9   Color/Sound....Red/"F."
Source 10A   Major Arcana Journey....The Hanged Man is the twelfth stop on the journey.
Source 10B   Journey in the Planes....The Hanged Man is the fourth stop on the progress through the Emotional Plane.

POSITION 13
Source 1A   Position 13 is number 13 in the series 1 to 22. It reduces to the number 4.
Source 1B   Position 13 is fourth number 4 and the fifth number 1 of the seven Stages series of 1 to 4.
Source 2   Major Arcana....Death.

Source 3   Consciousness Grid....Physical/Spiritual, changing to Physical/Higher Mental.
Source 4   Minor Arcana Grid....Pentacles/Wands, changing to Pentacles/Swords.
Source 5   Elements Grid....Earth/Fire, changing to Earth/Air.
Source 6   Real-Time Factor....Present/Thursday/Current Month, changing to Near
                Future/ Friday/ Next Month.
Source 7   Chakra....Heart, changing to Throat.
Source 8   Sense....Taste, changing to Smell.
Source 9   Color/Sound....Red/"F," changing to Orange/"G."
Source 10A   Major Arcana Journey....Death is the thirteenth stop on the journey.
Source 10B   Journey in the Planes....Death is the third stop on the progress through the
                Physical Plane.

POSITION 14
Source 1A   Position 14 is number 14 in the series 1 to 22. It reduces to the number 5.
Source 1B   Position 14 is the fifth number 2 of the seven Stages series of 1 to 4.
Source 2   Major Arcana....Temperance.
Source 3   Consciousness Grid....Emotional/Higher Mental.
Source 4   Minor Arcana Grid....Cups/Swords.
Source 5   Elements Grid....Water/Air.
Source 6   Real-Time Factor....Near Future/ Friday/ Next Month.
Source 7   Chakra....Throat.
Source 8   Sense....Taste.
Source 9   Color/Sound....Orange/"G."
Source 10A   Major Arcana Journey....Temperance is the fourteenth stop on the journey.
Source 10B   Journey in the Planes....Temperance is the fifth stop on the progress through
                the Emotional Plane.

POSITION 15
Source 1A   Position 15 is number 15 in the series 1 to 22. It reduces to the number 6.
Source 1B   Position 15 is the fifth number 3 of the seven Stages series of 1 to 4.
Source 2   Major Arcana....The Devil.
Source 3   Consciousness Grid....Mental/Higher Mental.
Source 4   Minor Arcana Grid.... Swords/Swords.
Source 5   Elements Grid....Air/Air.
Source 6   Real-Time Factor....Near Future/Friday/Next Month.
Source 7   Chakra....Throat.
Source 8   Sense....Taste.
Source 9   Color/Sound....Orange/"G."
Source 10A   Major Arcana Journey....The Devil is the fifteenth stop on the journey.
Source 10B   Journey in the Planes....The Devil is the fifth stop on the progress through the
                Mental Plane.

POSITION 16
Source 1A   Position 16 is number 16 in the series 1 to 22. It reduces to the number 7.

Source 1B	Position 16 is the fifth number 4 and the sixth number 1 of the seven Stages series of 1 to 4.
Source 2	Major Arcana....The Tower.
Source 3	Consciousness Grid....Spiritual/Higher Mental, changing to Spiritual/Higher Emotional.
Source 4	Minor Arcana Grid....Wands/Swords, changing to Wands/Cups.
Source 5	Elements Grid....Fire/Air, changing to Fire/Water.
Source 6	Real-Time Factor....Near Future/Friday/Next Month, changing to Mid-Future/Saturday/Second Month Hence.
Source 7	Chakra....Throat, changing to Third Eye.
Source 8	Sense....Taste, changing to Astral/Mental.
Source 9	Color/Sound....Orange/"G," changing to Indigo/"A."
Source 10A	Major Arcana Journey....The Tower is the sixteenth stop on the journey.
Source 10B	Journey in the Planes....The Tower is third stop on the progress through the Spiritual Plane.

Position 17

Source 1A	Position 17 is number 17 in the series 1 to 22. It reduces to the number 8.
Source 1B	Position 17 is the sixth number 2 of the seven Stages series of 1 to 4.
Source 2	Major Arcana....The Star.
Source 3	Consciousness Grid....Mental/ Higher Emotional.
Source 4	Minor Arcana Grid....Swords/Cups.
Source 5	Elements Grid....Air/Water.
Source 6	Real Time Factor....Mid-Future/Saturday/Second Month Hence.
Source 7	Chakra....Third Eye.
Source 8	Sense....Astral/Mental.
Source 9	Color/Sound....Indigo/"A."
Source 10A	Major Arcana Journey....The Star is the seventeenth stop on the journey.
Source 10B	Journey in the Planes....The Star is the sixth stop on the progress through the Mental Plane.

POSITION 18

Source 1A	Position 18 is number 18 in the series 1 to 22. It reduces to the number 9.
Source 1B	Position 18 is the sixth number 3 of the seven Stages series of 1 to 4.
Source 2	Major Arcana....The Moon.
Source 3	Consciousness Grid....Emotional/Higher Emotional.
Source 4	Minor Arcana Grid....Cups/Cups.
Source 5	Elements Grid....Water/Water.
Source 6	Real-Time Factor....Mid-Future/Saturday/Second Month Hence.
Source 7	Chakra....Third Eye.
Source 8	Sense....Astral/Mental.
Source 9	Color/Sound....Indigo/"A."

Source 10A   Major Arcana Journey....The Moon is the eighteenth stop on the journey.
Source 10B   Journey in the Planes....The Moon is the sixth stop on the progress through the Emotional Plane.

POSITION 19

Source 1A   Position 19 is number 19 in the series 1 to 22. It reduces to the number 1.
Source 1B   Position 19 is the sixth number 4 and the seventh number 1 of the seven Stages series of 1 to 4.
Source 2   Major Arcana....The Sun.
Source 3   Consciousness Grid....Physical/Higher Emotional, changing to Physical/Higher Physical.
Source 4   Minor Arcana Grid....Pentacles/Cups, changing to Pentacles/Pentacles.
Source 5   Elements Grid....Earth/Water, changing to Earth/Earth.
Source 6   Real-Time Factor....Mid-Future/Saturday/Second Month Hence, changing to Long-Term Future/Sunday/Third Month Hence.
Source 7   Chakra....Third Eye, changing to Crown.
Source 8   Sense....Astral/Mental, changing to Post-Mental.
Source 9   Color/Sound....Indigo/"A," changing to Purple/"B."
Source 10A   Major Arcana Journey....The Sun is the nineteenth stop on the journey.
Source 10B   Journey in the Planes....The Sun is the fourth stop on the progress through the Physical Plane.

POSITION 20

Source 1A   Position 20 is the number 20 in the series 1 to 22. It reduces to the number 2.
Source 1B   Position 20 is the seventh number 2 of the seven Stages series of 1 to 4.
Source 2   Major Arcana....Judgement.
Source 3   Consciousness Grid....Emotional/Higher Physical.
Source 4   Minor Arcana Grid....Cups/Pentacles
Source 5   Elements Grid....Water/Earth.
Source 6   Real-Time Factor....Long-Term Future/Sunday/Third Month Hence.
Source 7   Chakra....Crown.
Source 8   Sense....Post-Mental.
Source 9   Color/Sound....Purple/"B."
Source 10A   Major Arcana Journey....Judgement is the twentieth stop on the journey.
Source 10B   Journey in the Planes....Judgement is the seventh stop on the progress through the Emotional Plane.

Position 21

Source 1A   Position 21 is the number 21 in the series 1 to 22. It reduces to the number 3.
Source 1B   Position 21 is the seventh number 3 of the seven Stages series of 1 to 4.
Source 2   Major Arcana....The World.
Source 3   Consciousness Grid....Mental/Higher Physical.
Source 4   Minor Arcana Grid....Swords/Pentacles.
Source 5   Elements Grid....Air/Earth.

Source 6   Real-Time Factor....Long-Term Future/Sunday/Third Month Hence.
Source 7   Chakra....Crown.
Source 8   Sense....Post-Mental.
Source 9   Color/Sound....Purple/"B."
Source 10A   Major Arcana Journey....The World is the twenty-first stop on the journey.
Source 10B   Journey in the Planes....The World is the seventh stop on the progress through the Mental Plane.

POSITION 22

Source 1A   Position 22 is the number 22 in the series 1 to 22. It reduces to the number 4, but must also be considered for its value as a 22 as well. In addition, you must include its function as 0.
Source 1A.   Position 22 is the seventh number 4 of the seven Stages series of 1 to 4.
Source 2   Major Arcana....The Fool.
Source 3   Consciousness Grid....Spiritual/Higher Physical.
Source 4   Minor Arcana Grid....Wands/Pentacles.
Source 5   Elements Grid....Fire/Earth.
Source 6   Real-Time Factor....Long-Term Future/ Sunday/Third Month Hence.
Source 7   Chakra....Crown.
Source 8   Sense....Post-Mental.
Source 9   Color/Sound....Purple/"B."
Source 10A   Major Arcana Journey....The Fool is the final stop on the journey.
Source 10B   Journey in the Planes....The Fool is the fourth and final stop on the progress through the Spiritual Plane.

GLOSSARY

Arcana: The organization of the seventy-eight cards in classical Tarot decks is such that there are two groups; referred to as Arcana. One is called the Major Arcana; the other the Minor Arcana. Arcana means "secrets."

Card: Any of the seventy-eight drawings/illustrations that comprise a classical Tarot deck. These are rectangular in most decks, but may also be other shapes, such as square or round.

Chakra: *Chakra* is a Sanskrit word meaning "wheel." Used in Yoga disciplines, notably in reference to the *Kundalini* (the vital force lying dormant at the base of the spine until activated), and in the study of metaphysics and esoteric philosophy, to signify the principal centers or vortexes of spiritual energy along the body from an area near the base of the spine to the top of the head. Karmic Tarot refers to these seven chakras: Root (base of the spine...Adrenal); Genital (over the sex organs...Spleen); Solar Plexus (over the navel...Pancreas); Heart (over the heart...Thymus); Throat (front of the throat... Thyroid); Third Eye (between the eyebrows...Pituitary); and Crown (top of the Head...Pineal).

Classical Tarot Deck: Author's term for all decks that contain seventy-eight cards, consisting of a twenty-two-card Major Arcana and a fifty-six-card Minor Arcana.

Column: In all references to the seven stages in our evolution of consciousness and the seven Stages of the Karmic Spread, the organization of the information vertically is referred to as being in columns.

Court Cards: The sixteen cards, four each of the four suits that make up the Minor Arcana, through which the effects of personalities can be interpreted. They are Kings, Queens, Knights, and Pages.

Courts: Author's term for the sixteen Court cards.

Environment: The larger set to which anything belongs and upon which it depends for its identity and existence. It may be either physical, emotional, mental or spiritual.

Evolution of Consciousness: The continuing education of the soul through lessons learned in the experiences of chosen physical incarnations in numerous lifetimes on Earth.

God: That which is communicating with us continuously at each and every moment of our lives to help us learn our chosen lessons and advance along our path of evolving consciousness.

God Within: The aspect of the Divine with which the individual personality identifies and which exists deep inside each of us. Here is the feminine side of the Divine; the benevolent, the understanding, the forgiving God. At its extreme, it represents the infinitely small in the universe.

God Without: The aspect of the Divine which is conceived as external to the individual personality. Here is the masculine side of the Divine, the all-powerful, all-capable, the judgemental God. At its extreme, it represents the infinitely large in the universe.

Hierarchy: The concept in many schools of metaphysical thought that there is a group of advanced souls guiding man's progress on the incarnate plane, such guidance having required incarnating themselves from time to time. The Christian concept of archangels is similar.

Hooks: Author's term for the conventions, spreads/layouts, and card interpretations that every reader develops over time. Once a reader has established regular practices, they become the personal rules of grammar in their language of the Tarot, a grammar for the reader's personal dialect that can be used by God to deliver specific meanings/messages in any given reading.

Karma: The belief system which allows that the experiences of this lifetime, the lessons to be learned, are chosen in the context of and with the soul's knowledge of all prior incarnations. Karma is another word for our chosen path in toto. The popular notion of karma as punishment carried over to the present lifetime for wrongdoing in past lifetimes is incorrectly presented. The soul, from its overview, knows what it must do to advance efficiently along its path and will chose the work it needs to do. To the soul, no task or life position is worse or better than any other.

Karmic Contract: The first four cards in the Karmic Spread constitute the Karmic Contract, representing the readee's situation at birth. They show the physical, emotional, mental, and spiritual aspects of the work chosen for the present lifetime that are most applicable for the given reading.

Karmic Spread: The spread that accommodates a layout of twenty-two cards and which uses the information generated by the karma at work and visible in the structure of the Tarot itself, in particular the way in which the two Arcana interface graphically to reveal a four-fold aspect of the self moving through the seven stages of evolutionary growth in consciousness.

Karmic Tarot: The Tarot convention that uses a layout of twenty-two cards selected in each reading from a seventy-eight card classical Tarot deck and distributed over the spread pattern known as the Karmic Spread.

Layout: The distribution of cards in a designated pattern for a given reading using a predetermined spread convention. Each distribution of the cards is a layout.

Major Arcana: The group of twenty-two cards, numbered from 0 to 21, whose illustrations and meanings represent the archetypal lessons that the human race must experience and internalize. The author also refers to these twenty-two cards as the Majors.

Major Arcana Journey: The acquisition of the knowledge of the twenty-two Majors. This journey must be thought of on two levels: the path through the experiences of the present lifetime, and the path of growth in evolutionary consciousness through all our lifetimes—past, present and future.

Minor Arcana: The group of fifty-six cards, made up of four fourteen-card suits, each containing ten numbered cards (known as the Pips) and four face cards (known as the Court cards), and whose meanings represent the experiences in everyday life whereby we learn the archetypal lessons represented by the twenty-two Majors. The author also refers to these fifty-six cards as the Minors.

Mini-Journeys: The paths of experiences and lessons to be learned in the four Planes of the personality: Physical, Emotional, Mental, and Spiritual Journeys.

Path: The link through sequential events in the linear time of the present lifetime, whereby we are gaining the experience and knowledge of our chosen lessons and increasing our awareness of universal consciousness.

Pips: The forty numbered cards, Ace to 10, in each of the four suits of the Minor Arcana.

Planes: The four horizontal rows in the Karmic Spread: The Physical Plane, Emotional Plane, Mental Plane, and Spiritual Plane. They are the four aspects or levels of the personality.

Position: Any of the twenty-two locations on which cards fall in the Karmic Spread, such locations being created and defined by the grid formed by the intersection of the Planes (the horizontal rows) and the Stages (the vertical columns).

Provider: The divine source of all information given to the reader in the interpretation of any layout using the Karmic Spread.

Questions Index: The author's reference system for recording: 1) questions that you feel the Tarot should be able to provide answers to, and 2) where in the Karmic Tarot system (which positions in the Karmic Spread and which cards in the deck) you can expect to look for and find the answers to these questions.

Reader: The person receiving information from the Provider by interpretation of the twenty-two cards distributed in a layout using the Karmic Spread.

Readee: Known in most Tarot literature as the querent, this is the person for whom the Karmic Spread is being interpreted.

Reincarnation: The belief that we incarnate in a series of lifetimes that represent continuity in our education toward universal truth.

Row: In all references to the four planes of the personality and the four Planes of the Karmic Spread, the organization of the information horizontally is referred to as being in rows.

Royal Court: The four Court cards (Courts) that represent the strongest Court card in their respective suit; they are in essence the King of the Kings, the Queen of the Queens, the Knight of the Knights, and the Page of the Pages. Specifically, they are: the King of Pentacles, the Queen of Cups, the Knight of Swords, and the Page of Wands.

Sine Curve: Mathematically, an S-shaped curve described by the equation $y = \sin x$. But used by the author in reference to its shape and the connotation of oscillation, pulsation, up/down, phasing, rhythm, waves, duality, etc.

Soul: The innermost part of the human condition that seeks its identity in the identity of the Provider.

Source Definitions: Definitions of all the sources of influence from which are derived: 1) the meanings of the twenty-two cards of the Major Arcana and 2) the meanings of the twenty-two positions in the Karmic Spread.

Spread: Any pattern of positions designed to accept the laying out of Tarot cards for the purpose of interpreting a divine message from the Provider.

Stages: The seven vertical columns in the Karmic Spread representing the seven stages of development during the lifetime; used to mark chronological stages and stages of evolution of consciousness.

Suits: The four major groups that make up the fifty-six card Minor Arcana of a classical Tarot deck. They are the Pentacles, Cups, Swords, and Wands.

Swing Cards: The six cards that have fallen on the six swing positions in any layout using the Karmic Spread, which will have a dual interpretation as belonging to the end of one Stage and the beginning of the next.

Swing Position: The six positions in the Karmic Spread that represent the end of one Stage and the beginning of the next, and therefore carry a dual significance. These positions are 4, 7, 10, 13, 16, and 19.

Theosophists: Adherents of Theosophy, a school of teachings about God based on mystical insights that became a movement in the United States in 1875 It is based chiefly on Buddhist and Brahmanic theories, including pantheistic evolution and reincarnation.